X International Scientific and Technical Conference “Polytransport Systems” (PTS-2018)

AA003864

MATEC Web of Conferences Volume 216 (2018)

Tomsk, Russia
15 – 16 November 2018

Editors:

A.D. Abramov
A.L. Manakov
A.A. Klimov
V.I. Khabarov
V.I. Medvedev

ISBN: 978-1-5108-7308-7

Printed from e-media with permission by:

Curran Associates, Inc.
57 Morehouse Lane
Red Hook, NY 12571

proceedings.com

Some format issues inherent in the e-media version may also appear in this print version.

This work is licensed under a Creative Commons Attribution license:
http://creativecommons.org/licenses/by/2.0/
You are free to:
Share – copy and redistribute the material in any medium or format.
Adapt – remix, transform, and build upon the material for any purpose, even commercial.
The licensor cannot revoke these freedoms as long as you follow the license terms.
Under the following terms:
You must give appropriate credit, provide a link to the license, and indicate if changes were made. You may do so in any reasonable manner, but not in any way that suggests the licensor endorses you or your use. The copyright is retained by the corresponding authors.

Printed by Curran Associates, Inc. (2018)

For additional information, please contact EDP Sciences – Web of Conferences
at the address below.

EDP Sciences – Web of Conferences
17, Avenue du Hoggar
Parc d'Activité de Courtabœuf
BP 112
F-91944 Les Ulis Cedex A
France

Phone: +33 (0) 1 69 18 75 75
Fax: +33 (0) 1 69 28 84 91

contact-edps@webofconferences.org

Additional copies of this publication are available from:

Curran Associates, Inc.
57 Morehouse Lane
Red Hook, NY 12571 USA
Phone: 845-758-0400
Fax: 845-758-2633
Email: curran@proceedings.com
Web: www.proceedings.com

TABLE OF CONTENTS

Preface
X International Scientific and Technical Conference «Polytransport systems» (PTS-2018)

X International Scientific and Technical Conference «Polytransport systems» (PTS-2018) is held on 15-16 November 2018 at Siberian Transport University (Novosibirsk, Russia).

Program and Scientific Editorial Board:
Chairman
Aleksey L. Manakov, rector of Siberian Transport University, Dr. Tech. Sc. (Novosibirsk, Russia)
Key members:
Andrey D. Abramov – Dr. Tech. Sc., Prof., vice-rector for research, Prof. of the Department of Technologies of transport machine-building and exploitation of machines, Siberian Transport University (Novosibirsk, Russia), Chief Editor
Aleksander K. Golovnich – Dr. Tech. Sc., Prof., head of the Department of Transportation hubs, Belarusian State University of Transport (Gomel, Republic of Belarus)
Taisiya V. Shepitko – Dr. Tech. Sc., Prof., head of the Institute of track, construction and structures, Russian University of Transport (Moscow, Russia)
Vladimir V. Chervov – Dr. Tech. Sc., Prof., head of the Laboratory for mining mechanization, Chinakal Institute of Mining of the Siberian Branch of the Russian Academy of Sciences (Novosibirsk, Russia)
Vladimir N. Efimenko – Dr. Tech. Sc., Prof., Department of Automobile Roads, Tomsk State University of Architecture and Buildin (Tomsk, Russia)
Aleksander L. Isakov – Dr. Tech. Sc., Prof., head of the Department of Railway and highway surveying and design engineering, Siberian Transport University (Novosibirsk, Russia)
Evgeniy V. Boyarkin – Dr. Tech. Sc., Prof., Department of Electrical engineering, diagnostics and certification, Siberian Transport University (Novosibirsk, Russia)
Valeriy I. Khabarov – Dr. Tech. Sc., Prof., Department of Information technologies in transport, Siberian Transport University (Novosibirsk, Russia)
Vladimir I. Medvedev – Dr. Tech. Sc., Prof., Department of Life safety, Siberian Transport University (Novosibirsk, Russia)
Aleksander A. Klimov – Cand. Tech. Sc., Assoc. Prof., Department of Railway stations and junctions, Siberian Transport Univesity (Novosibirsk, Russia)
Evgeniy A. Grigoryev – Cand. Econ. Sc., Assoc. Prof., deputy dean of the faculty of Water transport management, Siberian State University of Water Transport (Novosibirsk, Russia)
Petr K. Rybin – Cand. Tech. Sc., Assoc. Prof., Department of Department of Railway stations and junctions, Emperor Alexander I St. Petersburg State Transport University (Saint Petersburg, Russia)
Sergei A. Maksimov – Cand. Tech. Sc., Assoc. Prof., president of Siberian Union of Transport, Freight Forwarders and Logistics Employees, Department of Systems analysis and project management, Siberian Transport University (Novosibirsk, Russia)
Diana Yu. Grishkova – Cand. Tech. Sc., Assoc. Prof., Department of Freight operation and rolling stock, Siberian Transport University (Novosibirsk, Russia)
Olga Yu. Chuykova – Cand. Tech. Sc., Assoc. Prof., Department of Freight operation and rolling stock, Siberian Transport University (Novosibirsk, Russia)
Maksim V. Korneev – Cand. Tech. Sc., Assoc. Prof., Department of Freight operation and rolling stock, Siberian Transport University (Novosibirsk, Russia)
Konstantin V. Zheldak – Cand. Tech. Sc., Assoc. Prof., Department of Freight operation and rolling stock, Siberian Transport University (Novosibirsk, Russia)
Nikolay A. Maslov – Cand. Tech. Sc., Assoc. Prof., Department of Mechanization of railway, loading/unloading and construction work, Siberian Transport University (Novosibirsk, Russia)
Evgeniy S. Tenitilov – Cand. Tech. Sc., Assoc. Prof., Department of Electrical engineering, diagnostics and certification, Siberian Transport University (Novosibirsk, Russia)
Sergey P. Sarychev – Cand. Tech. Sc., Assoc. Prof., Department of Information technologies in transport, Siberian Transport University (Novosibirsk, Russia)

X International Scientific and Technical Conference «Polytransport systems» is an interdisciplinary event dedicated to a wide range of relevant research topics such as problems of transport projects implementation: transport infrastructure facilities, transportation management and economy; infrastructure-related projects; modern systems of maintenance and repair of vehicles and rolling stock; non-destructive testing and technical diagnostics; intellectual control systems for transport; transportation safety; human resource-related safety aspects, etc.

The conference is held for the purpose of supporting research activities among research staff, specialists, young researchers, PhD students and undergraduate students by discussing relevant problems and research outcomes. The number of the conference participants has reached 240 people from 25 research and educational institutions, with 170 oral contributions.

The Chairman of the program and scientific editorial boards expresses his gratitude to the members of the organizational committee and secretariat of the event and all employees who help provide efficient work of the conference. Organizers acknowledge participants for their important contribution in the form of their oral reports and the present proceedings.

Editor of the Proceedings Volume,
Prof. Andrey D. Abramov,
Dr. Tech. Sc., Prof.
Novosibirsk, September, 2018

© The Authors, published by EDP Sciences. This is an open access article distributed under the terms of the Creative Commons Attribution License 4.0 (http://creativecommons.org/licenses/by/4.0/).

Statement of Peer review

In submitting conference proceedings to *Web of Conferences*, the editors of the proceedings certify to the Publisher that

1. They adhere to its **Policy on Publishing Integrity** in order to safeguard good scientific practice in publishing.
2. All articles have been subjected to peer review administered by the proceedings editors.
3. Reviews have been conducted by expert referees, who have been requested to provide unbiased and constructive comments aimed, whenever possible, at improving the work.
4. Proceedings editors have taken all reasonable steps to ensure the quality of the materials they publish and their decision to accept or reject a paper for publication has been based only on the merits of the work and the relevance to the journal.

Title, date and place of the conference

X International Scientific and Technical Conference «Polytransport systems»
November 15-16, 2018

Proceedings editor(s):

1. Andrey D. Abramov, Prof., Dr. (Chief Editor)
2. Aleksey L. Manakov, Prof., Dr.
3. Aleksander A. Klimov, Assoc. Prof., Cand. of Sc.
4. Valeriy I. Khabarov, Prof., Dr.
5. Vladimir I. Medvedev, Prof., Dr.

Date and editor's signature / Andrey Abramov, 24 September, 2018

GNSS availability monitoring method for railway transport

Vladislav Demyanov[1,*], *Boris* Shurygin[1], and *Olga* Imarova[1]

[1]Irkutsk State Transport University, 664074 Irkutsk, Russia

Abstract: The article studies relevant problem of real time monitoring - the availability of the required GNSS navigation characteristics, which is required for railway rolling stock traffic automation. As prototypes, the main approaches to monitoring the availability of the required navigation characteristics of WAAS EGNOS wide area differential systems users were analyzed. It was shown that the use of the total probability of violation of the required navigation characteristics without decomposition of an equivalent range error is an appropriate approach for building the algorithm for monitoring the availability of navigation support for transport applications. The method of monitoring the availability of required navigation characteristics was proposed for automated railway traffic control tasks.

Introduction

Full-scale introduction of GLONASS in railway transport is guided by widespread introduction of the coordinate method of automatic traffic control. This method is based on the use of "virtual traffic lights", mobile block sites and virtual zones of obstacle approaching.

There is a number of problems that prevent introduction of intelligent transport systems based on satellite navigation on the Russian Railways. These problems include the following: actual unpredictability of the current positioning accuracy; restrictions on the use of accurate geospatial data; insufficient availability of digital maps of railway facilities within territorial entities of the Russian Federation [1, 2]. Works of B. A. Lyovin, I. N. Rosenberg, S. I. Matveev, E. N. Rosenberg, A. S. Matveev are devoted to introduction of satellite navigation on domestic railways. [3-5].

The necessary prerequisite for ensuring the required navigation characteristics (RNC) in transport is the use of GLONASS functional add-ons, i.e., local and wide-area differential systems. Differential navigation means provide both high positioning accuracy and effective RNC availability real time monitoring [6]. Thus, full-scale introduction of differential navigation on railways opens wide prospects for using all potential benefits from introduction of GLONASS as the main element of intelligent transport systems.

Wide-area differential systems (WADS) have been sufficiently commissioned abroad long ago, e.g., WAAS (USA) and EGNOS (European Union). In most cases, these systems

* Corresponding author: sword1971@yandex.ru

© The Authors, published by EDP Sciences. This is an open access article distributed under the terms of the Creative Commons Attribution License 4.0 (http://creativecommons.org/licenses/by/4.0/).

ensure positioning accuracy with the residual error of 1-3 m with the RNC availability of not worse than 0.9999 with the user warning time of not more than 10 s [7]. Despite these high characteristics, insufficient reliability in the following conditions of irregular impacts remains the bottleneck of the WADS: geomagnetic disturbances of the ionosphere, electromagnetic interference, screening of signals of part of visible satellites by infrastructure facilities, etc. Unfortunately, the same can be stated about the domestic WADS GLONASS, known under abbreviation RSDKM [8].

The best solution for transport applications would be using local departmental differential systems. These are already widely used in radio engineering systems for aircraft guidance and landing [9]. But even here the issue of RNC monitoring with regard to irregular impacts has not been adequately elaborated. And so far the issue of full-scale use of differential navigation in railway transport for implementation of intelligent transport systems (ITS) has not been considered in practice yet.

In this paper, the issue of real time monitoring of RNC availability of GNSS users for transport applications is considered. Comparison of main advantages and disadvantages of the two main concepts of availability monitoring of the RNC used in WASS and EGNOS WADS is performed. The method of monitoring the availability of required navigation characteristics is proposed for automated railway traffic control tasks.

Concepts of RNC integrity monitoring used in WAAS and EGNOS systems

The RNC integrity monitoring algorithms of WAAS [10] (SBAS+GPS) and EGNOS (SBAS+Galileo) [11] were designed for use in aircraft navigation and landing systems [12]. Unfortunately, the similarly detailed technological information on the existing availability monitoring algorithms for RNC of RSDKM users (SBAS + GLONASS), is not generally available, therefore, it is not considered herein.

The general part of the algorithm for assessing the current availability of the RNC in the aforementioned foreign WADSs is as follows. The main station calculates the integrity parameters of the system segments and differential corrections within certain limits of the confidence intervals for components of range-errors of satellites in the zone of visibility. Based on this, current RNC integrity is evaluated in the system user's equipment. The integrity data is provided in the form of calculated current protection levels (PLs) in the horizontal and vertical plane in the local coordinate system. The user's receiver compares the calculated protection levels with the confidence intervals set for the horizontal plane (HAL) and the vertical plane (VAL) for the selected flight phase. If one of the protection levels goes beyond the confidence interval, the sign of the system integrity violation is generated.

However, the final technological algorithms for assessing the current RNC integrity in these systems differ. The WAAS technological algorithm assumes the following: 1) serviceability of visible navigation satellites, if the satellite itself does not produce the sign of "health" violation; 2) decomposition of the full range-error into separate components of the equivalent range-error: ionospheric error, tropospheric error, multipath error, and ephemeris error. With that, locally-dependent range-errors (ionospheric, tropospheric and multipath errors) are further converted into an averaged functionally-dependent form suitable for use anywhere in the wide work area [13].

The technological algorithm of integrity control in the EGNOS system works differently. It assumes independent monitoring of "health" of each of the visible satellites. Besides, this algorithm uses the full probability of the RNC violation without decomposition of the full range-error by main sources [14].

The RNC availability assessment used in WAAS in terms of plane and height is as follows:

$$HPL = K_H \cdot d_{major} \tag{1}$$

$$VPL = K_{V,PA} \cdot d_v \tag{2}$$

where:

K_H, K_V is the coefficient that indicates the margins of the confidence interval of the positioning error in terms of plane and height with the confidence probability of $P = 1\text{-}10^{-7}$;

d_{major} is the length of projection of the main ellipse projection semi-axis of dissipation of the error in positioning of the system user onto the plane in the local coordinate system, equal to the following:

$$d_{major} = \sqrt{\frac{d_{east}^2 + d_{north}^2}{2} + \sqrt{\left(\frac{d_{east}^2 + d_{norh}^2}{2}\right)^2 + d_{EN}^2}} \tag{3}$$

$$d_{EN} = \sqrt{d_{east}^2 + d_{north}^2} \tag{4}$$

d_{east} d_{north}, d_V are the semi-axes of the dissipation ellipse of the positioning error in the direction to the east, north and in height in the local coordinate system, respectively.

The RNC integrity monitoring algorithm, which is used as part of software and algorithmic support in the EGNOS system, directly estimates the expected probability of dangerous misalignment of the P_{HMI} (probability of hazardous misleading information) about the actual and expected positioning error. With that, the system performs calculation of the current value of the P_{HMI} probability and its comparison to the set permissible level. If the P_{HMI} exceeds the permissible set limit, this means that the estimated object state vector is outside the established RNC margins with the specified probability. The user must be immediately notified of this.

The mathematical notation of the algorithm for estimating the RNC availability in terms of plane and height in the EGNOS system is as follows:

$$P_{HMI}(VAL,HAL) = 1 - erf\left(\frac{VAL}{\sqrt{2}\cdot\sigma_{u,V,FF}}\right) + e^{\frac{HAL^2}{2\xi_{FF}^2}} + \frac{1}{2}\sum_{j=1}^{N} P_{fail,sat_j}\cdot\left(\left(1 - erf\left(\frac{VAL+\mu_{u,V}}{\sqrt{2}\cdot\sigma_{u,V,FM}}\right)\right) + \left(1 - erf\left(\frac{VAL-\mu_{u,V}}{\sqrt{2}\cdot\sigma_{u,V,FM}}\right)\right)\right) + \sum_{j=1}^{N}\left(P_{fail,sat_j}\cdot\left(1 - \chi^2_{2,\delta_{u,H}} cdf\left(\frac{HAL^2}{\xi_{FM}^2}\right)\right)\right) \tag{5}$$

Where:

$\mu_{u,V}$ is the permissible initial deviation of the positioning error in the vertical plane;

ξ is equivalent to d_{major} specified in (3);

$\sigma_{u,V,FM}$ are unaccounted range-errors;

$P_{fail,sat}$ is the probability of technical failure in the satellite operation.

The obvious disadvantage of the SBAS + GPS concept is that it is based on the health of all visible GPS satellites. In the case of unaccounted anomalies in the satellite operation, this can cause unpredictable deterioration in operation of the entire system.

The disadvantage of the SBAS+Galileo concept is that the main function for estimating the expected range-errors is shifted to the user equipment. On the one hand, it increases the availability and reliability of the RNC integrity monitoring, but, on the other hand, it puts the final result of the system operation in dependence on functioning peculiarities of the user navigation equipment of various manufacturers. That is, the possibility of strict unification, regulation and certification of the RNC integrity monitoring process, is violated, particularly for departmental users.

With consideration of the main ideas, as well as the disadvantages of the aforementioned RNC integrity monitoring algorithms, let us turn to consideration of the new algorithm. The algorithm proposed below is designed to monitor the RNC availability with positioning of the object on the plane with a rigidly defined motion path.

The RNC availability monitoring algorithm for the use in railway transport

The proposed method is based on the use of measurements of the full range-error of visible navigation satellites on the reference monitoring and correcting station of the local differential system (LDS). With that, no decomposition of range-errors is performed, and the RNC availability is monitored in the horizontal plane with consideration of motion along the rigidly defined path.

The availability of positioning must be determined from the standpoint of the full probability of the RNC availability in the LDS coverage area in the following form:

$$W = P(A) \cdot P(B) \cdot P(C|A, B) \cdot (1 - P_{FAULT}) \cdot W_{PDOP} \quad (6)$$

where A is the event at which GLONASS and LDS equipment is in the serviceable state;

B is the event at which GLONASS equipment is serviceable;

C is the event at which positioning accuracy corresponds to the RNC at the stage of solving a specific transport problem;

$(1 - P_{FAULT})$ is the probability of positioning failure at the stage of solving a specific transport task;

W_{PDOP} is the index that warns about the dangerous level of the expected positioning error, as a result of a sudden deterioration of geometric factor (PDOP).

Then, we believe that $P(A) = P(B) = 1$. This corresponds to the case if independent monitoring of the GLONASS+LDS system technical state is not provided.

The probability of positioning failure at the stage of solving the problem can be estimated as the probability of occurrence of k-events (failures) at random instants within the transport problem solution interval (ΔT) using the Poisson law as follows [15]:

$$P_{FAULT} = \frac{a^k}{k!} \cdot \exp(-a) \quad (7)$$

where k = 0, 1, 2,...n is the possible number of positioning failures within the monitoring period, ΔT, a is the Poisson distribution parameter.

The peculiarities of the proposed general methodology for use on the railway are as follows:

1) the train moves along a rigidly defined trajectory, therefore it is required to estimate not the unexpected positioning error in terms of plane, but the expected error in determining the current path ordinate (the braking distance length);

2) there is no need for warning the user of rapid deterioration of the positioning accuracy in the vertical plane, therefore, it is enough to estimate only the horizontal geometric factor for estimating of alarm index W_{PDOP}.

Thus, estimation of the RNC availability of in terms of the available positioning accuracy for navigational support of the railway transport takes the following form:

$$P(C|A,B) = exp\left(-0.5\cdot\left[\frac{(X_{BR}-m_X)^2}{\sigma_X^2}+\frac{\left(Y_{BR}-m_Y-c\cdot\frac{\sigma_Y}{\sigma_X}\cdot(X_{BR}-m_X)\right)^2}{\sigma_Y^2\cdot(1-c^2)}\right]\right) \quad (8)$$

where c is the coefficient of correlation between time ranges of positioning errors ΔX and ΔY; $m_X = x_{tl}^*, m_Y = y_{tl}^*, \sigma_X, \sigma_Y$ is the mathematical expectation and the RSD of errors in positioning of the tail of the train in front (the "virtual red traffic light" location point). See the explanation of other components of expression (8) in Figure 1.

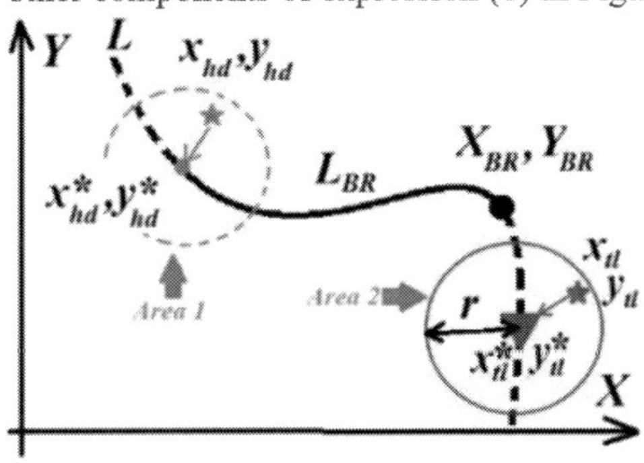

Fig.1. Elements of the train crash warning system.

The practical application of the method described by expression (8) is as follows. Firstly, one must learn the exact position of the path of movement along the railway (L) in the special railway coordinate system (X, Y). After learning coordinates L, one can calculate current braking distance L_{BR}) between point x^*_{hd}, y^*_{hd} and (X_{BR}, Y_{BR}) on the basis of the "speed-braking distance" normative curves known for this path section considering the train speed and mass. Coordinates of the forward train head (x_{hd}, y_{hd}) and tail (x_{tl}, y_{tl}) are estimated with the use of the GLONASS+LDS equipment. These coordinates are in the supposed center of the ellipses for dissipation of positioning errors (Area 1 and Area 2 in the figure). To calculate the length of the braking distance (L_{BR}), let us recalculate the current coordinates of the train head (x_{hd}, y_{hd}) for the nearest point on the railway path(x^*_{hd}, y^*_{hd}). After determination of length L_{BR} and the railway path coordinate, let us find the final point of the braking distance (X_{BR}, Y_{BR}) on the railway path. If it has been found out in the course of calculation by formula (8) that the coordinates of the final braking distance point (X_{BR}, Y_{BR}) fall within critical Region 2, it is necessary to issue a warning about the RNC violation, since the current state of the system does not allow adequate estimating of the size of the approach zone with a temporary obstacle. Area 2 radius depends on the confidence admissible collision probability, which is established a priori. For example, with the confidence probability of

"3 sigma" (1-0.997 = 0.003), the radius of Area 2 is $r \approx 3 \cdot \sigma_r$, where σ_r is the equivalent standard deviation of positioning errors in terms of plane, which is defined as: $\sigma_r^2 = \max\{\sigma_{\Delta X}^2, \sigma_{\Delta Y}^2\}$.

The remaining elements in original equation (6) are defined as follows. The distribution parameter in (7) depends on the duration of interval ΔT and distribution of the positioning errors time, which, in general, can be non-fixed during the ΔT period. Therefore, determination of the Poisson law parameter supposes accumulation of experimental histograms for the system put into operation, and then smoothing out the histogram data with the help of the theoretical Poisson law by the least squares method:

$$\sum_{k=0}^{n}\left(P_k - \frac{a^k}{k!} \cdot e^{-a}\right)^2 \to min \tag{9}$$

where n is the maximum number of positioning errors in the series of observations.

Current alarm index W_{PDOP} for the railway must be adopted to estimate the expected dangerous error only in terms of plane in the following form:

$$W_{PDOP} = \begin{cases} 1, & (HDOP \leq \Pi_{HDOP}) \\ 0, & (HDOP \geq \Pi_{HDOP}) \end{cases} \tag{10}$$

$$\Pi_{HDOP} \leq \frac{\left(\sqrt{\sigma_X^2 + \sigma_Y^2}\right)_{max}}{\sigma_{\Delta R}} \tag{11}$$

where the "max" index denotes the corresponding maximum allowable RSD of positioning errors on the plane in accordance with the RNC; $\sigma_{\Delta R}$ is the RSD of range-errors, which is calculated by direct measurements on the signals of visible satellites on the CCS of the LDS during the observation period, ΔT.

In general, as one can see, the proposed RNC availability monitoring method can be used for automated railway traffic control tasks. The method algorithm takes into consideration all possible irregular effects on the integrated GLONASS+LDS system, and also provides for the possibility of considering the technical state of segments of the system itself.

Conclusion

The method proposed is based on estimation of the current statistics of positioning errors and the full range-error (without its decomposition) on a time scale close to real time and within the LDS work zone. This approach makes it possible to count on high reliability of the RNC availability control algorithm, even taking into consideration the impacts of unpredictable and irregular factors. Such impacts can be geomagnetic disturbances, powerful electromagnetic interference and screening of signals from some satellites by infrastructure facilities. In method proposed ensures the possibility of estimating the expected sharp deterioration in the positioning accuracy due to screening of signals of some visible satellites. With that, the current range-error statistics is taken into consideration. This property of the method proposed allows adapting the operation of the GLONASS+LDS system as part of the complex of intelligent transport systems, taking into consideration the expected impact of known railway infrastructure facilities. The issues of estimating the LDS work zone dimensions, the range-errors stationarity interval and the behavior of the positioning error dissipation ellipse semi-axes on the plane are still open.

References

1. V.N. Tyapkin, E.N. Garin, *Metody opredelenija navigacionnyh parametrov podvizhnyh sredstv s ispol'zovaniem sputnikovoj radionavigacionnoj sistemy GLONASS* [Methods for determining navigational parameters of mobile assets using the GLONASS satellite radio navigation system] (SFU, Krasnoyarsk, 2012). (in Russian)
2. E.L. Afraymovich, Kosmicheskaja pogoda i kosmicheskij klimat [Space weather and space climate], **Vol. 3**, 427 (2013). (in Russian)
3. E.N. Rozenberg, A.S. Korovin, V.V. Batraev, *O razvitii bortovyh i napol'nyh sistem kontrolja bezopasnosti, minimizirujushhih vlijanie chelovecheskogo faktora* [Development of airborne and floor safety control systems, minimizing the impact of human factors] (Russian Railways JSC, Moscow, 2013). (in Russian)
4. S.I. Matveev, I.N. Rozenberg, *Grafy i navigacija* [Graphs and navigation] (Moscow, 2015). (in Russian)
5. I.D. Dolgiy, I.N. Rozenberg, S.V. Sokolov, V.I. Umanskiy, V.V. Kamenskiy, RU Patent 2468950 (16.05.2011). (in Russian)
6. A.I. Perov, V.N. Kharisova, *GLONASS: principy postroenija i funkcionirovanija* [GLONASS: principles of construction and operation] (Radiotehnika, Moscow, 2010). (in Russian)
7. Wide-Area Augmentation System Performance Analysis Report, 17 (William J. Hughes Technical Center, 2006), available at http://www.nstb.tc.faa.gov/REPORTS/waaspan17.pdf
8. V.V. Demyanov, Yu.V. Yasyukevich, *Solnechno-zemnaja fizika* [Solar-terrestrial physics] (ISU Pabl., Irkutsk, 2014). (in Russian)
9. Doc 9849 AN/457. *Global Navigation Satellite System (GNSS) Manual* (International Civil Aviation Organization, 2013). (in Russian)
10. Federal Aviation Administration, Satellite Navigation – WAAS – how it works (June 15, 2015), available at: https://www.faa.gov/about/office_org/headquarters_offices/ato/service_units/techops/navservices/gnss/waas/howitworks/.
11. European Global Navigation Satellite System Agency, About EGNOS, available at: https://egnos-user-support.essp-sas.eu/new_egnos_ops/egnos-system/about-egnos (May 09, 2018).
12. F. Kneissl, C. Stöber, Inside GNSS (January/February 2010).
13. V.V. Kurshin Doctoral thesis, Moscow Aviation Institute, Moscow, 2003. (in Russian)
14. EGNOS Safety of Life Service (SoL) SDD, Issue 3.1 (European GNSS Agency, 2016).
15. E.S. Venttsel, *Teorija verojatnostej* [Theory of probability] (Nauka, Moscow, 1969). (in Russian)

Technology of rail replacement at end stresses

Sergey Kosenko[1,*], *Sergey* Akimov[1], and *Pavel* Surovin[1]

[1]Siberian Transport University, 630049 Novosibirsk, Russia

Abstract. The paper focuses on topical issues relating to the maintenance of buffer spans and temporarily repaired sections of continuous welded rail (CWR) tracks. The paper is aimed at developing and studying the feasibility of a technology for replacing temperature-stressed continuous welded rails. For the purposes of this research, the analytical modeling method is used. A design model for moving the end of the stressed rail to the side is presented. Equations of deflections and bending moments arising when the rail is bent to the rated value were derived. Stresses on the rail bending length were determined and compared with the maximum allowable ones. A resource-saving technology has been developed for replacing temperature-stressed buffer rails of a CWR track using intermediate rail fastening Vossloh W-30.

Introduction

Due to operational advantages of continuous welded rail (CWR) tracks over jointed tracks, increasingly more CWR tracks are laid both on Russian railways and railways of other countries [1, 2]. At present, the total length of CWR tracks in the world has reached 500 thousand km, making up 1/3 of the total length of railway lines [3]. Despite the fact that this track is called "continuous", its design provides for joints with gaps. Gaps are necessary in buffer spans to compensate temperature strains of continuously welded rails.

Buffer spans are the weakest points in CWR tracks [4]. In conditions with a large annual temperature range, which is typical of many regions in the Russian Federation, buffer rails need to be replaced twice a year as part of seasonal maintenance [5]. A rise in temperatures in the spring season leads to the development of longitudinal compressive forces in continuously welded rails and their displacement [6]. Joint gaps in buffer spans are closed, and an end stress between rails arises [7], which makes it much more difficult to replace these rails for short ones.

There are several known technologies for replacing stressed rails. According to the existing technology [8], it is forbidden to change a stressed rail without cutting out its part with flame cutting. In this case, however, rails become unfit for relaying with initial parameters. There are also other ways to remove stressed buffer rails from the track. For example, the end stress of rails can be eliminated by nitrogen cooling of the CWR section adjacent to the buffer rail [9]. Another way of eliminating the end stress is to increase the length of the CWR section adjacent to the buffer rail by creating bending deflection [7].

* Corresponding author: kosenko.s.a@mail.ru

© The Authors, published by EDP Sciences. This is an open access article distributed under the terms of the Creative Commons Attribution License 4.0 (http://creativecommons.org/licenses/by/4.0/).

These methods are quite complex and cannot provide a sufficient level of occupational safety.

The paper is aimed at developing and studying the feasibility of a technology for replacing temperature-stressed continuous welded rails. The novelty of this research is the proposed technology of replacing stressed rails using a hydraulic rail replacement device, supported by equations of deflections and bending moments to move the rail to the rated value.

Research method

In order to ensure that a removed stressed rail preserves the initial parameters and can be reused many times, a hydraulic rail replacement device is proposed [10] (Fig. 1). The device is designed to replace stressed buffer rails and temporarily repaired sections of CWR tracks.

a

b

Fig. 1. The hydraulic rail replacement device with intermediate rail fastening: a – ZhBR-65Sh; b – Vossloh W-30.

In order to justify the feasibility of this device, it is necessary to derive equations of deflections and bending moments arising when the rail is bent to the rated value with the hydraulic rail replacement device. Then the stresses arising in the rail should be determined and compared with the maximum allowable ones. The required equations can be derived through analytical modeling.

In a design model, the rail is considered as a beam with a constant cross-section. The bending axis of the beam can be described by the following differential equation:

$$EJ_z \frac{d^4 v}{dx^4} = 0 \tag{1}$$

where E is the elastic modulus of the rail steel, Pa; J_z is the moment of inertia of the rail relative to the vertical axis, m^4.

When moving the end of the stressed rail to the side, the rail is exposed to a force P generated by the hydraulic device. The force P, located at an angle α to the rail axis, can be decomposed into two components:

$$N = -P\cos\alpha; \tag{2}$$

$$Q = -P\sin\alpha, \tag{3}$$

where N is the compressive longitudinal force, N; Q is the transverse force in the end section.

In this case, the rail will be subject to bending, and the differential equation of the bending axis can be written as:

$$EJ_z \frac{d^4 v}{dx^4} + P\cos\alpha \frac{d^2 v}{dx^2} = 0. \qquad (4)$$

The design model is shown in Figure 2.

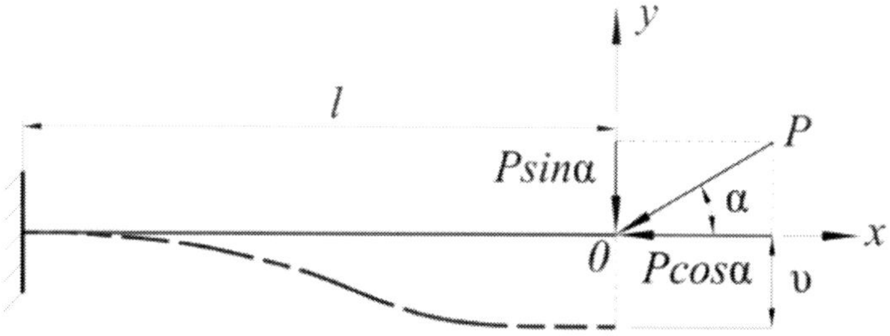

Fig. 2. The design model corresponding to the general solution of the differential equation that describes the bending axis of the beam.

Let us introduce a dimensionless coordinate $\xi = \frac{x}{l}$ and deflection $\mu = \frac{v}{b}$. Here, l is the length of a released section, m; b is the value of lateral shifting of a rail, m.

Let us find derivatives of the dimensionless coordinate ξ:

$$\frac{dv}{dx} = b\frac{d\mu}{dx} = b\frac{d\mu}{d\xi}\frac{d\xi}{dx} = \frac{b}{l}\frac{d\mu}{d\xi}; \quad \frac{d^2 v}{dx^2} = b\frac{d^2\mu}{dx^2} = b\frac{d^2\mu}{d\xi^2}\frac{d^2\xi}{dx^2} = \frac{b}{l^2}\frac{d^2\mu}{d\xi^2};$$

$$\frac{d^3 v}{dx^3} = b\frac{d^3\mu}{dx^3} = b\frac{d^3\mu}{d\xi^3}\frac{d^3\xi}{dx^3} = \frac{b}{l^3}\frac{d^3\mu}{d\xi^3}; \quad \frac{d^4 v}{dx^4} = b\frac{d^4\mu}{dx^4} = b\frac{d^4\mu}{d\xi^4}\frac{d^4\xi}{dx^4} = \frac{b}{l^4}\frac{d^4\mu}{d\xi^4}.$$

Then the equation (4) can be rewritten as:

$$EJ_z \frac{b}{l^4}\frac{d^4\mu}{d\xi^4} + P\cos\alpha \frac{b}{l^2}\frac{d^2\mu}{d\xi^2} = 0. \qquad (5)$$

By multiplying the derived equation by $\frac{l^4}{EJ_z b}$, we will obtain:

$$\frac{d^4\mu}{d\xi^4} + \frac{Pl^2\cos\alpha}{EJ_z}\frac{d^2\mu}{d\xi^2} = 0 \qquad (6)$$

Let us introduce a dimensionless coefficient $n^2 = \frac{Pl^2\cos\alpha}{EJ_z}$.

The general solution of this equation is a function

$$\mu(\xi) = C_1 + C_2\xi + C_3\cos n\xi + C_4\sin n\xi \qquad (7)$$

When the end of the stressed rail is moved to the side with the hydraulic rail replacement device, there is no contact between the rails at the joint and the end section of the rail cannot be turned. In this case, the boundary conditions can be defined as:

$$v(l)=0,\quad v'(l)=0,\quad v(0)=b,\quad v'(0)=0,$$

or in dimensionless form

$$\mu(1)=0,\quad \mu'(1)=0,\quad \mu(0)=1,\quad \mu'(0)=0.$$

System of boundary conditions:

$$\mu(1)=C_1+C_2+C_3\cos n+C_4\sin n=0;\ \mu'(1)=C_2-C_3n\sin n+C_4n\cos n=0;$$

$$\mu(0)=C_1+C_2\cdot 0+C_3\cos 0+C_4\sin 0=1;\ \mu'(0)=C_2-C_3n\sin 0+C_4n\cos 0=0.$$

Under these boundary conditions, we obtain the following system of equations:

$$C_1+C_2+C_3\cos n+C_4\sin n=0;$$

$$C_2-C_3n\sin n+C_4n\cos n=0;$$

$$C_1+C_3=1;\ C_2+C_4n=0.$$

After intermediate calculations and transformations, the constants of the equations can be determined as follows:

$$C_1=\frac{\cos n(\cos n-1)+\sin n(\sin n-n)}{(\cos n-1)^2+\sin n(\sin n-n)};\ C_2=\frac{n\sin n}{(\cos n-1)^2+\sin n(\sin n-n)};$$

$$C_3=\frac{1-\cos n}{(\cos n-1)^2+\sin n(\sin n-n)};\ C_4=\frac{-\sin n}{(\cos n-1)^2+\sin n(\sin n-n)}.$$

Then the expression for deflections will look like this:

$$\mu(\xi)=\frac{\cos n(\cos n-1)+\sin n(\sin n-n)+(n\sin n)\xi+(1-\cos n)\cos n\xi-\sin n\sin n\xi}{(\cos n-1)^2+\sin n(\sin n-n)}. \quad (8)$$

Let us write the second derivative

$$\mu''(\xi)=-n^2\frac{(1-\cos n)\cos n\xi-\sin n\sin n\xi}{(\cos n-1)^2+\sin n(\sin n-n)}. \quad (9)$$

The equation of the bending moment will look like this:

$$M=-EJ_z\frac{b}{l^2}\mu''(\xi)=-\frac{EJ_zb}{l^2}n^2\frac{-(1-\cos n)\cos n\xi-\sin n\sin n\xi}{(\cos n-1)^2+\sin n(\sin n-n)}=$$
$$=Pb\cos\alpha\frac{(1-\cos n)\cos n\xi-\sin n\sin n\xi}{(\cos n-1)^2+\sin n(\sin n-n)}. \quad (10)$$

The stresses arising in the buffer rail when one of its ends is moved to the rated value with the hydraulic rail replacement device are determined by the formula:

$$\sigma=\frac{N}{A}+\frac{M}{J_z}y, \quad (11)$$

where A is the cross-sectional area of the rail, equal to 82.65 cm^2, $J_z=564$ cm^4, y is the distance to the furthest point.

Results

Based on the derived equations of deflections and bending moments, stresses in different sections of the rail were determined. Their values are given in Table 1.

Table 1. Stresses arising in sections when one of ends of a stressed rail is released.

Parameter	Distance from the end, m:						
	0	1	2	3	4	5	6
Deflection, m	0.16	0.15	0.12	0.08	0.04	0.01	0.00
Bending moment, kN·m	-4.67	-5.05	-3.23	0.00	-3.23	-5.05	-4.67
Stress, MPa	-62.17	-67.16	-42.95	-0.06	-42.95	-67.16	-62.17

The maximum edge stresses arising in sections during the release of the stressed rail reach 67.16 MPa. They do not exceed the maximum allowable edge tensile stresses in the rail foot (240 MPa). Therefore, plastic deformations will not occur in the rail if the length of its bending part will be 6 m. The hydraulic rail replacement device can be used to replace temperature-stressed rails of CWR tracks.

The Department of Track and Track Facilities, Siberian Transport University, in collaboration with the Road Design and Engineering Office of the West Siberian Railway, developed a buffer rail replacement process for CWR tracks using KB-65 separate clip-bolt fastenings with plates, and then launched this process into production. A patent [11] was obtained. The features of this operating procedure are detailed in [12].

Over the past years, track sections with KB-65 fastenings throughout Russia have been replaced for fastenings that have a small number of elements and are less metal-intensive. These include Russian products – ZhBR fastenings of various modifications (for reinforced concrete sleepers) and APC-4 (anchor-type fastenings), as well as imported fastenings – *W*-30 (*Vossloh*) and *P*-350 (*Pandrol*).

Screw-dowel rail fastenings without plates, ZhBR-65Sh and *Vossloh* W-30, are of particular interest. These types of fastenings are promising: they ensure smooth movement and effective interaction of rolling stock with track superstructures.

In this connection, a technological process and a process chart were developed to replace temperature-stressed rails with screw-dowel fastenings (*W*-30 and ZhBR-65Sh). A schedule for replacement of stressed buffer rails with *W*-30 fastenings (*Vossloh*) is presented in Figure 3.

The work is carried out by a track repair team of eight members [13].

Prior to closing the relevant section for train traffic and beginning the replacement of buffer rails, preparatory steps should be taken: pulling screws of rail fastenings in anchoring sections (50 m away from the rail to be replaced in both directions) [9]; loosening and removal of four fish bolts (second and fifth ones) at two joints.

After the completion of the preparatory steps listed above, the relevant section is closed for train traffic. The work area is fenced in accordance with [14].

W-30 rail fastenings are dismantled from joint sleepers. The rail is lifted with a hydraulic jack. A pad is removed from the rail foot on the joint sleeper, which is on the side of the buffer rail.

The next steps are dismantling the rail joint and assembling the hydraulic rail replacement device. The device is activated. Pressure is created in the hydraulic system of the device. This transfers a separating force to wedge clamps. In this state, the hydraulic device functions as a joint plate. This prevents the rail from being released and ensures safety at work.

Then fastening elements are removed from the temperature-stressed buffer rail at 10 sleeper ends on the side of the hydraulic rail replacement device (on the inner side). On the outside of the rail, elastic clips are moved to the mounting position [15]. In this case, the length of the released rail will be 6 meters, which corresponds to the design model (Fig. 2) for determining edge stresses in the rail foot.

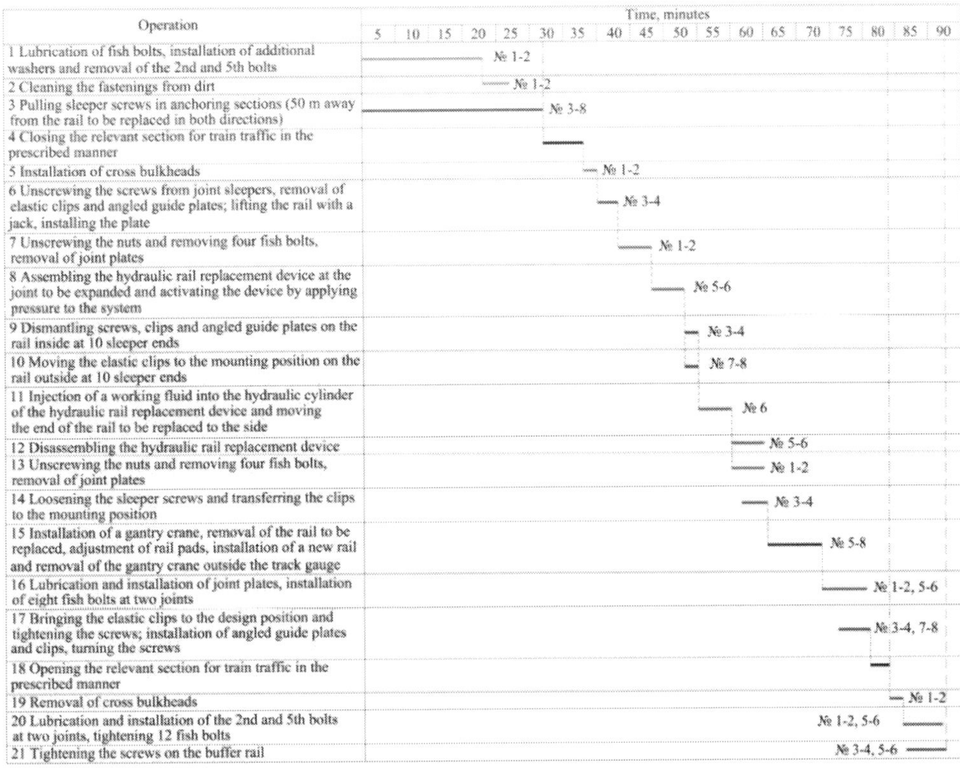

Fig. 3. A schedule for replacement of stressed buffer rails with the *W*-30 (*Vossloh*) screw=dowel rail fastening without plates.

After releasing a part of the rail from connections with the base, the end of the stressed rail can be moved to the side using the hydraulic rail replacement device. The end of the buffer rail is moved to the side up to the width of the rail foot and a small gap to ensure free longitudinal rail movement. In this case, the deformed axis of the bending part of the buffer rail will correspond to the design model (Fig. 2). Values of deflection are given in Table 1. Wedge clamps of the device are wedged. The hydraulic rail replacement device is disassembled.

Simultaneously with the removal of the hydraulic device, the joint plates on the second joint are dismantled. The elastic clips of the fastenings on the stressed part of the rail are moved to the mounting position [15].

Then the rail is replaced. A gantry crane is used to remove an old rail and install a new one [13].

After laying a new buffer rail of a shorter length, joint plates with four bolts at each joint are installed on both rail joints. Intermediate fastenings are installed along the entire length of the rail. Then track is opened for train traffic in the prescribed manner.

At the final stage, the remaining four bolts are installed. Nuts of all 12 fish bolts are tightened. In addition, the sleeper screws are tightened along the entire length of the buffer rail.

The total duration of on-track operations that require the section to be closed for train traffic is 55 minutes.

Conclusion

Using the derived equations of deflections and bending moments, as well as calculated edge stresses at the rail foot arising from its bending with the hydraulic rail replacement device, the feasibility of the proposed technology for replacing temperature-stressed continuous welded rails was justified. The developed technology will allow rails to be replaced without flame cutting. In this case, rails can be reused many times after seasonal replacements. The research results will contribute to timely maintenance of buffer spans and resource saving by increasing the life cycle of the basic element of track superstructures – the rail. The practical value of the proposed technology is that it ensures the safety and mechanization of work.

The technologies developed for KB-65, ZhBR-65Sh and *Vossloh W*-30 are applicable to 70% of the total length of continuous welded rail tracks in Russia. The proposed technologies are also applicable to railways of other countries that use similar fastenings. Further research may be aimed at improving the technology for replacing stressed rails for the considered and other types of intermediate fastenings. This will improve safety and reduce the time of maintenance.

References

1. P. Wang , K. Xie, L. Shao, L. Yan, J. Xu, R. Chen, Smart Materials and Structures, **25**, 015019 (2016).
2. H.-U. Bae, J.-Y. Choi, J. Moon, N.-H. Lim, Journal of Rail and Rapid Transit, **230**, 747-758 (2016).
3. P. Wang, K. Xie, R. Chen, L. Shao, L. Yan, H. Liu, M. Zhang, Journal of Sensors, **2016**, 3917604 (2016).
4. V.M. Ermakov, M.A. Egorov, Railway Track and Facilities, **9**, 25-29 (2015). (in Russian)
5. V.I. Novakovich, Railway Track and Facilities, **11**, 2-4 (2008). (in Russian)
6. N.Ö. Bezgin, 4th International Conference on Welding Technologies and Exhibition (Gaziantep, Turkey, 2016).
7. G.G. Zhulev, RU Patent 2045601 (1995). (in Russian)
8. Instrukcija po ustrojstvu, ukladke, soderzhaniju i remontu besstykovogo puti [Instructions for the installation, laying, maintenance and repair of a continuous welded path], of 14.12.16 No. 2544/p (Moscow, 2016). (in Russian)
9. G.G. Zhulev, RU Patent 2064027 (1996). (in Russian)
10. S.A. Kosenko, R.V. Shangin, A.S. Shurugin, S.S. Akimov, Modern Technologies. System Analysis. Modeling, **3(47)**, 187-190, (2015). (in Russian)
11. A.S. Shurugin, R.V. Shangin, S.A. Kosenko, S.S. Akimov, N.N. Starovoyt, RU Patent 2643324 (2018). (in Russian)
12. S.A. Kosenko, A.S. Shurugin, O.G. Yudin, S.S. Akimov, Transport of the Urals, **2(49)**, 44-47 (2016). (in Russian)

13. Tehnicheski obosnovannye normy vremeni na raboty po tekushhemu soderzhaniju puti [Technically justified time limits for work on the current track content], of 30.03.2009 (ed. 2015). (in Russian)
14. Instrukcija po obespecheniju bezopasnosti dvizhenija poezdov pri proizvodstve putevyh rabot [Instructions for ensuring the safety of train traffic in the manufacture of track works], of 14.12.16, No. 2540/p (Moscow, 2016). (in Russian)
15. Instrukcija na sborku, ukladku i jekspluataciju puti s promezhutochnym rel'sovym skrepleniem tipa W 30 na zhelezobetonnyh shpalah [Instruction for assembly, laying and operation of a track with an intermediate rail fastener type W 30 on reinforced concrete sleepers], of 31.01.2014, No. 225p (Moscow, 2014). (in Russian)

Linear structure taxonomy with the account of environmental polystructures impact

Tatyana Bobrova[1,*], and *Valeriy* Vorobyev[2]

[1]Siberian State Automobile and Highway University (SIBADI), 644080 Omsk, Russia
[2]Siberian Transport University, 630049 Novosibirsk, Russia

Abstract. One of the specific features of transportation facilities design is the necessity to account changing environmental conditions in considerable distances along the track. The purpose of the study is theoretical substantiation of structural decomposition of linear structures based on the degree of uniformity of environmental factors effect on the geotechnical system of an object. A new approach to linear road zoning is suggested on the basis of comprehensive assessment of multidimensional spatial data on the environment. Theory of pattern recognition is used as a classification tool. Linear structure taxonomy, as a part of this theory, is based on hierarchical agglomerative clustering algorithms which provide consequential merge of operating territorial units into uniform linear complexes. Application of taxonomy methods is considered for automated tasks solving on various levels of roads information modeling: when designing structures, organizing construction and operating a facility.

Introduction

Various aspects of the impact of environmental polystructures on a linear structure are considered with respect to the stage of its life cycle. For the purpose of control of road structures with the account of environmental factors impact, regulatory documents and design guidelines adopted in different countries provide the use of systematized territorial zoning data [1-5]. Today, development of reliable road structures requires building regional climatic models and using special software to include the optimization techniques in the design process [6-8].

Various approaches exist for solving road climatic zoning issues, they are based on assessment of various conditions, including environmental and climatic, geological and geographical, physico-climatic parameters of the territory [5, 9]. Differentiation methods (division of territories) used for transport infrastructure design are developed on the basis of the general theory of physico-geographic zoning with the account of the industry peculiarities. Road climatic zoning of the type "zone-subzone-district" is carried out with the application of structured approach principles using correlation and regression analysis methods, as well as methods of principal components analysis, parameters gradation and cluster analysis [10-12]. Weather stations and zero-dimensional objects located on the road

* Corresponding author: bobrova.tv@gmail.com

© The Authors, published by EDP Sciences. This is an open access article distributed under the terms of the Creative Commons Attribution License 4.0 (http://creativecommons.org/licenses/by/4.0/).

network are taken as structured space objects. Territorial zoning enables to assess the chosen route direction on the pre-project phase and to substantiate the essential structural solutions. At the same time, design faults related to underestimating of environmental factors variability in a certain geological and geomorphological situation lead to intolerable deformations and structural failures on the road sections during operation [13]. It is especially important to prevent faults and adopt adequate design solutions in complex climate conditions [9].

Bigger number and higher accuracy of parametric characteristics of environmental polystructures are required on the stage of designing certain elements of a linear object. Solving this task becomes ever more relevant with the development of road information modeling (RIM) technology. A new technological framework is formed in economics today in Russia and other countries which is related to information and digital technologies. The RIM technology differs considerably from on-site structures modeling. This technology is primarily aimed at providing automatic calculations of parameters in relation with multidimensional spatial data on natural environment at different design stages [14, 15].

The purpose of the study is theoretical substantiation of structural decomposition of a linear structure by the level of uniformity of environmental factors impact, and development of mathematical model for its implementation in a CAD system. In contrast to the previously applied zoning principles, the approach used in the study is based on unstructured data representation in the form of cluster of linear elements. The main input data for modeling in the form of environmental factors characteristics on elements (stations) are formed on the stage of surveying along the object trace.

Research methods

Multiple theoretical substantiations of zoning are based on hierarchical division of the studied objects into classes according to similarities and differences of their essential attributes. This approach takes its basis in the theory of pattern recognition (PRT), in which a pattern denotes a combination of data on an information object. The data include quantitative parameters obtained with the use of measurement systems or mathematical models [16]. Any recognition algorithm can be presented as an abstract functional system R consisting of thee components:

$$R = \{A, S, P\}\,, \tag{1}$$

where $A = \{A_k\}$, where $k = 1, \dots, K$ – alphabet of classes – aggregation of categories to which patterns are distributed, $S = \{S_j\}$, $j = 1, \dots, n$ – attributes dictionary – aggregation of characteristics which are used to describe the patterns, $P = \{P_l\}$, where $l = 1, \dots, L$ – number of rules for decision making.

Depending on the peculiarities of information components of system R three approaches to pattern recognition are distinguished: 1) template matching; 2) clusterization (taxonomy); 3) similarity of properties. In this system taxonomy is considered as a science dealing with classification and systematization of structures with complex organization. Choice of mathematical method depends on classification purposes applicable to components of "polystructural environment - linear transportation facility" system, as well as on the life cycle phase of the object: design, construction, operation.

Object of the study is a complex of a linear object and natural environment represented in CAD system using survey data. At this stage, calculations are highly detailed and are done with parametric modeling based on input data. For adopting reasonable structural solutions data of ground penetrating radar scanning along the axis of the road, right-of-way space and cross-section are used. Survey documentation includes detailed characteristics of engineering geological units (EGU) and their state. Road can be represented as an aggregate of structurally similar sections adapted to the geocomplex conditions.

According to the selected PRT method - taxonomy - let us define the peculiarities of this method that are related to linear extended elements of transportation facilities, primarily to subgrade and road pavement for motorways. The input data is presented in GIS for transportation in the form of multidimensional spatial data. The term "multidimensional" is related to attributive indicators (numerical and order ones) of various environment characteristics, whereas the term "spatial" specifies location of these data with a station mark on the road axis. To reduce the scale, transition to operational territorial units (OTU) was performed due to integration of station sequences. Integration is performed until the value of at least one indicator exceeds the standard values of coefficient of variation (for physical parameters - 0.15; for mechanical parameters - 0.30). Thus, before taxonomy procedure starts, the road is divided into discrete OTUs with the average values calculated on the stations integrated in a single OTU. Then, the input data are presented in the form of "OTU - attribute" incidence matrix. As a result of applying standard classification algorithm [17] OTUs are grouped into geographically distributed classes (taxa) with relatively uniform environmental conditions. With the account of the industry specificity, these taxa are denoted as linear road complexes (LRC), and the process of taxonomy development on the level of a CAD model – as linear road zoning.

Euclidean distance is used to assess similarities (differences) between OTUs in *N*-dimensional fuzzy attribute space. Classification is aimed at obtaining a certain predetermined number of groups (classes) of OTUs $S_1, \dots, S_K$. Within one group, OUTs shall possess the maximum degree of "similarity", and OTUs that belong to different groups - the maximum degree of "difference". The paper [18] gives the following mathematical interpretation of OTUs classing. If a set of OTUs is written as $O = \{o_1, \dots, o_N\}$, where o_i – ith OTU, N – number of OTUs, then the result of classing is represented by an *N*-dimensional vector $v = (v_1, \dots, v_N)$, $v_i \in \{1, \dots, K\}$ of OTU pertaining to one of the classes S_j:

$$v_i = j \Leftrightarrow o_i \in S_j,\ i \in \{1, \dots, N\},\ j \in \{1, \dots, K\}. \tag{2}$$

Various standard methods are used to make the final decision on the number of classes [16]. The experience of using taxonomies for road objects showed that formal criteria of classification can lead to excessive division of territorial units into classes, and consequently, to bigger number of LRCs of smaller length. The final decision on structural decomposition of a linear object according to environmental conditions (in other words, on the number of classes) shall be made by a design engineer on the basis of analytical data obtained when applying taxonomy algorithm. To fulfill the set task it is convenient to apply the method of automatic visualization of classification using the ER-model or relational data model [18]. Simpler models can be used, such as bar graph, to demonstrate average values of environment attributes and coefficient of attributes variation by placing them next to the corresponding class (LRC).

The result of linear taxonomy implementation is decrease in dispersion of environmental factors within a LRC. Quality indicators of a road structure such as strength, robustness, reliability, etc. are functionally connected with qualitative parameters of environment, which are the basis of the most part of design calculations. Using the formula for error propagation known from the probability theory, variance of a function (result) is defined based on the variance of its elements:

$$\sigma_F^2 = \sum_{i=1}^{n} \left(\frac{\partial F}{\partial x_i}\right)^2 \cdot \sigma_{x_i}^2, \tag{3}$$

where F – the considered function, variance of which σ_F^2 is sought; $x_i, \sigma_{x_i}^2$ – element of the function (argument) and its variance.

This formula indirectly defines the necessity of forming such structural units based on area or length, within which uniform road structures will possess similar strength and robustness parameters. Further research suggests assessment of output response parameters of road structures caused by changes in variation of environmental factors parameters. This may serve as a basis for control and optimization of LRC length on a linear structure.

Results and application

The described method was used for developing design documentation for a road section with the length of 47.4 km located in the permafrost region. The average coefficient of variation of environmental factors parameters on the LRC did not exceed 20%, with 80% and higher on the road in general. Due to this, design solutions with higher degree of reliability could be implemented [19]. Table 1 presents the formulated suggestions on the use and development of taxonomy methods for linear objects at various design stage.

When performing information modeling, 6 levels of development of information model elements (LOD) are considered: pre-design, schematic design, design development (CAD), construction documentation, construction stage, as built [15]. Processing of information contained in geographical environment shall be performed at each level.

Table 1. Taxonomy methods in road information modeling system.

LOD	Spatial grading of natural environment	Group of classification factors for natural and man-made environment	Classification methods / criteria	Groups and elements of RIM for design	Decision area
Schematic design	Zone, subzone, road district	Climate, relief, geomorphology, hydrology, soil design paramters	Hierarchical division algorithm (territory division); post-hoc analysis / key factor	Standard structures of the object elements	Feasibility study, Environmental assessment
Design development	Station, OTU, taxon, LRC	Engineering survey data, special conditions (permafrost, seismic activity, etc.)	Hierarchical agglomerative mechanism (OTU clustering) / proximity measure: Euclidean distance	Detailed design of all elements in LRC section	Technical project, structural design, production drawings
Construction documentation;	LRC	Type and scope of works, technology, seasonality, resources	Methods of PRT: template matching, similarity of properties	Methods of work performance. Resource provision	Process design (construction management plan and project execution plan)

As built	Zone, subzone, maintenance section	Physico-climatic factors, azonal factors, man-made structures	Division of area by negative conditions parameters (snowfalls, blizzard, ice).	Parameters and state of road elements	Cost regulation, recruiting employees for work performance, maintenance routes

Implementation of taxonomy algorithm of a transportation facility was performed automatically using MS Excel. However, more advanced software is known [18]. When changing environmental conditions, the necessity to adjust project solutions may arise. Application of taxonomy allows making corrections in the process of road information modeling, i.e. performing variable design, adjusting certain previous solutions on taxonomy considering changes in factors of geocomplexes.

The final decision on formation of LRC is made by a design engineer based on visual presentation of automated zoning results. The following variants are possible: 1. Group sections with significant deviations on any regional factor in a separate linear complex (taxon); 2. Group adjacent sections of LRC or OTU if the suggested structural solutions of structural elements fulfill the standard requirements; 3. Adjust the LRC length by suggesting measures on changing natural environment conditions, for instance, due to engineering of drainage system, lowering of ground water level, etc.

Not only structural solutions are connected with spatial decomposition of a linear object, but also the peculiarities of process design and operation of an object (Table 1). On the level of a construction model, differences in structural solutions for LRC are accounted while designing construction management. Variations may concern methods of organizing flows, list of special squads, terms of works execution. Application of parallel flow method when executing works on LRC enables to reduce terms of construction.

When designing as-built level of a road model, most significant climate indicators are defined which affect the traffic conditions in winter season. This way, zoning of Western Siberia region was performed by three classification groups of the following environmental polystructures: snowfalls, blizzards and ice [20]. Linear division of roads during operation is connected with zoning and is performed with the account of regional and azonal factors, both natural and human-made: shelter belts, crash barriers, heavy cuts, etc.

Conclusion

The method of linear structure taxonomy provides scientifically proven approach to an object division into sections with more uniform environmental parameters. Such structural decomposition results in increase of reliability level and efficiency of design solutions. Inclusion of linear objects taxonomy method in the road information modeling system contributes towards solving the scientific problem of improving the level of automation while designing transportation facilities on various levels of project model development.

Information modeling of transportation facilities currently is at the early stage of development. The paper demonstrates the possibilities of taxonomy as an automation tool for solving tasks of natural environment zoning and decomposition of linear objects for designing reliable road structures. Improvement and development of the method is planned for various levels of road parametric modeling. Further research in the field are primarily related to substantiation of optimum LRC parameters while designing standard subgrade structures, as well as to the issues of efficient computer implementation of taxonomy for the purpose of linear extended objects zoning.

References

1. SP 34.13330.2012. Avtomobil'nye dorogi [Automobile roads] (MinRegion, Moscow, 2012). (in Russian)
2. R. Kleiziene, A. Vaitkus, J. Zidanaviciute, E. Marcinkevicius, Proceedings of the 10th International Conference „Environmental Engineering“ (Vilnius Gediminas Technical University Lithuania, April 27–28, 2017).
3. L. Jukneviciute-Zilinskiene, Baltic Journal of Road and Bridge Engineering, **Vol. 5** (1), 62-68 (September, 2010).
4. M.M. Shallal, S.E.M. Ahmed, IOSR Journal of Engineering, **Vol. 4**, Issue 4 (April), 13-26 (2014).
5. M.A. Elshaeb, S.M. El-Badawy, E.A. Shawaly, American Journal of Civil Engineering and Architecture, **Vol. 2**, Issue 3, 115-121 (2014).
6. American Association of State Highway and Transportation Officials (AASHTO), *Mechanistic-Empirical Pavement Design Guide: A Manual of Practice. Interim Edition* (Washington D.C., 2008).
7. Q. Li, L. Mills, S. McNeil, The Implications of Climate Change on Pavement Performance and Design. UD-UTC Final Report (2011).
8. J. Saha, *Evaluation of Climatic Effects on Pavement Performance using MEPDG* (LAP LAMBERT Academic Publishing, 2011)
9. P.N. Kachroo, N.G.K. Raju, Freeze-thaw Effects on Roadways (Approach to Pavement Design with Special Reference to Roads in Mongolia), International Seminar on the Appropriate Use of Natural Materials in Road, Ulaan-Baator 18-21 June 2002.
10. C.E. Zapata, W.N. Houston, *Calibration and Validation of the Enhanced Integrated Climatic for Pavement Design* (Transportation Research Board, Washington, D.C., 2008).
11. V. Efimenko, S. Efimenko, A. Sukhorukov, A. Yankovskaya, *IOP Conf. Series: Materials Science and Engineering*, **Vol. 71**(1), 012049 (2015).
12. V. Efimenko, S. Efimenko, A. Sukhorukov, *MATEC Web of Conferences*, **Vol. 143**, 01012 (2018).
13. E.A. Bedrin, A.M. Zavyalov, M.A. Zavyalov, *Obespechenie termicheskoj ustojchivosti osnovanija zemljanogo polotna avtomobil'nyh dorog* [Providing thermal stability of the road bed] (SibADI, Omsk, 2012). (in Russian)
14. D.S. Sarychev, A.V. Skvortsov, CAD & GIS for roads, **1**(8), 9-12 (2017). (in Russian)
15. STO AVTODOR 8.6-2016. Organizacionnaja i tehnologicheskaja podderzhka processov formirovanija informacionnyh modelej avtomobil'nyh dorog na vseh jetapah zhiznennogo cikla [Organizational and technological support of the generation of information models for highways at all life cycle stages] (Avtodor, Moscow, 2016). (in Russian)
16. L.N. Chaban, *Teorija i algoritmy raspoznavanija obrazov* [Theory and algorithms of pattern recognition] (Moscow, 2004). (in Russian)
17. T.V. Bobrova, A.A. Dubenkov, Vestnik of Tomsk State University of Architecture and Building. English version appendix, **1-4**, 134-141 (2013).
18. A.V. Zavarzin, Thesis of Candidate of technical sciences, Lomonosov Moscow State University, Moscow, 2003. (in Russian)
19. A.A. Dubenkov, Vestnik SibADI, **4**(32), 46-52 (2013). (in Russian)

20. Yu.V. Kodentseva, Thesis of Candidate of technical sciences, Siberian State Automobile and Highway University, Omsk, 2007. (in Russian)

Increasing the operational stability of running surfaces of aluminothermic welded rail joints by hot grinding

Marina Galay[1,*] and *Eduard* Sidorov[1]

[1]Siberian Transport University, 630049 Novosibirsk, Russia

Abstract. Welded joints have traditionally been a weak point in a design of continuous welded rail (CWR) tracks. Grinding can be used as a resource-saving technology. The purpose of this paper is to study the grinding technology for welded rail joints at different temperatures. The temperature in the weld grinding zone varied from 560 to 850 °C. Using methods of microstructural analysis and hardness measurement, it has been established that different temperature conditions for weld grinding lead to the creation of non-identical mechanical properties of metal and a surface structure of the rail head in the weld zone. As a result of the research, an optimum temperature range, 600 ... 560 °C, was determined. This range is recommended for grinding aluminothermic welded joints.

Introduction

At present, contact or aluminothermic welding methods are used to weld rails throughout the railway network [1, 2]. The strength of aluminothermic rail welds is lower than that of joints welded by contact welding [3]. One of ways to increase the strength of welded rail joints proposed in [4, 5] is to modify a thermite powder by titanium or zirconium. It has been shown that the modification decreases grain content in the weld structure. Strength tests of modified welded joints have demonstrated that they have higher wear resistance and contact fatigue than unmodified welds.

Scientists of the Japanese Railway Technical Research Institute have proven that defects in welds and strength reduction are caused by incorrect installation of casting molds on rails prior to aluminothermic welding. They studied effects of the geometry of casting mold installation on filling a welding mold with liquid metal [6].

Papers [7–9] report the results of studies aimed at improving the quality of welded rail joints after welding through normalization and surface plastic deformation. Normalization of welded rail joints provided the best results. It has been established that normalization excludes harmful effects of overheating in the heat-affected zone. However, a problem of implementing the normalization process in real conditions has not been solved yet.

This paper proposes a method for hardening welded rail joints by hot grinding. The purpose of the paper is to study effects from grinding of welded rail joints, which have

* Corresponding author: galayms@mail.ru

© The Authors, published by EDP Sciences. This is an open access article distributed under the terms of the Creative Commons Attribution License 4.0 (http://creativecommons.org/licenses/by/4.0/).

different residual temperatures after aluminothermic welding, on hardness and roughness. It should be noted that aluminothermic welded joints are now ground in two stages: hot grinding (immediately after removing a casting mold and burring) and cold grinding (at a weld temperature of less than 100 °C). The regulatory documents that describe the welding process by aluminothermic method [10] do not specify the temperatures at which hot grinding should be carried out. Moreover, a review of literature sources has shown that there is insufficient information on hot grinding of materials [11].

In the context of the current trend towards increasing the length of continuous welded rail tracks all over the world, this study, aimed at improving the operational stability of welded joints, is relevant.

Materials and research methods

12 samples were prepared for the study. Samples were produced by aluminothermic welding of 0.25-meter long rails. Rails and a welding thermite consisting of powdered metal aluminum and scales were used as initial welding materials [10].

After the end of the welding process, the samples were burred with hydraulic shears. Then the samples were ground at a different residual post-weld temperature of the weld metal, which varied from 850 to 560 °C. The temperature range 850 ... 560 ° C was selected experimentally. A value of 850 °C, which was recorded immediately after burring, was taken as the maximum post-weld temperature of the welded joint. 560 °C was taken as a lower limit of the temperature range since phase transitions had completed at this temperature. The metal temperature in the weld zone was measured by non-contact method using a Mastech MS6550A digital pyrometer. Samples were ground with an SShG-1 hydraulic grinding machine manufactured by SNAGA at a speed of 3,000 rpm and a cutting depth of 0.2 mm.

To measure the hardness and roughness of running surfaces of a rail weld, templates were cut using a UE-350 SA semi-automatic horizontal band saw machine. The hardness was measured with a HBRV-187.5 multi-purpose hardness tester by Rockwell method described in [12]. An indentation scheme for hardness measurement is shown in Figure 1. The surface roughness was measured with a MarSurf PS1 roughness measuring instrument in accordance with the procedure described in [13]. Microstructural studies were performed using a Carl Zeiss EVO50 microscope.

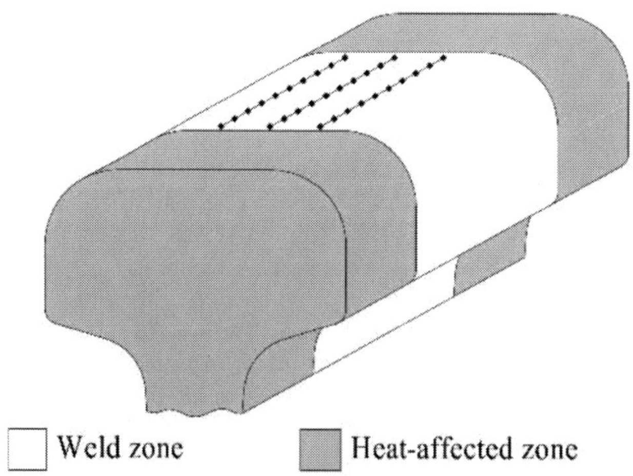

Fig. 1. Scheme of hardness test for welded rail joints.

Experimental data and results

Figure 2 shows hardness test results for the samples ground at different residual post-weld temperature of the rail. It should be noted that hardness values of the samples are in a wide range of 24 to 35 HRC.

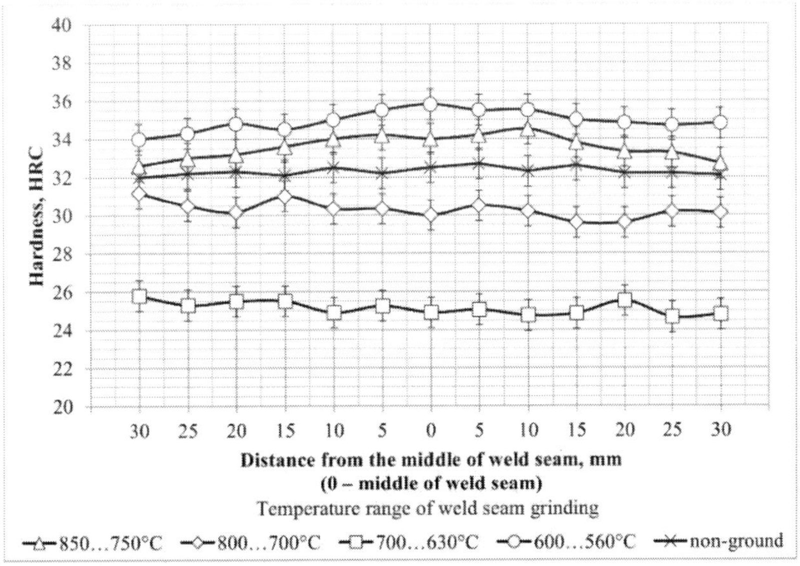

Fig. 2. Weld hardness distribution on the running surface of the rail head after grinding at different residual post-weld temperatures.

The maximum increase in the hardness up to 34...36 HRC is observed when a welded joint is ground at a temperature range of 600 to 560 °C. Since the pearlite structure deforms in this temperature range, work hardening is observed [14]. Grinding of welded rail joints in a temperature range of 850...750°C leads to the effect of high-temperature thermomechanical treatment, which is accompanied by deformation of austenite. However, the deformation of austenite does not persist due to dynamic recrystallization, which results in softening [15]. Therefore, when welded joints are ground in a temperature range 850...750°C, the hardness decreases to 24...26 HRC. Grinding of welded joints with a temperature of 800°C to 630 °C, leads to an increase to 4...6 HRC as compared to grinding in a temperature range 850...750 °C. A significant increase in the hardness seems to be due to the fact that the deformation is already taking place in the pearlite transformation zone, while the intensity of the dynamic recrystallization process is decreasing.

The microstructure of a weld that has not been mechanically treated during cooling is a cast structure of acicular low-carbon sorbite with ferrite in interdendritic layers (Fig. 3, a). The metal of welds exposed to hot grinding has a different structure (Fig. 3, b–e). Grinding in a temperature range of 850 ... 750 °C led to austenite deformation and, therefore, to the formation of a dispersed sorbitic structure. The exposure of the metal to lower temperatures in a range of 800 ... 700 °C was accompanied by deformation of austenite during its decomposition and the formation of an inhomogeneous microstructure with reduced hardness. Grinding in a temperature range of 700 ... 630 °C led to the formation of an inhomogeneous structure with globular pearlite sections and an increase in hardness as a result of the prevailing hardening process. The weld ground in a temperature range 600 ... 560 °C has a ferrite-perlite microstructure with grains stretched through deformation, which is confirmed by work hardening.

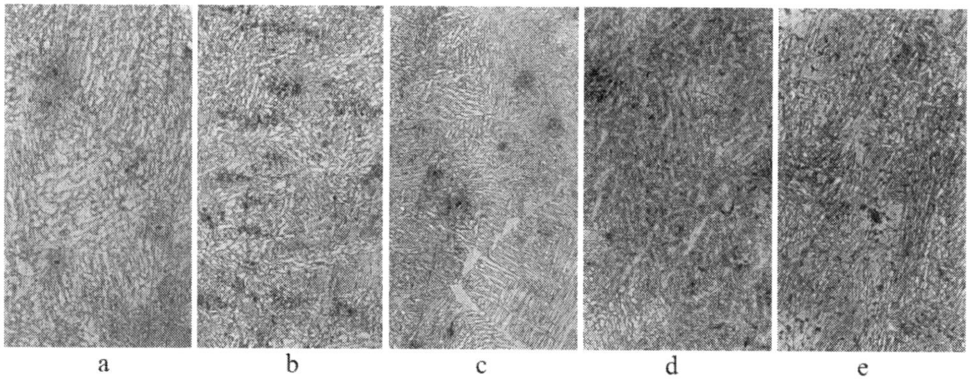

Fig. 3. Microstructure of an aluminothermic rail weld: a – without machining; b – after grinding in a temperature range of 850...750 °C; c – after grinding in a temperature range of 800 ... 700 ° C; d – after grinding in a range of 700 ... 630 °C; e – after grinding in the range of 600 ... 560 °C.

Effects from grinding of welded rail joints, which have different residual post-weld temperatures, on the surface roughness are presented in Figure 4.

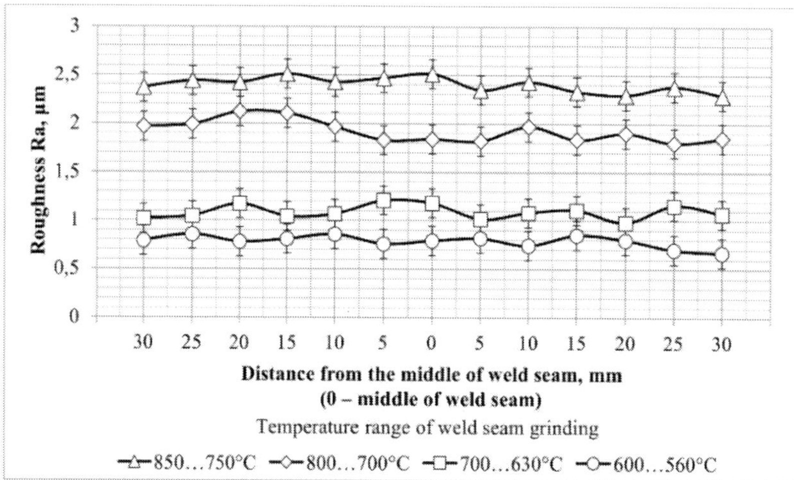

Fig. 4. Weld roughness distribution after grinding at different residual post-weld temperatures.

It can be seen from the graph that roughness values decrease with a decrease in the post-weld temperature of the weld. For example, when a welded joint with a residual post-weld temperature of 850...750°C is ground, the roughness varies from 2.3 to 2.6 μm. When a welded joint with a residual post-weld temperature of 600...560°C is ground, the roughness is equal to 0.6...0.8 μm. This is explained by the fact that in a range of 850...750 °C, much heat is concentrated in the cutting zone, which leads to significant softening of the metal in the surface layer and increase in the roughness. At grinding temperatures of 600...560°C, the thermal exposure decreases and the surface is deformed to a lesser extent.

Conclusion

As a result of completed studies, the authors developed a method to harden running surfaces of welded rail joints by grinding the material of the joint zone in hot condition. A recommended temperature range of a weld joint for post-weld grinding has been found to be 600...560 °C. It has been established that grinding of welded joints with this post-weld temperature provides a hardness level close to that of the base rail metal. Hardening of welds by hot grinding is a promising way to improving post-weld treatment processes for welded joints.

References

1. N.A. Kozyreva, A.A. Usoltsev, R.E. Kryukov, R.A. Shevchenko, P.E. Shishkin, *Innovacii v toplivno-jenergeticheskom komplekse i mashinostroenii* [Innovations in the fuel and energy complex and mechanical engineering (TEK - 2017)] Proceedings of the International scientific conference, 123-128 (Kemerovo, Russia, April 18-21, 2017).(in Russian)
2. S.E. Orlov, Railway Track and Facilities, 10, 26-28 (2016). (in Russian)
3. S.E. Aleksentseva, Vestnik of Samara State Technical University. Technical Sciences Series, **1(49)**, 130-137 (2016). (in Russian)
4. D.M. Costea, M.N. Gâman, G.T. Dumitru, Bulletin of the Transilvania University of Braşov CIBv, **Vol. 7(56),** Special Iss. 1, 285–288 (2014).
5. M. Brânzei, T. Coman, International Journal of Chemical, Molecular, Nuclear, Materials and Metallurgical Engineering, **Vol. 6,** 8, 745–748 (2012).
6. R. Yamamoto, Y. Terashita, M. Tatsumi, H. Itoh, K. Umenai, Quarterly Report of RTRI, **Vol. 57,** 2, 112–117 (2016).
7. V.A. Karguin, L.B. Tikhomirova, M.S. Galay, Ye.S. Kuznetsova, Welding International, **Vol. 29,** Iss. 2, 155–157 (2015).
8. L.B. Tikhomirova, A.S. Ilinykh, M.S. Galay, E.S. Sidorov, Obrabotka Metallov - Metal Working and Material Science, 1(70), 60–66 (2016). (in Russian)
9. V.A. Kargin, L.B. Tikhomirova, A.D. Abramov, M.S. Galai, Welding International, **Vol. 28 (3)**, 245-247 (2014).
10. TU 0921-337-01124323-2016. Railway rails welded in a thermite way. Technical specifications (Moscow, 2016). (in Russian)
11. N.I. Boyko, K.S. Fisenko, Engineering journal of Don, **T. 20** (2), 51-55 (2012). (in Russian)
12. GOST 9013-59. Metals. Method of measuring Rockwell hardness (Moscow, 2001). (in Russian)
13. GOST 2789-73. Surface roughness. Parameters and characteristics (Moscow, 2006). (in Russian)
14. L.M. Kaputkina, M.L. Bershteyn, V.A. Zaymovskiy, *Termomehanicheskaja obrabotka stali* [Thermomechanical treatment of steel] (Metallurgiya, Moscow, 1983). (in Russian)
15. L.I. Tushinskiy, A.A. Bataev, L.B. Tikhomirova, *Struktura perlita i konstruktuivnaja prochnost' stali* [Perlite structure and structural strength of steel] (Nauka, Novosibirsk, 1993). (in Russian)

Durability of operated reinforced concrete superstructures of railroad bridges

Stefan Efimov[1,*], *Sergey* Bokarev[1], and *Sergey* Pribytkov[1]

[1]Siberian Transport University, 630049 Novosibirsk, Russia

Abstract. The paper describes method to evaluate residual service life of reinforced concrete structures of railroad bridges, enabling to consider the presence of defects, operation history, and climatic factor to calculate probabilities of the structural state at any given moment of time. The model based on semi-Markov process was used to predict the state and calculate reliability indicators of structures and their elements. The data sources for reliability models are results of observations of the structural state, mathematical models of occurrence and development of defects. The example of determining residual service life of reinforced concrete superstructure is given based on the mathematical model of working reinforcement corrosion development.

Introduction

Over forty three thousand reinforced concrete superstructures are currently being operated on the railway network in the territory of the Russian Federation [1,2]. The major part is slab and ribbed structures which are mainly produced from conventional reinforced concrete and designed to sustain the loads of 1907, 1925, H7, H8, C14, etc. The range of the covered spans is from 1.3 to 16.5 m. The service life of 4.6% of superstructures, designed by the projects of 1911 to sustain the load of 1907 is >90-100 years. Superstructures designed to sustain the load of 1925 (2.6% of the total superstructures amount) are being under operation for 80-90 years, withstanding the load H7 (6.1%) and H8 (29.3%) – for 70-85 years. The service life of superstructures designed to sustain the load C14 (54.1%) does not exceed 50 years.

Apart from constant and temporary loads acting on reinforced concrete superstructures while operation they are also subjected to external environmental impacts, which generally have negative influence on reinforced concrete reducing its operation properties. Technical condition of the basic load bearing structures is generally determined by their service life, design features and operation conditions. According to the database of Automated Control System of Engineering Structures the relative number of superstructures on the network of "Russian Railways" JSC, having the following defects reducing the durability and load bearing capacity is as follows: the ballast depth under the tie above the admitted value – 20.9%; alkali washing of hardened cement paste – 20.1%; eccentricity of the railway over 5 cm – 19.6%; frost deterioration of concrete – 7.9%; delamination of reinforcement

* Corresponding author: esv@sgups.net

© The Authors, published by EDP Sciences. This is an open access article distributed under the terms of the Creative Commons Attribution License 4.0 (http://creativecommons.org/licenses/by/4.0/).

protective layer – 6.2%; longitudinal sidewall extended by over 20 cm – 4.8%; reinforcement corrosion – 2.4%; cracks along the rods of working reinforcement – 2.0%.

Considering the above data it can be noticed that the largest number of defects in maintenance of bridge deck is caused by such out-of-tolerance deviations [3] as ballast thickness layer and eccentricity of the railway. The next is negative water influence, as well as alternate freezing and thawing of concrete resulting in alkali washing and frost deterioration.

Materials and methods

Determining the residual service life is a required procedure in bridge operation. Up to date, this problem is not solved yet in the world practice [4, 5] and there are various approaches and ways to determine the standard and residual service life of reinforced concrete superstructures.

Foremost it should be clarified what residual service life means. Russian National State Standard GOST 32192-2013 [6] states that residual service life is operation time which is determined at the present moment of time before its transition into the limit state. This standard also defines that the limit state is the state when further operation is not possible and inappropriate due to risk assessment. Technical Regulations on Safety of Buildings and Structures (Federal Law No. 384) defines the limit state as the state when further operation is dangerous, constrained or inappropriate or recovering of operation condition is impossible or inappropriate. Keeping these definitions in mind it can be concluded that the limit state can be defined as non-operating state (further operation is not allowed) and the state when the recovery is not possible or irrational. This research was centered upon the assessment of the value of operation time before transition into non-operating state. Possibility and appropriateness to recover service life are the issues to be investigated.

The method to determine the residual service life suggested in the present work is based on the following background:

1. Adherence to the approach implemented in Instruction on State Estimation (scoring of the condition upon presence of defects of the superstructure) [7].
2. Complete correspondence to the National State Standard GOST 32192-2013 "Reliability of railroad engineering. The basic notions, terms and definitions" [6].
3. Implementation of the concept of methodology on resource, risks and reliability management at all the stages of lifecycle.

Let us define the parameters of objects under study, i.e. reinforced concrete superstructures. They are given as complex systems containing multiple elements. Each of the elements has its purpose and structure; each of them is generally subjected to the action of several factors and can have several various defects. There is an approach for engineering systems which consists in the use of particular reliability indicators (failure-free operation, durability, load bearing capacity, repair capability). These indicators characterize the ability of superstructure to fulfill the required functions.

During operation resulting from damages caused by various natural environment, climatic and man-made impacts defects occur in superstructures. Their condition deteriorates up to their complete failure. Thus, variety of possible states (Fig. 1) of both element and the structure on the whole includes:

1. Properly operating (index 0) – there are no defects, efficient, without speed limitations, complete residual service life;
2. Defective operating – completely operating states, characterized by presence of defects with various degree of development and reduced residual service life;
   - good (index 1) – defects with the least degree of development;
   - satisfactory (index 2) – defects with "medium" degree of development;

– unsatisfactory (index 3) – serious defects;

– pre-failure (index 4) – operating state with defects of maximum permissible degree of development, the residual service life is close to zero;

– when imposing speed limitation for the applied load or banning to pass separate types of rolling stock the object is considered as being in partly operating state (index 4.1);

3. Defective non-operating (index 5) – significant defects (up to destruction of load bearing structures), complete inability to fulfill its functions, the residual service life is over, moving is prohibited.

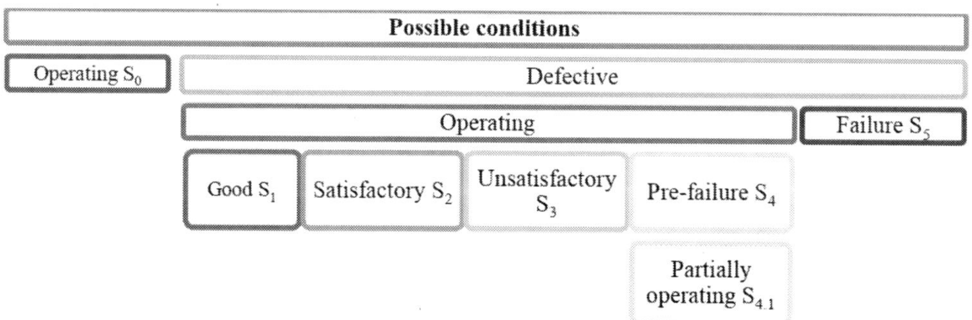

Fig. 1. Hierarchy of multiple possible states of the structure.

The residual service life of the element in operating state is equal to the standard one. Defective states differ by the degree of defects development. Pre-failure state is characterized by the borderline, maximum allowable degree of defects development. The structure could turn from pre-failure state into non-operating one. In pre-failure state the residual service life of the structure is almost over.

Deterioration of condition takes place due to occurrence of damages and growth of defects. The process of changing the condition is accidental. The possibility of failure leading to undesirable effects is defined according to the reliability models. In order to predict the state and calculate the reliability indicators of structures and their elements the model based on semi-Markov process is used.

The state model presented as semi-Markov process is set by distribution function matrix given in Figure 2. According to the model the probability of each of the possible states is determined at any pre-set moment of time.

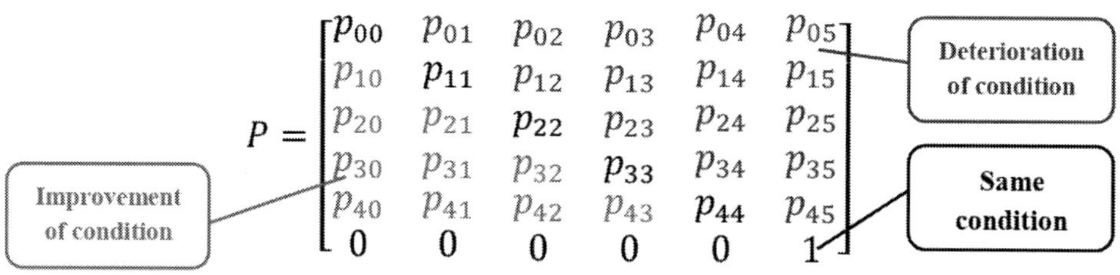

$$P = \begin{bmatrix} p_{00} & p_{01} & p_{02} & p_{03} & p_{04} & p_{05} \\ p_{10} & p_{11} & p_{12} & p_{13} & p_{14} & p_{15} \\ p_{20} & p_{21} & p_{22} & p_{23} & p_{24} & p_{25} \\ p_{30} & p_{31} & p_{32} & p_{33} & p_{34} & p_{35} \\ p_{40} & p_{41} & p_{42} & p_{43} & p_{44} & p_{45} \\ 0 & 0 & 0 & 0 & 0 & 1 \end{bmatrix}$$

Fig. 2. Transition probability matrix.

The data sources to build the reliability model can be results of observations from the database of Automated Control System of Engineering Structures (the observations mean inspections, surveying, testing and results of load bearing capacity calculations), mathematical models of occurrence and development of defects, as well as expert estimates. The preference should be given to statistics, as assessment based on the facts is better than experts' suppositions and theoretical conclusions. In case there is insufficient data on observations of the definite object, one needs to generalize observations of all the other objects similar to it. Provided that this data is also insufficient, one should appeal to mathematical models, and in the last turn to the experts' assessments. The calculation can determine the probability of failure during the pre-set time, the average time before failure, g-percentage service life (time before reaching the limit state with the given probability).

Results

Density of probability distribution of reinforced concrete superstructure being in one state before transition into the other state is complying with the distribution law of Veibull-Gnedenko with two parameters [8, 9, 10]. Probability density function looks as follows:

$$f(t) = \frac{\beta}{\eta}\left(\frac{t}{\eta}\right)^{\beta-1} e^{-\left(\frac{t}{\eta}\right)^{\beta}}, \quad (1)$$

where β is shape parameter;

η – scale parameter ("typical" service life).

The graphs of several of these functions *f(t)*, based on the statistical data processing of observing the state of reinforced concrete superstructures on the West Siberian railway according to database Automated Control System of Engineering Structures are given in Figure 3. It is rational to build these graphs for various roads or regions or to use climatic coefficient k_c.

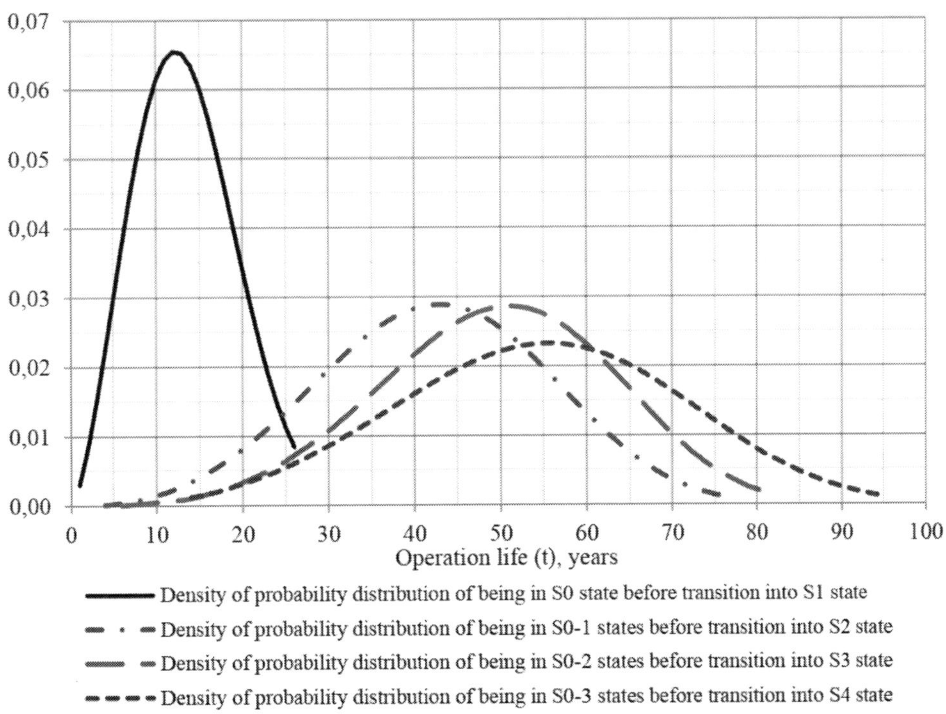

Fig. 3. Density of probability distribution of being in one state before transition into the other.

Let us consider the residual service life in details on the example of mathematical model of reinforcement corrosion development.

The time from the initiation of operation up to transition into S_4 state is determined according to the following formula [11, 12, 13]:

$$T_{0-4} = k_c(T_1 + T_4), \quad (2)$$

Where T_1 is the duration of corrosion initiation period), k_c – climatic coefficient, T_4 – time of corrosion development before the loss of reinforcing steel area reducing the load bearing capacity of the superstructure up to the level of applied loads (e.g. 10% of total area):

$$M_{prel} = M_{load}, \quad (3)$$

where $M_{prel} = f\{A_s(t)\}$, $M_{load} = f\{v(1+\mu)\}$.

In S_4 state the pass of load is only possible when the speed or mass is limited, when following the condition of:

$$M_{prel} > M_{load}. \quad (4)$$

The surface of reinforcement subjected to corrosion can be determined according to the following formula at any moment of time [11, 12, 13]:

$$A_s = A_{s,0}\left(1 - \frac{2}{d}C_э t^m\right), \quad (5)$$

where d is the diameter of working reinforcement, mm; $C_э$ – the velocity of reinforcement corrosion, within the interval of 0.08…0.3 mm/year; m – indicator of the corrosion degree, within the interval of 0.3…0.5; t – time from corrosion initiation up to the current or predicted state; $A_{s,0}$ – total reinforcement area not subjected to corrosion.

The condition of 10% loss of reinforcement surface area:

$$\frac{2}{d}C_э T_4^m \geq 0{,}1. \quad (6)$$

Thus, the time from initiation of corrosion development up to 10% loss of reinforcement surface area can be determined as follows:

$$T_4 = \left(\frac{0{,}05d}{C_э}\right)^{\frac{1}{m}}. \quad (7)$$

The time of transition from S_0 state into S_5 can be defined as:

$$T_{0-5} = T_1 + T_5, \quad (8)$$

where T_5 is the duration of corrosion development up to the loss of such reinforcement surface area when the ultimate force in the element will be equal to the force of train load not considering the dynamic coefficient $1 + \mu = 1{,}0$.

In S_5 state pass of the load is impossible.

Conclusion

As has been noted, reinforced concrete superstructures on the railway network are operated in various climatic zones and are to various extend subjected to the influence of negative environmental impacts. All these peculiar features are to be considered when determining the service life of reinforced concrete superstructures.

The suggested methods enable to account for the location region of reinforced concrete superstructure (e.g. by climatic coefficient), presence of existing defects (according to the acting Instruction [7] and Classifier [14]) and determine the probability of its state deterioration or failure. Based on the calculation, planning of the current maintenance is possible along with justification of the necessary repair works.

When conducting further studies it is necessary to take into account the economic feasibility of superstructures recovery with the aim of either their condition improvement or sustaining the current state of the structure up to its replacement. Apart from that, when calculating the residual service life of superstructures it is also required to account future planned reconstruction and repair works.

References

1. S.A. Bokarev, S.V. Efimov, Siberian Transport University Bulletin, 2, 10-20 (2016). (in Russian)
2. S.A. Bokarev, A.M. Karaulov, K.V. Korolev, S.V. Efimov, News of higher educational institutions. Construction, 4, 82-92 (2017). (in Russian)
3. CP-628. Instrukcija po soderzhaniju iskusstvennyh sooruzhenij [Instruction on the maintenance of artificial structures] (Ministry of Railways of Russian Federation, Moscow, 1998). (in Russian)
4. K. Gode, Construction science, **Vol. 15**, 11-18 (2014).
5. S. Rostam, Asian Journal of Civil Engineering (Building and Housing), **Vol. 6**, 15630854 (2005).
6. GOST 32192-2013. Dependability in railway technics. General concepts. Terms and definitions (Standartinform, Moscow, 2016). (in Russian)
7. Instrukcija po ocenke sostojanija i soderzhanija iskusstvennyh sooruzhenij na zheleznyh dorogah Rossijskoj Federacii [Instruction on the assessment of the state and content of artificial structures on the railways of the Russian Federation (OJSC "RZD", Moscow, 2006). (in Russian)
8. B.R. Levin, *Spravochnik po nadezhnosti* [Reliability Guide] (Mir, Moscow, 1969). (in Russian)
9. Metodicheskie ukazanija po ocenke riskov iskusstvennyh sooruzhenij [Methodological instructions for the assessment of risks of artificial structures] (OJSC "RZD", Moscow, 2018). (in Russian)
10. A.I. Orlov, *Matematika sluchaja. Verojatnost' i statistika – osnovnye fakty*, [Probability and statistics - basic facts] (Moscow, 2004). (in Russian)
11. A.I. Vasilyev, *Ocenka tehnicheskogo sostojanija mostovyh sooruzhenij* [Assessment of technical condition of bridge structures] (Knorus, Moscow, 2017). (in Russian)
12. V.P. Chirkov, *Osnovy teorii proektirovanija stroitel'nyh konstrukcij. Zhelezobetonnye konstrukcii* [Fundamentals of the theory of building structures design. Reinforced concrete structures] (Moscow, 1999). (in Russian)
13. V.P. Chirkov, *Prikladnye metody teorii nadezhnosti v raschetah stroitel'nyh konstrukcij* [Applied methods of reliability theory in calculations of building structures] (Marshrut, Moscow, 2006). (in Russian)
14. Klassifikator i normy porogovyh znachenij kriticheskih parametrov, harakterizujushhih predotkaznoe sostojanie iskusstvennyh sooruzhenij [Classifier and norms of threshold values of critical parameters characterizing the pre-failure state of artificial structures] (OJSC "RZD", Moscow, 2017). (in Russian)

Deformation properties of a subgrade in structures reinforced with full displacement piles

Alexey Lanis[1], *Denis* Razuvaev[1], and *Petr* Lomov[1,*]

[1]Siberian Transport University, 630049 Novosibirsk, Russia

Abstract. Construction of transport infrastructure facilities on weak subgrades requires special soil improvement measures. One of the advanced methods for deep subgrade soil compaction is known to be Full Displacement Piles (FDP). The purpose of this paper is to establish dependencies of subgrade deformation properties of a soil body reinforced with full displacement piles on reinforcement parameters and soil conditions. Using numerical simulation methods, the authors identified reinforcement parameters and initial soil indicators that have a significant effect on change in the deformation modulus of the reinforced body in the considered boundary conditions. Results of field experimental studies confirmed the reliability of the newly established relationships and regularities.

Introduction

When constructing a roadbed of transport infrastructure facilities in areas where weak clay soils prevail (with a deformation modulus of less than 5 MPa), including unfrozen subgrades [1], road builders face a problem of significant compressibility of a subgrade under operational loads and weight of facilities. In order to solve this problem and ensure stable operation of facilities, they use various methods to reinforce and compact subgrade soils.

A number of studies are underway to develop new and improve existing methods of soil reinforcement and compaction. They include reinforcement of soils with concrete piles [2, 3, 4], soil compaction using internal vibratory compactors [5], soil reinforcement by jet grouting [6, 8, 10], and combined reinforcement methods [13].

Deep compaction by Full Displacement Piles (FDP) is the most interesting method for transport construction [11]. This subgrade soil improvement method has proved to be effective in industrial and civil construction [11, 12]. The key barrier to wide-scale adoption of this reinforcement method in transport construction is lack of functional dependencies of deformation modulus on soil indicators, which can be used to determine deformation parameters of the reinforced body that are applicable to linear structures and take into account their features.

* Corresponding author: LomovPO@mail.ru

© The Authors, published by EDP Sciences. This is an open access article distributed under the terms of the Creative Commons Attribution License 4.0 (http://creativecommons.org/licenses/by/4.0/).

Subgrades of linear structures, including railways and motorways, are characterized by a wide variety of soil conditions, even within a single construction site. In this connection, theoretical justification and calculation of reinforcement parameters based on available geotechnical data is a highly relevant problem.

Since one of the key performance criteria for roadbeds on a weak subgrade is limited ultimate settlement of a structure, the purpose of this paper can be formulated as follows: to establish dependencies of deformation properties of a reinforced subgrade on FDP reinforcement parameters and initial soil conditions. In order to accomplish this purpose, it is reasonable to use numerical simulation and field experiments based on multivariate analysis of variance using a Latin square design [15]. This approach has proved to be highly effective [13] and can be used to identify, with sufficient accuracy, the reinforcement parameters that have a significant effect on the performance of the structure under study [15].

The novelty of the paper consists in theoretical justification and calculations for the FDP reinforcement method, which are required to select subgrade soil reinforcement parameters for linear transport structures (roadbeds) with initial soil conditions varying with length and, if necessary, a required deformation modulus.

Research methods

The performance of a subgrade reinforced with full displacement piles was studied by numerical modeling with GTS NX software and full-scale field experiments.

Numerical simulation enables to identify the reinforcement parameters that have a significant effect on the performance of the reinforced body, and establish the critical regularities. The reliability of numerical simulation data can be verified on the basis of field experiments.

A review of studies [11, 12, 14] shows that the reinforcement parameters that can influence soil reinforcement results include spacing l and diameter of reinforcing members d (hereinafter these parameters will be replaced with a reinforcement coefficient defined as $\xi=d/l$), as well as uniaxial compressive strength of pile material R. The key parameters that characterize change in initial soil indicators include void ratio e and liquidity index I_L.

The following varying boundary conditions (hereinafter referred to as the factors) were established for the selected reinforcement parameters and initial soil indicators: reinforcement coefficient — 0.25 to 0.50; strength of reinforcing member material — 0.2 to 1.0 MPa; soil liquidity index — 0.15 to 0.85 fractions; void ratio — 0.650 to 0.850.

When simulating the performance of the reinforced body, it is important to describe its properties adequately and reliably. A digital model of the reinforced body was constructed on the basis of field experiments, laboratory and theoretical studies [13, 14]. In the digital model, holes for full displacement piles were simulated with a varying diameter. An effective soil compaction zone around the holes was also taken into account.

In the model of a reinforced subgrade fragment, deformation modulus E was taken as an indicator of change in deformation properties of the body.

In order to estimate the compressibility of reinforced bodies and determine regularities of change in the deformation modulus, static load tests with a flat round plate were simulated in the digital model (Fig. 1).

Fig. 1. The digital model of the body reinforced ($\xi = 0.5$) with full displacement piles, and of the plate, built with the GTS NX software.

Field experimental studies of the reinforced bodies were conducted on experimental sites. The reinforced bodies were constructed with a GRO-250 soil compaction tool (Fig. 2 a) for soils with a liquidity index $I_L < 0.5$.

a b

Fig. 2. Displacement tools used to prepare experimental sites: *a* – GRO-250; *b* – displacement machine designed according to the RF Patent No. 147223.

For soils with a liquidity index $I_L > 0.5$, a special displacement machine with a hollow shaft (Fig. 2 b) was used. It was designed by the authors according to the RF Patent No. 147223 to fill holes with a grout, while lifting the displacement tool.

In order to study the compressibility of the soil bodies reinforced with full displacement piles, the authors used a flat round plate with an area of 5,000 cm^2, as shown in Figure 3.

Fig. 3. Flat round plate with an area of 5,000 cm^2.

Based on the results of numerical simulation and field experiments, the authors performed a correlation analysis to assess the reliability of the collected data.

Results of simulation and field experiments

The results of numerical simulation show that full displacement piles take up a major part of the stresses arising from plate loading. The highest stress release rate is observed at a depth of 2...2.5 times the diameter of the plate.

Vertical displacement diagrams for reference points of the digital model were used to determine the compressibility of the test fragment of the reinforced body at the subgrade (Fig. 4)

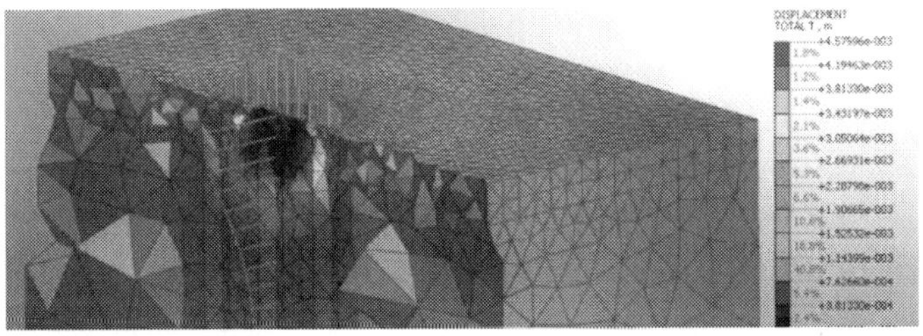

Fig. 4. Vertical displacement diagrams for reference points of the soil body reinforced with full displacement piles, in a plan view and in depth.

The vertical displacement diagrams for reference points were used to determine the deformation modulus of the reinforced body.

The analysis of the numerical simulation results shows that the effectiveness of soil reinforcement with full displacement piles depends directly on the reinforcement parameters and initial soil indicators. By relying on the obtained data, the authors assessed the influence and significance of individual factors on the performance of the reinforced body using an F-test according to the algorithm described in [15].

In soils with a liquidity index I_L of 0.45 to 0.85 fractions, the greatest effect of reinforcement can be achieved mainly by reducing reinforcement spacing and increasing the diameter of holes. The statistically processed results of numerical simulation are presented in Figure 5 as dependencies that reflect the influence of factors on the compressibility of the body.

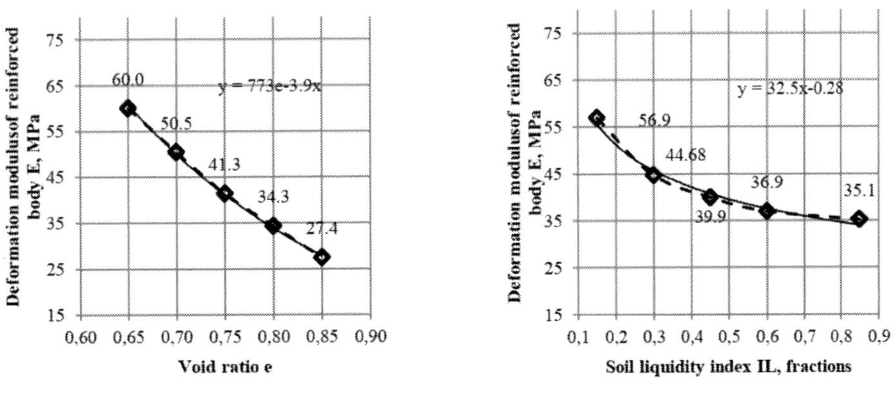

a b

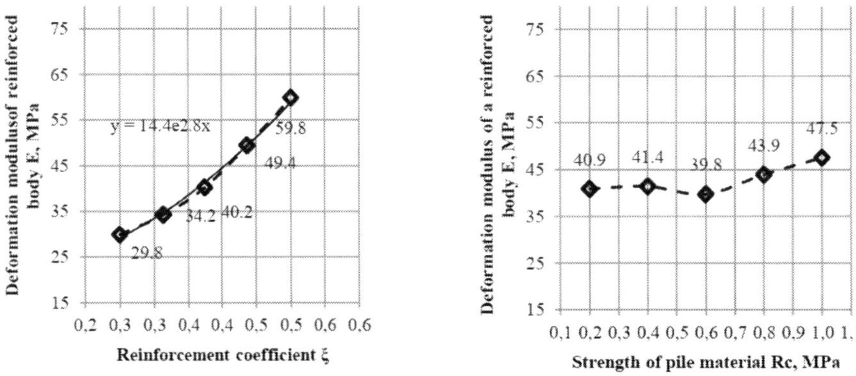

c d

Fig. 5. The dependencies that reflect the influence of reinforcement parameters and initial soil indicators on the deformation modulus of the body reinforced with full displacement piles: a – on void ratio; b – on liquidity index; c – on reinforcement coefficient; d – on pile material.

The F-test values [15] for the studied factors are given in Table 1. Using the obtained values, it is possible to determine the significant factors as follows: the factors whose test values exceed the critical value (for the purpose of this study F_{cr} = 3.2592) do not correlate with a mean of the sampled population and are significant for the tested mathematical model.

Table 1. F-test value.

Factor	F-test value	
	Actual, for E	Critical
Reinforcement coefficient	25.238	3.2592
Void ratio	28.963	
Liquidity index	13.167	
Material of full displacement piles (strength)	1.662	

By analyzing the obtained dependencies (Fig. 5) and F-test values (Table 1), we can conclude that soil conditions have a lesser effect on the compressibility of the reinforced body than spacing and diameter of full displacement piles. The strength of pile material has an insignificant effect as compared to other factors. Soil reinforcement by full displacement piles in soils with a liquidity index I_L exceeding 0.5 fractions is less effective. In such soil conditions, the greatest effect is achieved by reducing spacing and increasing diameter of piles. Three of the four studied factors contributed most to change in the deformation modulus of the reinforced body.

In order to use the results of numerical simulation in theoretical justification and calculation of reinforcement parameters for subgrade soils reinforced with full displacement piles, characteristic curves were plotted (Figs. 6 and 7).

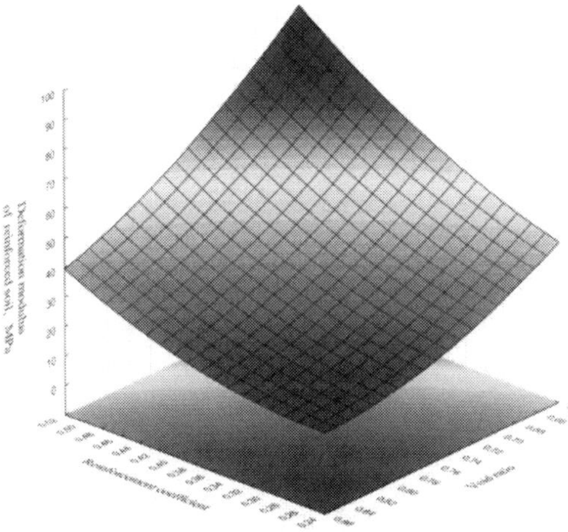

Fig. 6. Deformation modulus of the body reinforced with full displacement piles as a function of the reinforcement coefficient and initial void ratio.

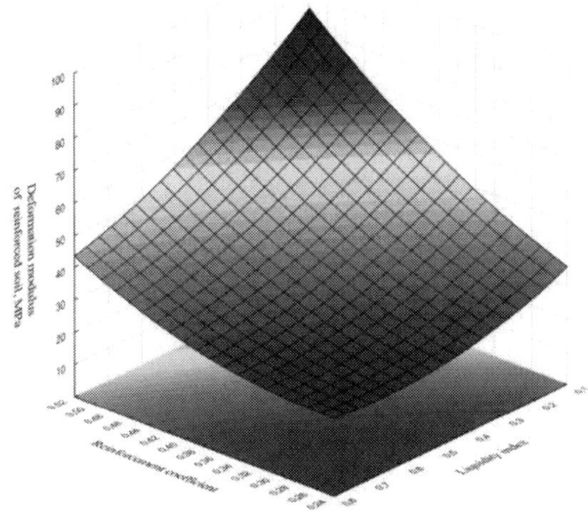

Fig. 7. Deformation modulus of the body reinforced with full displacement piles as a function of the reinforcement coefficient and initial soil liquidity index.

The results of field experiments are graphically represented in Figure 8 as dependencies that reflect the influence of reinforcement parameters and initial soil indicators on the deformation modulus of the reinforced body.

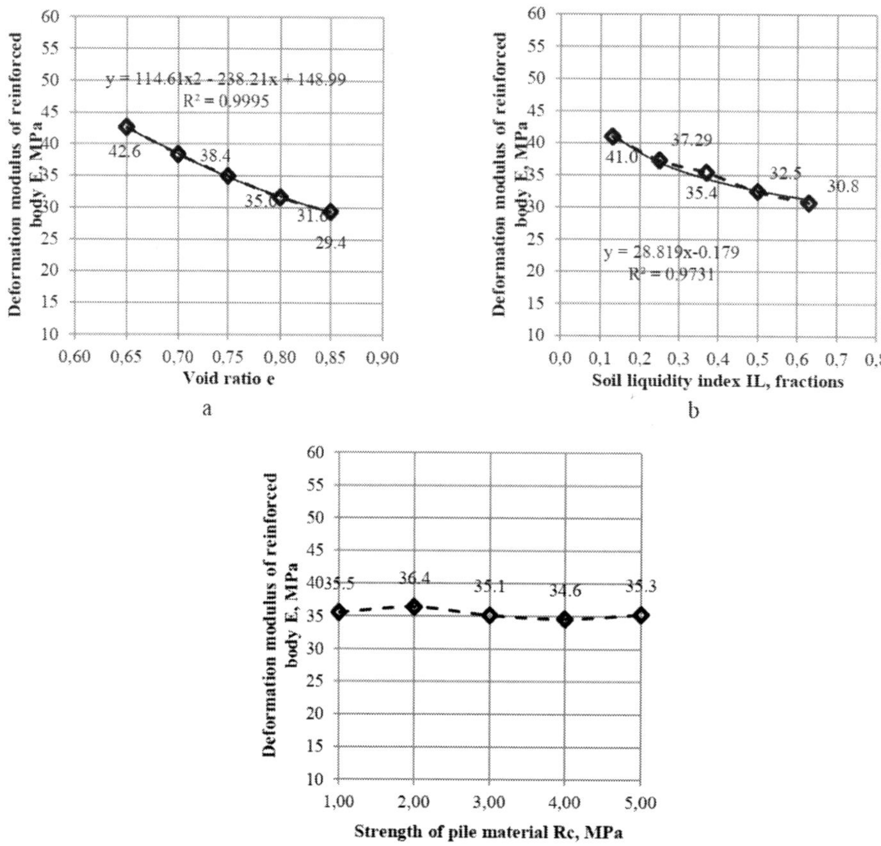

a b c

Fig. 8. Dependencies that reflect the influence of reinforcement parameters and initial soil indicators on the deformation modulus of the reinforced body, based on field experiments (at ξ=*0.25*): a – on void ratio; b – on liquidity index; c – on pile material.

The adequacy of digital models and correlation of numerical simulation data and experimental studies was assessed by the F-test. When performing a correlation analysis of the findings for soil reinforcement with full displacement piles, the authors considered sampled populations of deformations modules of the reinforced bodies, which were experimentally obtained and determined from the dependences shown in Figures 6 and 7 for the reinforcement coefficient ξ = 0.25 (at which all the experimental studies were conducted).

According to the correlation analysis, the F-test value for the deformation modulus E is equal to 1.314 at the critical value F_u=1.984. This suggests that the comparability of the results with the previously determined dependencies reaches 95%.

Conclusion

The performed studies of the full displacement piles (FDP) method allowed the authors to identify significant reinforcement parameters and establish functional dependencies of changes in deformation properties of the soil body reinforced with full displacement piles.

The obtained findings can be used to design reinforcements of subgrades with full displacement piles for linear transport structures with ground conditions varying with length and, if necessary, a required deformation modulus.

Further studies for developing the FDP method should be aimed at determining strength properties of a soil body reinforced with full displacement piles.

References

1. A.L. Lanis, D.A. Razuvaev, Sciences in Cold and Arid Regions, **9(3)**, 205-212 (2017).
2. T. Tronda, Proceedings of the International Conference on Deep Foundations, Seepage Control and Remediation, Deep Foundations, 225-231 (2016).
3. T. Tronda, Proceedings of the 8AYGEC, 155-158 (2016).
4. R.K. Kar, P.K. Pradhan, A. Naik, Electronic J. of Geotech., **17**, 3861-3874 (2012).
5. J. Grabe, E. Heins, T. Hamann, Sixth International Geotechnical Symposium on Disaster Mitigation in Special Geoenvironmental Conditions, 281–284 (2015).
6. K.M. Rollins, M. Herbst, M. Adsero, D. Brown, Advances in Analysis, *Modeling & Design*, Proceedings… ASCE, 1563-1572 (2010).
7. S.A. Tan, S. Tjahyono, K.K. Oo, Journal of Geotechnical and Geoenvironmental Engineering, **134**, 185-194 (2008).
8. J. Stacho, 16th International conference of PhD students with international participation, 1-8 (VUT in Brno, Czech Republic, 2014).
9. A.L. Gotman, M.N. Kharmatulin, SM&FE, **4**, 16-19 (2012).
10. G. Modoni, J. Bzowka, ASCE, **12**, 1442-1454 (2012).
11. A.N. Saurin, Papers of the International seminar on soil engineering, foundation engineering and transport works, 236–239 (2000). (in Russian)
12. A.L. Lanis, D.A. Razuvaev, P.O. Lomov, Vestnik SibADI, **2 (48)**, 110–120 (2016). (in Russian)
13. S.A. Ovchinnikov, Thesis of Candidate of technical sciences, Siberian Transport University, 2014. (in Russian)
14. A.L. Lanis, D.A. Razuvaev, P.O. Lomov, V.S. Vorobyev, News of higher educational institutions. Construction, **9** (705), 31-40 (2017). (in Russian)
15. K. Hartman, E. Letskiy, V. Shefer, *Planirovanie jeksperimentov v issledovanii tehnologicheskih processov* [Experiments planning in the study of technological processes] (Mir Publ., Moscow, 1977). (in Russian)

Use of the cross-type dowels when connecting elements of timber bridges

Anatoly Popov[1,*], and *Vladimir* Zinoviev[1]

[1]Siberian Transport University, 630049 Novosibirsk, Russia

Abstract. The use of cross-type dowels that are battered down with a gunshot method makes it possible to reduce labor intensity and speed up the process of erection and reconstruction of timber bridges. Objective of this paper is to develop a methodology for estimation of the permissible distance between dowels. For this purpose, the method of holographic interferometry in colliding beams was used. The resulting equations were obtained for the patterns of interference fringes observed in reflected light transmitted through the hologram. The investigations showed that the shear component of the strain tensor decreases exponentially with distance from the dowel. The concept of deformation attenuation constant was introduced, i.e. the distance at which the deformation decreases by e times. It is recommended to set dowels at a distance equal to eight attenuation constants.

Introduction

This paper [1] proposes to use dowels with x-shaped cross-section that are hammered by means of mounting guns. The gunshot method of making doweled connections can be fully appreciated by the builders who construct timber bridges in hard-to-reach areas. The spread of this method is promoted by the widespread use of mounting guns in the construction for the attachment of steel parts to brick or concrete structures. When hammering cross-sectioned dowels with knife sharpening with the mounting guns, a dense mortise is formed, which increases the reliability of the connection [2-3]. Until now, no methodology has been developed for determination of the permissible distances between dowels.
The study of the strain state of wood is complicated because of the large anisotropy of the material [4]. The optical methods for studying the strain state are used in the study of products made of various materials under various loading methods [5-6]. For the experimental determination of the permissible distance between the axes of the dowels, it is proposed to use the method of recording of holograms proposed by Yu. N. Denisyuk [7-11].

* Corresponding author: 47604@mail.ru

© The Authors, published by EDP Sciences. This is an open access article distributed under the terms of the Creative Commons Attribution License 4.0 (http://creativecommons.org/licenses/by/4.0/).

Study method

To derive the resulting equations of the patterns of the bands reconstructed by a double-exposure hologram, we consider the optical scheme for hologram recording shown in Figure 1. The path of the beams during the first exposure is represented by solid lines. During the second exposure, the lines are dotted. The photographic plate is located in front of the studied section of the product and is illuminated by a plane coherent light (Fig. 1). The pattern of the bands, which is recorded in the light passing through the recording medium, shall be determined by the interference of waves reflected from the surface of the product.

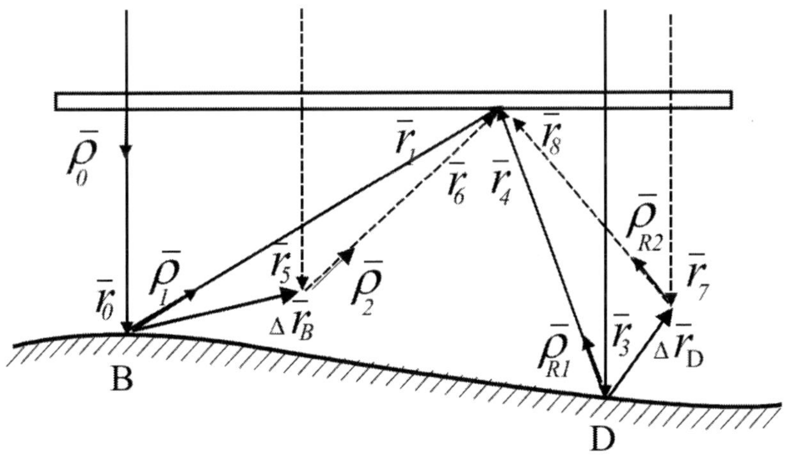

Fig. 1. Scheme of exposure optical path.

In the light reflected by a hologram, patterns are recorded that depend on the interference of the incident and reflected waves. Let us assume that $\vec{A}_{R1}$ is the wave vector of the reference wave, and $\vec{A}_1$ is the same for the object one. A photographic plate is illuminated by a light wave $\vec{A}_I$:

$$\vec{A}_I = \vec{A}_1 + \vec{A}_{R1} \tag{1}$$

The intensity of light is equal to the square of the modulus of the vector:

$$I_I = \vec{A}_I \cdot \vec{A}_I^* = \vec{A}_1^* \cdot \vec{A}_1 + \vec{A}_{R1}^* \cdot \vec{A}_1 + \vec{A}_1^* \cdot \vec{A}_{R1} + \vec{A}_{R1}^* \cdot \vec{A}_{R1} \tag{2}$$

Hereinafter, the symbol * denotes complex conjugation. Energy will enter the recording medium:

$$E_I = I_I t_1 \tag{3}$$

Here t_1 is the time of exposure.

Similarly to the second exposure:

$$\vec{A}_{II} = \vec{A}_2 + \vec{A}_{R2}\ ;\ I_{II} = \vec{A}_{II} \cdot \vec{A}^*_{II}\ ;\ E_{II} = I_{II} t_2 \tag{4}$$

Here $\vec{A}_2$ and $\vec{A}_{R2}$ are wave vectors of the object and reference wave; A_{II} -light wave illuminating the photographic plate; t_2 - second exposure time.

The coefficient of amplitude transmission T of the processed photographic plate is proportional to the obtained energy:

$$T \approx E = I_I t_1 + I_{II} t_2 \tag{5}$$

If the hologram is illuminated with light with a wave vector $\vec{A}_{RC}$, then it will reconstruct the light waves with the vector $\vec{A}_B$:

$$\begin{aligned} &\vec{A}_B = T\vec{A}_{RC} = (\vec{A}^*_I \cdot \vec{A}_I t_1 + \vec{A}^*_{II} \cdot \vec{A}_{II} t_2) \cdot \vec{A}_{RC} = \\ &[(\vec{A}^*_1 \cdot \vec{A}_1 t_1 + \vec{A}^*_2 \cdot \vec{A}_2 t_2 + \vec{A}^*_{R1} \cdot \vec{A}_{R1} \cdot t_1 + \vec{A}^*_{R2} \cdot \vec{A}_{R2} t_2) + \\ &+ (\vec{A}^*_{R1} \cdot \vec{A}_1 t_1 + \vec{A}^*_{R2} \cdot \vec{A}_2 t_2) + (\vec{A}^*_1 \cdot \vec{A}_{R1} t_1 + \vec{A}^*_2 \cdot \vec{A}_{R2} t_2] \cdot \vec{A}^*_{RC} \end{aligned} \tag{6}$$

Further, we will consider only the terms enclosed in the second brackets, they describe the virtual image, the third brackets describe the real one, and the first brackets describe the non-diffracted light:

$$\vec{A}_{BM} = [\vec{A}^*_{R1} \cdot \vec{A}_1 t_1 + \vec{A}^*_{R2} \cdot \vec{A}_2 t_2] \cdot \vec{A}_{RC} \tag{7}$$

The restored image will have an intensity:

$$\begin{aligned} &I = \left\{\left[\vec{A}^*_{R1} \cdot \vec{A}_1 t_1 + \vec{A}^*_{R2} \cdot \vec{A}_2 t_2\right]\vec{A}_{RC}\right\} \cdot \left\{\left[\vec{A}^*_{R1} \cdot \vec{A}_1 t_1 + \vec{A}^*_{R2} \cdot \vec{A}_2 t_2\right]\vec{A}_{RC}\right\}^* = \\ &= \left[\vec{A}^*_{R1} \cdot \vec{A}_1 t_1 + \vec{A}^*_{R2} \cdot \vec{A}_2 t_2\right] \cdot \left[\vec{A}^*_{R1} \cdot \vec{A}_1 t_1 + \vec{A}^*_{R2} \cdot \vec{A}_2 t_2\right]^* \cdot I_{RC}; \end{aligned} \tag{8}$$

Since, I_{RC} — the intensity of the reconstructing wave affects only the brightness of the image and having assumed $t_1 = t_2 = t$, then we will not take into account these parameters in the derivation of the resulting equations. In a complex form, the light wave vectors are represented as follows:

$$\vec{A}_1 = A_1 e^{i(-\vec{K}_1 \cdot \vec{r}_1 + \varphi_1)}\ ;\ \vec{A}_{R1} = \vec{A}_{R1} e^{i(-\vec{K}_{R1} \cdot \vec{r}_1 + \varphi_{R1})}\ ;$$

$$\vec{A}_2 = A_2 e^{i(-\vec{K}_2 \cdot \vec{r}_2 + \varphi_2)}\ ;\ \vec{A}_{R2} = \vec{A}_{R2} e^{i(-\vec{K}_{R2} \cdot \vec{r}_2 + \varphi_{R2})} \tag{9}$$

Here, the indices of the amplitudes A_k ($k =$ 1, R1, 2, R2), wave vectors $\vec{K}_k$ and initial phases φ_k indicate to which light vector they relate, $\vec{r}_i$ - the corresponding radius vectors. Let us denote:

$$-\vec{K}_1 \cdot \vec{r}_1 + \vec{K}_{R1} \cdot \vec{r}_1 + \varphi_1 - \varphi_{R1} = \alpha$$
$$-\vec{K}_2 \cdot \vec{r}_2 + \vec{K}_{R2} \cdot \vec{r}_2 + \varphi_2 - \varphi_{R2} = \beta \quad (10)$$

Then, if we assume that $A_1 A_{R1} \approx A_2 A_{R2} = A^2$:

$$\vec{A}_{R1} \cdot \vec{A}_1 = A^2 e^{i\alpha};\ \vec{A}_{R2} \cdot \vec{A}_2 = A^2 e^{i\beta} \quad (11)$$

In the virtual image, the intensity of light is described by the expression:

$$I \approx (e^{i\alpha} + e^{i\beta})^* \cdot (e^{i\alpha} + e^{i\beta}) = 2 + 2\cos(\alpha - \beta) \quad (12)$$

Maximum occurs under the following condition:

$$\alpha - \beta = 2\pi N, \quad (13)$$

Having substituted formula (10) into equation (13) and multiplying it by $\frac{\lambda}{2\pi}$, we obtain the following equation:

$$-\vec{\rho}_1 \cdot \vec{r}_1 + \vec{\rho}_{R1} \cdot \vec{r}_1 + (\varphi_1 - \varphi_{R1})\frac{\lambda}{2\pi} + \vec{\rho}_2 \cdot \vec{r}_2 - \vec{\rho}_{R2} \cdot \vec{r}_2 - (\varphi_2 - \varphi_{R2})\frac{\lambda}{2\pi} = N\lambda, \quad (14)$$

Here N is the number of the interference fringe; λ - length of the light wave; $\vec{\rho}_k$ - unit vectors directed along light waves.

The phase $\varphi_1 - \varphi_{R1}$ and $\varphi_2 - \varphi_{R2}$ differences in equation (14) are also constant and do not affect the distance between the bands. Therefore, they will not be taken into account. Then equation (14) takes the form:

$$(-\vec{\rho}_1 \cdot \vec{r}_1 + \vec{\rho}_{R1} \cdot \vec{r}_1) - (-\vec{\rho}_2 \cdot \vec{r}_2 + \vec{\rho}_{R2} \cdot \vec{r}_2) = N\lambda \quad (15)$$

Let us denote Δ_1, the terms in the first brackets (the path difference between the reference and object beam obtained at the first exposure), and in the second brackets - Δ_2 (the difference in the path of the same beams in the second exposure). Then, equation (15) takes the following form:

$$\Delta_1 - \Delta_2 = N\lambda \quad (16)$$

In accordance with Figure 1, the recording medium is illuminated by a plane wave with a unit vector $\vec{\rho}_0$, and the path difference of the light beams is calculated from it. The light waves corresponding to the first exposure are represented by solid lines, the second exposure - by dotted lines. It can be seen from the optical scheme that

$$\vec{r}_5 = \vec{r}_0 + \vec{W}_B; \quad \vec{r}_6 = \vec{r}_1 - \Delta\vec{r}_B; \ \vec{r}_7 = \vec{r}_3 + \vec{W}_D$$
$$\vec{r}_8 = \vec{r}_4 - \Delta\vec{r}_D; \ \vec{\rho}_2 = \vec{\rho}_1 + \Delta\vec{\rho}_{12}; \ \vec{\rho}_{R2} = \vec{\rho}_1 + \Delta\vec{\rho}_R \quad (17)$$

With this in mind, we determine the path differences Δ_1 and Δ_2:

$$\Delta_1 = \vec{\rho}_0 \cdot \vec{r}_0 + \vec{\rho}_1 \cdot \vec{r}_1 - \vec{r}_3 \cdot \vec{\rho}_0 - \vec{r}_4 \cdot \vec{\rho}_{R1}$$
$$\Delta_2 = \vec{r}_5 \cdot \vec{\rho}_0 + \vec{r}_6 \cdot \vec{\rho}_2 - \vec{r}_7 \cdot \vec{\rho}_0 - \vec{r}_8 \cdot \vec{\rho}_{R2} = (\vec{r}_0 + \vec{W}_B) \cdot \vec{\rho}_0 + \quad (18)$$
$$+ (\vec{r}_1 - \Delta\vec{r}_B) \cdot (\vec{\rho}_1 + \Delta\vec{\rho}_{12}) - \vec{\rho}_0 \cdot (\vec{r}_3 + \vec{W}_D) - (\vec{\rho}_{R1} + \Delta\vec{\rho}_R) \cdot (\vec{r}_4 - \Delta\vec{r}_D)$$

Substituting these expressions into equation (16), we obtain:

$$\vec{r}_0 \cdot \vec{\rho}_0 + \vec{\rho}_1 \cdot \vec{r}_1 - \vec{r}_3 \cdot \vec{\rho}_0 - \vec{r}_4 \cdot \vec{\rho}_{R1} - \vec{r}_0 \cdot \vec{\rho}_0 + \vec{W}_B \cdot \vec{\rho}_0 - \vec{r}_1 \cdot \vec{\rho}_1 + \Delta\vec{r}_B \cdot \vec{\rho}_1 - \quad (19)$$
$$- \Delta\vec{\rho}_{12} \cdot \vec{r}_6 + \vec{\rho}_0 \cdot \vec{r}_3 - \vec{W}_D \cdot \vec{\rho}_0 + \vec{\rho}_{R1} \cdot \vec{r}_4 - \vec{\rho}_{R1} \cdot \vec{r}_4 - \vec{\rho}_{R1} \cdot \Delta\vec{r}_D + \vec{\rho}_R \cdot \vec{r}_8 =$$
$$= (\vec{W}_B \cdot \vec{\rho}_0 + \Delta\vec{r}_B \cdot \vec{\rho}_1) - (\vec{W}_D \cdot \vec{\rho}_0 + \Delta\vec{r}_D \cdot \vec{\rho}_{R1}) - (\Delta\vec{\rho}_{12} \cdot \vec{r}_6 - \Delta\vec{\rho}_R \cdot \vec{r}_8) = N\lambda$$

Directions of vectors $\Delta\vec{\rho}_{12}$, $\vec{r}_6$ and $\Delta\vec{\rho}_R$, $\vec{r}_8$ are orthogonal in practice, therefore their products are equal to zero. Vectors $\vec{W}_B$, $\vec{W}_D$ and $\vec{\rho}_0$ are parallel, therefore their products $\vec{W}_B \cdot \vec{\rho}_0 = W_B$ and $\vec{W}_D \cdot \vec{\rho}_0 = W_D$. The path difference in the object beams during the time between the first and second exposure is described by the terms in the first brackets. The similar path difference in the reference beams is described by the second bracket.

For information recorded in reflected light, the reference beam does not change. The interference fringes observed in reflected light are described by the equation:

$$(W_B + \Delta\vec{r}_B \cdot \vec{\rho}_1) = U_B \cos\alpha + V_B \cos\beta + W_B(1 + \cos\gamma) = N\lambda \quad (20)$$

The pattern recorded in the light passing through the hologram is described by the equation:

$$(W_B + \Delta\vec{r}_B \cdot \vec{\rho}_1) - (W_D + \Delta\vec{r}_D \cdot \vec{\rho}_R) =$$
$$[U_B \cos\alpha + V_B \cos\beta + W_B(1 + \cos\gamma)] - \quad (21)$$
$$-[U_D \cos\alpha_R + V_D \cos\beta_R + W_D(1 + \cos\gamma_R) = N\lambda$$

In the course of the experiment, the angles α, β, γ are set (when choosing the direction of observation). The indicatrix of the scattering of the surface determines the angles α_R, β_R, and γ_R. When processing interference patterns, the order of the N band is determined. Using equations (20) and (21), the components of the displacement vector U, V and W are calculated. When studying flat surfaces $\alpha_R = 90^0$, $\beta_R = 90^0$, and $\gamma_R = 0$, the equation (21) takes the form:

$$U_B \cos\alpha + V_B \cos\beta + W_B(1 - \cos\gamma) - 2W_D = N\lambda \quad (22)$$

To determine the components of the displacement vector in reflected light, two patterns are recorded. The directions of their observation are symmetrical relative to the normal to the hologram. If the directions of observation are in the plane xoz, then the resulting equations have the form:

$$U_B \sin\gamma + W_B(1 + \cos\gamma) = N_1\lambda$$

$$-U_B \sin\gamma + W_B(1+\cos\gamma) = N_2\lambda \quad (23)$$

Here γ is the angle between the direction of observation and the normal to the surface of the product, N_1 and N_2 are the orders of the bands in the patterns observed at the angles γ and $-\gamma$. The displacement component lying in the plane of the sample and the recording plane shall be determined by the equation:

$$U_B = \frac{(N_1 - N_2)\lambda}{2\sin\gamma} \quad (24)$$

The determination of the displacement vector components lying in the plane along the interference patterns of bands recorded in the light passing through the hologram, is possible only with a small gap between the investigated surface and the recording medium.

Results

The method of holographic interferometry in colliding beams was used to determine the permissible distance between dowels. The reflectivity of the wood surface is small, so a reflective layer of aluminum powder was applied to the surface of the wooden beam. A dowel was hammered into the wooden beam. High-resolution holographic photographic plate was fixed on the surface of the beam. The photographic plate was exposed at two different loads applied to the dowel along the wood fibers. After the processing of the photographic plate, the patterns of interference fringes from two directions symmetrical with respect to the normal to the plate were recorded. Photos of these patterns are shown in Figure 2. The observation plane coincides with the direction of the wood fibers and is normal to the sample surface.

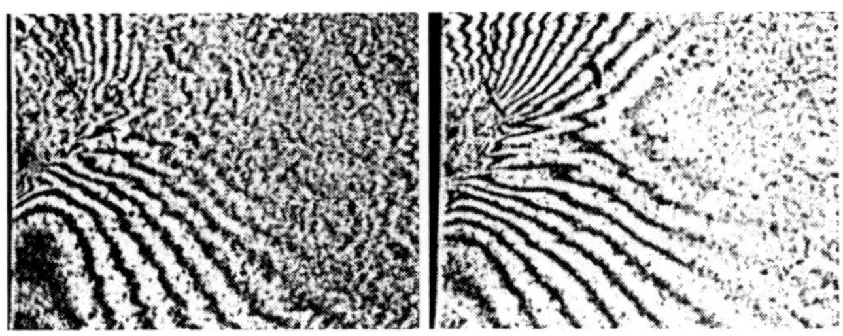

Fig. 2. Photographs of patterns of bands.

Photographs of the interferograms shown in Figure 2 were recorded when studying the strain state of wood near the dowel with the largest transverse dimension of 16 mm. When processing optical information, diagrams $N^* = \frac{N_1 - N_2}{2}$ were plotted along sections parallel to the fibers of wood. The value N^* is proportional to the component of the displacement vector U. The distance between the sections is 6 mm. To build the diagrams, we used the expression (24). Having made a linear assumption, it is possible to calculate a value proportional to the component of the shear deformation,

$$\frac{dU}{dy} \propto \frac{\Delta N}{d} \tag{25}$$

Here, d is the distance between the sections; ΔN - the difference between the values $\frac{N^*_1 - N^*_2}{2}$ calculated in different sections at points with the same coordinate x. The axis x coincides with the direction of the wood fibers. It is horizontal in Figure 2. It follows from (25) that $\ln\frac{dU}{dy} \propto \ln\Delta N - \ln d$.

Figure 3 shows the diagram $\ln\Delta N$, as you can see, it is almost straight.

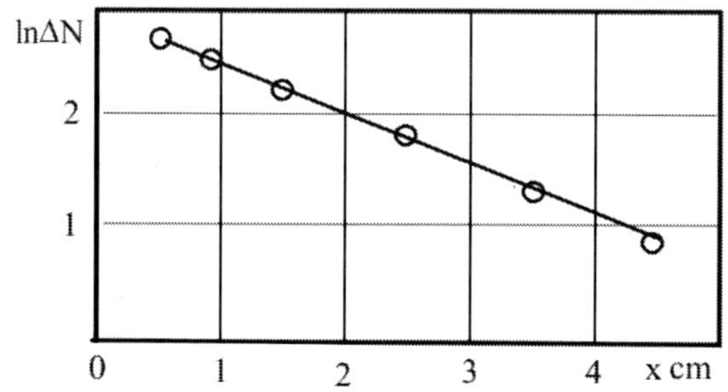

Fig. 3. Diagram $\ln\Delta N$.

So, $\frac{dU}{dy}$ and ΔN decrease exponentially [12] with distance from the axis of the dowel. Therefore, it can be assumed that the shear deformation component varies according to the law: $\frac{dU}{dy} = Ae^{-\frac{x}{\tau}}$, here τ - distance at which $\ln\frac{dN}{dy}$ and $\ln\Delta N$ decreases by unit (attenuation constant). For a dowel with a width of 16 mm, $\tau =$- 1.95 cm. The attenuation constant for a 14 mm dowel was determined in the same way, it turned out to be 1.75 cm.

Conclusion

For the reliable work of dowels, it is necessary that in the region of intersection of disturbances from adjacent dowels, the magnitude of the shear stresses does not exceed 2% of the maximum value. This is achieved at a distance equal 4τ, therefore, the distance between the axes of adjacent dowels should be equal 8τ. For a dowel in width of 16 mm, the distance between the axes should be 16 cm, and for 14 mm dowel - 14 cm. The developed technique allows determining the permissible distances between connecting elements in wooden structures.

References

1. V.I. Zhadanov, P.A. Dmitriev, V.N. Shvedov, G.A. Stolpovskiy, D.A. Ukrainchenko, RU Patent 2353830 (2007). (in Russian)
2. A.M. Popov, V.B. Zinovyev, Vestnik of TSUAB **2,** 235-238 (2012). (in Russian)
3. V.I. Zhadanov, M.A. Arkaev, V.G. Kotlov, Industrial and Civil Engineering **11,** 5-11 (2017). (in Russian)
4. Q.K. Cao, H.M. Xie, Experimental Mechanics, 1–16 (2018).
5. Y.L. Dong, B. Pan, Experimental Mechanics **8,** 1161-1161 (2017).
6. T.E.J. Edwards, F. Di Giacchino, H.P. Springbett, R.A. Oliver, Experimental Mechanics **9**, 1469-1482(2017).
7. Yu.N. Denisyuk, DAN SSSR **144** (1962). (in Russian)
8. Yu.N. Denisyuk, *Principy golografii* [Principles of holography] (Leningrad, 1979). (in Russian)
9. G.V. Ostrovskaya, Journal of Technical Physics **6,** 1-16 (2016). (in Russian)
10. A.M. Popov, V.B. Zinovyev, L.A. Spodareva, Scientific problems of transport in Siberia and the Far East 3, 77-80 (2015). (in Russian)
11. S.I. Gerasimov, V.A. Zhilkin, Applied Mechanics and Technical Physics **3,** 176-182 (2006). (in Russian)
12. A.G. Demeshkin, V.M. Kornev, Mechanics of Composite Materials **2**, 319-324 (1981). (in Russian)

Estimation of the life cycle cost of the upper railway track structure

Nikolai Karpuschenko[1,*], and *Pavel* Trukhanov[1]

[1]Siberian Transport University, 630049 Novosibirsk, Russia

Abstract. The length of tracks with excess tonnage was 14% in the territory of the Russian Federation in 2007, and it reached 20% by 2017. Removal of these restrictions is possible due to modernization of the upper railway track structure (URTS) with increasing its durability and lowering of the life cycle cost (LCC). The purpose of the study is building the LCC estimation model. This model includes the structure of the URTS, the categories and elements of the costs for its maintenance, identification (estimation) of costs, algorithms for their calculation. The average annual LCC of 1 km of the URTS includes the cost of reconstruction, maintenance, intermediate repairs, elimination of consequences of road failures and disposal in the form of the return value of old URS elements. The developed methodology was tested on the actual data of one of the sections of the West Siberian Infrastructure Directorate. The analysis of the obtained data made it possible to conclude that the adopted model of calculating the LCC of URTS adequately displays the categories and elements of the costs for maintenance of the railway track, their specific share in the LCC.

Introduction

Efficiency of a railway track as a railway transport infrastructure facility is determined by the level of reliability (failure-free operation, durability) and the cost of ownership (operation). Existing safety requirements affect the life cycle cost, as they determine the capacity and the type of the structure, norms and tolerances of railway track parameters in designing of maintenance [1]. In this regard, the subject of the study is a methodological tool for estimating the efficiency of design solutions for selection of the railway track design, its maintenance and life cycle duration.

The focus of this article is justification of the life cycle cost model of the upper railway structure, including the following: determining the facility structure (decomposition of the railway structure), selecting the category and cost elements for its modernization and maintenance, as well as presentation of costs.

The management system for the railway transport infrastructure technical condition is based on a concept that includes a set of risk management, resource management, reliability analysis (RRMRA) methods, estimation of the remaining resource (service life) of infrastructure facilities in operation and maintenance [2, 3]. In particular, this is due to the

* Corresponding author: pavelst07@mail.ru

© The Authors, published by EDP Sciences. This is an open access article distributed under the terms of the Creative Commons Attribution License 4.0 (http://creativecommons.org/licenses/by/4.0/).

requirements of the RAMS safety ensuring system and a number of European and Russian standards [4-6]. Existing traffic safety requirements significantly affect the life cycle cost when designing and maintaining the railway track [1].

The peculiarity of the research problem of calculating the LCC of railway infrastructure facilities is the complexity of determining the costs for the railway track maintenance. The review of foreign studies [7] performed earlier showed that they did not fully correspond to the conditions of the Russian railways, primarily in the field of maintenance of the URTS. Publications of Russian authors [8, 9] are general approaches to estimation of the LLC of innovative railway track designs and do not contain specific data on the categories and elements of the costs for the LCC and their identification methods.

In this connection, the essence of this study is development of a methodology, building a cost model and an algorithm for calculating the life cycle cost of the upper railway track structure. This represents the research novelty of this paper. In addition, new methods are private methods for determining the cost elements for the current road maintenance, elimination of railway track failures. These methods are developed on the basis of an array of statistical data obtained from the software package of the Russian Railways JSC, i.e., the Unified Corporate Automated Infrastructure Management System (UCAIMS). The empirical dependencies built on this basis take into consideration the specifics of operating conditions, development of tonnage and railway track failures in the track sections under consideration.

Research method

The life cycle cost (LCC) is the total cost of the facility during its entire life cycle. The main purpose of the LCC calculation is to provide input for making cost-effective decisions in the field of investment, renovation and maintenance of the railway infrastructure facility. Since the LCC analysis is presented as assistance for solutions of the reconstruction design, maintenance, etc., its use should be limited to the costs that can be controlled. To do this, it is necessary to identify the factors that affect the URTS operation and their interrelations [10, 11].

The LCC calculation process includes definition and estimation of the costs associated with development, acquisition (production), ownership and disposal of the facility during its life cycle. The LCC shall be calculated as the sum of its costs [12, 13]:

$$LCC = C_{\text{development}} + C_{\text{production}} + C_{\text{ownership}} + C_{\text{disposal}} \quad (1)$$

Cost elements are interrelations between the categories of costs and the facility structure by elements. This approach has the advantage, which manifests itself in the system and the exact method and provides a high level of confidence in the fact that all cost elements have been taken into consideration. In connection with this, let us adopt the following cost model:

$$\begin{cases} \overline{\text{LCC}} = \dfrac{S_{\text{rec}} + \sum_{i=1}^{n}\left(S_{\text{upkeep}}(i) + S_{\text{r}}(i) + S_{\text{fail}}(i)\right) - S_{\text{disp}}(n)}{n} \to \min; \\ \eta(n) \le C, \end{cases} \quad (2)$$

Where $\overline{\text{LCC}}$ is the average annual life cycle cost of 1 km of the URTS, thousand rubles; S_{rec} is the reconstructions cost (RC), thousand rubles; $S_{\text{upkeep}}(i)$ is the cost of current upkeep per year i, thousand rubles; $S_{\text{p}}(i)$ is the cost of intermediate repairs per year i, thousand rubles; $S_{\text{fail}}(i)$ is the cost of failures per year i, thousand rubles; $S_{\text{disp}}(n)$ is the cost of facility disposal (at the end of the service life), thousand rubles; n is the life cycle duration in years, thousand rubles; η is the function of failures *(reliability indicator); C is the required reliability method.

The sum of initial costs and reduced operating costs (taking into consideration the distance to the $\eta = \frac{1}{(1+d)^i}$ coefficient that is most recent) for the compared options can be represented with the following expression:

$$\mathrm{LCC} = S_{\mathrm{rec}} + \sum_{i=1}^{n} \frac{S_{\mathrm{upkeep}}(i)}{(1+d)^i} + \sum_{i=1}^{n} \frac{S_{\mathrm{r}}(i)}{(1+d)^i} + \sum_{i=1}^{n} \frac{S_{\mathrm{fail}}(i)}{(1+d)^i} + \frac{S_{\mathrm{disp}}(n)}{(1+d)^i}, \quad (3)$$

where LCC is the life cycle cost of 1 km of the railway track for the entire services life, thousand rubles; d is the discounting rate; i is the year of making costs.

Life cycle cost model. The life cycle of the railway track structure begins with reconstruction (or enhanced overhaul). Then, intermediate repairs are performed: average, continuous replacement of rails with the works in the scope of average repair, lifting repair, scheduled preventive repair. Grinding is also performed with certain frequency and continuous replacement of rails is performed depending on their condition (Fig.1). At the end of the life cycle, the railway track is recycled with a return value. Then, the second reconstruction (or major overhaul) is performed, which is the beginning of the life cycle of the newly laid track structure.

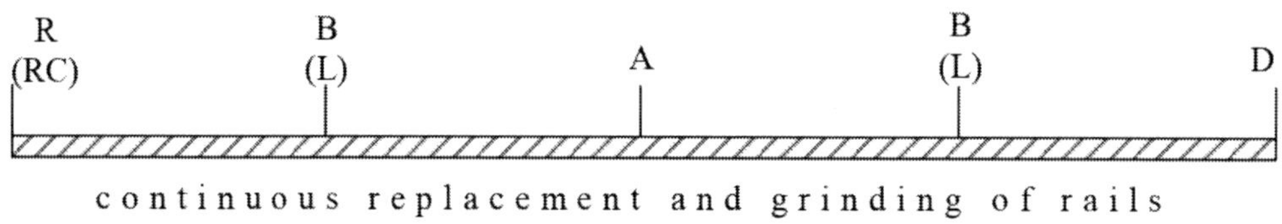

Fig. 1. Rehabilitation works performed during the railway track life cycle: R is track reconstruction; RC is enhanced overhaul; A is the average repair; B is scheduled preventive repair; L is lifting repair; D is the URTS disposal.

Cost elements calculation

The data for the LCC calculates has been taken from the UCAIMS of the West Siberian Infrastructure Directorate for 2017, after which it has been processed in accordance with the method made up.

Railway track reconstruction cost. According to the details of the track service of the West Siberian Infrastructure Directorate for 2017, the cost of reconstruction of the railway track with consideration of the cost of designing per 1 km comprises S_{rec} = 23 to 26 million rubles depending on the track section parameters.

Cost of current track upkeep. It is to be determined by the following formula

$$S_{\mathrm{upkeep}}(i) = S_{\mathrm{op}}(i) + S_{\mathrm{rm}}(i) + S_{\mathrm{mech}}(i), \text{ thousand rubles} \quad (4)$$

where $S_{\mathrm{op}}(i)$ is the costs for remuneration of labor, deductions, and special clothes of the workers involved in the current railway track upkeep, thousand rubles; $S_{\mathrm{rm}}(i)$ is the costs for replacement of the upper railway track structure materials, thousand rubles; $S_{\mathrm{mech}}(i)$ is the costs associated with operation of machines and mechanisms, thousand rubles.

Costs $S_{\mathrm{op}}(i)$ for remuneration of labor, deductions, and special clothes of the workers involved in the current railway track upkeep shall be determined by the following formula

$$S_{op}(i) = T + B + K_r + DSN + O + C,\ \text{thousand rubles} \tag{5}$$

where T is the annual tariff for remuneration of labor of the 3rd category workers that lay the track, thousand rubles; B is the bonus to the wage, thousand rubles; K_r is consideration of the district factor, thousand rubles; DSN is deductions for social needs, thousand rubles; O is overhead costs, thousand rubles; C is the cost of special clothes, thousand rubles.

Calculation of the components of formula (5) shall be performed according to the following algorithm.

Annual tariff for remuneration of labor of the 3rd category workers that lay the track

Tariff = (labor costs) x (hourly tariff rate), thousand rubles.

According to the method of calculation of labor costs with the district system of the current track upkeep [12], the calculation of labor costs for the railway track distance shall be performed assuming 2017 as the beginning of the life cycle of the upper railway track structure after reconstruction. The workload in the following years is planned based on the growth of the missed tonnage by the amount of freight traffic, which determines the accumulated tonnage for the year. Operating conditions and rail track design are permanent and adopted as of 01.01.2017.

To determine the labor cost for the current upkeep of the track, the authors introduce the concept of a reference kilometer [14].

Reference kilometer for a seamless track: a continuous track, rails of the P-65 type of unlimited length, reinforced concrete sleepers, KB type fasteners, crushed stone ballast; a section of the track equipped with automatic blocking, located at sites and inclines not steeper than 8 ‰, in straight or curved radii of more than 800 m; freight traffic is 26 to 50 million gross tons/km per year; passed tonnage is 201 to 400 million gross tons; trains speeds: 101 to 120 km/h for passenger trains / 81 to 90 km/h for freight trains.

With the help of regression analysis [14], the equations of dependencies of the labor cost norms of the workers involved in the current upkeep of the seamless path, in persons/year, on load-bearing capacity G, in million gross tons/km per year and tonnage T, million gross tons.

$$N_b = 0{,}055 + 2{,}7 \cdot 10^{-3} G + 2{,}2 \cdot 10^{-4} T,\ \text{pers./year} \tag{6}$$

The influence of structural peculiarities of the seamless structure on the labor cost norms is taken into consideration by the adjustment factors in accordance with [14].

Expenses for one-time replacement of materials of 1 km of the upper railway track structure. These costs shall be determined with the method represented in work [15]. Besides, the method contains parameters of the regression dependence of expenditure of materials

$$N_b = a + bG + c\mathrm{T} \tag{7}$$

where a, b and c are the parameters with the units of measurement in pers./year, pers./(million t·km (gross)/km per year) and pers./million gross tons; G and T are load-intensity, million t·km (gross)/km per year and passed tonnage, million gross tons.

See the total cost of the current upkeep of 1 km of a seamless track per year in Table 1.

Table 1. The aggregate costs for the current upkeep of 1 km of the seamless track (1 track, G = 115 million t·km (gross)/km per year).

Number of years of the LC	0	1	2	3	4	5	6
Year	2017	2018	2019	2020	2021	2022	2023
Tonnage, million gross tons	58	173	288	403	518	633	691
Remuneration of labor, deductions, and special clothes, thousand rubles	197.5	407.0	408.9	409.1	430.8	451.8	231.3
Cost of materials, thousand rubles	133.3	279.6	305.1	330.6	356.1	381.6	197.2
Total, thousand rubles	330.8	686.6	714.0	739.7	786.9	833.4	428.5

Track failures costs. The costs associated with elimination of the upper railway track structure failures $S_{fail}(i)$ include the costs for acceleration and deceleration of trains due to reduction in movement speeds S_{ss} and the costs of the trains idle time during a "window" S_w

$$S_{fail}(i) = S_{ss} + S_w. \tag{8}$$

Result of the life cycle cost research

Let us calculate the LCC in accordance with the aforementioned procedure. The calculation is performed in the 3 – A direction on a double-track section of the Central Siberian Railway, which has a complex layout and profile. The first and the second track differ in load-intensity by three times. As the first track has a high freight intensity and a short service life, two variants of repairs are considered along this track: according to the classical scheme (option 1) and with the continuous replacement of rails and straightening of the track in the scope of works of an average repair in the middle of the life cycle (option 2) to extend the life cycle. The final results of the LCC calculation can be found in Table 2 and in Figure 2.

Table 2. Total costs for maintenance and repair of 1 km of the track for the life cycle period.

No.	Type of costs	Cost					
		track 1 (option 1)		track 1 (option 2)		track 2	
		thousand rubles	percent	thousand rubles	percent	thousand rubles	percent
1	Reconstruction	25,000	65.9	25,000	40.2	25,000	63.1
2	Intermediate repairs and disposal	5,966	15.7	22,242	35.7	7,466	18.8
3	Current upkeep	4,520	11.9	10,004	16.1	5,356	13.5
4	Continuous replacement and grinding of rails	2,069	5.5	4,139	6.7	1,176	3.0
5	Track failures	392	1.0	784	1.3	652	1.6
	Total	37,947	100	62,169	100	39,650	100

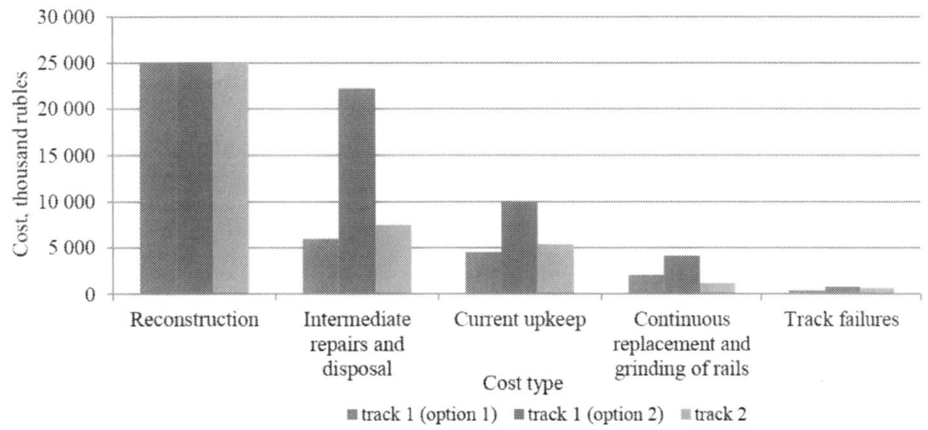

Fig. 2. Costs for maintenance and repair of 1 km of the railway track for the life cycle period.

As a result of the recalculation of the life cycle duration on the basis of tonnage operating units (million gross tons) per years, it was determined that the service life of the 1 track for the option 1 was 6 years; for the option 2 it was 12 years; and the life cycle of the 2 track is 20 years.

According to formula (2) and (3), the average annual cost of the life cycle and its cost for the entire service life is determined taking into consideration discount rate d = 10%. See the example of calculation for the track 1 with the rated resource of 675 million gross tons (option 2).

$$\overline{LCC} = \frac{25\,000 + 5\,966 + 4\,520 + 2\,069 + 392}{6} = 6\,325 \text{ thousand rubles.}$$

With consideration of the discount:

$$LCC_d = \frac{25536}{1} + \frac{1097}{(1+0,1)^1} + \frac{1874}{(1+0,1)^2} + \frac{6526}{(1+0,1)^3} + \frac{1197}{(1+0,1)^4} + \frac{1994}{(1+0,1)^5} + \frac{-276}{(1+0,1)^6} = 34884 \text{ thousand rubles;}$$

$$\overline{LCC_d} = \frac{34884}{6} = 5814 \text{ thousand rubles.}$$

See the results of calculation of the LCC and $\overline{LCC}$ for the rest of repair schemes in Table 3.

Table 3. LCC calculation.

Track	Without consideration of the discount		With consideration of the discount	
	LCC, thousand rubles	$\overline{LCC}$ (LCC), thousand rubles	LCC, thousand rubles	$\overline{LCC}$ (LCC), thousand rubles
1 (option 1)	37,947	6,325	34,884	5,814
1 (option 2)	62,169	5181	46,693	3,891
2	39,650	1,983	31,254	1,563

Analysis of the results obtained

The performed calculations for a particular section of the track showed that the largest average annual life cycle cost of the upper railway track structure is observed on the track 1 (option 1) with the repair scheme of RC B A B RC [16] (with the cycle duration of 6 years) is 5,814 thousand rubles taking into consideration the discount rate. The increase in the life cycle (up to 12 years) and the reduction of its average annual cost was achieved by continuous replacement of rails in the middle of the life cycle accompanied by the works in the scope of average track repair, as a result of which $\overline{LCC}$ (LCC) on the 1 track (2 option) was reduced to 3,891 thousand rubles. The economic effect of using such repair scheme with consideration of the discount will be

$$EE = 5\,814 - 3\,891 = 1\,923 \text{ thousand rubles per year.}$$

The lowest life cycle cost is observed on the 2 track of the section in connection with the low axial load and low traffic density, where the repair scheme of RC B B A B L RC is applied, amounting to 1,563 thousand rubles (the life cycle duration is 20 years).

The highest share in cost elements belongs to reconstruction: 65.9% on the track 1 (option 1), 40.2% on the track 1 (option 2) and 63.1 % on the track 2. The second place is held by the costs for intermediate repairs and disposal: track 1 (option 1) – 15.7 %, track 1 (option 2) – 35.7 %, track 2 – 18.8 %. The next lower share of the costs is attributed to the current upkeep: track 1 (option 1) – 11.9 %, track 1 (option 2) – 16.1 %, track 2 – 13.5 %.

Conclusion

The performed research on the method of engineering and economic evaluation of the efficiency of the upper railway track structure allowed developing the method for estimating its life cycle cost, including the cost model, specific methods for determining the cost elements, and the algorithm for calculating them [14-15].

A cost model has been adopted for estimating the LCC, which includes the costs of reconstruction (modernization), current upkeep, intermediate repairs, failures expressed in train delays and the speed of their movement, utilization of the rail-grille elements in the form of the return value of the old elements at the end of their service life, which is quite compliant with the formulated problem and the purpose of the study.

Calculations using the developed methodology have shown that it is fully adequate to the real operating conditions of the track. The greatest effect on reducing the average annual life cycle cost of the URTS provides an increase in its duration due to the continuous replacement of rails with implementation of straightening of the track in the scope of an average repair (in the middle of the life cycle), as well as in the areas with low freight intensity.

References

1. V.A. Gapanovich, Zheleznodorozhnyj transport [Railway transport] **6**, 26–34 (2013). (in Russian)
2. V.A. Aksenov, Izvestia Transsiba [Journal of Transsib Railway Studies] **4**, 115–123 (2013). (in Russian)
3. GOST P 54505–2011. Functional safety. Risk management on railway transport (Standartinform, Moscow, 2012). (in Russian)
4. BS EN 50126-1:2017. Railway Applications. The Specification and Demonstration of Reliability, Availability, Maintainability and Safety (RAMS). Generic RAMS Process (British Standards Institution, 2017).

5. A. Patra, RAMS and LCC in Rail Track Maintenance. Licentiate Thesis. Division of Operation and Maintenance Engineering (Lulea University of Technology, Lulea, 2009).
6. S. Kumar, A study of the rail degradation process to predict rail breaks. Licentiate Thesis, Division of Operation and Maintenance Engineering, (Lulea University of Technology, Lulea, 2006).
7. A. Wicken, W. Fleischer, H. Liesche, Eisenbahntechnische Rundschau **4**, 172–182 (2002).
8. A.V. Savin, *Bezballastnyj put'* [Non-ballast track] (Moscow, 2017). (in Russian)
9. M.A. Egorov, Collection of scientific papers of Rostov State Transport University: Transport and logistics: innovate development in the conditions of globalization of technological and economic rrelations **3 (36)**, 34–51 (2016).
10. A. Zoeteman, Doctoral thesis. Railway design and maintenance from a life-cycle cost perspective: A decision-support approach, Netherlands TRAIL Research School, 2004.
11. A.M. Zamyshljaev, M.Yu. Rachkovskiy, M.S. Nikiforova, Ekonomika zheleznyh dorog [Economy of railways], **12**, 11–22 (2012). (in Russian)
12. STO RZD 1.02.034–2010. Upravlenie resursami na jetapah zhiznennogo cikla, riskami i analizom nadezhnosti (URRAN). Obshhie pravila ocenki i upravlenija riskami [Resource management at life cycle stages, risks and reliability analysis (URRAN). General rules for risk assessment and management (Standartinform, Moscow, 2010). (in Russian)
13. STO RZD 1.05.509.15–2002. Sistema upravlenija jeffektivnost'ju postavok. Rukovodstvo po ocenke stoimosti zhiznennogo cikla produkcii [Supply Chain Management System. Guide to assessing the value of the life cycle of products] (Standartinform, Moscow, 2008). (in Russian)
14. N.I. Karpushhenko, A.V. Bystrov, P.S. Truhanov, Railway Track and Facilities, **1**, 2–7 (2016). (in Russian)
15. N.I. Karpushhenko, A.V. Bystrov, P.S. Truhanov, Ekonomika zheleznyh dorog [Economy of railways], **8**, 45–51 (2016). (in Russian)
16. Tehnicheskie uslovija na raboty po rekonstrukcii i remontu zheleznodorozhnogo puti [Technical conditions for work on the reconstruction and repair of the railway track]. (to be published). (in Russian)

Innovative aspects in developing bridge monitoring systems

Andrey Yashnov[1,*], and *Pavel* Kuzmenkov[1]

[1]Siberian Transport University, 630049 Novosibirsk, Russia

Abstract. The average age of bridges in operation and their accumulated damage are ever increasing, while design solutions of new bridges are increasingly complex. It is difficult to adequately reflect performance characteristics of these structures in design models. In order to prevent accidents during construction and operation, it is necessary to verify experimentally that the actual stress-strain behavior corresponds to design parameters. Special monitoring systems are developed and implemented to improve the operational reliability of structures. This study uses mathematical modeling and instrumental measurements to develop monitoring systems. A systematic approach has been implemented. The paper presents the results produced by modern automated measuring, recording and data processing equipment to provide online diagnostics and long-term status monitoring of bridge structures.

Introduction

In recent years, the road transportation of passengers and goods has been growing very fast. It is the most popular mode of transportation, accounting for more than 50% of the total traffic. Traffic speed and intensity, as well as cargo-carrying capacity of new cars and trucks are ever increasing. Rail transport accounts for 45% of the total freight turnover in Russia. On June 1, 2017, Russian Railways put high-capacity rolling stock (27 tonnes per axle) into pilot operation. The company also plans to continue increasing loads up to 30 tonnes per axle.

On the one hand, the average age of road and rail bridges in operation is increasing, as well as the number of damages accumulated during operation. There is a growing need for early detection of a tendency towards performance degradation in each particular structure. Automated monitoring is proposed as an innovative method [1–7]. On the other hand, new bridge construction is characterized by increasingly complex structures for bridging large spans and the introduction of poorly studied advanced materials, such as polymer composites, in designing new structures [8–11]. Therefore, new bridges also require automated monitoring.

The primary purpose of the proposed innovations is to increase the operational safety and maintenance efficiency of bridge structures on the basis of automated diagnostics and status monitoring. Taking into account the high cost of automated monitoring tools, it is

* Corresponding author: yan@stu.ru

© The Authors, published by EDP Sciences. This is an open access article distributed under the terms of the Creative Commons Attribution License 4.0 (http://creativecommons.org/licenses/by/4.0/).

necessary to select a minimum set of parameters that provide maximum information about the technical condition. The number of controlled parameters can be expanded without increasing the cost of the monitoring system, through periodic automated measurements [12]. All necessary parameters are recorded at certain intervals, rather than simultaneously. Excessive and insufficient information may reduce the efficiency of monitoring.

Research methodology

To illustrate the proposed approach, let us consider implementing periodic automated monitoring of tension strains of cable elements in a network arch (Fig. 1a). In parallel with periodic monitoring, a continuous automated monitoring station has been created (Fig. 1b) for continuous monitoring of integral parameters that reflect the overall technical condition of the structure. These controlled parameters are likely to include natural oscillation frequencies, movements of a reference point, stresses in the cross section of a structure that has the lowest capacity margin, etc. The continuous monitoring station can be used to determine stresses in cables, including invariant values and values independent of temporary loads.

a

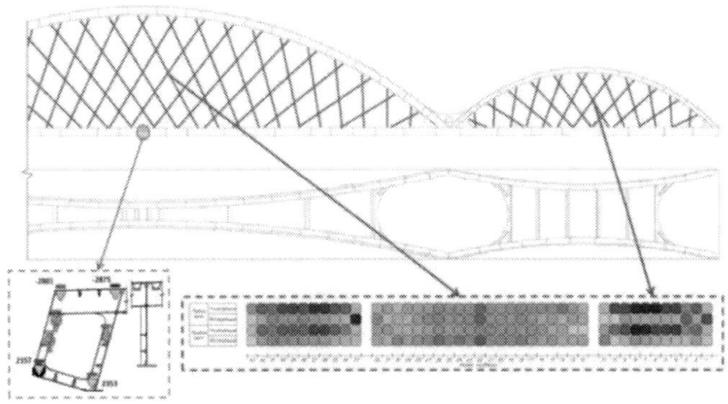

b

Fig. 1. Implementation of periodic automated monitoring: a – general view of a span structure; b – schematic diagram of the monitoring system.

The obtained values of stresses in cables can be conveniently represented as a color "digital portrait" [13] (Fig. 1b), where each strain value is marked with its own display color: green means no difference from calculated values; a red gradient indicates that the actual strain exceeds a design one; a blue gradient indicates a loss of tension. Periodic automated measurements with generation, comparison and analysis of "digital portraits" will make it possible to predict possible negative tendencies in the current state of structures. Thus, the primary objective of monitoring — to prevent limit states by taking preventive measures, rather than simply record their development — will be accomplished.

In order to ensure the correct operation of the monitoring system, it is necessary to implement it during construction. Information on the initial state of a structure will serve as the basis for a correct interpretation of field evidence. For example, control measurements may suggest there is some sagging of the structure, but it is impossible to make a correct conclusion without knowing its initial state. Or there may be another situation: a controlled element of the structure is subject to stresses from temporary loads that are much lower than the design resistance. However, there are load-induced cracks in this structure. These "inverse" problems can be solved by using modern automated instrumentation systems and software packages for calculating bridge structures. It is required to create a calculated finite element model that adequately reflects the actual operation of a bridge structure. For this purpose, it is necessary to conduct a cycle of measurements of stress-strain states under constant test load, and then adapt the developed model to test results.

Experimental data and results

Based on tests of a combined metal span structure, namely a continuous stiffening truss with a flexible arch and arched saddles (Fig. 2a), the developed finite element model was tested. The obtained actual stresses (Figs. 2b and 2c) confirm the adequacy of this model, which makes it possible to use it in numerical experiments.

Calculations and experimental studies of the stress-strain state performed on the basis of periodical monitoring provided the following results. Even under constant loads only, the level of stresses in short hangers (B1) is close to the design resistance of the metal. The existing vehicle loads were likely to lead to cracking, which actually occurred in the initial period of operation. The cracking process and the formation of an actual hinge at the point where the hanger B1 is attached to the arch is followed by redistribution of strains and increasing stresses in the nearest columns (H12). In general, however, the redistribution of strains does not create additional stress raisers. The hanger B1 will work as an element hinged to the arch and, therefore, have almost no bending moments and related stresses that can cause cracking. The total stresses in short columns also do not exceed the design resistances. At this stage, the structure is in a stable state, but we have identified some elements that may be subject to cracking. These findings will serve as the basis for making decisions relating to repairs of damaged elements and periodic control measurements of stress-strain states of structural elements.

a

Actual stress level Design stress level

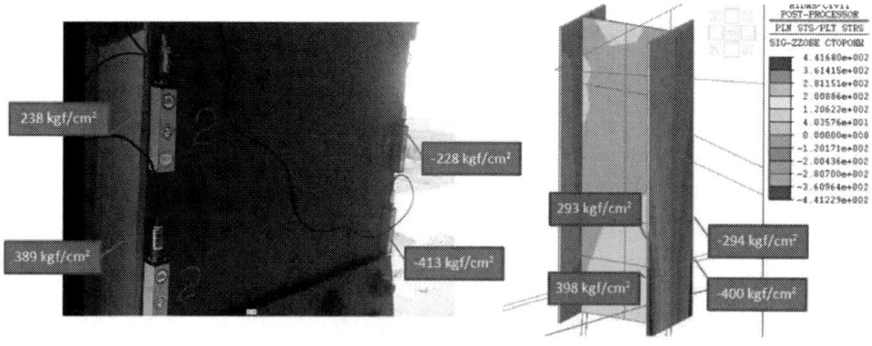

b

Actual crack width Design crack width

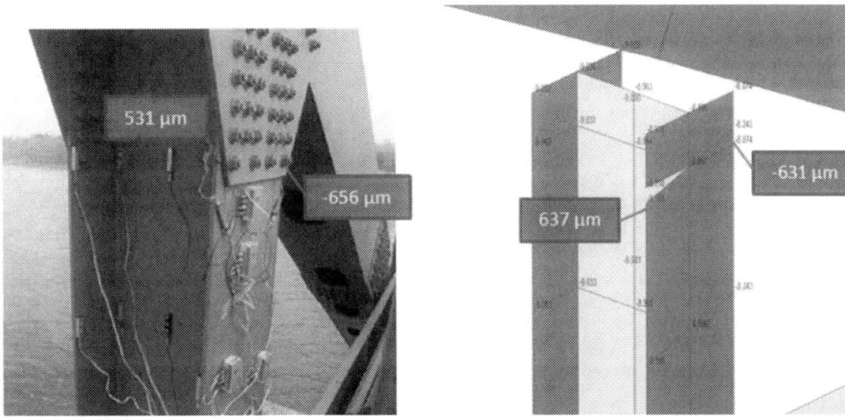

c

Fig. 2. Periodic automated monitoring: a – general view of the bridge span structure; b – performance of the column H3 under test load; c – performance of the hanger B1 under test load.

Conclusion

The findings of these studies confirm the possibility of increasing the operational safety and maintenance efficiency of bridge structures using innovative diagnostics and monitoring techniques. The studies are of practical significance because they demonstrate the possibility of using the developed methods and techniques for automated diagnostics and monitoring of stress-strain states in bridge maintenance systems.

References

1. J.J. Moughty, J.R. Casas, Applied Sciences, **7(5),** 510 (2017).
2. A.C. Neves, I. Gonzalez, J. Leander, R. Karoumi, Journal Civil Stract Health Monitoring, 689-702 (2017).
3. Ch. Tan, A. Elhattab, N. Uddin, Journal Civil Stract Health Monitoring, 615-625 (2017).
4. H.W. Shih, D.P. Thambiratnam, T.H.T. Chan, Structural Control and Health Monitoring, 20, 1271-1290 (2013).
5. T.M. Baranov, Thesis of Candidate of technical sciences, Irkutsk State Transport University, Irkutsk (2014). (in Russian)
6. VCE Vienna Consulting Engineers ZT GmbH, Life Cylce Management, available at: http://www.brimos.com/BRIMOS/HTML/en/services/lca.html (June 20, 2018).
7. Roctest, Our applications, available at: https://roctest.com/en/product-applications/ (June 20, 2018).
8. A.N. Ivanov, P.Yu. Kuzmenkov, Siberian Transport University Bulletin, 2 (2016). (in Russian)
9. A.N. Ivanov, B.V. Pyrinov, A.N. Yashnov, *Eksperimental'nye issledovanija gibridnogo proletnogo stroenija* [Experimental studies of a hybrid span structure] (Saarbrucken: LAP LAMBERT Academic Publishing, 2014). (in Russian)
10. A.N. Ivanov, E.A. Kuzmitskaya, Proceedings of the International scientific and practice conference (2016). (in Russian)
11. A.N. Ivanov, A.V. Martynov, Simvol nauki [Science Symbol], **6** (2015). (in Russian)

12. A.N. Jashnov, P.Yu. Kuzmenkov, *Transport infrastructure of the Siberian region,* Proceedings of the 7th International scientific conference (Irkutsk, 2016). (in Russian)
13. A.N. Yashnov, I.I. Snezhkov, S.L. Odnorog, P.Yu. Kuzmenkov, Certificate of official registration of computer programs No. 2017618579 (2017). (in Russian)

Determining strength of rubble masonry of bridges' supports being in operation

Ilya Zasukhin[1,*], and *Sergey* Bokarev[1]

[1]Siberian Transport University, 630049 Novosibirsk, Russia

Abstract. The purpose of this article is to create a methodology for determining the design strength of rubble masonry of bridge supports meeting the modern safety requirements for transport structures. The article contains data on the use of the rubble masonry in solid supports of railway bridges. Development of methodology of determining the permissible stresses on the rubble masonry, and the practice of applying the design strength of the rubble masonry in regulatory documents are considered. Analysis of the research works is carried out, according to which the design strength of the rubble masonry of solid supports is determined when calculating the load-bearing capacity. The experimental data of European scientists in the field of determining the strength characteristics of stone masonries are considered. A domestic method for determining the design values of strength characteristics for building materials used in transport construction is presented. The main deficiencies of the existing method for determining the design strength of rubble masonry are defined and suggestions are made for its clarification. The article concludes with the formulation of tasks required to be solved for clarification of strength characteristics of the operated railway supports made of rubble masonry.

Introduction

Stone masonry made of natural stones was widely used in the construction of structures from ancient times [1, 2]. In the late XIX, early XX centuries [3, 4], the only material used in the construction of railway bridge supports was a "trowel" masonry with a cladding of solid stones of regular shape. However, despite the age-old experience of using such structures, the nature of operation of stone structures has relatively recently become a subject of research. Most of the work is devoted to civil buildings, for which the nature of operation is different from the bridge structures [5, 6].

An important role in the development of the theory of performing the calculations for the rubble masonry was played by experimental studies carried out at the Central Research Institute of Building Materials by A.A. Shishkin and V.V. Shumitskaya under the guidance of Professor L.I. Onishchik. The first studies of the strength and elastic properties of the rubble masonry were performed in 1934-35 using the samples with cross-sections of 0.50 x 0.70 m [7]. In 1948, additional tests of samples with cross-section of 0.60 x 0.60 m were

* Corresponding author: zasukhiniv@mail.ru

© The Authors, published by EDP Sciences. This is an open access article distributed under the terms of the Creative Commons Attribution License 4.0 (http://creativecommons.org/licenses/by/4.0/).

carried out for the purpose of clarifying the features of the reinforced rubble masonry operation [8]. The results of studies were included into the new regulatory document covering the strength characteristics of stone structures NiTU 120-55 [9] which have never been clarified after that. As for the bridge structures, the design axial compression strength of the stone masonry was determined on the basis of the experiments carried out under the guidance of professor L.I. Onishchik. For the first time these results were reflected in the "Technical Specifications for Designing the Railway, Road and City Bridges and Pipes" SN 200-62 [10]. The purpose of this article is to create a methodology for determining the design strength of the rubble masonry of bridge supports. Such a methodology should meet the modern safety requirements applicable to transport structures.

Research methods

Construction Codes and Regulations SNiP II-22-81 [11] contain the specification of ultimate compression strength of the masonry determined according to the empirical formula (1) derived by A.A. Shishkin in 1934-1948 on the basis of tests [7, 8]. Its application is described in the manual on the design of stone and reinforced stone structures [12] issued on the occasion of publication of the Construction Codes and Regulations SNiP II-22-81 [9].

$$R_u = A \cdot R_1 \left(1 - \frac{0,2}{0,25 + \frac{R_2}{2R_1}} \right) \gamma, \tag{1}$$

Where R_u is a masonry compression strength, kgf/cm^2;

R_1 is a compression strength of the filler (rubble stone), kgf/cm^2;

R_2 is a compression strength of the mortar (cubic strength), kgf/cm^2;

A is a constructive coefficient of masonry determined according to the formula:

$$A = \frac{100 + R_1}{250 + 8R_1}, \tag{2}$$

γ is a coefficient taken into account for the strength of the masonry on solutions of grades 25 and below, which is determined according to the formula:

$$\gamma = \frac{0,02R_1 + 2,75R_2}{0,08R_1 + 2R_2}. \tag{3}$$

Basic information about the tests carried out by A.A. Shishkin in 1934-1948 [7, 8] is given in Table 1. Referring to the test results the formulas (1 to 3) are valid only until the strength of the stone (R_1) does not exceed 900-1000 kgf/cm^2. Therefore, if the limit of strength of the rubble is higher than the indicated value, when performing the calculations according to formula (1), R_1 is conventionally assumed equal to 900 kgf/cm^2. In Table 1 these data are marked with (*).

Table 1. An extract from the results of test carried out by A.A. Shishkin.

Rubble type	Rubble strength R_1, kgf/cm^2	Mortar strength R_2, kgf/cm^2	Ultimate strength of the masonry according to the test results R_u, kgf/cm^2	Ultimate strength of the masonry R_u, kgf/cm^2 (according to formula 1) / Relative inaccuracy, %
Compact limestone	490	30.0	18.8	18.5 / -2
Compact limestone	490	118.0	27.8	31.9 / +15
Limestone	450	14.0	11.5	11.8 / +3
Compact limestone	670	18.0	14.0	15.5 / +11
Granodiorite	2900*	18.0	16.0	17.4 / +9
Granodiorite	2900*	50.0	39.0	30.5 / -22
Compact limestone	450	70.0	23.5	25.0 / +6

One can see from the Table 1 that deviations of the experimental data from the theoretical data calculated according to the formulas (1 to 3) reach 35%. At the same time, the design value does not always include the strength reserve. Consequently, the design formula, in which the breaking strength of the rubble masonry depends only on the strength of the rubble and mortar, does not accurately reflect the studied dependence. The authors of the tests made a suggestion that one of the factors having a great influence on the load-bearing capacity of the masonry is the strength of the rubble for splitting, however, insufficient experimental data were collected in this regard.

Unfortunately, no regulatory document [11, 12] contains the information about the size of the samples to be used for determining the compression strength of the rubble and the mortar (R_1 and R_2, respectively). According to the experiments carried out by Shishkin [7, 8], when deriving the calculation formulas (1 to 3), R_1 was used as an ultimate compression strength of stone samples having the form of a cube of 7x7x7 cm with the strength less than 800 kgf/cm^2 and cube of 5x5x5 cm with higher strength. The cubes of 7x7x7 cm were used for testing the mortars.

When carrying out a survey of the bridge supports, it was found out that in practice the sampling of the mortar and rubble from the structure represented as a rubble masonry was very labour-intensive process. Sampling of cores from the body of supports is easily carried out using the diamond drill with core drills with a diameter of at least 100 mm. The obtained samples could be used in a laboratory conditions for preparing the reference samples of the mortar in the form of cubes with faces of 20-30 mm and samples of rubble in the form of cylinders with a diameter and height of 40-50 mm. Obviously, for the purpose of performing the transition from the deign strength of the obtained samples to R_1 and R_2 values, it is necessary to use the requirements of GOST 8462-85 and GOST 5802-86, respectively.

R. Senthivel and P.B. Lourenço, obtained the deformation characteristics of rubble masonry materials on the basis of numerous experimental data, which were used for creation of finite element models [13]. This approach enables the authors to accurately predict the appearance of cracks. In their experiments the authors used samples with a cross-section of 0.20x1.0 m. The influence of the form and bricklaying method was also considered. Figure 1 shows the experimental samples used in the experiments of R. Senthivel and P.B. Lourenço.

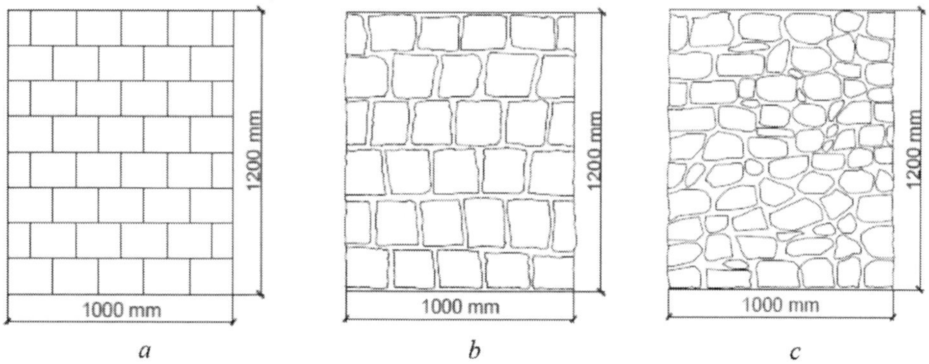

Fig. 1. Experimental samples used in the experiments of R. Senthivel and P.B. Lourenço: *a* – dry stone masonry; *b* – uncoursed masonry with mortar; *c* – coarse stone masonry.

The strength of the stone and mortar in the experimental samples was 692 kgf/cm^2 and 30 kgf/cm^2, respectively. Substituting the known values into formulas (1 to 3), the ultimate strength of masonries of types b and c (Figure 1) should be 210 kgf/cm^2. However, the experimental samples were broken down when the stress level for the dry stone masonry reached 370 kgf/cm^2 and only 61 kgf/cm^2 for coarse stone masonry. Such a wide range of values indicates the necessity to take into account a number of additional parameters for more accurate assessment of the load-bearing capacity of the rubble masonry.

It should be noted that ultimate compression strength of the rubble masonry is determined by the formulas (1 to 3). For the purpose of performing the transition to the permissible stresses for all the structures made of a stone masonry L.I. Onishchik proposed to use a safety factor equal to three [14]. In 1955, after transition to the method of calculation according to the limit states, the safety factor $\gamma=2$ was adopted for the transition from the ultimate compression strength of the stone masonries to the design strength [9]. The characteristic strength of materials associated with the defective or control characteristic of the batch was not applied to the masonry, since its strength was not established by the standards.

The basic design characteristics of materials for transport structures are designated by the Recommendations on the Assessment and Ensuring the Reliability of Transport Structures [15]. The design axial compression strength of materials is determined based on the standard values of the strength ($R_{standard}$) taking into account the corresponding safety factor for the material γ_m (Ym) and its intended purpose γ_n (Yn):

$$R_{design} = \frac{\gamma_n R_{standard}}{\gamma_m} . \quad (4)$$

It follows from here that the safety factor for the material without taking into account the safety factor for its intended purpose is determined as follows:

$$\gamma_m = \frac{R_{standard}}{R_{design}} . \quad (5)$$

Standard material strength values are assigned based on the condition of availability of at least 0.95:

$$R_{standard} = \bar{R}(1-1,64\nu), \quad (6)$$

Where $\bar{R}$ is arithmetic mean value of an ultimate strength of the material;
ν is a variation factor calculated according to the following formula (7):

$$\nu = \frac{S}{\bar{R}} \cdot 100\%, \quad (7)$$

Where S is the mean square deviation of an ultimate strength of the material.

The design strength of the materials is assigned based on the condition of availability of at least 0.9986:

$$R_{design} = \bar{R}(1-3\nu) \quad (8)$$

Using the expressions (5), (6), (8) the safety factor for the material is:

$$\gamma_m = \frac{1-1,64\nu}{1-3\nu} \quad (9)$$

As for the bridge structures the value of the standard structural safety shall be 0.99997, which may be achieved by introduction of operating condition factors.

As for the rubble masonry there are no GOST standards for testing and determining the strength characteristics. However, all the experiments, on the result of which the formulas (1 to 3) were derived, were carried out using the samples 1 m high with a cross-section of 0.50 x 0.40 m. These dimensions may be taken as reference ones. Table 2 contains the detained information about the experiments of A.A. Shishkin and the results characterizing the distribution of strength characteristics.

Table 2. Static Parameters of the Strength Distribution for Rubble Masonry Samples.

No.	R_1, kgf/cm^2	R_2, kgf/cm^2	Ultimate strength of the masonry R_u, kgf/cm^2	$\bar{R}$, kgf/cm^2	S	ν, %	γ_m (Ym)
1	490	30.0	17.2	18.1	3.92	21.6	1.84
			20.1				
			22.1				
			13.1				
2	490	118	31.2	27.8	4.72	17.0	1.47
			24.5				
3	750	30.5	30.0	33.5	4.95	14.8	1.36
			37.0				
4	450	14.0	12.8	11.4	1.40	12.3	1.26
			10.0				
			11.4				
5	670	18.0	15.7	14.0	2.40	17.2	1.48
			12.3				
6	670	50.0	30.0	31.5	3.74	11.9	1.25
			28.7				
			35.7				
7	130	5.5	2.6	3.00	0.57	18.9	1.59
			3.4				
8	130	40.0	8.8	8.50	0.42	5.0	1.08
			8.2				

The total number of experimental samples used for processing is 32 pieces. The maximum value of the variation factor is 21.6%, and the average value is 11%. The safety factor for the material varies over a wide range from 1.04 to 1.84. Taking into account a small amount of experimental data and a wide range of the strength distribution parameters, it is possible to take a variation factor for rubble masonry equal to 20%, and safety factor for the material of 2.0. The factor of operating conditions, as for the intended purpose γ_n when performing calculation according to the limit states of the first group for railway bridge structures, is taken equal to 0.9.

Results

Thus, the design strength of the rubble masonry for the railway bridge supports should be calculated according to the following formula:

$$R_{design} = \frac{R_u(1-1,64\text{v})}{\gamma_m} = 0,33R_u\gamma_n \qquad (10)$$

Although the safety factor for the material did not change in comparison with the requirements of the regulatory document [19], the design strength became 1.7 times smaller than that shown in Table 4.5 [19]. Thus, the safety level to be ensured for transport structures was reached [15]

As for the historical buildings, it was also confirmed that the actual strength and deformation properties of the rubble masonry were lower than the design values specified in the regulatory document [16]. In 2013-2017 a group of European scientists carried out a large number of tests of walls made of a stone masonry with a rubble of various shapes and sizes [17, 18]. According to the experimental data, when determining the ultimate strength of the masonry, the variation factor was within 0.14-0.30, which corresponds to the results of A.A. Shishkin [7].

At present, the design strength of the rubble masonry of the supports of operated railway bridges is determined in accordance with Table 4.5 of the "Guidelines for Determining the Load Capacity of Railway Bridge Supports" [19]. A similar table is presented in Construction Rules SP 15.13330.2012 "Stone and Reinforced Stone Structures" [20, Table 9]. However, as for the railway structures when performing the transition from the ultimate compression strength of the rubble masonry to design strength it is not sufficient to use the safety factor γ=2.

Conclusion

Based on the analysis of regulatory and technical literature, it is possible to make the following conclusions: (1) When considering the experimental data of the authors of formulas (1 to 3), it can be seen that the deviation of the load-bearing capacity of the masonry obtained according to the test results from the design capacity according to formulas (1 to 3) and Tables 9 [18], 4.5 [17] can reach 35 %. A.A. Shishkin observed that there was a connection between the ultimate strength of the rubble masonry and the ultimate strength of the rubble for splitting. In addition, as it was shown by the experiments [11], it is necessary to take into account the influence of the dimensions of the structure. Accounting for these factors can help to clarify the calculation formulas, but this requires additional experiments, including numerical experiments using finite element methods; (2) the design strength characteristics of the rubble masonry for railway bridges are currently calculated according to Table 4.5 presented in the regulatory document [17]. This article shows that the table values do not meet the modern requirements for ensuring the safety of the transport structures. Therefore, for the purpose of performing the transition from the ultimate strength of the rubble masonry to be calculated according to the formulas (1 to 3) to the design strength of the railway bridge supports the factor of 0.3 should be introduced. In addition, the static parameters for the distribution of the strength of the rubble masonry samples have a wide range of values, which requires the additional experiments for clarifying these parameters.

References

1. A.N. Badak, I.E. Vojnich, N.M. Volchek, *Istorija Drevnego mira. Drevnij Rim* [History of ancient world. Ancient Rome] (Harvest Publ., Minsk, 2005). (in Russia)
2. A.M. Rozenbljumas, *Kamennye konstrukcii* [Masonry structures] (Vysshaya Shkola Publ., Moscow, 1964). (in Russian)
3. L.F. Nikolai, *Mosty: krat. ruk.* (Tip. Ju.N. Jerlih Publ., Saint Petersburg, 1907) (in Russian)
4. A.N. Tetior, *Zhelezobetonnye i kamennye konstrukcii* [Reinforced concrete and masonry structures] (Moscow, 2016). (in Russian)
5. B.S. Sokolov, A.B. Antakov, News of the Kazan State University of Architecture and Engineering 3, 75-81 (2014). (in Russian)
6. *Sooruzhenie Srednesibirskoj zheleznoj dorogi, 1893-1898 g. Sbornik tehnicheskih uslovij, instrukcij i pojasnitel'nyh zapisok* [Mid-Siberian railway structures, 1893-1898. Collection of specifications, instructions and clarifications] (Russkaja Pechatnja Publ., Saint Petersburg, 1901). (in Russian)
7. A.A. Shishkin, *Prochnost' kladok iz estestvennyh kamnej po jeksperimental'nym dannym. Issledovanija po kamennym konstrukcijam: sb. statej* [Strength of natural stones masonry based on experimental data. Masonry structures research: collection of papers] (Strojizdat Publ., Moscow, 1938). (in Russian)
8. A.A. Shishkin, *Prochnost' kladok iz estestvennyh kamnej po jeksperimental'nym dannym* [Strength of natural stones masonry based on experimental data] (Strojizdat Publ., 1949). (in Russian)
9. NiTU 120-55. Normy i tehnicheskie uslovija proektirovanija kamennyh i armokamennyh konstrukcij [Standards and specifications of masonry and reinforced masonry structures design] (Moscow, 1955). (in Russian)
10. SN 200-62. *Tehnicheskie uslovija proektirovanija zheleznodorozhnyh, avtodorozhnyh i gorodskih mostov i trub* [Specifications for design of railway, motorway and urban bridges and pipes] (Transzheldorizdat, Moscow, 1961). (in Russian)
11. SNiP II-22-81. *Kamennye i armokamennye konstrukcii* [Masonry and reinforced masonry structures] (Strojizdat Publ., Moscow, 1983). (in Russian)
12. *Posobie po proektirovaniju kamennyh i armokamennyh konstrukcij* [Reference guide for masonry and reinforced masonry structures design, to SNiP II-22-81) (Strojizdat Publ., Moscow, 1985). (in Russian)
13. R. Senthivel, P.B. Laurence, Engineering Structures 31, 1930-1943 (2009).
14. L.I. Onishchik, *Prochnost' i ustojchivost' kamennyh konstrukcij* [Strength and robustness of masonry structures] (Leningrad, 1937). (in Russian)
15. *Rekomendacii po ocenke i obespecheniju nadezhnosti transportnyh sooruzhenij* [Recommendations on evaluation and ensuring reliability of transport structures] (USSR Transport Ministry Publ., Moscow, 1989). (in Russian)
16. A.S. Chesnokov, B.I. Pinus, Bulletin of Irkutsk State Technical University 3, 162-165 (2015). (in Russian)
17. B. Silva, PhD thesis, University of Padova, Italy, 2012.

18. F. Vanin, D. Zaganelli, A. Penna, K. Beyer, Bulletin of Earthquake Engineering **15,** 5435-5479 (2017).
19. Rukovodstvo po opredeleniju gruzopodjemnosti opor zheleznodorozhnyh mostov [Reference guide for defining bearing capacity of railway bridges supports] (Moscow, 2015). (in Russian)
20. SP 15.13330.2012. *Kamennye i armokamennye konstrukcii* [Masonry and reinforced masonry structures] (Moscow, 2012). (in Russian)

Simulation of stresses in asphalt-concrete pavement with frost heaving

Vladimir Churilin[1,*], *Sergei* Efimenko[1], *Oleg* Matvienko[1], and *Viktor* Bazuev[1]

[1]Tomsk State University of Architecture and Building, 634003 Tomsk, Russia

Abstract. The article reviews the issue of the stress-strain state of the road surface in the winter period as a result of roadbed soil heaving. The main purpose of the work is to determine the stress fields in the asphalt-concrete pavement, which is necessary for designing of frost-resistant roadbeds in the areas with seasonal freezing of roadbed soils. The following research methods were used: theoretical, laboratory, field. With consideration of different properties of materials and geometric dimensions of the road surface section, stress fields in the asphalt-concrete pavement during freezing were obtained with the use of the software product. Comparison of theoretical studies with the results of experimental and full-scale tests showed that the forms of theoretical solutions describe the stress fields in the freezing asphalt-concrete pavement quite accurately.

Introduction

Strains in the form of cracks, which are often formed during the first three years of highway operation, are widespread in northern districts [1, 2]. Occurrence of cracks on the pavement in winter can be caused by low-temperature cracking [3, 4] or uneven elevation of the pavement surface as a result of frost heaving of soils. In areas with deep seasonal freezing of soils, cracks formed as a result of uneven elevation of the road surface due to frost heaving of soils were most widely spread [5 - 7].

To forecast the future state of highways and minimize operating costs for their maintenance, large-scale studies were performed as described in [8]. In this work, occurrence of cracks on the surface of the asphalt-concrete pavement is described by the mathematical model based on statistical study methods. This allows predicting arising of cracks on the road surface with a certain accuracy, but does not explain the process of crack formation.

It is necessary to study the stress-strain state of roadbed in winter for the purpose to increase frost resistance of road surfaces. Works in this field [9 - 12] are focused on studying the impact of the automobile wheels on the road surface. At present, the topic of the stress-strain state of roadbed as a result of frost heaving remains poorly studied.

To achieve this goal, a mathematical model of stresses of asphalt-concrete pavements caused by frost heaving was built with consideration of elastoplastic strain by the Huber-Mises criterion [13].

* Corresponding author: lex-16-2008@mail.ru

© The Authors, published by EDP Sciences. This is an open access article distributed under the terms of the Creative Commons Attribution License 4.0 (http://creativecommons.org/licenses/by/4.0/).

Study methods

Soil conditions of the existing highway network were studied and monitoring of strain in asphalt-concrete pavement in winter was performed at the first stage. Observations were performed at specially prepared posts (sections) of the operated road for three calculation schemes for wetting the ground roadbed. Points for monitoring of the pavement strain were fixed with dowels and painted over (Fig. 1). Roadbed was opened at each site to determine the number of layers and their thickness. The material of each layer was also determined. Soils were sampled to determine their characteristics and heaving properties [14]. To ensure the invariability of the reference point during freezing and heaving of soils, freezing reference points were set up, which were used to measure the roadbed surface in winter [15].

Laboratory experimental studies of asphalt-concrete samples (in the form of small beams) were performed at the second stage. Bending tension tests were performed at negative temperatures. As a result, tensile strength characteristics of asphalt-concete of the A and BI type with 90/130 bitumen were obtained in the range of temperatures from -21^{0}C to -35^{0}C [16].

Fig. 1. Examples of roadbed strain monitoring section "Teguldet – B. Dorokhovo, km 19+400, in Tomsk region".

The third stage is building a mathematical model for determination of stresses in asphalt-concrete pavement as a result of freezing soils heaving in the roadbed based on the available exact solutions of the mechanics of the rigid strained body (elasticity and plasticity theory) [17]. Critical stresses for asphalt-concrete pavement were determined based on the strain strength characteristics of asphalt-concrete of the A and BI type with 90/130 bitumen obtained as a result of the experiments. Critical stresses were compared to the field measurements. Stree fields were built on the example of the 1st area type by the wettening condition of "Teguldet – B. Dorokhovo, km 19+400, in Tomsk region", where winter monitoring over the pavement strain was performed.

Results

Winter monitoring over the pavement strain as a result of roadbed soils heaving was performed during 2017 to 2018 (Table 1).

Table 1. Results of displacements of pavement points at heaving at highwway section "Teguldet – B. Dorokhovo, km 19+400, in Tomsk region".

Row No. / section No.	Displacement, mm										
	1	2	3	4	5	6	7	8	9	10	11
1	28	28	27	26	24	25	26	25	21	23	23
2	26	27	24	24	24	20	21	22	22	22	20
3	25	23	20	20	20	20	18	18	20	19	21
4	27	24	23	21	24	20	18	19	18	20	18
5	27	20	24	22	19	21	18	21	19	24	28
6	29	26	27	20	19	19	19	19	21	25	27
7	33	29	27	25	26	27	25	25	28	29	31

Note: see distances between points in a row and in a section in Figure 1.

On the basis of these results, it is possible to determine the components of gradient tensor of displacement $\frac{\partial u_i}{\partial x_j}$ ($i=1$ – complies with axis x in the longitudinal direction, $i=2$ – complies with axis y in the transverse direction, $i=3$ – complies with axis z in the vertical directions). The antisymmetric part of the displacement gradient tensor $\Phi_{ij}=\frac{1}{2}\left(\frac{\partial u_i}{\partial x_j}-\frac{\partial u_j}{\partial x_i}\right)$ characterizes rotations (deflections). The symmetric part of this tensor $\varepsilon_{ij}^{C}=\frac{1}{2}\left(\frac{\partial u_i}{\partial x_j}+\frac{\partial u_j}{\partial x_i}\right)$ characterizes the stretching/compression and shear strain (the Cauchy strain) and can be used in case of small deflections. In case of large deflections, the use of the Cauchy strain measure becomes incorrect. It is necessary to use nonlinear Green's ratios [18] to describe the stress-strain state at large deflections:

$$\varepsilon_{ij}^{G}=\frac{1}{2}\left(\frac{\partial u_i}{\partial x_j}+\frac{\partial u_j}{\partial x_i}+\frac{\partial u_k}{\partial x_i}\frac{\partial u_k}{\partial x_j}\right). \tag{1}$$

If the displacement field is characterized with one component u_z ($u_x=0$, $u_y=0$), then Green's strain tensor components may be expressed as follows:

$$\varepsilon_{xx}^{G}=\frac{1}{2}\left(\frac{\partial u_z}{\partial x}\right)^2, \varepsilon_{yy}^{G}=\frac{1}{2}\left(\frac{\partial u_z}{\partial y}\right)^2, \varepsilon_{xy}^{G}=\frac{1}{2}\left(\frac{\partial u_z}{\partial x}\frac{\partial u_z}{\partial y}\right), \tag{2}$$

$$\varepsilon_{xz}^{G}=\frac{1}{2}\left(\frac{\partial u_z}{\partial x}\right), \varepsilon_{iz}^{G}=\frac{1}{2}\left(\frac{\partial u_z}{\partial y}\right), \quad \varepsilon_{zz}^{G}=\frac{1}{2}\left(\left(\frac{\partial u_x}{\partial z}\right)^2+\left(\frac{\partial u_y}{\partial z}\right)^2\right). \tag{3}$$

Equation (2, 3) was received on the basis of formula (1) on condition that the displacement field is characterized with one component u_z.

The stress field can be determined after determination of strains.

If the strain is elastic, then Hooke's law is observed, which is as follows in the index form [19]:

$$\sigma_{xx} = \frac{\nu E}{(1+\nu)(1-2\nu)}\left(\varepsilon_{xx}^{G} + \varepsilon_{yy}^{G} + \varepsilon_{zz}^{G}\right) + \frac{\nu E}{(1+\nu)}\varepsilon_{xx}^{G}, \tag{4}$$

$$\sigma_{yy} = \frac{\nu E}{(1+\nu)(1-2\nu)}\left(\varepsilon_{xx}^{G} + \varepsilon_{yy}^{G} + \varepsilon_{zz}^{G}\right) + \frac{\nu E}{(1+\nu)}\varepsilon_{yy}^{G}, \tag{5}$$

$$\sigma_{zz} = \frac{\nu E}{(1+\nu)(1-2\nu)}\left(\varepsilon_{xx}^{G} + \varepsilon_{yy}^{G} + \varepsilon_{zz}^{G}\right) + \frac{\nu E}{(1+\nu)}\varepsilon_{zz}^{G}, \tag{6}$$

$$\sigma_{xy} = \frac{\nu E}{(1+\nu)}\varepsilon_{xy}^{G}, \qquad \sigma_{xz} = \frac{\nu E}{(1+\nu)}\varepsilon_{xz}^{G}, \qquad \sigma_{yz} = \frac{\nu E}{(1+\nu)}\varepsilon_{yz}^{G}. \tag{7}$$

where E is the pavement elasticity module (assumed to be $E = 3000$ MPa in the calculations on the basis of design pavement temperature at section "Teguldet – B. Dorokhovo, km 19+400, in Tomsk region" of -21 ^{0}C), $\nu = 0{,}30$ is the Poison's ratio.

The design pavement temperature was assumed based on the air temperature regime in the area where the monitoring of pavement strain in winter was monitored and was determined by formula [20]:

$$T_{n}^{\min} = 0{,}859T_{\min} + 1{,}7,, \tag{8}$$

where $T_{\min}$ is the 5-day minimum air temperature, ^{0}C,

The invariant measure of strain is intensity of shear deformations:

$$U = \sqrt{2\left(\varepsilon_{ij}^{G} - \frac{1}{3}\varepsilon_{kk}^{G}\delta_{ij}\right)\left(\varepsilon_{ji}^{G} - \frac{1}{3}\varepsilon_{kk}^{G}\delta_{ij}\right)}. \tag{9}$$

As the stress invariant, shear stress intensity can be considered [21]:

$$S = \sqrt{\frac{1}{2}\left(\sigma_{ij} - \frac{1}{3}\sigma_{kk}\delta_{ij}\right)\left(\sigma_{ji} - \frac{1}{3}\sigma_{kk}\delta_{ij}\right)}. \tag{10}$$

According to the Huber-Mises-Henki condition, the transition from the elastic state to the plastic state occurs when the $\tau_Y = S$ condition is met [22]. In this case, stress tensor components may be determined from the following equations [18]:

$$\sigma_{xx} = \frac{\nu E}{(1+\nu)(1-2\nu)}\left(\varepsilon_{xx}^{G} + \varepsilon_{yy}^{G} + \varepsilon_{zz}^{G}\right) + \min\left[\frac{\nu E}{(1+\nu)}, 2\frac{\tau_Y}{U}\right]\varepsilon_{xx}^{G}, \tag{11}$$

$$\sigma_{yy} = \frac{\nu E}{(1+\nu)(1-2\nu)}\left(\varepsilon_{xx}^{G} + \varepsilon_{yy}^{G} + \varepsilon_{zz}^{G}\right) + \min\left[\frac{\nu E}{(1+\nu)}, 2\frac{\tau_Y}{U}\right]\varepsilon_{yy}^{G}, \tag{12}$$

$$\sigma_{zz} = \frac{\nu E}{(1+\nu)(1-2\nu)}\left(\varepsilon_{xx}^{G} + \varepsilon_{yy}^{G} + \varepsilon_{zz}^{G}\right) + \min\left[\frac{\nu E}{(1+\nu)}, 2\frac{\tau_Y}{U}\right]\varepsilon_{zz}^{G}, \tag{13}$$

$$\sigma_{xy} = \min\left[\frac{\nu E}{(1+\nu)}, 2\frac{\tau_{Y}}{U}\right]\varepsilon_{xy}^{G}, \quad (14)$$

$$\sigma_{xz} = \min\left[\frac{\nu E}{(1+\nu)}, 2\frac{\tau_{Y}}{U}\right]\varepsilon_{xz}^{G}, \quad (15)$$

$$\sigma_{yz} = \min\left[\frac{\nu E}{(1+\nu)}, 2\frac{\tau_{Y}}{U}\right]\varepsilon_{yz}^{G}. \quad (16)$$

The results of calculations of stress fields of the asphalt-concrete pavement are presented in Figures 2 to 7. In Figures 2 and 7, maximum shear displacement arise at the beginning and at the end of pavement section "Teguldet – B. Dorokhovo, km 19+400, in Tomsk region" in the *xz* vertical plane. The cracks that appeared on the pavement did not reach the monitoring area (Fig. 1). Perhaps, a greater increase in shear stresses caused formation of a transverse crack on the road surface.

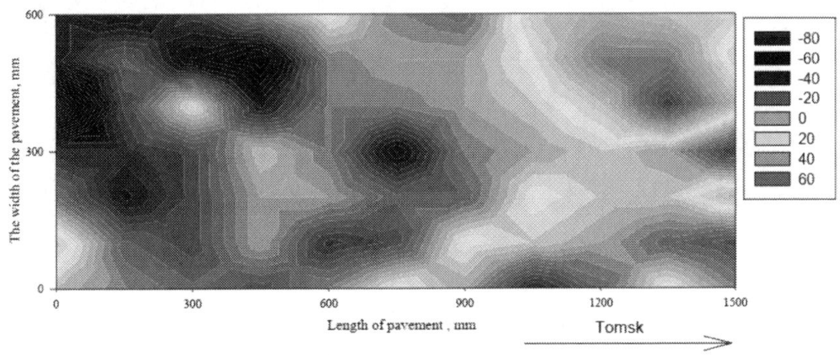

Fig. 2. Distribution of shear stresses on the roadbed surface in the *xz plane*.

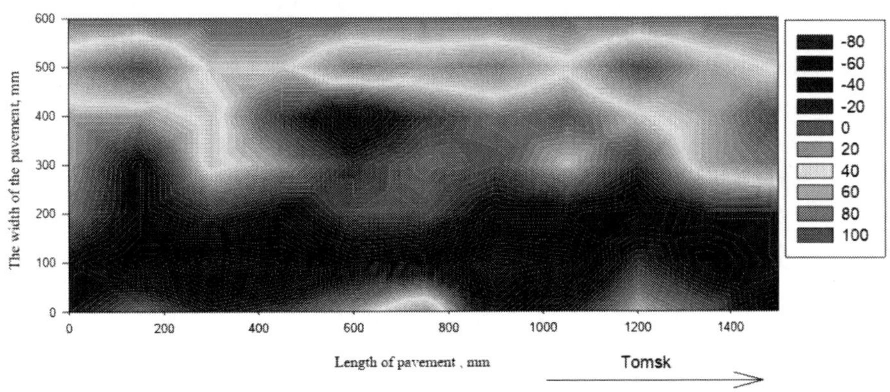

Fig. 3. Distribution of shear stresses on the roadbed surface in the *yz* plane.

The stresses (Fig. 3) that arose in the *yz* plane were caused by irregular freezing of soils under the roadbed and roadside verges. The condition for irregular freezing of the roadbed is large amount of snow on the roadside verges and the absence of snow on the pavement.

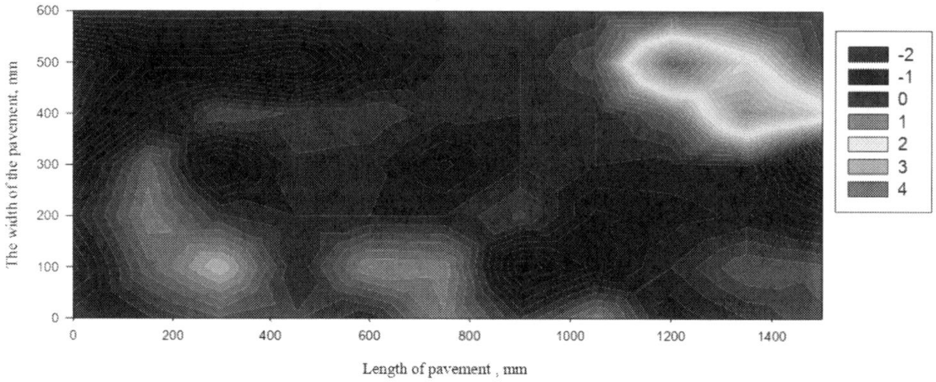

Fig. 4. Distribution of tensile stresses on the roadbed surface in the *xy plane*.

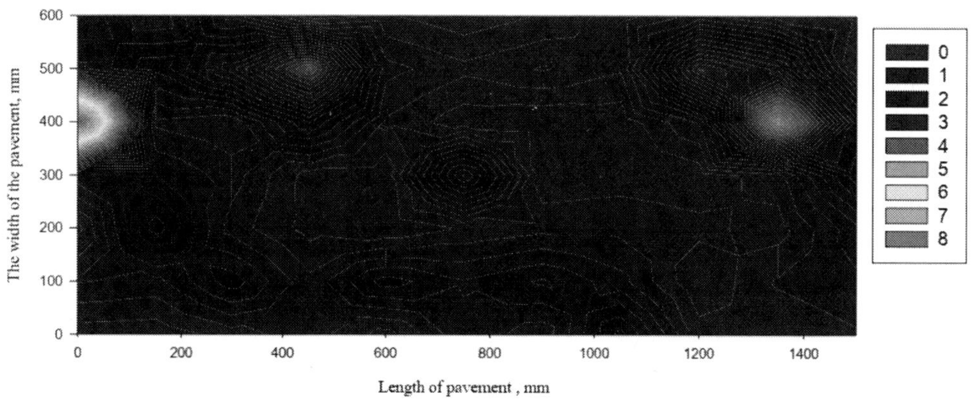

Fig. 5. Distribution of tensile stresses on the roadbed surface along the *xx* axis.

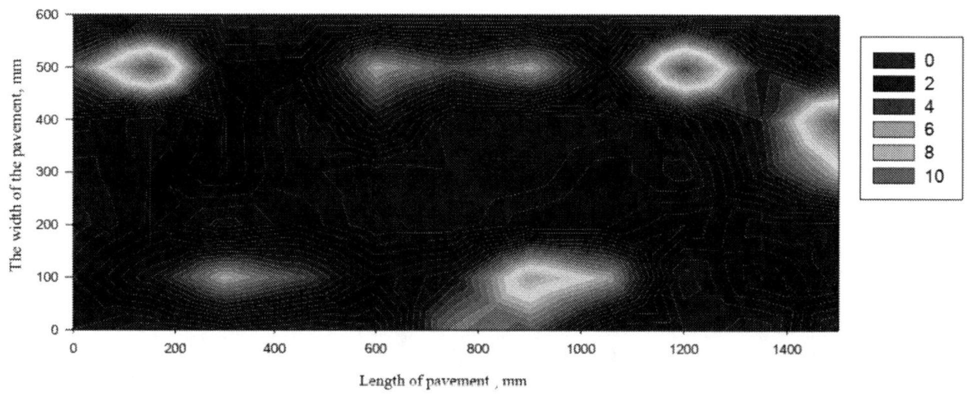

Fig. 6. Distribution of tensile stresses on the roadbed surface along the *yy* axis.

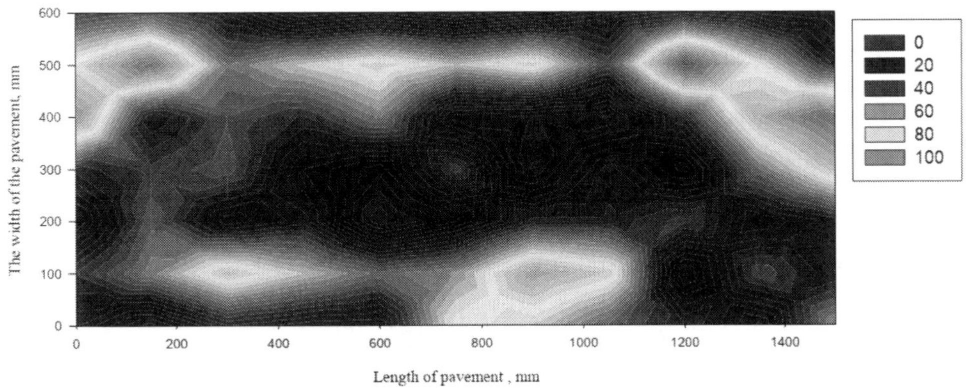

Fig. 7. Total intensity of shear stresses on the roadbed surface.

In Figure 4, stresses in the *xy* plane are insignificant as compared to the obtained value of asphalt-concrete bending strength of 6.8 MPa (at the design negative temperature of -21 ^{0}C) for this area. The adequacy of the model is confirmed by the results of field studies of pavements and laboratory experiments (Table 2).

Table 2. Comparison of tensile stresses in the proposed mathematical model with the critical stresses obtained in laboratory conditions for asphalt-concrete and field monitoring of the road pavement.

Section title	Section No.	Design tensile stresses according to the proposed mathematical model, MPa	Critical tensile stresses, MPa	Surface condition
Melnikovo – Kozhevnikovo km 22+620	5	8.0	7.1	transverse crack
Parabel – Kargasok km 166+400	4	10.0	8.2	longitudinal crack
Molchanovo - Chazhemto km 231+500	1	12.0	8.5	transverse crack
Teguldet - B. Dorokhovo km 3+844	7	8.0	7.5	diagonal crack

It must be noted that there are small areas in Figures 5 and 6 that exceed limit values of the bending strength. Cracks of local nature and not long cracks were not registered. It was very difficult to visually regster formation of micro cracks.

Conclusion

Development of the pavement stress prediction model allows considering material characteristics and determining the most critical conditions of the pavement during operation of roads in winter. Based on the results of the study, the model was built that adequately predicted stresses in pavement. Application of the model will ensure the quality of designing frost-resistant roadbeds in areas with deep seasonal freezing. However, the model requires further calibration and continued monitoring of strains in road pavement in winter. To ensure that the model conforms to the actual conditions of pavement operation, more initial information on the pavement material is needed. For example, the effect of aging of bitumen on the strain strength characteristics of asphalt-concrete. Development of a model for predicting behavior of materials of the underlying layers of pavement as a result of frosty soils heaving in the roadbed is not less important.

References

1. M. Sarady, Licentiate thesis, Uppsala University, Uppsala 2014.
2. Premature asphalt concrete pavement cracking. Final report (Oregon Department of Transportation, 2015)
3. B.B. Teltaev, Reports of the National Academy of the Republic of Kazakhstan **302,** 40–65 (2015). (in Russian)
4. Wu, Zhong, and Danny X. Xiao. Development of DARWin-ME Design Guideline for Louisiana Pavement Design. No. FHWA/LA. 11/551. 2016
5. S.V. Bel'kovskij, *Proektirovanie gruntovyh osnovanij usovershenstvovannyh pokrytij s uchjotom ih raboty v zimnih uslovijah* [Design of soil bases for improved coatings, taking into account their work in winter conditions], 53 – 114 (1953). (in Russian)
6. F. Rengmark, Highway Research Board **33**, 137-157 (1963).
7. Summary report of a cooperative analysis by teams from Iowa, Kansas, Nebraska North Dakota and Oklahoma. Transverse cracking of asphalt pavements. Final report (U.S. Department of Transportation, 1982).
8. N.G. Göransson, Uppföljning av vägars tekniska tillstånd: lägesrapport för observationssträckor ingående i LTPP-projektet till och med december 2017, 1-2018, (Swedish National Road and Transport Research Institute, Linköping, 2018).
9. B.S. Radovskiy, A.S. Suprun, *Proektirovanie dorozhnyh odezhd dlja dvizhenija bol'shegruznyh avtomobilej* [Designing of road clothes for the heavy vehicles (Budivelnik, 1989). (in Russian)
10. B.B. Teltaev, Doctoral thesis, Institute of Mechanics and Engineering, National Academy of Sciences of the Republic of Kazakhstan (Almaty, 1998). (in Russian)
11. A.V. Smirnov, Raschjot dorozhnyh i ajerodromnyh konstrukcij na dinamicheskie vozdejstvija [Calculation of road and airfield structures for dynamic impacts] (SibADI, Omsk, 2008). (in Russian)
12. M. Li, H. Wang, American society of civil engineers, **Vol. 144**(2), 04018014 (2018).
13. J. Lubliner, *Plasticity theory* (Courier Corporation, 2008).
14. S. Efimenko, V. Efimenko, A. Sukhorukov, *AIP Conference Proceedings*, **1698**, 1 (2016).
15. V.S. Churilin, A.V. Sukhorukov, M.B. Badina, *Youth, science, technology: new ideas and perspectives (YSIP-2017),* Proceedings of the IV International scientific conference, 334 – 336 (Tomsk, 2017). (in Russian)
16. V.S. Churilin, Vestnik of TSUAB, **5** (2015). (in Russian)
17. O.V. Matvienko, V.P. Bazuev, V.S. Churilin, Dorogi i mostyi [Roads and Bridges], **36** (2017). (in Russian)
18. V.V. Novozhilov, *Osnovy nelinejnoj teorii uprugosti* [Fundamentals of the nonlinear theory of elasticity] (Moscow, 2003). (in Russian)
19. A.G. Gorshkov, E.I. Starovojtov, D.V Tarlakovskiy, *Teorija uprugosti i plastichnosti* [Theory of elasticity and plasticity] (Fizmatlit, Moscow, 2002). (in Russian)

20. Superpave Performance Graded Asphalt Binder Specification and Testing. Asphalt Institute Superpave. Series **1** (1997).
21. O.V. Matvienko, V.P. Bazuev, V.N. Venik, Vestnik of TSUAB, **4,** 165 - 176 (2017). (in Russian)
22. D.M. Klimov, A.G. Petrov, D.V. Georgievskiy, *Vjazkoplasticheskie techenija. Dinamicheskij haos, ustojchivost', peremeshivanie* [Viscous plastic flows. Dynamic chaos, stability, mixing] (Nauka, Moscow, 2005). (in Russian)

Features of dynamic loading of transport vehicles in intensive operation

Andrey Eliseev[1,*], *Sergey* Eliseev[1], and *Alexey* Orlenko[2]

[1]Irkutsk State Transport University, 664074 Irkutsk, Russia
[2]Krasnoyarsk Institute of Railway Transport, branch of the Irkutsk State Transport University, 660028 Krasnoyarsk, Russia

Abstract. The paper proposes a method to construct mathematical models of technical objects exposed to intense vibrational interactions, which is typical for assemblies of transport vehicles. A technique has been developed to construct structural mathematical models in the form of structural diagrams, which are dynamically equivalent to automatic control systems. Analytical tools have been adopted from the theory of automatic control. The paper demonstrates the possibilities of changing dynamic properties of technical objects, design schemes of which are represented by mechanical oscillatory systems. Changes in the dynamic effects arising from the introduction of additional inertial couplings have been estimated. Effects of new dynamic properties have been considered. Analytic relations have been proposed for detailed estimates.

Introduction

Maintaining operational reliability and safety of railway rolling stock is one of the most important and relevant scientific and engineering problems, which have been reflected in studies of Russian scientists [1–3]. The development prospects of transport systems require that a special attention is given to developing a methodological basis for dynamics and operation of vehicles under intense dynamic loading. It is important to assess dynamic states of transport vehicles because this assessment plays an important role in developing principles and specific techniques to be implemented in the systems that ensure the general operational safety of transport vehicles and reliability of their major units and assemblies [4–6].

An increase in speeds and axle loads has a significant effect on the dynamic state of a traction motor. This can be attributed to a change in dynamic stiffness and generation of dynamic bursts produced by a combination of disturbing factors. Some aspects of these issues are considered in [7–10]. The available studies show that motions with increased velocities initiate the development of oscillatory processes with increasing oscillation amplitudes and resulting impact interactions. Passive means of adjusting dynamic states of motor mounting at high speeds of vehicles are not effective enough, especially in situations where natural frequencies and dynamic damping of oscillations are sufficiently close to

* Corresponding author: eliseew_aw@irgups.ru

© The Authors, published by EDP Sciences. This is an open access article distributed under the terms of the Creative Commons Attribution License 4.0 (http://creativecommons.org/licenses/by/4.0/).

each other. A promising solution in these situations is using motion conversion devices that are capable to widely vary the reduced mass of an object with a controlled dynamic state.

Traction electric motors of electric locomotives are among the technical devices that are subject to a lot of mechanical factors arising from both wheel–rail contacts and interactions with the entire complex mechanical system as a whole, which is determined by structural and engineering characteristics of a locomotive [11–12].

The novelty of this study is in examining scientific foundations underlying mechanisms of dynamic bursts or a certain bunch of oscillatory processes that arise in contacts between the traction motor case and elements connected to the truck frame. The authors put forward the idea of constructing frequency diagrams with families of frequency parameters (partial and natural frequencies, dynamic damping frequencies) constructed according to a parameter to be adjusted. The physical meaning of the burst generation mechanism implies uncontrolled convergence of frequency parameters due to simultaneous action of several external disturbances.

This study focuses on methodological aspects in the development of methods and tools aimed at maintaining the operational safety of locomotive traction motors. The key feature of the approach is that it takes into account possibilities of changing dynamic states of a motor mounting system in transport vehicles by introducing additional couplings. The paper gives a special focus to connectivity between parameters of mounting elements and simultaneous action of several external disturbances so that these aspects are taken into account in the approach.

Problem statement

Design diagrams representing mechanical oscillatory systems with lumped parameters and several degrees of freedom are used to assess dynamic properties of technical objects, including traction motors. Depending on tasks assigned, traction motors can be represented as mechanical chain systems with two or three degrees of freedom, as well as mechanical oscillatory systems with an object in the form of a solid body on elastic supports, which is in planar motion (Fig. 1). External influences on the traction motor are generated not only as external kinematic disturbances on the side of the bearing surface, but also can be created by irregular electrical loads on the traction motor armature and periodic force disturbances of a different nature [6].

Dynamics of traction motor units can be detailed according to the notions of vibrational effects from the traction motor case on the operation of the commutator-and-brush assembly. The commutator-and-brush assembly is subject to a large number of mechanical factors, among which contacts with surface roughnesses of the armature commutator are of particular importance. At the same time, vibrations from the case of the commutator-and-brush assembly significantly affect the operation of the traction electric motor [2, 11].

Figure 1 shows the design diagram of a frame- and axle-mounted traction electric motor. A special feature of the design scheme is the introduction of additional couplings in the mechanical oscillatory system (Fig. 1) in the form of motion conversion devices with reduced masses L_1 and L_2. Values of these parameters may change if the following condition is fulfilled:

$$L_2 = \alpha L_1, \tag{1}$$

where α is the connectivity coefficient for parameters L_1 and L_2. It is assumed that α is a positive quantity and can vary in a sufficiently wide range [13].

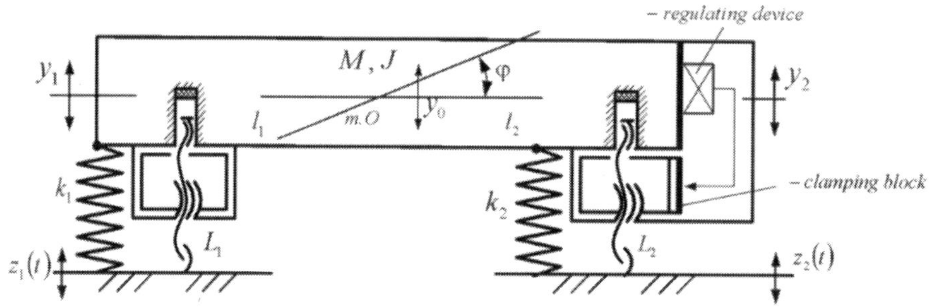

Fig. 1. The design diagram of a frame- and axle-mounted traction electric motor for motion conversion.

The authors are developing an approach within the framework of structural mathematical modeling [14]. The mathematical model of the initial system (Fig. 1) is presented in Figure 2. It is represented as a structural scheme that is dynamically equivalent to the automatic control system.

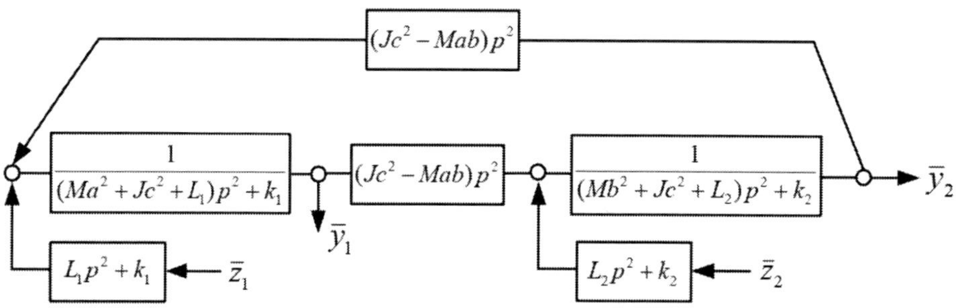

Fig. 2. The structural mathematical model of the initial system taken from Figure 1 with kinematic disturbances.

Figure 2 assumes that $p = j\omega$ as a complex variable; symbol "–" over the variable means its Laplace transform under zero initial conditions [15 ÷ 16]. The system has two input actions: $\bar{z}_1$ and $\bar{z}_2$. The dynamic state is estimated with variables $\bar{y}_1$, $\bar{y}_2$; M, J — weight and moment of inertia of the solid body, respectively; a, b, c — the geometric parameters of the system.

The purpose of the study is to assess the features of a dynamic system, which is simultaneously excited by several disturbances that create some specific dynamic effects.

Mathematical modeling

Taking into account the simultaneous action of external disturbances, transfer functions of the system can be represented as

$$W_1(p)\Big|_{\bar{z}_1=\bar{z}_2=\bar{z}} = \frac{\bar{y}_1}{\bar{z}} = \frac{(L_1p^2+k_1)[(Mb^2+Jc^2+L_2)p^2+k_2]+(L_2p^2+k_2)(Jc^2-Mab)p^2}{A(p)}, \quad (2)$$

$$W_2(p)\big|_{\bar{z}_1=\bar{z}_2=\bar{z}}=\frac{\bar{y}_2}{\bar{z}}=$$
$$=\frac{(L_2p^2+k_2)[(Ma^2+Jc^2+L_1)p^2+k_1]+(L_1p^2+k_1)(Jc^2-Mab)p^2}{A(p)}, \quad (3)$$

where

$$A(p)=[(Ma^2+Jc^2+L_1)p^2+k_1]\cdot[(Mb^2+Jc^2+L_2)p^2+k_2]-$$
$$-[(Jc^2-Mab)p^2]^2, \quad (4)$$

a, b, c are the geometric parameters.

From (2) ÷ (4) it follows that the system has two frequencies at which resonant phenomena are possible. Frequencies of such processes can be determined from equation (4). In turn, the system for each coordinate $\bar{y}_1$, $\bar{y}_2$ may be subject to the dynamic oscillation damping mode. The respective oscillation frequencies can be determined by setting the numerators of the transfer functions (2) and (3) to zero.

Using (1), (2) ÷ (4) can be transformed as follows

$$W_1'(p)\big|_{L_2=\alpha L_1}=\frac{\bar{y}_1}{\bar{z}}=$$
$$=\frac{(L_1p^2+k_1)[(Mb^2+Jc^2+\alpha L_1)p^2+k_2]+(\alpha L_1p^2+k_2)(Jc^2-Mab)p^2}{A_1(p)}, \quad (5)$$

$$W_1'(p)\big|_{L_2=\alpha L_1}=\frac{\bar{y}_2}{\bar{z}}=$$
$$=\frac{(\alpha L_1p^2+k_2)[(Ma^2+Jc^2+L_1)p^2+k_1]+(L_1p^2+k_1)(Jc^2-Mab)p^2}{A_1(p)}, \quad (6)$$

where

$$A_1(p)=[(Ma^2+Jc^2+L_1)p^2+k_1]\cdot[(Mb^2+Jc^2+\alpha L_1)p^2+k_2]-$$
$$-[(Jc^2-Mab)p^2]^2. \quad (7)$$

In this case, the partial frequencies of the system are given by expressions

$$n_1^2=\frac{k_1}{Ma^2+Jc^2+L_1}, \quad (8)$$

$$n_2^2=\frac{k_2}{Mb^2+Jc^2+\alpha L_1}, \quad (9)$$

from which it follows that the partial frequency n_2 depends on the connectivity coefficient α. In our case, in contrast to conventional approaches [13, 14], dynamic damping frequencies will no longer coincide with values of partial frequencies, but will be determined from the "zeroing" condition, i.e. setting the numerators of the rational expressions in the corresponding transfer functions to zero. This can be attributed, in particular, to features of solutions to two biquadratic equations.

$$p^4[L_1(Mb^2+Jc^2+\alpha L_1)+\alpha L_1(Jc^2-Mab)]+p^2[k_1(Mb^2+Jc^2+\alpha L_1)+ \\ +k_2(L_1+Jc^2-Mab)]+k_1k_2=0, \tag{10}$$

$$p^4[\alpha L_1(Ma^2+Jc^2+L_1)+L_1(Jc^2-Mab)]+p^2[k_2(Ma^2+Jc^2+L_1)+ \\ +k_1(\alpha L_1+Jc^2-Mab)]+k_1k_2=0. \tag{11}$$

Thus, the probability of dynamic damping conditions of oscillations will be assessed according to the corresponding roots of equations (10) and (11). In this respect, a grapho-analytical method has some capabilities and could be called a "frequency diagram construction method".

This diagram is constructed as a set of dependency graphs $n_1^2(\alpha)$, $n_2^2(\alpha)$, $\omega_{1\,dyn}^2(\alpha)$, $\omega_{2\,dyn}^2(\alpha)$, $\omega_{1\,nat}^2(\alpha)$, $\omega_{2\,nat}^2(\alpha)$. The dependency graphs $\omega_{1\,dyn}^2(\alpha)$ $\omega_{2\,dyn}^2(\alpha)$ show relationships between dynamic oscillation damping conditions. Conventional interaction schemes, in which $L_1 = 0$, $L_2 = 0$ in the coordinate system y_1 and y_2, with only a single external disturbance (e.g., $z_1(t) \neq 0$, $z_2(t) = 0$), the dynamic oscillation damping mode can be realized only with respect to the coordinate $\bar{y}_1$. In this case, the dynamic damping frequency coincides with the partial frequency n_1, i.e. $\omega_{1\,dyn}^2 = n_2^2$. In the case where $z_1(t) = 0$, $z_2(t) \neq 0$, only one disturbing factor will be involved as well. In this connection, the dynamic damping frequency will also coincide with the corresponding partial frequency, i.e., the condition $\omega_{2\,dyn}^2 = n_1^2$ will be satisfied.

With the simultaneous action of two kinematic perturbations, $\bar{z}_1 = \bar{z}_2 = \bar{z}$ and $L_1 = 0$, $L_2 = 0$, dynamic damping frequencies can be realized with respect to both coordinates — $\bar{y}_1$ and $\bar{y}_2$, which is defined by expressions:

$$\omega_{1\,dyn}^2 = \frac{k_1k_2}{Jc^2(k_1+k_2)+Mb(k_1b-k_2a)}, \tag{12}$$

$$\omega_{2\,dyn}^2 = \frac{k_1k_2}{Jc^2(k_1+k_2)+Ma(k_2a-k_1b)}. \tag{13}$$

Provided that $k_1b - k_2a = 0$, two dynamic damping frequency modes can coincide with each other at a single frequency, which corresponds to certain symmetry relations of system properties (at $a = b$, the condition $k_1 = k_2$ is satisfied; this case needs to be addressed separately).

Estimation of dynamic properties based on the frequency diagram of the system

The following system parameters are selected to construct a frequency diagram for the model problem. M = 7,000 *kg*; J = 2,000 *kg.m*^{2}; a = 0.57; b = 0.43; c = 0.71; k_1= 1,000 *kN/m*; k_2 = 2,000 *kN/m*; l_1 = 0.6 *m*; l_2 = 0.8 *m*; L_1= 100 *kg*.

The dynamic damping frequency at which simultaneous dynamic damping of oscillations will occur is identified by intersection of the dependence graphs $\omega_{1\,dyn}^2(\alpha)$ and

$\omega^2_{2\,dyn}(\alpha)$ on the frequency diagram (Fig. 3). Two graphs $\omega^2_{1\,dyn}(\alpha)$ and $\omega^2_{2\,dyn}(\alpha)$ intersect at point (2), which simultaneously determines the coefficient of connectivity α and a frequency at which simultaneous dynamic damping occurs with respect to coordinates y_1 and y_2. Point (1') determines the dynamic damping case only with respect to the coordinate y_2. In both cases, points (1) and (1') can be projected to the y-axis in parallel to determine the respective dynamic damping frequencies. Moreover, point (2) is an intersection point between the dependency graphs $\omega^2_{1\,dyn}(\alpha)$ and $\omega^2_{2\,dyn}(\alpha)$, which determines the dynamic damping mode with respect to both coordinates. This occurs at $\alpha = 31{,}205$. The dynamic damping frequency can be found in the same way — by projecting the points to the y-axis. Points (3), (3') and (4) are representative of the effects of a significant change in the dependence graphs $\omega^2_{1\,dyn}(\alpha)$ and $\omega^2_{2\,dyn}(\alpha)$, which is associated with the corresponding frequency responses of the system [13].

The frequency diagram (Fig. 3) shows partial, natural and dynamic damping frequencies as a function of α (symbols used on the dependency graphs are explained in Fig. 3). In order to show the system properties, representative points of the graphs are introduced. In this case, points (1), (2), (3), and (4) are considered.

In order to estimate the features of the frequency diagram in the vicinity of points (3) and (3'), point (5) with a value $\alpha = 0.93$, marked on the x-axis of the dependence curve $\omega^2_{1\,dyn}(\alpha)$ (Fig. 3), is used. Point (4) corresponds to bends on the dependence curve $\omega^2_{2\,dyn}(\alpha)$. For point (1), which corresponds to $\alpha = 2$ (on the x-axis), the frequency diagram reflects specific dynamic properties: both coordinates $\bar{y}_1$, $\bar{y}_2$ become equal to zero simultaneously at the same frequency.

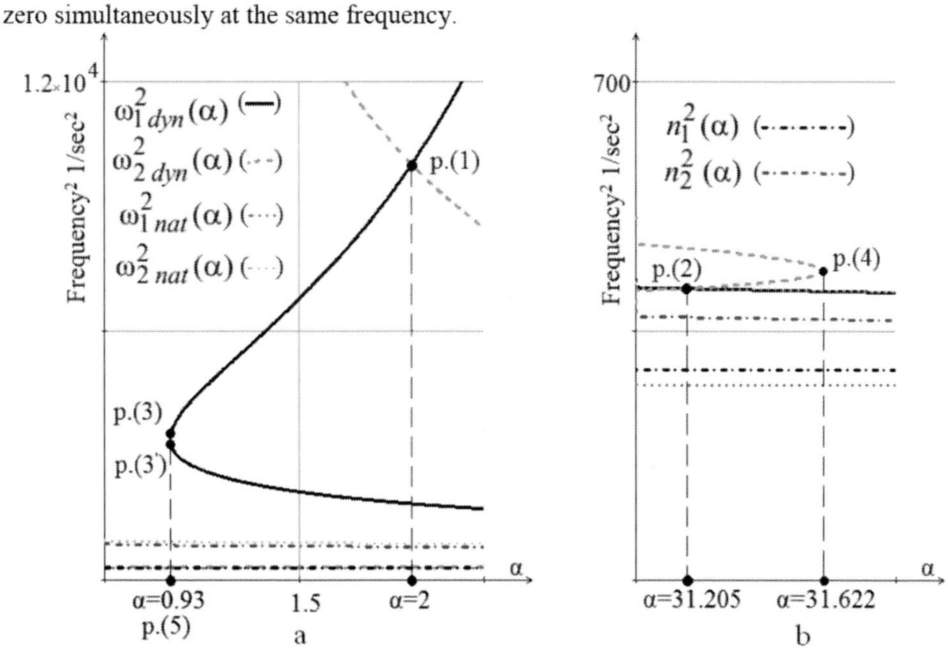

Fig. 3. The frequency diagram for determining dynamic damping modes at $L_1 \neq 0$, $L_2 \neq 0$ and different values of the connectivity coefficient α: a - a range of the y-coordinate (0.1.2x10^4); b - a range of the y-coordinate (0, 700).

Thus, the frequency diagram gives an integral representation of distribution dynamics for characteristic frequencies of the system and the possibilities of realizing certain dynamic effects.

Conclusion

The authors have developed a method to construct mathematical models aimed at estimating dynamic properties of systems with several degrees of freedom under the combined action of several external in-phase harmonic disturbances. They propose a method for constructing frequency diagrams of mechanical oscillation systems. These methods have been used to study possible dynamic properties of systems under the simultaneous action of two disturbances in dynamic damping modes. Possibilities of generating dynamic damping modes with respect to two coordinates simultaneously, as well as change modes of frequency response with variation of the connectivity coefficient α, have been identified. It has been shown that changes in dynamic properties of the system can be obtained by introducing additional links or devices for motion conversion. Physically, the connectivity coefficient determines the ratio between reduced masses of motion conversion devices.

The authors have developed an original method to estimate the potential for generating various instability modes in processes where natural frequencies and dynamic damping of oscillations converge to each other. They have proposed a method based on the construction of frequency diagrams that can be used to find possible frequency zones of unstable operation. It has been shown that dynamic bursts are shown to be predetermined by a combination of disturbing factors. Physically, this phenomenon is equivalent to a change in the reduced dynamic stiffness. Change in the reduced mass, whose value is generated by a special motion conversion mechanism can be controlled, thereby maintaining the level of oscillations of traction motors within a normal range and avoiding collisions of the motor case against stops.

A feasibility study of active mounting systems for traction motors, which are capable to prevent dynamic bursts exceeding the recommended limits in terms of quantity and qualitative parameters, can be proposed as one of further research areas.

References

1. O.S. Valinsky, Zheleznodorozhnyj transport [Railway transport] **2,** 48-51 (2018). (In Russian)
2. A.I. Orlenko, M.N. Petrov, O.A. Teregulov, *Kompleksnaja diagnostika tjagovogo jelektrodvigatelja jelektrovoza* [Comprehensive diagnostics of locomotive traction electric motor] (OOO Polikom, Krasnoyarsk, 2016). (In Russian)
3. V.V. Kharlamov, P.K. Shkodun, A.V. Dolgova, D.A. Akhunov, *Sovershenstvovanie tehnologii diagnostirovanija tehnicheskogo sostojanija kollektorno-shhetochnogo uzla tjagovyh jelektrodvigatelej jelektrovozov* [Improvement of diagnistics technologies for operational condition of a collector-and-brush assembly unit of locomotive traction electric motor] (OSTU, Omsk, 2015) (In Russian).
4. A.N. Savoskin, Y.S. Romen, A.A. Akishin, World of Transport and Transportation **13** 1 (56), (2015). (In Russian)
5. Y.S. Romen, Zheleznodorozhnyj transport [Railway transport] **11,** 62-64 (2017). (In Russian)
6. A.N. Smalev, Candidate of sciences thesis, Omsk, 2011. (In Russian)
7. A. Sladkowski, *Rail Transport—Systems Approach* (Cham: Springer, 2017).

8. A. S. Girnik, A. L. Fedyanin, A. V. Kiselev, E, S. Dorokhina, J. Mach. Manuf. Reliab. **46,** 240-245 (2017)
9. D. Ya. Antipin, D. A. Bondarenko, O. V. Izmerov, Procedia Engineering **206**, 1583-6 (2017).
10. I. Galiev, A. Shiler, A. Kildibekov, I. Kukushkin, Procedia Engineering **100,** 1724-31 (2015).
11. S.K. Ismailov, Doctoral thesis, Omsk, 2004. (In Russian)
12. I.I. Galiev, V.A. Nekhaev, V.A. Nikolaev, *Metody i sredstva vibrozashhity zheleznodorozhnyh jekipazhej* [Methods and means of vibration protection of railway carriages] (Moscow, 2010). (In Russian)
13. S.V. Eliseev, A.I. Orlenko, *V sbornike: Kulaginskie chtenija: tehnika i tehnologii proizvodstvennyh processov* [Proceedings of Kulaginskie readings: methods and technologies of production processes], 142-148 (Transbaikal State University Publ., Chita, 2017). (In Russian)
14. S.V. Eliseev, A.I. Artyunin, *Prikladnaja teorija kolebanij v zadachah dinamiki linejnyh mehanicheskih sistem* [Applied theory of vibrations in problems of linear mechanical systems dynamics] (Nauka Publ., Novosibirsk, 2016). (In Russian)
15. de Silva, Clarence W.,*Vibration. Fundamentals and Practice* (Boca Raton, London, New York, Washington, D.C.: CRC Press, 2000).
16. I.A. Karnovsky, E. Lebed. *Theory of vibration protection.* (Switzerland: Springer, 2016).

Asphalt concrete pavement reinforced with chemical fibers

Viktor Lukashevich[1,*], *Igor* Efanov[1], *Viktor* Vlasov[1], and *Olga* Lukashevich[1]

[1]Tomsk State University of Architecture and Building, 634003 Tomsk, Russia

Abstract. Asphalt concrete pavement which is currently built in accordance with the existing requirements does not withstand the standard service life. Various kinds of damages occur. Fiber reinforcement of asphalt concretes is one of the effective means to deal with deformations and fractures of road pavements, such as rutting, buckling, crack formation and shear. Chemical fibers serving as reinforcement are of great concern herein. The major purpose of this work was evaluation of reinforcement fibers resistance to natural environment and climatic impacts within the conditions of experimental production construction and studying compactibility of asphalt concrete mixture with fiber reinforcement. Infrared spectroscopy and physical-chemical investigations of fibers were used to study changing properties of fiber-forming polymer. Compactibility of asphalt concrete mixture with fiber reinforcement was determined upon compaction factor. Research results revealed insignificant influence of natural environment and climatic impacts on the properties of fiber reinforcement material. In order to obtain the standard compaction factor of asphalt concrete additional compacting impact is not required.

Introduction

Asphalt concrete pavements have been distinguished with economic feasibility, simplicity of construction, maintenance and repair and possibility of the material to be recovered and reused, thus resulting in their wide application on the roads of the majority of world countries. However, their strength properties are largely dependent on the ambient temperature which makes it one of the major shortages of pavements of such kinds. At high positive temperatures asphalt concrete possesses low resistance to shear load, while under negative temperatures it lacks sufficient crack resistance. Hence, it results in occurring deformations of asphalt concrete pavements (rutting, crack formation, buckling and shear).

Both processing and constructive techniques are applied to reduce the intensity of deformations occurrence. Fiber reinforcement of asphalt concrete mixtures has been proven to be the most effective technique among them, as confirmed by the studies in [1-3]. Belarusian and Russian scientists A.V. Akulich, I.P. Gamelyak, Y.N. Kovalev proved that fiber-reinforced asphalt concretes (FRAC) have higher shear strength at high temperatures,

*Corresponding author: vnluc@yandex.ru

© The Authors, published by EDP Sciences. This is an open access article distributed under the terms of the Creative Commons Attribution License 4.0 (http://creativecommons.org/licenses/by/4.0/).

better tensile strength and enhanced deformability under negative temperatures and they are more resilient to fatigue failures [4-9].

In spite of the fact that a significant amount of studies are devoted to FRAC, still there are a number of issues to be investigated. The influence of natural environment and climate on the properties of reinforcement fibers is insufficiently studied. The issues of compactibility of asphalt concrete mixtures subject to chemical fiber reinforcement have also not been investigated yet. The present paper aims to study the influence of natural environment and climate on physical-chemical properties of fiber reinforcement; and to determine compactibility of FRAC mixture within the conditions of experimental production construction.

Materials and methods

The resistance of reinforcement fibers was investigated in laboratory and experimental production conditions. Rope-shaped nylon fibers with the linear density 250 tex. were randomly selected. They were further divided into four groups of specimens, 50 meters long each. The specimens in the first group were reference ones and they were not subjected to treatment. Specimens of the other groups were placed in bitumen, then taken out and purified in hexane. Oil bitumen (Russian grade BND 90/130) was used for treatment, as it is most commonly used in road-construction companies of West Siberia. Hexane was used for purification of fibers from oil bitumen due to its being the most pure product having clearly distinctive characteristic absorption bands as seen from infrared spectroscopy investigations; moreover, hexane has slight influence on the general nature of changes in specimens under study.

Ageing of specimens was performed using artificial weather apparatus IP-1-3 brand, (weathering machine). The influence of atmospheric factors of moderately continental, subtropical and northern climates was imitated with the aid of this machine. The machine looks like an isolated chamber. Inside the chamber a cylinder is mounted (a drum to fasten and move the specimens) which rotates with the velocity of 1 circle per minute. In the center of the drum there are two arc lamps and two mercury quartz lamps PRK-2 of ultraviolet lighting. They provide emission which is close to sunlight by its spectral composition. The integrated radiant flux surface density (730±130) W/m^2 is provided inside the machine while flux density of ultraviolet lighting per unit area is (30±5) W/m^2. The machine has two spray systems: the first is for simulating humidity conditions in the chamber, the second is for watering of the specimens. The machine has panel board, electric motor for drum drive, gear box, resistors for arc lamps, fan, manometric thermometers (self-recording and indicating), nozzles for watering of the specimens, automatic valve, cycle timer to set the watering mode. The fibers were tested in artificial weather apparatus at the mode simulating northern climatic conditions. The number of impact cycles of climatic factors corresponded to pavement service life of 18 years. After treatment in climatic chamber, the specimens were purified from bitumen by hexane.

Degree of compaction of FRAC mixture was determined in the conditions of experimental production works. Compaction factor was determined according to the methodology stated by the regulatory documents [10]. Infrared spectra of the fibers were recorded using "Specord M-80" spectrophotometer. Spectra identification was performed with the aid of the reference data [11].

Results

The properties of asphalt concrete obtained according to the conventional technologies are characterized by interactions within the system "mineral – bitumen". The adhesion between the particles of mineral material in asphalt concrete mixture and therefore, the strength of asphalt concrete is primarily provided by absorption-solvation bitumen shells which are there on the surface of mineral particles. It should be noted that the adhesion of each particle is performed only by the neighboring particles surrounding it (short-range order adhesion). There is no adhesion between the mineral particle and the particles separated from it by the rows of other particles (long-range order adhesion). The nature of these interactions changes in the presence of reinforcement fibers.

The basic factor enabling to lower the intensity of occurrence of such road pavements deformations as rutting, crack formation, buckling and shear is the presence of fiber reinforcement in asphalt concrete composition. These segments of reinforcement are placed between the grains of mineral material and are in the absorption-solvation bitumen shells. Passing through the patterned bitumen layers surrounding several particles, reinforcement fibers are hooked in them thus providing additional adhesion between these particles. In this way, adhesion between the particles of fiber-reinforced materials is basically provided by the two types of cohesion: by the patterned bitumen layers and by the fiber reinforcement hooked in these layers. Moreover, each particle in fiber-reinforced materials is bonded not only with the surrounding particles (short-range order adhesion) but also with the particles separated from it by several rows of other particles (long-range order adhesion). Reinforcement fibers are bonded with each other due to their location in the patterned bitumen layer. Thus, they form space lattice in asphalt concrete mixture which encircles mineral particles within the conglomerate composition. It results in substantial improvement of all the properties of asphalt concrete mixture.

Fiber reinforcement of asphalt concrete requires provision of established space lattice from segments of chemical fibers, uniformly distributed throughout the total volume. In case this condition is not followed, the asphalt concrete layer will not be equal in strength, as separate parts of pavement will not be covered by reinforcing space lattice. The lower strength properties of such areas will cause initiation of fractures, specifically in these areas; the effect of fiber reinforcement will not be accomplished.

The increase of strength and rheological properties in fiber reinforcement occurs in consequence of extended structures formation from reinforcement fibers. Closely spaced fibers are bonded into single structures – strength clusters. The size and shape of such structures (clusters) and the strength of fibers determine the properties of reinforced materials [9]. In this regard, it is of great importance to study the resistance of reinforcement fibers to the impact of oil bitumen and natural environment and climatic impacts. This refers in particular to periodical moistening and drying, heating and cooling, freezing and thawing. One of the major factors leading to destruction of polymer materials is ultraviolet lighting impact.

Investigations of resistance of reinforcement fibers to the impact of oil bitumen and natural environment and climatic impacts were carried out in laboratory and in the conditions of experimental production works.

The properties of four groups of reinforcement specimens from nylon rope-shaped fibers were investigated:

1 – reference specimens (without treatment);

2 – specimens placed in bitumen, taken out and purified in hexane;

3 – specimens placed in bitumen, aged in weathering machine for 18 hours, purified in hexane;

4 – specimens placed in asphalt concrete on the experimental plot of road pavement and taken out after 7 years of operation.

The fourth group of specimens was used in the process of experimental production works on construction of experimental plot of road pavement. Fine-grained fiber-reinforced dense asphalt concrete of B type was used for that purpose. It was compacted from hot mixture and its properties coincided to the requirements of Russian National State Standard GOST 9128[12]. Experimental production works on construction of experimental plot were carried out on the basis of the republican automobile road department "Gorno-Altayavtodor" in 2010 by the Road Operator No.217 on the approach to Gorno-Altaysk. In 2017 reinforcement fibers were taken out from the road pavement and subjected to laboratory studies. During experimental production works compactibility of fiber-reinforced asphalt mixtures was also investigated. In these conditions, the intensity of compacting impact was identical to the intensity used while compacting asphalt concrete mixtures of conventional composition (unreinforced mixtures).

All four groups of specimens of nylon rope-shaped fibers were subjected to chemical and physical-mechanical testing. The results of physical-mechanical testing of nylon rope-shaped fibers are given in Table 1.

Table 1. Results of physical-mechanical testing of nylon rope-shaped fibers.

Parameter	Unit of measurement	Specimen No.1	Specimen No.2	Specimen No.3	Specimen No.4
Specific viscosity	-	2.456	2.5	2.52	2.51
Content of extractable	%	2.6	2.0	1.5	1.8
substances		0.2	0.2	0.7	0.5
Thermal stability	^{0}C	215	215	216	216
Melting temperature	g/tex	15.9	19.3	8.1	14.7
Breaking strength	%	45.6	47.7	26.9	34.8
Breaking elongation					

Analyzing the data given in the table it can be noted that specific viscosity and thermal stability in all four specimens changed insignificantly. After fiber treatment with bitumen the value of breaking strength increased, however, after 18 years simulated in the chamber, this value decreased by almost 50%. This can be explained by the fact that artificial weather apparatus provides more severe conditions than the real ones. In the weather machine ultraviolet emission impacts the nylon fiber, which is protected just by the adsorption layer of oil bitumen. However, in the real conditions it is protected by the asphalt concrete layer, which reduces significantly the intensity of natural environment and climatic impacts. In the real conditions breaking strength decreased by only 8%. The processes of fibers ageing also resulted in decrease in breaking elongation. After weather machine this value decreased by 65% and in the real conditions by 31%. The results of investigations of fiber specimens using infrared spectroscopy are given in Figure 1.

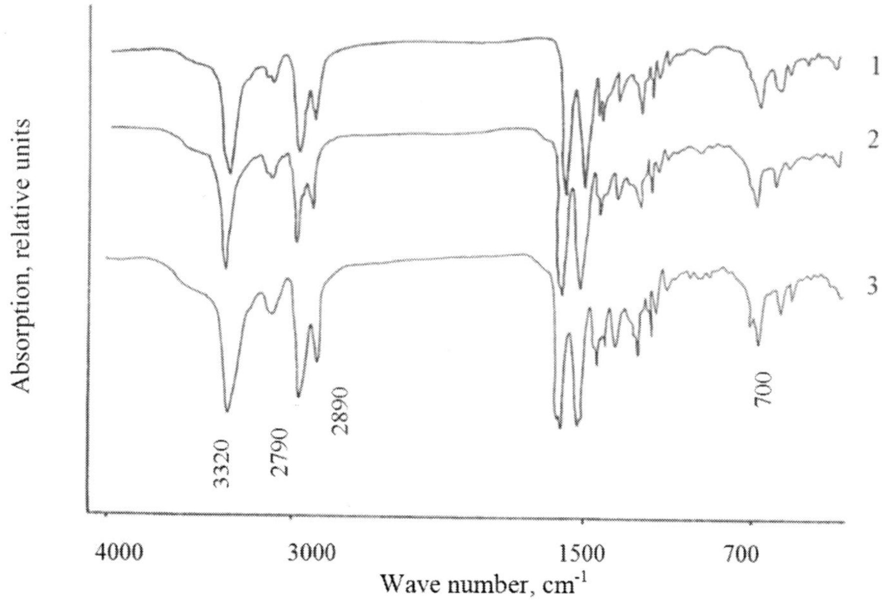

Fig. 1. IR spectra of nylon rope-shaped fibers: 1 – reference nylon fiber; 2 – nylon rope-shaped fiber treated with bitumen, hexane purified; 3 – nylon rope-shaped fiber taken out from asphalt concrete pavement, hexane purified.

It can be seen from Figure 1 that IR spectra of the initial fiber and the one taken out from the road pavement is characterized by absorption bands in the area 1640-1690 cm^{-1} (the peak with absorption bands 1660 cm^{-1} - "amide I band" of carbonyl group C=O). The free group N-H conditions in addition to the band C=O. The same bands of stretch vibrations as N-H when 3050-3550 cm^{-1} (the peak is undertaken by transform with absorption band 3320 cm^{-1}) and deformation vibrations –NH- when 1530-1570 cm^{-1} (the peak 1560 cm^{-1}). Absorption with the band 1300 cm^{-1} is mostly connected with the vibrations C-N. This vibration is also overlapped with the vibrations NH "amide III band". Deformation vibrations N-H provide rather intensive wide brand in the area 650-900 cm^{-1} (the peak 700 cm^{-1}). Weak bands in the area 1030-1230 cm^{-1} correspond to stretch vibrations CN. Their location slightly differs from the stretch vibrations C-C. Brands 2970 and 2890 cm^{-1} (duplet) can be referred to the stretch vibrations C-H. As an indirect proof of such reference the increase in intensity of these bands of nylon fiber specimen treated by bitumen, aged and hexane purified may serve. These data testify that during natural environment and climatic impacts fiber-forming polymer did not experience any significant changes.

Upon the completion of experimental production works the compaction factor of fiber-reinforced asphalt concrete and asphalt concrete made according to the conventional technology was determined. It was established that the compaction factor in both cases satisfied the value established in the regulatory documents, i.e. 0.98 [10].

Conclusion

As a result of experimental production works on construction of experimental plot of road pavement from FRAC the following conclusions were made. The layer of asphalt concrete pavement serves as a screen protecting reinforcement fibers from natural environment and climatic impacts. The properties of reinforcement fibers do not undertake significant changes herewith. In the real conditions of road pavement operation the value of breaking strength decreased by only 8%.

The obtained results testify that fiber reinforcement from nylon rope-shaped fiber can fulfill the reinforcing functions during the whole lifecycle of asphalt concrete pavement. In order to obtain the reference compaction factor of asphalt concrete additional compacting impact is not required. Further research will be focused on experimental works determining the influence of various reinforcement factors on compactibility of fiber-reinforced asphalt concrete mixtures.

References

1. M. Amuchi, S.M. Abtahi, B. Koosha, M. Hejazi, H. Sheikhzeinoddin, Journal of industrial textile, **44**(4), 526–41 (2015).
2. M. Vadood, M.S Johari, A.R. Rahai, Journal of central south university, **22**, 1937–46 (2015).
3. N. Gibson, X. Li, Journal of transportation research board, 2507, 57–66 (2015).
4. A.V. Akulich, author's abstract of Candidate of technical sciences thesis (1987). (in Russian)
5. I.P. Gamelyak, author's abstract of Candidate of technical sciences thesis (1992). (in Russian)
6. Y.N. Kovalev et al., Avtomobil'nyj transport i dorogi [Automobile transport and roads], **8**, 73-78 (Vyshejshaja shkola Publ., Minsk, 1981). (in Russian)
7. A.E. Merzlikin, I.P. Gamelyak, *Konstruirovanie, raschet i ispytanie dorozhnyh odezhd* [Design, calculation and testing of road pavements] (Sojuzdornii, Moscow, 1990). (in Russian)
8. V.I. Solomatov, A.V. Akulich, *Povyshenie kachestva stroitel'stva avtomobil'nyh dorog v Nechernozemnoj zone RSFSR* [Improvement of automobile road construction quality in Nonchernozem belt, proceedings of scientific and technical conference] (Vladimir, 1987). (in Russian)
9. V.N. Lukashevich, I.N. Efanov, G.I. Prokofyeva, I.V. Vaks, Vestnik of TSUAB, **6**, 177-185, (2015). (in Russian)
10. SP 78.13330 – 2012. Ministry of Regional Development of the Russian Federation. Construction standards and regulations of the Russian Federation. Automobile roads (Standartinform, Moscow, 2013). (in Russian)
11. L. J. Bellamy, The Infra-red Spectra of Complex Molecules (Mir Publ., Moscow, 1971). (in Russian)
12. GOST 9128 – 2013. State standard of the Russian Federation. Mixtures for asphalt concrete, polymere asphalt concrete for automobile roads and airdromes construction. Specifications (Standartinform Publ., Moscow, 2014). (in Russian)

Interaction in transportation as the basis for implementation of intergovernmental cooperation

Natalia Popova[1,*], *Marina* Kvint[1], and *Aleksei* Dementyev[1]

[1]Siberian Transport University, 630049 Novosibirsk, Russia

Abstract. The purpose of this paper is to define the role and place of the transportation component of the adjacent subjects of two countries in their economic potential for implementation of intergovernmental cooperation. The role and place of the transportation component in estimation of the benefits of the transportation and geographical position becomes evident only when the population, resources and economy of the border regions are jointly analyzed. The analysis of such parameters of the border regions of Russia (Western Siberia) and Kazakhstan performed by means of comparison and association of their economic and transportation potentials, showed that territorial production complexes in them have been developed, and the prospective development within the framework of the Eurasian Economic Union will be determined by the joint use of the benefits of the transportation and geographic position implemented with participation of railway transport.

Introduction

Interaction in transportation has always been considered an integrating factor that determined the *implementation* of the transportation process within the scope of international exchange. The parameters of interaction in transportation in intergovernmental cooperation are determined by the simultaneous presence of geographic or territorial, technical, socio-economic, resource-economic and other factors.

One of the parameters that determine interaction of participants in implementation of transportation services is the geographical factor or the location factor (Bugromenko, 1987; Golts, 1984; Bezrukov, 2004).

The essence of the research problem is that interaction, both as a process and as a result, has territorial boundaries within which this phenomenon can be studied, understood, simulated and estimated for the future. Thus, in paper [1], the authors considered the complex problem of transport development in the east of Russia, paying considerable attention to new directions in the railway network, to their structure, subsequent operation and "integration" into the system of regional transport and economic connection. The models of interaction and the value of the railway transport component within the scope of implementation of the economic potential have been considered within the borders of

* Corresponding author: pnb1512@yandex.ru

© The Authors, published by EDP Sciences. This is an open access article distributed under the terms of the Creative Commons Attribution License 4.0 (http://creativecommons.org/licenses/by/4.0/).

Russian in the "west-east" and "north-south" direction. In paper [2], the author takes into consideration theoretical foundations of the economic and geographical position (Baransky, 1980) and shows the simulation peculiarities of the transport-geographical position (TGP) as part of the EGP.

This paper shows that the transportation component is a parameter of comprehensive estimation of the economic potential, along with socio-economic, resource-economic and other factors. The TGP of territorially close subjects of countries acts as the prerequisite for creation of a transportation cluster for implementation of intergovernmental cooperation.

The border regions of Russia and Kazakhstan, the territorial production complexes (TPCs) of which are similar and can interact between each other, are viewed as the testing ground for the research. The interaction factors are the socio-demographic, natural-resource and economic potential of the territories. The cooperation conditions are technical capabilities, in this case, railway border crossings (RBCs) or stations where customs clearance, transfer of freight carriages and containers, technical works are performed. Availability of a unity of factors and conditions shall be the basis and the problem of interaction, the research and practical content of which has not been studied yet. Judging by [3], a comprehensive analysis of these issues within the scope of the EGP estimation to understand the role and the place of the transportation component in estimating the TGP benefits has not been performed to date. Separate economic and geographical problems are considered in works of domestic and foreign authors [4–6]. The issues of international cooperation through railway logistics are revealed in paper [5] but without estimation of the interaction subjects' economic potential. Paper [6] shows the potential of transportation routes but only natural and economic factors in interaction are taken into consideration. Strategic documents [7, 8] designate the technical component as a condition for arrangement of interaction between subjects but do not pay attention to demographic, resource and economic factors.

The novelty of this study is revealed in the peculiarities of applying a single methodological approach, i.e., in selection of parameters and indicators from literature references, mapping and statistical sources, in their comparison and association, in approbation of the methodology for specific border subjects.

Study method

The methodological approach consists in a comparative-analytical association of the social, resource, economic and transport potentials of the border areas, namely, Omsk and Novosibirsk region, the Altai territory and the Altai Republic; of Pavlodar and East Kazakhstan region. Initially, according to the transport-geographical maps published in [11] and to earlier mapping products published, it was found out that several dozens of transportation customs clearance points were key points for the interstate deliveries in the east of Russia. Only 20 out of them are RBCs where carriages and containers are transferred.

The longest section is the border with Kazakhstan, which determines the vector of the study. The initial data for the research analysis were the topical maps of regions published in the geographical atlases of the USSR, Russia and Kazakhstan. Then, territories were selected that had direct access to the borders of the neighboring state within each of the four constituent entities of the Russian Federation. Those were 6 districts in Novosibirsk region, 7 districts in the Altai Territory, 8 districts in Omsk region. The Altai Republic is not connected with Kazakhstan with railway routes. All subsequent actions to estimate social, resource, economic potential were taken on the basis of comparison, association and analysis of tables in statistical reference books as related to those districts. Similarly, two territories of Kazakhstan, which had access to the borders of the West Siberian regions, were studied.

In selecting significant information, the following main principles of the economic and geographical characteristics of economic entities were taken into consideration: location and availability of common borders, administrative and territorial status, availability of comparable information on demographic, resource, production and transportation indicators [9: Section 4,15,16,17,25 , 26; 10: Section 2,4,6,7,8,14; 12].

Indicators of population density, length of railways, transport availability in the territory, etc., were calculated using known formulas. Reliability and comparability of the initial data was ensured by the fact that the information had been obtained from official published sources. Estimation of the "natural resources" and "production" parameters was performed by the method of sampling information, both from statistical and other sources [9,13,14,16]. Regarding the natural-resource potential, the information obtained from research and monographic publications published 10 or more years ago was used. Names were assigned to resource types based on the generally accepted classification (A. A. Minz, 1972; I. V. Komar, 1975). The nomenclature adopted in statistical sources was used in names of industries. The time limit for selection and analysis of production indicators was selected for the 3 to 5 year period. The "last date", but not later than three years ago, was used for demographic indicators. The registration parameters were taken in traditional units of measurement, i.e., square and linear kilometers when estimating the areas of entities and the extent of transport routes; absolute and relative meters when assessing the population, resource availability and production in the TPC.

In the region under consideration, the territorial-production complexes of the eastern regions of Russia (Western Siberia) and territorial socio-economic systems of the border areas of eastern Kazakhstan were integrated into a single transportation and logistic chain.

Results

The main results of implementation of the methodology adopted for determining the role and the place of the transportation component in assessing the benefits of the TGP are summarized in Table 1. It represents the social, natural-resource and economic characteristics of the border territories of the two states, i.e., Russia (within the Siberian Federal District) and Kazakhstan. The role and the place of the transportation component in the total economic potential of the regions become apparent when taking into consideration the demographic, natural-resource and economic peculiarities of geographically close subjects of the two countries. The mapping analysis showed that the length of the border lines of the Siberian regions with Kazakhstan in Omsk region was 1,020 km, in Novosibirsk region, it was 317 km, in the Altai Territory, it was about 850 km, and in the Altai Republic, it was more than 500 km.

Statistically, the demographic potential of these regions of Russia is more than three times higher than that of the regions of the Republic of Kazakhstan. Almost 13% of the country's population live in the border regions of Kazakhstan, and about 5% of the country's population live in the regions of Russia under consideration, but it is more than 38% of the number of residents of the constituent entities of the Siberian Federal District (SFD).

Table 1. Socio-Demographic, Natural-Resource, Economic and Transportation Potential of Border Territories Sources of data: [8-11].

Indicators	Border regions	
	Russia	Kazakhstan
Districts of border states	Omsk, Novosibirsk region, the Altai territory. the Altai Republic	Pavlodar, East Kazakhstan region
Quantity of population	more than 7.3 million people	about 2.2 million people
Natural resources	coal, iron ore and non-ferrous metal ores, non-metallic industrial raw materials, timber, hydro resources	coal and slates, iron ore and non-ferrous metal ores, hydro resources, non-metallic industrial raw materials, timber
Production	mining, processing, power engineering	mining, processing, power engineering
Transportation availability, km (railways)	over 4.1 thousand km	about 2.0 thousand km

The values of the population living in the "nearest neighborhood" regions have the following indicators by districts.

In the south-west of Novosibirsk region, where the border with Pavlodar region of the Republic of Kazakhstan runs, the population density does not exceed 5 people/sq.km, on average. In the districts of the Altai territory that have access to the border with Kazakhstan, the population density also does not exceed 5 people/sq.km. The longest segment of the Russian-Kazakh border belongs to Omsk region. Railways are laid closer to the southern part of the region, where the population density is 5 to 10 people/sq.km on an average. The population density in the Altai Republic is 2 people/sq.km and below, but the region is not connected with the neighboring East Kazakhstan region by railway lines.

Analysis of various literature references revealed that the resource availability of border entities of Russia and Kazakhstan has similar structural characteristics, but the types of natural raw materials of the Altai territory, Novosibirsk and Omsk region of Russia is largely complementary. Thus, the Altai territory is rich in mineral and raw materials base, namely, polymetallic ores, iron ore, coals and non-metallic minerals, mainly developed and used. In the Altai Republic, connected with the Altai territory by roads, the resource potential is extremely diverse in terms of natural raw materials, but the main deposits are mostly explored, evaluated and prepared for mining. There are more than 500 deposits of various types of natural raw materials In Novosibirsk region, about a third of which is concentrated in the railway zone of gravity and is operated. Omsk region does not have major deposits of non-metallic industrial raw materials in the proximity zone.

The resource supply of Pavlodar and East Kazakhstan regions is characterized by great diversity and integrity of the mineral and raw materials complex. More than a third of reserves of energy coals, polymetallic ores, rare metal ores and non-metallic industrial raw materials is concentrated here [12–14]. The scale of deposits' operation largely depends on their relevance to the complex of processing industries in the country. Processing and mining industries of the border regions of both countries also have their own peculiarities. See the structure of the economic complex of the West Siberia regions in Figure 1.

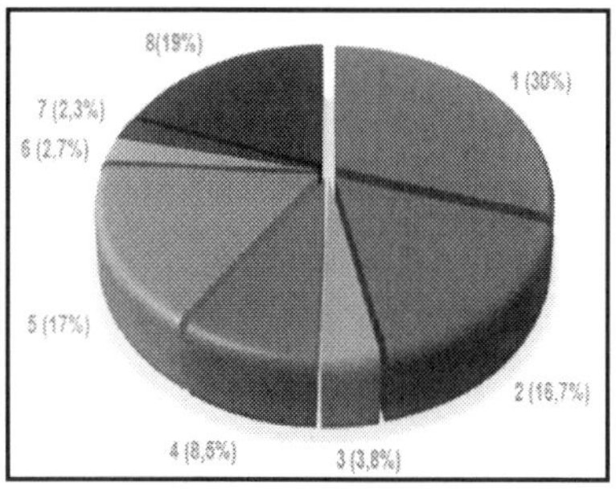

1. Chemical production, production of petroleum products, rubber products and mineral products;
2. Production of machinery, various equipment, agricultural equipment and other equipment;
3. Manufacture of metal products;
4. Production of building materials and cement;
5. Production of food and consumer goods;
6. Production of wood and products from it;
7. Production of other products;
8. Production of agricultural and industrial complex (grain, flax, livestock, feed production).

Fig. 1. The economic complex structure of border regions of Russia (Western Siberia).

According to petrochemical production and many types of machine-building and agricultural production, Omsk region's own production exceeds the level of domestic consumption, while the energy potential of this region is clearly not sufficient. The region is energy-deficient, therefore, supplies from neighboring regions of Siberia and the nearest regions of Kazakhstan are an important condition for the future development of the multi-profiled industrial structure of the region [9]. Industrial specialization of enterprises in Novosibirsk region is more balanced and unites, both with its own resources and raw materials, and with the benefits of the TGP. The profile of enterprises of Novosibirsk region was formed due to machine-building products, agricultural enterprises, chemical, woodworking industries and cement production. There are electricity and power generating capacities in Novosibirsk region, but the production area is based on the fuel imported from Kemerovo region and the Khakassia [9]. The Altai territory participates in interregional exchange in agricultural and textile products, food products, agricultural accessories, various chemical products with nanotechnological characteristics. Electric power engineering facilities of the region (thermal power plants and gas turbine power plants) are operated on imported and local coal [9].

The structure of industry in the border regions of Kazakhstan, namely, Pavlodar and East Kazakhstan, was mainly formed in the "Soviet era" and the profile of industrial enterprises is largely preserved at present. See the structure of the economic complex of Kazakhstan regions in Figure 2.

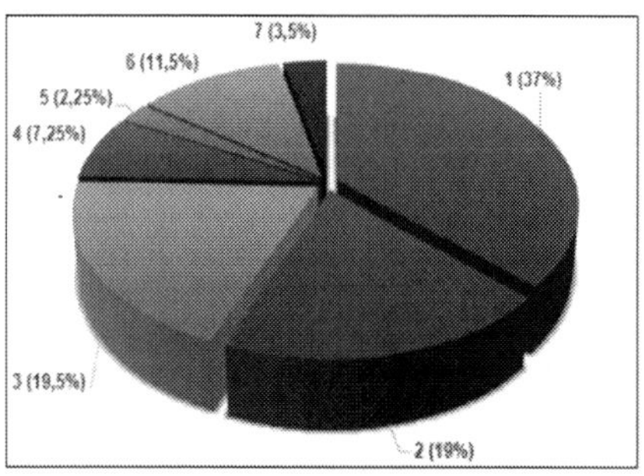

1. Production of mining and processing plants, coalmines;
2. Metallurgical and metal-working products;
3. Mechanical engineering products (equipment, tools, valves);
4. Mineral production;
5. Agricultural products;
6. Production of food and consumer goods;
7. Production of wood and products from it.

Fig. 2. The structure of economic complex of border regions of Kazakhstan.

Mining enterprises of Pavlodar region are developing coal and other deposits, mainly of polymetallic ores. Significant volumes of GRP are formed in processing industries specialized in metallurgy and metal working, production of manufacturing equipment and tools. The share of agricultural industry is less than 5% in the GRP structure and the increase in this indicator is virtually impossible due to inadequate hydration of the region.

Power engineering and electric generating capacities of the region are characterized by their development and self-sufficiency. Overhead power transmission lines connect the region with adjacent regions of Kazakhstan and Russia. Production is also the leading branch of the economy in the East Kazakhstan region. The developed and operated mineral resource base of the region is the basis for development of mining industries. Production at processing enterprises is associated with production of ore concentrates, refined gold and silver, cement, silicate bricks, reinforcement, equipment and wood products. Specialization of enterprises in production of food and products and a wide range of consumer goods is due to the availability of the agricultural production base and the socio-economic needs of the population that resides in the region. The energy potential of the East Kazakhstan region is significant. There are hydroelectric power plants and facilities for generation of electric and thermal power in the region [12–14].

Thus, with all unification of the products manufactured in economic complexes of the border states, a number of commodity groups remain unique. Mutual deliveries could create the commodity basis for the transportation and economic cluster, the ability of which is largely determined by the transportation availability in the border regions. [15]

The transportation component of the economic potential has its own peculiarities. From the standpoint of the railway transport development, almost all border entities, both in Kazakhstan and Russia (with the exception of the Altai Republic), are provided with railways with the 1,520 mm tracks, but the TGP benefits for arrangement of mutual social, economic and transport links are more typical of geographically close border districts of the border entities. Thus, the southeastern and the southwestern parts of Novosibirsk region, the central and southern parts of Omsk region, the central, western and southwestern parts of the Altai territory have railway connections with the districts of Central and Eastern Kazakhstan, and the Irtysh-Karasuk line directly crosses a section of Kazakhstan territory. The Kurgan-Petropavlovsk-Omsk railway line also runs through Kazakhstan territory. The southern line, which runs from Novosibirsk through the Altai territory, is a branch of the railway line from the Tatarskaya station that crosses the extreme west of Novosibirsk region and the Altai territory and also "emerges" at the border with Kazakhstan, is connected with Kazakh railways. By the length of the railway lines, the indicator of the West Siberian border regions of the Russian Federation is a quarter of the SFD index and, in fact, it is twice as large as the one for the regions of the Republic of Kazakhstan.

The key railways of Pavlodar and East Kazakhstan region have the "north-south" direction. A line in the "west-east" direction was built not long ago. Railway branches ensure connection of the northern and the eastern Kazakhstan with both inner regions of the Republic of Kazakhstan and with the border regions of the Russian Federation [11]. The total length of the railway lines of Pavlodar and East Kazakhstan region is more than 13% of the country's railway network.

Conclusion

Analysis of mapping materials, statistical data and information from literature references on the resource availability, population and peculiarities of the economy of the border territories of the two states showed that the TPCs of the regions are mainly formed and are conditioned by the peculiarities of the available natural conditions and resources. The comparative analytical association of the indicators made it possible to state the special significance of the transportation component in the economic potential of the proximity of the entities of the two countries for implementation of intergovernmental cooperation. It was possible to show that the border regions have all the prerequisites, i.e., industrial, economic, social, organizational ones, for uniting and interaction in the form of the transportation and the economic cluster.

Taking into consideration the intercontinental position of this transportation and economic cluster, railway transport can initially play the core role in arrangement of the transportation flow and "connection" to the European transportation routes. Research of the activities of the transportation and economic cluster will prove to be very productive in simulation of new managerial approaches to intergovernmental uniting of productive forces and the expansion of foreign economic relations of the geopolitically united states of the continent [16].

References

1. V.A. Lamin, V.Y. Plenkin, V.Y. Tkachenko, *Global track: development of transport system in the East of the country* (Ural branch of the Russian Academy of Sciences, Yekaterinburg, 1999). (in Russian)
2. Y. Kanemoto, Evaluating benefits of transportation in models of new economic geography, **J, E 2 (2-3)**, p.53-62 (2013).
3. D. Snidal, M. Sampson, Interstate Cooperation Theory and International Institutions. Oxford Bibliographies (2017), available at: http://www.oxfordbibliographies.com/view/document/obo-9780199743292/obo-9780199743292-0093.xml (May 20, 2018).
4. N.B. Popova, Y.M. Buintseva, E.A. Sidenkova, M.S Chikinova, E.A. Korchovaya, *Integrated transport system* (STU Publishing house, Novosibirsk, 2014).
5. N.K. Isingarin, *Logistics of international rail transport* (Economtransconsulting Publ., Almaty, 2006). (in Russian)
6. S.E. Rakisheva, A.A. Saipov, *Geography of integration of the transport system of Kazakhstan into the world transport and communication system*, **Vol. 1,** International scientific conference on Geosystem approach to the study of the natural environment of the Republic of Kazakhstan, Eurasian national University, Astana, 2018, 251-254.
7. Transport strategy of the Russian Federation for the period up to 2030: order of the government of the Russian Federation from 22 November, 2008 № 1734-R (as amended on June 11, 2014). (in Russian)
8. KazPortal.kz, Transport system of Kazakhstan, available at: kazportal.kz›transportnaya-sistema-kazahstana (Febryary 23, 2018). (in Russian)
9. Russian statistical yearbook. 2017 (Rosstat, Moscow, 2017). (in Russian)
10. Russia and the world. 2016 (Rosstat, Moscow, 2016).
11. Atlas Railways (Omsk cartographic factory, Omsk, 2012). (in Russian)
12. WWW.LIBRARY/PUBLICATIONS/THE-WORLD-FACTBOOK. The World Factbook – East&Southeast Asia, available at: http://www.library/publications/the-world-factbook (April 24, 2018).
13. WWW.ECONOMY.GOV.KZ. Ministry of national economy of the Republic of Kazakhstan: available at: http://economy.gov.kz/ru/kategorii/itogi-socialno-ekonomicheskogo-razvitiya-rk (April 24, 2018).
14. WWW.STAT.GOV.KZ. Official website of the state statistics service of Kazakhstan: available at: http://stat.gov.kz/faces/wcnav_externalId/publicationsCompilations?(April 24, 2018).
15. S.U. Niyazbekova, I.T. Grekov, T.K. Blokhina, Economy of Region, **J, E 4**, 1263-1273 (2016).
16. A. Lesh, *Spatial organization of economy* (Nauka, Moscow, 2007). (in Russian)

Damping of vertical and horizontal transverse vibrations in the bridge span structures

Darya Provornaya[1,*], *Sergey* Glushkov[1], and *Leonid* Solovyev[1]

[1]Siberian Transport University, 630049 Novosibirsk, Russia

Abstract. The paper considers the issues of vibration isolation of railway bridge units on high-speed lines and seismic protection using dynamic vibration dampers. The purpose of the research is to justify the efficiency of damping the dynamic vibrations of the bridge supports with seismic insulating support parts. The research methodology involves building mathematical models of the systems under consideration and their numerical analysis. The methods of structural mechanics and dynamics of structures were used for solving the assigned tasks. The basic mathematical dependences of the vibration system with two seismic masses were developed. The rolling stock was represented by concentrated forces moving along the span structure. As a result, a new scheme for dynamic damping of vibration of the bridge supports was proposed according to which the span structure used as the dynamic vibration damper has an additional fastening on a rigid abutment.

Introduction

The design of railway bridges on high-speed lines and bridges in seismic areas shall be carried out with the account of special requirements to the dynamic characteristics of span structures and supports [1, 2]. Such requirements may be deemed critical when choosing the structural solutions. But if for the bridges on high-speed lines the tasks to be solved relate to the prevention of lifting-off (unloading) of truck wheels of the rolling stock and travelling comfort, the main problems concerning the issues on seismic protection relate to prevention of throwing down the span structures from supports and elimination of occurrence of excessive forces in the support sections. In other cases, the requirements of the design standards [3] to dynamic characteristics of the span structures are not critical and are usually ensured.

According to recent research all seismic isolation systems are divided into stationary and adaptive ones [6]. Stationary systems retain their elastic and damping characteristics in case of vibration, and the adaptive systems irreversibly change their parameters thus adapting to the loading program (seismic impact). Stationary seismic isolation systems may be subdivided into systems with and without restoring force. The last type of seismic isolation is arranged by the use of a seismic insulating sliding belt (seismic belt). In such systems load exceeding the frictional force in the seismic belt cannot be transferred to the seismic insulating part of the structure. Designs of seismic insulating belts were proposed

* Corresponding author: molokovada@gmail.com

© The Authors, published by EDP Sciences. This is an open access article distributed under the terms of the Creative Commons Attribution License 4.0 (http://creativecommons.org/licenses/by/4.0/).

by many experts, but they were studied in more details in the works of L.S. Kilimnik, V.P. Chudnetsov and L.A. Soldatova [16]. A new method of seismic isolation is considered on the basis of the previous studies.

Dynamic calculations of bridges on the high-speed lines require consideration of the mechanical vibration system such as "bridge-moving train" having energy dissipation properties. Repeated loads from the oncoming trucks of a moving train cause the forced vibrations of the span structures in a certain speed range. Vibrations with frequencies close enough to the natural structure vibration frequencies may cause resonance effect. The resonance effect for high-speed lines is a much greater problem than the movement of trains with normal speeds (up to 160-200 km/h) because of the danger of losing contact between the wheel and the rail [8].

For the purpose of eliminating the resonance in the existing design practice, the method of adjustment of the span structure mass is applied upwards (in comparison with the solutions providing only the strength of the structures). This entails an increase in expenses both for the span structure, and for supports and foundations, as well as the complication of conditions of installation of structures [4]. The use of dynamic vibration dampers allows us to achieve compliance with the requirements for bridges on the high-speed lines in terms of safety of operation even with the use of span structures of standard design solutions [5].

The scientific problem is that with regard to calculation and design of all kinds of structures for seismic regions the calculation of seismic resistance of bridges falls back the calculations of joint seismic resistance because the demolition of bridges by percentage takes not the first place on the total scale of destructions after the earthquake [7]. Existing recommendations on the assigning of calculation models for bridges when calculating the seismic impacts do not provide for the basis for multilevel design. The system created during the last 10 years includes the updated systems of anti-seismic reinforcement of bridges based on the principles of seismic isolation and seismic damping [16].

The purpose of the research is to justify the efficiency of damping the dynamic vibrations of the bridge supports with seismic insulating support parts. The scientific novelty of the research results includes:

1. use of vibration dampers of a new type for improvement of operational characteristics of the bridge span structures;
2. study of vibrations of support assemblies in span structures;
3. development of the span structure design concept with dynamic vibration damper considered in this research work.

Mathematical research model

Let us consider a beam of a span structure which is exposed to rectilinear vibrations under the influence of a harmonic force with amplitude F_0 and frequency ω. Assume that $x_0(t)$ is the displacement of the span structure in the horizontal or vertical plane, and $x_1(t)$ is the displacement of damper.

On the basis of the obtained calculation model, we are going to develop a mathematical model for it, which may most fully describe the behaviour of the system: span structure beam – dynamic vibration damper – support. Differential equations of the system movement can be written in the form as follows:

$$\begin{cases} m_0\ddot{x}_0 + (C_0 + C_1)x_0 - C_1x_1 + (h_0 + h_1)\dot{x}_0 - h_1\dot{x}_1 = F\sin\omega t; \\ m_1\ddot{x}_1 - C_1x_0 + (C_1 + C_2)x_1 + (h_1 + h_2)\dot{x}_1 - h_1\dot{x}_0 = 0. \end{cases} \quad (1)$$

The system is solved using the method of complex amplitudes. For this purpose let us write down the system of equations in the same way as (1) thus denoting in the left part x_0 and x_1 through y_0 and y_1 respectively, and specifying F_0 cos in the right part. The initial system (1) is added to the resulting system of equations multiplied by $i = \sqrt{-1}$, and we obtain a system of equations relative to the complex variables $z_0 = ix_0 + y_0$ и $z_1 = ix_1 + y_1$:

$$\begin{cases} m_0 \ddot{z}_0 + (C_0 + C_1)z_0 - C_1 z_1 + (h_0 + h_1)\dot{z}_0 - h_1 \dot{z}_1 = Fe^{i\omega t}; \\ m_1 \ddot{z}_1 - C_1 z_0 + (C_1 + C_2)z_1 + (h_1 + h_2)\dot{z}_1 - h_1 \dot{z}_0 = 0. \end{cases} \quad (2)$$

The system (2) is solved as follows:

$$z_0(t) = A_0 e^{i\omega t}; \quad z_1(t) = A_1 e^{i\omega t}. \quad (3)$$

Taking into account the expression (3) we obtain from (2) a system of linear algebraic equations for the complex amplitudes A_0 and A_1:

$$\begin{cases} \left[-m_0 \omega^2 + C_0 + C_1 + i(h_0 + h)_1 \omega\right] A_0 - \left[C_1 + ih_1\omega\right] A_1 = F; \\ \left[-m_1 \omega^2{}_1 + C_1 + C_2 + i(h_1 + h_2)\omega\right] A_0 - \left[C_1 + ih_1\omega\right] A_0 = 0. \end{cases} \quad (4)$$

or in non-dimensional form

$$\begin{cases} \left[1 - \Omega^2 + iq_0\Omega\right]\bar{A}_0 - \left[iq_{01}\Omega + \lambda\right]\bar{A}_1 = 1; \\ \left[\mu(\upsilon^2 - \Omega^2) + iq_1\upsilon\mu\Omega\right]\bar{A}_1 - \left[iq_{01}\Omega + \lambda\right]\bar{A}_0 = 0, \end{cases} \quad (5)$$

where $\mu = m_1/m_0$ is the mass ratio of the damper and the beam; $\upsilon^2 = \omega_1^2/\omega_0^2$ – damper adjustment; $\omega_0 = \sqrt{(C_0 + C_1)/m_0}$ – natural frequency of the span structure beam; $\omega_1 = \sqrt{(C_1 + C_2)/m_1}$ – partial frequency of the damper; $= /\ _0$ – non-dimensional excitation frequency; $q_0 = 2(h_0 + h_1)/h_{0кр}$, $q_{01} = 2h_1 / h_{0кр}$, $q_1 = 2(h_1 + h_2)/h_{1кр}$ – non-dimensional ratios of resilient friction; $\bar{A}_0 = A_0/A_{0C}$, $\bar{A}_1 = A_1/A_{0C}$ – non-dimensional amplitudes of vibrations of the span structure beam and the damper, respectively; $A_{0C} = F_0 / C_0$ – conditionally static movement of the span beam during passage of the travelling load.

Since the forced vibrations are considered, it is sufficient to determine only the amplitudes of these vibrations, that is, the modules of complex amplitudes. When solving the system of equations (5), we obtain

$$|\bar{A}_0| = \sqrt{\frac{\mu(\upsilon^2 - \Omega^2)^2 + (q_1\upsilon\mu\Omega)^2}{A^2 + iB^2}}, \quad (6)$$

$$|\bar{A}_1| = \sqrt{\frac{(q_{01}\Omega)^2 + \lambda^2}{A^2 + iB^2}}, \quad (7)$$

where A is the real part and B is imaginary part defined by formulas

$$A = \mu\Omega^4 - \Omega^2\left[\mu(1 + +q_0 q_1 \upsilon) - q_0^2\right] + \mu\upsilon^2 - \lambda^2, \quad (8)$$

$$B = -\mu\Omega^3\left(q_0 + q_1\upsilon\right) + \Omega\left(q_0\mu\upsilon^2 + q_1\mu\upsilon - q_{01}\lambda^2\right). \quad (9)$$

Solution of the research model

Expressions (6) and (7) are equations for the determination of vibration amplitudes on the support of the span structure and the dynamic damper, respectively. Analysis of expression (6) allows us to conclude that, for any type of adjustment of the damper, the amplitude of the span structure beam does not go to zero. But if $q_1 = 0$ (there is no damping in the damper), then $\left|\bar{A}\right| = 0$ with any $\upsilon = \Omega$ ($\omega_1 = \omega$). Consequently, the vertical and horizontal vibrations of the span structure beam will be damped by the additional mass at a partial frequency of the damper equal to the excitation frequency. The vibration amplitude of the damper itself differs from zero and finite in this case.

According to the classical theory [15], there are three ways to prevent the vibrations and oscillations such as: reduction of the level of vibration in the source, reduction of its level along the path of extension, and change of the resonance properties of the protected objects. One of the effective methods for reducing vibrations of span structures is the creation of passive multi-resonance dynamic vibration dampers. Dynamic damping of vibrations involves the adding to the main vibrating mass of the additional mass which forms a certain part of the main mass.

Depending on the properties of connections, there are dynamic vibration dampers [9, 10] having a form of an additional mass applied to the mass of the main structure by means of an elastic element or pendulum scheme. The additional mass is applied to the mass of the main structure using the viscous or friction elements, namely, the dampers (impact absorbers). Also the additional mass may be applied to the main structure mass by means of resilient and viscous elements. Depending on the amount of additional mass the dynamic vibration damper may be [11] of a small mass (the damper mass is 10% of the mass of the structure); equal (commensurate) mass (the damper mass is equal to the mass of the structure); large mass, when the damper mas exceeds the mass of the structure by two or more times.

The dynamic vibration damper of small mass is effective for adjusting the vibrations of span structures according to the conditions for passing high-speed traffic. Taking into account the complex spectrum of the impact of moveable loads on the bridges, it is advisable to create the unified passive dynamic vibration dampers, which can be set for elimination of any resonance effects. The dynamic vibration damper of small mass used for damping the vibration in case of seismic impacts has its disadvantages since such a damper is very sensitive to setting and there can be no damping effect in the event of relatively small deviations caused by inaccuracies in mounting [14].

A device for damping vertical and horizontal transverse vibrations can be used as a dynamic vibration damper of small mass. Such device consists of a supporting elastic element in the form of a coil spring (Fig. 1) [12, 13]. Such a design can be installed either directly on the span structure (as applicable to reference to the high-speed lines), or between the support and the span structure beam (for seismic impacts). In the latter case, the rigidity of the spring 1 will mainly be determined according to the requirements for vertical displacement of the path.

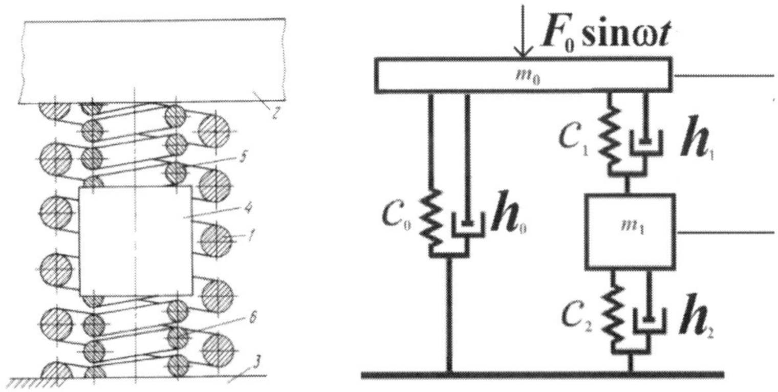

a b

Fig. 1. Dynamic vibration damper (a) and its design scheme (b) C0 - stiffness of the main carrier spring; C1 and C2 - the stiffness of the main and additional springs of the absorber, respectively; h1, h2, h3 - damping factors; m0, m1 - mass of beam and dynamic absorber, respectively.

The device under consideration is a supporting elastic member 1 in the form of a coil spring installed between the supports 2 and 3 and a dynamic damper in the form of a coaxially installed inertial mass connected to the supports by the springs 5 and 6. Such installation of the inertial masses of the damper enables to change the interaction of the support and the span structure at operating frequencies of the span structure beam.

It is possible to change this interaction by compensating the periodic forces and moments transmitted by the supporting elastic elements, forces and moments of the opposite direction from the inertial masses vibrating in the opposite direction. It should be noted that if mass 4 is taken as the mass of a span structure, then such a damper becomes a damper of equal (commensurate) mass and can be effectively used for seismic protection in this form.

Results

On the basis of the expressions obtained a support part enabling the use of the span structure mass as a dynamic vibration damper (Fig. 2) was constructed. As for the conditional initial data (a beam of pre-stressed reinforced concrete, load C14, estimated seismicity in 9, maximum permissible vertical movements according to the railway operation rules), the spring parameters were selected in accordance with GOST 13765-86. The same stiffness was assigned for all springs for uniform activation.

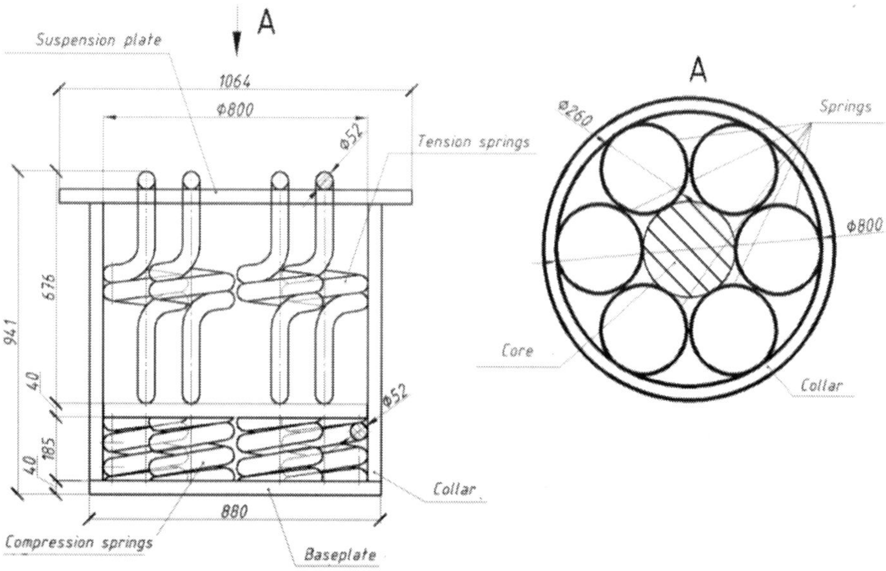

Fig. 2. Schematic diagram of the support part.

The developed support part does not exceed the overall dimensions of the existing seismic insulating support parts, and can be placed both above the bearing block (pier cap) of the supports, and in a special niche in the pinnacle. Such a support part is serviceable and, if necessary, can be replaced entirely. It works on the principle of the device, considered in Figure 1.

Conclusion

The support part obtained according to the results of calculations makes it possible to change the interaction of the support and the span structure at operating frequencies of the span structure beam. It will solve the problem of lack of modern calculations and recommendations for designing seismic isolation of bridges.

It is possible to change this interaction by compensating the periodic forces and moments transmitted by the supporting elastic elements, forces and moments of the opposite direction from the inertial masses vibrating in the opposite direction. The developed support part consists of compression and extension springs working together for bearing both vertical and horizontal loads arising from permanent, temporary and seismic impacts. In addition to the main task of bearing vertical and horizontal loads, such a support part is able to return the span structure to the initial position after having been exposed to the seismic impact. Also, it eliminated the resonance that does not increase the expenses both for the span structure, and for supports and foundations, and does not complicate the conditions of installation of structures. The use of such supports allows us to achieve compliance with the requirements for bridges on the high-speed lines in terms of traffic safety even with the use of span structures of standard design solutions.

References

1. STU-4. Engineering structures of Moscow-Kazan section of high-speed railway track

Moscow – Kazan – Yekaterinburg. Technical regulations and requirements todesign and construction (St.-Petersburg Publ., 2016). (in Russian)
2. SP 14.13330.2011. Construction in seismic regions. Revised edition of SNiP II-7-81* (Moscow, 2011). (in Russian)
3. SP 35.13330-2011. Bridges and pipes. Revised edition of SNiP 2.05.03-84* (Moscow, 2011). (in Russian)
4. A.V. Romanov, E.I. Shehtman, Bulletin of research results, 3(8), 48-53 (2013). (in Russian)
5. L. Fryba, *Dynamics of Railway Bridges* (Thomas Telford, London, 1996).
6. V.M. Kruglov, Naukovedenie, **Vol. 5** (24), (2014). (in Russian)
7. L.K. Dyachenko, Author's abstract of candidate of science thesis (Saint-Petersburg, 2017). (in Russian)
8. Y.B. Yang, *Vehicle-bridge interaction dynamics with applications to high-speed railway* (World Scientific, 2004).
9. A.L. Zakora, Science and transport progress. Bulletin of Dnipropetrovsk National University of Railway Transport named after Academician V. Lazaryan, 6, 118-123 (2005). (in Russian)
10. U.Z. Shermuhamedov, I.O. Kuznetsova, Science and transport progress. Bulletin of Dnipropetrovsk National University of Railway Transport named after Academician V. Lazaryan, 41, 175-180 (2012). (in Russian)
11. S.P. Glushkov, A.M. Baranovsky, RU Patent 2082907 (1997). (in Russian)
12. S.P. Glushkov, Author's abstract of candidate of science thesis (Novosibirsk, 1999). (in Russian)
13. S.P. Glushkov, L.U. Solovyev, N.A. Donets, Vestnik of TSUAB, 4, 27–34 (2011). (in Russian)
14. V. Hajbin'. Author's abstract of candidate of science thesis (Moscow, 2010). (in Russian)
15. U.Z. Shermuhamedov, Author's abstract of candidate of science thesis (Saint-Petersburg, 2010). (in Russian)
16. T.V. Sukonnikova, Author's abstract of candidate of science thesis (Saint-Petersburg, 2017). (in Russian)

Road surface quality as the basis of safe operation of transport systems

Pavel Grekhov[1,*], *Sergey* Levashov[2], *Vladimir* Shkrabak[3], and *Roman* Shkrabak[3]

[1]Kurgan State Agricultural Academy by T.S. Maltsev, 641000 Kurgan, Russia
[2]Kurgan State University, 641000 Kurgan, Russia
[3]Saint-Petersburg State Agrarian University, 196661 Saint-Petersburg, Pushkin, Russia

Abstract. The safe functioning of the transport system mainly depends on the quality of road surfaces. Therefore, improvement of the physical and mechanical characteristics of roads will ensure the effective protection of health and safety of people engaged in this field. Consequently, modification of the physical and mechanical characteristics of road surfaces will ensure safety in the field of transport systems. Bitumen-salt mass was used as a modifier of the road bitumen emulsions and such a mass was obtained by means of destructing the chemical weapons of the organophosphorus class of compounds since they have an effect of surface-active substances. Studying of the modified road surface parameters was carried out according to the dispersion parameters and using the method of mathematical design of the experiment. As a result, the positive effect of the bitumen-salt mass on the dispersion distribution of the bitumen phase in the bitumen emulsion was determined. The proposed method of modification of the bitumen emulsions allowed us to improve the operational parameters of the road surfaces, and thus the safety of road transport systems as a whole.

Introduction

During the Cold War, large quantities of chemical weapons containing the organophosphorus class of toxic substances (sarin, soman, VX-gases) as the main component were stored in the Soviet Union. After Russia signed the "Convention on the Prohibition of the Development, Production, Stockpiling and Use of the Chemical Weapons and on their Destruction" it was decided to destroy the chemical weapons. Warehousing and storage was arranged at the sites of destruction of chemical weapons. Various options for further utilization of wastes obtained after such destruction were considered, and one of them was using in the road construction, since roads and quality of road surfaces are the most important elements ensuring the safety and reliability of the transport system in Russia.

In January 1993, the question of how to handle 40,000 tons of toxic substances arose. When destructing the arsenal of chemical weapons stored at several sites and having different chemical bases, it was required to determine the mode of decomposition. After the

* Corresponding author: grehov-pgs@yandex.ru

© The Authors, published by EDP Sciences. This is an open access article distributed under the terms of the Creative Commons Attribution License 4.0 (http://creativecommons.org/licenses/by/4.0/).

announcement of competition, the method for destructing the Chemical Weapons of the organophosphorus class of compounds proposed by the State Research Institute of Organic Chemistry and Technology (GosNIIOKhT) (Moscow) was selected, since this class of compounds is contained in the great bulk of all the Chemical Weapons of approximately 32,200 t. [1-3]. This method provides for a two-stage technology involving the initial neutralization of toxic substances such as sarin, soman, VX-gases and obtaining of a reaction mass which is bitumenized at the second stage (mixed with petroleum bitumen). As a result, the bitumen-salt mass of the third hazard category is obtained [4-6]. It should be noted that the amount of the bitumen-salt mass increases compared to the initial amount of toxic substances by 3.5 times. Thus, significant volumes of the bitumen-salt mass may and should be used for industrial purposes.

Due to the significant content of petroleum bitumen in the bitumen-salt mass, it is possible to use these wastes for the production of waterproofing materials (for coating and covering) and in road construction [9]. Analysis of the reaction mass components showed that it can have an effect of surface-active substances [7, 8]. Introduction of surface-active substances into the composition of structural elements of road surfaces will not only improve the mechanical characteristics, but also significantly reduce a number of road accidents. The latter circumstance will ensure an improvement of safety of drivers on the roads, as well as all related infrastructure of road transport systems. This is particularly significant for the roads in rural areas, namely, for the agricultural industry complex, where the machinery of large mass and carrying capacity is used. It also should be noted that these roads have periods of intensive exploitation, such as sowing season, harvesting and transportation of crops.

For the purpose of ensuring high strength and performance of road surfaces, an optimal ratio of various components of the system under consideration is required. One of the main factors is interaction of the bitumen binder with the inert components of the dispersion system of road surfaces [11, 12]. A high degree of adhesion and spreading of bitumen over the gravel and sand is possible only with the use of bitumen emulsions (BE) [7, 10]. The efficiency of the bitumen emulsion is determined by the efficiency of emulsifiers, namely, surface-active substances, introduced into its composition. Therefore, when introducing the bitumen emulsion and petroleum bitumen into the composition the bitumen-salt mass can ensure an improvement of physical and mechanical properties of asphalt concrete [9]. In view of the fact that the bitumen emulsion is a multiphase system, the surface-active substances will influence the dispersion of the dimensional parameters of the bitumen phase, and, consequently, the resistance to delamination and spreading capacity. Similar experiments were carried out with the use of conventional Surface-Active Substances but experiment with the use of the bitumen-salt mass was carried out for the first time. Determination of the dispersion parameters of the bitumen emulsion was carried out according to the compositions using the experiment design theory and preparing a simplex design as per the "composition-property" scheme according to Table 1 below. Whereupon, a mathematical model was created with verification by Kohren and Fisher criteria. Bitumen of BND 60/90 grade was used as one of the Bitumen Emulsion phases.

Study method

For determining the dispersion parameters, the SHIMADZU SALD-7101 unit was used. This unit is suitable for determining the dimensional and quantity characteristics of the bitumen phase in the bitumen emulsion. Analysis of the differential parameters of the bitumen emulsion compositions being studied was evaluated taking into account predefined parameters of spreading capacity, since in compliance with the normative documentation the mineral components should be covered with a bitumen component by at least two-thirds of the surface area of the mineral component. In addition, the disperse range of dimensional parameters of the bitumen phase increases thus leading to a decrease in the contacting number of bitumen micro-droplets. An increase in the dimensional parameters range (minimum dimensions) leads to an increase in the surface area of the phase boundaries, which activates the processes of chemical dispersion and micellar catalysis.

Table 1. Disperse system stability index depending on the amount of introduced Bitumen-salt mass.

Component description and time index of the disperse system	Numbering and ratios of components of experimental compositions									
	1	2	3	4	5	6	7	8	9	10
Bitumen, %	60	50	50	53.3	56.6	56.6	53.3	50	50	53.3
Water, %	40	50	40	40	40	43.3	46.6	46.6	43.3	43.3
Modifying additive (Bitumen-salt mass), %	0	0	10	6.6	3.3	0	0	3.3	6.6	3.3
Hydrochloric acid, HCL, %	0.20									
Emulsifier Redicote EM44, %	1.5									
Time to the moment of delamination, h	409	527	0.15	333	501	379	547	145	0.3	337

Results

While comparing the dimensional and quantity parameters of the bitumen phase with or without bitumen-salt mass in the bitumen emulsion composition, one may note the significant differences. Thus, in compositions without bitumen-salt mass there are significant changes in quantitative parameters (%) of some sizes of micro-droplets of the bitumen emulsion of 8-9μ (Fig. 1) and 8-10μ (Fig. 2) respectively. The presence of bitumen-salt mass in such compositions leads to changes in the distribution of dimensional and percentage parameters of the bitumen phase distribution. It proves that the reaction mass exhibits the properties of the surface-active substances expressed in the appearance of smaller micro-droplets of bitumen in the emulsion. Thus, in the composition No. 5 (Fig. 3) the presence of micro-droplets with size of less than 1μ and more uniform distribution of particles within the range from 3-15μ are observed. In composition No. 10 (Fig. 4) including bitumen-salt mass the appearance of micro-droplets with size starting from 0.8μ is observed as opposed to the compositions without bitumen-salt mass (Figs. 1 and 2).

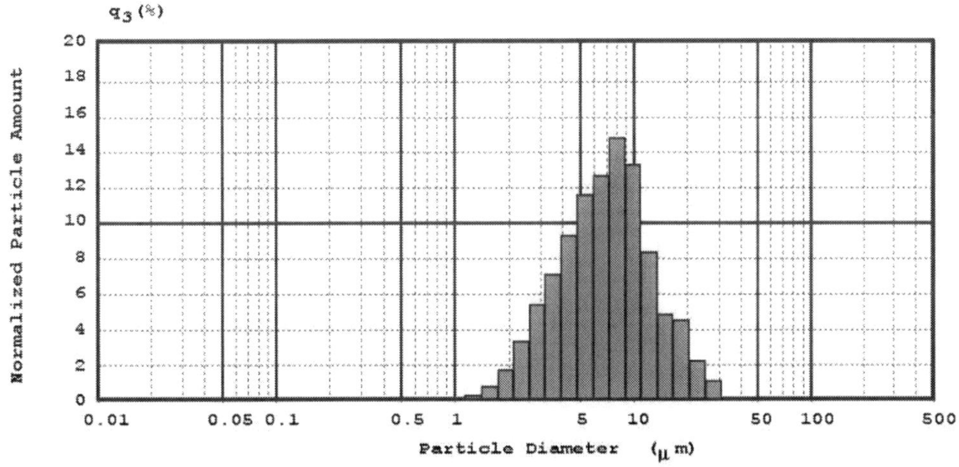

Fig. 1. Dispersion parameters of the bitumen phase of composition No. 6 (Table 1).

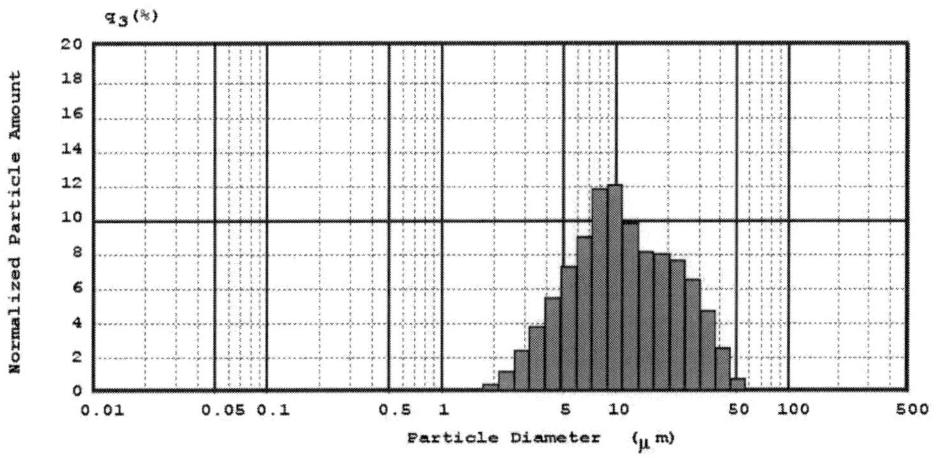

Fig. 2. Dispersion parameters of the bitumen phase of composition No. 7 (Table 1).

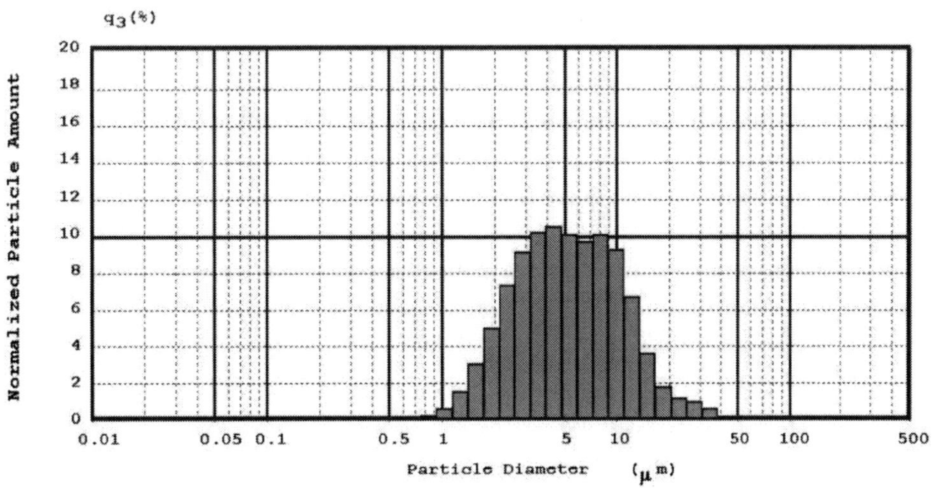

Fig. 3. Dispersion parameters of the bitumen phase of composition No. 5 (Table 1).

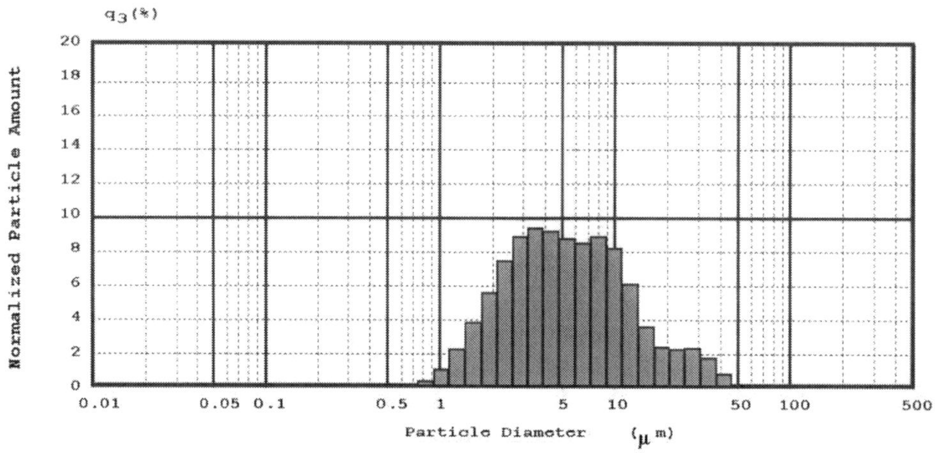

Fig. 4. Dispersion parameters of the bitumen phase of composition No. 10 (Table 1).

Since the spreading capacity and delaminatability of the bitumen emulsion relate to the thixotropic characteristics, and the bitumen phase in the oil-in-water system has the shape of a sphere or something close to it, consideration of the effect of internal interactions is impossible without application of the closest packing theory. According to this theory, the maximum filling volume of a single cell with identical spheres is possible only by 75.05%, and in this case, there will be voids, one octahedral and two tetrahedral [7]. However, the bitumen emulsion has spheres of bitumen phase of different diameters, which will cause a change in the contacting number in the dispersion system. Ideally, the contacting number is maximal, but if the dispersion of spheres by size and quantity does not correspond to the closest packing theory, then the contacting number decreases. Therefore, for increasing the time before delamination it is necessary to strive for decreasing the contacting number of spheres of the bitumen phase in the bitumen emulsion, since the surface-active substances are displaced at the contact points of the bitumen spheres to other surfaces thus accelerating the processes of coalescence.

When considering the ratio of components in the bitumen emulsion as indicated in Table 1, it can be seen that the amount of bitumen phase does not exceed 60%, therefore, the micro-droplets do not contact each other and are completely washed by the liquid (water) phase. Particularly it is possible to distinguish the compositions No. 3 and No. 9, where the stability indicators related to time differ (by several orders of magnitude) from those of other compositions. These compositions are characterized by a high content of the bitumen-salt mass in the bitumen phase; therefore, the concentration of the reaction mass on the surface of bitumen micro-droplets will be maximal. The amount of bitumen is minimal for the interval under consideration, which entails a decrease in the surface area and increase in the concentration of the reaction mass of the Bitumen-salt mass at the inter-phase boundary. Then a rapid reduction of the bitumen emulsion stability time is explained by the formation of micelles of surface-active substances at the inter-phase boundary between the "bitumen-water" phases and the subsequent occurrence of micellar catalysis [8].

Compatibility of Redicote EM44 emulsifier and bitumen-salt mass in bitumen emulsions is proved, which will improve the quality of the joint operation of different layers of road surface. The amount of the bitumen-salt mass in the bitumen phase should not exceed 6.6% - this will ensure the optimal formation of the dispersed structure of the bitumen emulsion. When performing further selection of the disperse system compositions, the amount of hydrochloric acid and emulsifier may be significantly reduced, which will positively affect the economic indicators.

Conclusion

Thus, the introduction of the bitumen-salt mass into the composition of the bitumen emulsion will allow us to modify the dispersion parameters, which will ensure high performance characteristics of the road surfaces. It will ensure improvement of transport systems safety. The obtained results may be applied for industrial complexes producing elements of road surface. Further studies are relevant to insulating and binding materials (reinforcement of roadsides and road slopes).

References

1. V.M. Kolodkina, I.I. Manilo, *Shhuchanskij arsenal himicheskogo oruzhija. Predvaritel'nyj prognoz ugrozy naseleniju* [Shhuchanskij chemical weapon arsenal. Preliminary forecast of threat to civilians] (IPP «DAMMI» Publ., 1997). (in Russian)
2. N.I. Kalinina, *Himija ili zhizn'? Vybiraem zhizn'* [Chemistry or life? We choose life] (Kurgan, 1997). (in Russian)
3. Y.I. Livanov, I.I. Manilo, *Zadacha optimal'nogo upravlenija tehnologicheskoj sistemoj objekta po unichtozheniju himicheskogo oruzhija* [Task of optimal control of technological system of chemistry weapon destruction facility] (NCSP "Ekonomika i Reformy" Publ., Kurgan, 1998). (in Russian)
4. U.I. Musijchuk, *Medicinskie problemy unichtozhenija himicheskogo oruzhija* [Medical issues of chemical weapon destruction] (Kurgan, 1997). (in Russian)
5. V.A. Petrunin, V.V. Sheluchenko, V.V. Demidjuk, *Problemy Rossii v realizacii konvencii po zapreshheniju himicheskogo oruzhija: sostojanie i perspektivy k koncu 2000 goda* [Problems of Russia in implementation of the Convention on prohibition of chemical weapons: state and prospects by the end of 2000] (Agentstvo Rakurs Publ., Moscow, 2001). (in Russian)
6. V.A. Petrunin, V.V. Sheluchenko, V.V. Demidjuk, Federal'nye i regional'nye problemy unichtozhenija himicheskogo oruzhija. Informacionnyj sbornik [Federal and regional problems of chemical weapons destruction], **Vol. 1** (VNIITI Publ., Moscow, 1999). (in Russian)
7. P.I. Grekhov, V.S. Shkrabak, Bulletin of Saint-Petersburg State Agrarian University, 40 (2015). (in Russian)
8. M.I. Kuchma, *Poverhnostno-aktivnye veshhestva v dorozhnom stroitel'stve* [Surface-active substances in road construction] (Transport Publ., Moscow, 1980). (in Russian).
9. P.I. Grekhov, V.S. Shkrabak, RU Patent 2579128 (2014). (in Russian)
10. P.I. Grekhov, V.S. Shkrabak, RU Patent Application No. 2017106846 (2017). (in Russian)
11. A.I. Kitajgorodskij, *Vvedenie v fiziku* [Introduction to physics] (Nauka Publ., Moscow, 1973). (in Russian)
12. I.V. Berezin, K. Martinek, A.K. Jacimirskij, Russian Chemical Reviews, 42 (10), (1973). (in Russian)

Energy-efficient power regulators for electric railway vehicles

Leonid Astrakhantsev[1,*], *Natalya* Ryabchyonok[1], *Tatyana* Alekseeva[1], *Andrey* Khomenko[1], and *Aleksey* Martusov[1]

[1]Irkutsk State Transport University, 664074 Irkutsk, Russia

Abstract. This study aims at validation of the power regulation parameter for electric railway vehicles for effective use of electrical potential of energy sources. Based on analysis of electromagnetic processes with the use of suggested energy parameters and mathematical modeling method the assessment of energy efficiency was performed for semiconductor power regulators for alternating and direct current electric traction drives. Power balance and obtained mathematical equations for calculation of its components allow improving the education content of educational institutions due to eliminating methodological inconsistencies. The suggested technical solutions for continuous and full use of the electrical potential of overhead systems and self-generated power supply sources ensure their advantage in terms of structure, energy efficiency and electromagnetic compatibility.

Introduction

Average energy costs of transport work amount to 12% of operating costs of the whole transportation process [1]. Global productions of power regulators for electric power consumers, which are used in all economy sectors, is characterized by the use of pulse-type utilization of the electric potential of power sources and power supply systems. Electric energy is inefficiently used to perform work in various industrial processes, emitting electromagnetic interference into the environment. This inefficiency harms both the society and the environment, hindering the development of technologies for energy-efficient use of expensive but convenient energy carriers. For the purpose of cost reduction some research are done on boosting the electric energy use by applying semiconductor devices [2-3].

The conventional technical solutions are aimed at improving the quality parameters of energy processes, however they don't eliminate the cause of unsatisfactory operation of equipment. With this aim algorithms for semiconductor converters regulation are developed based on feedbacks [4], and additional equipment is produced. Active filters and peak load compensators [5, 6] are used for improving electromagnetic compatibility of electric power system components. Subject of this study is energy processes in electric circuits. Specifically, the study focuses on defining and eliminating causes for decrease of their energy efficiency and increasing electromagnetic compatibility of semiconductor power regulators of electric drives for electric railway vehicles.

* Corresponding author: astrahancev1943@mail.ru

© The Authors, published by EDP Sciences. This is an open access article distributed under the terms of the Creative Commons Attribution License 4.0 (http://creativecommons.org/licenses/by/4.0/).

Scientific substantiation of energy processes theory, which is studied in educational institutions in Russia and abroad, is based on Poynting's theorem (1885). The change in the duration of the irreversible transformation of electrical energy into another type of energy is accounted for by the conventional law of conservation of energy in the electromagnetic field [7]. However, this issue is often disregarded in the educational process, when the teachers fail to bring it to notice of their students. Power regulation in electric drives today is performed using controlled power semiconductor devices (PSD). The duration of the use of the electrical potential of energy sources for the performance of work is reduced due to current switching in PSD regulators.

The scientific problem consists in lack of mathematical dependences using which one can account the effect of PSD regulators on the duration of use of energy sources electric potential

for task performance. This study aims to develop analytical equations which account variation in the duration of use of energy sources electric potential by power regulators. The power balance at the input of a semiconductor power regulator (SPR) of the electric traction drive is suggested based on the revised energy conservation law in electromagnetic field. New energy parameters enable to eliminate methodological inconsistencies in educational process and to perform differential assessment of energy efficiency of electric power system elements. Mathematical dependences are obtained for calculating the power factor in direct current (DC) circuits. A new parameter for electric engine power control is suggested based on activating of input electrical resistance of electric traction drive.

The power factor F_p for alternating current (AC) electric railway vehicles with a rectifier-inverter converter (RIC) and pulse phase thyristor control method can be calculated [8] using the quality attributes of the energy process ν and cosφ (1)

$$F_P = \nu \cdot cos\varphi,\ \nu = \frac{2\cdot\sqrt{2}\cdot cos\frac{\alpha}{2}}{\pi\cdot\sqrt{\frac{\pi-\alpha}{\pi}}},\ cos\varphi = \cos\left(\frac{\alpha}{2} + \frac{\gamma_1+\gamma_2}{4}\right), \quad (1)$$

where ν – is the current total harmonic distortion (THDi),

$cos\varphi$ – is the displacement factor,

α – is the angle of thyristor regulation of the RIC,

γ_1, γ_2 – are the switching angles of RIC thyristors.

The use of formulas (1) to calculate the power factor and its dependence on α, γ1, γ2 makes it possible to achieve satisfactory accuracy for engineering calculations. But the calculated dependences are applied in practice as a way to find technical solutions for increasing the current total harmonic distortion (ν → 1) and for increasing the displacement factor (cosφ → 1).

Frequency control of asynchronous traction motors (ATM) is performed using an autonomous inverter and pulse width modulation (PWM) at the stator windings [9, 10]. Duration of the use of the electrical potential of the power supply system shortens in the rated ATM operating conditions due to the pauses between rectangular voltage pulses (Fig.1).

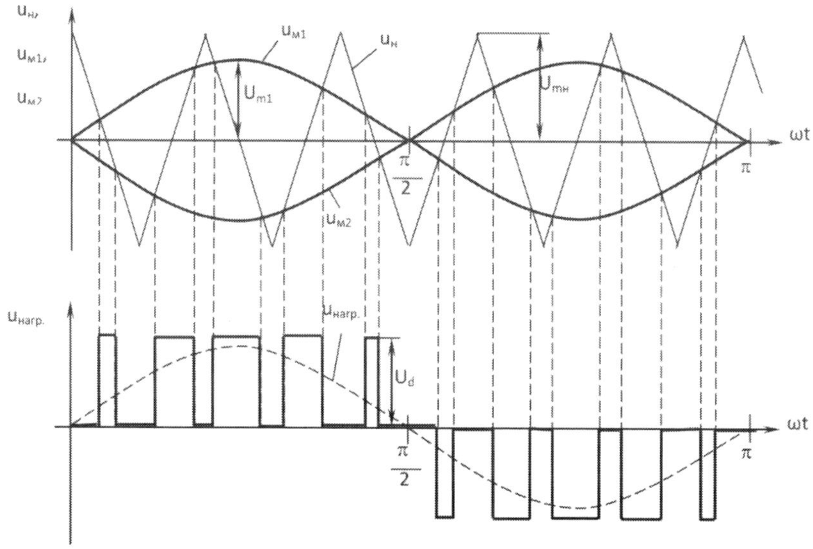

Fig. 1. Voltage timing diagrams for pulse width modulation.

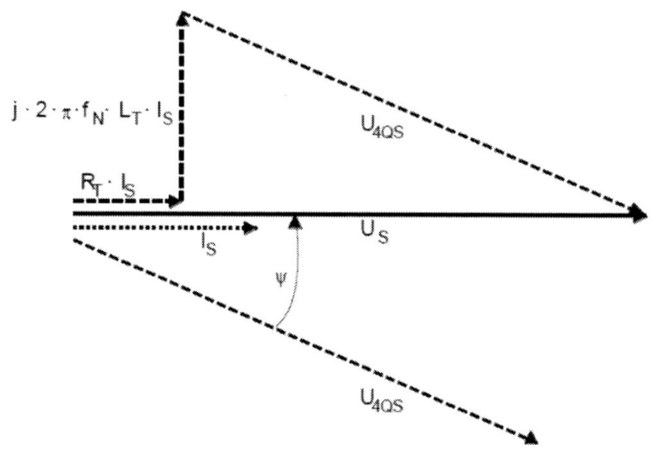

Fig. 2. Vector diagram of voltages and currents when the 4qS converter is operating in the rectifier mode.

ATM starting and output torque ramping are carried out with a reduced effective voltage at the stator windings and decreased frequency. To provide that the pauses between rectangular voltage pulses are increased. This approach makes it possible to reduce the duration of the irreversible transformation of electrical energy into another type of energy. PWM is used to control PSDs of four-quadrant 4qS converters. The pulse current envelope IS at the input of the converter ($\varphi = 0$) is matched with the instantaneous AC voltage curve U_S in the traction mode (Fig. 2). Phase displacement occurs by the angle π of the pulse current envelope at the converter input with the instantaneous AC voltage curve for the regeneration mode [11].

Research methods

The validation of the reason for unsatisfactory energy efficiency and electromagnetic compatibility of pulse semiconductor power regulators was carried out by refining the energy conservation law in the electromagnetic field [12, 13]. The revised version of the law takes into account the reduction of the duration of irreversible conversion of electrical energy not only by reactive elements of the electrical circuit, but also by semiconductor devices. The power balance at the input of a semiconductor power regulator (SPR) of the electric traction drive of an electric railway vehicle (2) was obtained and new energy characteristics were

$$\sqrt{S_{in}^2 - \Delta S^2} = \sqrt{P^2 + Q^2}. \tag{2}$$

The total power at the regulator input S_{in}

$$S_{in} = U \cdot I, \tag{3}$$

where U, I are the effective voltage, current at the input of the power regulator.

The component of the total power at the input of the SPR for the non-conductive state of the PSD

$$\Delta S = \sqrt{\sum_{k=0}^{n} U_{pk}^2 \cdot I_k^2} = U_p \cdot I, \tag{4}$$

where U_{Pk} – is the effective voltage of the kth component of Fourier series at the input of the power regulator during the non-conductive state of the PSD;

I_k – is the effective value of current of the k-th harmonic at the input of the SPR;

U_P – is the effective voltage at the input of the SPR during the non-conductive state of the PSD;

k – is the number of terms of the Fourier series, integers only;

n – is the number of the last harmonic counted.

Active power at the regulator input

$$P = U_{c0} \cdot I_0 + \sum_{k=1}^{n} U_{ck} \cdot I_k \cdot \cos \varphi_k \tag{5}$$

where U_{c0}, U_{ck} – are respectively the average voltage and the effective value of voltage of the kth harmonic at the input of the SPR in the conductive state of the PSD;

I_0, I_k – are respectively the average current and the effective value of current of the kth harmonic at the input of the SPR.

Reactive power at the regulator input

$$Q = \mp \sqrt{\sum_{k=1}^{n} U_{ck}^2 \cdot I_k^2 \cdot \sin^2 \varphi_k} \tag{6}$$

Phase angle φ_Σ of the total power and electrical resistance at the input of the PSD

$$\varphi_{\sum} = arctg\left(\frac{\mp\sqrt{\sum_{k=1}^{n} U_{ck}^2 \cdot I_k^2 \cdot \sin^2 \varphi_k}}{U_{c0} \cdot I_0 + \sum_{k=1}^{n} U_{ck} \cdot I_k \cdot \cos \varphi_k} \right) \quad (7)$$

The developed energy characteristics allow eliminating methodological contradictions in the process of specialist training, they also comply with the provisions of fundamental electrical engineering [14-16]. These characteristics account the influence of nonlinear distortions of voltage and current on the active and reactive power and the phase angle of the input electrical resistance (7) of the power regulator with a load. All components of the power balance (2) can be calculated and checked for the accuracy of calculation and measurement.

The power factor can be applied to estimate the energy efficiency of the use of electrical energy in direct and alternating current circuits. An assessment method is proposed for the operation of a power regulator K_C and the effect of reactive elements of the electrical circuit K_Q on the efficiency of the energy process (8)

$$F_P = \frac{P}{S_{in}} = \frac{\sqrt{P^2+Q^2}}{\sqrt{P^2+Q^2+\Delta S^2}} \cdot \frac{P}{\sqrt{P^2+Q^2}} = K_C \cdot K_Q\,, \quad (8)$$

where $K_C = \frac{\sqrt{P^2+Q^2}}{\sqrt{P^2+Q^2+\Delta S^2}}$ – is a coefficient that accounts changing by the electric railway vehicle power regulator of duration of using the electrical potential of the overhead system for train traction,

$K_Q = \frac{P}{\sqrt{P^2+Q^2}}$ – is a coefficient that takes into account the change in the reactive elements of the electrical circuit the duration of the irreversible conversion of electrical energy into another form of energy.

It is possible to justify the introduction of a new parameter for controlling the power of the electric traction drive of an electric railway vehicle by expressing the current at the input of the power regulator using (2) and taking into account the expressions (3 - 6)

$$\mathrm{I} = \frac{\sqrt{P^2+Q^2}}{\sqrt{U^2-U_P^2}}. \quad (9)$$

It follows from the expression (9) that in order to create an energy-efficient electric traction technology, instead of the known pulse power regulators one should use electric potential of energy sources completely and continuously ($U_P = 0$). A new technical solution is achieved when changing the value of input electrical resistance for power regulation and making active ($\varphi_{\sum} = 0$) input electric resistance of the electric traction drive. The application of the new power control parameter for electric traction drives becomes particularly relevant for mainline electric railway vehicles with a limited self-generated power supply. Regulators changing the power of the electric traction drive by controlling the input electrical resistance are discussed in detail in [17], and their effectiveness can be verified by mathematical modeling.

The mathematical model accounts the parameters of traction substation, overhead system, traction transformer of an electric railway vehicle, power regulator, traction electric drives and load. The results of calculation of the basic performance indicators of a traction drive were obtained using the expressions (2 – 8), using Simulink environment and MATLAB software package.

Results

The mathematical model of operation of an electric traction drive (Fig. 3) of a DC electric railway vehicle with an input electrical resistance for regulator controlling the electric traction motor (ETM) collector with a rated voltage of 1000 V provides the load on the overhead system with the current I_{in} = 462.4 A, and current I_d = 815.1 A in ETM windings.

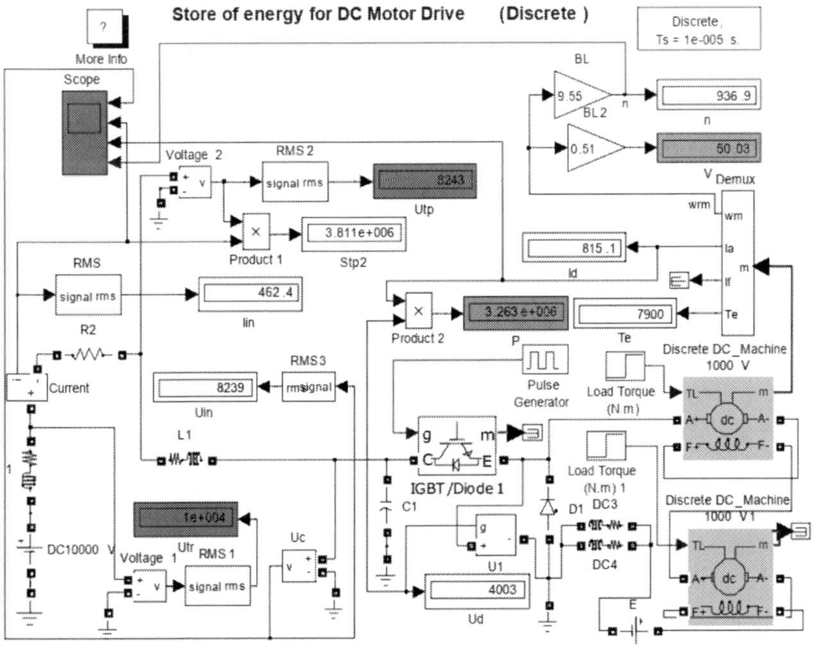

Fig. 3. Mathematical model of a DC motor drive of an electric railway vehicle with U_H = 10 000 V, rated traction and V = 50 km/h.

This regulator can function as an electric semiconductor variator (ESV), as the total voltage on ETM windings U_d = 4003 V, which is almost two times lower than the voltage on the bow current collector U_{tp} = 8243 V in the middle of the feeder zone of the overhead system. The power factor is F_P = 0.86, the efficiency is 93.3 %. The power factor can be increased to 1 by successive enabling the electric traction motors of 2 sections of the electric railway vehicle to an intermediate storage C_1. Start, breakaway and acceleration of an electric traction drive (Fig. 4) significantly differ from those in operation of drives with conditional pulse power regulators. Once the current collector is lifted to the contact wire, the intermediate storage is charged up to the voltage u_C = 10 kV (the first oscillogram, Fig. 4). With the voltage supplied to the windings of the electric traction motor, the current in the windings increases to i_d = 1000 A (the third oscillogram, see Fig. 4) and the current is consumed in the overhead system i_{in} (the second oscillogram, Fig. 4) to charge the intermediate energy storage. At the end of the acceleration, the consumed input current from the overhead system iin = 46.36 A, and the current in ETM windings id = 802.2 A. The moment of resistance on the shaft torque of the ETM 7772 N · m and the shaft rotation frequency n = 94 rpm (the fourth oscillogram, Fig. 4). The power factor of a electric traction motor F_P = 0.99 at the electric railway vehicle speed of 5 km/h, efficiency η = 67%, mainly depending on the efficiency of the ETM in this mode of operation.

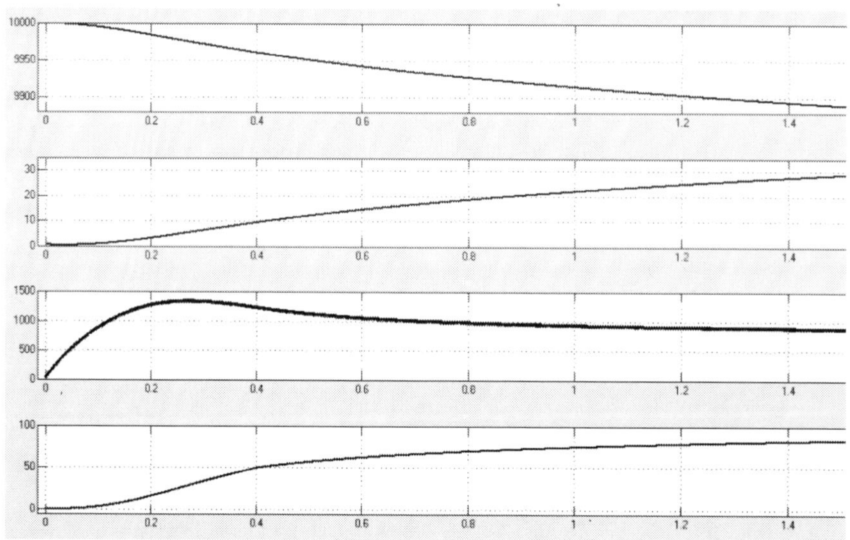

Fig. 4. Oscillograms showing the voltage u_C, input current i_m at the input of the ESV, ETM current I_d and the speed of rotation n of the motor shaft.

A study of operation of a section of an alternating current electric railway vehicle with ATD-1200 asynchronous traction motors at the current collector voltage of 26960 V in the middle of the feeder zone of the overhead system of the direct current. It is made it possible to establish that at a current of 144.8 A consumed from the overhead system, the total phase current of the 4 ATMs was 1977 A at the vehicle movement speed of 51 km/h and the ATM shaft drag torque of 7772 N · m. The power factor of the traction drive is 0.9, the efficiency is 90%.

When starting, breaking away and accelerating, the electric traction drive of the section of the electric railway vehicles of the alternating current ESV and ATM the current consumed from the overhead system does not exceed 32 A in the steady state when moving at a speed of 5 km/h and the ATM shaft drag torque of 7772 N · m. The power factor is 0.91, the power efficiency is 40.3 %.

Conclusion

The reason for the reduction in energy efficiency and electromagnetic compatibility of semiconductor power regulators is the reduction in the duration of irreversible conversion of electrical energy into another type of energy. The refinement of the law of conservation of energy in the electromagnetic field eliminates certain teaching problems in the educational process are eliminated. Specialists are focused on developing new engineering solutions to eliminate the cause of drawbacks of currently produced equipment. The proposed power characteristics of an electric traction drive are suitable for studies of direct and alternating current circuits with any form of instantaneous curves of voltage and current. The developed engineering solutions contribute to further development of innovative technologies in energy-efficient electric traction.

References

1. A.T. Burkov, *Elektronika i preobrazovatel'naja tehnika*, [Electronics and Converter Equipment] (UMCZDT, Moscow, 2015). (in Russian)
2. M.S. Jaya Kumar, G. Ajeesh, International Journal of Electrical & Computer Engineering, **Vol. 2** (3), 339-344 (2012).
3. P.V. Prasuna, J.V.G. Rama Rao, Ch.M. Lakshmi, International Journal of Engineering Research and Applications (IJERA), **Vol. 2** (4), 2368-3376 (2013).
4. K. Mohanraj, C. Lanya Bersis, S. Sekhar, *Power Electronics and Renewable Energy Systems*, Proceedings of ICPERES, 29-38 (2014).
5. S. Jenella, V. Radj Kumar, *Power Electronics and Renewable Energy Systems*, Proceedings of ICPERES, 225-236 (2014).
6. J.H. Poynting, *Proceedings of the Royal Society* (London, 1884).
7. O.A. Maevskiy, *Energeticheskie harakteristiki ventil'nyh preobrazovatelej* [Energetic characteristics of valve inverters] (Energiya, Moscow, 1978). (in Russian)
8. R.T. Shreyner, *Matematicheskoe modelirovanie jelektroprivodov peremennogo toka s poluprovodnikovymi preobrazovateljami chastoty* [Mathematical Simulation of Alternating Current Drives with Semiconductor Frequency] (Ural Branch of Russian Academy of Sciences, Ekaterinburg, 2000). (in Russian)
9. Yu.A. Bakhvalov, G.A. Buzalo, A.A. Zarifyan, *Dinamicheskie processy v asinhronnom tjagovom privode magistral'nyh jelektrovozov* [Dynamic Processes in an Asynchronous Pulling Drive of Mainline Electric Locomotives] (Marshrut, Moscow, 2006). (in Russian)
10. J. Teigelkotter, D. Sprenger, *Moshhnyj preobrazovatel' na IGBT-tranzistorah dlja primenenija na zheleznodorozhnom podvizhnom sostave* [Powerful converter on IGBT-transistors for use on railway rolling stock] (Siemens AG, Munich, 2000). (in Russian)
11. N.L. Ryabchyonok, T.L. Alekseeva, K.P. Yakobchuk, L.A. Astrakhantsev, Tehnicheskie Nauki. Energetika [Technical Sciencies. Power Engineering] No. 5 (2016). (in Russian)
12. T.L. Alekseeva, N.L. Ryabchyonok, L.A. Astrakhantsev, Technology of Electric Power Efficient Use in Transport, In: *International Scientific Conference Energy Management of Municipal Transportation Facilities and Transport EMMFT 2017*, 120-133 (2017).
13. P.A. Ionkin, *Teoreticheskie osnovy elektrotehniki* [Theoretical Basis of Electrical Engineering] (Vysshaja shkola, Moscow, 1976). (in Russian)
14. L.A. Bessonov, *Teoreticheskie osnovy jelektrotehniki* [Theoretical Basis of Electrical Engineering] (Vysshaja shkola, Moscow, 1996). (in Russian)
15. K.S. Demirchan, L.R. Neyman, N.V. Korovkin, *Teoreticheskie osnovy jelektrotehniki* [Theoretical Basis of Electrical Engineering] (Piter, St. Petersburg, 2009). (in Russian)
16. A.V. Vorotilkin, N.L. Mikhalchuk, N.L. Ryabchenok, T.L. Alekseeva, Science And Engineering, **Vol. 13**, No. 6, 62-76 (2015). (in Russian)

Financial aspects of transport infrastructure development in regions

Vyacheslav Bubnov[1,*], and *Yulia* Bubnova[2]

[1]Irkutsk State University of Railway Engineering, 664074 Irkutsk, Russia
[2]Baikal State University, 664003 Irkutsk, Russia

Abstract. The level of economic development depends on many factors, among which infrastructure, including railway transport, is the key one. Financing of infrastructure-related projects on the regional level encourages economic growth. However, different level of overall development of subject of the Russian Federation causes inequality in the level of transport infrastructure development and makes common approach to its financing inapplicable. The necessity appears to build a model of financing for transport-related infrastructure with the use of statistical data and mathematical approach with the account of regional market peculiarities. Due to selection of indicators affecting economic growth and building parametric factor model, classification of financing on subfederal level was carried out, which makes it applicable for states with federal structure.

Introduction

Current state of world economy reveals rather serious disproportions in economic development of certain regions. Usually, the main part of financial resources is concentrated in financial centers where the key infrastructure-related investment projects are implemented. Divergent development of big territorial entities occurs [1], which causes subsequent flow of labor, material, intellectual and other resources from the periphery to the center. It results in slowdown of growth rate in both leading global economies and developing countries.

The problems of economic growth in developing countries are vastly studied. The works of A. Elekes and P. Halmai [2] revealed that the model of economic growth and convergence effective up to 2008, is inapplicable for current conditions in these countries. Study of the Bank for International Settlements demonstrated why too rapid growth of financial sector has negative effect on the overall economy [3]. Particularly, the resource supply of economic growth leads to the deficit of public finances. According to D. Mauldin and D. Tepper [4], if one fails to get control of the USA budget deficit, it will reach 200% of the GDP by 2025, which will bring the leading global financial system in an unstable position. The main factor of financial capital allocation in such conditions is not the reliability of capital maintenance, but the proximity to functioning markets [5]. According

* Corresponding author: bubnovva13@gmail.com

© The Authors, published by EDP Sciences. This is an open access article distributed under the terms of the Creative Commons Attribution License 4.0 (http://creativecommons.org/licenses/by/4.0/).

to Ph. Hugon [6], this leads the global economy to asymmetry and contradictions between periphery and center.

As a result, the role of corporate finances in economic growth is enhanced, to meet the needs of such capitals offshore companies are formed. The initial purpose of creating tax shelters to enable transnational corporations to enter new markets [7] transformed into "black holes in the global economy" [8], which has a detrimental effect on public finances disturbing their sovereignty [9]. Deep contradictions are formed between public and corporate finances.

Some authors believe in the ability to unite financial systems [10], others prove negative effect on the economic development caused by incompatible national finances [11-13]. According to W. Van Lear and J. Sisk [14], major corporations switched from performance strategy mainly based on the national economy framework to the strategy of direct foreign investments, which according to M. Woodford [15] requires unconventional measures.

Active and rational participation of the government in financing is necessary to overcome these negative tendencies [16]. Development and growth of national economy is only possible when based on subfederal level development.

Research methods

When studying subfederal level, a reasonable suggestion shall be made, that regions have different levels of development, which makes common approach to financing of economic development inapplicable. Consequently, it is important to classify regions on the basis of factors affecting economic growth and development from the viewpoint of financing.

A parametric model is used to build a factor model of financing, it enables to interpret the results obtained in research and practical activities. Per capita gross regional product (internal factor – y) was taken as a target parameter, which depends on external variables – $x_1, x_2, \ldots, x_m$, given in Table 1. In order to provide comparability of the economic growth parameter on the subfederal level it was recalculated as per capita gross regional product for a certain region and chosen time period (Table 1). The given calculations showed that in various regions economic growth is affected by different factors, which became the basis for classification [17].

Table 1. Classification of financing in regions with regard to the effect on economic growth.

Region type	Factor affecting economic growth
Quasi-corporation region	x_3 – investments in fixed capital per capita x_4 – capital/labor ratio in all organizations x_5 – organizational demography x_6 – railway transportation of cargo
Quasi-state region	x_1 – per capita expenses of consolidated regional budget x_2 – per capita expenses of state non-budgetary funds x_{10} – per capita share of public employees
Society region	x_7 – annual per capita income x_8 – annual level of occupation x_9 – level of citizens' economic activity

Official data on subjects of the Russian Federation and federal districts for the period 2000-2014 were taken as a statistical basis for calculations. Software products were used when solving computational problems, and the best model was selected based on multicriteria approach (Table 2), which allowed defining factors financing of which affect economic growth. Additionally, factors having negative effect on economic growth were defined. The obtained results became the basis for shaping state finance policy in the conditions of limited financial resources of the Russian society.

Table 2. Federal districts of the Russian Federation factor model of financing economic growth in 2000-2014 [17].

Federal district	Model
Central	$y = -1.05e^5 + 3.49x_2 + 5.61x_3 - 42.9x_4 - 0.321x_7 + 1.74e^5x_{10}$
Northwest	$y = -1.10e^{05} + 2.46x_1 + 129x_4 + 709x_6$
South	$y = -2.37e^4 + 5.72x_1 - 55.9x_4 + 598x_6$
North Caucasus	$y = -1.40e^4 + 1.04x_1 + 2.14x_2 + 1.30e^3x_6$
Volga	$y = -359895 - 3.858x_1 + 3.132x_3 + 177.46x_4 + 156.33x_6 + 180.64x_8 + 4899.94x_9$
Ural	$y = -3.43e^5 + 1.80x_1 + 4.81x_2 + 1.35e^{03}x_6 + 2.68e^5x_{10}$
Siberia	$y = -1.03e^5 + 2.40x_2 + 1.21x_3 + 258x_6 + 4.56e^4x_{10}$
Far East	$y = -2.56e^4 + 3.45x_2 + 0.786x_3 + 32.7x_4 + 0.0567x_7 + 3.45e^{04}x_{10}$

Experimental data and results

Classification of economic growth financing was performed with regard to subjects of the Russian Federation, it includes: quasi-corporation regions - 44; quasi-state regions - 23; society-regions - 13; non-defined - 2 [17], which enables to make the following conclusions:

- subjects of the Russian Federation significantly differ in their level of development;
- comparability of factors affecting economic growth and development are non-existent, even with regard to federal districts;
- the selected factors have both positive and negative effect on economic growth (Table 3), which proves inability to apply a common approach to financing;
- the existing division into federal districts is carried out formally and is based on geographical characteristics, which hampers growth of financing efficiency.

Financing of economic growth shall be performed on the basis of the suggested classification of financing of subjects of the Russian Federation.

Table 3. Synthesis of factors affecting economic growth on subfederal level (without the account of federal districts) [18].

Indicator	x_1	x_2	x_3	x_4	x_5	x_6	x_7	x_8	x_9	x_{10}	Total
Number of factors with positive effect	21	24	26	19	0	17	29	15	7	11	169
Number of factors with negative effect	9	12	18	15	0	17	16	6	18	19	130
Total number of factors	30	36	44	34	0	34	45	21	25	30	299
% of positive effect	26.3	30.0	32.5	23.8	0.0	21.3	36.3	18.8	8.8	13.8	21.1
% of negative effect	11.3	15.0	22.5	18.8	0.0	21.3	20.0	7.5	22.5	23.8	16.3

When financing on the subfederal level, the following peculiarities found while model testing shall be accounted (Table 4):

- increase in financing of small and medium-sized enterprises is only reasonable for the purpose of social development, since organizational demography factor has no effect on economic growth in any of the regions;

– railway transportation of cargo can have both positive and negative effect on economic growth depending on the region, therefore, financing of railway transport development may affect the uncontrolled finance reallocation on the subfederal level;

– shadow market and tax evasion by self-employed civilians (factor of level of citizens' economic activity) effect economic growth negatively;

– reformation of finance allocation on payments for government employees is necessary when reaching a quasi-state level, since in this case the share of government employees is a negative factor.

The performed analysis showed that subjects of Siberian federal district belong to quasi-corporations (8 subjects) and quasi-states (4 subjects), which makes common policy of reasonable financing applicable. Let us consider factor model of economic growth financing in more detail (Table 4).

Table 4. Factor model of financing economic growth in subjects of the Russian Federation included in Siberian federal district, for 2000-2014 [17].

Region	Model	Determination criterion
Altai Republic	$y = -2.12e^4 + 19.7x_4 + 9.33e^5x_{10}$	$R^2 = 0.275$
Republic of Buryatia	$y = -1.01e^5 + 4.17x_2 + 1.66e^3x_6 - 0.0552x_7 + 6.13e^6x_{10}$	$R^2 = 0.909$
Tyva Republic	$y = -5143.46 - 0.484x_1 + 0.186x_3 + 0.21x_7 +$ $+ 486.83x_8 - 253.34x_9 - 124015x_{10}$	$R^2 = 0.987$
Republic of Khakassia	$y = -3.33e^4 + 0.720x_3 + 0.636x_7$	$R^2 = 0.957$
Altai Krai	$y = -1.04e^6 + 684x_4 - 0.163x_7 + 7.69e^3x_8 + 6.35e^3x_9$	$R^2 = 0.958$
Zabaykalsky Krai	$y = -9.83e^4 + 25.6x_1 - 2.26x_2 - 16.7x_3$	$R^2 = 0.720$
Krasnoyarsk Krai	$y = 4.56e^5 + 222x_2 - 63.4x_3 - 1.07e^4x_4 + 45.7x_7$	$R^2 = 0.925$
Irkutsk region	$y = -72031.3 + 3.58133x_2 + 0.28136x_7 +$ $+ 16160.7x_8 - 12941.2x_9$	$R^2 = 0.999$
Kemerovo region	$y = -2.43e^5 + 25.7x_1 - 3.31x_2$	$R^2 = 0.705$
Novosibirsk region	$y = -1.28e^5 + 14.5x_3 + 5.71e^3x_6 - 0.403x_7$	$R^2 = 0.946$
Omsk region	$y = 3733780 - 36,45x_1 + 12,23x_3 + 2472,36x_4 -$ $- 64598,8x_6 - 2,28x_7 - 23586,8x_9 - 110316000x_{10}$	$R^2 = 1$
Tomsk region	$y = 1.75e^5 - 4.15x_3 + 5.85e^4x_6 + 5.47x_7 - 5.37e^7x_{10}$	$R^2 = 0.966$

Having analyzed the data in Table 4, a valid conclusion can be made that there are no regions with identical models in Siberian federal district. Besides, Altai Republic and Kemerovo region have low determination criteria and require in-depth study.

Reasonable financing can be focused on both enhancing factors with positive effect on economic growth and minimizing those with negative effect. Below is suggested the conceptual approach applied to subjects of Siberian federal district (Table 5).

Table 5. Conceptual approaches to reasonable financing [17].

Type of subject of the Russian Federation	Subject of the Russian Federation	Conceptual approaches to reasonable financing
Quasi-corporation	Altai Republic	Corporate tax exemptions, development of loyal business environment
	Republic of Buryatia	Financing of social sphere, corporate tax exemptions
	Tyva Republic	Public-private projects, corporate tax exemptions, financing of creating jobs, rationalized approach to regional budget allocation
	Republic of Khakassia	Corporate tax exemptions, financing of creating jobs
	Altai Krai	Corporate tax exemptions, financing of creating jobs, financing of social sphere
	Novosibirsk region	Corporate tax exemptions, financing of social sphere
	Omsk region	Corporate tax exemptions, rationalized approach to regional budget allocation, financing of social sphere
	Tomsk region	Corporate tax exemptions, development of loyal business environment
Quasi-state	Zabaykalsky Krai	Creation of comfortable business environment and social infrastructure, increase of federal budget subsidies
	Krasnoyarsk Krai	Financing of social sphere by increasing costs of state non-budgetary foundations, financing of creating jobs, creation of comfortable business environment
	Irkutsk region	Financing of social sphere by increasing costs of state non-budgetary foundations, financing of creating jobs, financing law enforcement authorities working against shadow market
	Kemerovo region	Increase of federal budget subsidies and grants, financing of social sphere

Rational financing is impossible without attracting corporate finances of railway transport industry. The key member of this industry is Russian Railways JSC which has the following structure of project finance sources (Table 6).

Table 6. Structure of project finance sources in Russian Railways JSC in 2017 (%) [19].

Indicator	2013	2014	2015	2016	2017
Amount of profit	0.1	-4.5	0.0	0.6	1.4
Increase of authorized capital	12.6	5.4	10.1	5.0	5.4
Financial resources of budget and non-budgetary foundations	0.136	5.898	0.230	0.048	0.136
Finance lease	3.4	5.1	5.5	6.8	6.9
Credits	35.4	49.6	42.3	40.2	43.3
Bonded loans	48.4	38.5	41.8	47.4	42.8
Total amount	100	100	100	100	100

The projects are financed from various sources: own resources (income and depreciation reserve), government support (also by increasing the capital of Russian Railways JSC), loaned funds (credits, bonded loans). The major part is represented by loaned funds (more than 90%) including credits, bonded loans and leasing. However, these resources are obviously insufficient. It shall be noted that in 2018 capital investments in Eastern operating domain alone exceed 1.5 billion rubles [20].

Table 7. Capital investment of Russian Railways JSC in development of Eastern operation domain (million rubles, excl. VAT).

Project title	2013	2014	2015	2016	2017	2018
	actual				plan	
Improvement of railway infrastructure of Baikal-Amur Mainline and Trans-Siberian Railway with enhanced traffic and freight-carrying capacity	4,072.8	21,656.1	64,208.8	83,526.2	70,999.4	86,200.3
Complex development of the Mezhdurechensk - Taishet section of Krasnoyarsk railway	1,709.0	4,639.7	5,949.4	4,766.5	3,646.4	6,756.1
Improvement of Baikal-Amur Mainline and Trans-Siberian Railway						270.0
Increase of traffic capacity of Artysh - Mezhdurechensk - Taishet section						1,275.4

Search of new financial instruments is a relevant task. Infrastructure mortgage may become one of public-private partnership tools. The essence of this option consists in the possibility to use part of future tax revenues from project implementation for covering mortgage payments. Capital investments of a company may be made with the government support in the form of guarantees and further payment for this infrastructure while using it. When such system is applied, a bank shall offer affordable credits to the construction companies who shall build infrastructure facilities at the lowest possible cost. Then, the government starts paying the companies for them to repay the credit using the finances of the infrastructure beneficiary, with the minimum increase in taxes and payments. In fact, such infrastructure facilities are purchased on loaned funds from private investors and the users of the facility gradually repay this loan.

Conclusion

As the result of the study the recommendations were elaborated for financing development on subfederal level. It was proved that the use of common financing model on the subfederal level is impossible. Therefore, relevant models shall be chosen depending on classification of the region financing and the funding streams with confirmation of efficiency using the described factor model; this also applies to financing of railway infrastructure projects. Due to the classification of economic growth financing, conceptual approaches to reasonable financing were formulated which shall be accounted in transport infrastructure development.

The existing division of the economy into public and private (based on recommendation of Anglo-Saxon economists) is obsolete and doesn't meet economic development interests. The sector of public interests shall be defined and include systemically important financial institutions (like Russian Railways JSC), the activity of which impact the overall country development.

To reach the development goals new financial tools should be used, including infrastructure mortgage which is a public-private partnership instrument. This will provide additional tax revenues and development of finance and credit sector, as well as economic growth on the regional level.

Some additional research are required before practical use of the obtained results of the study, which will concern reciprocal effect of transport infrastructure and finance and credit system on the regional level. However, the outcomes of the study define the direction for further reserach.

References

1. RosStat, Gosudarstvo, obshhestvennye organizacii [The State, public organizations], Available at: http://www.gks.ru/wps/wcm/connect/rosstat_main/rosstat/ru/statistics/state/# (May 14, 2018). (in Russian)
2. A. Elekes, P. Halmai, Intereconomics, **Vol. 48**, 2, 124-130 (2013).
3. Vesti. Ekonomika, The Economist: finansovyj bum meshaet rostu jekonomiki [The Economist: financial boom hinders economic growth], Available at: http://www.vestifinance.ru/articles/53638 (20.02.2015).
4. D. Mauldin, D. Tepper, Endgame: The End of the Debt Supercycle and How It Changes Everything (Mif, Moscow, 2013). (in Russian)
5. S. Pavoni, The Banker, 16-17 (2011).
6. Ph. Hugon, Problemes econ P., 3011, 41-48 (2011).
7. Frère Albert. Le site des gros PatriMoines, Les paradis fiscaux, source d'enfer social et fiscal, Available at: http://www.frerealbert.be/fiscalite/fraude-fiscale/les-paradis-fiscaux-source-denfer-social-et-fiscal-/ (July, 2018).
8. Stop paradis fiscaux, Available at: http://www.partidegauche66.over-blog.fr/ (July, 2018).
9. Y. Steiner, M. Ruf, Les paradis fiscaux expirent lentement, Available at: http://www.hedbo.ch/_44246_.html (July, 2018).
10. P.A. Samuelson, W.D. Nordhaus, *Ekonomika* [Economics] (Binom, Moscow 1997). (in Russian)
11. R.G. Rajan, *Linii razloma: skrytye treshhiny, vsjo eshhjo ugrozhajushhie mirovoj ekonomike* [Fault Lines: How Hidden Fractures Still Threaten the World Economy] (Gaidar Institute Press, Moscow, 2013). (in Russian)
12. C. Borio, P. Disyatat, *Global imbalances and the financial crisis: Link or no link?* BIS working papers **346**, 43 (Bank for International Settlements Communications, Basel, 2011).
13. J. Ramos-Tallada, Bull. de la Banque de France, 184 (2011).
14. W. Van Lear, J. Sisk, Journal of Economic Issues, **Vol. 44** (3), 779-793 (2010).
15. M. Woodford, Journal of Economic Perspectives, **Vol. 24** (4), 21-44 (2010).
16. E.S. Rosengren, Defining financial stability, and some policy implications of applying the definition (Boston, 2011).
17. V.A. Bubnov, Thesis of Candidate of economic sciences, Novosibirsk State University of Economics and Management, Novosibirsk, 2017. (in Russian)
18. V.A. Bubnov, Scientific journal Vestnik NSUEM, 2, 312-327 (2017). (in Russian)
19. RZD to Investors, Company Reporting, Available at: http://ir.rzd.ru/static/public/ru?STRUCTURE_ID=32 (May, 2018). (in Russian)
20. RZD to Investors, Borrowing policy and debt obligations, Available at: http://ir.rzd.ru/static/public/ru?STRUCTURE_ID=65 (May 14, 2018). (in Russian)

Automated control system to monitor dielectric losses in polymers

Denis Butorin[1,*]

[1]Irkutsk State Transport University, 664074 Irkutsk, Russia

Abstract. The basic property of the processed polymers when it comes to high-frequency heat treatment is their dielectric losses. The purpose of the present study is elaboration of automated control system to monitor dielectric losses in polymers during heating. The technique developed in the given paper implies linear uniform heating of the studied material by contact method with the given velocity and when heating is off, periodic short-term action of high-frequency electric field on the polymer after each temperature growth of polymer per preset degree. The studies conducted in the automatic mode allowed obtaining new knowledge on changing electro-physical properties of polymers during heat treatment; and determining the new parameter to control polymer state while high-frequency processing; distinguishing and identifying different relaxation transitions of polymer materials during heating and thus broadening applicability of high-frequency heat treatment.

Introduction

High-frequency (HF) heat treatment is currently one of the most common among insignificant number of polymer heat treatment techniques (convective, contact, vacuum, infrared and compound); and it is considered as the most advanced, energy and resource saving processing technique of polymer components [1-4]. HF heat treatment technique is based on the polymer ability to dissipate energy in the electric field [2, 5-8]. Dielectric loss angle δ and its tangent $tg\delta$ are used to describe this ability [9, 10].

Russian and foreign scientists [1, 2, 5, 6, 11, 12] made a significant progress in HF heat treatment technique development, particularly regarding diagnostics, drying, welding and recovery of the strength properties of polymer products. Furthermore, literature review indicates that control of HF treatment quality and relaxation state of polymer during treatment can be performed based on the single parameter of electric thermal equipment operation – anode current I_a of HF generator connected analytically with $tg\delta$. The research in [1, 2, 6, 12-14] uses this parameter (I_a) as a controlled one. At this point it should be noted that due to few previous studies of HF influence on the polymer and the fact that polymer polarity was not considered, control of the polymer state in existing process procedures of HF treatment is attached just to the two relaxation transitions (maximum and

* Corresponding author: den_butorin@mail.ru

© The Authors, published by EDP Sciences. This is an open access article distributed under the terms of the Creative Commons Attribution License 4.0 (http://creativecommons.org/licenses/by/4.0/).

minimum $I_a(T)$). The temperature dependency $tg\delta$ contains several extreme values divided into dipole-segmental losses (α) and dipole-group losses (β, γ, δ) [1, 9, 10].

To provide quality control of process procedures of polymers HF heat treatment it is required to develop a technique for controlling their dielectric losses described by the dependency $tg\delta(T)$. This will allow establishing new controlled parameters of treatment, broadening the list of treated polymer materials, getting new knowledge on changing of their electro-physical parameters during treatment and widening applicability of HF heat treatment. Therefore, the present study aims to elaborate an automated technique to control dielectric losses in polymers during heating.

Materials and methods

To control dielectric losses in polymers a technique was developed which suggests linear uniform heating of the material under study by contact method with the velocity of 2 °C/min and periodic short-term (1 second) impact on the polymer, when heating is off, by HF electric field (voltage U_p = 4000 W) after each temperature growth of polymer specimen by 2 °C.

The technique was implemented on the improved and automated experimental setup ASNI VC (automated system for research studies of high-frequency treatment) [1, 6, 12-14]. Hardware component of the improved setup differed from the existing setup by exception of the press influence on heating and deformations of the specimen under study. Press unit (force 0…400 kg) was turned off, while the weight P of upper moving plate of operating capacitor was taken up by elastic members up to $P \geq F_{TPon}$, where F_{TPon} – friction force in supports. The final scheme of experimental setup is shown in Figure 1.

In simplified form the developed technique includes the following operations. The specimen from polymer material 1 is placed between electrodes 3 of a parallel plate operating capacitor connected to a HF generator 4, while a thermal-electrical insulator 2 is placed between the studied specimen 1 and electrode 3. The lower electrode as a whole is an electrical heating element 6, providing heating of the specimen up to melting temperature T_m (determined experimentally) with the velocity of 2 °C/min. Device 5 has a hole with inserted heat and electrical insulation layer and a thermocouple 7 to control surface temperature of the studied specimen 1. Anode current on the operating capacitor is measured automatically using the current sensor 8-1 after switch-on of the HF generator. Specimen temperature compared to the existing ASNI VC [1, 6, 12-14], is controlled using the thermocouple 7-1 only when HF generator is switched off, thus, measuring of temperature and current I_a are synchronized automatically in phase opposition. Output signals from the thermocouple 7-1 and current sensor 8-1 enter a computing unit 10, given as micro controller, connected to the personal computer via COM-port. Computing unit 10 includes the following sub-units:

- temperature control sub-unit 6-2;
- anode current control sub-unit 8-2;
- linear thermal expansion control sub-unit 11-2.

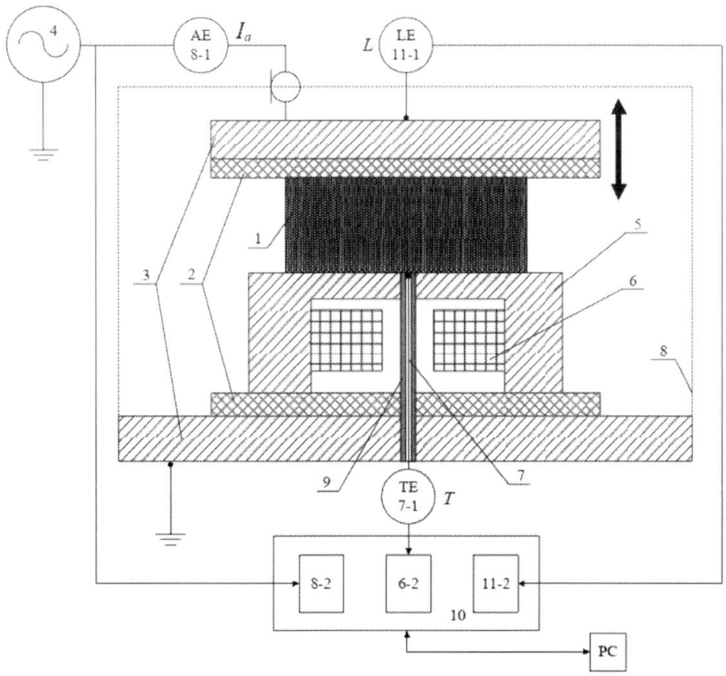

Fig. 1. Scheme of automated experimental setup to define amperometric dependency of dielectric losses in polymer materials, where 1 is polymer specimen under study; 2, 9 are thermal-electrical insulators; 3 is electrodes of operating capacitor; 4 is HF generator; 5 is a device for specimen heating; 6 is electrical heating element; 6-2 is temperature control sub-unit; 7 is a thermocouple; 7-1 is a thermocouple-temperature gauge; 8 is a protective screen; 8-1 is a current sensor; 8-2 is an anode current control sub-unit; 10 is a computing unit; 11-1 is a linear thermal expansion sensor; 11-2 is a linear thermal expansion control subunit.

To record the moment when the specimen reaches melting temperature, Balluff Micropulse BIW inductive linear position sensor with analog output signal 0...+10 W was attached to the mechanism of upper moving plate of the operating capacitor; the data was received by the computing unit 10. The software component of ASNI VC was improved by the developed algorithm for controlling the research process. Its flow-diagram is shown in Figure 2.

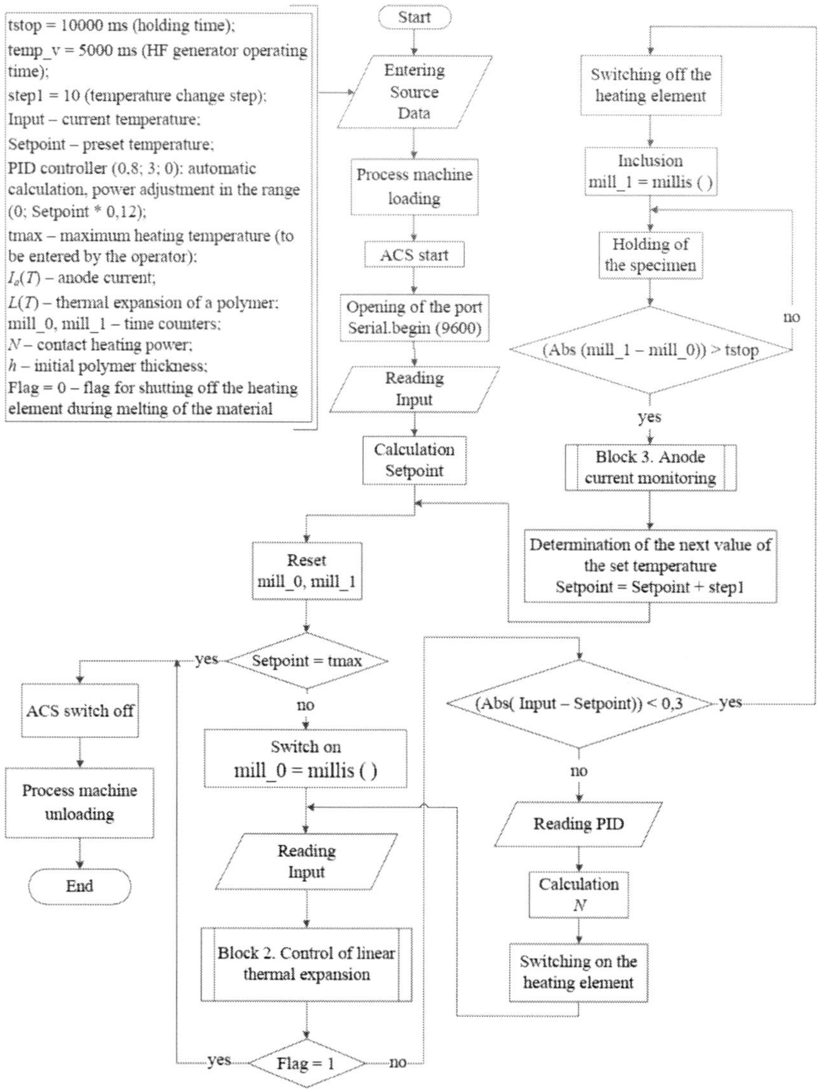

Fig. 2. Flow-diagram of the algorithm for controlling the process of linear homogenous heating of material under study and periodic short-term action of HF electric field when heating is off.

The elaborated control algorithm consists of three units:

- unit 1 of uniform heating of the material under study (basic unit);
- unit 2 of linear thermal expansion control during automated research (Fig. 3, a);
- unit 3 of anode current control (Fig. 3, b).

The given algorithm takes surface temperature of polymer specimen T_{surf}, its linear thermal expansion L and anode current of HF generator as the controlled parameters; while contact heating capacity N was accepted as a parameter-driven.

Resulting from the value of I_a of HF generator the studies were conducted on dielectric losses of some strong-polar polymer materials (PVC-plasticate OMB-60) and polar polymer materials (polyamide PA6) according to the elaborated technique on the improved experimental setup of brand UZP 2500 with operating capacity of HF generator 27.12 MHz. The specimens' sizes were chosen due to the criteria of maximum efficiency treatment on HF setup and were presented as round discs 60 mm in diameter and 4 mm thick. 7 tests were conducted on each of the materials to get valid results.

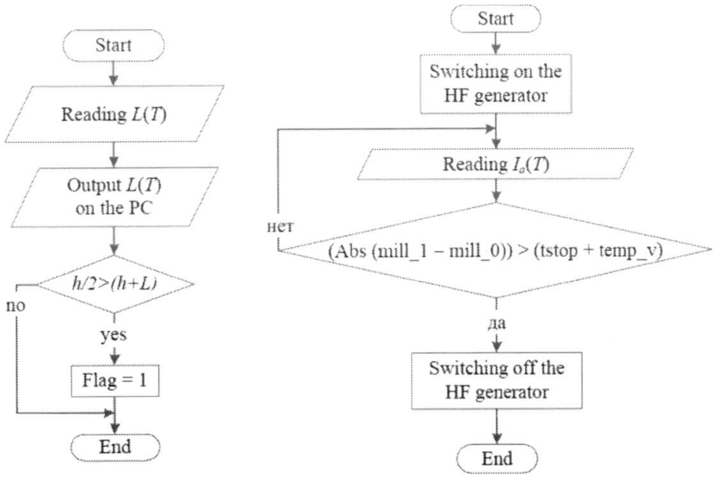

a b

Fig. 3. Flow-diagram of sub-units: a – unit 2 linear thermal expansion control; b – unit 3 anode current control.

Experiment and results

Resulting from the obtained experimental data dependency graphs between $I_a(T)$ and $L(T)$ were built for the given polymer materials (Fig. 4). Analysis of the given dependencies $I_a(T)$ and $L(T)$ provides interesting data. The dependency graph $I_a(T)$ (Fig. 4, a), obtained while polyamide treatment shows two extreme values (maximum and minimum points of I_a), while during PVC treatment I_a extreme values were not observed (Fig. 4, b).

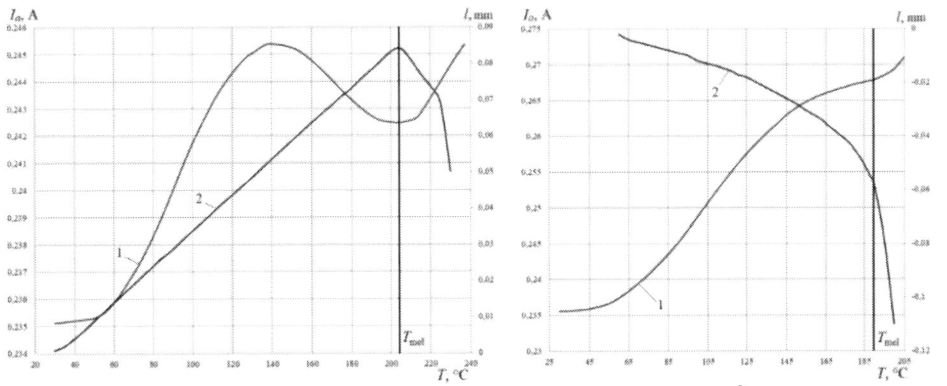

a b

Fig. 4. Dependency graphs of $I_a(T)$ (1) and $L(T)$ (2) obtained during treatment of polyamide PA6 (a) and PVC-plasticate OMB-60 (b).

Combining the dependency graphs of $I_a(T)$ and $L(T)$ obtained during polyamide treatment (Fig. 4, a) enables to identify the minimum of I_a as the moment when polymer reaches the melting temperature, its temperature value corresponds to the reference data.

Maximum of $I_a(T)$, as described in literature sources reflects the state when polymer reaches high-elastic state (dipole-segmental losses).

It also should be noted that for certain polymers the curve $L(T)$ has monotonic dropdown nature (PVC-plasticate), for other materials (polyamide PA6) it looks like a curve with a bending point. It is obvious that this fact depends on materials properties which vary during heating process, thus, it can be used for polymer identification.

Supported by previous studies [1] and analyzing the dynamics of anode current change the velocity of anode current change dI_a/dT was defined using differential operator of left finite difference of the first approximation order. The graph showing the velocity of anode current change dI_a/dT for the mentioned materials is given in Figure 5.

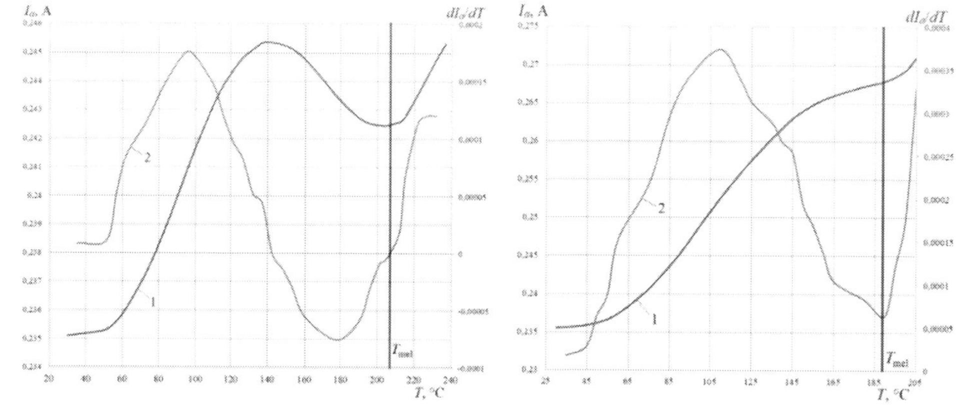

a b

Fig. 5. Dependency graphs of $I_a(T)$ (1) and dI_a/dT (2) obtained during treatment of polyamide PA6 (a) and PVC-plasticate OMB-60 (b).

Data analysis (dI_a/dT) revealed that the velocity of anode current change can be also used as the controlled parameter of treatment. During processes of HF treatment of polar polymers, such as polyamide PA6 (Fig. 5, a), as compared to strong-polar polymers (PVC-plasticate OMB-60), their melting state (minimum I_a) or dipole-segmental mobility (maximum I_a) can be defined by dI_a/dT passing through zero and reaching first the negative value, and then the positive value.

During HF-treatment of PVC-plasticate (Fig. 5, b), which shows no extreme values I_a, calculation of dI_a/dT reveals new reference points (extreme values dI_a/dT), and along with them new opportunities to organize process procedures of HF heat treatment and automation of their control. Minimum dI_a/dT during treatment of PVC-plasticate was first identified in this study as the moment when plasticate reaches the melting state. Maximum dI_a/dT obtained during treatment of both studied polymers was identified as reaching the state of dipole-group losses β ($tg\delta$).

Conclusion

The present study allowed developing and automating the technique to control dielectric losses in polymers through anode current of HF generator. In the course of experimental data analysis the new data was obtained on changing electrical and physical properties of polymers during heat treatment. The new controlled parameter in HF treatment was established, i.e. the velocity of anode current change dI_a/dT.

The developed technique enabled to determine and identify different relaxation transitions of polymer materials during heating along the extreme values I_a and dI_a/dT, as well as the dependencies $L(T)$. From the viewpoint of extremal systems controlling the process of polymer HF treatment each relaxation transition possesses practical importance. Thus, the maximum state I_a corresponds to the effective temperature of drying and recovering the strength properties of products from polar polymers. The minimum state I_a corresponds to the temperature of welding and adhesive bonding processes during treatment of polar polymers; while the minimum state dI_a/dT refers to treatment of strong-polar polymers. The maximum dI_a/dT can be applied as the reference point while impregnating polymer with various substances, e.g. motor oils. All this broadens the application field of high-frequency heat treatment.

Further research will be focused on distinguishing new classification of polymer materials considering their controllability when building extremal systems and elaboration of automated control systems of high-frequency treatment processes.

References

1. A.V. Livshits, Doctoral thesis, Irkutsk State Transport University, Irkutsk (2016). (in Russian)
2. N.G. Filippenko, Thesis of Candidate of technical sciences, Irkutsk State Transport University, Irkutsk (2012). (in Russian)
3. Yu.S. Arkhangelskiy, Vestnik of Saratov State Technical University, **4**, Issue 3, 5–15 (2011). (in Russian)
4. A.V. Markov, Yu.P. Yulenets, Elektrotehnika [Russian Electrical Engineering] **7**, 60–64 (2007). (in Russian)
5. S.N. Rumynskiy, Thesis of Candidate of technical sciences, Saint-Petersburg State Institute of Technology, Saint-Petersburg (2005). (in Russian)
6. A.G. Larchenko, Thesis of Candidate of technical sciences, Irkutsk State Transport University, Irkutsk (2014). (in Russian)
7. T. Ohe, Y. Yoshimura, Sen'i Gakkaishi, **1(65)**, 64–70 (2009).
8. W.R. Tinga, S.O. Nilson, The Journal of microwave power, **1**, 27–33 (1973).
9. V.K. Kryzhanovskiy, V.V. Burlov, A.D. Panimatchenko, Yu.V. Kryzhanovskaya, *Tehnicheskie svojstva polimernyh materialov* [Technical properties of polymeric materials] (Professiya, St-Petersburg, 2005). (in Russian)
10. A.A. Tager, *Fiziko-himija polimerov* [Physicochemistry of polymers] (Nauchnyj mir, Moscow, 2007). (in Russian)
11. A.V. Livshits, JP Journal of Heat and Mass Transfer **14(2)**, 219–226 (2017).
12. S.I. Popov, Thesis of Candidate of technical sciences, Irkutsk State Transport University, Irkutsk (2013). (in Russian)
13. A.V. Livshits, *Proceedings of the International Scientific Conference «Science and practice: new discoveries»*, 106–114 (Czech Republic, Karlovy Vary – Russia, Moscow, 2015). (in Russian)
14. A.V. Livshits, Engineering and Automation Problems, **4**, 54–60 (2015). (in Russian)

Application of probability and statistics methods in arrangement of railway transportation

Grigory Gefan[1,*]

[1]Irkutsk State University of Railway Engineering, 634074 Irkutsk, Russia

Abstract. Complex economic and mathematical methods are becoming more widespread in training of specialists in the field of railroad communication arrangement. The purpose of this study is to develop an effective methodology for mathematical training of railway transportation specialists on the basis of active training methods. The article deals with application of probabilistic and statistical methods to problems in design of railway transportation, for example, fluctuations in loading of railway stations and distribution of the time interval between arrival of trains. Using the example of the flow of arriving trains, the technology of testing the hypothesis that the time between arrival of trains is distributed according to the exponential law and the hypothesis of independence of events in the flow is displayed in detail. When confirming each of these hypotheses, it must be concluded that the flow of trains arriving at the station is according to the simplest (Poisson's) model. This conclusion allows using the apparatus of Markov chains to describe a random process.

Introduction

Mathematical and probabilistic models are used in various tasks related to functioning of transport (for example, [1-9]). The role of probabilistic methods in designing and analyzing the operation of railway communication is determined primarily by the fact that these methods are an effective tool for minimizing costs and ensuring traffic continuity. This is associated with the use of the traffic density concept, i.e., the number of cargoes and/or passengers per 1 km of the operated railway line or section per unit of time [10].

Average values are used when describing the density of traffic on the line or in the transport node: average number of transportation units, average time interval, average distance, etc. These values do not describe fluctuations in the traffic density. The irregularity factor is introduced to eliminate this disadvantage: it is the ratio of the largest (peak) value of the traffic density to the mean value. Determination of the irregularity factor depends on additional assumptions related to the nature of the oscillations in the traffic density. Exactly this is provided by application of probabilistic methods.

Application of probabilistic and statistical methods to problems arising in the design of railway transport is considered in this article. For example, fluctuations in loading of

* Corresponding author: grigef@rambler.ru

© The Authors, published by EDP Sciences. This is an open access article distributed under the terms of the Creative Commons Attribution License 4.0 (http://creativecommons.org/licenses/by/4.0/).

railway stations, distribution of the time interval between arrival of trains are among the topics considered. The first works in the field of applying the probability theory to solve the problems of railway traffic appeared before the Second World War, and monographs [11, 12] covering many issues of the mathematical theory of transport flows were published in 1960's. Then, books of German and Polish authors [13, 10] appeared in translations into Russian.

Application of probabilistic and statistical methods in arrangement of transportation is considered from the standpoint of training railway transportation specialists in this article. One can improve the efficiency of training of specialists with the following: (1) when studying the probability theory and mathematical statistics, considering specific railway tasks; (2) by applying active training methods. This determines the novelty and the main study objective - to develop the efficient methodology for mathematical training of railway transportation specialists on the basis of active training methods (business games).

It is considered mandatory that the use of active training methods is consistent with the nature of the future professional tasks and the functions of trainee, including the nature of official and job relations (the so-called contextual training theory of A. A. Verbitsky [14]). In particular, when organizing business games, there should be a "simulation of the process of activity of managers and specialists of enterprises and organizations in developing managerial decisions" [15]. It is much more difficult to ensure this in teaching mathematics or physics than when teaching professional technical or economic disciplines.

As compared to the number of attempts to use business games in such areas as economics, management, pedagogy, psychology, engineering disciplines, military science, ecology, medicine, the use of business games in mathematics is scarce. There is experience of arranging business games in the simplest sections of probability theory for students of humanitarian specialties [16], on optimization of problems for future economists [17].

A business game is an imitative gaming method of active training. In this regard, a business game developer has two main tasks. First, they must create an imitation model that would reflect the actual reality that is relevant to the professional activities of the specialist to a certain extent. Secondly, a game model must be created, which is a description of the work of participants with the simulation model. Thus, both objective and social context of the specialist's professional activity is ensured [14]. The solution of two problems related to application of probabilistic and statistical methods in design of railway transportation is considered in this article as an example of the business game structure.

Study method. Imitation probabilistic model

Let us briefly consider the essence of the probabilistic methodology as applied to the traffic density concept. One of the most important concepts of the probability theory and the theory of random processes, related, in particular, to operation of transport is the flow of events. It can be considered as a sequence of moments of onset of these events: $t_1, \ldots, t_i, \ldots$ For example, it may be the moments when the train arrives at the station. It is commonly believed that simultaneous occurrence of events is almost impossible (in this case, the flow of events is called ordinary). The stationary flow assumption is accepted, which means that the probability of occurrence of an event in time t depends only on itself t, but does not depend on the time of beginning of this interval. Therefore, if occurrence of an event is reliable within a limited period of time τ, then the probability of occurrence of this event in time t $(0<t<\tau)$ is equal to $p(t)=t/\tau$. If, during time τ, each of the available n trains reliably arrived at the station, the probability of the event that exactly k trains ($0\leq k\leq n$) will arrive at the station within time t is determined by the Bernoulli formula [18]:

$$p_k(t) = C_n^k (t/\tau)^k (1 - t/\tau)^{n-k} \,. \tag{1}$$

If we consider the number of trains arriving at to the station within time t as a discrete random value K, then formula (1), with $p_k(t) \equiv P(K = k)$, will describe the binomial distribution.

However, binomial distribution of the number of events within the time interval is very inconvenient for use. It is distribution (1) with two parameters (n and t/τ). In practice, the possibility of replacing the binomial distribution by another distribution of a discrete random variable (the Poisson's distribution) is often used. As it is well known, the Poisson's distribution is the limiting case of binomial distribution as the number of tests tends to infinity and the probability of occurrence of an event in a separate test tends to zero [18]. Therefore, we must admit the following in the considered problem of the arrival of trains: $n \to \infty$; $t/\tau \to 0$; $0 < nt/\tau \equiv \lambda t < \infty$. Practical research in the field of railway transport usually meets the following requirements $n > 40$, $t/\tau < 0.1$ [10]. Value $\lambda = n/\tau$ represents the average intensity of onset of events (the average number of trains arriving per unit time), and value λt is the average number of events occurring within the time interval with the duration of t. The very Poisson's distribution has the form of [18]

$$P(X = k) \equiv p_k(t) = \frac{(\lambda t)^k e^{-\lambda t}}{k!}, \quad k = 0, 1, \ \ldots \tag{2}$$

Unlike binomial distribution, this is a distribution with one parameter λt, which makes composing of tables much easier.

Wide use of analytical methods for solving problems using queuing theory tools is possible when assuming the hypothesis of the flow of Poisson's applications. To do this, it is necessary to confirm the correspondence of the real empirical data to assume the so-called simplest flow of events, which has three properties. The first two properties (ordinariness and stationarity) have already been mentioned above. The third property is the absence of post-effect: events occur independently of each other; the onset of the event does not affect the onset of other events.

Substitution of the binomial distribution with the Poisson's distribution is the transition from the model in which n points are scattered over a segment of finite length τ to the model with points scattered on the infinite time line with constant intensity λ. The Poisson's distribution of the number of trains arriving within interval t is the distribution describing an unlimited flow of events and arising in the event of rejection of the condition of a deterministic number of events in time τ. The Poisson's flow is the simplest flow, i.e., stationary, ordinary flow without a post-effect.

Random value T, which is the time interval between onset of two events in the simplest flow, has the distribution function

$$F(t) = P(T < t) = 1 - p_0(t) = 1 - e^{-\lambda t} \ , \ t > 0 \,, \tag{3}$$

and the probability distribution density $f(t) = F'(t) = \lambda e^{-\lambda t}$, $t > 0$.

Assuming that there is a simple flow of events, one can test the hypothesis of the exponential distribution of time between events. In this case, time between events has mathematical expectation $M(T) = 1/\lambda$, (λ the flow intensity), and the probability of hitting the random variable in interval (a, b) is equal to $P(a < T < b) = e^{-\lambda a} - e^{-\lambda b}$. Therefore, the statistic assessment of parameter λ will be the value opposite to the selected mean $\lambda^* = 1/\bar{t}$, and the theoretical frequency of hitting interval number i should be calculated by formula

$$n_i' = n\left(e^{-\lambda^* t_{i-1/2}} - e^{-\lambda^* t_{i+1/2}}\right). \quad (4)$$

After this, the hypothesis of exponential distribution is tested using the Pearson's criterion. However, this is not yet equivalent to confirming the statistical hypothesis that the flow of events is the simplest (Poisson's) one. It is also required that all time intervals between events are independent random variables. Let us describe the procedure required [10]. Let the entire range of values of random variable T (the time interval between arrival of trains) be divided into partial intervals and the frequencies of hitting these intervals are known. Let us assume the following:

(a) the moment of arrival of this train is such that it is separated from the previous train by the time interval falling into partial interval i;

(b) the moment of arrival of the next train is such that it is separated from this train by the time interval falling into partial interval j;

The probability of event (a) may be assessed through its relative frequency as $p_i^* = n_i/n$; the probability of event (b) may be assessed as $p_j^* = n_j/n$. The probability of the product of these events is assessed as $p_{ij}^* = n_{ij}/n$, where n_{ij} is the frequency of the event that for two "adjacent" observations, interval i will be followed by interval j. If events (a) and (b) are independent, then $p_{ij} = p_i p_j$. In other words, "empirical" frequencies of n_{ij} must be close to "theoretical" frequencies of $n_i n_j/n$. With that, the partial intervals should be selected so that the frequencies of hitting them are not low. It is believed [10] that each frequency should be not less than $\sqrt{n}$. Comparison of empirical and theoretical frequencies in this case can also be performed using the Pearson criterion.

Source data and results

Below is the solution of two problems related to application of probabilistic and statistical methods in design of railway transportation.

1. Trains arrive at the station in accordance with the Poisson's flow of events: on an average, within τ hours, n trains arrive (i.e., the average arrival intensity is $\lambda = n/\tau$ trains per hour), and the probabilities of arrival of k trains within 1 hour are distributed in accordance with the Poisson's law. It is required to make a decision on the need to build additional arrival and departure ways in accordance with the following criterion: the probability of arrival of 6 or more trains at the station within 1 hour should not exceed a certain critical value of p_{cr}.

For example, if for $\tau = 16$ hours, $n = 25$ trains arrive (i.e., the average arrival intensity will comprise $\lambda = 25/16$ trains per hour), then the probability of arrival of 0 to 5 trains within 1 hour in accordance with formula (2) is equal to $p_0(1) = 0.210$, $p_1(1) = 0.328$, $p_2(1) = 0.256$, $p_3(1) = 0.133$, $p_4(1) = 0.052$, $p_5(1) = 0.016$, and the probability of arrival of 6 and more trains at the station within 1 hour is equal to $P(K \geq 6) = 1 - 0.995 = 0.005$. If this value exceeds the critical probability value p_{cr}, then a decision must be made on the necessity of constructing additional arrival and departure tracks.

2. Within a day, i.e., during the time of $\tau = 1440$ minutes, n trains arrive at the station: intervals between consecutive arrival time values are known (each gap is calculated as the difference between the arrival time of the train and the arrival time of the previous train). Having input the partial intervals, the hypothesis that the time between arrival of trains is distributed according to the exponential law and the hypothesis of independence of events in the flow must be tested. When confirming each of these hypotheses, it must be concluded that the flow of trains arriving at the station is according to the simplest (Poisson's) model. This conclusion is important, as it allows using the apparatus of Markov chains to describe a random process.

Table 1. Planned moments of arrival of trains at the station ($n = 84$, $\tau = 1440$).

hours	minutes	Interval (min)	hours	minutes	Interval (min)	hours	minutes	Interval (min)	hours	minutes	Interval (min)
00	07	8	07	19	3	14	23	75	19	15	18
00	14	7	07	29	10	14	52	29	19	27	12
00	37	23	07	32	3	14	58	6	19	33	6
01	03	26	07	37	5	15	02	4	19	43	10
01	07	4	07	44	7	15	08	6	19	58	15
01	19	12	08	24	40	15	15	7	20	14	16
02	10	51	08	30	6	16	01	46	20	25	11
03	19	69	08	31	1	16	07	6	20	44	19
04	23	64	08	57	26	16	30	23	20	59	15
05	16	53	09	02	5	16	32	2	21	09	10
05	18	2	09	03	1	16	42	10	21	45	36
05	32	14	09	26	23	16	56	14	22	01	16
05	58	26	09	46	20	17	00	4	22	21	20
05	59	1	10	18	32	17	06	6	22	27	6
06	04	5	10	39	21	17	10	4	22	35	8
06	09	5	10	59	20	18	08	58	22	58	23
06	09	0	11	09	10	18	16	8	23	06	8
06	19	10	11	12	3	18	41	25	23	09	3
06	27	8	11	51	39	18	43	2	23	32	23
07	15	48	13	05	74	18	48	5	23	47	15
07	16	1	13	08	3	18	57	9	23	59	12

The information on arrival of trains at the station (per day) is shown in Table 1. We could estimate the average time interval between the arrival of trains and the average intensity of events directly by this data. However, when testing the hypothesis of the distribution type, one will have to use the grouped data. Therefore, in order for the calculations to be internally consistent, let us assess the values of $\bar{t}$ and λ after grouping the data into partial intervals. Let each interval have the duration of 4 min (0-4, 4-8, ...). Let us calculate the frequencies of hitting t each interval. After this, we will get the assessment $\bar{t} = \frac{1}{n}\sum_{i=1}^{k} t_i n_i = 16.57$, where $k = 19$ is the number of partial intervals, n_i are empirical frequencies, and medium values of intervals are assumed as variants of t_i. Estimation of intensity of events is $\lambda^* = 1/\bar{t} \approx 0.06$. Now, let us calculate theoretical frequency (4) for each interval. Calculation of the Pearson criterion $\chi^2 = \sum_{i=1}^{k} \frac{(n_i - n_i')^2}{n_i'}$ gives the value of 23.47 at critical point $\chi^2_{cr}(0.05, 17) = 27.59$ (0.05 is the level of significance of the hypothesis, 17 is the number of degrees of freedom). The hypothesis is accepted: the time between arrival of trains is distributed according to the exponential law.

To test the second hypothesis, let us set three partial intervals (0-8, 8-20, 20-76) and calculate the frequencies of hitting them according to Table 1. Then, let us determine theoretical frequencies $n_{ij}' = n_i n_j / n$ and empirical frequencies n_{ij} (Table 2).

Table 2. Empirical n_{ij} and theoretical n_{ij}' frequencies.

n_{ij} / n_{ij}'	$j = 1$	$j = 2$	$j = 3$	n_i
$i = 1$	17 / 16.30	7 / 10.13	13 / 10.57	37
$i = 2$	7 / 10.13	12 / 6.30	4 / 6.57	23
$i = 3$	13 / 10.57	4 / 6.57	7 / 6.86	24
n_j	37	23	24	$n = 84$

The observed value of the criterion in our case is $\chi^2 = 10.26$. When determining the critical point of distribution χ^2, it is necessary to determine the number of degrees of freedom. In this case, it is the number of frequencies n_{ij} independent of each other. For this, let us take 5 rigid links into consideration: the sum of frequencies in the first line; the sum of frequencies in the second line; the sum of frequencies in the first column; the sum of frequencies in the second column; total frequencies. Thus, the number of degrees of freedom is equal to $m = 9 - 5 = 4$. According to the level of significance $\alpha = 0.05$, critical point $\chi^2_{cr}(0.05, 4) = 9.49 < \chi^2$; the hypothesis of independence of events in the flow must be rejected. However, with $\alpha = 0.01$ $\chi^2_{cr}(0.01, 4) = 13.28 > \chi^2$, the hypothesis of independence of events in the flow is accepted.

Conclusion

The recommended use of the aforementioned study is primarily related to improvement of mathematical training methods for railway transportation specialists. These materials can be used to develop business games and other methods of contextual training. The preferred method is to divide students into teams. 2-3 weeks prior to commencement of the game, captains are appointed from among the most enterprising students, who select the composition of the teams. The work with methodological material for the business game [19] begins, during which the captains distribute roles between team members. At the beginning of a business game, each team receives the source data (for joint analysis of the results, all teams should have the same data). On expiration of the time allotted for the task, each team presents the protocol on a special form. The teacher arranges comparison and analysis of the results of the teams and joint discussion of errors.

Results of pedagogical experiments [20] have shown that playing a business game using probabilistic and statistical methods significantly improves the quality of training, which is confirmed by the results of intermediate testing and final examination grades. Preparation and attitude of students towards a business game is significantly different from their attitude to traditional events (workshops, control and graphic works), which is explained by emergence of a new psychological situation. In the course of this event, students not only receive the skills of independent work with references, but are also trained in disciplined team work with distribution of roles, responsibility for results of the calculations and for the decisions made. This is an effective means of translating abstract theoretical knowledge into the activity context, which makes it possible to shorten the time required for gaining practical experience drastically.

References

1. H.M. Repolho, A.P. Antunes, R.L. Church, Transportation Science, 47, 330–343 (2013).
2. D.V. Ratobylskaya, Mathematical Machines and Systems, **18**, 162-169 (2013) (in Russian).
3. G.B. Titov, Izvestia of Emperor Alexander I St. Petersburg State Transport University, **35**, 81-86 (2013) (in Russian).
4. A.V. Gasnikov, S.L. Klenov, E.A. Nurminskiy, Ya.A. Kholodov, N.B. Shamray, *Vvedenie v matematicheskoe modelirovanie transportnyh potokov* [Introduction to mathematical simulation of transport flows] (Moscow, 2013) (in Russian).
5. O.A. Sidorov, A.N. Smerdin, A.S. Golubkov, Izvestia Transsiba [Journal of Transsib Railway Studies], **31**, 123-131 (2017) (in Russian).
6. D.N. Shevchenko, Vestnik of BelSUT: Science and Transport, **35**, 37-39 (2017) (in Russian).
7. I.A. Elovoy, E.N. Potylkin, Vestnik of BelSUT: Science and Transport, **35**, 80-85 (2017) (in Russian).
8. A.A. Mihalchenko, E.P. Gurskiy, Vestnik of BelSUT: Science and Transport, **35**, 86-90 (2017) (in Russian).
9. J. Shi, L. Yang, J. Yang, Z. Gao, Transportation Research Part B: Methodological, **110**, 26-59 (2018).
10. E. Vengerskiy, *Verojatnostnye metody v proektirovanii transporta* [Probabilistic methods in the design of transport] (Transport, Moscow, 1979) (in Russian).
11. F. Height, *Mathematical theories of traffic flow* (Academic Press Ink., New York-London, 1963).
12. W. Ashton, *The theory of road traffic flow* (Methuen, London-New York, 1966).
13. G. Pottgoff, *Uchenie o transportnyh potokah* [The doctrine on transport flows] (Transport, Moscow, 1975) (in Russian).
14. A.A. Verbickiy, *Aktivnoe obuchenie v vysshej shkole: kontekstnyj podhod* [Active learning in higher education: contextual approach] (Vysshaya shkola, Moscow, 1991) (in Russian).
15. Ya.M. Belchikov, M.M. Birshteyn, Delovye igry [Business games] (Avots, Riga, 1989) (in Russian).
16. O.N. Sakharova, Vestnik Vysshey Shkoly [High School Herald], **7**, 38-44 (2008) (in Russian).
17. M.B. Sukhanov, Izvestia: Herzen University Journal of Humanities & Science, **152**, 195-202 (2012) (in Russian).

18. E.S. Venttsel, *Teorija verojatnostej* [Probability Theory] (Vysshaya shkola, Moscow, 2001) (in Russian).
19. G.D. Gefan, *Verojatnostno-statisticheskie metody na primere zadach issledovanija raboty zheleznodorozhnogo transporta* [Probabilistic-statistical methods on an example of research problems of work in railway transportation] (IrGUPS Publ., Irkutsk, 2015) (in Russian).
20. G.D. Gefan, O.V. Kuzmin, Tomsk State Pedagogical University Bulletin, **181**, 49-56 (2017) (in Russian).

Cost management in track facilities of railway transport infrastructure

Irina Solskaya[1,*], and *Sergei* Belomestnykh[2]

[1]Irkutsk State Railway Transport Engineering University, 664074 Irkutsk, Russia
[2]Russian Railways JSC, 664005 Irkutsk, Russia

Abstract. The purpose of the study is definition and substantiation of the main development points of assessment and planning functions in the cost management system of railway transport infrastructure. Methods used in the study include general scientific analysis and synthesis, dynamic and structural analysis of economic indicators, as well as textual analysis of regulatory documents. Such approach enables to formulate industry-specific peculiarities of cost assessment based on general theoretical concepts of effective use of factors of production. The result of this study is an author's developed approach to cost management system for railway transport infrastructure.

Introduction

Limited resources is the main problem of all economic activities. On the theoretical level, solution to the problem is based on improvement of cost management methods. The results of studies on cost management published in [1-4] characterize common system factors of this process. Works [5-8] describe the peculiarities of cost management in transport industry. However, the authors do not present a complete solution on cost assessment as a progressive factor of manufacturing and economic sustainability and operating safety of transport.

This study is aimed at defining and substantiating the key development points of assessment and planning functions in the cost management system. Subject of the study is an infrastructure complex of railway transport. The study is particularly focused on increasing investment opportunities for updating and improvement of infrastructure based on cost assessment and planning. Relatively low profitability of transportation activities of railway companies is the main system constraint for applying the existing cost management methods. Novelty of the obtained results is proved by their applicability for the companies operating at the break-even point. Conclusions and results of the study have practical value due to their relevance in the conditions of fast growing prices on the resources consumed by transport industry and decrease of the amount of transportation services caused by the economic crisis.

* Corresponding author: irina_solskaya_@mail.ru

© The Authors, published by EDP Sciences. This is an open access article distributed under the terms of the Creative Commons Attribution License 4.0 (http://creativecommons.org/licenses/by/4.0/).

Research methods

The research methods used in the study are based on institutional approach to assessment of improvement opportunities for cost management system of transportation services market participants. The study includes scientific achievements in economics, best national and international practices on cost effectiveness improvement in transport industry, such as: control theory, systems theory, and other undertakings of Russian Railways JSC on improving operational efficiency [9-13]. Methods used in the study include general scientific analysis and synthesis, specific methods applied for economic studies, such as dynamic and structural analysis of economic indicators [14], as well as textual analysis of regulatory documents. Regulatory and report materials of Russian Railways JSC served as information basis for implementing the study [15].

Results

The analysis of legal framework and its application allowed assessing a number of peculiarities of cost management system for railway transport infrastructure, as well as types of transport activities and governmental support of infrastructure development. This commitment has been implemented also due to development of corporate regulatory framework for cost management (Table 1).

Such low-profit sphere of business as infrastructure is the primary subject that shall be assessed for cost planning effectiveness [16]. In this study, the subject of research focused on development of cost management system was West-Siberian infrastructure department - the branch of Central Directorate for Infrastructure of Russian Railways JSC located in the territory of West-Siberian Railway.

The analysis of business activities demonstrated that the Directorate for Infrastructure, as a vertically-integrated branch, provides a more effective infrastructure cost management system due to the following factors:

1. organization of a single center responsible for the state of infrastructure objects and their development;
2. item-by-item planning of works and current maintenance costs based on the assessment of actual state of infrastructure objects by means of diagnosis and complex systems with the account of reliability, level of physical deterioration and risk;
3. reduction of unit costs on current maintenance compared to the overhaul and retrofit costs;
4. higher quality of all types of repair of infrastructure objects due to ordering services and their acceptance;
5. organization of resource allocation on priority routes on the basis of the infrastructure reliability and availability with the account of its current state and wear of fixed assets;
6. modification in effectiveness and performance assessment system for infrastructure complex activities.

Table 1. Corporate regulatory framework for cost management of Russian Railways JSC.

No.	Introduced	Canceled
1.	Order of the Ministry of Transport of the RF as of 08/17/2007 No.124 "On approval of introduction procedure for separate accounting of revenues, costs and financial performance for different types of activities, tariff components and aggregate activity types of Russian Railways JSC"; effective of 01/01/2008 (resolution of the Government of the Russian Federation as of 50/21/2007, No. 640-p)	Order of the Ministry of Transport of the RF as of 08/17/2007 No.124 ceased to be in force because of the order of the Ministry of Transport of the Russian Federation as of 12/31/2010 No.31

2.	Order of the Ministry of Transport of the RF as of 12/26/2011 No.330 "On the introduction procedure for separate accounting of costs and revenues by natural monopoly entities in the field of railway transportation"; accepted by the order of the Ministry of Transport of the RF as of 12/31/2010 No.311 "On approval of introduction procedure for separate accounting of revenues, costs and financial performance for different types of activities, tariff components and aggregate activity types of Russian Railways JSC"	Order of the Ministry of Transport of the RF as of 12/31/2010 No.124 ceased to be in force since 10/26/2015 because of the order of the Ministry of Transport of the Russian Federation as of 09/15/2015 No.271
3.	Order of the Ministry of Transport of the RF as of 08/12/2014 No.225 "On the introduction procedure for separate accounting of costs and revenues by natural monopoly entities in the field of railway transportation" (hereinafter referred to as "Procedure") came into force since 01/09/2015	Effective to date

It should be noted that providing evidence for effectiveness and performance assessment is one of the essential points in improvement of effectiveness for current infrastructure maintenance. For more in-depth studies of the cost formation and planning processes in West-Siberian Directorate for Infrastructure a separate directorate department is formed - track maintenance service.

The track maintenance service is a key department of the Directorate of Infrastructure, because with the help of maintenance divisions (MD) is organizes railroad tracks services [17]. In the context of decreasing the planned preventive maintenance (PPM) volume since 2021 and reconstruction of 20 thsd km of rail tracks it is planned to increase the effect of substantial investments in renovation of mechanical equipment of track complex by 110 billion rubles (around 1,8 billion USD). The problems of railway transport infrastructure are emphasized as a result of considerable difference in operational performance of MDs: 50% of costs are spent on 168 MDs which provide 75% of traffic load, and the rest 50% of costs are spent on 211 MDs providing only 25% of the load [15].

It is found that the economic efficiency of operation of Russian Railways transport infrastructure is largely defined by the costs on tracks maintenance and repair. The main internal factors also influence the costs of railway complex, they can become the basis for effective managerial decisions on costs optimization [18]. Table 2 presents the classification of the main factors that influence railway complex costs.

Table 2. Classification of the main factors that influence railway complex costs.

Group attribute	Factor
1. Operational conditions defined by natural and macroeconomic factors	1.1. Climate conditions 1.2. Tax attributed to costs 1.3. Social welfare payments
2. Operational conditions defined by the product and labor market conditions	2.1. Salary level 2.2. Prices for material resources, fuel and energy resources
3. Conditions defined by the transportation market situation	3.1. Structure of transportation by traffic type (passenger, freight) 3.2. Structure of transportation by freight type
4. Operational conditions defined by the level of technical equipment of railway transport	4.1. Traffic flow 4.2. Structure of railroad line by the number of tracks 4.3. Plan and profile of tracks (grades and curves) 4.4. Track structure by railway track

	superstructure (type of rails and ties, type of ballast, share of continuous welded rails, etc.) 4.5. Number and type of artificial structures 4.6. Number of guarded and unguarded level railway crossings 4.7. Number of items of railway equipment, motor transport, structure of industrial buildings 4.8. Operational reliability of technical facilities, incl. track and its facilities 4.9. Level of physical wear and obsolescence of main assets
5. Transportation and facilities maintenance technology, quality of operation	5.1. Trains velocities 5.2. Mechanization of track operations 5.3. Unit labor requirement

The conducted studies demonstrated that it is reasonable to group the cost items for the planning purpose in the following way:

1. maintenance costs;
2. repair and improvement costs;
3. amortization costs;
4. other costs.

These costs are annually planned, which means that the Central Directorate for Infrastructure allocates planned funding for these purposes when forming the budget for each of the existing units. Consequently, cost planning activities in railway transport industry is done in cycles.

The biggest part of costs of track facilities are spent on maintenance, complete rebuild or repair. Such costs are defined according to the following regulatory provisions:

1. Classification of capital assets subject to amortization, Decree of the Government of the RF as of 01/01/2002 No. 1;

2. Resolution of Russian Railways JSC as of 10/30/2003 No.43 "On the procedure for defining useful life of capital assets when accounting in Russian Railways JSC";

3. Catalog of capital assets inventory items of Russian Railways JSC approved by the resolution of Russian Railways JSC as of 03/13/2007 No.395p.

Capital assets and related operational costs take the second position in the cost structure of MD (Table 3), therefore, more attention shall be given to better use of capital assets of track facilities, including tracks, machines and equipment [11, 20]. Along with mechanization, machines are widely introduced in track operations, which enables to perform up to 70% of operations with the help of machines and mechanisms.

Table 3. Item-by-item cost analysis of maintenance division of West-Siberian Directorate for Infrastructure.

No.	Cost items of MD West-Siberian Directorate for Infrastructure, million rubles	2014	2015	2016	2017
1.	Materials	398.02.	438.21.	447.83.	624.21.
2.	Fuel	112.23.	138.22.	139.76.	140.10.
3.	Energy	35.98.	36.45.	37.53.	39.01.
4.	Other costs, services performance	302.45.	310.78.	311.99.	322.10.
5.	Labor costs	2897.21.	3023.47.	3287.19.	3321.55.
6.	Social welfare payments	901.01.	947.12.	956.60.	980.20.
7.	Amortization	2348.87.	2423.11.	2103.12.	2233.98.
8.	Other costs	1232.56.	1423.90.	1542.91.	1324.02.
	Total costs	8228.33.	8741.26.	8826.93.	8985.17.

The key measures to enhance intensity of use of the existing infrastructure include improvement of maintenance stations operation technology, optimization of distances between maintenance points, elimination of temporary repair areas using rail-welding machines. At the stage of technology development for elimination of temporary repair areas and rail defects, many repair facilities of Russian Railways JSC (maintenance sections, track machine stations) faced the problem of high amount of such faults.

The most cases of rail faults and single rail renewal occur because of insufficient rolling contact fatigue of rails metal (defects 21, 26, 30); higher dynamic loading in the rail joints (defects 53, 56, 46, 43); rail head shelling and longitudinal cracking (defects 14, 16, 24) after slipping or sliding, as well as after rolling of wheels with big flat spots or chatter marks. In 2017, costs for single rail renewal and faults repair amounted to 211 million rubles (around 3,4 million UDS) (Table 4).

Table 4. Dynamics of rail faults elimination in the territory of West-Siberian Directorate for Infrastructure.

	2014	**2015**	**2016**	**2017**
Number of eliminated faults, pcs	3,124	3,517	3,657	3,824
Costs for faults elimination, million rubles	149.85	177.48	194.33	211.23

In recent years, global studies have been conducted on reasons for formation of rail faults, measures of faults elimination, extension of service life of rail facilities and equipment (Table 5).

Table 5. Dynamics of increase in number of joints that require welding, exemplified with West-Siberian Directorate for Infrastructure.

No.	Period	Length of continuous welded rails, km	Number of joints that require welding, pcs
1.	as of 01/01/2007	924.	1,602
2.	as of 01/01/2008	1,173.5	3,138
3.	as of 01/01/2009	1,362.6	5,867
4.	as of 1/1/2010	1,573.4	7,863
5.	as of 01/01/2011	1,763.3	9,648
6.	as of 01/01/2012	1,968.2	11,613
7.	as of 01/01/2013	2,163.7	11,308
8.	as of 01/01/2014	2,325	14,792
9.	as of 01/01/2015	2,502	14,500
10.	as of 01/01/2016	2,620	14,603
11.	as of 01/01/2017	2,870	14,102

At the stage of technology development for elimination of temporary repair areas and rail defects, many repair facilities of Russian Railways JSC (maintenance sections, track machine stations) faced the problem of high amount of such faults (Table 6).

Table 6. Comparative analysis of existing temporary repair areas on the level of Directorates for Infrastructure.

No.	Directorate for Infrastructure	Length of continuous welded rails, km of tracks	Number of joints that require welding, pcs
		as of 01/01/2017	
1.	October	10,223	59,058
2.	Kaliningrad	746	3,870
3.	Moscow	10,599	52,928
4.	Gorky	6,454	26,648

5.	Northern	5,604	11,548
6.	North Caucasus	6,443	17,582
7.	South-Eastern	5,733.	21,300
8.	Privolzhsk	5,245	27,066
9.	Kuibyshev	5,688	18,230
10.	Sverdlovsk	5,580	19,566
11.	South Ural	6,016	20,824
12.	West-Siberian	7,068	17,936
13.	Krasnoyarsk	2,441	9,086
14.	East-Siberian	2,870	14,102
15.	Zabaikal	3,075	15,924
16.	Far Eastern	3,245	10,362
		Total:	346,030

Along with conventional approach to elimination of rail faults, there are some advanced solutions, like aluminothermic rail welding and wide gap welding technologies.

To reveal practicability of using new means of railway transport repair comprehensive proof shall be provided. This process starts with the project design stage, when the preliminary feasibility assessment is performed [19].

Introduction of aluminothermic rail welding and wide gap welding technologies in production process of the Russian Railways JSC chain is an important factor that affects the results of business activities, such as quality, completeness and timeliness of all operations and, consequently, the amount of services, their prime cost and financial position of the company.

In order to improve cost management system it is suggested to use the economically feasible costs approach, based on the fact that due to transformation of costs (sphere of purchase of factors of production) into expenses (sphere of end products sales) the cost of production are formed, in other words, promotion expenses shall provide functioning of production costs [1].

On the example of West-Siberian Directorate for Infrastructure, cost management model was suggested based on capital functioning. Practical implementation of this model is based on comparison of the two existing technologies – single rail renewal and rail repair technologies, like build-up weld, welding and grinding.

Conclusion

The main outcome of the conducted study consists in the developed methodical approach to cost assessment and planning for track facilities of railway transport infrastructure. The author's approach to cost efficiency analysis is based on the use of aggregate benefit-cost ratio. It enables to define the cost planning procedure [21].

Practical relevance of the results of benefit-cost ratio for contracts between the railway institutions and third parties consists in the ability to solve two prospective tasks:

1) performance of multiple-criteria analysis of any method of rail repair assignment depending on the return on costs;

2) Assessment of practicability of the used rail repair and definition of limits for assigning such types of repair.

Analysis of the key factors defined as a result of the study showed dependence of these factors on the type and intensity of transportation activities, as well as on lay-out and length of continuous welded rails.

Proof of conclusions and results of the study suggests that further research on adaptation of the author's approach to cost efficiency assessment and planning for other infrastructure components might be perspective.

References

1. A. Mas-Colell, M.D. Whinston, J. Green, *Microeconomic Theory,* Book 1 (Delo Publ., Moscow, 2016). (in Russian)
2. C.R. McConnell, S.L. Brue, *Economics: Principles, Problems, and Policies*. (INFRA-M, Moscow, 2009). (in Russian)
3. T. Copeland, T. Koller, J. Murrin, *Measuring & Managing the Value of Companies* (Olimp-Biznes, Moscow, 2008). (in Russian)
4. N.A. Lumpov, Financial Management, No. 4, 11-16 (2007). (in Russian)
5. D.N. Boyarkin, N.I. Novikov, Vestnik of Chelyabinsk State University, 14(195), 127-132 (2010). (in Russian)
6. E.I. Zorina, Bulletin of Scientific Research Results, 4(9), 76–84 (2013). (in Russian)
7. V.A. Shamis, Electronic Scientific & Practical Journal "Modern Scientific Researches and Innovations, 5 (2016).
8. S. Kot, PROMET – Traffic & Transportation, 27(5), 387-394 (2015).
9. S.M. Vasin, Vector of Sciences. Togliatti State University, 4(22), 34-37 (2012). (in Russian)
10. E.M. Panevina, Rossijskoe predprinimatel'stvo [Russian Journal of Entrepreneurship], **11**, Issue 2 (147), 56-62 (2009). (in Russian)
11. I.Yu. Solskaya, N.V.Trubina, D.A. Dinec, *Analiz i ocenka jeffektivnosti v sisteme upravlenija predprijatiem zheleznodorozhnogo transporta* [Analysis and efficiency evaluation in the railway enterprise management system] (Irkutsk State Railway Transport Engineering University, Irkutsk, 2009). (in Russian)
12. I. Oborilova, V. Melichar, *SGEM 2015 Conference Proceedings,* Book 2, **Vol. 3**, 211-218 (2015).
13. J.A. Gomez-Ibanez, *Regulating Infrastructure: Monopoly, Contracts and Discretio.* (Mass. Harvard University Press, Cambridge, 2003).
14. A. Baublys, Computer Modelling & New Technologies, **Vol. 6** (1), 72-81 (2002).
15. Annual report of Russian Railways for 2016: assets, capital, liabilities of Russian Railways, available at: https://ar2016.rzd.ru/en/financial-results/key-results (February 27, 2018).
16. Yu. Krupnov, Transport of the Russian Federation, No. 2, 4-5 (2010).
17. V.S. Poryadin, Vestnik of Pushkin Leningrad State University, 4(6), 16-24 (2011). (in Russian)
18. A.A. Kostin, E.A. Posmetukhina, Rossijskoe predprinimatel'stvo [Russian Journal of Entrepreneurship], 3(249) (2014). (in Russian)
19. A.V. Bondarenko, Marketolog [Marketing Consultant], 8(82) (2006). (in Russian)
20. European Conference of Ministers of Transport (ECMT), Railway Reform and Charges for the Use of Infrastructure (OECD Publications Service, Paris, 2005).
21. A.V. Vasilyev, Voprosy Ekonomiki [Economic Matters], 15 (2011). (in Russian)

Modeling of traction power supply systems for movement of high-speed trains

Aleksandr Cherepanov[1,*], *Vasily* Zakaryukin[1], and *Andrey* Kryukov[1,2]

[1]Irkutsk State Transport University, 664074 Irkutsk, Russia
[2]Irkutsk National Research Technical University, 664074 Irkutsk, Russia

Abstract. Upgrading of traction power supply systems will be required to transfer electrified railway lines to high-speed traffic. Coaxial cables and balancing transformers can be used as technical upgrading means. The article presents the results of computer simulation in the Fazonord software complex of the traditional 2x25 kV traction system, as well as systems with coaxial cables and Woodbridge symmetric transformers. Simulation results showed that the use of cables contributes to a significant increase in the level of voltage on current collectors of electric rolling stock. Use of modified Woodbridge transformers makes it possible to reduce the imbalance coefficient by the reverse sequence on high voltage buses of traction substations. However, the reduction is insignificant and depends on the modes of movement of trains in adjacent inter-station zones. The biggest positive effects occur in the integrated application of balancing transformers and coaxial cables.

Introduction

Currently, railway lines for the traffic speeds of over 160 km/h are being operated and built, which are electrified primarily by alternating current [1 - 4]. To ensure efficient power supply for transferring of electrified lines to high-speed traffic, upgrading of the traction network (TN) is required, the purpose of which is to ensure that the voltage levels on the rolling stock current collectors (ERS) lie in the range from 24 to 29 kV in the normal mode of operation [1].

To select rational ways to upgrade the TN for high-speed traffic conditions, computer modeling facilities shall be required for the railway power supply systems (RPSS) modes including three-phase and single-phase subsystems and the systems actively interacting with each other. Availability of such subsystems makes it much more complicated to create an adequate computer model based on traditional approaches to determination of the RPSS modes, which are based on the use of the symmetric components method (SCM) [5-7]. Due to multiple longitudinal and transverse asymmetries in the RPSS, the use of the SCM becomes almost impossible with the formation of models of real systems with thousands of nodal points. It is associated with the algorithmic difficulties caused by the need to take numerous imbalances into consideration. Resolving of this problem is complicated due to

* Corresponding author: santela89@mail.ru

© The Authors, published by EDP Sciences. This is an open access article distributed under the terms of the Creative Commons Attribution License 4.0 (http://creativecommons.org/licenses/by/4.0/).

the specific nature of the RPSS that consists in the movement of traction loads [5-10], which is particularly pronounced on high-speed lines.

The second problem that arises in simulation of high-speed railways is the use of non-traditional devices, for example, Woodbridge synchronizing transformers and coaxial cables, to strengthen their traction networks [1]. This requires creation of universal modeling technologies that ensure adequate consideration of any amplifying elements that are acceptable in practice.

The objective of the study was to develop the methods and tools that provide adequate simulation of modes of high-speed lines with high gain elements. The proposed simulation methods for the modes are based on the use of phase coordinates and allow adequately simulation of high-speed railways RPSS and choosing the most rational means of their upgrading.

The novelty of the proposed methods is that they are of the multiphase, multi-modal and multitask nature. The first factor provides consideration of multiphase systems: single-phase, three-phase, four-phase, six-phase, and their combinations. The second distinctive feature makes it possible to determine a wide range of modes: normal, emergency, non-sinusoidal, and limiting. The third feature provides solution of additional tasks that are relevant in the practice of design and operation of the RPSS: determination of induced voltages on adjacent power lines; calculation of electromagnetic field strengths created by the TN; parametric identification of power supply lines and transformers; accounting for the proximity effect in simulation of massive current-conducting parts. Another important distinguishing feature of the proposed methods is joint simulation of the traction power supply system and the high-voltage power supply network, which allows implementing a systemic approach to the analysis of RPSS modes of alternating current.

Research methods

Irkutsk State Transport University (Russia) developed the methods for simulation of RPSS in phase coordinates [11] based on the use of lattice replacement schemes (LRS) of multi-conductor elements, which are the RLC elements joined into complete graph schemes. The following formalized determination may be provided for the LRS:

$$TEC : hub \bigcup con, \forall i, j \subset hub \to con_{i,j} \subset con ,$$

where TEC is determination of the LRS; hub is the totality of nodes; con is the totality of branches. By combining LRS of individual elements, the lattice structure is implemented that corresponds to the three-phase and single-phase network of the RPSS:

$$TEC_{\Sigma} = \bigcup_{k=1}^{n} TEC_{k} ,$$

where $\bigcup$ denotes joining of LRS of individual elements on the basis of the specific network topology.

The conducting matrix of the calculation model is formed on the basis of TEC_{Σ}.

$$\text{A} : TEC_{\Sigma} \to \underline{\mathbf{Y}}_{\Sigma} = \mathbf{M}_0 \underline{\mathbf{Y}}_{V} \mathbf{M}_0^{T} ,$$

where $\underline{\mathbf{Y}}_{V}$ is the block-diagonal matrix, blocks of which correspond to conductivity matrices of individual elements; $\mathbf{M}_0$ is the generalized incidence matrix. Non-linear equations that describe the totality of RPSS modes for movement of trains are formed with the use of $\underline{\mathbf{Y}}_{\Sigma}$ [11]:

$$\underline{\mathbf{Y}}_{\Sigma}(t_k)\dot{\mathbf{U}}(t_k) = \operatorname{diag} \frac{1}{\widetilde{U}_j(t_k)} \cdot \widetilde{\mathbf{S}}(t_k), j = \overline{1..n}; k = 1..m ,$$

where $\dot{\mathbf{U}}$ is the vector of angular strains; $\widetilde{\mathbf{S}} = \left[\widetilde{S}_1 \quad \widetilde{S}_2 \quad \ldots \quad \widetilde{S}_j \quad \ldots \quad \widetilde{S}_n\right]^T$; $\widetilde{S}_j$, $\widetilde{U}_j$ are adjacent complex of power and voltage of the jth network node. A small number of variables corresponding to the balancing nodes, in which the $\dot{U}_j$ parameters are assumed to be a priori set, are excluded from this system. After separation of real and imaginary components, the final model is formed, which can be written as follows in the general form

$$\mathbf{F}_k\left[\mathbf{V}(t_k), \mathbf{X}(t_k)\right] = \mathbf{0}, k = 1..m,$$

where $\mathbf{F}$ is the non-linear vector function; $\mathbf{V}$ is the vector of regulated parameters (independent variables); $\mathbf{X}$ is the vector of non-regulated parameters (dependent variables).

The described simulation technology is implemented within the scope of the Fazonord industrial software package [11], which has passed a large-scale approbation. To verify the adequacy of the simulation, the simulation results were compared repeatedly to instrumental measurements at real facilities. The maximum differences between the calculated and the experimental data did not exceed 3 to 5%, which is a sufficient result for problems of this grade characterized with the presence of inaccuracies in the initial information.

Fazonord software package allows simulating modes of RPSS of various design, for example, RPSS with reinforcing elements used in upgrading of high-speed lines. The following systems may be attributed to such RPSS systems [1]:

- 2x25 kV RPSS with Woodsbridge synchronizing transformers (ST) [12] (Fig. 1);
- RPSS with coaxial cables (Fig. 2) [1].

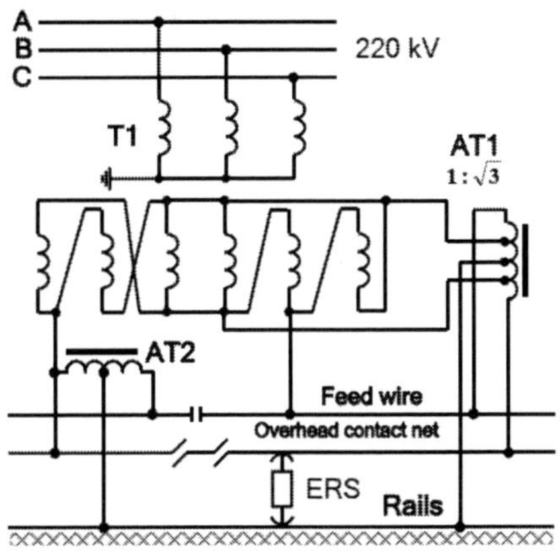

Fig. 1. 2x25 kV RPSS with modified Woodsbridge transformers [12]: AT – automobile transformers; ERS - electrical rolling stock.

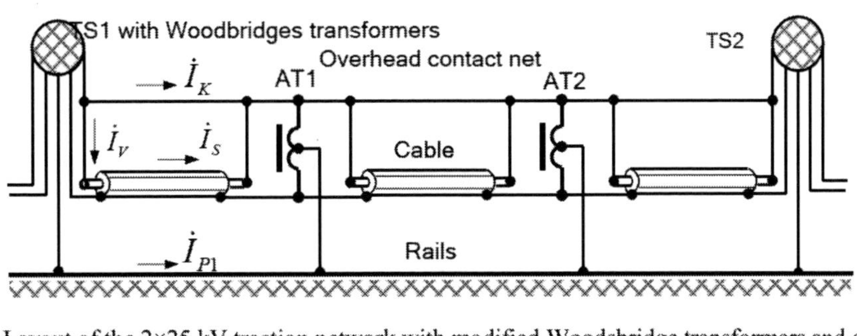

Fig. 2. Layout of the 2×25 kV traction network with modified Woodsbridge transformers and coaxial cables [1].

The coaxial cable can be represented by a multi-wire model. This model assumes a relative dielectric permeability of the medium equal to one, therefore, it is possible to reduce the distance between the core and the conductors of the screen to obtain the required equivalent generation of reactive power. With that, the induction of the core-screen loop is changed insignificantly. The required internal diameter of screen D can be calculated from the formula for the capacitance of a cylindrical capacitor:

$$D = d\exp\left(\frac{2\pi\varepsilon_0}{C}\right),$$

where d is the core diameter; C is the linear reservoir. See the coordinates of location of current conducting parts of the TN model on Figure 3.

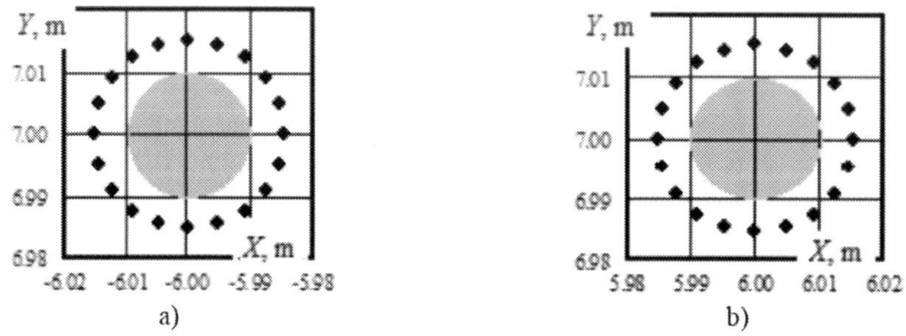

Fig. 3. Coordinates of the model wires: a is the section of the left cable conductors, b is the right cable section.

At the first stage of the simulation, which was performed on the basis of the Fazonord software package, a traditional 2x25 kV traction network of the 85 km long section of the railroad with three traction substations and 220 kV power supply was considered for movement of four conventional passenger trains with electric VL-65 locomotives and the same number of the Sapsan electric trains [13, 14]. The average segment speed for the first variant was 60 km/h, and for the second variant the speed was 230 km/h. The aforementioned variants of upgrading of the traction network are considered at the second stage.

Simulation results

See the simulation results in Table 1 and 2 and on Figure 4 to 6.

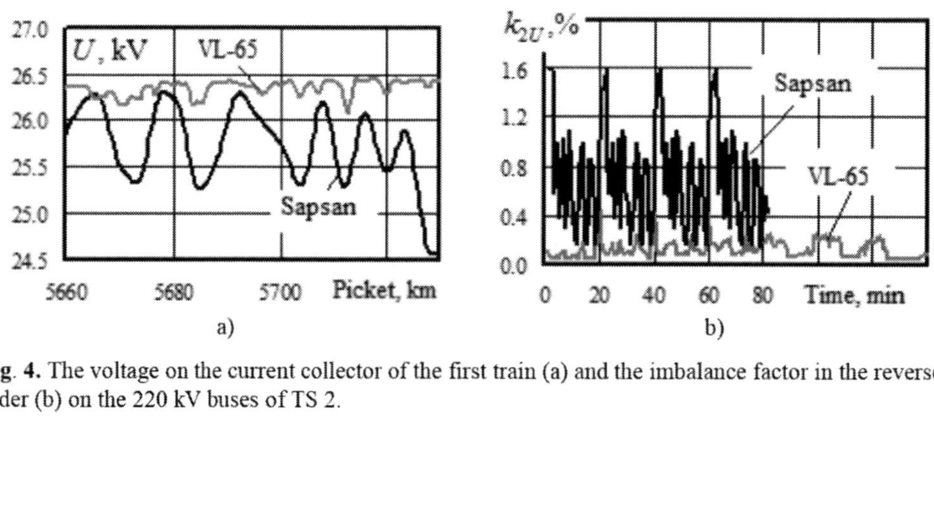

Fig. 4. The voltage on the current collector of the first train (a) and the imbalance factor in the reverse order (b) on the 220 kV buses of TS 2.

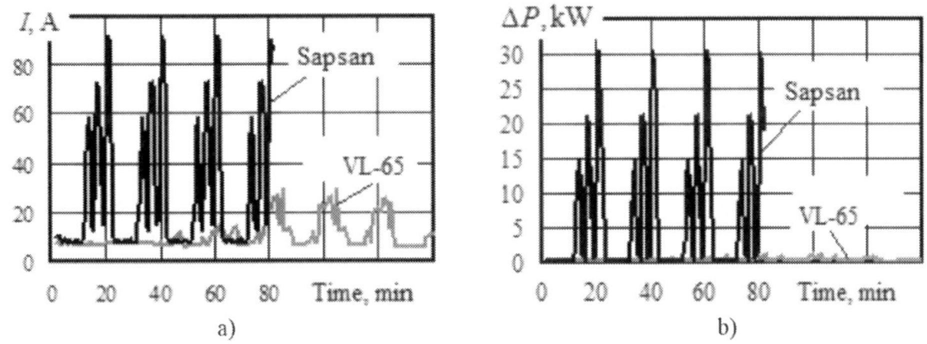

Fig. 5. Currents of the TS-1 contact network feeder (a) and losses of power on the first segment of the contract network (b)

Table 1. Transfers of active and reactive energy (W_a, W_r) and losses (ΔW_a) at the head segment of the feeding overhead power transmission line.

Parameter	VL 65	Sapsan	Difference, %
ΔW_a, kWh	232	141	-39
W_a, kWh	3,000	8,120	170
W_r, kvar·h	-61,100	-32,200	47

Table 2. Summarized indicators.

Paramet er	Minimum			Average value			Maximum		
	VL 65	Sapsan	Difference, %	VL 65	Sapsan	Difference, %	VL 65	Sapsan	Difference , %
k_{2U}, %	–	–	–	0.1	0.7	600	0.5	1.6	220
U, kV	26.1	24.6	–5.7	26.4	25.6	–3.0	26.5	26.3	–0.8

Notes: k_{2U} is the imbalance coefficient by reverse sequence on 220 kV buses of TS2; U is the voltage on the current collector of the first train.

A high-speed train generates traction loads of much greater magnitude than a conventional passenger train. The currents that flow through the contact wires (Fig.5a) are increased approximately threefold. The growth of traction loads causes reduction in the voltage on the current collectors of electric locomotives (Fig. 4, a), to a significant increase in asymmetry (Fig. 4, b) on high-voltage buses of traction substations, as well as losses in the traction network (Fig. 5, b).

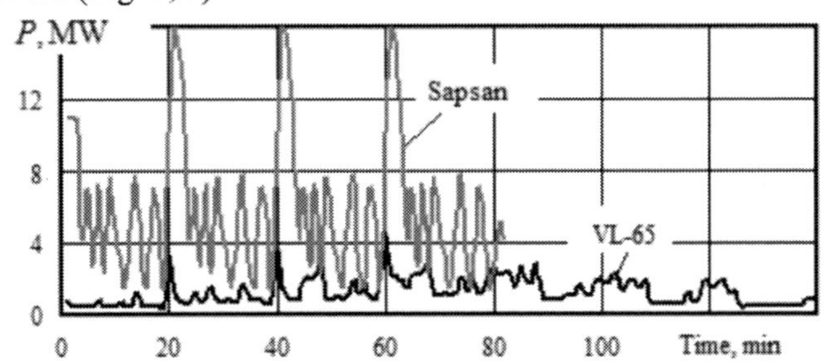

Fig. 6. Active capacity flows in the trunk OPTL 1.

The increased loads created by trains with Sapsan locomotives cause a significant increase in the active power flow in the trunk overhead power transmission line (Fig. 6). However, the total losses of ΔW_a are reduced due to redistribution of reactive transfers (Table 1).

The results of simulating the movement of high-speed trains in the RPSS equipped with Woodbridge transformers and coaxial cables are summarized in Table 3 and are illustrated in Figures 7, 8.

Table 3. Imbalance in 220 kV buses of TS2 and voltage in the current collector of the train.

Indicator	Parameter	Value			Difference, %	
		T	**W**	**W+C**	Between the poles 2 and 1	Between the poles 3 and 1
		1	**2**	**3**		
k_{2U}, %	Average	0.7	0.7	0.7	0	0
	Maximum	1.6	1.6	1.4	0	−12.5
U, kV	Minimum	24.6	24.8	27.2	0.8	10.6
	Average	25.6	25.6	27.7	0	8.2
	Maximum	26.3	26.2	28.3	−0.4	7.6

Note: T – traditional 2x25 kV RPSS; W – RPSS with Woodbridge transformers; W+C– RPSS with Woodbridge transformers and coaxial cables.

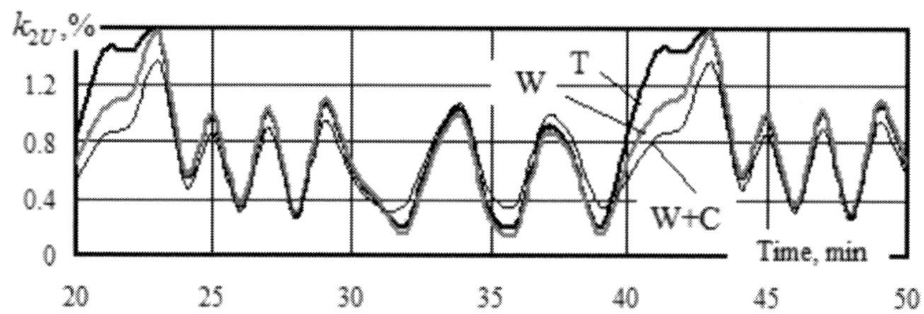

Fig. 7. Imbalance coefficients on reverse order on 220 kV buses of TS 2: T – traditional 2x25 kV RPSS; W – RPSS with Woodbridge transformers; W+C– RPSS with Woodbridge transformers and coaxial cables.

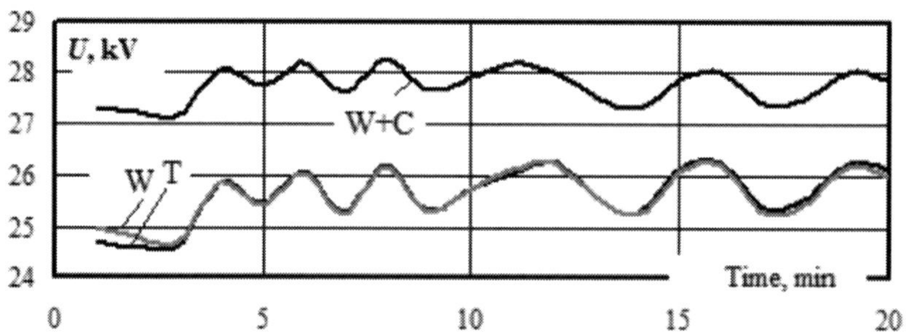

Fig. 8. Voltage on the current collector of the first train.

The results obtained demonstrate that the use of coaxial cables contributes to a significant increase in the level of voltage on ERS current collectors, which is particularly important for high-speed lines.

Use of modified Woodbridge transformers in 2x25 kV RPSS makes it possible to reduce the imbalance coefficient by the reverse sequence on high voltage buses of traction substations. The biggest positive effects occur in the integrated application of balancing transformers and coaxial cables.

Conclusion

The results obtained indicate that the problem of simulating modes of traction power systems of high-speed AC railways can be solved on the basis of the methods proposed. The described computer technologies can be used in practice to select the most rational ways to strengthen traction networks. It is expedient to perform further studies in the direction of development of the technologies for simulation of modes of the RPSS equipped with automatic mode regulating means [14 – 17].

References

1. I.P. Kiselev, L.S. Blazhko, A.T. Burkov, et al., *Vysokoskorostnoj zheleznodorozhnyj transport* [High-Speed Railway Transport] (UMCZDT, Moscow, 2014). (in Russian)
2. I.P. Kiselev, Zheleznodorozhnyj transport [Journal of Rail Transport], No. 5, 6-7 (2011). (in Russian)
3. B.M. Lapidus, Zheleznodorozhnyj transport [Journal of Rail Transport], No. 9 (2014). (in Russian)
4. V.A. Gapanovich, Zheleznodorozhnyj transport [Journal of Rail Transport], No. 9 (2014). (in Russian)
5. A. Steimel, *Electric traction motive power and energy supply. Basics and practical experience* (Oldenbourg Industrieverlag, Munchen, 2008).
6. H. Biesenack, E. Braun, G. George, et al., *Energieversorgung elektrischer bannen* (B.G. Teubner Verlag, Wiesbaden, 2006).
7. A. Ogunsola, A. Mariscotti, *Electromagnetic Compatibility in Railways* (Springer, 2013).
8. R.J. Hill, *Transactions on the Built Environment,* **Vol. 6** (1994).
9. M. Mandić, I. Uglešić, V. Milardić, Tehnički vjesnik, No. 20, 3 (2013).
10. M.G. Shalimov, G.P. Maslov, G.S. Magay, *Sovremennoe sostojanie i puti sovershenstvovanija sistem jelektrosnabzhenija jelektricheskih zheleznyh dorog*, [Current state and ways to improve the electric power supply systems for electric railways] (OSTU, Omsk, 2002). (in Russian)
11. V.P. Zakaryukin, A.V. Kryukov, *Innovation & Sustainability of Modern Railway – Proceedings of ISMR'2008* (Beijing: China, 2008).
12. Y. Hase, Handbook of power system engineering (John Wiley & Sons Ltd, 2007).
13. V. Zakaryukin, A. Kryukov, A. Cherepanov, International Scientific Conference Energy Management of Municipal Transportation Facilities and Transport EMMFT 2017 (EMMFT 2017), *Advances in Intelligent Systems and Computing,* **Vol. 692** (Springer, 2017).
14. V.P. Zakarjukin, A.V. Krjukov, I.M. Avdienko, et al., Modern technologies. System analysis. Modeling, No. 3(55) (2017). (in Russian)
15. A. Alsulami, MSc Thesis, Chalmers University of Technology (Goteborg, Sweden, 2014).

16. A. Pana, Active Load Balancing in a Three-Phase Network by Reactive Power Compensation, in: *Power Quality and Monitoring, Analysis and Enhancement* (2011).
17. M.M. Saied, Electrical Power Quality and Utilisation, **Vol. XVI**, No. 1 (2013).

Use of the relative indicator for estimation of railway blocks capacity

Sergei Bessonenko[1,*], and *Ekaterina* Klimova[1], and *Aleksei* Dementyev[1]

[1]Siberian Transport University, 630049 Novosibirsk, Russia

Abstract. Capacity of railway blocks and sections is one of the most important parameters of railway transport operation. The purpose of the study is to find a universal parameter of railway blocks and sections capacity that would allow maximum use of the reserves available. This paper proposes to use "partial capacity filling factors", which are defined as the ratio of the changed capacity factor to the existing value, as a relative indicator. The methodology of application of this indicator has been elaborated, examples of calculations have been provided. There are nomograms in the paper that allow determining the maximum number of trains that can be passed through the section taking into consideration all conditions of operation.

Introduction

Correct estimation of the capacity of railway blocks and sections allows ensuring the maximum traffic for each block. At the present stage of the development of the methodology for assessing and analyzing the capacity, domestic and foreign scientists use various methods [1] based on the following: mathematical dependencies for set infrastructure parameters and parameters of the train traffic arrangement system (analytical methods) [2, 3]; determination of the change in capacity with variation of the infrastructure parameters and parameters of the train traffic arrangement system, taking into consideration possible delays of trains (parametric methods) [4, 5, 6, 7]; transportation process parameters optimization principles [8, 9]; simulation of a railway block operation [7, 9, 11]. Absolute values or capacity filling factors, which take into account the initial parameters considered, for example [12, 13], are used with the existing estimation and analysis methods.

Railway operation conditions often require rapid estimation of the change in the line capacity value by the resulting value. The value of this indicator depends on many initial parameters: intervals between stations and trains, block usage time, duration of provision of the technological "window", number of trains of various categories, coefficients of removal of freight trains with other categories. With that, such parameter as the infrastructure reliability factor that depends on the number of main tracks in the block and the thrust type is assumed to be conditionally constant.

The purpose of the study is to search for a universal indicator for estimating railway blocks capacity in conditions of changing the initial parameters. The subject of the study is

* Corresponding author: bessonenkosa@mail.ru

© The Authors, published by EDP Sciences. This is an open access article distributed under the terms of the Creative Commons Attribution License 4.0 (http://creativecommons.org/licenses/by/4.0/).

railway blocks capacity, the object of the study is railway blocks, sections and operating domains. The novelty of this study consists in the use of a relative indicator that depends on the minimum set of variable parameters.

Research methods

At present, determination of intervals between stations and trains and of the railway section capacity is performed in accordance with the applicable Instructions [114, 2]. The final result of the calculations is the capacity filling factor that shows the proportion of scheduled graph threads occupied by real trains. Factor analysis of the effect of the following initial parameters for the i-th version of the block operation on the capacity filling factor has been performed within the scope of the study:

1) time parameter that characterizes the type of the train traffic schedule used T_i (for example, for single-track blocks, schedule period, T^i_{fr}, for double-track blocks, the estimated interval between trains in the package, I^i_p), minutes;

2) estimated freight trains traffic parameters - N^i_{fr}, passenger trains traffic parameters - N^i_{ps}, etc., of the k-th category N^i_k;

3) coefficient of freight trains removal by passenger trains, ε^i_{ps}, etc., of the k-th category ε^i_k;

4) duration of provisioning of technological infrastructure breaks, t^i_{tech}, minutes.

It is proposed to use the relative indicator of "$k_{r.i}$", the quotient of capacity filling factors as the ratio between the changed capacity filling factor and the existing value" to estimate the effect of the initial parameters on the final result. The indicator shall be calculated by the following formula:

$$k_{r.i} = \frac{k_{ch}}{k_{exis}}, \qquad (1)$$

where k_{ch}, k_{exis} are the values of the capacity filling factor for new (changed) and existing railway block operation conditions, respectively.

This indicator is a dimensionless value and reflects how many times the block capacity filling factor will change with the change in the initial parameters.

With that, all calculations are performed regarding the initial conditions that correspond to the minimum set of parameter values.

Thus, the generalized formula for calculation of the relative indicator in conditions of changing of all the aforementioned initial parameters will take the following form:

$$k_{r.i} = \frac{N^{ch}_n \cdot N^{exis}_н}{N^{exis}_n \cdot N^{ch}_н} = \frac{(1440 - t^{exis}_{tech}) \cdot T_{ch} \cdot (N^{ch}_{fr} + \varepsilon^{ch}_{ps} \cdot N^{ch}_{ps} + \sum \varepsilon^{ch}_k \cdot N^{ch}_k)}{(1440 - t^{ch}_{tech}) \cdot T_{exis} \cdot (N^{exis}_{fr} + \varepsilon^{exis}_{ps} \cdot N^{exis}_{ps} + \sum \varepsilon^{exis}_k \cdot N^{exis}_k)}, \qquad (2)$$

where N^i_n is the required capacity for the i-th variant of operation of the railway block, trains or pairs of trains;

$N^i_н$ is the existing capacity for the i-th variant of operation of the railway block, trains or pairs of trains.

The following are special cases:

A) change of the existing blocks capacity as a result of varying of the following:
- the time parameter and the duration of provisioning of technological "windows":

$$k_{r.i} = \frac{N_н^{exis}}{N_н^{ch}} = \frac{(1440 - t_{tech}^{exis}) \cdot T_{ch}}{(1440 - t_{tech}^{ch}) \cdot T_{exisi}} , \tag{3}$$

- the time parameter:

$$k_{r.i.} = \frac{T_{ch}}{T_{exis}} , \tag{4}$$

- the duration of provisioning of technological "windows":

$$k_{r.i} = \frac{(1440 - t_{tech}^{exis})}{(1440 - t_{tech}^{ch})} ; \tag{5}$$

B) change of the required blocks capacity as a result of varying of the following:
- the number of trains of various categories and the freight trains removal coefficients:

$$k_{r.i} = \frac{N_n^{ch}}{N_n^{exis}} = \frac{N_{fr}^{ch} + \varepsilon_{ps}^{ch} \cdot N_{ps}^{ch} + \sum \varepsilon_k^{ch} \cdot N_k^{ch}}{N_{fr}^{exis} + \varepsilon_{ps}^{exis} \cdot N_{ps}^{exis} + \sum \varepsilon_k^{exis} \cdot N_k^{exis}} , \tag{6}$$

- the number of trains of various categories:

$$k_{r.i.} = \frac{N_{fr}^{ch} + \varepsilon_{ps}^{exis} \cdot N_{ps}^{ch} + \sum \varepsilon_k^{exis} \cdot N_k^{ch}}{N_{fr}^{exis} + \varepsilon_{ps}^{exis} \cdot N_{ps}^{exis} + \sum \varepsilon_k^{exis} \cdot N_k^{exis}} , \tag{7}$$

- the freight trains removal coefficients:

$$k_{r.i} = \frac{N_{fr}^{exis} + \varepsilon_{ps}^{ch} \cdot N_{ps}^{exis} + \sum \varepsilon_k^{ch} \cdot N_k^{exis}}{N_{fr}^{exis} + \varepsilon_{ps}^{exis} \cdot N_{ps}^{exis} + \sum \varepsilon_k^{exis} \cdot N_k^{exis}} . \tag{8}$$

The methodology described was used to perform calculations to estimate the use of the capacity of a number of railway blocks and sections. The calculated data showed that a more efficient use of capacity reserves was possible in a number of cases.

A conditional railway section, the characteristics of which are as close as possible to the real railway line is adopted as the object of approbation in the article: a double-track section equipped with automatic block system, electrified, only allows two categories of trains, namely, freight and passenger trains.

See the characteristics of changes in the initial values in Table 1.

Table 1. Characteristics of changes in the initial values.

Initial parameter	UOM	Minimum value	Maximum value	Step of changing
calculated interval between freight trains, minutes	min	7	11	1
calculated traffic intensity of freight trains	train	40	90	10
calculated traffic intensity of passenger trains	train	5	30	5
coefficient of removal of freight trains by passenger trains	-	1	5	0.1

Results

The study results showed that the dependence of the quotient of capacity filling factors (or the relative indicator)

A) only on the time parameter (design interval between trains) is direct, linear, and proportional, i.e., as value I_p is increased by 2 times, value $k_{o.n}$ is increased by 2 times;

B) only on the "window" duration is direct, non-linear, and non-proportional;

C) on other possible cases of changing of the initial parameters is direct, linear, and non-proportional.

Nomograms for the following special cases were built as an example that illustrates the dependency of the relative indicator on the initial parameters:

- in conditions of the growth in the estimated number of freight trains with the fixed number of passenger train equal to 15 (Fig. 1);
- in conditions of the growth in the number of passenger trains with the fixed number of freight train equal to 60 (Fig. 2).

In both cases, the coefficient of removal of freight trains by passenger trains also varies.

Besides, horizontal lines on the graphs show the limiting values of the permissible capacity filling factor referred to the initial value of the section capacity filling factor. This makes it possible to determine the limiting values of the removal coefficient and/or the number of trains, provided that the capacity filling factor for this variant of combinations of parameters does not exceed the limiting value.

For example, with the freight trains traffic intensity of 50 and the design interval between trains of 10 minutes, reliable passing of trains through the section is only ensured if the coefficient of removal of freight trains by passenger trains does not exceed the value of 4. Otherwise, the absolute value of the capacity filling factor will exceed the permissible value (0.99 for double-track blocks).

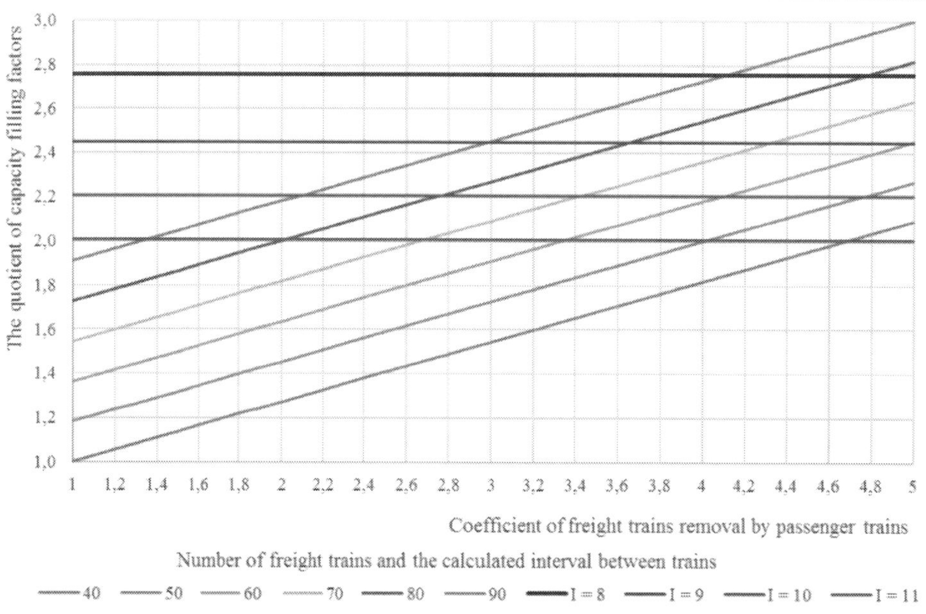

Fig. 1. Graphs of dependency of the relative indicator on changes in removal coefficients with the variable number of freight trains and the fixed number of passenger trains (15 trains).

However, it must be noted here that the interval between trains in the package must be taken into consideration when calculating the absolute value of the capacity loss due to increasing of the removal coefficient, as it affects the existing capacity of the section.

The following are initial conditions on the graphs presented:

- for Figure 1: the number of passenger trains is 15, the number of freight trains is 40, the coefficient of removal of freight trains by passenger trains is 1;
- for Figure 2: the number of passenger trains is 5, the number of freight trains is 60, the coefficient of removal of freight trains by passenger trains is 1.

Graphs allow quick determining the number of times by which the capacity filling factor will grow with increasing of the coefficient of removal of freight trains by passenger trains (with the fixed number of freight and passenger trains).

With that, in conditions of changing the number of freight trains, the graph threads will be parallel to each other at the same distance (Fig.1). With changes in the number of passenger trains, the graph threads will be crossed in the negative zone of the coefficient of removal of freight trains by passenger trains (Fig.2).

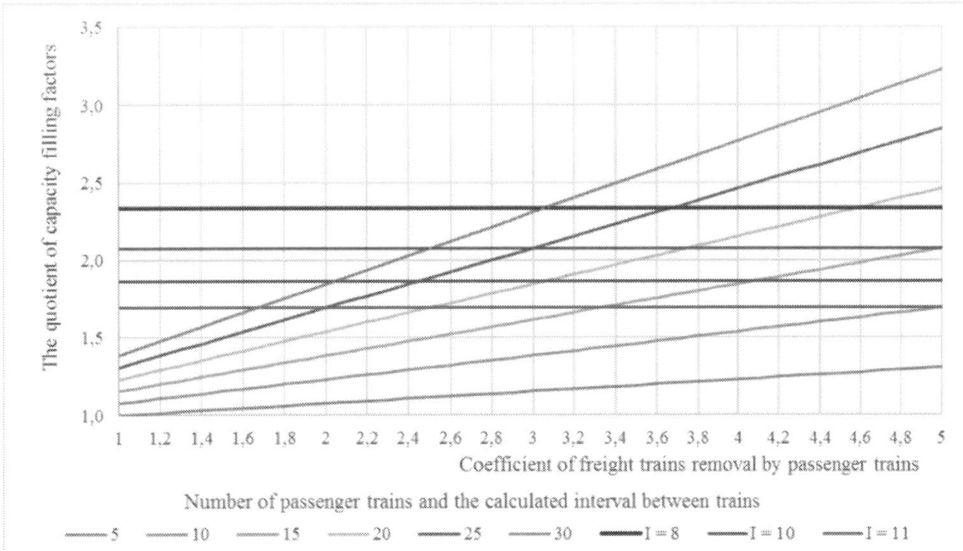

Fig. 2. Graphs of dependency of the relative indicator on changes in removal coefficients with the variable number of passenger trains and the fixed number of freight trains (60 trains).

In conditions of transition from the parallel graph type to the non-parallel type, the coefficient of removal of freight trains by passenger trains may be changed from 1 to 2.5, which corresponds to the quotient of capacity filling factors equal to 1.409 (Fig.1, with 40 freight trains and 15 passenger trains. It means that the required capacity will grow by 1.409 times, from the value of 55 trains to the value of 77.5 trains, the capacity filling factor will change from 0.359 to 0.506 with the interval between trains in the package equal to 8 minutes.

In conditions of increasing of the coefficient of removal of freight trains by passenger trains from 1.5 to 2.5, the quotient of capacity filling factors will increase from 1.136 to 1.409. It means that the required capacity will grow by 1.409/1.136 = 1.24 times, from the value of 62.5 trains to the value of 77.5 trains, the capacity filling factor will change from 0.359 to 0.506.

Besides, the graphs presented allow determining the change in the capacity filling factor in the case of changing of both parameters For example, the first condition corresponds to 10 passenger trains with the removal coefficient equal to 3, the second condition corresponds to 15 passenger trains with the removal coefficient equal to 2. Figure 2 is used to determine the change in the filling factor regarding the initial conditions (the number of passenger trains is 5, the number of freight trains is 60, the coefficient of removal of freight trains by passenger trains is 1). In accordance with the first condition, it is 1.385, in accordance with the second condition, it is also 1.385. I.e., the specified combinations of the initial parameters have equal values for the capacity filling factors and the transition from one variant to the other one will be equivalent and will not cause an increase in the capacity filling factor.

The graph of changing of the coefficient of removal of freight trains by high-speed trains from 1 to 9 with the number of passenger trains of 25, the coefficient of removal of freight trains by passenger trains equal to 2 and the number of freight trains of 60 was built for modeling the change in the capacity in conditions of introduction of high-speed passenger trains (Fig.3).

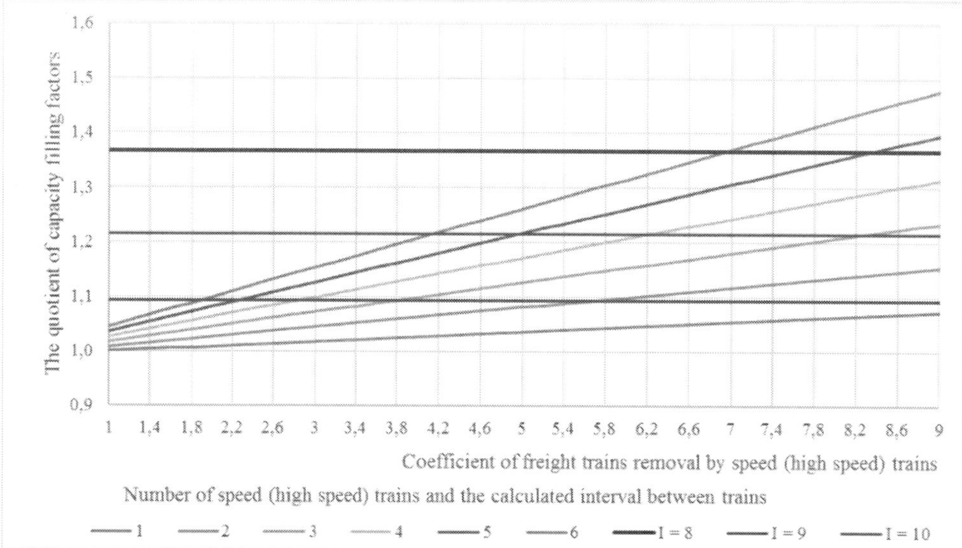

Fig. 3. Graphs of dependency of the relative indicator on changes in removal coefficients with the variable number of high-speed trains and the fixed number of passenger trains (25 trains) and freight trains (60 trains).

The graph built shows that if 2 high-speed trains run on the section, the removal coefficient must not exceed 5.6, if the design interval between trains is 10 minutes. Otherwise, the absolute value of the capacity filling factor will exceed the permissible value. No reliable passing of trains through the section will be ensured.

Besides, the graph allows determining the maximum values of the number of high-speed trains and removal coefficients on condition of provision of reliable passing of trains through the block, section or the operating domain. With the design interval between trains equal to 8 minutes, the maximum number of high-speed trains is 6 with the removal coefficient of not more than 6.9.

Conclusion

The paper proposes a new relative indicator for estimating railway blocks capacity - the quotient of the capacity filling factors. The use of the relative indicator allows estimating the change in railway blocks capacity with the change in the number of trains and the intervals between them, including the conditions of circulation of high-speed passenger trains and during provisioning of technological "windows" of various duration.

The use of the proposed indicator allows making simple calculation, on the basis of which graphs can be developed. The graphs are used to determine the limiting values of freight and passenger trains on the block as well as intervals between them on condition of reliable passing of trains through the section. This indicator is universal and can be used in estimation of the capacity of single-track and double-track blocks with various technical equipment and schedule types. Its application will allow maximum use of the capacity reserves, which will cause significant improvement of railway transport operation. The results obtained may be used in all software and hardware packages for development of train traffic schedules.

References:

1. S.A. Branishtov, A.M. Shirvanyan, D.A. Tumchenok С.А. Браништов, Information and Control Systems, 5, 51 – 57 (2014). (in Russian)
2. Instrukcija po raschetu nalichnoj propusknoj sposobnosti zheleznyh dorog: utv. OAO «RZD» 10.11.2010 [Instruction for the calculation of the available railway capacity] (Tehinform, Moscow, 2011). (in Russian)
3. *UIC Code 406. Capacity* (International Union of Railways (UIC), Paris, 2013).
4. A.M. Makarochkin, Yu.V. Dyakov, *Ispol'zovanie i razvitie propusknoj sposobnosti zheleznyh dorog* [Use and development of railway capacity] (Transport, Moscow, 1981). (in Russian)
5. I.T. Kozlov, *Propusknaja sposobnost' transportnyh sistem* [Capacity of transport systems] (Transport, Moscow, 1985). (in Russian)
6. Y.C. Lai, PhD-thesis, University of Illinois, Urbana-Champaign, 2008.
7. S.A. Branishtov, A.M. Shirvanyan, D.A. Tumchenok, Information and Control Systems, 6, 68 – 74 (2014). (in Russian)
8. R. Lusby, J. Larsen, M. Ehrgott, D. Ryan, OR Spectrum, 3, 843 – 883 (2009).
9. J. Yuan, I.A. Hansen, Transportation research. Part B: methodological, **Vol. 41**(2), 202 – 217 (2007).
10. J. Pachl, *Railway operation and control* (VTD rail publishing, Mountlake Terrace (USA), 2015.
11. V.S. Timchenko, *Informatics: Problems, methodology, technologies*, Proceedings of the XVI International scientific conference, Voronezh, 502 – 506 (2016). (in Russian)
12. A. Lindfieldt, Doctoral thesis, KTH Royal Institute of Technology, Stockholm, 2015.
13. H. Pouryousef, P. Lautala, T. White, Journal of Modern Transportation, 23(1), 30 - 42, (2015).
14. CD-361. Instruction for the determination of station and inter-train intervals (Tehinform, Moscow, 1995). (in Russian)

Conceptual framework of economic reliability of production processes

Tatyana Vladimirova[1,*], *Aleksey* Manakov[1], and *Viktor* Sokolov[1]
[1]Siberian Transport University, 630049 Novosibirsk, Russia

Abstract. The study presents the authors' approach to defining economic reliability of production processes; interpretation of the essence, content and mathematical implementation of its parameters. The methodology of study includes classical scientific methods like observation, analysis, synthesis, formalization and logic. Also, some special methods were used like knowledge base and database creation, variance analysis, economical and statistical methods of data processing, economical and mathematical modeling. The authors' approach to control of economic reliability of production processes suggests transition from classical elasticity coefficients of relations between two factors to elasticity functions, including multidimensional ones. Rigidity functions are introduced as a counter-concept of elasticity functions. As a result of the study the following notions are defined: extreme technologies, basic principle of the technology extremality; assessment of production process reliability, as well as essence, content and mathematical implementation of its parameters. The suggested method is implemented in a number of large-scale projects in various branches of Russian national economics.

Introduction

When making decisions on economic systems management the economists mainly use the category of economic reliability as a tool for assessing competitiveness of economic systems starting with Michael Porter [1]. Many authors, including V. Nechiporenko, interpret economic reliability as the state of an organization which provides reasonable use of its resources, effective and sustainable development, meeting of the stakeholders' interests within the tolerable risk limits [2]. B. Prykin, A. Raikin and J. Forrester define economic reliability as "integration of internal and external actions of a system by means of cybernetic model functioning" [3, 4, 5], which they present as a set of actual balanced parameters at a given moment of time.

For quantitative assessment of economic reliability of an organization V. Kabanov and N. Zheglova suggest defining an integral parameter as a comprehensive result of a diagnostic assessment of production processes [6] and a complex parameter of its financial state [7].

Similar approaches to quantitative assessment of economic reliability are demonstrated by foreign authors who suggest using systems of indicators (tests): in quality control [8]; in statistical assessment of economic reliability [9], for defining reliability variation vector

*Corresponding author: vladimirovatat@yandex.ru

© The Authors, published by EDP Sciences. This is an open access article distributed under the terms of the Creative Commons Attribution License 4.0 (http://creativecommons.org/licenses/by/4.0/).

(calculation of company indicators related to industry, general economy, reputation) [10]; for assessing reliability by the costs related to reliability procedures [11].

The mentioned approaches to interpretation of the notion of economic reliability and its assessment reduce the possibility of its application as a parameter for managing economic systems, considering today's soaring uncertainty. Literature review in the field showed that the methodical instruments and model mechanisms for providing economic reliability of the made decisions for economic systems is little developed. This research problem is characterized by the following factors: large scale of information required for making a decision; high subjectivity of the decisions made and uncertainty of conditions for decision making which significantly exceeds the uncertainty of decision making in technical systems.

First, the category of "reliability" appeared as an important parameter of technical systems management, where in practice reliability is provided by including predetermined elements of counteractions against negative disturbing effects in management mechanisms. Unfortunately, in practice of economic systems management such mechanisms are not always developed in advance, more often "struggle against risks" occurs [12].

Reliability of technical systems is determined as a system's ability to perform certain functions within a given period of time or as a probability of achieving a certain goal. Reliability can be assessed in two ways: (1) with a system of quantitative parameters of reliability properties of an object [13] or (2) with a system of statistical parameters of variation. In production process and technology management this approach is reflected in the "input – output" categories of production process or a technology.

The authors of this study support the second approach to defining reliability and interpret reliability of production systems as "probability of performing a given task within a required period of time with a required quality level and provided resources" [14].

When forecasting production processes the uniqueness of parameters for decisions to be made is lost, which forces to consider a lot of various scenarios. In the end of the day, whichever number of scenarios has been considered, only one can be recommended for implementation, in most cases it differs from the actual scenario. In such circumstances certain stock-piles and mechanisms shall be provided to compensate for the existing inconsistency.

To describe the management procedures for production processes such categories as economic reliability, economic manoeuvre, and flexibility are used. But in most cases they cannot be implemented in operational use, one of the reasons is poor mathematical training of specialists in the field, which raises a serious issue in the conditions of digital economy development.

The experience of managing economic components of complex production processes shows that there are three types of reactions to negative disturbing effects: flexibility, mobility and stability. These reactions are implemented in a system of parameters with a common economic reliability parameter. When managing technical aspects of production processes some mechanisms are developed for their adaptation to negative effects, whereas in economic management such mechanisms are not provided, especially for extreme production processes.

Contribution to the development of mechanisms for production processes adaptation to negative effect and methodical tools for providing economic reliability has been made by V. Smirnov and V. Sokolov. First in 1975, V. Smirnov and V. Sokolov in their article "Adaptive Parameters of a Plan" suggested a conceptual framework and quantitative parameters of a new subject domain which was economic reliability. Later, computing technology advances made it possible to use these parameters in practice of economic systems management. Today such possibilities has increased manifold.

The methodical framework for providing economic reliability of decision making has been developed in the following monographs of the authors: Assessment of Plan Reliability and Manoeuvre Parameters (1978), System Modeling of Planning Reliability (1984), Study of Flexibility and Reliability of Economic Systems (1990), Justification of Resource Provision in Innovative Projects (2008), Economic Reliability of Investment Management in Construction (2013).

The purpose of this study is presentation of the authors' approach to defining economic reliability of production processes, and interpretation of essence, content and mathematical implementation of its parameters.

Research methods

The research methods include classical scientific methods like observation, analysis, synthesis, formalization and logic; and some special methods like knowledge base and database creation, post-hoc analysis of the level of production process goal achievement, variance analysis of input parameters variation for this processes such as technology and resource provision or standard performance parameters. Also, economical and statistical methods of data processing were applied for post-hoc assessment of production processes reliability; economical and mathematical modeling was performed for production processes of certain companies, branches and the national economics in general.

Results

Any production process is understood as an aggregate of technologies applied for solving practical tasks, including product manufacturing, performance of works and services. The modern period of technological development is characterized by the growing extremality level. By extreme technology the authors mean such technologies that provide the maximum output per resource unit in comparison with other ones.

The growing number of extreme innovative technologies considerably enhances the production processes efficiency, as well as the risks. The following principle arises: when some technology provides a better output per resource unit than the other, this technology will suffer bigger losses in case of the resource deficiency. The authors call this principle the basic one in extreme technologies.

Losses of extreme technologies are especially detrimental for innovative production processes. Technical failures in managing production processes sometimes cause considerable financial losses. However, the records show that damage caused by faults in providing economic reliability of the processes is much higher.

The paradox arises that proves the extremality principle of technology: the lower technological efficiency is the less loss it brings to the production process in case of negative effects (disturbances). For instance, the coal stock at a central heating and power plant can be considered as one of the least efficient technologies, for it doesn't provide products manufacturing.

However, in case of extreme disturbing effect like non-delivery of coal this stock will transit from the category of cold standby to a fully-fledged technology. Due to external factors this paradox is consciously or subconsciously ignored in production processes management, since the society cannot reject scientific and technological advances, i.e. extreme yet more efficient technologies.

Assessment of economic reliability of a production process means mathematical expectation of the level of completion of a planned task or of some other controlled parameter of the process. To provide reliability one shall organize control of deviations or variations of possible parameter values of a production process from the mean value. It shall be noted that languages of technical and economic components do not coincide and their information bases have almost no common data. These factors require a specific approach to providing production process reliability taken as an integral whole of technology + economics.

On the one hand, economic reliability of a production process performs as a single parameter (mathematical expectation of the level of achievement of a planned value of a certain controlled parameter). On the other hand, it is a complex parameter which includes several properties of reliability: mobility, adaptability, flexibility, elasticity, stability, rigidity, reversibility, etc. These parameters are only implemented in quantitative forms. They are easily integrated in interaction charts for generally used economic categories of production processes management. Quantitative assessment of a production process economic reliability can be expressed by a "potential probability of performing a planned task for the kth parameter" [15, p.61].

Let us assume that the value P_k^0 is the value of some k^{th} output plan parameter of the process development and functioning, failure to achieve this parameter at a certain period can be interpreted as maloperation. P_k is assumed to be a probable actual value of this parameter. It may differ from the planned one due to possible change in the conditions of process implementation. Then, the probability of $P_k > P_k^0$ occurring within the studied period of time shall indicate reliability of the project task performance for the kth parameter. This definition of a potential reliability can be implemented as follows:

$$q_k = q\,(P_k > P_k^0), \tag{1}$$

where $q\,(P_k > P_k^0)$ – probability of $P_k > P_k^0$.

The most important requirements to economic reliability parameters are the possibility of their quantitative assessment and interpretability. This primarily concerns certain parameters of economic decision. The basic parameter that retrospectively characterizes reliability of economic decision is the degree of its performance (percent, share). Using the previously introduced nomenclature this parameter can be expressed as follows:

$$H_k = 1 - E\,[(P_k^0 - P_k) / P_k^0],\ k = 1,\dots,K, \tag{2}$$

where H_k – reliability performance for k^{th} parameter of economic decision; E – mathematical expectation; K – nomenclature of parameters; P_k^0- design (planned) value of the kth parameter; P_k – its probable actual value.

It is natural that the reliability assessment (1) is formally inconsistent with assessment (2). What is more, in some cases H_k can formally be greater than 1. Nevertheless, it is useful to apply it in economic components of production processes in the form approximate to assessment (1) in a sense that their qualitative assessments vary synchronically.

Moreover, for defining the sufficient level of economic reliability of a production process retrospective assessments in the form (2) are acceptable. In this case reliability of a production process becomes a controllable parameter. One of important factors of its control is elasticity function applying which enables one to use technological, structural, material, financial, organizational and other reserves. Positive correlation exists between the reliability assessments (1) and (2) for production processes.

For extreme production processes the complex parameter of adaptability is especially important, it denotes their ability to adapt and adequately react to changes of internal and external environment. Adaptability is motivated by natural substitution of conventional processes and technologies with new and extreme ones.

In this case we observe the rigidity parameter of production process economic reliability. Rigidity occurs under the influence of firmly established competences, experience, traditions, information support system for document flow, habits. The more resources are invested in the production process the more rigid this process is.

Reduction of production processes rigidity is achieved by actively effecting both internal and external environment, and adapting to it. It is an implementation of adaptability. Parameters of economic reliability of production processes related to adaptability are flexibility and mobility. Flexibility of the process, which means the ability to adapt without changing technological and organizational structure, mostly reveals under little disturbances. Whereas mobility of the production process, or its ability to adapt by means of technological, structural and organizational changes, is manifested under strong disturbances.

Stability of a multistage production process is reflected in its ability to eliminate negative disturbances, for example, in a logistics chain of freight and passenger transportation. Here, the basic extremality principle is implemented: the elimination of disturbances comes faster in non-efficient technologies because of smaller number of stages, such technologies are characterized by a high stability level.

Conclusion

The issue of formation of economical and mathematical framework for providing economic reliability of production processes can be solved by using the suggested approach to its understanding and implementation, especially when applicable to extreme technologies. During the study the following notions were defined: extreme technologies, basic principle of the technology extremality; assessment of production process reliability, as well as essence, content and mathematical implementation of its parameters.

The suggested approach has practical value for controlling economic reliability parameters of production processes, which is validated by implementing certain projects in various branches of economics: gas flows optimization while planning the development of a unified gas supply system of the country with the account of economic reliability; optimization of dynamic input-output balance of the country; optimization of development plans for iron and steel industry infrastructure in Western Siberia; flexible pricing and tariffs formation for production and transportation systems with the account of economic reliability; interactive model of reliability assessment for long-term target program implementation, etc.

Prospective direction for further research in this field can be development of universal adaptive systems for providing economic reliability and adaptability of production processes to negative effects – economic robots. Such robots are unit-based economical and mathematical models, with each unit corresponding to a certain scenario. The general system constraints are requirements on reliability of achieving the required goals like volume of production, amount of revenue, etc.

The central unit of such robot may correspond to the most probable conditions for decision making. Other units will correspond to different scenarios with less probable conditions. The connection between the central unit and a certain scenario is implemented by constraints for adaptation of a decision corresponding to the central unit to another unit.

These constraints are related to flexibility and mobility. At the same time, mobility implies change of production process structure, like replacement of some production technology or its cancelling. Mobility constraints will enable to make the process stable to, for example, fluctuations of prices or demand on the market.

References

1. M.E. Porter, *Competitive Strategy: Techniques for Analyzing Industries and Competitors* (Moscow, 2006). (in Russian)
2. V.I. Nechiporenko, *Strukturnyj analiz sistem (jeffektivnost' i nadezhnost')* [Structural analysis of systems (efficiency and reliability)] (Sovetskoe radio, Moscow, 1977). (in Russian)
3. B.V. Prykin, *Tehniko-jekonomicheskij analiz proizvodstva* [Technical and economic analysis of production] (Yuniti, Moscow, 2000). (in Russian)
4. A.L. Raykin, *Elementy teorii nadezhnosti tehnicheskih sistem* [Elements of the theory of reliability of technical systems] (Sovetskoe radio, Moscow, 1978). (in Russian)
5. J.W. Forrester, *Osnovy kibernetiki predprijatija* [Industrial Dynamics] (Progress, Moscow, 1971). (in Russian)
6. V.N. Kabanov, Russian Journal of Entrepreneurship, **Vol. 9**, 1, 163-167 (2008). (in Russian)
7. N.V. Zheglova, Naukovedenie [Science studies], **Vol. 8**, 3 (2016). (in Russian)
8. M. Aslam, M.Q. Shahbaz, Journal of Statistics, 14(1), 53-60 (2007).
9. R.R.L. Kantam, G. Srinivasa Rao, B. Sriram, Journal of Applied Statistics, 33(3), 291-296 (2006).
10. A. Gorobnyak, Procedia Engineering, **Vol. 165**, 1203-1210 (2016).
11. K.K. Aggarwal, Economics of Reliability Engineering, In: *Reliability Engineering. Topics in Safety, Reliability and Quality*, **Vol. 3** (Springer, Dordrecht, 1993).
12. A.L. Manakov, Doctoral thesis, Moscow State University of Railway Engineering, Moscow, 2013. (in Russian)
13. K. Kapur, L. Lamberson, *Reliability and design of freight traffic systems* (Mir, Moscow, 1980). (in Russian)
14. Cyberpedia, Nadezhnost' proizvodstvennyh sistem [Reliability of production systems] Available at: https://cyberpedia.su/9xe7f.html (July, 2018). (in Russian)
15. V.G. Sokolov, V.A. Smirnov, *Issledovanie gibkosti i nadezhnosti jekonomicheskih sistem* [The study of the flexibility and reliability of economic systems] (Nauka, Novosibirsk, 1990). (in Russian)

Optimization of processes in railways based on the cost management model

Valery Vorobyov[1,*], *Aleksey* Manakov[1], *Anatoly* Reger[2], and Iuliia Tanaino[1]

[1]Siberian Transport University, 630049 Novosibirsk, Russia
[2]West-Siberian Railway - branch of Russian Railways JSC, 630004 Novosibirsk, Russia

Abstract. The main aim of activities of the branches of vertically integrated Russian Railways JSC is enhancing of manageability and efficiency of business operations. At the current stage, the issue of optimization of costs for product transportation and facilities maintenance in the system of production and technological processes of the railway network has gained relevance. The purpose of this study is development of a mathematical model for the logistic system of transportation, storage, cargo-handling operations, facilities maintenance and reconstruction. Methods of spatial and dynamic modeling in the structure of end-to-end planning of operations were used in the study. Optimization criterion is aggregate cost minimization. Cost function is proposed in the form of local functions of multiple sections along the railway network. The modeling result consists in determining the plans of transportation and supply with minimum costs.

Introduction

Public railway transport keeps the leading position in Russian transportation system. It has no alternative in handling massive and stable freight traffic delivered on middle and long distances [1]. Railway transportation is meant to provide delivery of raw materials and primary products.

The system of freight transportations are subject to delays which impact the investment decisions. In turn, costs depend on correct and timely input data [2, 3, 4, 5].

Considerable growth in the number of freight trains in sections of Trans-Siberian Railway (in the direction Kuzbass - Far East) is provided until 2020 (Table 1).

* Corresponding author: decansgd@stu.ru

© The Authors, published by EDP Sciences. This is an open access article distributed under the terms of the Creative Commons Attribution License 4.0 (http://creativecommons.org/licenses/by/4.0/).

Table 1. Target indicators of freight transportations until 2020.

Zone	Number of freight trains per year, piece		
	2018	2019	2020
Inskaya – Mariinks	6	6	12
Mariinks –Taishet	6	6	12
Mezhdurechensk –Taishet	1	3	8
Taishet – Karymskaya	7	9	20
Karymskaya – Khabarovsk	7	9	20
Khabarovsk – Smolyaninovo	7	9	20

Increase of the number of trains with the weight of 7,100 tones from the initial point of freight traffic (Kuzbass) till the destination point (seaports of Primorsky region) is possible in case of implementing investment projects of Eastern railway polygon development until 2020. Implementation of such projects, as well as maintenance of Russian railway network requires considerable economic costs related to supporting reliability of infrastructure facilities and providing safety of transportation process [6-7].

According to conservative scenario of the Transport Strategy of the Russian Federation until 2030, the estimate amount of financial resources is 72 trillion 465 billion rubles, including federal budget funds in the amount of 20 trillion, 40 billion rubles are funds of legal entities in the framework of public-private partnership. Business operations play a significant role in organization of production activities and managerial structures operation, which became the reason for major reorganization in railway transport [8-9]. The issue of business interest agreement between transportation process organizers and infrastructure facilities owners, as well as alignment of indicators of quality and amount of work keep their relevance.

A number of unsolved systemic problems still exists in the transportation system in general and in its certain divisions, which is conditioned by the increasing demand for transportation services ever growing in the predicted perspective. The required integration in managing development and operation of transportation system is not provided; dynamics of the environment expressed in functioning of modern enterprises in high complexity and uncertainty conditions is not accounted; new low-cost methods for interaction between the manufacturer, operating company, transportation service provider, and customer are insufficiently developed; a new paradigm of scientific knowledge is not formed to provide the gound for common understanding of new notions, categories, methods and principles of organizational and managerial changes in a railway network in time and space [10-11].

Among the above issues, a relevant scientific problem is cost optimization in production, technological and organizational processes in railways operation based on modeling and forecasting of goods supply via local transport network. Methods and model of solutions for similar tasks exist [5, 12]. However, they do not consider differentiation of planning horizons in the railway polygon represented by local transport network, including take-off points, classification yards, destination points and the connecting sections (hereinafter mentioned as "sections") with rolling mode of end-to-end planning, which provides regular development of plans with a shift on a certain time unit. Maximum efficiency of problem solving shall be reached by permanent final goal orientation when performing all types of managerial actions, such as: developing product supply plan that provides minimization of aggregate cost of freight transportation on track sections; organization of product supply on sections; product storage while loading, transporting and unloading; maintenance, repair, reconstruction, retrofit and development of transport infrastructure (railway tracks, stations, cargo-handling equipment, etc.). The existing research in the field of cost management in industrial processes of transportation with the use of spatial and dynamic modeling methods are insufficient.

The purpose of this study is development of a model for transport and logistic system of transportation, storage, cargo-handling operations, facilities maintenance and reconstruction.

Scientific novelty of the study is provided by integral use of spatial and dynamic methods of representation of transport systems for defining the optimum number of supply batches while planning transportations with lowest possible costs.

Research methods

The problem of cost optimization in production, technological and organizational processes is conditioned by the paradigm of labor productivity increase as the main category of economic development and growth in prosperity under the influence of human factor. Object of the study is a railway polygon, subject is costs of technological and organizational processes. The research hypothesis is as follows: cost minimization on the railway polygon is possible and can be reached when developing a transportation plan by mathematical modeling of technological and organizational processes.

The study has the following tasks:

1. define informational parameters of transportations in the railway polygon;
2. define the main assumptions related to freight transportation costs in the polygon of railway network;
3. review mathematical models and methods for determining the extent of their applicability to transport systems presentation.
4. develop a mathematical model of a transport and logistic system including cost functions in the transportation polygon of the railway network;
5. formulate a task for defining freight transportations plan with minimum cost functions and satisfactory balance: accumulation of cargo and traffic in original points, transit and terminal points with the account of existence of sections in railway network with and without preset amount of time consumed;
6. determine the economic order quantity with the account of the above hypotheses.

In theory and practice, the following assumptions related to freight transportation costs in the polygon of railway network are accepted:

1. Costs for freight transportation are directly proportional to tonne-kilometer performance.
2. Costs for organization of supply are directly proportional to the number of batches (sets, cars, etc.) on the studied section.
3. Costs for storage of one product batch at the point during cargo-handling operations or when transporting is directly proportional to the product of storage time multiplied by volume.
4. Costs for infrastructure maintenance and development on the section of the area are directly proportional to the number of product batches (freight traffic density) per unit of time.
5. Costs for developing cargo-handling equipment of a certain point of delivery/receipt are directly proportional to the amount of cargo delivered/received per unit of time.

The existing simulation models of production processes, as well as methods of linear and dynamic programming of transportation processes have been studied [12]. It is known that statistical models reflect the state of technological process at a given moment of time, stationary models account time intervals between the initial moment of input disturbance and the current moment of time under external actions, nonstationary models allow simulating production process the parameters of which depend on the current time and the initial time of input disturbances action [13]. In continuous models, production parameters are defined for any moment of time, in discrete models the production parameters are defined in discrete moments of time. Spatial models represent technological process in space (continuous linear objects, spatial objects), whereas lumped parameter models disregard spatial coordinates of an object. Deterministic models are clearly defined by input parameters, constraints and the target function, stochastic (probabilistic) models account impact of random factors on the technological process.

The approach to developing a cost management model for production processes in the railway network based on spatial and dynamic models that represent space and time of their occurrence, is considered the most efficient.

The railway polygon is characterized by the following informational parameters: the total operation time of the network is unlimited; the intensity of cargo-handling operations at each point of the network is permanent; the transport network includes only points of loading, handling and unloading (transit points are excluded); the costs for product storage in the facilities of any network point during the setup time, and the costs for developing facilities and equipment for storage and setup operations are considered negligible and will not be accounted further on.

Results

The purpose of the study is implemented in the following model, for its description the following nomenclature is used:

Let us assume that Y1, Y2, Y3 are a multitude of loading points, classification yards, and destination stations respectively.

$$Y_1 \cup Y_2 \cup Y_3 = Y; \qquad Y_1 \cap Y_2 = \emptyset;$$

q_i – volume of loaded product at the i-th point ($I \in Y_1$);

B_j – volume of unloaded product at the j-th point ($j \in Y_2$);

S_j – multitude of sections in the railway network, <ij>, adjacent to the point j ($j \in Y$);

q_{ij} – freight traffic on <ij> section (<ij> $\in S_j$, $j \in Y$);

n_{ij} – number of load batches (sets, cars, etc.), on <ij> section of the network (<ij> $\in S_j$, $j \in Y$);

f_{ij} (q_{ij}, n_{ij}) – costs function <ij> of the section (<ij> $\in S_j$, $j \in Y$);

C_{ij} – transportation costs per unit of product on <ij> section;

Z^p_i – costs for developing cargo-handling facilities and equipment at the i-th point of <ij> section per unit of loading/unloading intensity. By loading/unloading intensity we shall mean the amount of load handled at the i-th point per unit of time;

Z^c_{ij} – costs for maintenance and development of infrastructure of section <ij> per unit of freight traffic intensity which denotes the number of load batches (sets, cars, etc.) transported on this section per unit of time;

Z^n_{ij} – costs for organization of transportation on <ij> section per one load batch;

Z^x_i, Z^x_j, Z^x_{ij} – product storage costs per unit of time at the initial (i) and terminal (j) points and on the section <ij> during cargo-handling operations and transportation respectively;

t_{ij}, t'_{ij}, t''_{ij} – total time of load transportation on <ij> section, loading at the i-th point and unloading at the j-th point respectively.

Let us put down the cost function for the transportation polygon of the network as follows:

$$F(Q,N)=\sum_{j\in Y}\sum_{C_{ij}\in S_j}\left[C_{ij}\cdot q_{ij}+Z_{ij}^{\Pi}\cdot n_{ij}+\frac{Z_{ij}^{c}}{t_{ij}}n_{ij}+\left(\frac{Z_i^{p}}{t_{ij}^{'}}+\frac{Z_j^{p}}{t_{ij}^{"}}\right)\cdot q_{ij}+\frac{1}{2}\left(Z_i^{x}t_{ij}^{'}+Z_j^{x}t_{ij}^{"}+2Z_{ij}^{x}t_{ij}\right)\cdot\frac{q_{ij}}{n_{ij}}\right] \quad (1)$$

The function *F(Q,N)* can be presented in the form of sum of local functions of costs on certain sections f_{ij} (q_{ij}, n_{ij}) due to its separability for multiple sections of the transport network.

$$F(Q,N)=\sum_{j\in Y}\sum_{C_{ij}\in S_j}f(q_{ij}n_{ij}) \quad (2)$$

The task of determining the plans for transportation and supply can be formulated as follows: determine transportation plan $Q=\|q_{ij}\|$ and supply plan $N=\|n_{ij}\|$ that provide minimum of the function satisfying the conditions below:

– freight traffic at loading points:

$$\sum_{<ij>\in S_j} q_{ij}+q_j=\sum_{<ji>\in S_j} q_{ji},\ j\in Y_1;$$

– freight traffic at transit points (classification yards):

$$\sum_{<ij>\in S_j} q_{ij}=\sum_{<ji>\in S_j} q_{ji},\ j\in Y_2;$$

– freight traffic at destination points:

$$\sum_{<ij>\in S_j} q_{ij}=\sum_{<ji>\in S_j} q_{ji}+B_j,\ j\in Y_3;$$

– nonnegativity of transportations:

$q_{ij}\geq 0$, $i,j\in Y$;

– integrality and nonnegativity of the number of load batches:

n_{ij} – integer; $n_{ij}\geq 0$; $i,j\in Y$.

– The task is approached based on the following assumptions:

– The railway polygon contain sections with preset amount of time consumed $t_{ij}, t_{ij}^{'}, t_{ij}^{"}$;

– The railway polygon contains sections for which the specified values are linear functions of total amount of loaded and unloaded products:

$t_{ij}^{'}=\varphi_{ij}^{'}\cdot q_{ij}$, $t_{ij}^{"}=\varphi_{ij}^{"}\cdot q_{ij}$, $t_{ij}=\varphi_{ij}\cdot q_{ij}$.

Here, $\varphi_{ij}^{'}$, $\varphi_{ij}^{"}$, φ_{ij} are coefficients that characterize speed of loading, transportation and unloading.

1. The network also contains sections $<i,j>$ with preset time parameters $t_{ij}, t_{ij}^{'}, t_{ij}^{"}$.

A local cost function for a random section can be put as follows (for the convenience purpose we omit indices of section $<i,j>$):

$$f(q,n)=\alpha\cdot q+\gamma\cdot n+\left(\frac{z^{c}}{t_1}+\frac{z^{p}}{t_2}\right)\cdot q+\frac{z^{n}}{t_3}\cdot n+\frac{1}{2}\left(Z_1^{x}t_1+Z_2^{x}t_2+2Z_3^{x}t_3\right)\cdot\frac{q}{n} \quad (3)$$

Here, the parameters with index 1 and 2 characterize initial and terminal points respectively, whereas parameters with index 3 denote the section itself.

In case the conditions of hypothesis 1 are satisfied with $q > 0$ for some section, then the optimum number of batches on such section can be defined by the formula

$$n = \sqrt{\frac{(Z_1^x t_1 + Z_2^x t_2 + 2Z_3^x t_3)\cdot t_3 q}{2(z^n + \gamma t_3)}}, \tag{4}$$

And the local cost function is brought to the following:

$$f = \alpha \cdot q + \left(\frac{z^c}{t_1} + \frac{z^p}{t_2}\right)\cdot q + \sqrt{Z_1^x \frac{t_1}{t_3} + Z_2^x \frac{t_2}{t_3} + 2Z_3^x} \cdot \sqrt{(z^n + \gamma t_3)q} \tag{5}$$

In case the conditions of hypothesis 2 are satisfied with $q > 0$ for some section, then the optimum number of batches on such section can be defined by the formula

$$n = q\sqrt{\frac{(Z_1^x \varphi_1 + Z_2^x \varphi_2 + 2Z_3^x \varphi_3)\cdot \varphi_3}{2(\frac{z^n}{q} + \gamma\varphi_3)}}, \tag{6}$$

And the local cost function is brought to the following:

$$f(q) = \alpha \cdot q + \left(\frac{z^c}{\varphi_1} + \frac{z^p}{\varphi_2}\right) + \sqrt{Z_1^x \frac{\varphi_1}{\varphi_3} + Z_2^x \frac{\varphi_2}{\varphi_3} + 2Z_3^x} \cdot \sqrt{z^n q + \gamma\varphi_3 q^2} \tag{7}$$

In case all sections of the network satisfy the conditions of hypothesis 2, the optimum freight traffic depends on costs for development of production and distribution points.

In case the conditions of hypothesis 3 are satisfied with $q > 0$ for some section, then the optimum number of batches, and time for loading, transportation and unloading can be defined by the formulas

$$n = \sqrt{\frac{q^2}{\gamma^2}\left(\sqrt{\frac{Z_1^x z^c}{2}} + \frac{Z_2^x z^n}{2}\right)^2} \tag{8}$$

$$t_1 = \sqrt{q}\cdot\sqrt{\frac{2z^c}{Z_1^x}}; \qquad t_2 = \sqrt{q}\cdot\sqrt{\frac{2z^p}{Z_2^x}}; \qquad t_3 = n\cdot\sqrt{\frac{z^n}{Z_3^x q}} \tag{9}$$

And the local cost function is brought to the following:

$$f(q) = \alpha \cdot q + \sqrt{Z_3^x z^n q} + \sqrt[3]{4\gamma(\sqrt{Z_1^x z^c} + \sqrt{Z_2^x z^p})q^2} \tag{10}$$

In today's state of economy, special importance is gained by railway transport that forms tariff component in the products pricing structure. Reduction of this component is provided by optimizing costs for production and technological processes in railways. Agreement of economical and business interests of transportation process organizers and infrastructure facilities owners can be reached due to optimization of cost management based on modeling and forecasting of products supply on a local transport network.

Conclusion

As a result of the study the model of cost management for technological processes in railways has been developed. It is based on splitting and rationalization of costs for freight transportation, supply organization on sections of a transport network, loads storage and cargo-handling operations, maintenance and development of infrastructure. The obtained cost functions enable to determine the optimum number of load batches distribution of which is ensured by agreement of business interests of market players in the economic system of the country and its regions. Further research shall be focused on parametric (digital) modeling of processes in polygon technologies.

References

1. Strategija razvitija zheleznodorozhnogo transporta v Rossijskoj Federacii do 2030 goda ot 17 ijunja 2008 № 877-p [Strategy for the development of railway transport in the Russian Federation until 2030 of June 17, 2008, No. 877-p]. (in Russian).
2. M. Andersson, M. Berglund, J. Flodén, C. Persson, J. Waidringer, Research in Transportation Economics, **66,** 59-69 (2017).
3. G. Zembri-Mary, European Transport Research Review 2017, 9:51 (2017).
4. L. Márquez, V. Cantillo, Journal Transportation Planning and Technology, **36**(6), 529-546 (2013).
5. K. Kerkman, K. Martens, H. Meurs, Journal of Transport Geography, **60**, 155-166 (2017)
6. A.A. Reger, Zheleznodorozhnyj transport [Railway transport], **2,** 62-65 (2014). (in Russian)
7. I.B. Repina, Nauchnye problemy transporta Sibiri i Dal'nego Vostoka [Scientific problems of transport in Siberia and the Far East], **1**, 114-117 (2013). (in Russian)
8. A.E. Bashirov, D.S. Rubchenko, Zheleznodorozhnyj transport [Railway transport], **8,** 46-50 (2017). (in Russian)
9. A.N. Smorodin, Zheleznodorozhnyj transport [Railway transport], **6,** 56-59 (2016). (in Russian)
10. J–M.A. Hiltrop, Europ. Management, **14**(3), 243-254 (1996).
11. V.A. Bystrov, T.N. Borisova, N.Yu. Grekova, O.G. Tregubova, P.K. Dyakov, Fundamental'nye issledovanija [Basic research], **7-1,** 66-71 (2016). (in Russian)
12. V.S. Vorobyev, A.L. Lanis, Yu.V. Popova, News of higher educational institutions. Construction, **7**(703), 100-109 **(**2017). (in Russian)
13. L. Li, R.R. Negenborn, B. De Schutter, *Proceedings ITSC* **6728399**, IEEE Conference on Intelligent Transportation Systems, 1224-1230 (2013).

Estimation of conditions of using combined single-track and double-track railways at high-speed traffic

Alexei Dmitrenko[1,*], *Sergei* Karasev[1], *Alexandra* Kalidova[1], and *Dmitry* Sivitsky[1]

[1]Siberian Transport University, 630049 Novosibirsk, Russia

Abstract. An important condition when arranging high-speed railway transportation with insignificant traffic is saving of capital investments in construction of new lines or the reconstruction the existing ones. Development of methods for multi-criteria estimation of the possibility of using fully single-track blocks on a line with high-speed traffic, as well as single-track blocks with double-track inserts, is a relevant issue. The purpose of the study is to develop the criteria and the method for estimation of the feasibility of using single-track elements on a line with high-speed traffic. Methods of simulation modeling, mathematical statistics, regression analysis were used. A method that includes estimation of the technological conditions of using single-track elements on a line with high-speed traffic instead of double-track blocks was developed. The method can be used for multi-criteria optimization of the configuration of a combined single-track and a double-track line using single-track elements in high-cost areas.

Introduction

One of the most urgent tasks that railway transport faces is the need for a planned increase in traffic speeds, introduction of high-speed transportation in both passenger and freight traffic [1]. Considering high cost of high-speed transport infrastructure, it is urgent to develop scientifically sound solutions related to the use of combined single-track and double-track lines [2].

The subject of the study is to determine the development logic of single-track lines, to study the influence of parameters of blocks and separate points on the capacity and speed of the train traffic. The scientific problem is in the lack of scientifically justified technical and technological solutions for arrangement of high-speed traffic using combined single-track and double-track lines, which requires development of methods for estimating the use of single-track blocks and artificial structures on specialized lines with high-speed traffic as well as mixed traffic lines.

The lines intended for high-speed traffic are designed to be double-track. This is due to a significant passenger flow, which requires high intensity of traffic of high-speed trains [3]. As a rule, such lines are only specialized in high-speed traffic. High cost of

* Corresponding author: gdsu@rambler.ru

© The Authors, published by EDP Sciences. This is an open access article distributed under the terms of the Creative Commons Attribution License 4.0 (http://creativecommons.org/licenses/by/4.0/).

infrastructure of specialized double-track lines pays off due to the significant traffic volume [4]. With that, in a number of countries in Eastern Europe, Central Asia, South America, as well as in Russia, the volume of passenger traffic is insufficient for development of high-speed traffic under such scheme. In these conditions, creation of a high-speed railway system requires finding ways to reduce the amount of required investments [5, 6].

One of the possibilities is the use of single-track distances and artificial structures, separating points [7]. Such solutions ensure significant saving on costs. However, there is almost no scientific research in this direction in the countries that occupy the leading positions in the field of high-speed transportation. The reason is the difference in the volume of passenger traffic: with a large passenger flow, development of single-track lines for high-speed traffic is not considered to be a promising technical solution.

The research is based on findings of a number of authors [1, 2, 6, 7] devoted to the use of single-track elements on high-speed railways, which reduces the infrastructure cost. The experience of using fully or partially single-track lines on the railway network shows that in a number of cases they provide significant saving on capital investments with a sufficient level of capacity [8, 9]. These studies deal with arrangement of train traffic, scheduling, as well as technical solutions for railway construction.

The authors of this article make an attempt to develop scientific solutions aimed at determining the rational layout of the line. The purpose of the study was to develop the criteria and the method for estimation of the feasibility of using single-track elements on a line with high-speed traffic. The novelty of the study is to consider the problem of using single-track elements on railway lines with high-speed traffic in a multi-criteria setting. The criteria are capacity, train speed, capital costs of line development.

Research methods

General scientific methods of analysis and synthesis, methods of simulation modeling, mathematical statistics methods are used. The use of single-track blocks with increasing traffic volumes and speed may cause lack of line capacity. This creates the task of estimating the design conditions for single-track blocks.

The method of computer simulation was used to estimate the conditions of single-track elements. Unlike traditional methods of analytical calculation of capacity, the method used provides the possibility of variant calculations with arbitrary parameters of train traffic in both directions. IM Barrier-1 software was developed [10]. Passing of trains through a single-track infrastructure element is simulated (block, artificial construction). The model takes into consideration the structure of missed train traffic, the difference in speed, the duration of occupation of the element, the delay of trains on the approaches and the costs associated with the slowdown in passage of trains.

Approaching of trains to the single-path element can be considered as a stream of demands [5], while the intervals between trains and the duration of occupation of approaches and the element itself can vary. The duration of occupation of the element is directly proportional to its length. It is necessary to assess the influence of single-track blocks parameters on the delays of train traffic and the increase in the transit time of trains.

The program can simulate passing of train traffic in the graphical and analytical form with an arbitrary approach of trains in each direction. Package and non-package schedule is modeled with any given inter-train intervals for an arbitrary time of single-track element occupation by a train in each direction. The incoming flow can be specified as a set of trait attributes $\{\Pi_i\}$ as an object with a set of properties that determine the order of its passing through a single-track element. Such attributes can be, for instance, a high-speed train category, weight and length, a given priority of passing.

The algorithm of the model is based on combining two incoming train flows from different directions into the general flow, either with or without prioritizing of passing of individual trains (Fig. 1). Selection of the direction priority depends on the following factors: the priority of the train itself; the sequence of approach of trains to a single-track element determined by the schedule or the traffic graph; the train approach speed to the one-track element; the intensity of arrival of trains from each direction.

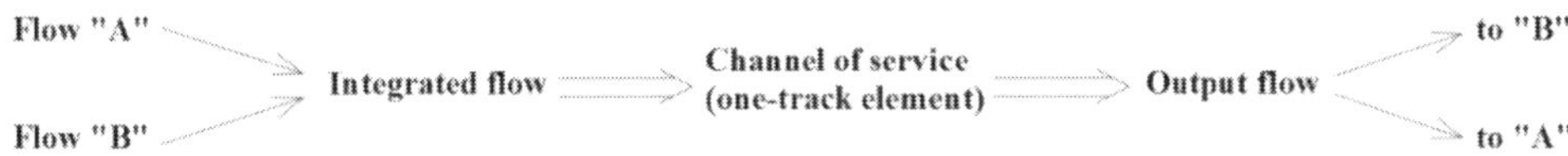

Fig. 1. A single-track element in the form of mass servicing system.

Results of simulation of passing of counter traffic flows are displayed in numerical form. The graph of train passing is also formed, taking into consideration the increase in time on the approaches to the single-track element (Fig. 2).

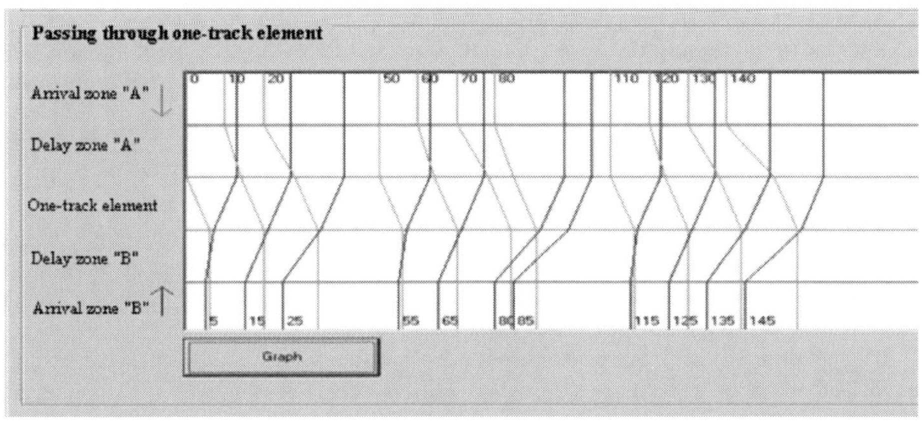

Fig. 2. The graph of passing the counter-moving trains through a one-track block, taking into consideration possible delays due to route hostility.

Results

The possibility of using single-track or combined single-track and double-track lines is determined by the design and conditions of use of separate points and blocks. One of the obstacles to increase the traffic speed on single-track lines is the design of separate points. The analysis showed that development of increasing volumes of transportation at various stages of development of railway transport took place in the following main ways:

1. By increasing technical equipment of stations, increasing the length of station tracks, taking into consideration the increase in the average weight of freight trains and traffic irregularity, particularly when performing works on the track overhaul.

2. By increasing the capacity of the blocks, first of all, due to construction of double-track inserts, and, subsequently, second main tracks.

Passing loops allow increasing the capacity of single-track railway lines. Increase in the number of passing loops reduces the distance between them, reduces the period of the train traffic graph and causes an increase in the line capacity. The nature of passing trains along the main single-track lines is influenced not only by the locations of passing loops, but also by their layout solutions.

In conditions of growth of transportation volumes on single-track railway lines, it is possible to distinguish two basic stages in development of passing loops design. At the first stage, in the absence of automated means of communication regarding train traffic, the increase in capacity was ensured by the use of layouts of passing loops and stations with the transverse arrangement of receipt and departure tracks (Fig. 3a). With small initial traffic intensity, the costs associated with stopping of low-weight trains and lengths under crossings at such passing loops are small.

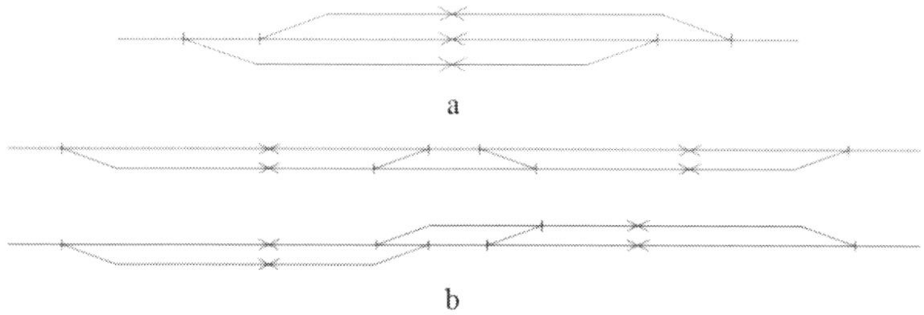

Fig. 3. Major passing loops layouts: a – transverse type passing loop; b – longitudinal type passing loop.

At the next stage, development of increasing transportation volumes took place due to the increase in the train traffic speed, the introduction of electric and diesel traction, heavy-duty carriages. Non-stop crossing of trains was arranged on single-track railway lines. Development of transportation was also performed through construction of double-track inserts, continuous second main tracks on existing lines. The use of passing loops with the longitudinal arrangement of tracks (Fig. 3b), which provided good opportunities for increasing the speed of passing trains due to non-stop crossing, became more active.

The layout shown in Figure 3a allows crossing with stopping of freight trains of standard length coming from both even and odd direction. Availability of passing loops with several parallel tracks allows reducing the time spent on preparing tracks for receiving and departure of freight and passenger trains.

It is determined that such passing loops are inefficient in conditions of increasing the length and speed of trains because of the additional costs associated with stopping trains when they cross on single-track lines due to increase in the following:

a) time costs associated with idle trains on the crossing;

b) energy costs associated with braking and acceleration of trains at crossings;

c) total number of crossings due to reduction in traffic speed.

Then, there was an increase in transportation volumes, traffic speed, introduction of new means of communication with trains participating in the traffic. As a result, the efficiency of the use of longitudinal-type passing loops (Fig. 3b) and double-track inserts has increased. Construction of second main tracks became more widespread. However, this measure was not enough to improve the economic performance of single-track railway lines in the face of increasing traffic volumes and the required increase in traffic speed [11, 12].

The analysis of the technology of trains passing for layout with transverse arrangement of receiving and departure tracks was performed. The most effective option is when one train stops and the second train passes without stopping (Fig. 4). A completely different situation will arise for highly intensive traffic, when in conditions of crossing irregularity two trains of the opposite traffic direction arrive simultaneously. This will cause the situation when losses of time for parking at crossings will be increased for each of the trains in the layout of passing loops with transverse arrangement of tracks.

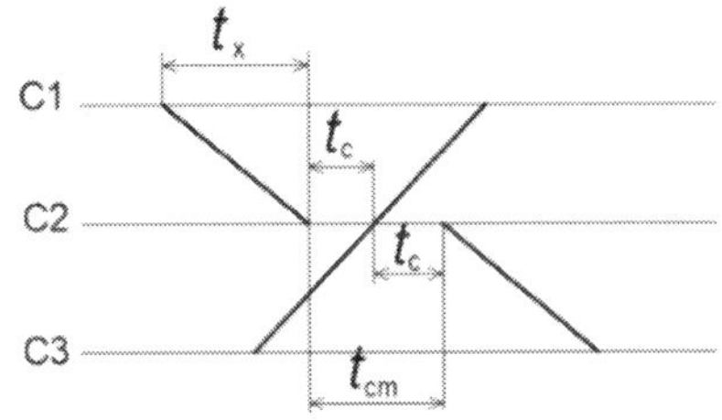

t_x – travelling time; t_c – crossing interval; t_{cm}– delay at crossing

Fig. 4. Parking layout in the case of simultaneous receiving of trains at their crossing at the station.

Comparison of efficiency of the variants showed that simultaneous receiving at the station is less beneficial for layouts of passing loops with transverse arrangement of tracks. For layouts with longitudinal track arrangement, simultaneous receiving of trains provides a significant reduction in energy costs and the time spent when trains are at the crossing. Besides, if there are transverse-type passing loops, additional tracks are usually not used in the case of subsequent laying of the second main track.

Designing of passing loops with displaced and sequential arrangement of tracks makes it possible to reduce the costs associated with stops. It is of particular importance in the case of simultaneous receiving of trains for crossing.

For the proposed schemes of development of the main single-track railway lines, it is expedient to use long double-track inserts instead of construction of separate passing loop points. They will turn separate blocks or their series into double-track sections (Fig. 5). In this case, there arises the possibility of non-stop crossing of trains running at high speed, as well as long trains. The possibility of trains crossing during package passing will also be improved.

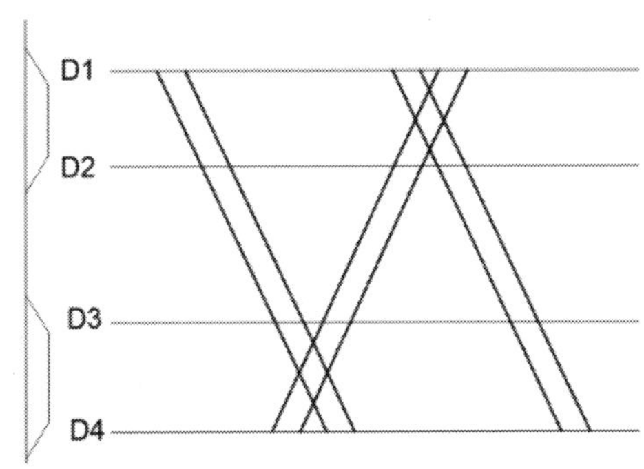

Fig. 5. Train traffic layout in situations of availability of blocks with double-track inserts.

Theoretical analysis of layouts of separate points allows concluding that it is expedient to use passing loops of the longitudinal type in conditions of increasing the traffic speed and development of high-speed traffic. Passing loops with sequential arrangement of tracks on the same side of the main track allows non-stop crossing of trains. It forms good conditions for staged transition to a double-track line. Construction of double-track inserts is recommended at separate stages with a light profile and simple construction conditions. This will allow increasing the train traffic speed with consideration of their crossing without stops. Thus, the subsequent transition from a fully single-track to a combined single-track and double-track line will be performed. Later, it may easily be developed into a double-track line.

The element that limits the capacity of combined single-track and double-track lines is single-track blocks and other elements (in particular, single-track artificial structures). It is expedient to use simulation methods to determine the possibility of their use in conditions of high-speed traffic. The model allows determining the available capacity of a single-track element (block, artificial structure) for high-speed traffic conditions (Fig. 6).

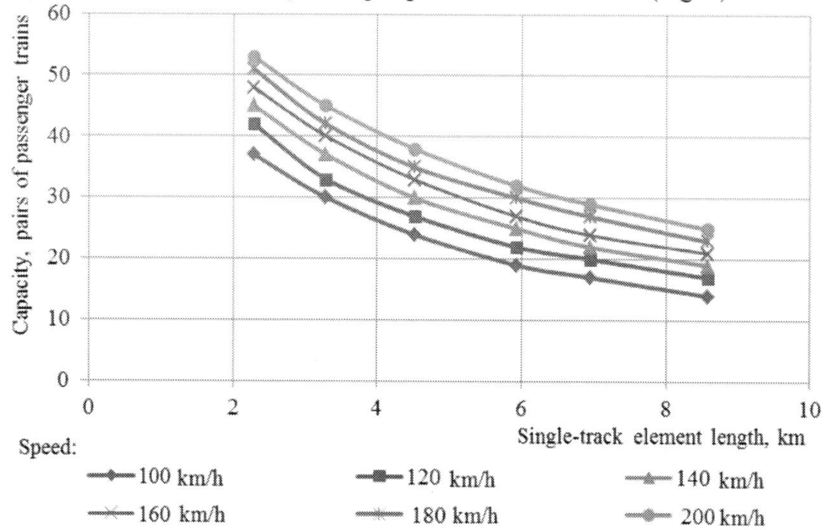

Fig. 6. Graphic dependence of the available capacity on the length of a single-track element.

The dependences obtained can be used to estimate the possibility of using single-track elements on a combined single-track and double-track line. It is also possible to apply them for estimating the capacity level.

The performed theoretical studies and simulation results show that the use of combined single-track and double-track lines can be quite effective at low required capacity. Their application with justified parameters of layouts of separate points and single-track blocks can provide a significant reduction in capital investments at the sufficient level of available capacity.

Arrangement of passing of trains through a single-track element at possible delays depends on the length of the element and the time of its occupation. With consecutive passing of trains, it is necessary to determine the possible delays associated with the route hostility of passing trains. Such delays affect the capacity of a certain element and section. With that, the delay may also be not associated with train stopping. Then, it is necessary to ensure reduction in speed and, correspondingly, increasing in the traveling time on the approach to the single-track element for the period of time equal to the estimated delay time. In this case, the need for a feasibility study for additional development of separate points arises.

In order to ensure the optimal passage of trains, it is necessary to adjust the rate of their approach to single-track blocks. It is achieved by adjusting the intervals between trains. Estimation of conditions of use of single-track elements can be performed by solving the problem of rational distribution of homogeneous resources. Such resources are capital investments or the total travel time of the train over the section. The capacity of line elements in this case is taken into consideration in the form of constraints and can determine the need for conversion of certain single-track elements into double-track ones.

The proposed method makes it possible to reasonably approach making decisions on development of railway networks and individual operating domains, including the conditions of increasing traffic speeds. Justified use of combined single-track and double-track lines, including the conditions of high-speed traffic will provide a significant reduction in the required investments, make it more realistic to implement similar projects on feeder and other low-loaded lines.

Conclusion

The results obtained confirm the possibility of using single-track elements on the lines with high-speed train traffic. Single-track elements can provide sufficient capacity for the length of up to several kilometers. The biggest effect in the form of cost savings will be observed on lines with a large number of artificial structures and separating points. The significance of the results obtained lies in the possibility of using them in justifying the infrastructure development of new or reconstructed lines with high-speed traffic. Further research will be devoted to refinement and specification of the results obtained, taking into consideration various means of communication on the train traffic, as well as the forms of the traffic schedule.

References

1. A.V. Dmitrenko, Vestnik transporta, **10** (2010). (in Russian)
2. E. Castillo, M. Nogal, Z. Grande, Computer-Aided Civil and Infrastructure Engineering, **30** (2015).
3. C Martani, Y Jin, K Soga, S. Scholtes, Computer-Aided Civil and Infrastructure Engineering, **10** (2016).
4. S. Sogin, C.P.L. Barkan, M.R. Saat, *Proc. of the Winter Simulation Conference*, **Vol. 16** (Arizona, 2011)
5. Problems with China's high-speed trains: high costs, safety issues and corruption. Available at: http://factsanddetails.com/china/cat13/sub86/item1848.html (Accessed July 26, 2018).
6. D.Yu. Levin, Mir transporta [World of Transport and Transportation Journal], **2** (2014). (in Russian)
7. S.V. Karasev, A.D. Kalidova, Vestnik of the Railway Research Institute, **1** (2018). (in Russian)
8. X. He, T. Wu, Y. Zou, Y.F. Chen, H. Guo, Structure and Infrastructure Engineering Maintenance, Management, Life-Cycle Design and Performance, **Vol. 13** (2017).
9. Sh.-L. Shaw, Zh. Fang, Sh. Lu, R. Tao, Journal of Transport Geography, **Vol. 40** (2014).
10. J.E. Doomernik, 13th World Conference on Transportation Research (Rio de Janeiro, Brazil, 2013).
11. M.A. Caldas, F.R. Carvahal, P.D. Gabriele, T.G. Ramos, 13th World Conference on Transportation Research (Rio de Janeiro, Brazil, 2013).
12. M. Nogal, A. O'Connor, B. Caulfield, B. Martinez-Pastor, Rel. Eng. & Sys. Safety, **156** (2016).

Method for calculating the maximum number of railway cars in a cut

Aleksandr Klimov[1,*], *Anton* Gunbin[1], *Dmitry* Osipov[1], and *Pavel* Burdyak[1]

[1]Siberian Transport University, 630049 Novosibirsk, Russia

Abstract. A shunting process in hump yards has a number of technical and technological constraints, one of which is the maximum permissible number of cars in a cut. This constraint increases the number of cuts, time of shunting, operating costs of car handling operations in a railways network, while reducing the safety level of classification. The purpose of the paper is to maximize the handling capacity of hump yards by reasonably increasing the permissible length of cuts. The current methods of calculation do not take into account some features of classification operations with long cuts of cars. The proposed method is based on probability calculations and simulation modeling of the shunting process in hump yards. The authors identified the critical factors limiting the maximum permissible number of cars in a cut and developed a method to determine this limitation.

Introduction

Car handling operations in railway networks around the world are concentrated in classification yards. Technical and technological constraints of hump yards are connected with safety requirements. One of such constraints in railway networks of Russia and other countries is the maximum permissible number of cars in a cut. This increases the time of shunting and reduces the handling capacity of a hump yard.

The subject of the study is a controlled rolling-down process for cuts of varied length. The research focuses on determining the maximum number of cars in a cut.

The existing method for calculating the maximum number of cars in a cut used by classification yards of Russia's common railway network is based on energy parameters of a cut rolling down from the hump [1]. The total power of retarder positions in a decreasing part of the hump and in the classification yard as well as the permissible entry speed of a multi-car cut to the classification yard are considered as constraints. Specialists calculate these parameters by analytical methods, without taking into account some features of calculations for hump yard operations, which are described in the applicable standards [2–3].

Rolling-down parameters are calculated subject to forces of resistance to train movement. Different countries of the world use several types of uncontrolled resistance forces to calculate parameters of hump yard operations. These include net resistance,

* Corresponding author: aklimov@ngs.ru

© The Authors, published by EDP Sciences. This is an open access article distributed under the terms of the Creative Commons Attribution License 4.0 (http://creativecommons.org/licenses/by/4.0/).

resistance from the environment and wind, resistance from railway switches and curves, snow and frost, etc. [4–13].

Studies [14–15] describe a process of passing long cuts through a hump crest and confirm that the total specific energy stored by these cuts decreases with a decrease in the center of mass relative to the hump crest.

In general, the existing methods for calculating the maximum number of cars in a cut can be used to quickly determine a required parameter for any hump yard. However, there are some controversial issues in the calculation. Several empirical coefficients and experience of similar calculations in different countries make it necessary to develop a new method for determining the maximum permissible number of cars in a cut.

The calculations made in this study are aimed at increasing the handling capacity of hump yards to reduce operating costs of car handling operations, while reducing the safety level of the classification process.

Research method

The existing calculation method [1] has the following drawbacks:

1. Acceleration of gravity $g = 9.8$ m/s^2 is used in calculation. However, the method does not take into account the inertia of rotating parts of cars, which is expressed as g' in conventional calculations for hump yard operations.

2. The method does not take into account the energy loss from overcoming uncontrolled forces of resistance to the movement by the cut, as well as the dependence of the maximum number of cars in the cut on its weight.

3. The method does not specify requirements for environmental parameters to be calculated, and necessary conditions for these calculations.

4. The shunting speed v_o is proposed to be taken from local guidelines. The Design Rules and Regulations for Shunting Facilities [2] give specific instructions for determining the shunting speed depending on the capacity of a hump yard and tasks to be solved.

5. The total specific energy stored by a cut of cars includes Δh – the maximum difference between a hump crest and a yard retarder position. For long multi-car cuts, the center of mass is always below the hump crest, which should be taken into account when studying rolling-down dynamics of cuts with varied length.

A review of experience in studying the hump yard performance shows that the rotating inertia of wheelsets should be taken into account in calculation of parameters for hump yards. This leads to a decrease in acceleration to values $g' = \{9.11 - 9.65\}$ m/s^2 [16, 17]. Both in Russia and abroad, weight and running performance of cuts are taken into account [2, 3]. In addition, weight distribution within a cut of varied length is important for multi-car cuts [18].

The proposed method for calculating the maximum number of cars in a cut N_{max} is based on the current safety principle of the classification process — the maximum kinetic energy of a cut H_{max} must not exceed the energy that can be absorbed by available hump retarders H_{ret}, i. e.:

$$H_{ret} \geq H_{max} , \tag{1}$$

There should be a possibility to retard a rolling-down cut of cars with all available hump retarder positions. The estimated exit speed of the cut to the classification track is limited to 1.38 m/s, which corresponds to the permissible impact velocity of cars on the railways of the Russian Federation.

This case can be described by the following expression:

$$h_{\text{diff}} + h_0 = h_w + H_{\text{ret}} + h_{\text{end}}, \tag{2}$$

where h_{diff} is the difference between elevation of the hump crest and the minimum elevation of the end of the yard retarder position, m; h_0 is the specific energy corresponding to the initial running speed (shunting speed = v_o, m/s), MeV; h_w is the specific energy equivalent to the total work of uncontrolled forces of resistance to the movement of a multi-car cut, MeV; h_{end} is the specific energy corresponding to the end running speed in a given section (v_k = no more than 1.38 m/s), MeV

Consequently:

$$h_{\text{diff}} + h_0 - h_w - h_{\text{end}} = H_{\text{ret}} \text{ or } h_{\text{diff}} + h_0 - h_w - h_{\text{end}} \le H_{\max}. \tag{3}$$

Values h_{diff} and H_{ret} not depend on the number of cars in a cut. The power of hump retarders is determined by the following formula:

$$H_{ret} = (0{,}5 \cdot n_{ret}^{RP-I} \cdot h_{ret}^{RP-I} + n_{ret}^{RP-II} \cdot h_{ret}^{RP-II} + n_{ret}^{YRP} \cdot h_{ret}^{YRP}) \cdot K_{\text{ret}}, \tag{4}$$

where 0.5 is the factor that takes into account the need of breaking down trains when one of the retarders in the first retarder position (RP-I) is switched off for scheduled maintenance and repair [2]; $n_{ret}^{RP-I}, n_{ret}^{RP-II}, n_{ret}^{YRP}$ is the number of retarders on retarder positions of the decreasing part (RP-I and RP-II) and in the classification yard (yard retarder position); $h_{ret}^{RP-I}, h_{ret}^{RP-II}, h_{ret}^{YRP}$ is the available power per retarder placed on RP-I, RP-II and yard retarder position (YRP), respectively, MeV; K_{ret} is the utilization factor of retarding facilities related to the location of retarder positions and the retarding characteristics of long cuts at which wheelsets cannot be squeezed out from retarders.

The number of cars in a cut and their weight are taken into account in calculating the specific energy corresponding to the speed of the cut h_v, as well as loss of energy consumed to overcome forces of resistance to the movement h_w. According to the current methodology, h_v in general form is calculated by the following formula:

$$h_v = \frac{v^2}{2g'} = \frac{v^2}{2 \cdot (1 + 0.42 \cdot \frac{n}{q})}, \tag{5}$$

where n is the number of axles in the cut; q is the weight of the cut, tonnes.

In calculating the loss of energy consumed to overcome forces of resistance to movement h_w, the number of cars and weight of the cut should be taken into account [2]. According to the calculation method proposed by the authors, it is necessary to perform a number of iterative calculations to determine the maximum number of cars in a cut. Therefore, in order to calculate $H_{\max}$ (parameters h_{diff}, h_0, h_w, h_k) and test condition 1, it is necessary to simulate the rolling-down process [15].

When simulating the movement of the cut, projections of both accelerating and retarding forces on the rolling-down axle are taken into account. Axles of wheelsets are taken as application points of forces in the cut. In order to calculate car-to-car connections, all specific forces should be considered from car to car. Thus, when each car enters a particular section of the hump, several types of forces are applicable to this car. These include the specific driving force (f), the net specific resistance (w_o), resistance from switches and curves (w_{sc}), resistance from the environment and wind (w_{ew}), snow and frost (w_{sf}), and retarder positions (w_{ret}).

Cars with uniformly distributed axle load are used for simulation. A point of separation of the cut from the approaching train is assumed to be a section of the moving part of the hump, which fulfills the following condition:

$$v_{cut} > v_{train}, \tag{6}$$

where v_{cut} is the running speed of the cut, m/s; v_{train} is the running speed of the approaching train, m/s.

In addition, the working zone of a yard conductor (uncoupling device) is taken into account, since the cut cannot be separated before the beginning of the uncoupling zone. The calculations were performed using the Skat-Otsep software package [15].

Experimental data and results

The object of the study is a real high-capacity hump yard, parameters of the layout and longitudinal section, and the power of retarding facilities that are used in the simulation.

Initially, the authors conduced a number of experiments to calculate the minimum required power of retarder positions, depending on the number of cars in a cut (Fig. 1). The minimum required power should be sufficient to stop a cut of loaded cars at the exit from the yard retarder. The calculation was performed for favorable rolling-down conditions:

– rolling-down route: "easy" track of a hump neck;
– maximum shunting speed: 2.5 m/s;
– the cut consists of full-weight loaded cars;
– climatic conditions: favorable;
– utilization factor of retarder positions: assumed to be 0.67 in accordance with the applicable guidelines [1].

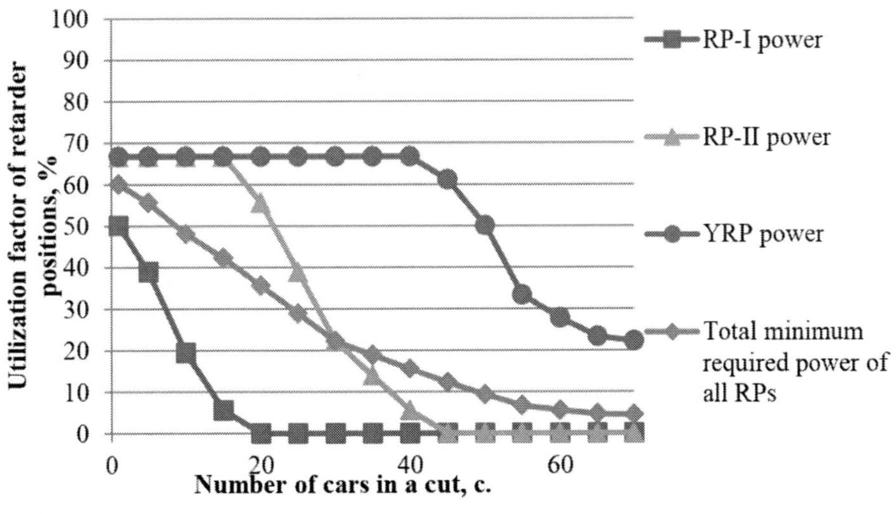

Fig. 1. Dependence of the required power of hump retarders on the number of cars in a cut.

The results of the experiment show that the required power level of retarder positions decreases with an increase in the number of cars in a cut. This effect can be attributed to a distribution pattern of cut weight in the vertical plane: the conditional center of mass of the entire cut decreases relative to the hump crest with an increase in the number of cars in the cut (Fig. 2). Therefore, the total specific energy stored by the cut decreases with an increase in the number of cars.

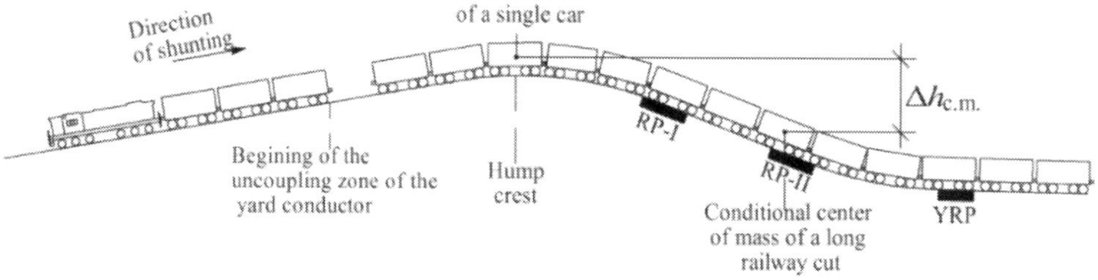

Fig. 2. Schematic diagram for determining the conditional center of mass of the cut with several cars.

At the second stage, the authors conducted experiments by rolling down cuts of empty cars with the worst running properties. Cuts were rolled down without retardation. During the simulation, the exit speed of the cut from the yard retarder position (v_{exit}) and the probability that the cut will overcome the yard retarder position (P_{exit}) were determined (Table 1). The experiments were performed for the following conditions:

– rolling-down route: "difficult" track of a hump neck;
– climatic conditions: severe;
– net specific resistance to the movement of a single very bad runner: 4.5 N/kN;
– the net specific resistance to the movement of a single-car cut is assumed to be moderate for the lightweight category (1.75 N/kN);
– the net specific resistance to the movement of a multi-car cut is derived from the distribution law of a random variable for cars of the lightweight category [2];
– the probability (P_{exit}) that the last car in the cut will overcome the yard retarder position is determined by repeated simulation of the rolling-down process for various multi-car cuts of the lightweight category with a specified length;
– the average exit speed from the yard retarder position is determined by simulating the rolling-down process for various multi-car cuts of the lightweight category, unless the cuts fail to reach a target point.

The values in Table 1 suggest that the probability that the cut of cars will overcome the yard retarder position in a given hump (P_{exit}) begins to decrease for cuts with 40 cars and more. Therefore, cuts with more than 40 cars is subject to risk of being stopped on the decreasing part of the hump. This may interrupt hump yard operations and increase the probability of incidents, including collisions between cars at high speeds.

Table 1. The average exit speed of empty cars from the yard retarder position, rolling down without retardation.

v_{shunt}, m/s	Number of cars in a cut											
	A very bad runner		1		30		40		50		60	
	P_{exit}	v_{exit}, m/s	P_{exit}	v_{exit}, m/s	P_{exit}	v_{exit}, m/s	P_{exit}	v_{exit}, m/s	P_{exit}	v_{exit}, m/s	P_{exit}	v_{exit}, m/s
1.0	1.00	1.79	1.00	4.30	1.00	2.61	0.98	1.30	0.09	0.58	0.00	-
1.5	1.00	1.90	1.00	4.35	1.00	2.70	1.00	1.48	0.26	0.59	0.00	-
2.0	1.00	2.05	1.00	4.42	1.00	2.89	1.00	1.84	0.71	0.87	0.00	-
2.5	1.00	2.23	1.00	4.53	1.00	3.09	1.00	2.17	0.98	1.26	0.25	0.64

Table 2 shows the results of similar experiments for cuts of loaded cars. The calculation is based on the same conditions with the following exceptions:

– the net specific resistance to the movement of a single very good runner is assumed to be minimum for the heavyweight category of cars (0.5 N/kN);

– the net specific resistance to the movement of a single-car cut is assumed to be moderate for the heavyweight category of cars (1.25 N/kN);

– the net specific resistance to the movement of a multi-car cut is derived from the distribution law of a random variable for cars of the heavyweight category [2];

– the probability that the last car in the cut overcomes the yard retarder position is determined by repeated simulation of the rolling-down process for various multi-car cuts of the heavyweight category with a specified length;

– the average exit speed from the yard retarder position is determined by simulating the rolling-down process for various multi-car cuts of the heavyweight category, unless the cuts fail to reach a target point.

Table 2. The average exit speed of loaded cars from the yard retarder position, without retarding at all retarder positions.

v_{shunt}, m/s	Number of cars in a cut											
	A very good runner		1		30		40		50		60	
	P_{exit}	v_{exit}, m/s	P_{exit}	v_{exit}, m/s	P_{exit}	v_{exit}, m/s	P_{exit}	v_{exit}, m/s	P_{exit}	v_{exit}, m/s	P_{exit}	v_{exit}, m/s
1.0	1.00	7.35	1.00	6.93	1.00	4.80	1.00	4.09	1.00	3.56	1.00	3.11
1.5	1.00	7.38	1.00	6.99	1.00	4.89	1.00	4.20	1.00	3.68	1.00	3.27
2.0	1.00	7.46	1.00	7.09	1.00	5.02	1.00	4.37	1.00	3.87	1.00	3.48
2.5	1.00	7.55	1.00	7.16	1.00	5.17	1.00	4.55	1.00	4.08	1.00	3.72

The data in Table 2 suggest that cuts of loaded cars are not subject to any limitation in terms of the number of cars. Therefore, shunting of multi-car loaded cuts can be performed without limiting the number of cars in a cut.

Conclusion

This paper proposes a new method for calculating the maximum number of cars in a cut based on probability calculations and simulation modeling of the shunting process in hump yards. The findings show that the maximum number of cars in a cut depends on the longitudinal section and equipment of a hump yard, as well as on climatic conditions of the area where it is located. In this case, shunting of loaded multi-car cuts to a clear classification track is not subject to any restriction on length of a cut.

It has been established that the permissible number of cars in a cut can be limited by the total kinetic energy stored by an empty multi-car cut, rather than by the required power level of hump retarders. Therefore, in addition to checking the power of hump retarders, it is necessary to check rolling down of cuts with empty cars to the classification yard (outside the yard retarder position). The proposed method of calculation is more advanced than the method currently used on the railways of the Russian Federation and a number of other countries. By using the proposed method, it is possible to increase or even remove the restriction on the maximum number of cars in a cut, which should be calculated for each specific hump yard.

References

1. Instrukcija po raschetu maksimal'no dopustimoj dliny otcepa pri rospuske na sortirovochnyh gorkah [Instructions on calculating the maximum allowable length of the uncoupling by disbanding on the hump yards] (Moscow, 2012). (in Russian)
2. Pravila i normy proektirovanija sortirovochnyh ustrojstv na zheleznyh dorogah kolei 1520 mm [Rules and design standards for assorting works on railways with track 1520 mm] (Tehinform, Moscow, 2003). (in Russian)
3. M. Kutz, *Handbook of transportation engineering* (McGraw-Hill Professional, Boston, 2004).
4. E.R. Kraft, Journal of Transportation Research Forum, **Vol. 39** (4), 95–115 (2000).
5. H. Khadilkar, S.K. Sinha, Proceedings of the International Conference on Industrial Engineering and Engineering Management, 1151–1155 (IEEE, Bali, 2016).
6. K. Kube, Progressive Railroading, **7**, 50–52 (2002).
7. P. Logan, *Role of Yard or Terminal in Operating Performance and Capacity* (Transportation Research Board, Washington D.C., 2006).
8. J. Prokop, Sh. Myojin, Memoirs of the Faculty of Engineering, **Vol. 27**, 41–58 (1993).
9. G. Ribeill, La Vie du Rail, **3529,** 13–25 (2015).
10. J.T. Haahr, R.M. Lusby, Networks, **Vol. 67** (2), 126–138 (2016).
11. J.T. Haahr, R.M. Lusby, *A Matheuristic Approach for Solving the Railroad Hump Yard Block-to-Track Assignment* (DTU Management Engineering, 2015).
12. Z. Wang, A. Ceder, Journal of the Operational Research Society, **1**, 1600-1619 (2017).
13. M. Rhodes, *German Marshalling Yard Directory* (Blurb, Incorporated, 2016).
14. A.A. Gunbin, The Siberian Transport University Bulletin, **1** (44), 5–14 (2018). (in Russian)
15. A.A. Klimov, A.A. Gunbin, Scientific problems of transportation in Siberia and the Far East, **2**, 88–91 (2011). (in Russian)
16. S.A. Bessonenko, Doctoral thesis, Moscow State University of Railway Engineering, Moscow, 2011. (in Russian)
17. V.I. Bobrovskiy, D.N. Kozachenko, *Sbornik nauchyh trudov GETUT* [Collection of scientific papers of Kyiv University of Economics and Transport Technologies], **Vol. 16,** 20–29 (2010). (in Ukraine)
18. V.I. Bobrovskiy, D.N. Kozachenko, N.P. Bozhko, N.V. Rogov, N.I. Berezovy, A.V. Kudryashov, *Optimizacija rezhimov tormozhenija otcepov na sortirovochnyh gorkah* [Optimization of uncoupling braking modes on the hump yard] (Makoveckiy Pabl., Dnepropetrovsk, 2010). (in Ukraine)

Effect of the sorting track profile change on the it's occupancy quality at train humping

Konstantin Kornienko[1,*], and *Sergei* Bessonenko[1]

[1]Siberian Transport University, 630049 Novosibirsk, Russia

Abstract. To increase the hump yard capacity, it is necessary to ensure high quality of sorting track occupancy. The purpose of this paper is to study the effect of changing the track profile on the quality of its occupancy. The simulation model developed for occupancy of sorting tracks based on the calculation of the speed of the cut and taking the following into consideration was used for the study: the possibility of starting the cut movement after a stop, errors in operation of the devices in charge of the speed of releasing the cut to the track, the possibility of displacement of the cars when the next cut collides with them. A real profile of the sorting facility track was analyzed as an example of it. It was determined that the profile caused strong effect on the track occupancy quality. The sagging of the profile causes an increase in the probability of collision of the cuts with exceeding the permissible speed. An increase in the up-gradient reduces the range of the run-off distance, which in turn causes an increase in the number of car back-ins. Profile correction will allow increasing the track occupancy quality.

Introduction

Hump yards are one of the most important elements of the transport network, therefore, upgrading of the humps is viewed as one of the main goals of transport development in Russia [1] and in Western Europe [2-5]. This is due to the fact that most of the time required for delivery of goods falls on shunting operations performed at hump yards [6-8]. To reduce this time, it is necessary to increase the hump yard capacity. However, the capacity in the Russian Federation is already 4-5 times higher than in the countries of Western Europe and America [9], so further increase in capacity is possible by increasing the humping speed, introduction of new technologies or reduction of the time spent for performing additional operations.

The third method is most economical. The time is mostly spent for backing-in cars, working with hazardous cargo [10-11], elimination of commercial defects, etc. Reduction of this time is possible with improving the sorting track occupancy quality. The following is understood within the scope of it: minimization of gaps and collision of cuts with the permissible speed [12-13].

To date, a large number of works are devoted to calculation of the sorting track as the main element in terms of quality of its occupancy. Equipping a sorting track with additional

* Corresponding author: Kkonstantini@mail.ru

© The Authors, published by EDP Sciences. This is an open access article distributed under the terms of the Creative Commons Attribution License 4.0 (http://creativecommons.org/licenses/by/4.0/).

devices is one of the most effective ways to improve the track occupancy quality [13-17]. But this method requires large capital expenses and is complicated in technical implementation and maintenance. The facility braking position also significantly affects the track occupancy quality [18-23]. Incorrect operation of the retarder causes deterioration in the track occupancy quality.

Based on the aforementioned, it can be concluded that there are currently many factors affecting the sorting track occupancy quality, but the effect of the track profile change during operation has not been fully understood. The purpose of this study is to investigate the effect of the track profile on its occupancy quality and the efficiency of profile correction.

Research methods

The simulating model of track occupancy was used for the study [24-27]. This model considers the possibility of starting the cut movement after a stop, errors in operation of the devices controlling the speed of releasing the cut to the track and operation of the retarder, the possibility of displacement of the cars when the next cut collides with them [25]. Calculation of the speed of the cuts was checked by its comparison to the actual motion speed. Distribution curves were plotted by running this model 100,000 times. The flow of cars and cuts was set with random distribution. The ambient air temperature, wind speed and direction were set for Novosibirsk region, taking into account the correction for the track. The track (Fig. 1) was reviewed within the borders from tangent retarders to insulating joints at the end of the track. The profile survey was performed each 50 meters. The rated values comply with [28-29].

The subject of the study is tracks of the sorting facility. The study object is effect of the track profile on the track occupancy quality.

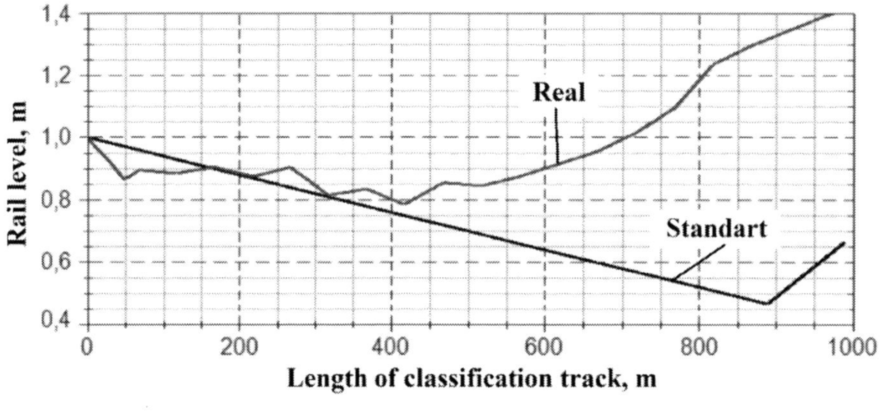

Fig. 1. Track profile of the sorting track.

Effect of the track profile on the cut stop point

One of the important parameters for traffic safety is calculation of the cut stop point at the sorting track. If this point is defined incorrectly and the next cut is released on track, there is a possibility that the cars will collide at the speed exceeding the permissible value and, consequently, damage cars or cargo. It is also important that the cut can move backwards under the action of gravity, if the cut stops at the up-gradient. The study [25] indicated that the cut full stop point must meet the following two conditions: the speed of the cut at the point is equal to zero and the displacement condition is not met including movement in the opposite direction *(not taken into consideration today).*

In addition to these factors, the track profile also affects the cut stop point, and, consequently, the track profile also affects the range of the cut run at the sorting track [24, 26]. Increase of down-gradient of the track causes an increase in the speed of the cut movement, which causes an increase in the probability of car collision with the increased speed. Increase of the length and steepness of the up-gradient affects the distance of the cut run, since it lowers the cut speed and increases the probability of the cut moving backwards, towards the hump top, and, consequently, increases the gaps, which increases number of backing-out and increases the hump interval, which reduces the hump yard capacity.

Imitation simulation of cut movement on the standard and real profile was performed on the basis of Figure 1. Figure 2 shows distribution curves of the probability of cuts stopping depending on the distance traveled.

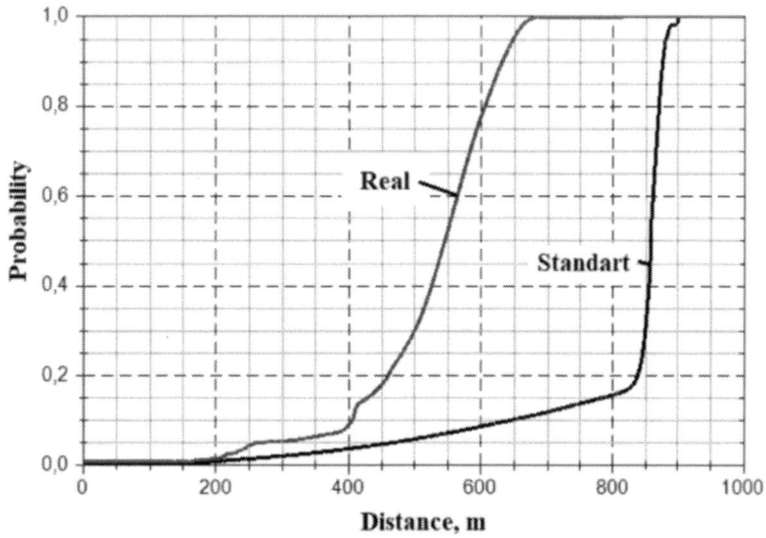

Fig. 2. Distribution of the probability of cars stopping on the track.

The following conclusions can be made on the basis of Figure 2:

- profile changes affects the cut run distance significantly;
- the average cut run range for the standard profile is 813 m with standard deviation of 137 m;
- the average distance for the real profile is 524 m with the real of 106 m, therefore, the run distance has been reduced by 289 meters due to the change in the up-gradient.
- None of the cuts released on track with the standard profile has overcome the distance of 840 meters. According to the rules, there is an up-gradient at the end of the track, due to which the cuts roll back. The useful track length is reduced due to this up-gradient, therefore, it is necessary to develop other stop devices at the end of the track to increase the useful track length.

Effect of the profile on the track occupancy quality

In connection with displacement of the cut stop point, it can be assumed that the track occupancy level will be below the permissible value. The track occupancy level can be presented with the following formula [30]:

$$K^{i}_{OCC} = \frac{N^{i}_{CAR} * L_{CAR}}{L^{i}_{TRACK}} \quad (1)$$

where N^{i}_{CAR} is the number of cars released on track, pcs;

L_{CAR} – conditional car length, 14 m;

L^{i}_{TRACK} – length of the free zone of the sorting track after backing-out, m.

Imitation simulation of the track occupancy with cuts of various length and weight in various conditions was performed for the profile. Results of this simulation, and, in particular, distribution curves of the track occupancy quality for the standard and real profile are presented in Figure 2. This Figure also shows distribution of the track occupancy quality when humping to the free track. Table 1 shows results of the experiment.

Table 1. Experimental results.

Study parameter	Rated profile	Actual profile
Average track quality level	0.8724	0.5775
Average track level coefficient for a free track	0.8637	0.3388
Average number of backing-outs for accumulation of one train	2.32	4.263
Possibility of reverse movement of the cut	0.079	0.314
Possibility of collision of cuts with exceeding of the collision speed	0.016	0.039

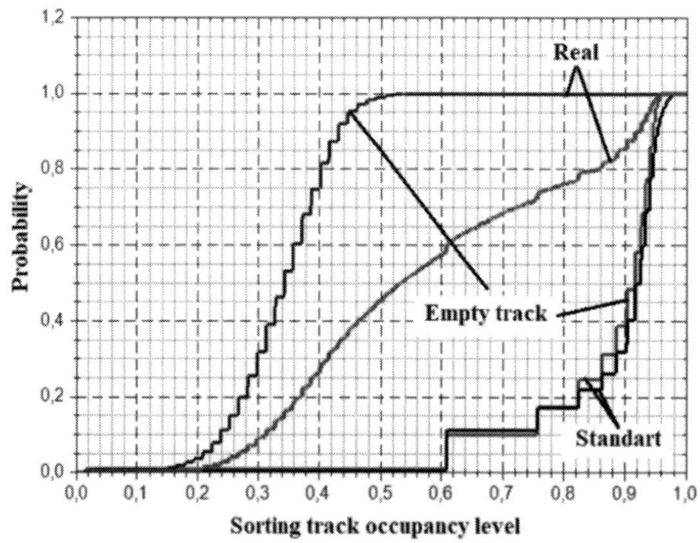

Fig. 3. Track occupancy level distribution.

The following conclusions can be made on the basis of Table 1 and Figure 3:

- The profile change affects the sorting track occupancy level.
- Experimental results confirm the conclusion that the track occupancy quality for the first breaking up of the train on the free track will be below the permissible value due to the displacement of average cut stop point.
- The average track occupancy level when breaking up to the free track for the real profile is 3 times less than for the standard profile. This means that the standard profile accumulates on an average 36 cars more before the first backing-out.
- [30] indicates that the track occupancy level must be within 0.8 to 1 according to the regulatory documents. This condition is satisfied in most cases for the standard profile, both during humping at the free track and in the course of accumulation of cars on the track, on which cars are already located. This condition is not met in most cases for the track with real profile. When cuts are humping to the free track, the maximum track occupancy level does not exceed 0.5. This means that almost half of the track in this case will not be used until the first backing-outs.
- The average number of backing-outs per one train at the real track is by 2 backing-outs more than the one with the standard track. It means that the train accumulation at the real profile requires double time as compared to the standard profile. This causes growth of the hump interval, and, consequently, reduction of the hump yard capacity.
- The probability of reverse movement for the real profile is three time higher than for the standard one. It means that each third cut will not reach the standing cars.
- The probability of collision with increased speed for the real profile is much higher than for the standard one.
- On the basis of the last two points, it can be concluded that the profile significantly reduced the track occupancy quality by increasing gaps and collisions with increased speed.

Conclusion

Change of down-gradient causes increase in the probability of collision with increased speed between the cut and the cars standing ahead. The change in the up-gradient is the reason for reduction in the distance of the cut run and the useful path length at the first breaking up on the free track. Moreover, after stopping on the up-gradient, the cut starts moving backwards under the effect of the gravity force. When the next cut is released to such track, collision between the cuts with increased speed may take place, unless the first cut has stopped yet. The track occupancy level is less than permissible at tracks with long up-gradient. The tendency of increasing the number of backing-outs for accumulation of one train is also observed when increasing the up-gradient length.

Analysis of real profiles of the sorting track shows that the track occupancy level on many tracks is significantly lower than permissible. This causes shortening of the time period between backing-outs, hence, increasing of the hump interval. Correction of profiles will allow increasing the track occupancy level and reducing the number of backing-outs. The issues of economic efficiency of profile correction or use of other means for increasing the hump yard capacity require further studying.

The authors would like to express their gratitude to the "Operational Work Management" and "Stations and junctions" Department of the Siberian Transport University and employees of the Insk Signaling Division for assistance in writing this article. This study was performed with support of the Novosibirsk Region Government.

References

1 Strategija razvitija holdinga RZhD na period do 2030 goda [Development strategy of the Russian Railways for the period until 2030] (16.04.2014). (in Russian)
2 D.M.Z. Islam, S. Ricci, B.L. Nelldal, Eur. Transp. Res. Rev., 8, 18 (2016).
3 P. Mortimer, D.M.Z. Islam, Eur. Transp. Res. Rev., 6, 503 (2014).
4 U. Clausen, R. Voll, Eur. Transp. Res. Rev., 5, 129 (2013).
5 N. Boysen, M. Fliendner, F. Jaehn, E. Pesch, European Journal of Operational Research, 220, 1 – 14 (2012).
6 O.P. Yugrina, Yu.A. Tanayno, Transport of the Urals, 4(51), 83-86 (2016). (in Russian)
7 V.A. Gapanovich, A.N. Shabelnikov, Zheleznodorozhnyj transport [Railway transport], 8 (2010). (in Russian)
8 O.P. Yugrina, S.Yu. Sosnin, Herald of the Ural State University of Railway Transport, 1(33), 84-90 (2017). (in Russian)
9 V.N. Sokolov, Automation, Communication and Informatics, 2 (2011). (in Russian)
10 A.M. Ostrovskiy, A.M. Lisyutin, Scientific papers SWorld, **Vol. 2**(1), 38–41 (2012). (in Russian)
11 A.F. Borodin, R.V. Ageev, A.S. Krylov, M.B. Sirotich, Zheleznodorozhnyj transport [Railway transport], 7, 20–27 (2010). (in Russian)
12 S.V. Karasev, Thesis of Candidate of technical sciences, Siberian Transport University, Novosibirsk, 2003 (in Russian)
13 S.V. Karasev, V.I. Zhukov, O.V. Kutsenko, Sovershenstvovanie ekspluatacionnoj raboty zheleznyh dorog [Improving the field operation of railways], 119–129 (Novosibirsk, 2002). (In Russian)
14 C. Zhang, Y. Wei, G. Xiao, Z. Wang, J. Fu, *Proc. of Second Intern. Conf. on Transportation and Traffic Studies*, 285-290 (2000).
15 S. Zarecky, J. Grun, J. Zilka, Transport Problems, **Vol. 3**(4), 1, 87-95 (2008).
16 V.I. Bobrovskiy, D.N. Kozachenko, N.V. Rogov, Vestnik of Dnepropetrovsk National University of Railway Transport named after V. Lazaryan, 11, 103–111 (2006).
17 D. Kozachenko, V. Bobrovskyi, Y.J. Demchenko, Mod. Transport, 1-11 (2018).
18 V.A. Kobzev, Automation, Communication and Informatics, 10, 30–33 (1996). (in Russian)
19 D.N. Kozachenko, S.V. Grevtsov, T.V. Bolvanovskaya, Vestnik of Dnepropetrovsk National University of Railway Transport named after V. Lazaryan, 4(64), 37-46 (2016).
20 V. Bobrovskyi, D. Kozachenko, A. Dorosh, E. Demchenko, T. Bolvanovska, A. Kolesnik, Transport Problems, **Vol. 11**(1), 147-155 (2016).
21 C. Worrell, Railway Age, 11, 36-28 (2015).
22 O. Bardas, I. Skovron, Y. Demchenko, A. Dorosh, S. Buriak, Transport Problems, **Vol. 12** (1), 151-158 (2017).
23 S.A. Bessonenko, Doctoral thesis, Moscow State University of Railway Engineering, Москва, 2011. (in Russian)
24 E.A. Akhmaev, S.A. Bessonenko, V.V. Borisov, K.I. Kornienko, Transport of the Urals, 4(55), 49-53 (2017). (in Russian)
25 K.I. Kornienko, Transport: Science, Equipment, Management, 11, 36–40 (2017). (in Russian)
26 E.A. Akhmaev, S.A. Bessonenko, V.V. Borisov, K.I. Kornienko, Siberian Transport University Bulletin, 1(40), 13-18 (2017). (In Russian)
27 K.I. Kornienko, Transport of the Urals, 2(57), 35-22 (2018). (in Russian)
28 Yu.A. Mukha, L.B. Tishkov, V.P. Sheykin, et al., *Posobie po primeneniju pravil i*

norm proektirovanija sortirovochnyh ustrojstv [Manual on the application of rules and norms for design of assorting works] (Transport, Moscow, 1994). (in Russian)
29 Pravila i normy proektirovanija sortirovochnyh ustrojstv na zheleznyh dorogah kolei 1520 mm [Rules and norms for the design of sorting works on railways with gauge 1520 mm] (Moscow, 2003). (in Russian)
30 A.N. Shabelnikov, V.R. Odikadze, Automation, Communication and Informatics, 3, 9-11 (2009). (in Russian)

Method for determining the acceptability of transport operations involving dangerous goods

Vladimir Medvedev[1,*], *Igor* Teslenko[1], and *Sergey* Karasev[1]

[1]Siberian Transport University, 630049 Novosibirsk, Russia

Abstract. Due to transport incidents and accidents involving dangerous goods, which cause significant damage to the infrastructure and environment, there is a need to study ways of preventing losses from these accidents and minimizing their costs. The purpose of the paper is to develop a method for determining the acceptability of transport operations involving dangerous goods under normal conditions. The methods used in the study include analysis and synthesis, risk management and Delphi methods. The key outcome of the study is a developed method founded on an integrated generalized criterion for acceptability of the main transport operations involving dangerous goods. This criterion is based on risk assessment. It has been established that the safety of transportation is determined by the maximum level of dynamic loads, impact velocity, energy absorption efficiency, braking mode of railway cars, and degree of risk.

Introduction

The development of railway transport is determined by socio-economic needs of the country. As compared to more economically developed countries, the railway transport in Russia has a number of important features, primarily in terms of technical and economic parameters. Shunting operations constitute a significant part of the lifecycle of freight services, making up 1 to 10% of the total transportation time [1]. In the existing network structure of the federal railway transport, the possibility to increase freight traffic volumes is limited by handling capacities of classification yards. This limiting factor is expressed mainly in handling of car traffic volumes in hump yards. Handling of dangerous goods is the most complicated process.

Some studies [1–4] show that the most common cause of safety violations in transportation of dangerous goods is excessive dynamic loads on rolling stock, containers, packaging, and cargoes. Breaking up trains loaded with hazardous goods in hump yards is the most critical step in transportation of dangerous goods by rail, which accounts for the greatest number of safety violations [1, 5–7].

In order to ensure trouble-free and continuous transport operations, competent authorities have established standards and conditions [8–10] to govern classification

[*] Corresponding author: MedvedevVI2017@yandex.ru

© The Authors, published by EDP Sciences. This is an open access article distributed under the terms of the Creative Commons Attribution License 4.0 (http://creativecommons.org/licenses/by/4.0/).

operations. The Russian Railways have three shunting modes: the normal mode (with a maximum impact velocity of 5 km/h [8]); with special caution (with a maximum coupling velocity of 3 km/h); passage of cars through a hump yard only with a locomotive.

In foreign countries, there are no equivalents of these three shunting modes [5, 9]. This can be explained by the fact that a number of countries (USA, Canada, Australia) use cars with high-capacity draft gears, which allow safe impacts between cars at a speed of up to 10 km/h or more [1, 3–5]. In European countries [5], car handling volumes in hump yards are low; car fleets consist of lightweight two-axle cars. Shunting operations are carried out at a low rate, while the impact velocity does not reach threshold values. The problem of safety in handling cars with dangerous goods can be fundamentally solved through comprehensive routing of car traffic. In particular, such solutions are used in Japan [4–6]. At the same time, a worldwide trend towards increasing the traffic of dangerous goods [5] by high-capacity cars dictates the need to improve transportation safety even in these countries.

The subject of this study is transportation of dangerous goods by rail. The object of the study is linear facilities of the railway network. The scientific problem raised by this paper is a feasibility study of shunting conditions for cars with dangerous goods in the hump yards that support necessary parameters, such as train handling rate and acceptable level of accident risk. Dynamic and other loads can affect the technical condition of a car and initiate dangerous properties of goods.

The purpose of this study is to develop a method for determining the acceptability of shunting operations involving dangerous goods based on a feasibility study of shunting modes. Complex risk of transport operations involving dangerous goods is used as a criterion to assess a solution to the problem defined in this paper. A science-based approach proposed by the authors is based on a comprehensive risk assessment of transportation of dangerous goods by rail, taking into account technical and technological characteristics of rolling stock and infrastructure facilities. This approach is novel: no other research team has yet defined and solved this problem in such a broad setting.

Research methods

The research stages correspond to stages of a transportation process involving dangerous goods, from loading to unloading, since the risk can be expressed at any stage of transportation. The study focused on the factors that affect the transportation safety, such as rolling stock, cargo, and transportation procedure. Using an analysis and synthesis method, the authors studied a car fleet, dangerous goods transported by cars of appropriate types, and shunting modes. The analysis and synthesis method was used to review the regulatory documents governing the transportation of dangerous goods and operating procedures of hump yards [5, 7–11] to identify specific features in handling the cars with dangerous goods. The analysis of shunting modes was based on a sample of seven main classes, ten subclasses and 3,152 types of dangerous goods. The Delphi method was used to identify possible hazards of elements in the transportation procedure for dangerous goods. Risk management methods were applied in the final research stage to develop an integrated risk assessment method. For the purposes of this study, the risk is defined in a conventional way, as a combination of the probability of a hazardous event and the severity of damage [7, 12].

Results

It has been established that special shunting modes for cars with dangerous goods in hump yards apply to special goods of various hazard classes. Shunting modes for cars with dangerous goods are summarized in Table 1.

Table 1. Structure of shunting modes for cars with dangerous goods.

Class, subclass according to GOST R57478-2017		Type of car				Unrestricted
		box car, general-purpose container		tank car, tank container		
		Prohibited	Caution	Prohibited	Caution	
Class 2, subclasses	2.1	2	61	73	0	7
	2.2	0	65	63	0	9
	2.3	24	56	52	0	14
Total for class:		26	182	187	0	30
Class 3		7	2	13	2	761
Class 4, subclasses	4.1	0	1	0	0	123
	4.2	2	0	3	0	74
	4.3	4	0	2	0	81
Total for class:		6	1	5	0	278
Class 5, subclasses	5.1	3	0	2	0	149
	5.2	152	0	10	0	0
Total for class:		155	0	12	0	149
Class 6, subclasses	6.1	7	19	3	17	570
	6.2	0	0	0	0	5
Total for class:		7	19	3	17	575
Class 8		2	1	3	0	400
Class 9		0	0	0	0	309
TOTAL		203	205	223	19	2,502
Share of goods subject to this mode, %		6.44	6.50	7.07	0.60	79.38

Thus, 20% of dangerous goods are subject to shunting restrictions, some of which are obviously excessive [3–5]. In international practice, instead of restrictions, a risk transfer method is used in the form of carrier liability insurance [9, 13]. Using the Delphi method, the authors have established that, in addition to dangerous properties of goods, such characteristics as rolling stock, technical parameters of hump yards, and a handling procedure influence the transportation safety. Types of railway cars accepted for the carriage of dangerous goods represent a wide range of vehicles [9, 11]. There is a variety of transportation options depending on types of vehicle, dangerous cargo, container and packaging (Fig. 1). Factors that affect dangerous goods can be classified into two groups:

1. depending on the level of technological development;
2. not depending on the level of technological development.

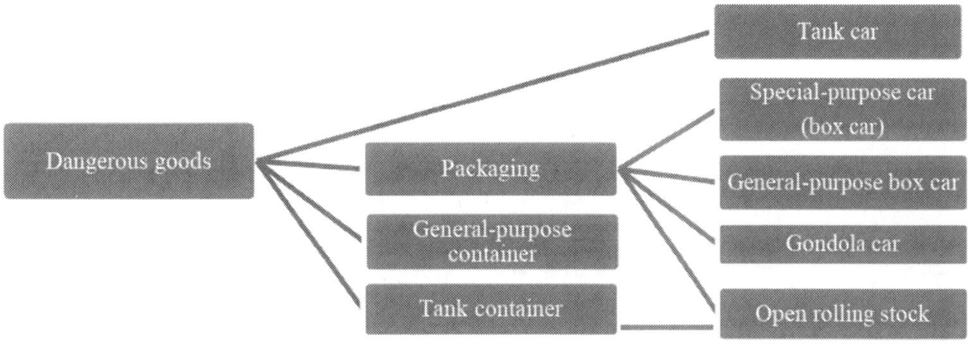

Fig. 1. Transport support options for dangerous goods.

The proposed classification of factors of the first category is presented in Figure 2.

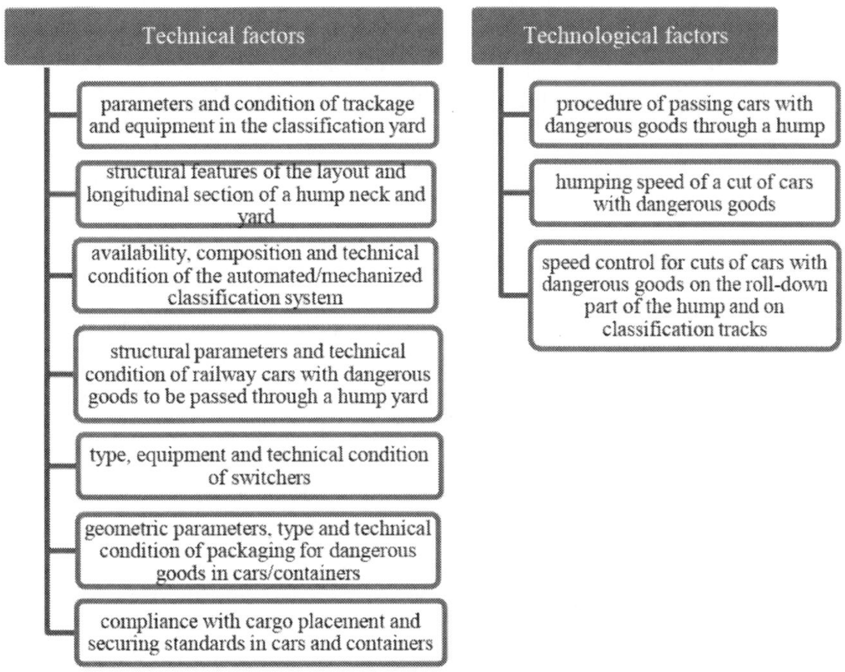

Fig. 2. Classification of technical and technological factors that determine the safe conditions for the transportation of dangerous goods.

The second category includes physicochemical (physical, chemical and hazardous properties, aggregate state of a dangerous cargo) and other factors that characterize a dangerous cargo. Other factors influencing the safety of shunting the cars with dangerous goods include parameters of the natural environment and human factor [1, 2].

All these factors have a significant influence on a combination of energy impacts that accompany the carriage of dangerous goods. Most transport operations are significantly influenced by kinetic, potential and thermal energy. Normal carriage conditions are the conditions under which a deviation in changes of all types of energy influencing transport operations does not exceed the maximum permissible levels (MPL).

$$\Delta E^{0}_{en-i} \le \Delta E_{en-i}(t) \le \Delta E^{MPL}_{en-i} , \quad (1)$$

where ΔE^{0}_{en-i} is the value of the ith type of energy in the initial condition of the transportation process (before loading into a car);

$\Delta E_{en-i}(t)$ is the change in the ith type of energy in transport operations during the entire period of (t) transportation;

ΔE^{MPL}_{en-i} is the maximum permissible levels of change in the ith type of energy.

The expression (1) corresponds to the risk management principle according to which the actual degree of risk should not exceed the permissible level [7, 12]. When implementing a sequence N of transport operations, it is obvious that the degree of level R_j $(j=\overline{1,N})$ at each jth stage should not exceed the acceptable level of risk for this stage. Taking into account that a hazardous situation may occur (regardless of a transportation stage) due to the exceeded permissible level of energy impact on a dangerous cargo, we can assume that the acceptable level of risk is equal for all stages and determined by tolerance of the maximum permissible level. Then, critical risks are those risks that correspond to the exceeded maximum permissible level. Risk management activities should be implemented for the relevant transportation stages. They should be aimed at minimizing the probability of a hazardous event and/or the severity of its consequences/damage.

During the transportation, the energy changes $\Delta E_{en-i}(t)$ in a certain time interval t_k under the influence of a short-term impact $W_i^{en}(t_k)$. In most cases, this impact is caused by technical and technological factors. The probability of changing the state in the jth stage of transportation process can be defined as:

$$P_j(t) = P_{i,j} ln \frac{W_i^{en}(t)}{W_{i,j}} , \quad (2)$$

where $P_{i,j}$ is the probability that the ith type of energy will influence the jth stage of transportation;

$W_{i,j}$ is the time of impact of the ith type of energy during the transportation of goods.

The risk of violation of safety conditions is determined by the formula:

$$R_j = Y^* \cdot P_j(t) = Y^* \cdot P_{i,j} \cdot ln \frac{W_i^{en}(t)}{W_i}, \quad (3)$$

where Y^* is the severity of the consequences of a hazardous situation/damage.

Safety targets are presented in Table 2.

Table 2. Traffic safety indicators.

Deviation indicator	Deviation from normal carriage conditions		
	incident	accident	emergency situation
Standard risk, R	10^{-5}	10^{-6}	10^{-7}
Minimum possible risk, R_{min}	10^{-4}	10^{-5}	10^{-6}

Expression (3) can be used as an integrated generalized criterion for acceptability of main transport operations involving dangerous goods. Thus, the key outcome of the study is the method that includes the following components: the integrated generalized criterion (indicator) of acceptability of the main transport operations involving dangerous goods, such as loading, shunting operations, including hump shunting, movement in the train, unloading; risk assessment for transportation of dangerous goods. This method can be used to draft a technical regulatory document to govern changes in the current rules and conditions of transportation.

Conclusion

The proposed classification of the factors that determine the safe transportation of dangerous goods can be a basis for comprehensive risk assessment. Based on the solution to the scientific problem considered in this paper, this approach can be used to take into account the influence of technical and technological factors on car handling conditions and to review hump shunting conditions for 20% of cars loaded with dangerous goods which do not pose a significant danger to personnel, infrastructure and environment. The risk assessment method is applicable not only to railway, but also to other modes of transport, as well as to multimodal transportation.

By developing engineering solutions using condition (1), research teams and manufacturing enterprises will be able to focus on the creation of effective technical and technological proposals. This approach will significantly reduce risks in transportation of dangerous goods. Adoption of the relevant amendments to the Rules for Transportation of Dangerous Goods will reduce the time of classification by 2.5–5%. Complex risks, including risks of failure on hump yards and late delivery, will be reduced.

Further research will be aimed at quantifying the risks of transport operations with all dangerous goods. As a result, science-based solutions for the Russian rail carrier, as well as carriers of the United Nations member states will be developed.

The authors are grateful to the University's administration, including Rector A.L. Manakov and Vice-Rector of Academic Affairs S.A. Bokarev, for their assistance in this research.

References

1. V.I. Medvedev, I.O. Teslenko, V. D. Sumina, Proceedings of the VIII International Scientific and Technical Conference within the Russia – EU year « Scientific problems of the implementation of transport projects in Siberia and the Far East», 263-265 (STU, Novosibirsk, 2017). (in Russian)
2. J. Forigua, L.L. Barrera, Transportation Research Procedia, **Vol. 12,** 842-850 (2016).
3. X. Liu, M.R. Saat, C.P. Barkan, Journal of Hazardous Materials, **260**,131-140 (2013).
4. M.R. Saat, C.J. Werth, D. Schaeffer, H. Yoon, C.P.L. Barkan, Journal of Hazardous Materials, **264**, 560-569 (2014).
5. ST/SG/AC.10/1 l/Rev.5. UN Recommendations on the transport of dangerous goods. Manual of Tests and Criteria (United Nations, Geneva, 2009).
6. E. Zio, T. Aven, Process Safety and Environmental Protection, **91** (2013).
7. GOST 33433-2015. Functional safety. Risk Management in Railway Transport (Standartinform, Moscow, 2016). (in Russian)
8. Pravila tehnicheskoj ekspluatacii zheleznyh dorog Rossijskoj Federacii [Rules for Technical Operation of Railways in the Russian Federation] (RZD JSC, Moscow, 2011). (in Russian)
9. ST/SG/AC.10/1/Rev. 18. UN Recommendations on the Transport of Dangerous Goods – Model Regulations (United Nations, Geneva, 2013).
10. Pravila perevozok opasnyh gruzov po zheleznym dorogam [Rules for the transportation of dangerous goods by railways (Transport, Moscow, 2009). (in Russian)

11. Tehnicheskie uslovija razmeshhenija i kreplenija gruzov v vagonah i kontejnerah [Technic specifications for the placement and fastening of goods in wagons and containers] (Transport, Moscow, 2003). (in Russian)
12. ISO/IEC 31010:2009. Ed. 1.0. Risk Management – Risk Assessment Techniques. (International Organization for Standardization, Geneva, 2009).
13. S. Dekker, E. Hollnagel, D. Woods, R. Cook, *Resilience Engineering: New directions for measuring and maintaining safety in complex systems*. Final Report (Lund University School of Aviation, 2008).

Terminalistics as the methodology of integrated assessment of transportation and warehousing systems

Oksana Pokrovskaya[1,*]

[1]Siberian Transport University, 630049 Novosibirsk, Russia

Abstract. The increasing integrated nature of logistics systems services and their role in global chains increases the relevance of the development of a multifactorial methodology for the evaluation of transport-warehouse systems. The study is aimed at development of the methodology of the multidisciplinary study of the terminal and warehousing infrastructure (the author's name is "terminalistics"). Approaches of logistics, transport geography and operation of transportation nodes were used when developing the concept of the methodology. The theory of decision making and the systems theory was used to develop standardized indicators. Programming was used for automatation of decision making. A system of indicators was proposed for comprehensive assessment of operation of transportation and warehousing systems. The characteristics of the new integrated section of the transportation and logistics science was given. A system of logistic normalization of logistics facilities activities was described. Some graphical dependencies based on the proposed indicators were obtained by calculation in real conditions.

1. Introduction

At least 5 thousand logistics facilities of various types, which provide a wide range of terminal and logistics services, are working in the Russian railway network today. In 2017, the share of such services in the Russian Railways holding portfolio was 20%. With that, operation of logistics facilities is not systematically regulated or normalized, which complicates monitoring of the logistics chain. On the one hand, the Russian Railways holding company allocates two separate divisions for transportation management and the terminal and warehousing complex management. On the other hand, it performs integrated transportation and logistics services for customers. When Russian Railways is transformed from a transportation and infrastructure company to a logistics company, elimination of this contradiction acquires special urgency for research and practice. The situation is complicated by the need to solve a number of diverse tasks on integrated design, audit and regulation of logistics facilities in the aggregate. The complexity of creation of such integrated approach is associated with the following: 1) the multidimensional essence of the logistics facility as an integrated transportation and warehousing system; 2) a

* Corresponding author: insight1986@inbox.ru

© The Authors, published by EDP Sciences. This is an open access article distributed under the terms of the Creative Commons Attribution License 4.0 (http://creativecommons.org/licenses/by/4.0/).

multifunctional role in the logistics chain; 3) the variety of types of such facility and formats of their businesses.

Most modern scientists [1-16] consider facilities of the terminal and warehousing infrastructure only in certain aspects/perspectives: as transportation nodes [1, 3, 9] or as warehouse distribution systems [2, 4, 5, 7, 9, 10], or as spatial logistic entities [6, 13, 14], but not as transportation and warehousing systems. Besides, the following separate groups of tasks are resolved in analyzed studies [1-16]: designing [1, 3, 4, 6, 11, 16], integration with global transport systems and corridors [2, 5, 8, 9, 10], economic and spatial development [12, 13, 14], etc. However, the issue of developing a methodology for integrated assessment of transportation and warehousing systems remains open taking into consideration these tasks. It is possible to solve these problems within the scope of the integrated applied methodology, in the field of study of which there would be logistic facilities of all formats. This will allow considering all aspects of operation and various forms of such facilities, which will increase the efficiency of their design and management.

The study objective is to develop a new methodology for studying and evaluating complex logistics facilities. The research novelty of the study consists in the following: separation of an independent interdisciplinary section from the overall logistics structure; development of a system of indicators for logistic normalization of transportation and warehousing systems operation normalization parameters.

2. Study methodology

A new interdisciplinary methodology for integrated study and evaluation of transportation and warehousing systems will be called "terminalistics" [17-19]. It includes tools and methods of such related scientific disciplines as logistics, regional and sector economy, transport geography, design and operation of cargo terminals and transport hubs. One of the applied tools of terminalistics methodology is the system of logistic rationing of the terminal and warehousing infrastructure.

2.1. Terminalistics methodology characteristics

The name of the methodology is associated with its purpose. The scope of research in terminalistics is interlinking the issues of transportation arrangement and operation of terminal and warehousing infrastructure facilities (warehouses, cargo terminals and other logistics facilities) using methods and tools of the transportation, economic and logistic science.

Terminalistics is logistics of terminal networks and terminal and warehousing infrastructure. Terminalistics can be considered as a methodology for comprehensive assessment of the parameters of the terminal and warehousing infrastructure. The integrated nature of the assessment consists in solving the problems of determining the number and dislocations of the terminal network nodes, their composition, their stages of development and functions, taking into consideration the flow processes of transportation, technological and economic origin and the associated multiplicative effect. The word formation logics is integration of the notions of "terminal" + "logistics" = "terminalistics". Let us introduce the terms used in this methodology.

Logistic facilities (LF) is a type of transportation and warehousing systems (TWS), which physically render transportation and warehousing services to customers and are geographically concentrated in one area.

The logistic normalization system (LNS) is a new system of indicators (some of them are introduced for the first time) to assess the key parameters of functioning and development of terminal and warehousing infrastructure of railway transport.

Let us show the interdisciplinary connections of terminalistics and basic composition of its methodological foundations. First of all, terminalistics is conceptually close to the theory of logistics, and is its independent branch. However, unlike logistics, which considers all types of flows as its object, regardless of their origin in the delivery chain, terminology restricts the study object only to the flows generated and transformed in the logistics infrastructure. Besides, terminalistics develops and supplements O.B. Malikov's warehousing systems theory. This is to expand the scope of research not only by rational designing of transportation and warehousing systems, but also by solving complex audit tasks and rationing of such systems. As a methodology, terminalistics is close to foreign studies on Rodrigue [14], Nottebum [13] – "transportation geography". At the same time, terminalistics is not limited to configuration of transportation and logistics systems from the standpoint of logistics and geography. Terminalistics is aimed at the set of solvable tasks of designing and evaluating various TWSs using transport, economic and logistic theories.

The issue of comprehensive assessment of transportation and warehousing systems as the basis for the logistics infrastructure has not been sufficiently studied in Russia. This is largely due to inadequate development of the domestic logistics infrastructure, the scarcity of Grade A quality warehousing facilities as well as relatively young age of the logistics concept in Russia. The issues of formation of transport and logistics systems are reflected in the works of [6-15] and other authors.

The methodological basis of terminalistics is based on the works of scientists in the field of logistics, economics and design of transport nodes [1, 2, 4, 11, 14, 16]. The position of terminalistics is interdisciplinary. This means that it is not located above or below the existing theories, but in the position associating them with a single area of effective design, research and operation of TWSs. On the one hand, such position of terminalistics is auxiliary, since it allows linking and concentrating various areas of scientific knowledge in the complex TWS study. On the other hand, it is independent, as it formulates a new set of tasks, proposes new means and methods for obtaining logistical solutions. See other detailed information on the methodology of terminalistics in the author's earlier works [17-18].

2.2. Characteristics of the logistics normalization methodology

LNS is a system of parameters for integrated assessment of parameters and setting the reasonable norms of parameters for design and operation of the LNS. Methods of logistics, economics, planning of operational work of railway transport are used in the LNS logistics normalization system. Besides, the LNS integrates transportation, operational, logistical and economic indicators of the TWS functioning. LNS takes into consideration the logistic work not previously displayed in the statistics of railway transport in the terminal and warehousing servicing of cargo transportation. In particular, there are no parameters and tools useful for logistical audit of TWSs. For example, it is provided for assessment from the perspective of the client orientation and the economic efficiency of operation of LFs and TWSs; their structure and complexity; integrated nature of logistics operations with cargo units (and, consequently, appreciation of the value added for the end customer); configuration of terminal networks and dislocation of LFs in them. Certain parameters offered by the author are characterized in Table 1.

Table 1. Characteristics of Certain Parameters Offered in the LNS.

Parameter and its value	Description	Purpose	Decision-maker	Taking the decision
Logistic work, in ton-operations/day.	The number of individual logistics operations performed by LFs for 1 ton of the i-th cargo per a unit of time.	It displays the range of operations with 1 ton of cargo not only in the process of transshipment, but during the entire term of keeping of the cargo in the TWS, including operations of added value.	LF and/or TWS owner.	The parameter is normalized according to the planned handling indicators. The higher the value of the parameter, the more efficient it is from the qualitative perspective of the LF.
The LF logistic utility factor is dimensionless.	The ratio of the total value of goods processed at the LF to the change in their added value, taking into consideration the number of logistical operations performed independently by the LF per a unit of cargo.	It reflects the ability of the LF to render complex logistics services for cargo flows independently and completely.	LF and/or TWS owner, client.	The parameter is normalized according to the planned handling indicators. The higher is the value of the parameter, the more useful is logistic work.
Logistical rating of the network section, thousand rubles*LF	The ratio of the total volume of basic and additional logistics services to logistics utility taking into consideration the integrated nature of the service on the LFs (the ratio of the volume of the extended (complex) logistics services to the total volume, taking into consideration their combinations).	It shows the availability of high-quality logistic customer services of the certain economic and geographical area, in which the section of the common railways network under consideration is located.	LF and/or TWS owner, regional authority.	The parameter is maximized. The higher is the value of the parameter, the higher is the supply of high-quality logistics services to customers of this economic and geographical area.
Client service efficiency indicator, in ton-operations per client.	The ratio of the volume of LF cargo handling taking into consideration the logistic utility ratio, the volume of logistics operations taking into consideration the integrated nature of the service and logistical independence of the LFs.	It displays the integrated nature of the transportation and logistical services rendered to a certain client with the LFs.	Investor, client.	The parameter is maximized. The higher is the value of the parameter, the higher is the integrated nature of the services offered to an individual client as a single whole package and without intermediaries
The parameter of availability of transportation and logistical services in the region, in qualitative LFs (units).	The ratio between the parameter of quality of terminal and warehousing services to the number of LFs of Russian Railways JSC within the total number of LFs in the region.	It displays the average weighted share of qualitative areas of LFs in the region (international class A and A+) in the total value of all LFs in the region.	Investor, railway carrier, regional authority	The parameter is maximized. The higher is the value of the parameter, the less is the number of railway LFs required for servicing this region.

The object of the LNS is the totality of economic, logistical and operational (technical and technological) parameters of the terminal and warehousing infrastructure, which determine its state and development. LNS distinctive features: integrated, logistic and client-oriented standardization of TWS parameters. The LNS implements the following management functions: planning, accounting, monitoring, analysis, and assessment of the TWS operations. The known TWS parameters only display the perfection of design solutions and the technology of cargo processing. These indicators are only economic (accounting for operational or investment costs, etc.) or only technical (internal zoning, calculation of freight fronts, etc.). However, they do not reflect the interests of other participants of the delivery system (clients, warehouse tenants) and do not assess the increase in the added value of goods, LF dislocations, the integrated nature of servicing, usefulness of logistics operations, etc.

The LNS objective is synthesis of client oriented tools and interlinking them with the technical regulations of railway transportation. The practical purpose is development of applied tools for rationing, control, analysis and audit of LFs and TWSs in general. Logistic norms are suggested to determine the parameters for establishing and maintaining the required level of transportation and logistics services. The calculation capacity of the LNS is the mathematical support of terminalistics. There are totally 85 parameters to be calculated within the scope of the LNS, including 41 author's parameters. See other issues of application of the LNS methodology, its composition and the methods of decision taking in the author's earlier work [19].

3. Experimental data and results

The composition of theoretical foundations of the terminology was considered in the course of this work (Fig. 1). The composition of LNS parameters was also considered (Fig.2). The methodology of terminalistics was tested in real conditions (Novosibirsk region, Russia).

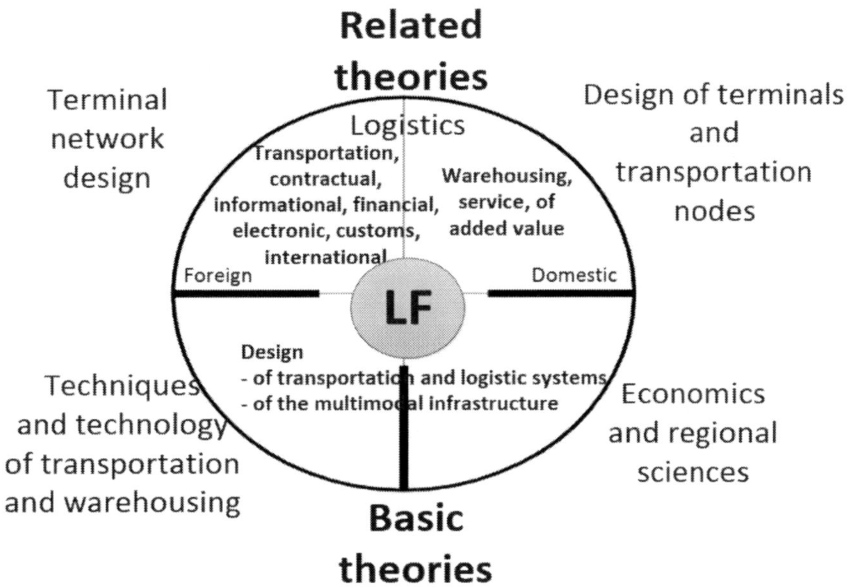

Fig. 1. Study object of terminalistics.

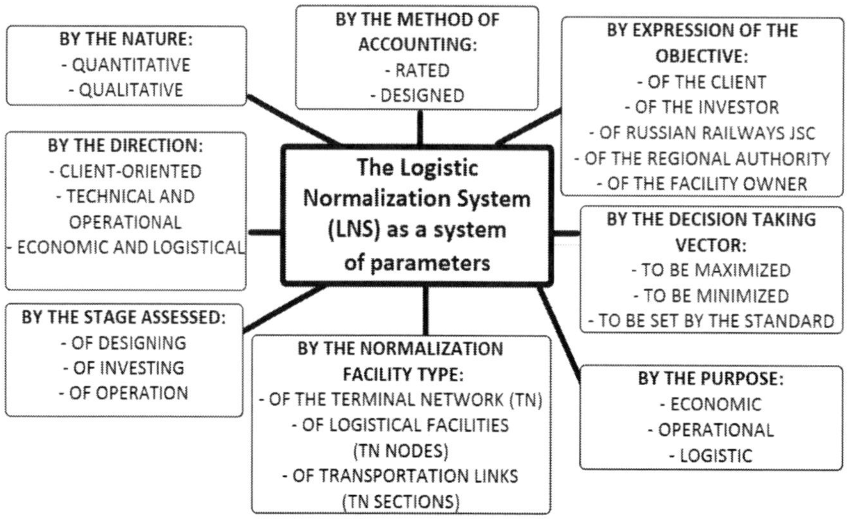

Fig. 2. LNS parameters composition.

Graphical dependencies on a number of LNS parameters were built in accordance with the calculations: dependency of the logistic utility coefficient of the LF on the LF capacity (Fig. 3); dependency of availability of transportation and logistic services in the region on the quality of logistic services (Fig. 4); dependency of the potential number of LFs on the logistics rating of the railway network section (Fig. 5); dependency of the logistic utility coefficient of the LF on the total cost of cargo processed (Fig. 6); dependency of the prospective capacity of the terminal network on the number of stations in the node (Fig. 7); dependency of the LF service integration coefficient on the coefficient of combining the logistics operations (Fig. 8). The values and dependencies comply with the trends of the Russian market, which allows considerating the results valid.

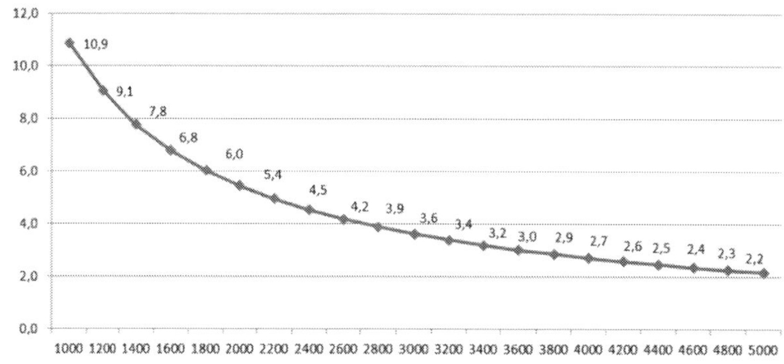

Fig. 3. Dependency of the logistic utility coefficient of the LF, LOG*, on the LF capacity.

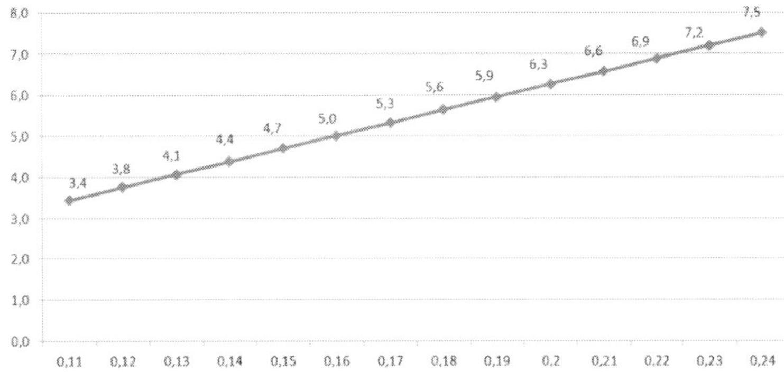

Fig. 4. Dependency of availability of transportation and logistic services in the region, Ktla*, on the quality of logistic services.

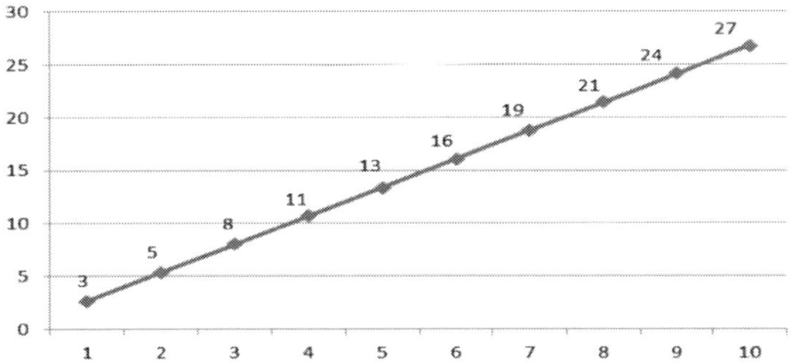

Fig. 5. Dependency of the potential number of LFs, Plf*, on the logistics rating of the railway network section.

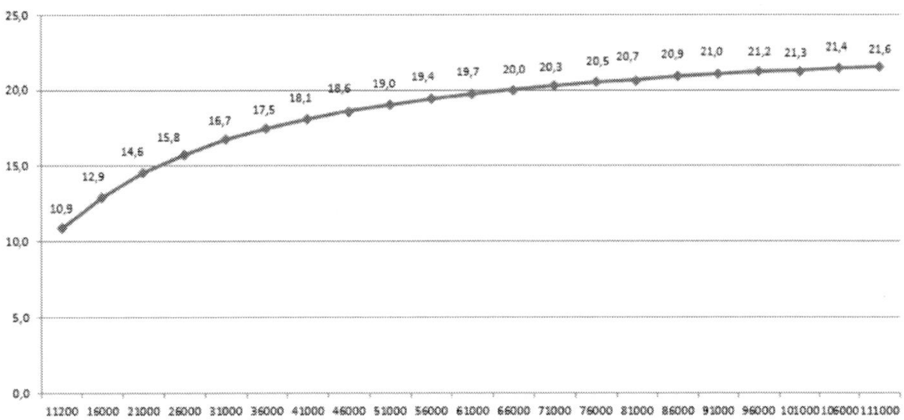

Fig. 6. Dependency of the logistic utility coefficient of the LF, LOG*, on the total cost of cargo processed.

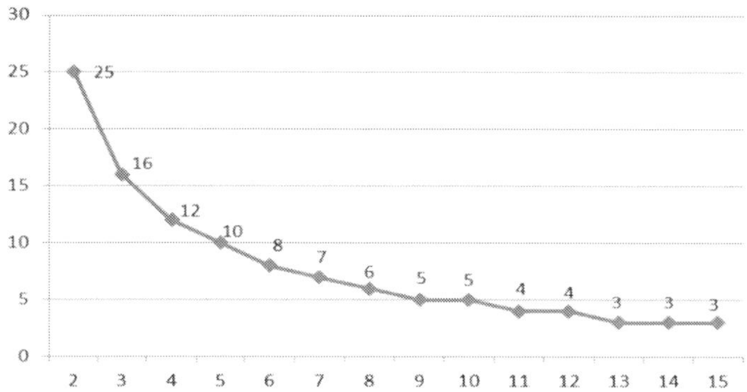

Fig. 7. Dependency of the prospective capacity of the terminal network on the number of stations in the node.

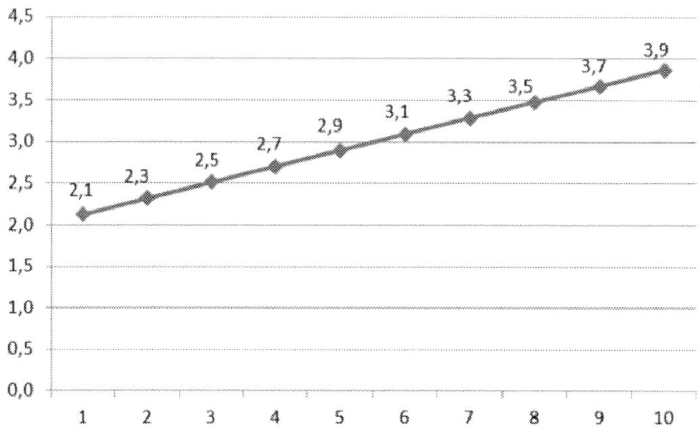

Fig. 8. Dependency of the LF service integration coefficient on the coefficient of combining the logistics operations.

* along the vertical axis

Conclusion

The study objective was achieved, in particular, the methodology of terminalistics and the system of logistic parameters was proposed. In future, it is possible to expand the scope of the terminalistics problematic fields by incorporating new research disciplines into it and applying innovative methods to solve a variety of design and assessment problems. The study results may be applied for the following: 1) LF identification taking into consideration the design, type of storage, dimensions, technical equipment, etc.; 2) LF selection taking into consideration its functional capabilities, etc.; 3) appraisal of construction and reconstruction projects for railway terminal and warehousing infrastructure; 4) assessment of logistics activities; 5) supervising and audit of TWSs; 6) designing LF with optimal parameters; 8) planning operation of railway transport, which will ensure the growth of revenues gained from logistic activities.

The study is performed within the scope of the Russian Railways JSC grant for development of research and pedagogical schools in the field of railway transport (see minutes No.36 of 07.09.2017, approved by President of Russian Railways JSC O.V. Belozerov on 11.10.2017).

References

1. O.B. Malikov, *Kontejnernye terminaly: ustrojstvo, oborudovanie, proektirovanie, issledovanija* [Container terminals: arrangement, equipment, design, research (Lambert Academic Publishing, Saarbruecken, 2014) (in Russian).
2. S.M. Rezer, *Mezhdunarodnye transportnye koridory: problemy formirovanija i razvitija* [International Transport Corridors: Problems of Formation and Development] (Moscow, 2014) (in Russian).
3. O.N. Chislov, V.V. Trapenov, Vestnik RGUPS, **1(61)**, 87-97 (2016) (in Russian).
4. V. Dybskaya, P. Sverchkov, Transport and Telecommunication, **Vol. 18(3)** (2017) (in Russian).
5. T.A. Prokofyeva, V.I. Sergeev, *Perspektivy razvitija logistiki i upravlenija cepjami postavok* [Prospects for the logistics development and supply chain management] **1**, VII th International scientific conference, Moscow, 2017, (2017) (in Russian).
6. D.J. Bowersox, D.J. Closs, *Logistical Management: The Integrated Supply Chain Process* (Olimp-Biznes, Moscow, 2017) (in Russian).
7. I. Fechner, *LogForum,* **Vol. 6,** Issue 2(2) (2010).
8. C.D. Higgins, M.R. Ferguson, *An Exploration of the Freight Village Concept and its Applicability to Ontario* (McMaster University, Hamilton, 2011).
9. M. Leenders, F. Johnson, A. Flynn, H. Fearon, *Purchasing & Supply Management: With 50 Supply Chain Cases* (Moscow, 2014) (in Russian).
10. Y. Zhang, S. Wen, *ICETMS 2013* **1**, *I th International conference on Educational Technology and Management Science,* Nanjing, Jiangsu, 2013 (2013).
11. D. Middendorf, *Intermodal Terminals Database: Concepts, Design, Implementation, and Maintenance* (Bureau of Transportation Statistics U.S. Department of Transportation, Washington DC, 1998).
12. A. Musso, *Progetto di Terminali ed Impianti di Trasporto,* Chapter 2 (Sapienza Università di Roma, Rome, 2010).
13. L.C. Nguyen, T. Notteboom, World Review of Intermodal Transportation Research, **Vol. 6 (3)**, 229-250 (2017).
14. J.-P. Rodrigue, *The Geography of Transport Systems*, 4th Ed. (Routledge, London, 2017).
15. A. Rushton, Ph. Croucher, P. Baker, *The Handbook of Logistics and Distribution Management* (Kogan Page Publishers, London, 2014).
16. N.V. Pravdin, S.P. Vakulenko, A.K. Golovnich, *Proektirovanie infrastruktury zheleznodorozhnogo transporta* [Design of railway transport infrastructure] (Marshrut, Moscow, 2014) (in Russian).
17. O.D. Pokrovskaya, V.M. Samuylov, Innotrans Journal, **4 (18)**, 13-24 (2015) (in Russian).
18. O.D. Pokrovskaya, *Logisticheskoe rukovodstvo* [Logistics Guide] (Buk, Kazan, 2017) (in Russian).
19. O.D. Pokrovskaya, Italian Science Review, **1(34)**, 112-115 (2016).

Assessment criteria for decisions in the field of rail freight transportation

Iuliia Tanaino[1,*], *Olga* Yugrina[1], and *Larisa* Zharikova[1]

[1]Siberian Transport University, 630049 Novosibirsk, Russia

Abstract. Timely relocation of empty cars to loading stations plays an important role in rail freight transport logistics. The purpose of the study is to determine the criteria for identifying a need for reserved station tracks while minimizing operating costs. The authors used special methods to study freight transport operations and mathematically modeled the transportation process subject to the developed technological measures, such as concentrating the car traffic at stations and yards with sufficient technical capabilities, minimizing the number of handling operations in transit, and differentiating cars according to their respective operators. As a result, the authors identified the criteria underlying the decision-making algorithm for managing rail transport operations, while minimizing costs throughout the service area.

Introduction

Technical regulation of rail transport operations is a way of managing the entire transportation process that helps to achieve optimal distribution of vehicles. Standard indicators of car fleet utilization are determined through a technical regulation process. The efficiency of transport operations management is determined by estimating utilization indicators for locomotive and car fleets. However, in the context of the ongoing privatization of car fleets in Russia, only two criteria can be used to assess the quality of rail transport operations: speed and transit time of cars.

Reliable technical standards, such as objective criteria for transport operations, contribute to the development of sustainable solutions in planning of rail transport operations. These solutions, in turn, contribute to increasing the stability of car traffic and providing loading operations with necessary facilities. Operations with empty cars are significantly streamlined. The current methods for technical regulation of quantitative and qualitative indicators have a number of shortcomings. Such qualitative indicators as service speed, waiting times for transit and local cars at stations and yards, and waiting times for cars per cargo operation, are determined without taking into account their dependence on traffic volume and utilization rate of the infrastructure. Due to shortcomings in the current technical regulation system, operational management methods come to the fore. This approach has a negative impact on the entire transportation process [1–3].

* Corresponding author: chechulinau@gmail.com

© The Authors, published by EDP Sciences. This is an open access article distributed under the terms of the Creative Commons Attribution License 4.0 (http://creativecommons.org/licenses/by/4.0/).

From the above, it can be concluded that efficient car traffic management, especially for empty cars, with cost minimization is an important problem for freight transportation and sustainable use of the railway infrastructure. At present, the technology has fundamentally changed in the context of private fleets of empty cars. This has led to a higher utilization rate of the infrastructure and changed the interaction between carriers and owners of rolling stock. There are no effective measures in place to optimize this process [4–12].

In other countries, rail freight logistics faces a strong competition from other modes of transport. In this context, operators need to focus primarily on interests of cargo owners and plan just-in-time deliveries by following a train schedule with maximum routing [13, 14]. The following methods are used: an individual approach to delivery times; reducing the total handling time of cars at stations and yards; increasing the weight of freight trains (if this measure can reduce operating costs); door-to-door delivery services; separating a core of freight trains with accelerated turnaround in a schedule [15, 16]. In Russia, due to long distances (more than six thousand km), rail transport operations create a significant load on the infrastructure: the utilization rate is 2.7 times higher than that in other countries. However, the fact that the railway infrastructure belongs to a single owner allows minimal reserves and costs to be managed [17].

Thus, it is important to study this problem since its solution will increase the competitiveness of railways by allowing carriers and owners of car fleets to reduce the delivery time, develop regulations for empty cars adapted to the new conditions and, therefore, minimize their operating costs. The subject of the study is logistics principles for empty private cars that take into account the freight transport technology and operating costs of rail transport. The purpose of the study is to refine the criteria for identifying a need for reserved station and yard tracks while minimizing operating costs. These criteria will make it possible to comprehensively assess feasible utilization of capacities of railway sections based on available infrastructure and traction facilities, and to identify priorities in development of the rail freight transport technology. The paper proposes an algorithm based on the refined criteria to perform an integrated assessment of infrastructure capabilities and select options of station infrastructure utilization by redistributing classification operations among railway stations and yards.

Research methods

In order to determine optimization measures in transportation of empty private cars, the authors analyzed operations with cars during the delivery using special methods for studying freight operations. Taking into account the railway transport technology, they developed a transportation flow chart with constituent elements and time inputs [18]. It has been established that there are some difficulties in operating empty cars in cooperation with rolling stock operators:

1) due to excessive saturation of stations and yards with cars, some of their tracks remain inactive. This reduces traffic and handling capacities of stations and yards;

2) due to oversaturation of sections with trains, part of trains are left at wayside stations without locomotives, which reduces the number of tracks for crossing and passing trains and removes some train paths.

A relationship between station fleets, locomotives, freight traffic and service speed indicates that the maximum freight traffic volumes with maximum limits of park fleets increases the need for reserved tracks at stations and yards. Based on these relationships, it is possible to comprehensively estimate the feasible utilization of capacities of railway sections, taking into account the availability of infrastructure and traction facilities. They can be represented as a cause-and-effect loop (Fig. 1). In order to break this loop and overcome difficulties, it is necessary to fill a gap of track capacity by physically expanding the number of tracks (extensive method) or improving the technology that can replace the reserved track capacity with management reserves (intensive method).

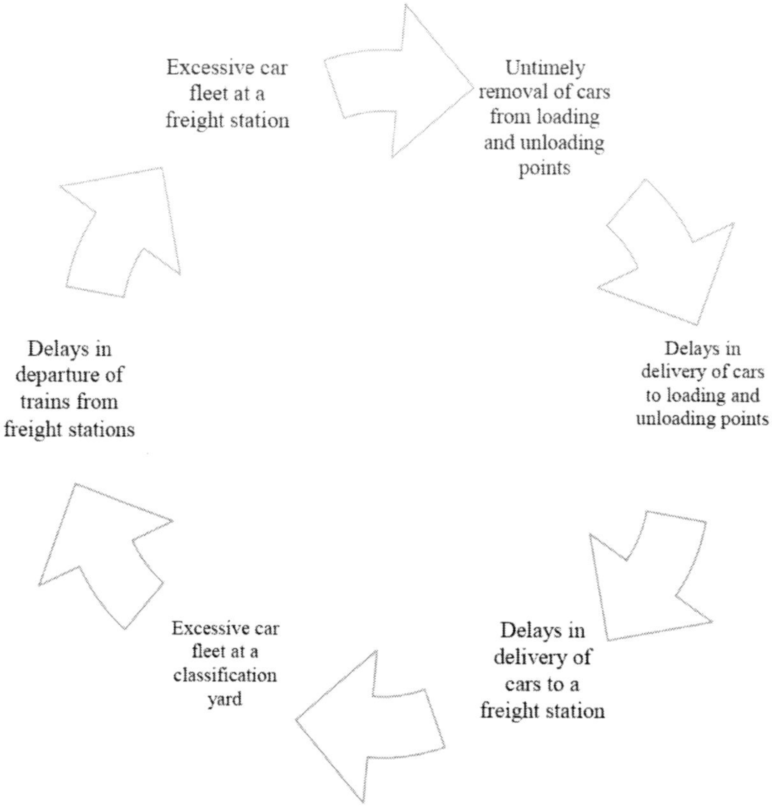

Fig. 1. Cause-and-effect loop.

By optimizing the technology (intensive method), it is possible to accelerate the car turnaround and increase a fleet of cars in a hold yard, i. e. the utilization of track capacity can be reduced while maintaining the same number of cars. One of the research methods used by the authors is mathematical modeling, which allows the system (in our case, the process of rail freight transportation) to be described in general terms and presented as a formula. Using this approach, the economic result for a carrier from the introduction of technological measures can be presented as a solution to the problem with the objective function of minimizing related operating costs for transportation:

$$E_{ec} = \sum E = E_{tr} + E_{not\,handled} + E_{handled} + E_{load} \rightarrow \min , \qquad (1)$$

where E_{tr} are the operating costs for transportation of cars in trains in railway sections; $E_{not\,handled}$, $E_{handled}$ are the operating costs incurred by a carrier when cars remain idle at technical stations without and with handling, respectively; E_{load} are the operating costs incurred by a carrier when cars are idle at loading/unloading stations.

The solution to this function depends on how efficiently the following criteria are implemented in practice: trains follow the shortest path with the minimum possible number of car handling operations, subject to rated limits of classification yards; the car traffic is differentiated by type of cargo, type of rolling stock, and owner.

As noted by leading scientists [18], one of the decisive technological measures is to manage transportation of empty gondola cars by various types of route trains. Due to uneven intake of cars and loading, rolling stock operators need a reserve of cars. Instead of keeping necessary reserves, it is possible to manage the intake of empty cars.

It has been found that reserves are not created in static conditions (waiting times at marshaling yards increase). By creating routes for breaking up trains, we can quickly manage the intake of empty cars, taking into account a departure sequence of trains for loading stations.

Trains are made up from empty cars: (1) on non-public railways; (2) at large unloading stations; (3) at classification yards and section stations from cars coming from other stations.

Possible making-up options:

1) through trains from empty cars of a certain fleet involved by a carrier are made up at technical stations and bulk unloading stations, and then delivered to a loading station according to a loading order.

2) designation of trains from empty cars, including:

- through trains from empty cars of any origin to certain destination stations,
- direct technical routes of trains from empty cars in loading stations or hold yards belonging to certain rolling stock operators or their associations,
- technical routes for breaking up,
- forwarder routes of trains from empty cars of certain rolling stock operators from unloading stations, relocation stations or hold yards.

The study of the existing car traffic structure has revealed that empty cars, including gondola cars, are delivered to a loading station with a considerable number of handling operations at classification yards and technical stations in transit. In order to reduce the number of these handling operations, it is necessary to concentrate a selection of empty gondola cars at a smaller number of stations, taking into account their location throughout the service area. It is reasonable to use the stations and yards located at the entrance to a coal loading region to create technical routes in a number of directions. By using better equipped yards, it is possible to use classification facilities to a fuller extent and reduce operating costs for rail transportation of goods. A comparison can be based on information on operating processes in stations and yards. Their performance parameters and time inputs that determine the utilization of stations and yards should be kept up-to-date. Capabilities of classification yards and systems are limited to allowable handling volumes according to a making-up plan and train schedule. In other words, technical capabilities of classification yards are one of the criteria that influence the choice of a car traffic management option for the service area.

Results

Thus, in order to increase the transit traffic of cars, it is necessary to consider various routing options. A choice of transport operations management options should be based on the criteria that make it possible to minimize costs throughout the service area. The decision-making algorithm for transport operations management includes the following steps:

1) At first, feasibility of delivering goods with the shortest possible routes should be studied. Choice of routes that are not the shortest ones may be reasonable if they are associated with a lower cost of passing trains (use of parallel tracks with better performance parameters, such as type of traction, throughput capacity, possibility of passing heavier

trains without weight reduction). If the capacity of sections is sufficient, it is reasonable to select a route with minimal operating costs:

$$E_{tr} \rightarrow \min \quad (2)$$

2) Geographical location of handling stations: the possibility of concentrating car traffic and combining directions at entry and exit of handling stations. Otherwise, there is a need for additional handling operations at trailing stations, and a train fails to follow the shortest possible route. A possibility of reducing the number of handling operations in transit and excluding backhaul of cars is considered:

$$E_{tr} + E_{handled} \rightarrow \min \quad (3)$$

3) Mandatory inspection of technical capabilities (rated limits) involved in car handing. Excessive traffic will require some operational measures, which always increase costs. Technical capabilities of car handing stations are considered subject to the number of destinations:

$$E_{handled} \rightarrow \min \quad (4)$$

4) Minimization of handling operations in transit. This measure will reduce car turnaround and minimize costs by reducing a load on the infrastructure and a required fleet of cars to be maintained by car owners. An increase in the transit traffic, achieved through en-route transportation and reduction of car handling operations, is taken into account as well:

$$E_{handled} \rightarrow \min \quad (5)$$

5) At present, it is reasonable to differentiate the traffic of loaded and empty cars. The traffic of loaded cars should be analyzed taking into account types of goods transported, such as coal or oil products. When analyzing the traffic of empty cars, it is reasonable to consider type of rolling stock. This approach makes it possible to differentiate the car traffic according to the characteristics mentioned above and designate different types of traffic to specific stations, thereby reducing handling operations at destination stations. It is also necessary to consider preparing trains for loading stations (empty cars) and unloading stations (loaded cars) at large classification yards subject to customer requirements. This will reduce costs of operations at freight stations, since marshalling operations at hump yards are cheaper:

$$E_{load} \rightarrow \min \quad (6)$$

6) Taking into account that cars belong to different owners or lessees, there should be a possibility of making up trains from empty cars of certain types and certain rolling stock operators at specially designated classification yards. For large operators, the concentration of empty cars at certain yards speeds up the delivery of cars and allows operators to accurately predict the time of arrival for loading, without burdening infrastructures of destination stations. Moreover, this approach makes it possible to plan a sequence in which empty cars are delivered to several stations in a region of loading. It also allows loading stations to satisfy their needs for cars of specific operators according to customer requests, thereby reducing costs of operations at freight stations due to a lower cost of marshalling at hump yards:

$$E_{handled} + E_{load} \rightarrow \min \quad (7)$$

By implementing the transportation process in accordance with the rail transport technology, it is possible to predict the delivery time with a sufficient degree of accuracy [19]. By reducing the turnaround of a freight car on an empty leg and predicting delivery time, rolling stock operators will reduce their costs for maintaining a reserve of cars, which is required due to uneven intake and loading:

$$E_{operators} = \Delta n \cdot C_{car} \rightarrow \min \ , \quad (8)$$

where Δn is the change in the active car fleet from the introduction of technological measures; C_{car} is the unit cost per car used by a rolling stock operator.

Based on the Siberian and Far Eastern Federal districts of the Russian Federation, the authors considered redeploying classification operations to a yard T, in which empty cars are differentiated by owner and direction. It is difficult to create loop routes for empty gondola cars at port railway stations due to their remoteness. By introducing technical routes to the classification yard T for breaking up, operators will avoid unnecessary handling in their service area. By making up trains from empty gondola cars at the same yard, they will avoid unnecessary handling in transit.

If a rolling stock operator is interested, cars can be sent to the yard T for loading only from stations of individual railways. In this case, the operator can reduce the car turnaround on an empty leg and the delivery time of cars, and, most importantly, implement the just-in-time delivery principle that allows it to determine the transit time with sufficient accuracy. Therefore, while introducing technical routes, operators should conclude contracts to standardize the delivery time, taking into account the rail freight transport technology. By taking the just-in-time approach to the proposed en-route deliveries, operators will reduce the car turnaround and free up 1,045 cars/day. This, in turn, will reduce a load on their infrastructures by freeing up tracks of the classification yards listed above and open-line tracks.

Conclusion

The developed criteria for selecting car traffic management options, which allow operating costs to be minimized throughout the service area, make it possible to optimize railway transport operations. This will make it possible to efficiently use tracks of stations and yards, as well as reduce the required rolling stock and minimize costs for railway infrastructure development. In order to efficiently manage the traffic of empty cars, it is necessary to prioritize the making-up process on non-public tracks or tracks of unloading stations and classification yards in transit. By reducing the car turnaround and predicting the delivery time of cars to a point of destination, operators can significantly facilitate their activities. Therefore, it is reasonable to identify incentive measures for creating different types of routes from empty cars after unloading of bulk goods. Further research by the authors will be aimed at developing a criterion for minimizing operating costs by reducing the number of car handling operations in transit.

References

1. Instructions on the organization of railroad car flows on the railways of Russian Railways JSC, 16.10.06 (2007). (in Russian)

2. A.F. Borodin, Trudy VNIIAS, 6 (2008). (in Russian)
3. K.P. Shenfeld, Doctoral thesis, Moscow State University of Railway Engineering, Moscow, 2014. (in Russian)
4. O.P. Yugrina, Zheleznodorozhnyj transport [Railway transport], 10, 25-30 (2010). (in Russian)
5. A.F. Borodin, Bjulleten' Objedinennogo uchenogo soveta OAO RZhD [Bulletin of the Joint Scientific Council of Russian Railways JSC], **2,** 65-73 (2017). (in Russian)
6. O.P. Yugrina, Nauchnye problemy transporta Sibiri i Dal'nego Vostoka [Scientific transport problems in Siberia and the Far East], 4, 14-17 (2015). (in Russian)
7. S.Yu. Eliseev, Zheleznodorozhnyj transport [Railway transport], 10, 30-33 (2015). (in Russian)
8. A.F. Borodin, Mir transporta [World of Transport and Transportation Journal], 1(68), 6-17 (2017). (in Russian)
9. V.G. Lemeshko, V.A. Sharov, Zheleznodorozhnyj transport [Railway transport], 11, 12-20 (2010). (in Russian)
10. N.P. Shipulin, Zheleznodorozhnyj transport [Railway transport], 2, 52-55 (2012). (in Russian)
11. Yu.A. Chechulina, Nauchnye problemy transporta Sibiri i Dal'nego Vostoka [Scientific transport problems in Siberia and the Far East], 2, 92-95 (2013). (in Russian)
12. V.A. Sharov, Zheleznodorozhnyj transport [Railway transport], 3, 33-35 (2017). (in Russian)
13. M. Bielli, A. Bielli, R. Rossi, Procedia Social and Behavioral Sciences, **Vol. 20,** 4-18 (2011).
14. M. Demers, Saving Time, Saving Dollars (2014), available at: https://wasteadvantagemag.com/saving-time-saving-dollars
15. P. Zhang, Journal of Railway Engineering Society, **32(6),** 81-86 (2015).
16. T. Mai, E. Frejinger, M. Fosgerau, Transportation Research. Part B: Methodological, **75,** 100-112 (2015).
17. P.V. Kurenkov, F.I. Khusainov, A.A. Sechkarev, Vestnik transporta, 4, 10-16 (2014). (in Russian)
18. V.V. Panin, E.S. Prokofyeva, D.V. Rubtsov, Bjulleten' Objedinennogo uchenogo soveta OAO RZhD [Bulletin of the Joint Scientific Council of Russian Railways JSC], 2, 57-64 (2017). (in Russian)
19. L.S. Kazantseva, Nauchnye problemy transporta Sibiri i Dal'nego Vostoka [Scientific transport problems in Siberia and the Far East], **2**, 39-43 (2013). (in Russian)

Modern approaches to product competitiveness evaluation for companies of various industries

Elena Tyunyukova[1,*], *Vladimir* Ruban[1], and *Vladimir* Burovtsev[1]

[1]Siberian Transport University, 630049 Novosibirsk, Russia

Abstract. This study is aimed at forming modern approaches to product competitiveness evaluation for companies of various industries. Relevant task is to obtain a quantitative evaluation parameter for product competitiveness that enables to adequately compare competing products. The study was performed using the methods of systems and structural analysis, strategic modeling and general principles of economic studies. The paper includes review of the existing approaches to product competitiveness evaluation based on its qualitative and quantitative assessment. Key groups of parameters that effect competitiveness of the manufactured product were determined, and an approach based on Harrington desirability function was suggested for its evaluation.

Introduction

Evaluation of product competitiveness for companies of different industries is the key factor for their success on the market. The field of studies is related to industrial management and focuses on competitiveness evaluation for the manufactured product.

The authors note lack of a uniform method that enables to clearly evaluate product competitiveness. V. Faltsman suggests defining product effectiveness through indices that connect import and export parameters [1]. L. Rodionova and O. Kantor offer to introduce a balance criterion for competitiveness parameters [2]. Practically all authors agree on the necessity to obtain adequate quantitative assessments of product competitiveness based on which strategic marketing decisions could be made. The preferable variant of such assessments will be their representation in the form of an index using which general evaluation of competitiveness can be performed [3].

The purpose of this research is related to obtaining quantitative assessments of product competitiveness based on the product's qualitative parameters. Novelty of the research consists in the approach to obtaining a uniform quantitative parameter for competitiveness of product manufactured by companies from various industries.

Efficiency of production activity of a company is defined by multiple factors, one of the key parameters being competitiveness of the manufactured product. In the end of the day, competitive product affects competitive position the company occupies on the market. Traditional approaches to defining this position use the notions of market share or relative market share [4-5]. These parameters to some extent characterize state of a company and its

* Corresponding author: evtun@ngs.ru

© The Authors, published by EDP Sciences. This is an open access article distributed under the terms of the Creative Commons Attribution License 4.0 (http://creativecommons.org/licenses/by/4.0/).

competitive practices. An important role in defining a company's state is played by the level of novelty and quality of the competitive product. Distinguishing participants by the occupied market share enables to assign them certain roles. M. Porter's classification of industry market participants includes leaders, companies with about 40% of the market share, challengers having 30% of the market share, followers with 20% and nichers whose market share is about 10% [4].

The key factor of success for all cases is choice of the right marketing strategy and presence of competitive advantage related either to the company or to its product. It shall be noted that such advantage is ideally copyrighted and shouldn't be easy for competitors to copy.

Competitive advantage of a company's product can be represented in many ways, but mostly it consists in characteristics or attributes of the product not noticed by the competitors [5]. Competitiveness is the parameter that indicates presence of such peculiarities and allows forecasting the future success of marketing activities of a company related to the product.

Research methods

The study was performed using the methods of systems and structural analysis, strategic modeling and general principles of economic studies. The conducted research is exploratory and uses secondary information for forming a set of parameters for evaluation of product competitiveness for companies from various industries.

Usually, the notion of product competitiveness is related to consumer and defined as the level of attractiveness of a certain product for an actual consumer [6]. Therefore the customer's requirements to the product are the key ones.

Besides, competitiveness is often related to such notions as quality, cost and quality level [7]. Quality and technical level of the product are to some extent constants related to the product's peculiar characteristics and the the level of scientific and technical development of the studied market. The parameter of competitiveness is a much wider notion, it may significantly vary for the same product quality depending on the market state, competitors' activities, their marketing strategies, appearance of new products in the studied product group [8]. Nevertheless, quality and technical level of the product are inherent parts of competitiveness and shall be accounted in its evaluation; however, the overall product attractiveness is defined by the customer. The main groups of parameters accounted when evaluating competitiveness are given in Figure 1.

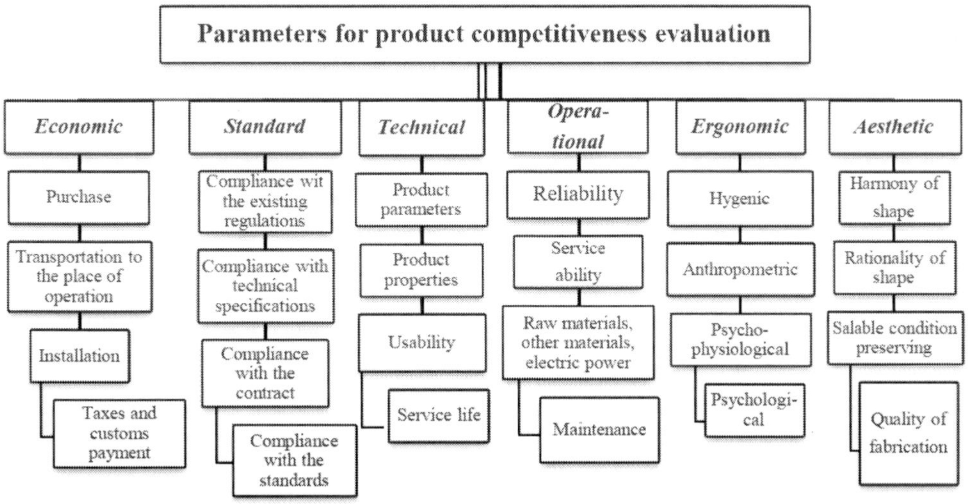

Fig.1. Parameters for product competitiveness evaluation.

Further actions are related to selection of meaningful parameters of the product in question, selection of the reference sample with ideal parameters and comparison of the studied sample with the reference one.

All methods applied for comparing the samples can be categorized by the parameter of qualitative or quantitative evaluation of competitiveness. The so-called mixed or combined evaluation methods are represented by assessments (obtained by means of surveying experts and customers) transformed into quantitative parameters using some mathematical tools. Quantitative assessment is usually performed by calculating single, group and integral indices [9].

Single index is defined by the formula (1)

$$g = \frac{P}{P_{100}} \times 100, \tag{1}$$

where g – single parameter index;
P – parameter level for the studied product;
P_{100} – parameter level for the reference product sample which 100% satisfies the need.

After finding single parameter indices a group parameter G can be calculated by the formula (2) which enables to integrate single indices for a uniform group of parameters – economic, standard, technical, operational, ergonomic and aesthetic (Fig.1). Single indices can be integrated using weight factor set during expert survey.

$$G = \sum a_i \times g_i, \tag{2}$$

where a_i – weight factor;
g_i – single index.

Integral index is usually calculated (formula (3)) in the format "selected group of parameters / economic parameters", which in fact provides the parameter evaluation in relation to its cost characteristics.

$$I = \frac{G_{techn}}{G_{econ}}, \tag{3}$$

where G_{techn} – group index for group of technical parameters;

G_{econ} – group index for group of economic parameters.

Then, the conclusion is made: if $I < 1$, then the studied product is inferior to the reference sample, in case of $I > 1$, the reference sample has higher competitiveness.

Significant drawback of such approach consists in the fact that only those parameters can be used for comparison, which have numerical value, i.e. physical parameters of a product.

Results

Optimized product competitiveness index is the most accurate one. This index shall account qualitative parameters of competitiveness, such as harmony of a product's shape, serviceability and other parameters relevant for the studied product.

Such optimized index can be obtained using generalized Harrington desirability function [10] which allows transforming several qualitative attributes into a single quantitative parameter. Application of Harrington desirability function for search of optimum conditions is proved in the study [11]. Harrington desirability function uses transformation of single responses expressed by natural values into a desirability scale, Table 1.

Table 1. Transition from quantitative to qualitative values.

Desirability	Scale marks
Very good	1.00 - 080
Good	0.80 - 0.63
Satisfactory	0.63 - 0.37
Bad	0.37 - 0.20
Very bad	0.20 - 0.00

The scale marks given in the Table 1 correspond to the curve presented in Figure 2 which is conditioned by the equation (4)

$$k = exp[-exp(-y)], \quad (4)$$

The y axis contains desirability values k which vary from 0 to 1. The k axis contains response values in the form of coded scale. The k axis contains response values in the form of coded scale. They are selected in the range from 3 to 6 and the number of intervals defines the curve steepness in the middle zone.

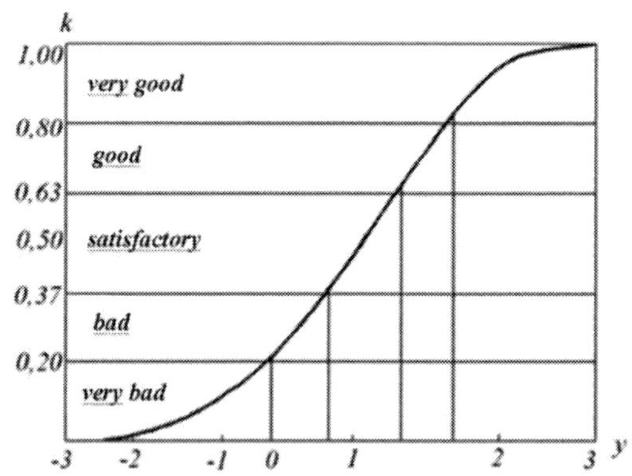

Fig. 2. Desirability function.

The 0.37 mark on the desirability scale is critical, as below this value the studied factor has unsatisfactory value. The desirability scale can be used as a quite simple and handy tool for obtaining quantitative expression of any parameters, including qualitative ones. It is enough to match responses with a coded scale. The possibility of applying such approach to assess communication strategy and competitiveness of a company was proved in the studies [12-13].

Then, either groups of competitiveness evaluation parameters or single indices out of these groups, i.e. single responses, are selected. The next step is connected with obtaining qualitative assessments of these parameters on the basis of experts survey. The assessment is given both to the product under study and to that produced by the closest competitor. Based on the qualitative assessment given in the form "very good", "good", "satisfactory", "bad" and "very bad" to each of the parameters, coded scales by the number of parameters are built (k axis).

The number of experts involved in the survey can be equal to the number of assessed parameters [14]. After transforming single responses into particular desirability functions the optimized competitiveness index K_{prod} will be obtained, formula (5):

$$K_{prod} = \sqrt[n]{\prod_{i=1}^{n} k_i}, \quad (5)$$

where k_i – individual desirabilities.

Conclusion

Due to the use of the described approach to product competitiveness evaluation the process of its defining can be unified. It enables to obtain a unified quantitative evaluation of competitiveness based on qualitative assessments of certain parameters. Considering that competitiveness is a multicomponent index influenced by marketing activities of companies, and new competitive advantages that appear, for example, when using unforeseeable marketing strategies, other groups of parameters for product competitiveness evaluation can be introduced for calculating an optimized product competitiveness index. Further research is related to formation of specifications for product competitiveness indices.

References

1. V.K. Faltsman, ECO Journal (2016). (in Russian)
2. L.N. Rodionova, O.G. Kantor, Economy of Region, 3, 257-264 (2014). (in Russian)
3. O. Notta, A. Vlachvei, Advances in Panel Data Analysis in Applied Economic Research, 693-705 (2018).
4. M.E. Porter, *Konkurentnaja strategija: Metodika analiza otraslej i konkurentov* [Competitive Strategy Techniques for Analyzing Industries and Competitors] (Alpina Publ., Moscow, 2016). (in Russian)
5. A.A. Thompson, A.J. Strickland, *Strategicheskij menedzhment. Iskusstvo razrabotki i realizacii strategii* [Strategic Management: Concepts and Cases] (Moscow, 1998). (in Russian)
6. A.D. Yudanov, *Konkurencija: teorija i praktika* [Competition: theory and practice] (Izdatel'stvo Gnom i D, Moscow, 2001). (in Russian)
7. M.N. Grigoryev, Marketing (Urait Publ., Moscow, 2010). (in Russian)
8. A.N. Romanov, G.A. Zhukov, S.I. Mayorov, et al., Marketing (Moscow, 1996). (in Russian)

9. G.V. Savitskaya, *Ekonomicheskij analiz* [Economic analysis] (Novoe znanie, Moscow, 2004). (in Russian)
10. E.C.Jr. Harrington, Industrial Quality Control, **21**, 494–498 (1965).
11. Yu.P. Adler, E.V. Markova, Yu.V. Granovskiy, *Planirovanie eksperimenta pri poiske optimal'nyh uslovij* [Planning an experiment when searching for optimal conditions] (Nauka, Moscow, 1976). (in Russian)
12. E.V. Tyunyukova, *Kommunikacionnye strategii organizacii* [Communication strategies of the organization] (STU Publ., Novosibirsk, 2001). (in Russian)
13. E.V. Tyunyukova, P.Yu. Bondarenko, *Aktualnye problemy kommercii i marketinga v potrebitelskoj kooperacii* [Problems of commerce and marketing in consumer cooperation], 288-292 (Novosibirsk, 2004). (in Russian)
14. E.P. Golubkov, *Marketingovye issledovanija: teorija, praktika i metodologija* [Marketing research: theory, practice and methodology] (Finpress, Moscow, 1998). (in Russian)

Design of the railway track infrastructure of the subpolar and northern regions

Gennady Akkerman[1,*], *Sergei* Akkerman[1], and *Aleksandr* Mironov[2]

[1]Ural State University of Railway Transport, 620034 Yekaterinburg, Russia
[2]Infotex AT LLC, 620049 Yekaterinburg, Russia

Abstract. The interest in the development of the Subpolar and Northern regions of the Eurasian and the American continent has sharply increased recently, which is reflected, among other things, in construction of railways. This construction is associated with large resource costs. The purpose of this work is to study the possibility of using "new" materials - ice, sulfur concrete for construction of railway beds. The paper presents results of computer simulation of the "wheel-rail" interaction, which made it possible to investigate the loads onto the ice base, in the "Universal Mechanism" software package. It was determined that the load was less than permissible. The technique of laboratory (with the help of a jack) and field (moving by a steam locomotive) tests of the ice base was described. It was determined that the geometry of the track was not changed under the load. This observation and the computer simulation allows believing that the ice railway beds can be used in the Subpolar and Northern regions.

Introduction

About 70% of the territory of Russia belongs to the Northern and Arctic zone, which is characterized by permafrost and severe climate. For comparison, in Canada this territory occupies 40%. The Northern and Arctic territories of Russia are rich in natural resources: oil and gas, coal, non-ferrous and rare metals, diamonds, etc. There are also ports of the Northern Sea Route, which is the shortest sea link from the East to the West. Development of the northern regions of the Eurasian and American continents [1–4] is a special governmental task.

The shape of the railway transport system in this region is formed on the basis of the analysis of design and construction of roads in such conditions: China-Tibet Railway, the Labrador Railway in Canada, northern railway lines of Russia. Computer simulation results, laboratory and full-scale tests performedat the "Tracks and Constructions of Railways" Department of the Ural State University of Railway Transport in Yekaterinburg, Russia, allowed proposing a new track infrastructure design.

Studies have shown that construction and operation of railways in the area considered faces a number of differences as compared to other areas. In particular, this is extremely high cost of infrastructure construction. For example, costs for construction of the Northern Latitudinal Way is 334 ÷ 404 million rubles/km, and the construction cost of the railway to

* Corresponding author: GAkkerman@usurt.ru

© The Authors, published by EDP Sciences. This is an open access article distributed under the terms of the Creative Commons Attribution License 4.0 (http://creativecommons.org/licenses/by/4.0/).

the Obskaya-Bovynenko-Karskaya railway to the Yamal peninsula is 227 million rubles/km [5, 6].

The existing approaches to design and construction of railways in these conditions are based on increasing the required resources, which causes an increase in their cost. Therefore, there is a need to create alternative, reliable and economically viable approaches to designing the railway infrastructure for the subpolar and northern regions, which is the purpose of this paper. The results of studies in the design and construction of railways in the Northern regions do not "radically" affect the material of which the railway bed is built, its layout and profile [3–5].

The work is devoted to computer simulation of loads on the ice sheet of the railway with the "wheel-rail" interaction. Confirmation of computer results was obtained by laboratory and field tests, which proved the invariability of the geometry of the ice rail track under real loads from the rolling stock.

In [3–6, 8], the emphasis is on preserving the consistency of the permafrost soils in earth railway beds. Nothing is discussed about the "ice beds", "non-melting ice" or sulfur concrete in construction of track infrastructure, about the possibility of changing the track "geometry". This work is performed with the purpose of reducing the resources required for railway communication in the Subpolar and Northern regions.

Various types of transport often operate in the transportation system of northern regions, such as rail, road, river and sea. With small initial cargo flows, in order to reduce the construction cost, road automobile traffic including road trains is arranged along the route of the future railway [7]. With the increase of cargo flow, the upper railway track structure is laid and the road traffic is replaced by railway traffic.

The role of the railway is sharply increased if it is part of the international transportation corridor. For example, it can be part of the South-North international corridor (Azerbaijan, India, Iran, Russian Federation are interested in it) [8]. Belkomur is part of this corridor. Unpredictable weather conditions in the north can often disrupt the operation rate of the multimodal transport chain (for example, sea-railway). It is necessary to create multimodal transportation and logistic centers (MTLCs) to manage the risks of failures. The following are positive features of MTLCs: (1) intermodality (multimodality); (2) synergistic effect, the effect of combining and managing the links of supply chains. Logistical services in northern areas can reach up to 50% of the value of goods in the cost of production [9, 10]. It is desirable to use intelligent transport systems (ITS) to reduce the cost of multimodal transportation in the North. Due to high cost of construction and operation, the payback period of certain railways of this area exceeds 20 years. For example, due to the long payback period, the sale of the Obskaya-Bovynenko-Karskaya railway (with the book value of ~130 billion rubles) to the Yamal peninsula (Russia) from Gazprom to Russian Railways JSC is complicated.

To reduce the railway construction cost, it is possible to use materials that are not quite usual, but are applicable in the conditions of the extreme North. In the absence of local soil to fill the railway bed, it is proposed to use ice instead.

Cryolithozone has been developed for more than 100 years. The Labrador railway (Canada), the Alaska railway (USA), the Norilsk railway (Russia), the Yamal railway (Russia), the Qinghai-Tibet railway (China), the Baikal-Amur Mainline, the AYAM (Amur-Yakut railway, Russia), etc., were partly built on the permafrost. The main disadvantage of ice soils is subsidence during thawing or heaving during freezing [10, 11].

Mechanical properties of ice are important [10–14]. Elastic properties of ice are manifested at short-term loads. With constant exposure (even small), plastic strain of ice is observed (for example, the slow "flow" of the glacier in the mountains). The destruction of ice in bending begins at pressure P_{LL}=1.5 MPa, and with compression $P_{LL} \approx 3$ MPa (30 kg/cm^2) [12–14].

It should be noted that the average pressure along the axis of the railway bed from the upper railway track structure P_{URTS} = 0.016 MPa and from the rolling stock P_{RS} = 0.84 MPa, i.e., total

$$P=P_{URTS}+P_{RS}=0.86\text{ MPa}, \tag{1}$$

$$\text{i.e., } P_{LL}>P. \tag{2}$$

Significant strength of ice was assumed when building the following ice crossings: across LakeBaikal (with the "initial" operation of the Trans-Siberian Railway), across the Volga near Saratov in 1928, across the Northern Dvina in Arkhangelsk (1943 to 1944), across Lake Ladoga (the "Road of Life", etc.) .

The strength of ice can be increased technologically, using the "thin films" principle and by changing its composition. Thin films of crystallized water are stronger than "ordinary" ice: they do not have heat shrinkable shells and cracks. The thin films principle is reduced to rapid freezing of granular ice layer by layer.

Thus, in mid-November 1981, ice was frozen on a ferry across the Lena at the air temperature of -32 to -34°C near Yakutsk, Russia. Mobile pumping stations (with the head of 100 m) with sprinkler nozzles created a drip cone. The droplets were partially frozen (ice in the cone, approximately 40 to 67%) in ice balls on the surface and formed granulated ice, more uniform than natural ice, with water.

The thin films principle is used in Yakutia when building structures: ice is quickly frozen on an inflatable formwork in the form of an arch, layer by layer. The strength of the construction obtained is not less strong than concrete.

Ice concrete, which is ice consisting of pebbles (gravel), sand and water [15], is often used for construction in polar regions. Its strength is equal to "ordinary" concrete, and its bending strength is 2 to 4 times higher than that of concrete or bricks. Ice with inclusion of sawdust, various fibers is 2 to 3 times stronger than "pure" ice [16, 17]. It withstands the pressure of up to 5 MPa. Ice reinforcement with fiberglass increases its strength by almost 8 times.

Non-melting (a chemically inert substance, sulfur concrete) can melt and freeze repeatedly. The melting point is about 150°C, it retains strength and hardness up to 70°C and conducts heat poorly. It is not hazardous to humans. Laboratory and full-scale tests of ice-frozen rails were performed at the static load of 10 tons at our department.

Research method

The test bench was a frame welded of steel channels with the following dimensions: height - 160 mm, width - 64 mm, thickness - 5 mm. The frame corners were reinforced with gussets. The frame was buried vertically into the ground to the depth of 50 cm. In winter, at the air temperature of minus 20 ° C, an ice prism (instead of a ballast prism) was built (on layers of 4-5 cm) on frozen soil, 30 cm high and 122 cm wide on both sides of its axis. A rail with the length of 12.5 m of mark P-50 (height of 150 mm, sole width of 132 mm, head height of 33 mm) was laid on the prism by dragging through the frame. The rail was frozen into the ice by layers on one side to the level of the rolling track and on the other side on the rail head. The width of the ice prism along the top of the rail axis was 76 cm on one side (half of the track width) and 50 cm on the other side.

The load on the rail, measured with a manometer, was created by a hydraulic jack with the maximum force of 10 tons, which corresponds to the pressure on the crew axis of 20 tons. Rail deformations were determined: vertical ones by an optical level; horizontal ones by a metal ruler from the basis set earlier. The experiment was performed 5 times at negative air temperature: 8°C, 11°C, 14°C, 21°C, 16°C.

Results

The rail geometry remained unchanged for all tests. The same result was obtained for the load from the locomotive (at speeds of 5, 10, 15 km/h, the load of 16 tons per axis). The steam locomotive ran three times on ice-frozen rails 12.5 m long without sleepers. If it is assumed that only one running meter of the rail works under one axis, then the pressure on the ice is less than 0.4 MPa.

Tram tracks that consisted of rails without sleepers, filled with plastic (polypropylene) were tested in Strasbourg (France) with positive results. The filling thickness was about 40 cm.

In construction of railway beds not of earth but of ice in the Subpolar regions, the "thin films" technology must be applied. It is desirable to reinforce ice with geogrids, better (but not necessarily) with the ones manufactured by German company "HUESKER". For example, it can be rigid FOZTZAC geogrid with the strength of up to 3,000 kN/m. To the south, the width of the main site must be increased for thermal insulation at least 0.5 m. It is possible to use the "non-melting ice" (sulfur concrete). The basis of sulfur concrete is "sulfur polymer cement" or elemental sulfur with a large proportion of its polymeric allotropes and a small percentage of additives (stabilizers) [18].

See the comparison of sulfur concrete and cement concrete in Table 1.

Table 1. Comparison of sulfur concrete and cement concrete.

Indicators	Units of measurement	Sulfur concrete	Cement concrete
Frost resistance	%	200	100
Thermal conductivity	%	66	100
Strength: compression	MPa	55 – 65	10 – 60 (up to 100)
bending	MPa	10 – 15	5 – 8
elongation	MPa	5 – 7	0.5 – 4
Time required to reach 50% strength	hours	0.3	24
Cost of 1 m^3	%	50	100

Portland cement concrete is based on irreversible chemical reaction of hydration, and sulfur concrete is based on a reversible process of cooling the liquid melt (the melting temperature is 120 to 150°C).

Embankment construction: ice is built up to the required mark using thin film technology in accordance with the previously installed back slopers, the ice layers are reinforced with a geogrid at a given location. "Non-melting ice" is applied onto back slopers by layers. Since this melt is applied in thin layers from the top downwards, the ice of the railway bed does not have time to melt (the thickness of the "shell" made of sulfur concrete is 15-20 cm).

Variants of construction of the "ice bed" can be different: first the it is framed with "non-melting ice", and then its core is filled with ice. The embankment can be made of previously harvested ice cubes "frozen" with each other.

Artificial structures are corrugated metal pipes, or arched pipes made of sulfur concrete, built on inflatable formwork. Film formwork, for example, made of polyvinyl chloride, withstands the temperature of +120 to +150°C. The first layers of the melt is poured with cold water, which is evaporated almost immediately. Pipe openings are determined by the estimated water flow with the probability of exceeding of 1/300. Such flow rate is adopted to avoid accumulation of water near the artificial structure.

The ballast prism is also made of reinforced ice or "non-melted" ice under the rail 20 to 25 cm thick. The rails are frozen into ice without sleepers. As reinforced ice holds a "vertical wall" well, the slopes of the bed are made 1:1, i.e., steeper than for existing railways. Excavation is not desirable.

The rails are frozen from the inside of the track to the head, and from the outside - along the walkway (similar to how the city tram ways are "drowned" in the asphalt). The ice-free head of the rail, except for the rolling track, is covered with white paint. Our research has shown that this coating is a good heat insulator.

All surfaces except for the northern exposure to reflect the sun rays are covered with the 0.5 cm layer of "white" ice, i.e., water plus chalk powder. Construction of the ice sheet of the railway must be performed in winter. For example, summer on the Taimyr Peninsula lasts for only 6 weeks with the maximum air temperature of + 10°C. Therefore, it is desirable to protect the slopes of embankments and excavations of the southern exposure from the sun by canopies, just in case.

Sun canopies were used on the Qinghai-Tibet railway in China, in some sections of the Baikal-Amur Railway, the Amur-Yakutsk Railway of Russia [5, 9, 19]. It is supposed to make canopies of sandwich panels over the snow-free surface. By protecting the latter from sunlight, the canopy reduces the temperature of the surface underneath it by 3 to 5°C and protects it from summer precipitation [20]. Naturally, a system of engineering and climatological monitoring [6] must be created behind ice structures, similar to monitoring the stressed state of a seamless railway track using balises [21]. Implementation of the proposed designs must be preceded by a program of experimental works.

1. As already noted, the subpolar regions are a severe region for human habitation and, therefore, with low population density. Therefore, railways in these areas must be equipped with low amount of personnel, taking into consideration the arrangement of works in shifts both during construction and particularly during operation. That is why it must have a stable layout and profile that do not change its design outline (or low-changeable) under the influence of passing trains (resources will not be required for their straightening). The efficiency of the biclotoidal design of the railway layout and profile was proved by simulation in the "Universal Mechanism" software package (UM) created at the Bryansk State Technical University. UM is an effective tool for simulation of the dynamics of machine behavior. This requirement is met by the biclotoidal design of the curvilinear sections of the layout and profile (the transverse forces are reduced by two times, on average) [22]. There is no need to comply with the existing requirements for the mismatch of the vertical curve in the profile with the transition curves in the layout [23, 24]. Based on the reducing dynamics of the wheel-rail interaction, the track geometry must meet the design requirements, and it is desirable to keep train speeds under 60 km/h (16.7 m/s), and then the the radius of the vertical curve at the clotoids conjugation point will be as follows with the minimum vertical acceleration of a_v=0.1 m/s^2:

$$R_в = \frac{V^2}{a_в};\ R_в = 2800 \text{ м} \tag{3}$$

or, after rounding, R_v=3,000 m.

The value of the limiting (leading) slope must not exceed 25‰. Weight of train Q with locomotive traction 2TE-10 Q=1,630 n, $Q_п$=1,150 t.

In other words, 24 trains/day will be required for every 10 million tons of cargo per year. Then, it is necessary to arrange passing loops every 35 km with the average speed of 40 km/h.

Conclusion

Thus, under appropriate conditions, the railway transportation system of the Subpolar regions is single-track railways. The layout and the profile are with the minimum number of curves designed by biclotoids. The minimum radius of the vertical curve R_v = 3,000 m at the clotoid conjugation point in the vertical plane, i_p = 25‰, the profile breaks are unlimited and may coincide with the transition curves in the layout. Excavations are not desirable. The lower structure of the path is made of ice, the upper structure is without sleepers, the rails are "drowned" in the ice. With a freight turnover of 10 million tons per km per year, diesel locomotion and the average speed of trains of 40 km/h, passing loops must be made each 35 km. Culvert are metal corrugated pipes or pipes made of non-melting ice. Automatic blocking is provided on the basis of the "axis counter".

The nature of the railway transportation system is significantly changing in subpolar and northern regions. Technologies that require low number of personnel are used in the design, construction and operation of railways, therefore:

- design of the layout and the profile of the curvilinear sections reduces the wheel-rail interaction forces by 2 times on average, the track stability is increased;
- it is different from the usual track structure: the lower railway track structure is built of ice in a "shell" of sulfur concrete, the upper railway track structure is without sleepers, the rails are "drowned" in ice;
- maximum automation of transport process control and monitoring. The latter requires GIS (geoinformation systems) and radio tags (balises) installed along the railway at certain distances between them. As a pilot project, traffic of trains without a locomotive crew must be performed in Subpolar regions.

References

1. The State Program of the Yamalo-Nenets Autonomous District "Development of International Foreign Economic and Interregional Activities for 2014-2020" of 25.12.13 No. 1133-П (2013). (in Russian)
2. Northern strategy of Canada: Our North, Our Heritage, Our Future. Document of Government of Canada (2009). (in Russian)
3. G.A Gross, *Yron ore deposits of Canada and the West Yudies* (Survey of World iron ore resources, New York, 1970).
4. V.M. Nazarenko, K.S Nazarenko, *Transportnoe obespechenie vneshnejekonomicheskoj dejatel'nosti* [Transport support of foreign economic activity] (UNITI, Moscow, 2005).
5. V.G. Kondratyev, *Collection of reports of the 1st Congress of Russian geocryologists* (MSU, Moscow, 1996). (in Russian)
6. V.G. Kondratyev, V.A. Pozin, *Koncepcija sistemy inzhenerno-geokriologicheskogo monitoringa strojashhegosja zheleznodorozhnogo puti Barkakit – Tommot – Jakutsk* [The concept of the system of engineering-geocryological monitoring of the railway Barkakit-Tommot-Yakutsk] (Zabtrans, Chita, 2000). (in Russian)
7. G.L. Akkerman, S.G. Akkerman, Transport of the Urals, **3**, 27 – 32 (2016). (in Russian)
8. W.J. Fend, W. Ma, Z.Z. Sun, G.Y. Li, W.B. Yu., I.E. Zheny. *Conf. Proc. IX International Symposium on Perm a frod Engineering*, **1** (Mirny, Russia. 2011). (in Russian)
9. N.A. Valiev, V.E. Kondratyev, *Inzhenernaja geologija* [Engineering geology], **4**, 56–63 (2015). (in Russian)

10. SNiP 2.05.07-85. Building regulations. Manual for the design of railways and highways of industrial enterprises in permafrost regions (Gosstroy SSSR, 1990). (in Russian)
11. SP-25-13330. Set of rules. Foundations and foundations on permafrost soils. Updated version of SNiP 2.02.04-88 (Rosstandart, 2012). (in Russian)
12. I.S. Peschanskiy, *Inzhenernaja gljaciologija* [Engineering Glaciology] (Moscow, 1976). (in Russian)
13. K.F. Voytkovskiy, *Mehanicheskie svojstva l'da* [Mechanical properties of ice] (Moscow, 1960). (in Russian)
14. I.S. Peschanskiy, *Ledovedenie i ledotehnika* [Ice science and ice engineering] (Leningrad, 1963). (in Russian)
15. Stroitel'nyj jekspert [Construction expert]. Ice - building material of the past, present and future. Available at: https://ardexpert.ru/article/8185 (December 12, 2016). (in Russian)
16. A.M. Chekotilo, *Primenenie snega, l'da i merzlogo grunta v fortifikacii* [The use of snow, ice and frozen ground in fortification] (Moscow, 1943). (in Russian)
17. Yu. Semenov, S. Silin, *Innovacionnye tehnologii ispol'zovanija l'do-kompozitnyh materialov v stroitel'stve i jekspluatacii plavuchih objektov* [Innovative technologies for the use of ice-composite materials in the construction and operation of floating facilities] (Moscow, 2011). (in Russian)
18. PNST 105-2016. Technical conditions. Preliminary national standard. Sulphur concrete mixes and sulphur concrete (Stroitel'stvo, 2016). (in Russian)
19. V. Kondratyev, *Inzhenernaja zashhita* [Engineering protection] (Moscow, 2015). (in Russian)
20. N. Enjin, Sh. Yongping, *Cuide of Field Excursion after Asian Conference on* Permafros (Lanshon, China, 2006).
21. G.L. Akkerman, M.A. Skutina, Herald of the Ural State University of Railway Transport, **1**, 28-35 (2017). (in Russian)
22. G.L. Akkerman, S.G. Akkerman, O.A. Kravchenko, Zheleznodorozhnyj transport [Railway transport], **5**, 41 – 42 (2011). (in Russian)
23. G.L. Akkerman, S.G. Akkerman, V.A. Kopylenko, A.V. Zamuhovskiy, Transport Rossijskoj Federacii [Transport of Russian Federation], **1**, 22 – 25 (2018). (in Russian)
24. SP 119.13330.2012. Set of rules. Railways with gauge 1520 mm. Updated version of SNiP 32-01-95. (Stroitel'stvo, 2012) (in Russian)

Model of passenger rolling stock maintenance

Dmitry Bannikov[1,*], and *Nina* Sirina[1]

[1]Ural State University of Railway Transport, 620034 Yekaterinburg, Russia

Abstract. In order to improve the quality of maintenance and repair of a passenger rolling stock, Russian Railways JSC requires transition to routine maintenance. The paper studies the main stages of building a discrete-event model of a passenger rolling stock maintenance using AnyLogic environment. The following key parameters of maintenance are used: maintenance facilities location, rolling stock operability index, probability index for operational efficiency (downtime and failure probability), maintenance and repair costs. The maintenance model is implemented in the integrated modeling library. Simulation model enables to implement the modeled system and obtain performance indicators of routine maintenance system operation. By simulating various conditions it is possible to evaluate efficiency of the studied maintenance system for a high-speed passenger rolling stock.

Introduction

Reorganization of Russian transportation system, particularly federal railways, caused significant changes in structure of transportation services. The number of transportation companies increased, including those with own rolling stock. Today, clients on the transportation market have higher demands in respect to the quality of transportation services [1].

Scientific support of maintenance system presently fails to provide accurate operational readiness assessments of a passenger rolling stock. There is lack of the ability to forecast the level of operational readiness considering the existing limits of finance, passenger flow, failure intensity [2,3]. The known methods are not integrated into a single complex model of maintenance system.

Time and financial parameters, as well as variation of maintenance and repair intensity are not fully accounted, hence, the obtained predictive estimates are incomplete. For optimization purpose, it is suggested to perform system modeling that includes simulation of routine maintenance of a passenger rolling stock. The built simulation model will represent a system that allows multiple implementation of various production scenarios, thus simplifying evaluation and forecasting of the maintenance system condition.

In [4], the model of maintenance planning is based on the probability of technical failures in a certain moment of time. The model is built of the following constituents: planning a facility, purchasing spare parts, defining the maintenance and repair intervals. The studies of Pierskalla and Voelker [5], Osaki and Nakagawa [6], Sherif and Smith [7],

* Corresponding author: bannikov_d@mail.ru

© The Authors, published by EDP Sciences. This is an open access article distributed under the terms of the Creative Commons Attribution License 4.0 (http://creativecommons.org/licenses/by/4.0/).

Valdez-Flores and Feldman [8], Cho and Parlar [9] are focused on defining optimum maintenance resources and finding minimum economic life cycle. The authors distinguish traditional methods of problem solving by linear and dynamic programming, stochastic models and present value analysis.

Campbell [10] declares that there is no correct maintenance, but there are strategies that allow effective use of resources in certain situations. Anyway, organization of maintenance and repair shall be flexible.

Russian researchers pay a lot of attention to the use of mathematical methods for solving tasks of organization and management of rolling stock maintenance and repair. Wide application of statistical methods with the use of mathematical tools of queuing theory and theory of random processes for locating car-repair facilities on the railway network is described in the studies of V. Tsyganov, N. Sirina, M. Bolotin [11-13].

Scientific support of maintenance and repair management consists in development and application of routine maintenance model. This will facilitate transition from maintenance and repair of existing and high-speed passenger rolling stock to routine maintenance. The overall estimate of model implementation capacity enables to reasonably plan and organize maintenance and repair system. For that reason, development of routine maintenance model will provide accuracy of predictive estimates of operation and repair parameters which largely define the effectiveness of passenger rolling stock life cycle management.

Modeling method

Object of the developed simulation model is a passenger maintenance facility performing several functional operations on maintenance and repair of passenger rolling stock. Therefore, the model provides collection of statistical data on the following parameters:

- maintenance queuing time;
- average maintenance and repair time;
- distance between the operation location and maintenance facility;
- share of rolling stock serviced by the maintenance facility.

Simulation modeling of technological processes is based on the mathematical tool of the described process. Since the model is simplified and idealized during its development it is necessary to rationally define the level of assumptions in the described mathematical model. One of the accepted assumptions in the suggested model is distance between the operation location and maintenance facility. The distance is accepted as constant from the first scheduled repair of passenger rolling stock.

In general, maintenance and repair system [14-15] of passenger rolling stock is a queuing system. The flow of passenger cars subjected to maintenance and repair is complex and consists of two flows: 1 – the flow defined by failures in rolling stock; 2 – the flow of passenger cars assigned for maintenance and repair after the end of duration of time between repairs. The queuing theory provides analytical assessment and solution with system research limitations. The key data for describing queuing system operation are: flow of service applications, queue and output flow.

Building of the model was performed using system dynamics tools of the simulation model. This tool includes both discrete-event and agent-based modeling in AnyLogic environment. System dynamics is a simulation modeling approach, methods and tools of which allow understanding the structure and dynamics of the designed model. System dynamics is characterized by a high level of abstraction and can be used for strategic system modeling.

Discrete-event modeling presents the modeled system as a process, i.e. a sequence of operations performed with modeling agents. The model is graphically represented as a process diagram, with each block standing for a certain operation.

Agent-based modeling is an alternative view of the modeled system behavior. Structure of the agent-based model can be described both graphically and with the preset scenario. The agent behavior can be preset by various actions upon occurrence of certain events.

Simulation model is the one that builds the trajectory of system condition variation. We can say that simulation model is a set of rules according to which the system passes from one state into another. These rules are set by means of differential equations and statecharts. Using output data of the model the system behavior can be analyzed within the set parameters.

Model structure

Let us consider the model of routine maintenance of rolling stock as a queuing system with the applications flow λ (failure intensity) and service flow μ (repair intensity). System state graph is presented in Figure 1.

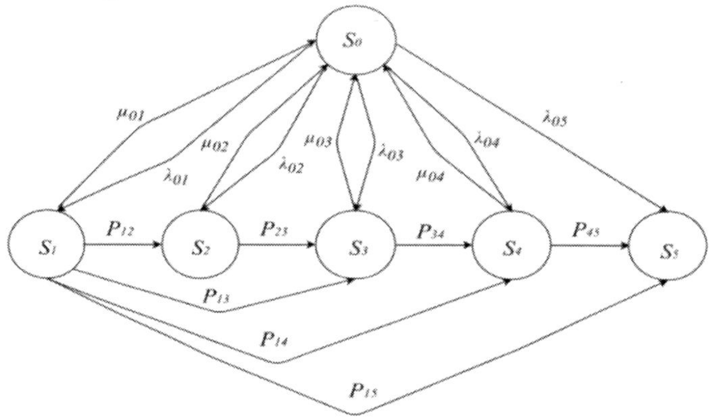

Fig. 1. Car state graph in a system.

Let us define the states in the graph as follows: S_0 – serviceable and in good operating condition; S_1 – out of service in operating condition; S_2 – out of service and nonoperable; S_3 – limit state retrievable after scheduled maintenance; S_4 – limit state retrievable after roundhouse servicing or overhaul repair; S_5 – ultimate limit state. *Pi* is the probability of car state transition. The state graph is described by the system of differential equations:

$$\begin{cases} \dfrac{dn_0(t)}{dt} = -\lambda_{01}n_0(t) + \mu_{10}n_0(t) - \lambda_{02}n_0(t) + \mu_{20}n_2(t) - \lambda_{03}n_0(t) + \mu_{30}n_3(t) - \\ \quad - \lambda_{04}n_0(t) + \mu_{40}n_4(t) - \lambda_{05}n_0(t); n_0(0) = N_0; \\ \dfrac{dn_1(t)}{dt} = \lambda_{01}n_0(t) - \mu_{10}n_1(t); n_1(0) = N_1; \\ \dfrac{dn_2(t)}{dt} = \lambda_{02}n_0(t) - \mu_{20}n_2(t); n_2(0) = N_2; \\ \dfrac{dn_3(t)}{dt} = \lambda_{03}n_0(t) - \mu_{30}n_3(t); n_3(0) = N_3; \\ \dfrac{dn_4(t)}{dt} = \lambda_{04}n_0(t) - \mu_{40}n_4(t); n_4(0) = N_4; \\ \dfrac{dn_5(t)}{dt} = \lambda_{05}n_0(t); n_5(0) = N_5; \\ n_0(t) + n_1(t) + n_2(t) + n_3(t) + n_4(t) + n_5(t) = N(t). \end{cases} \quad (1)$$

Solution of the suggested system in AnyLogic environment includes the following stages. Solution of each stage depends on input data specified in the model. On the first stage of model building several classes of agents were introduced from the process modeling library, as well as statechart and elements of system dynamics of the agent. In this case the operating passenger rolling stock is taken as an agent. Simulation modeling of the maintenance system of passenger rolling stock cannot exist without creating algorithm for processing data and calculations. The second stage of building the model is a structured flow diagram of the model presented in Figure 2.

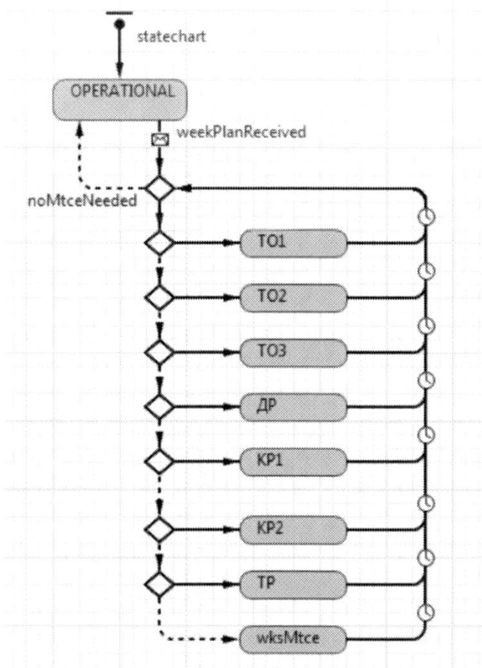

Fig. 2. Flow diagram of the maintenance model.

The built flow diagram represents a function of passing passenger rolling stock for maintenance and repair. The "Operational" statechart defines the agent behavior. The rolling stock is passed for maintenance after receiving the message «weekPlanReceived» which satisfies the set parameters. Then, branching and passage for required maintenance or repair occur. Each type of maintenance and repair is performed in certain period of time, after which the rolling stock will be serviced and put in operation.

The interface of the experiment "Planning of maintenance of passenger cars" (Fig. 3) includes elements of control and input of parameter values. The main parameters will be: car mileage, time between repairs, and the ability to change the downtime during maintenance depending on the rolling stock type.

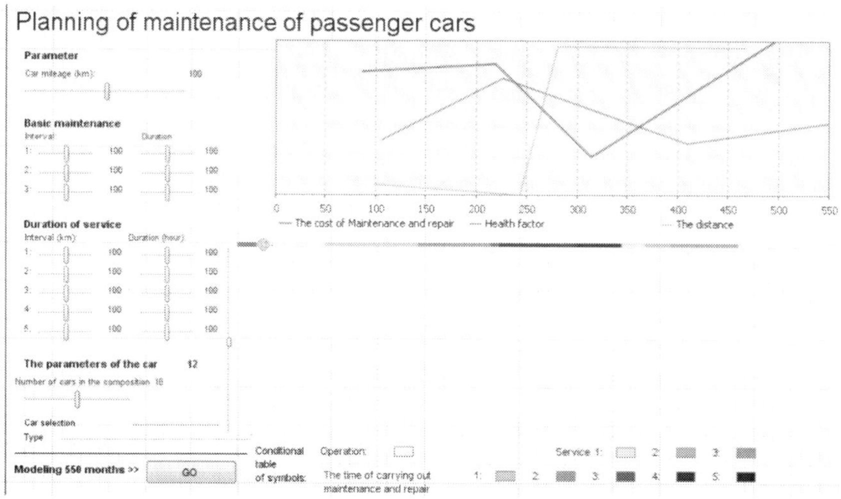

Fig. 3. Interface of the experiment "Planning of maintenance of passenger cars".

Modeling results

As a result of modeling the following data were obtained: an operability index variation graph (Fig. 4) for rolling stock, the level of costs for maintenance and repair, the average distance between the maintenance facility and the operation location of the rolling stock.

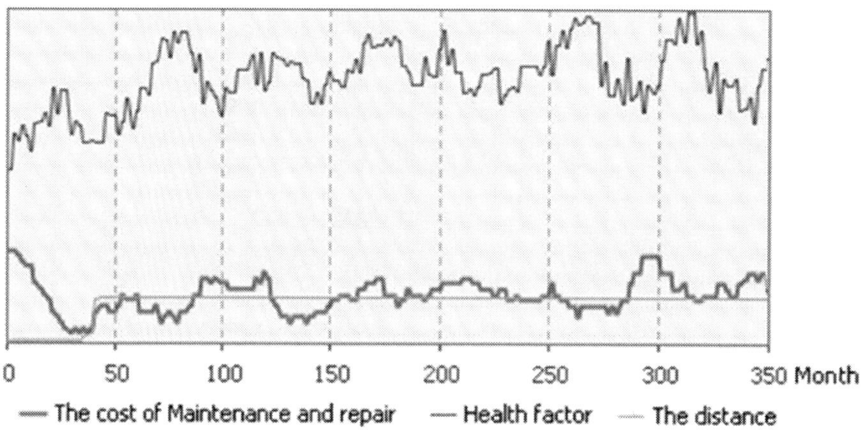

Fig. 4. Modeling results.

Variation of operability index is defined by periodic pulse function of repair intensity μ of passenger rolling stock. Repair intensity depends on the type of performed maintenance or repair of rolling stock. In this model, repair intensity is constant and is characterized by the average repair time.

Maintenance and repair cost also depends on the type of performed maintenance and repair, and repair time. Besides, cost variation can be explained by the fact that the model accounts both scheduled types of passenger rolling stock repair and ordinary repair. Ordinary repair is accounted in the model at an arbitrary point of time defined by the function in the flow diagram of the system.

The developed simulation model of passenger rolling stock maintenance enables to schedule and manage maintenance and repair along with the analysis of maintenance service development on the railway network. One can track the dynamics of variations in the modeling process by varying the input data of the model.

This simulation model will become the basis for maintenance optimization model. Optimization will allow defining the optimum location of maintenance facilities and finding the readiness index of passenger rolling stock for providing high-quality maintenance.

Conclusion

Variations occurring for different values can be compared by varying mileage between repairs and the duration parameter of maintenance and repair in the model. It is also possible to evaluate the impact of each parameter on the model behavior. The output of modeling is represented by the information required for developing predictive estimates of a system operation, which, in turn, influences managerial decision making.

Discrete-event modeling is an alternative method for modeling various processes in maintenance and repair of passenger rolling stock. When using all options of AnyLogic software the modeled situation can be implemented in its full range with demonstration of the model behavior and characteristics. This model is designed for defining optimum locations of maintenance facilities to provide high operational readiness index of passenger rolling stock and minimum time and financial expenditures for maintenance and repair.

The facilities will provide maintenance and repair services for passenger rolling stock. The services in the facilities are provided either by the passenger rolling stock manufacturer or by a private operating company upon agreement with the manufacturer. Such structure will provide stability of serviceable and good operating condition of rolling stock during the whole life cycle.

The developed model will be used as a foundation for building a simulation model of operating capacity of maintenance and repair facilities for passenger cars. The model will enable to forecast equal distribution of rolling stock among enterprises. For further development of the model, elaboration of the optimization model is suggested which will include statistical data of rolling stock failures. Based on these data, the possibility of downtime occurrence when expecting maintenance can be studied, as well as the impact on the operational readiness index and financial expenditures.

References

1. A. Rakhmangulov, A. Kolga, N. Osintsev, I. Stolpovskikh, A. Sladkowski, Transport Problems, **Vol. 9**, 125-132 (2014).
2. V.S. Timchenko, Vestnik transporta Povolzhya, **Vol. 4**, 59–66 (2017). (in Russian)
3. D.G. Evseev, K.G. Shcherbakov, Mir transporta [World of Transport and Transportation Journal], **Vol. 3**, 134–139 (2014). (in Russian)
4. A. Crespo Marquez, P. Moreu de Leon, J. Gomez Fernandez, C. Parra Marquez, V. Gonzalez, *Safety, Reliability and Risk Analysis: Theory, Methods and Applications* (Martorell et al. Taylor & Francis Group, London2009).
5. W.J. Pierskalla, J.A. Voelker, Naval Research Logistics Quarterly, 23, 353–388 (1976).
6. S. Osaki, T. Nakagawa, IEEE Transactions on Reliability, 25, 284–287 (1976).
7. Y.S. Sherif, M.L. Smith, Naval Research Logistics Quarterly, 28, 47–74 (1981).
8. C. Valdez-Flores, R.M. Feldman, Naval Research Logistics, 36, 419–446 (1989).
9. D.I. Cho, M. Parlar, European Journal of Operational Research, 51, 1–23 (1991).

10. J.D. Campbell, *Uptime* (Productivity Press, Portland, 1995).
11. N.F. Sirina, V.V. Tsyganov, Problema upravlenija [Management problems], **6,** 93-95 (2006). (in Russian)
12. N.F. Sirina, Doctoral thesis, Ural State University of Railway Transport, Ekaterinburg, 2009. (in Russian)
13. M.M. Bolotin, Mir transporta [World of Transport and Transportation Journal], **Vol. 3**, 4–15 (2005). (in Russian)
14. Order of the Ministry of Railways of the Russian Federation No. 9, 04.04.1997 (ed. on 13.01.2011). Introduction of a new system of maintenance and repair of passenger cars (1997). (in Russian)
15. Normativnye sroki sluzhby mashin i oborudovanija [Normative service life of machines and equipment]. (in Russian)

Integrated development of carrying capacities of the Baikal-Amur Mainline and Trans-Siberian Railway

Andrey Borodin[1,*], *Petr* Kozlov[2], and *Anatoly* Kalinichenko[3]

[1]Institute of Transport Economics and Development JSC, 105066 Moscow, Russia
[2]Transportny Algorithm LLC, 109029 Moscow, Russia
[2]INTEGRAL Company LLC, 121099 Moscow, Russia

Abstract. The paper considers actual technical and technological problems in the development of the Eastern polygon of the Russian railway network. The purpose of the study is to develop a methodology and software tools that ensure the search for effective solutions for given resource and logistical constraints. Methods of simulation modeling, distribution of flows on networks and graphs are used. The result of the study is a hybrid set of model calculations.

Introduction

The integrated investment project "Modernization of the Railway Infrastructure of the Baikal-Amur Mainline and Trans-Siberian Railway with the Development of Throughput and Carrying Capacities" is among high-priority projects aimed at developing the Russian transport system. Its implementation since 2013 has already provided major results in logistics support of the national economy and its export potential [1]. Volumes of goods shipped from the major mineral deposits on the Eastern polygon are expected to increase from 58.1 million tonnes in 2012 to 124.9 million tonnes in 2020 and to 184.7 million tonnes in 2024.

The scale and complexity of the problems to be solved by the project require a significant scientific and methodological support, new algorithms and software for calculating effective parameters, as well as a database for decision-making. The key methodological problems include:

1. limited investment resources and possibilities to construct and reconstruct the railway infrastructure to the extent and within the time frames as required under the integrated project.

2. The boundaries of the polygon within which investment activities are carried out do not coincide with the boundaries in which technological, commercial, socioeconomic and budgetary effects and losses should be calculated.

3. Integrated investment projects for railway infrastructure development contain target indicators, such as traffic capacity of railway sections; carrying capacity of railway sections

* Corresponding author: borodinaf@mail.ru

© The Authors, published by EDP Sciences. This is an open access article distributed under the terms of the Creative Commons Attribution License 4.0 (http://creativecommons.org/licenses/by/4.0/).

in freight transportation directions; standard and average weights of freight trains; sectional speed of freight trains; route speed of passenger trains.

The applicable regulations set forth requirements for parameters of channels in the transport system (as defined in [2]), but do not contain any requirements for parameters of bunkers. Parameters of channels (as defined in the railway terminology) include traffic capacities of stations, sections and junction tracks, handling capacities of classification yards and cargo terminals. Bunkers are characterized by capacities of tracks used for accumulating trains and regulating their departures.

The paper [3] shows the consequences of underestimated properties and parameters of bunkers in the development of a railway network. In case of excess car fleet, part of yard tracks is excluded from traffic and handling operations with trains and cars. At the same time, the resulting traffic capacity of the railway infrastructure is significantly reduced relative to rated values calculated in accordance with the applicable instruction [4]. In order to take these factors into account, methodological provisions of studies [5–9] should be further developed. The existing flow control models are aimed at building some optimal dynamic processes. They include a dynamic transportation problem for managing empty car flows in dynamics [10]; a dynamic matching method for designing coordinated delivery of goods to ports [11]; a software package ELBRUS for generating an optimal multivariate train schedule according to a specified criterion [12].

It is only imitation models that can verify the effectiveness of these methods at specific polygons and in close-to-real conditions. The novelty of the study is in solving the methodological problems listed above. The purpose of the study is to develop a methodology, algorithms and software tools that ensure the search for effective solutions for given resource and time constraints in delivery of goods and empty cars.

Research methods

Bottlenecks of the railway infrastructure are classified in the applicable regulations. The concept of "bottleneck" is used in the General Railway Network Development Scheme [5, 6] and in supporting materials of investment projects: it is defined as a railway section whose traffic capacity is utilized above the allowable level set by the applicable instruction [4]. As shown in [1], the length of these bottlenecks will be increasing (as compared to 2013) and reach over 8,000 km (75% of the total length of the Baikal-Amur Mainline and Trans-Siberian Railway) in 2020 and about 10,000 km (more than 90% of their total length) in 2025.

At the same time, it has been proved [2] that the greatest delays in transport flows do not always arise from the most loaded infrastructure element. Therefore, it is proposed to distinguish between (Fig. 1):

a bottleneck of the first kind (an element loaded above the allowable level according to [4]);

a bottleneck of the second kind (an element that causes delays in acceptance of trains by railway stations or neighboring railway units);

a bottleneck of the third kind (a process operation that causes the greatest or unacceptable delays).

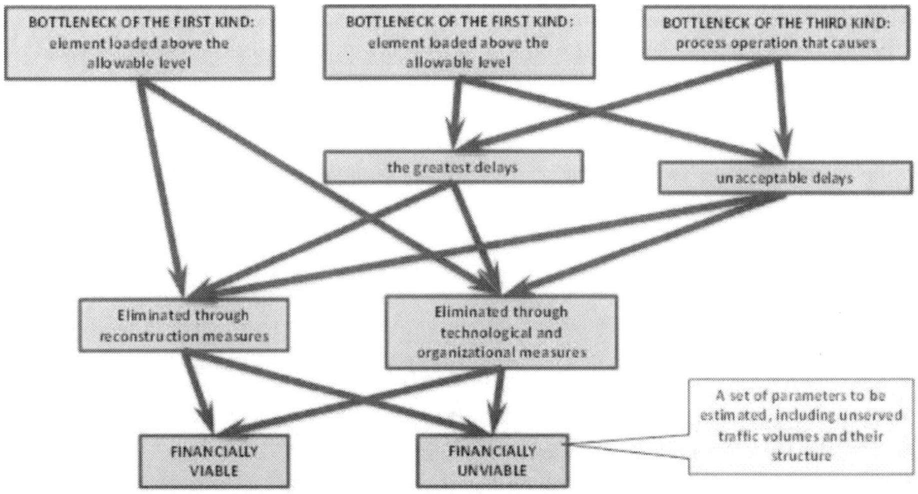

Fig. 1. Classification of bottlenecks and methods to remove them.

Removal of all bottlenecks only through reconstruction may lead to excessive need for investments and higher costs of subsequent operation. This solution is unacceptable.

Therefore, a methodical approach to solving a problem development and operation of the railway infrastructure and transportation resources in an integrated way was formulated and applied. The components of the solution contain controlled variables of three categories: (1) investment in infrastructure development; (2) adjustment of the number and structure of locomotive and car fleets; (3) improvement of a traffic management technique to minimize non-productive use of rolling stock and infrastructure capacities.

The solution must meet the following requirements. Sets of reconstruction measures should be sufficiently invariable to fluctuations of traffic flows (cargo base, passenger flows, car fleet management system). Infrastructure should allow railway carriers to regulate car traffic in the current operating conditions by redistributing car flows among its elements. This regulation involves using parallel railway routes, redistribution of classification operations among railway stations and yards, etc.

The following categories of process solutions aimed at maximizing the utilization of available traffic capacities of bottleneck sections were tested for the polygon of the Baikal-Amur Mainline and Trans-Siberian Railway.

1. To reduce standard processing time of trains in receiving-departure yards of technical stations.
2. To install parallel inputs and outputs (three-track insert rails) on the sections adjacent to technical stations.
3. To accelerate turnover of innovative high-capacity cars for reducing the total required volume of freight traffic.
4. To increase loaded train traffic passing through sections of the Baikal-Amur Mainline under an unpaired traffic schedule by returning empty car traffic through the sections of the Trans-Siberian Railway in trains of 100 conditional cars.

Results

The result of the study is a set of hybrid mathematical models developed and applied to solve the problems described above. Statistical analysis and forecasting components of this set are designed to calculate dynamics and structure of traffic flows. Network flow models allow traffic flows to be distributed. Simulation models can be used to calculate performance indicators.

Based on the results of the study, a simulation modeling technique was prepared and then approved by Russian Railways in 2018. It contains clear requirements for simulation systems and resulting models of stations and polygons. Automated simulation systems ISTRA (for stations) and IMETRA (for polygons) best meet these requirements. The models based on these systems can be used to assess the effectiveness of measures aimed at developing transport infrastructure and technological improvements.

Outputs of the model simulation are real traffic and handling capacities of a simulated object, utilization rate of individual devices, and related delays. Models provide additional information to designers and technologists. This information includes, for example, representation of processes in dynamics. A mimic diagram representing the station model demonstrates train and shunting movements, location of locomotives and track loading (Fig. 2).

On a mimic diagram representing the polygon model, traffic of trains on sections and their location at stations are marked with arrows (Fig. 3). As clearly seen from the presented fragment, station 3 is obviously overloaded. When switching to a graph of completed traffic, one can see how this overloading causes significant waiting times (Fig. 4).

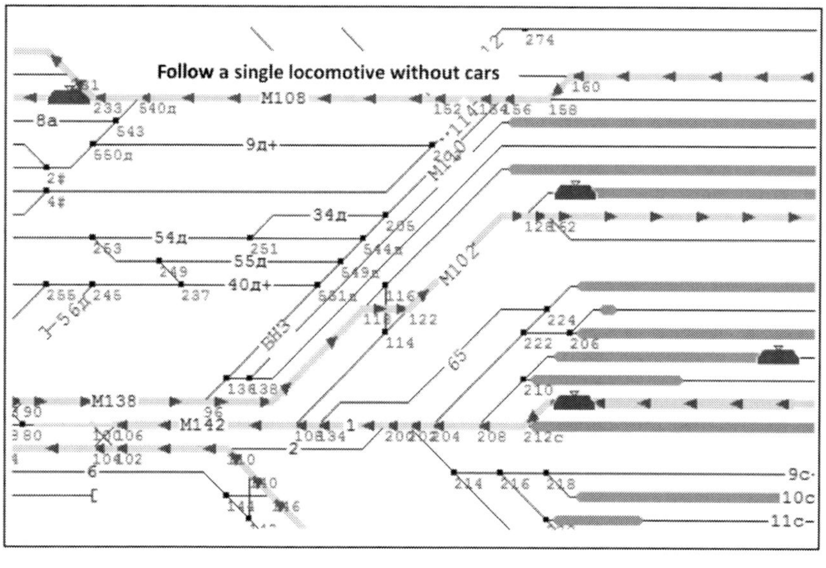

Fig. 2. Dynamics of processes in the station model.

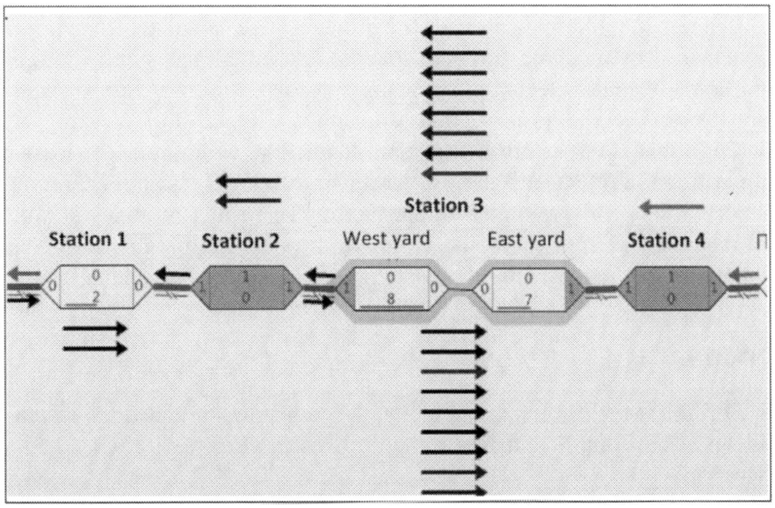

Fig. 3. Dynamics of processes in the polygon model.

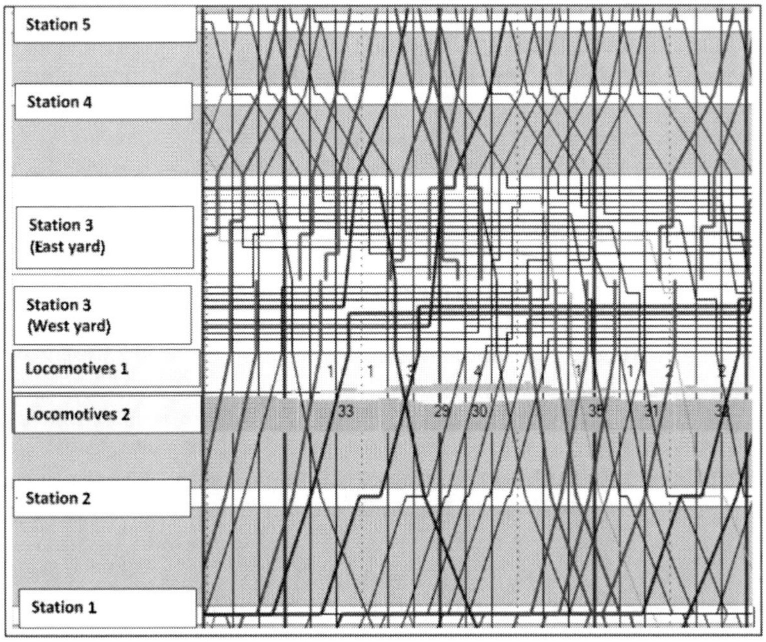

Fig. 4. A fragment of graph representing completed traffic in the polygon model.

Conclusion

The supporting materials for the integrated project "Modernization of the Railway Infrastructure of the Baikal-Amur Mainline and Trans-Siberian Railway with the Development of Throughput and Carrying Capacities" were elaborated in detail using the presented methodological solutions and software tools. The results contain multivariate calculations and an integrated selection of parameters for managing passenger and freight flows. The proposed traffic management technique includes traffic interchanges, a junction technology with non-public tracks, choice of routes for car traffic, standard weight and length of trains, traffic routing, a train making-up plan, traction facilities, and a train schedule. As a result, target indicators of the projects were calculated. The progress towards their achievement was synchronized with specific investment measures.

The traffic management technique is being considered jointly with Russian Railways, a technology auditor of the project, and Consumer Council for Working with Russian Railways. Coordinated issues are being submitted to the Committee for Russian Railways Priority Investment Projects of the Government of the Russian Federation. Thus, the practical calculations and preliminary approval of the results by experts confirm that the developed methods are applicable and effective in justifying parameters of upgrading the railway infrastructure, in particular the Eastern polygon of the Russian railway network.

References

1. A.F. Borodin, M.V. Storchak, Bjulleten' Obyedinennogo uchenogo soveta OAO RZD [Bulletin of the Joint Scientific Council of Russian Railways JSC], 2, 65 – 73 (2017). (in Russian)
2. P.A. Kozlov, Mir transporta [World of Transport and Transportation Journal], **12,** 2(51), 30 – 37 (2014). (in Russian).
3. E.A. Sotnikov, *Ekspluatacionnaja rabota zheleznyh dorog (sostojanie, problemy, perspektivy)* [Operational work of railways (condition, problems, prospects)] (Transport, Moscow, 1986). (in Russian)
4. Russian Railways JSC, *Instrukcija po raschetu nalichnoj propusknoj sposobnosti zheleznyh dorog* [Instructions for calculating the available capacity of railways] (Techinform, Moscow, 2011). (in Russian)
5. F.S. Pekhterev, Zheleznodorozhnyj transport [Railway transport], 5, 4 – 9 (2012). (in Russian)
6. F.S. Pekhterev, Bjulleten' Obyedinennogo uchenogo soveta OAO RZD [Bulletin of the Joint Scientific Council of Russian Railways JSC], 13 – 22 (2015). (in Russian)
7. A.A. Assad, Transportation Research Part B: Methodological, **14**, Issues 1–2, 101-114 (1980).
8. X. Wang, Q. Meng, Transportation Research. Part B: Methodological, **95**, 76-104 (2017).
9. A. Petraska, A. Jarasuniene, K. Ciziuniene, Procedia Engineering, **178**, 589-596 (2017).
10. I.P. Vladimirskaya, Doctoral thesis, Moscow State University of Railway Engineering, Moscow, 2011. (in Russian)
11. P.A. Novikov, Transport of the Urals, 2 (17), 72-75 (2008). (in Russian)
12. L.A. Muginshteyn, A.Yu. Anfinogenov, V.Yu. Kiryakin, S.A. Vinogradov, O.V. Lyashko, L.N. Ponarin, *Imitacionnoe modelirovanie v zadachah organizacii dvizhenija poezdov* [Simulation modeling in the tasks of organizing train traffic] (Intekst, Moscow, 2012). (in Russian)

Calculation of hardening process parameters for locomotive parts

Alexander Buynosov[1,*], *Vasily* Lapshin[1], *Alexander* Smolyaninov[1], and *Albert* Dinislamov[1]

[1]Ural State University of Railway Transport, 620034 Yekaterinburg, Russia

Abstract. The existing theoretical models of heating by concentrated sources with a high energy density generally describe processes with deep penetration welding of part surfaces. The purpose of this study is to identify the factors that have a major effect on hardening of parts through heat treatment with a high-speed or pulsed scanning stationary heat source, which creates a uniform temperature field. Using methods of regression analysis, the authors derived equations for calculating the hardening depth in the proposed hardening process, the rate and time of steel cooling in a critical temperature range. The paper presents the calculated parameters of the hardening process in which parts, including wheel flanges of locomotives, are heated by a plasma arc in nitrogen. The findings can be used to reduce costs of complex experiments aimed at selecting surface heat hardening parameters to increase the service life of locomotive mechanical parts.

Introduction

Different types of hardening are used to improve the reliability of steel parts throughout the entire life cycle. At present, surface hardening of steels by powerful concentrated energy sources, such as a laser beam and plasma arc, have been widely adopted. In order to avoid surface melting and increasing the area to be treated, heat source scanning is used. A plasma arc with transverse electromagnetic oscillations is widely used to harden various mechanical parts of locomotives made of carbon steels, including wheel flanges [1].

A review of foreign [1–8] and Russian [9–12] studies shows that heating parameters for concentrated sources with a high energy density are chosen on the basis of deep penetration welding procedures [2–4] or determined empirically [5]. After a part is hardened, a hardness profile of the hardened layer is measured using a destructive method. The procedure is repeated until the required depth and hardness of the thermally hardened layer are achieved. This requires considerable time and money. The most common techniques include low-temperature plasma nitriding [2, 3] and plasma heat treatment [4, 11]. The key factors influencing hardening of steel parts, however, have not yet been established.

The purpose of this study is to identify the factors that have a major effect on hardening a part through heat treatment with a high-speed or pulsed scanning stationary heat source.

* Corresponding author: byinosov@mail.ru

© The Authors, published by EDP Sciences. This is an open access article distributed under the terms of the Creative Commons Attribution License 4.0 (http://creativecommons.org/licenses/by/4.0/).

The scientific novelty of the paper is a method designed to calculate steel hardening parameters for locomotive parts through heat treatment with a high-speed or pulsed scanning stationary heat source, which creates a uniform temperature field.

Selection of a calculation methodology

To calculate parameters of temperature fields, we can use an equation [4] that describes heating of a semi-infinite body for an instantaneous source:

$$T = \frac{Q}{c\gamma \cdot \sqrt{a\pi t}} \cdot e^{\frac{z^2}{4at}}, \tag{1}$$

where T is the temperature; Q is the energy density; c is the specific heat capacity; γ is the density of steel; a is the coefficient of thermal diffusivity; t is the time of heat propagation; z is the depth from the body surface.

When different mechanical parts of the locomotive are hardened with a plasma arc (K = 1.4 cm/s; δ = 2.8 cm; a = 0.08 cm^2/s [10]), the conditions $K{\cdot}\delta/4\ a$ = 12.25 is satisfied. Therefore, the solution to the equation (1) can be used. The same solution is applicable to deep layers. For example, the thickness of a hardened layer (2 mm) for wheelsets is small compared to the thickness of a flange (maximum: 33, minimum: 25–28 mm).

Define a heat flux as $q = \eta{\cdot}N/S$ and the arc time as t_0, where η is the efficiency of a heat source; N is the power of a heat source; S is the area of heat treatment. For a heat source moving at a speed V, $N = U{\cdot}I$, (U is the voltage, I is the arc current), $S = b{\cdot}d$ (b is the oscillation width of the arc, d is the effective arc diameter, $t_0 = d/V$).

During the operation of the plasma arc that generates the heat flux q, at a time point t, for the period dt', the energy $dQ = q{\cdot}dt'$ will be emitted (Fig. 1).

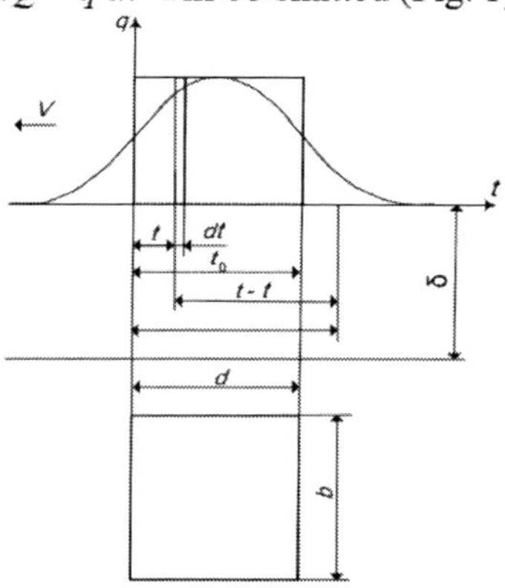

Fig. 1. Diagram of heating by a normally distributed source reduced to a uniformly distributed source.

By substituting dQ into (1), we obtain an equation for temperature change

$$T - T_0 = \frac{q}{c\gamma\sqrt{\pi a}} \int_0^B \frac{dt'}{\sqrt{t-t'}} \cdot e^{-\frac{z^2}{4a\cdot(t-t')}}, \tag{2}$$

where $B = t$ at $t < t_0$ and $B = t_0$ at $t \geq t_0$; T_0 is the initial temperature; t' is the heating time.

It is clear that the maximum temperature (T_m) is reached on the surface (at $z = 0$) at the end of heat treatment $t = t_0$. We can easily obtain it by integrating (2):

$$T_m - T_0 = \frac{2q}{c\gamma} \cdot \sqrt{\frac{t_0}{\pi a}}. \tag{3}$$

Let us introduce relative parameters: time $\tau = t/t_0$; operating time of the source $\tau' = t'/t_0$; depth $Z = z/(4 < a \cdot t_0)^{1/2}$; temperature $\theta = (T - T_0)/(T_m - T_0)$. The expression (2) can be written as:

$$\theta = \frac{1}{2}\int_0^B \frac{d\tau'}{\sqrt{\tau - \tau'}} e^{-\frac{Z^2}{\tau - \tau'}}, \tag{4}$$

where $B = \tau$ at $\tau < 1$ and $B = 1$ at $\tau \geq 1$.

For the surface $Z = 0$, the integral (4) can be finally expressed as:

$$\theta = \sqrt{\tau} - \sqrt{\tau - 1} \tag{5}$$

$$\theta = \sqrt{\tau} \text{ for } \tau < 1. \tag{6}$$

The expressions (4), (5) and (6) have the same form for stationary pulsed and high-speed sources.

Calculation of heat hardening parameters

It is reasonable to use numerical methods for calculating thermal conductivity parameters. Results of calculations with the equations (4), (5) and (6) are presented in Figure 2.

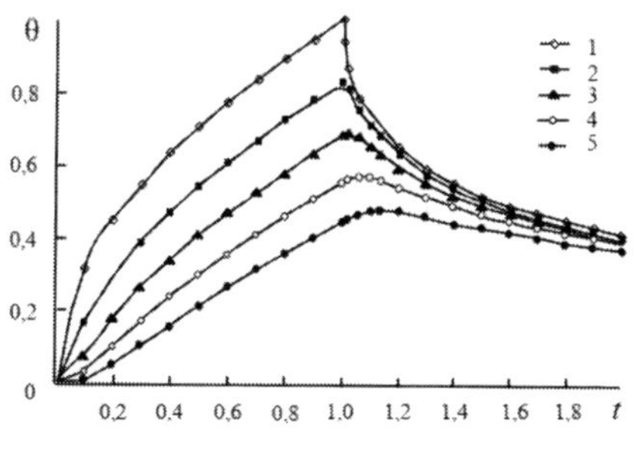

Fig. 2. Dependence of the relative temperature (τ) on the relative temperature (θ) for different depths: 1 – Z = 0; 2 – Z = 0.1; 3 – Z = 0.2; 4 – Z = 0.3; 5 – Z = 0.4.

For a moving heat source, it is more convenient to count the time from the end of the exposure to the source (the surface temperature is maximal). The relative temperature in a new coordinate system can be written as:

$$\theta = \frac{1}{2}\int_0^1 \frac{dt'}{\sqrt{\tau + \tau'}} \cdot e^{-\frac{Z^2}{\tau + \tau'}}, \tag{7}$$

for points at a certain depth of the part (body), and

$$\theta = \sqrt{\tau + 1} - \sqrt{\tau}, \tag{8}$$

$$\tau = \frac{1}{4}\left(\frac{1}{\theta} - \theta\right)^2 \tag{9}$$

for points on the surface of the part (body).

The residence time of metal in austenite state t_a is very important in the heat hardening process for locomotive mechanical parts [12]:

$$\tau_a = \frac{t_a}{t_0} = \frac{1}{4} \cdot \left(2 + \frac{1}{\theta_a^2} - 3 \cdot \theta_a^2\right). \tag{10}$$

In the equation (10), the relative temperature $\theta = (T_a - T_0)/(T_m - T_0)$.

When the maximum temperature θ_m is reached at a depth Z, in order to determine the relative time τ_m, it is necessary that $d\theta/d\tau$=0, then:

$$\tau_m = 2 \cdot Z^2 - \frac{\int_0^1 \frac{\tau' d\tau'}{\sqrt{(\tau_m + \tau')^5}} \cdot e^{-\frac{Z^2}{\tau_m + \tau'}}}{\int_0^1 \frac{d\tau'}{\sqrt{(\tau_m + \tau')^5}} \cdot e^{-\frac{Z^2}{\tau_m + \tau'}}}. \tag{11}$$

By substituting (11) into (7), we can determine θ_m. The relative parameters calculated with the equations (7) and (11) are given in Table 1. In this case, the hardening depth can be limited to$Z$ = 0.4.

Table 1. Values of relative parameters Z, τ_m and θ_m.

Z	τ_m	θ_m
0	0	1
0.05	0.0006857	0.914149
0.10	0.0035267	0.834054
0.20	0.0199325	0.691799
0.30	0.0588132	0.573651
0.40	0.1313577	0.478503

Figures 3a and 3b show dependences $\tau_m(Z)$ and $\theta_m(Z)$, respectively. For the data given in Table 1, these dependences can be approximated by nonlinear functions $\tau_m = 1.235 \cdot Z^{2.522}$ and $\theta_m = 1 - 1.2089 \cdot Z^{0,8729}$, respectively.

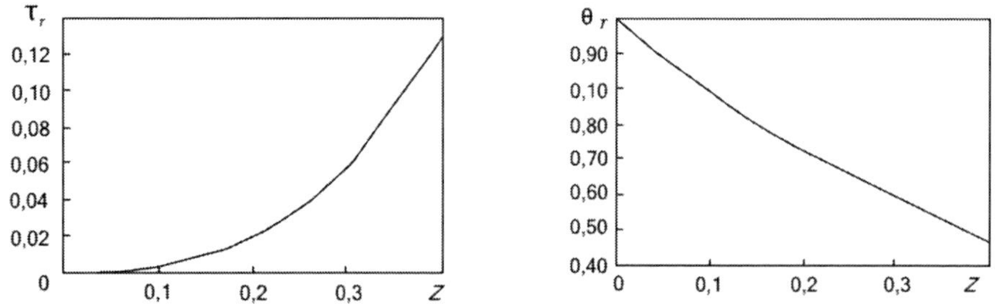

a b

Fig. 3. Dependence on the relative depth Z for: a – relative time τ_m; b – relative maximum temperature θ_m.

The relative time τ_m and maximum relative heating depth Z_m calculated at $T_0 = 950$ °C and $T_m = 1{,}000–1{,}500$ °C are given in Table 2.

Table 2. Values of temperature T_m, and relative parameters Z, τ_m and θ_m.

T_m, °C	$\theta_m = 950/T_m$	τ_m	Z_m
1,000	0.950000	0.00019995	0.0287207
1,100	0.863636	0.00213545	0.0810998
1,200	0.791666	0.00645315	0.1280839
1,300	0.730769	0.01329445	0.1708493
1,400	0.678571	0.02271107	0.2102661
1,500	0.633330	0.03473166	0.2469703
1,600	0.593750	0.49409390	0.2814682

Figures 4a and 4b present dependences $\tau_m(T_m)$ and $Z_m(T_m)$, respectively.

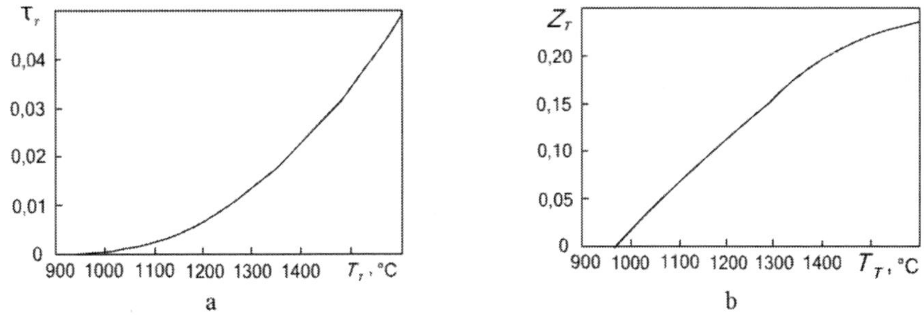

Fig. 4. Dependence on the maximum surface heating temperature T_m for: a – relative time τ_m; b – relative depth of the hardened layer Z_m.

As it can be seen from Table 2 and Figure 4b, when the heating surface temperature of the part falls from 1,500 to 1,000 °C, the heating depth decreases tenfold. Therefore, maintaining the required surface temperature is the key factor for high-quality hardening of locomotive mechanical parts.

Based on the calculated values given in Tables 1 and 2, an equation for calculating the hardening depth was derived using regression analysis [5, 13].

$$Z_m = 0{,}7838 \cdot (1-\theta)^{1.1485}. \qquad (12)$$

When using the approximate equation (12) in calculations, the maximum relative error is equal to 0.003 in the most common depth range $Z = 0.1–0.3$.

When analyzing the hardening process for a band of grade 2 in [14], the authors of the study [15] consider the cooling time $t_{8/5}$ in a temperature range of 800 to 500 °C and the band cooling rate in a temperature range of 600 to 500 °C. The relative cooling time in the body (at a depth) can be expressed by the relation $\tau_{8/5} = \tau_{500} - \tau_{800}$. Relative times τ_{500}, τ_{550} and τ_{800} are calculated by the formulas (9) and (10). The relative cooling rate of the part in the body can be defined as:

$$W_{550} = \frac{d\theta}{d\tau} = \frac{1}{4} \cdot \int_0^1 \frac{\left[2Z^2 - (\tau_{550} + \tau')\right] d\tau'}{\sqrt{(\tau_{550} + \tau')^5}} \cdot e^{-\frac{Z^2}{\tau_{550}+\tau'}}. \qquad (13)$$

The relative values of time $\tau_{8/5}$ and rate W_{550}, determined as a function of the maximum surface heating temperature T_m at T_a = 950 °C and T_0 = 0 °C, are given in Table 3 and Figure 5.

Table 3. Relative time and rate as a function of the maximum surface heating temperature.

T, °C	τ_{500}	τ_{550}	τ_{800}	in the body		on the surface	
				$\tau_{8/5}$	W_{550}	$\tau_{8/5}$	W_{550}
1,000	0.5608	0.4004	0.049	0.5118	0.3663	0.5119	0.3663
1,100	0.7484	0.5492	0.0913	0.6571	0.2666	0.6568	0.2667
1,200	0.9502	0.7093	0.1389	0.8113	0.2014	0.8098	0.2015
1,300	1.1675	0.8817	0.1918	0.9757	0.1563	0.9722	0.1565
1,400	1.4013	1.0672	0.2500	1.5371	0.1240	1.1446	0.1242
1,500	1.6521	1.2665	0.3138	1.3383	0.1001	1.3278	0.1004
1,600	1.9205	1.4799	0.3834	1.5371	0.0821	1.5219	0.0824

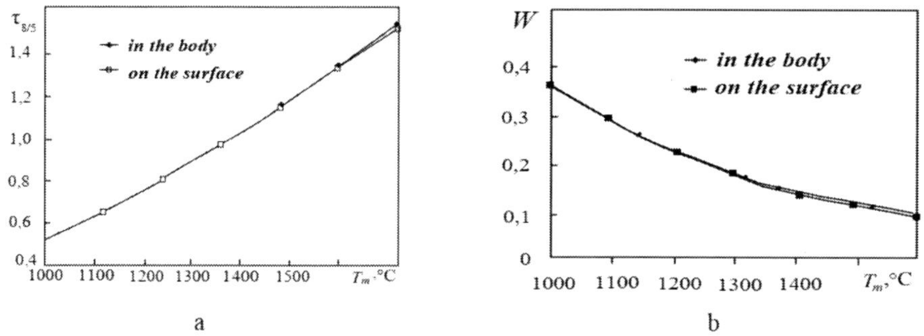

Fig. 5. Dependence on the maximum surface heating temperature T_m for: a – relative cooling time $\tau_{8/5}$ in a temperature range 800–500 °C; b – relative cooling rate W at 550 °C.

As it can be seen from Figure 5, the dependences in the body and on the surface are almost identical. This means that various layers of the part follow a similar cooling pattern at different heating temperatures. Hence, hardening of the part through heat treatment with a high-speed or pulsed scanning stationary heat source is mainly determined by two factors: the maximum temperature and the surface heating time.

Since the heating time is defined as a ratio of the diameter of the heat source to the speed of the source itself, the following parameters should be maintained constant to ensure the high-quality hardening process: 1) arc current and voltage that affect the effective diameter of the heat source; 2) constant speed of the source.

Conclusion

As a result of the studies, the key factors that influence hardening of steel locomotive parts were determined. Mathematical expressions were obtained for calculating the hardening depth, cooling time and rate of steels in a critical temperature range generated by a scanning stationary heat source, which creates a uniform temperature field. These findings should be compared with experimental data, results of computer-aided 3D modeling of dynamics and kinematics of the hardening process, and other hardening methods (e.g., electric arc).

References

1. S. Radchenko, D. Dorokhov, I. Gryadunov, Journal of Chemical Technology and Metallurgy, J. E **1**, 50, 104112 (2015).
2. T. Aizawa, K. Wasa, Micromachines, J. E **8**, 157 (2017).
3. V.A. Korotkov, M.V. Zlokazov, Journal of Friction and Wear, J. E **2**, 133136 (2014).
4. M. Zhang, C. Chen, X. Wang, J. Hou, S. Zhang, G. Zhu, H. Jing, Acta Metallurgica Sinica (English Letters), J. E **3**, 27, 521529 (2014).
5. V. Ivantsivsky, K. Parts, V. Popov, Applied Mechanics and Materials, J. E **788** (2015).
6. V.I. Pyndak, A.E. Novikov, Metal Science and Heat Treatment, J. E **3-4**, 58, 226230 (2016).
7. G.M. Zhuravlev, A.E. Gvozdev, A.E. Cheglov, N.N. Sergeev, O.M. Gubanov, Steel in Translation, J. E **6**, 47, 399411 (2017).
8. A.S. Kolpakov, N.I. Kardonina, Thermal Engineering, J. E **2**, 63, 150155 (2016).
9. D.N. Trushnikov, D.S. Belinin, Y.D. Shitsyn, Modern problems of science and education, 2, 95 (2014). (in Russian)
10. S.A. Mikaeva, A.S. Mikaeva, M.S. Rodyukov, Uprochnjajushhie tehnologii i pokrytija [Strengthening Technologies and Coatings], 3, 128–131 (2018). (in Russian)
11. S.Yu. Petrov, R.V. Kokorin, S.M Baban, Tekhnologiya Mashinostroeniya [Technology of Mechanical Engineering], 4, 37-44 (2017). (in Russian)
12. V.V. Muravyev, S.Yu. Petrov, L.V. Volkova, Defektoskopija [Russian Journal of Nondestructive Testing], 10, 64-74 (2015). (in Russian)
13. O.V. Pilipenko, S.J. Radchenko, D.O. Dorokhov, I.M. Gryadunov, International Journal of Applied Engineering Research, J. E **13** (2017).
14. GOST 398–2010. Rough tyres for railway rolling stock. Specifications (Standartinform, Moscow, 2011). (in Russian)
15. V.V. Girzhon, A.V. Ovchinnikov, Metal Science and Heat Treatment, J. E **11-12**, 58, 719723 (2017).

Survivability of the locomotive cabin at interval estimation of obstacle parameters

Alexander Smolyaninov[1,*], *Igor* Emel'yanov[1,2], *Vladimir* Mironov[2], *Alexei* Kuznetsov[2], and *Vasily* Lapshin[1]

[1]Ural State University of Railway Transport, 620034 Yekaterinburg, Russia
[2]Institute of Engineering Science, Ural Branch of the Russian Academy of Sciences, 620049 Yekaterinburg, Russia

Abstract. The article considers the multiparameter problem of the mechanical system behavior and its survivability when destructing individual elements. The technique for constructing the area of safe operation of the cabin of the GT1-h gas turbine locomotive was illustrated on the example of collision of a locomotive with an obstacle at a crossing. The main parameters determining the energy of interaction between the cabin and the obstacle was singled out, and their influence on the survivability of the structure was analyzed. The finite element method was used to calculate the load-bearing capacity of a power frame with a buffer device in the initial state and after the destruction of individual structural elements by the dynamic strength criterion. The force of elastic interaction between the locomotive and the obstacle was estimated through the spring, the rigidity of which was estimated on the basis of the finite element calculation results. As a result of the calculations, proposals were developed to strengthen the cabin frame to ensure the safety of the crew and the instrument part in case of unauthorized collision with an obstacle of considerable mass and violation of the speed regime.

Introduction

The problem of maintaining the load-bearing capacity of a metal structure after destruction of individual elements is known as the problem of the survivability of structures. Estimation of a real structure survivability is reduced to solving a nontrivial multiparameter problem of constructing a safe operation area in a certain functional space [1-5]. The task of such a large scale can have an ambiguous solution, different levels of strictness in formulation of particular problems, and ways of presenting the results. The situation is complicated by the fact that the initial data on the design and the nature of external impact are almost never sufficiently complete. For this reason, there is no single scheme or any single-valued algorithm for solving such problems. In connection with this, the search for approaches to a more accurate estimation of the survivability of real mechanical systems under operating conditions and, in particular, under excessive loads is relevant. An example

* Corresponding author: ASmolyaninov@usurt.ru

© The Authors, published by EDP Sciences. This is an open access article distributed under the terms of the Creative Commons Attribution License 4.0 (http://creativecommons.org/licenses/by/4.0/).

is the problem of survivability of a locomotive cabin in a collision with an obstacle on a crossing, which is considered in this article.

Methods for estimation of protection of the cabin's power frame from destruction in collisions with obstacles are reduced to calculating the efficiency of buffer devices [6-8]. With that, the obstacle appears as an absolutely rigid body, which causes incorrect estimation of the interaction effort. To clarify the effort, the locomotive and obstacle are treated as two point masses interacting through a spring of equivalent rigidity, which is determined taking into consideration of compliances of the cabin with the buffer device and the obstacle. Since the type of obstacle is not known in advance, interval estimation of its structure rigidity is given. The studied area of safe combinations of obstacle parameters is determined by the equality of the determined interaction force in a collision and the load of the limiting state of the cabin power frame determined with the finite element calculation.

It is believed that the most reliable information about the consequences of such external influences and possible scenarios of destruction is provided by performing field tests and crash tests [9-12]. But such information is possible for relatively inexpensive objects. It is often statistically unreliable and is not comprehensive, since it is rarely possible to provide space-time synchronization of loads due to the random nature of the external impact. For these reasons, the task of calculating the quantitative estimation of the extreme loads spectrum of the structure that limits the area of safe operation is actual at the design stage. The purpose of this work is to develop and implement an algorithm for quasistatic calculation of the limiting state of the cabin structure, in which the kinetic energy of the impact, the compliance of the cabin structure and obstacles is taken into consideration in addition to the masses and the velocity of the composition.

Study methods

GT1-h gas turbine locomotive with a buffer device of passive protection was selected as a specific object for the proposed demonstration of the approach [1, 10]. The power frame of the gas turbine locomotive cabin is a three-dimensional beam-rod structure made up of more than a hundred bent profiles and open-ended beams (Fig. 1). The buffer device consists of a frontal beam, fastening braces and six honeycomb elements between the frontal beam and the header. Experimental study of such systems with a review of the loading conditions is not possible. Costly field tests are very informative, but they cannot give a statistically reliable result. The most affordable way to calculate the carrying capacity of a complex design is mathematical simulation and computational experiments to determine the stress state.

The ANSYS-14 calculation package, the Uranus supercomputer of the Institute of Engineering Science, Ural Branch of the Russian Academy of Sciences and the quasistatic approach to solving dynamic problems was used in this work. Such approach is typical, for example, for the catastrophe theory [13], where dynamic phenomena in a mechanical system are predicted on the basis of equilibrium surfaces analysis. The carrying capacity of the cabin was determined in calculation of the stress state under various loading conditions. As the elements of the cabin are basically thin-walled structures, the SHELL-181 finite element [14-19] is used in the shape model that consists of over 450 thousand finite elements.

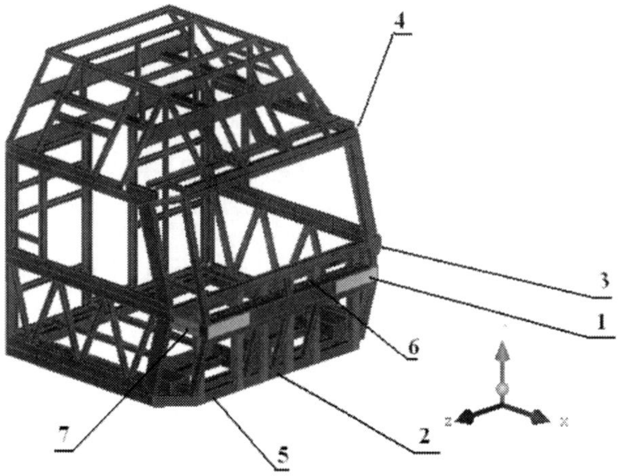

Fig. 1. The design layout of the GT1h gas turbine locomotive cabin drawn in the ANSYS ICEM CFD 14.0 application, where 1 is the frontal beam, 2 is fastening elements, 3 is the power belt, 4 is the upper harness of the cabin, 5 is the lower frame of the cabin, 6 is the set of honeycomb elements, 7 is side stops.

The dynamic nature of impact interaction between the cabin and the obstacle at a crossing is taken into consideration in the material model. It was assumed that the material of the cabin elements (3sp5 steel with the tensile strength of $\sigma_V = 500$ MPa) remains elastic until the failure at the dynamic yield point of $\sigma_{DY} = 1{,}3\sigma_V = 650$ MPa [20]. The strength criterion of a single structural element is adopted in the form of

$$\sigma_V \geq \sigma_{DY} \tag{1}$$

where σ_V is Mises' equivalent strain.

Calculation of the stress state of the cabin with destruction of individual elements by criterion (1) showed that the limiting state of the entire structure is only reached when the buffer device is completely destroyed. The corresponding limiting load on the frontal beam for a given value of contact area S_f integrally determines the resistance to damage to the entire cabin structure

$$P_{prel} = \iint_{S_f} q dxdy \tag{2}$$

where q is the contact load at the moment of impact.

On the other hand, the maximum force of interaction between the locomotive and the obstacle as two point masses can be estimated by the formula [1, 10]

$$F_{\max} = v\sqrt{cm_2} + F_T \tag{3}$$

Here, c is the equivalent rigidity of the system, which is determined from following expression by analogy with the successive connection of two springs

$$c^{-1} = c_c^{-1} + c_{ob}^{-1} \quad (4)$$

where c_c is the rigidity of the cabin with a buffer devices determined at the calculation of P_{prel} by the results of the finite element analysis. The mass m_1 of the train with the gas turbine locomotive reaches four thousand tons and more. Formula (3) output assumed $m_1 >> m_2$.

Obstacle rigidity c_{ob} can be determined in a similar calculation in the specific case. As the parameters of a potential obstacle are not known before the collision, c_{ob} can only be estimated by the interval value of ratio $r = c_{ob}/c_c$, $r \in [0,1;1]$ By changing this ratio, it is possible to predict possible interaction force F_{max} with obstacles of different design. This includes the conditions regulated by European standard EN 15227:2008 [11].

Equality of formula (2) and (3) allows revealing the area of safe combinations of obstacle parameters, in which the power frame of the cabin does not collapse. Therefore, the safety of machinists and the instrumental part will be ensured. The results of calculations are presented in the form of a limiting surface in the three-dimensional space, the mapping of which on the obstacle parameters plane gives the required area of safe operation of the cabin.

Results

The calculated dependences of force P on displacement w of the cross section at the center of the frontal beam for various states of the system are represented by straight lines 1, 2 and 3 in Figure 2.

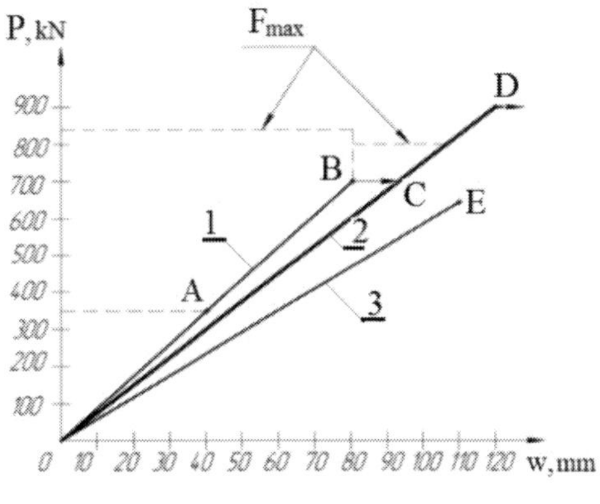

Fig. 2. To limit load calculation algorithm P_{prel}.

The calculated straight lines are built for various states of the system. Straight line 1 in Figure 2 was built for the initial state; the destruction of the anchoring struts (point A) did not affect the system rigidity. Straight line 2 was built for a cabin without honeycomb elements that collapsed under load P_B (straight line 1). Straight line 3 was built for a power frame without honeycomb elements that collapsed under load P_D (straight line 2). Destruction of honeycomb elements causes transition of the BC to new load line 2. At the same time, no destruction of the power frame occurs. The transition dynamics must be neglected in view of the overall impact stress nature. Transition from point D is impossible, as the destruction of the frontal beam will cause destruction of the cabin power frame. Therefore, the carrying capacity of the cabin will be determined by the value of the ultimate integral load $P_{prel} = P_D$ =920 kN.

It should be noted that the destruction of the system elements causes a reduction in cabin rigidity c_c and, in accordance with expression (4), to the reduction of the equivalent rigidity of the "cabin-obstacle" system. Then, according to expression (3), the value of the maximum interaction force F_{max} is also reduced. In the example considered, this reduction is small (see the dashed line in Figure 2) and can be neglected. In the general case, using the equality of expressions (2) and (3) to construct the desired boundary G_q, the calculated stiffness c_c shall be determined by the slope of the line on which value P_{prel} is determined.

Let us not down the equality of expression (2) and (3) that connects the parameters of the cabin and obstacles in the form of an implicit function

$$v\sqrt{c(f)m_2} + F_T(m_2) - P_{prel}(\sigma_{DY}, f) = 0 \quad (5)$$

Such function defines a certain hypersurface in the multidimensional space of the parameters studied. Visual representation of such surface can be obtained for three or four variables. For the example considered, coefficient of the the frontal beam area overlapping f=1. Surface (5) is presented in Figure 3 (a) at the set intervals of $m_2 \in [1000;20000]$ kg and $r \in [0,1;1]$.

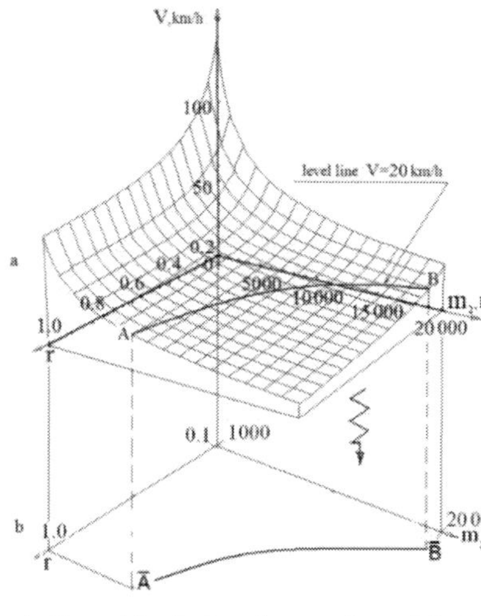

Fig. 3. Design hypersurface: *a* is the cabin destruction surface; *b* is the projection of the level line onto the obstacle parameters plane.

According to the rules for the operation of the rolling stock of railways [6], the recommended speed of the train at a crossing must not exceed 20 km/hour. Level line AB is assigned on the surface corresponding to the given speed value, and Figure 3 (b) shows its projection $\overline{A}\overline{B}$ onto the obstacle parameters plane. Line $\overline{A}\overline{B}$ is the studied boundary G_q of the area of safe operation of the cabin at a crossing within the specified ranges of the mass change and the obstacle structure rigidity. The structure will be survivable until the obstacle parameters are located within the area bounded by G_q. Destruction of the cabin with the combination of obstacle parameters within this area is only possible because of exceeding of the recommended speed at a crossing.

Conclusion

The performed calculations of the gas turbine locomotive cabin allowed making a reasoned conclusion about the need to strengthen the structural frame of the structure. The calculation algorithm and the developed finite element model of the cabin with a buffer device can be adapted to structural changes without large expenditures. The procedure for calculating the boundary between the structure and the sacrificial elements will not change with another set of investigated parameters, including standard variants. A significant complication in calculations of the load is possible if the material model becomes more complex. In general, a relatively simple quasistatic approach allowed solving the task set and finding the area of safe combinations of the main obstacle parameters for the cabin. Unlike standard approaches, the presented calculation takes into consideration the rigidity of the cabin and obstacles.

The guaranteed area of safe operation of the structure is clearly indicated by the assumptions, limitations and criteria of the limiting states of a particular methodology for a typical calculation for regulated combinations of loads. When an over-normative load is applied, the definition of the area of safe operation of a specific object that provides protection for personnel and equipment is associated with solution of a number of new non-trivial tasks. First of all, this is due to incompleteness of studies of the phenomenon of destruction of materials and structures, as well as due to the fact that the parameters of external influence in a non-emergency situation have not been fully determined in advance. In the absence of rigorous solutions to statistical dynamics in computational practice, deterministic engineering estimates of the limiting state of the entire complex structure will be in demand.

Further studies of this problem are related to refinement of dynamic properties of the structure material under impact loading. They are also related to refinement of the input parameters of the problem in accordance with possible scenarios of collision of the locomotive with various obstacles. Consideration of physical and geometric nonlinearity of the problem can provide a certain refinement of survivability prediction.

References

1. I.G. Emel'yanov, V.I. Mironov, A.V. Kuznetsov, Journal of Machinery Manufacture and Reliability, **Vol. 44(5)**, 449 – 454 (2015).
2. S.A. Timashev, A.V. Bushinskaya, Proceedings of the 6th All-Russian conference "Safety of Critical Infrastructures and Territories", 212-222 (AMB, 2014). (in Russian)
3. N.E. Naumenko, I.Yu. Khizha, Tehnicheskaja mehanika [Technical mechanics], 4, 65–74 (2014). (in Russian)
4. M.B. Sobolevskaya, S.A. Sirota, Tehnicheskaja mehanika [Technical mechanics], 1, 84–96 (2015). (in Russian)
5. P. Llana, R. Stringfellow, R. Mayville, *Proc. of the ASME/IEEE 2013 Joint Rail Conf.*, 1–11, Knoxville, TN, USA, April 15-18, 2013.
6. Normy dlja rascheta i ocenki prochnosti nesushhih jelementov, dinamicheskih kachestv i vozdejstvij na put' jekipazhnoj chasti lokomotivov zheleznyh dorog MPS RF kolei 1520 [Norms for calculating and evaluating the strength of load-bearing

elements, dynamic qualities and impacts on the way of the crew part of locomotives of the railways with gauge 1520] (Moscow, 1998). (in Russian)
7. E.M. Ryazanov, M.V. Zhuykov, A.E. Pavlyukov, Transport of the Urals, **4(43),** 44-49 (2014). (in Russian)
8. N.M. Zhuravlev, Thesis of Candidate of sciences, Moscow Institute of Transport Engineers, Moscow, 2006. (in Russian)
9. Y.Q. Sun, C. Cole, M. Dhanasekar, D.P. Thambiratnam, Vehicle System Dynamics: Intern. J. of Vehicle Mechanics and Mobility, **Vol. 50** (7), 1137–1155 (2012).
10. I.G. Emel'yanov, V.I. Mironov, A.V. Kuznetsov, *AIP Conf. Proc.* **1785**, 040014 (2016).
11. EN 15227. Railway applications – Crash worthmess requirement sforrail way vehicle bodies (European committee for standardization, Brussel, 2008).
12. ГОСТ 32410-2013. Emergency crash-systems railway rolling stock for passenger transportations. Technical requirements and methods of control (Standartinform, Moscow, 2013). (in Russian)
13. V.M. Markochev, Strength of Materials Journal **7**, 43-46 (1985). (in Russian)
14. I.G. Emel'janov, V.I. Mironov, *Dolgovechnost' obolochechnyh konstrukcij* [Durability of shell structures] (Yekaterinburg, 2012). (in Russian)
15. I. Copaci, A. Tanasoiu, B. Tanasoiu, *Proceedings of Invited Papers*, 3th WSEAS International Conference on Finite Differences - Finite Elements - Finite Volumes - Boundary Elements (F-and-B '11), Bucharest, Romania, 2010.
16. T. Manescu, N. Zaharia, D. Avram, N. Tiganasu, M. Stroia, *Proceedings of Invited Papers*, 4th International Conference on Finite Differences - Finite Elements - Finite Volumes - Boundary Elements (F-and-B '11), Paris, France, 2011.
17. M.B. Sobolevskaja, I.B. Telichko, I.K. Hrushh, D.V. Gorobets, Yu.A. Klyk, Tehnicheskaja mehanika [Technical mechanics], **2**, 19 – 28 (2010). (in Russian)
18. M.B. Sobolevskaya, I.B. Telichko, Tehnicheskaja mehanika [Technical mechanics], **2**, 49–62 (2011). (in Russian)
19. A.A. Alyamovskiy, A.A. Sobachkin, E.V. Odincova et al., *Solid Works komp'juternoe modelirovanie v inzhenernoj praktike* [Solid Works computer simulation in engineering practice] (BHV-Peterburg, St. Petersburg, 2005). (in Russian)
20. Kh.A. Rakhmatulin, Yu.A. Demyanov, *Prochnost pri intensivnykh kratkovremennykh nagruzkakh* [Strength under Intensive Momentary Loads] (Gos. izd-vo fiz.-mat. lit. Publ., Moscow, 1961). (in Russian)

Estimation of container system development in a region

Daria Kochneva[1,*], *Vasily* Say[1], and *Valentina* Parshina[1]

[1]Ural State University of Railway Transport, 620034 Yekaterinburg, Russia

Abstract. A relevant problem of scientific research is formalization of the processes of interaction between transportation systems and the region in the context of modern ideas of synergetic approach. The purpose of this article is to develop a methodology for assessing and forecasting the needs of a region for container transport system development. The methodology includes two elements. First is the model for forecasting region's demand for container transportation based on the methods of correlation-regression analysis, index prediction and the Monte Carlo method. Second is the imitation model for assessing the needs of the region in the technical and organizational development of the container system. Organizational development is achieved due to system integration of market players, coordinated management of container flows, which makes it possible to establish the synergistic effect availability.

Introduction

Container transportation has been the most dynamically developing type of cargo transportation in recent years. The average level of containerization in the world is 60-70% of the total volume of dry cargo transportations [1]. In Russia, this indicator is significantly behind the global level and presently amounts to 6.2% only, but it has been growing at a rapid pace over the past decade and the containerization factor on the railway network has more than doubled [2].

The reasons for rapid development of the container market in the regions of Russia are growth of industrial production, intensification of foreign trade with the countries of the Asia-Pacific region, redistribution of freight traffic from other types of rolling stock towards containers. This caused a significant increase in the need for container infrastructure in the regions and formation of a competitive container market.

At the same time, there is currently no single coordination approach to assessing the need for regions to develop container infrastructure, so formation of regional container systems is often spontaneous. Each transport market player pursues only its own economic interests, which causes an imbalance in development of terminal capacities in the region, the emergence of irrational empty container flows, and the inefficient use of rolling stock. In its turn, the reduction in the efficiency of operation of the container system has negative effects on development of the regional economy.

* Corresponding author: dana_rich@mail.ru

© The Authors, published by EDP Sciences. This is an open access article distributed under the terms of the Creative Commons Attribution License 4.0 (http://creativecommons.org/licenses/by/4.0/).

Arrangement of interaction between the links of the container transport system under market conditions has been the subject of a large number of modern studies. Various methods and models are used in this area, for example, cluster analysis [3], game theory models [4], supply chain management concept [5], agent-based simulation modeling [6], etc. However, the basis of these approaches primarily consists in the interests of certain companies, while the interests of the container system in general and in the specific region, the needs of which such system meets, do not receive due attention.

This determines the relevance and novelty of developing approaches to assessing the need of the region for developing the container transport system based on the balance of interests of suppliers and consumers of transport services, taking into consideration territorial economic characteristics. The basis for development of the model is the modern understanding of the system approach in logistics [7-8].

Study method

The volume of container transportations in the region is mainly determined by the following two factors: demand of enterprises for container transportation and technical development of the container infrastructure. Therefore, let us express the region's containerization level in the following function:

$$k_t = F(D_t; R_t), \tag{1}$$

where D_t is the demand of enterprises of the region for container transportation at moment of time t,
R_t is the technical and technological development of the container infrastructure in the region at moment of time t.

Thus, solution to this task includes the following two main stages: forecasting the region's demand for container transportation and assessing the need for development of the container system to meet this demand.

Forecasting of the region's demand for container transportation can be performed with various methods. There are the following main methods of traffic forecasting among many methods proposed in the references: extrapolation of time series [9], index prediction method [10], expert methods [11], correlation-regression analysis methods [12-13], simulation modeling methods [14].

The following author's model for forecasting the demand for container transportation is proposed on the basis of the index method, regression modeling and the Monte Carlo method. First, considering the fact that the demand for container shipments is limited by the volume of the cargo fit for containers, we have the following function:

$$D_t = w_t \cdot G_t, \tag{2}$$

where w_t is the share of cargo fit for containers in the region at moment of time t;

G_t is the total value of the region's demand for freight traffic (total freight traffic of all transport types in the region), tons.

Second, let us use the index method and put down the expression for forecasting the total freight traffic on the basis of information about the past:

$$G_t = I_{Gt} \cdot G_{t-1}, \tag{3}$$

where I_{Gt} is the index of growth of the total cargo flow of the region.

Third, given that the growth of the region's freight traffic is determined by the dynamics of its economic indicators, the regression model can be used:

$$I_{Gt} = f(I_{1t}, I_{2t}...I_{nt}), \tag{4}$$

where $I_{1t}, I_{2t}...I_{nt}$ are indices of growth of economic indicators of the region. The latter can be indices of the GRP physical volume, the index of output of goods and services, production indexes, physical turnover volume indexes, etc., can be used. Selection of indices in the proposed regression model is determined by the structure of the GRP of the region, the availability of information on the investigated parameters, the regional economy specifics. The decision to include or exclude parameters in the model is taken on the basis of the analysis of regression significance indicators (correlation coefficient, determination coefficient, Student's test, Fisher test, etc.).

Fourth, let us take into consideration the fact that the change in the growth indices in the region's economic indicators is a random variable, which is determined by a large number of difficultly predictable external factors. Therefore, the Monte Carlo method is used to express each growth index of economic indicators of the region I_i as a random variable with the established distribution law.

Thus, taking into account expression (2) to (4), the model for forecasting the demand for container transportation in the region in general terms shall be expressed as follows:

$$D_t = w_t \cdot G_{t-1} \cdot f(I_1, I_2...I_n). \tag{5}$$

Let us determine the regression equation (4), establish the law and the distribution parameters of the random variable I_i in the example of the Sverdlovsk region.

To find the regression equation, let us use the step-by-step algorithm, the essence of which is selection of a small number of variables from the large number of factor attributes (in our case, region development indices I_i), which contribute the most to the variation of the dependent variable (in our case, the I_G freight traffic growth index) [15].

The following two statistically significant indicators were selected in accordance with the Student's criterion based on the regression analysis of information on the volume of freight traffic and economic indicators of the Sverdlovsk region for 25 years [16]: the GRP physical volume index in the "Processing Manufacturing" section (I_1, %) and the GRP physical volume index under the "Wholesale and Retail Trade" section (I_2, %). Then, the multiple regression linear equation will be as follows:

$$I_G = 0.8067\, I_1 + 0.3016\, I_2 - 7.5712. \tag{6}$$

With that, the multiple coefficient of determination (R^2) for the model obtained is 0.953, which means that in 95.3% of cases the model explains the change in the volume of freight traffic and can be used for forecasting.

In accordance with the Monte Carlo method algorithm, the laws and distribution parameters for variable I_1, I_2 are determined, and the calculation was performed with the help of the STATISTICA software (see Table 1).

Figure 1 shows the algorithm for predicting optimistic, pessimistic and expected level of demand for container transportations for the set forecasting horizon T based on N trials with a given probability of the output reliability.

Table 1. Statistical characteristics of distribution of random values I_1, I_2.

Variable	I_1	I_2
Random variable distribution law	Normal	Log-normal
Pearson criterion	$X^2 = 7,07; X^2_{crit}(9;0,05) = 16,92$ $X^2 < X^2_{crit}(9;0,05)$	$X^2 = 5,62; X^2_{crit}(7;0,05) = 14,06$ $X^2 < X^2_{crit}(7;0,05)$
Kolmogorov-Smirnov criterion	$\lambda = 0,198; \lambda_{crit}(0,05) = 1,358$ $\lambda < \lambda_{crit}(0,05)$	$\lambda = 0,082; \lambda_{crit}(0,05) = 1,358$ $\lambda < \lambda_{crit}(0,05)$
Statistical distribution parameters	Mathematical expectation: μ=103.05 Standard deviation: σ =8.43	Median: Me = 101.31 Standard deviation: σ =12.71
Expression for calculation of the random value	$I_1 = 103,05 + 8,43Z$, where Z is the random number regularly distributed within the interval from -3 to 3.	$X = 101,31 \cdot e^{12,71 \cdot \lg(\sum_1^{12} Z_i - 6)}$, where Z_i is the random number regularly distributed within the interval from 0 to 1.

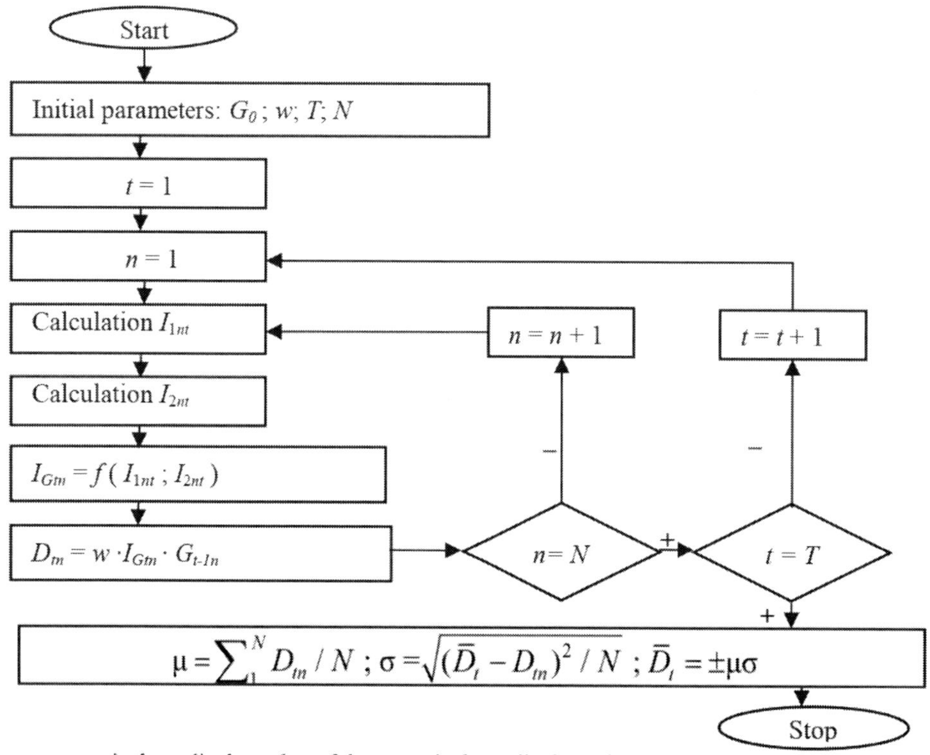

n is the ordinal number of the test; t is the ordinal number of the forecast period;
λ is the normalizing factor

Fig. 1. Design algorithm for forecasting the demand for container transportation.

Based on the forecast value of demand, it is possible to estimate the need for resources of the container transport system in the region, namely: the container fleet, terminals, rolling stock. To do this, let us use the imitation model of the regional container transportation and logistics system developed by the authors in [17-18].

Ehe general view of the aforementioned imitation model can be seen in Figure 2.

The regional container system in the model representation combines a complex of technical and technological resources and a subsystem of integrated management of container traffic. Technical and technological resources of the container system shall include the following:

– the totality of terminals with the throughput of P_{kt} at moment of time t, various owners k located in the territory of the region;

– the totality of containers A_t and fitting platforms P_t located in the territory of the region at moment of time t that belong to various owner k.

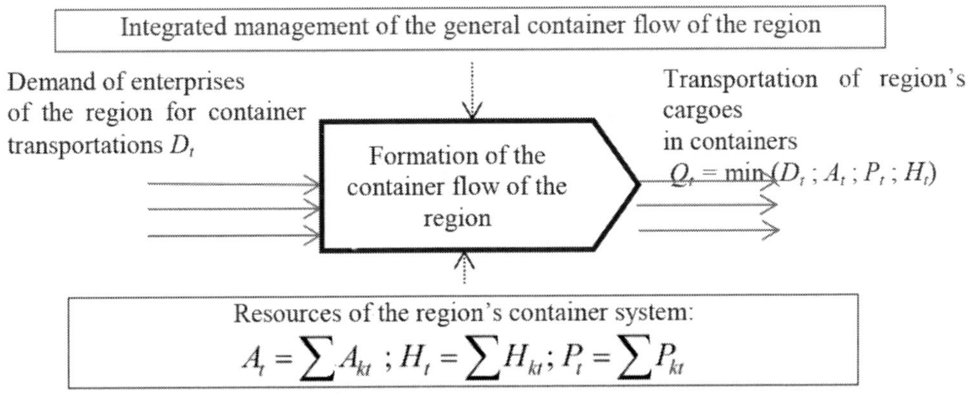

Fig. 2. General model representation of the container system of the region.

The maximum volume of container transportations provided by the system cannot exceed the demand for container transportations and the available resource constraints, that is:

$$Q_t = \min(D_t, A_t, P_t, H_t), \tag{7}$$

The equation $Q_t = D_t$ within a given period of time means that the demand for container transportation is fully satisfied, the container system is able to ensure the export of the products fit for transportation in containers. Otherwise, it is required either to create a reserve of resources (within the available opportunities) or to invest into development of a particular resource.

A special role in the presented model is played by the function of integrated control of container traffic: the model allows analyzing two states of the system, i.e., in the absence or presence of integration. In the absence of integration, the activities of the competing links of the regional organizational network are considered separate, and, as a result, many isolated and non-coordinated container flows are formed. It causes the imbalance in loading of container capacities; the emergence of resources shortage in some elements of the container system, with the reserves of others.

The availability of system integration assumes that the organizational network efficiency criterion is not the individual indicators of its individual components, but the system-wide result, which is expressed in maximizing the satisfaction of the region's demand with minimal terms of container traffic processing.

Experimental data and results

Let us try the proposed model on the example of the Sverdlovsk region. Figure 3 shows the results of numerical experiments with the Monte Carlo method for forecasting the demand for container transportations. The experiment on the model showed that the region's demand for transportations in containers will not exceed 8,806.7 thousand tons and will not be less than 3,085.3 thousand tons with the probability of the 95% reliability.

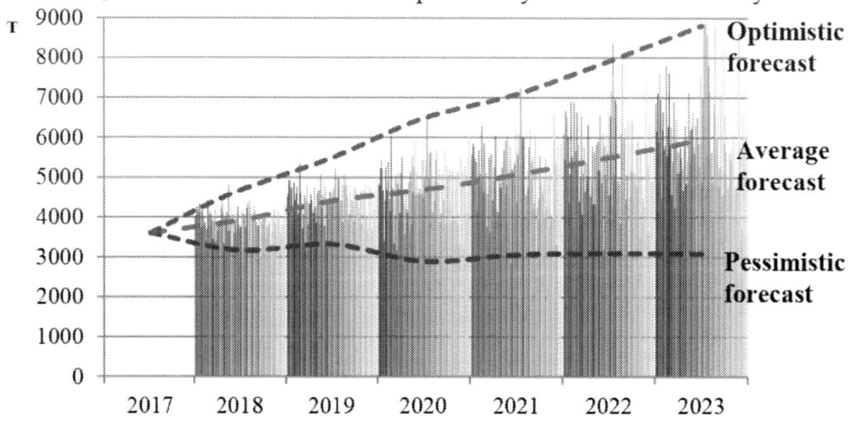

Fig. 3. Results of numerical experiments on forecasting the region's demand for container transportations.

Using model [17-18], the capacity of the container transportation network of the region was assessed with the presence and absence of system integration of links. The result of the system resource development estimation is comparable with the established forecast level of the region's demand for transportations (Fig. 4).

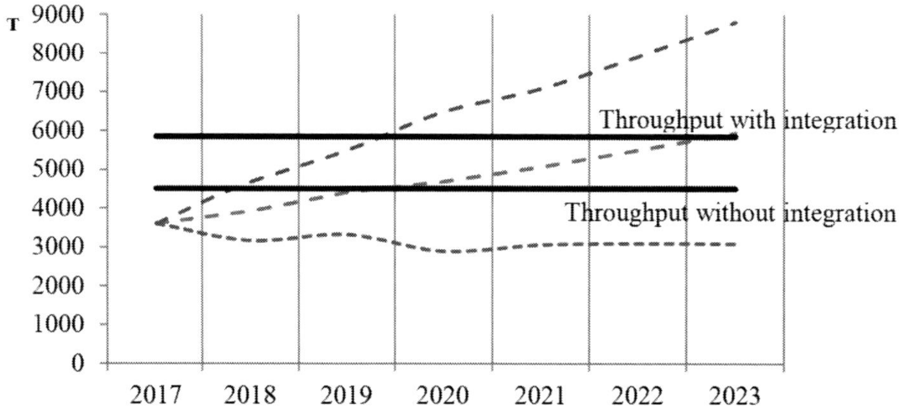

Fig. 4. Results of numerical experiments to estimate the need for development of the container system.

The results of numerical experiments on the model showed that the throughput of the container system in the absence of integration would fully meet the region's demand for transportations until 2019, with the expected containerization growth forecast.

Formation of a system-integrated container network in the region will increase the capacity of the system by 30% (according to the data of experiments [17]), which will increase the period of its uninterrupted operation without additional investments in the terminal infrastructure until 2023.

Conclusion

The method for forecasting the region's demand for container transportations was proposed depending on the dynamics of the region's economic indices, taking into consideration the random nature of their changes. With the help of the simulation model, the estimation of the required development of the region's container resources was performed to meet the forecast demand. The experiment on the model showed that the integrated flow control allows increasing the container system capacity. Thus, it was determined that the need for technical development of container resources was reduced due to the organizational development of the network.

Implementation of the model in practice will allow making well-founded management decisions regarding expansion of the terminal infrastructure, estimation of prospects and constraints of containerization development taking into consideration the needs and resource possibilities of the region. Further research must be focused on developing approaches to arrangement of interaction of the container organizational network elements based on the system integrator formation in the region.

References

1. R. Boşneagu, C.E. Coca, F. Sorescu, *EIRP Proceedings* 10, 360 – 368 (2015).
2. The official web-site of TransContainer JSC, available at: https://trcont.com/en/main (April 10, 2018).
3. S.M. Rezer, O.V. Moskvichev, E.E. Moskvicheva, Transport: science, equipment, management 7, 3-7 (2016). (in Russian)
4. X. Chen, X. Zhu, O. Zhou, Y.D. Wong, Journal of Advanced Transportation **2017**, 3128372 (2017).
5. H. Belbo , B. Talbot, Forests **5**, 2084-2105 (2014).
6. M. Intihar, T. Kramberger, D. Dragan, PROMET – Traffic&Transportation **5**, 529–542 (2017).
7. B. O'Kane, Computer-Aided Design and Applications **11,** 44 – 53 (2014).
8. T. Keeffe, G. Ormsby, Development in Practice, 25, 843-855 (2015).
9. D. Teodorovic, M. Janic, *Transportation Engineering* (Butterworth-Heinemann, 2016).
10. N.Yu. Yaroshevich, V.Zh. Dubrovskiy, Izvestia of the USUE **6**, 54 – 61 (2014). (in Russian)
11. Yu.V. Dorokhova, N.S. Goncharuk, Central Russian Journal of Social Sciences **1,** 34-44 (2013). (in Russian)
12. T. Tsekeris, C. Tsekeris, Economic Research **24**, 82 – 94 (2011).
13. E.G. Varagouli, T.E. Simos, G.S. Xeidakis, Mathematical and Computer Modelling **42**, 817-836 (2005).
14. K. Aksyonov, B. Klebanov, A. Hrenov, *Proceedings of the 4th IMACS Symposium on Mathematical Modeling* **24,** 1414–1420 (2003).
15. V.P. Borovikov, G.I. Ivchenko, *Prognozirovanie v sisteme STATISTICA* [Forecasting in the STATISTICA system] (Finansy i statistka, Moscow, 2000). (in Russian)
16. Federal State Statistics Service. Russian Federation, available at: http://www.gks.ru/wps/wcm/connect/rosstat_main/rosstat/en/main/ (April 20, 2018)

17. D.I. Kochneva, Thesis of Candidate of technical sciences, Ural State University of Railway, Yekaterinburg, 2012. (in Russian)
18. D.I. Kochneva, V.M. Say, Herald of the Ural State University of Railway Transport **4**, 65–75 (2016). (in Russian)

Increasing the traffic capacity of railway blocks

Boris Sergeev[1,*], *Vitaly* Dontsov[1], and *Boris* Arzhannikov[1]

[1]Ural State University of Railway Transport, 620034 Yekaterinburg, Russia

Abstract. The paper considers ways of increasing the traffic capacity of railway sections equipped with automatic block signaling systems, with a discrete variable number of block sections. Simultaneous traffic of long and short trains on a single block is analyzed. The paper highlights shortcomings and limitations of the existing automatic block signaling systems, including low traffic capacity and non-compliance with traffic safety requirements for railway sections. The study is aimed at removing these shortcomings and limitations. For this purpose, a reasonable technical solution has been presented, analyzed and scientifically grounded. System analysis techniques have been used to study the performance of traffic control devices.

Introduction

The key technical and economic indicator of railway sections is their traffic capacity, which is ensured by using various types of automatic block signaling systems with a discrete separation of the block length into several block sections. Issues related to improving the performance of such systems are studied by a number of Russian and international scientists and engineers [1–9]. Based on a scientific analysis, various technical solutions have been developed to improve the performance of automatic block signaling systems. In particular, a system that uses devices with a variable number of block sections is presented as one of optimal systems [10, 11]. However, as shown by the study of well-known devices, they are not free of shortcomings. The purpose of this study is to create scientific foundations and develop general principles aimed at increasing the traffic capacity of railroad sections as related to trains of different lengths.

Research methods

The current methodology aimed at studying train traffic in railway sections is based on a system timing analysis of the processes that occur when trains move according to "proceed" or "stop" indications of the automatic block signaling system. In this case, the length of block sections on the Russian railways is determined in accordance with the applicable guidelines [7, 8], while the traffic capacity of the railway section can be calculated by the following formula [5]:

$$N_{\text{block}} = 1{,}440/t_{\text{int}}, \quad (1)$$

* Corresponding author: sergeew@uralmail.com

© The Authors, published by EDP Sciences. This is an open access article distributed under the terms of the Creative Commons Attribution License 4.0 (http://creativecommons.org/licenses/by/4.0/).

where: 1,440 is the number of minutes in a day, minutes; t_{int} is the inter-train interval, minutes.

For the most common three-aspect automatic block signaling system, the minimum inter-train interval is defined as:

$$t_{int} = 0.06(3L_{bs} + l_t)/V_t, \tag{2}$$

where $3L_{bs}$ is the total length of block sections lying ahead of a moving train with length l_t; V_t is the sectional speed of the train.

The length of each block section depends not only on the train speed, but also on a number of rated parameters of moving trains. This interaction of parameters can be presented in a generalized form as:

$$L_{bs} = kl_p, \tag{3}$$

where k is the coefficient that determines a set of parameters and is used in calculations performed in accordance with the standard [7]. These automatic block signaling systems are designed in such a way that any characteristics of trains moving along a designed block will meet the applicable traffic safety requirements as related to the braking distance and the maximum permissible speed. It is assumed that trains must move according to the green indication of the nearest traffic light lying ahead, i. e. at least three block sections L_{bs} ahead of a moving train must be clear. The number of reference cars (car with a standard length of 15 m) moving along blocks ranges from 71 to 100 or 140 [8]. This range determines standard lengths of trains on different railway sections.

The calculated maximum length of a block section $L_{bs\ max}$ will be reached at the maximum train length $l_{t\ max}$ and respective values of the set of parameters $\Sigma\Pi_i$. This applies to freight trains, including long and heavy trains consisting of 100 or more reference cars. However, passenger or electric trains consisting of 6 to 26 reference cars move along the same railway section. Geometric, braking and traction characteristics of such trains ($\Sigma\Pi_i$) are significantly different from those of freight trains [10].

Obviously, if practical lengths of block sections are determined by parameters of long trains, this will decrease the traffic capacity for passenger or electric trains.

Thus, there is a certain disproportion between possibilities of reaching a sufficiently high traffic for different types and lengths of rolling stock, which is determined by expressions (1) and (2).

Works [10, 11] propose a method to remove this disproportion. This method assumes that the number of block sections on the block varies with the length of the train that enters the block from a departure station. In other words, the number of signaling points switched on or off on the block varies with the train length. In order to implement this method at the departure station, it is necessary to determine the train length l_t using known axle counters on a track [6]. The collected information is transmitted to all signaling points of the block, some of which are switched off or on depending on l_t of the train leaving the departure station. In this case, inactive signaling points of the automatic block signaling system switch to the translation mode to translate the relevant codes through a rail circuit or channels of axle counters.

This method can be illustrated with a diagram of a block and a station with two trains whose lengths are l_{t1} and l_{t2} (Fig. 1). Information on the train length S_{ax} is transmitted from the axle counter to a signal box. It is converted into a signal S, which is sent to all signaling points of the block. According to this signal, the relevant signaling points of the automatic block signaling system are switched on or off. In the general case, as it clearly follows from the performed traction calculations based on the set of parameters $\Sigma\Pi_i$, the lengths of different block sections l_{bsi}, according to the expression (3), will be different and close to the most efficient ones.

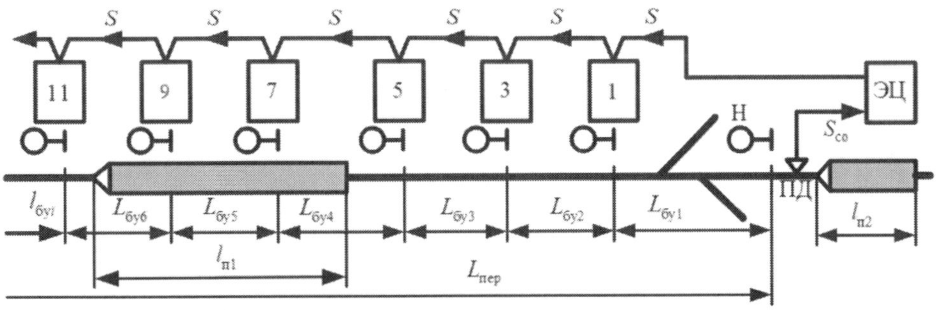

Fig. 1. Diagram of a block with simultaneous switching of all signaling points in the automatic block signaling system.

The practical application of this method can not only increase the traffic capacity of railway sections, but also optimize traffic control for heavy freight trains, in particular twin trains, based on signals of the automatic block signaling system. However, this approach to increasing the traffic capacity of blocks has some shortcomings. Let us illustrate them on the basis of the block diagram shown in Figure 1.

Suppose that the first long train with length l_{t1} is moving along the block, covering the common length of several block sections: $l_{t1} \leq L_{bs6} + L_{bs5} + L_{bs4}$; l_{bs1}. The second train leaving the station according to an exit signal H has a short length l_{t2}, which corresponds, e. g., to an electric train: $l_{t2} \leq l_{ts\ min}$, where $l_{ts\ min}$ is the minimum length i^{th} of the block section that lies, e. g., between signaling points 1 and 3.

In this case, until the first train completely leaves the entire block L_{block}, all signaling points of the block will be in the initialization mode to initialize the long block sections whose total length in our case is equal to: $L_{ts\Sigma} = L_{ts6} + L_{ts5} + L_{ts4}$.

Therefore, if several trains of different lengths are moving along the block and the first of them is a long train, then lengths of block sections for the second short train, which follows the first one, will correspond to lengths of the long train l_{t1}. Obviously, this restricts the speed of the second train along the block and its traffic capacity.

Another shortcoming of the existing method can be demonstrated on the same example with two trains moving along the block, the first of which is short, while the second one is long. In this case, when the first train with length $l_{t\ min}$ leaves the station and enters the block, active / inactive signaling points will be configured in the form of various short block sections along the entire block. Obviously, the departure of the long train from the station will be impossible until the first train leaves the entire block. Only then, according to the signal S (Fig. 1), signaling points of the block will be switched to a greater length $l_{t2} > l_{t1}$. Failure to comply with this condition will not ensure the compliance with traffic safety requirements and, therefore, must be avoided.

Thus, this approach to increasing the traffic capacity can be optimized subject to the constraints arising from the fact that the approach is valid only in the presence and during movement of long trains along the block.

Results

The results of the scientific analysis indicated the possibility of eliminating these shortcomings. Let us consider this possibility using the example of the block in Figure 2, which shows the location and movement of two trains l_{t1} and l_{t2} of a specified length. The diagram in Figure 2 differs from the diagram in Figure 1 by the presence of information channels S_{1H}, S_{3-1},... S_{11-9}..., which transmit data from signaling points of the block to adjacent signaling points and the signal box.

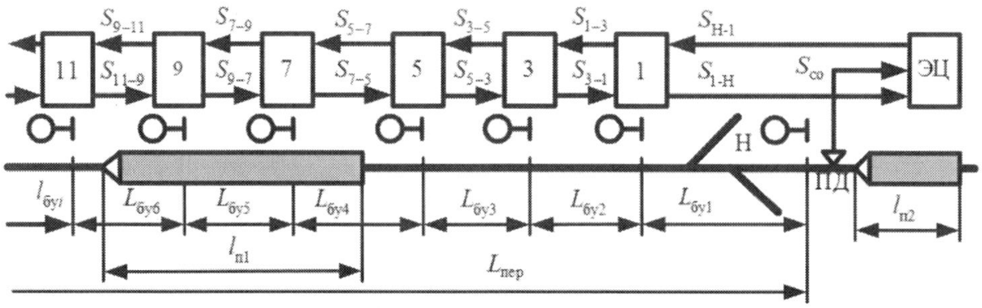

Fig. 2. Diagram of a block with selective switching of all signaling points in the automatic block signaling system.

The structural diagram of the block shown in Figure 2 works as follows. When the first, e. g., a long train of length l_{t1} leaves the station and the block is clear according to signals S_{H-1}, S_{1-3},...S_{9-11}, all signaling points receive the relevant information. This leads to initialization of only those signaling points that match the calculated set of parameters $\Sigma\Pi_i$ for this train.

When the train moves along the block and its tail end clears the relevant block sections, devices of signaling points generate the signals that are transmitted to adjacent signaling points and the signal box. Therefore, the station receives real-time information about leaving block sections by the tail end of the first train of length l_{t1}.

When the second train arrives at the station and is ready for departure, the axle counter transmits information about its length l_{t2}. This leads to the generation of signals S_{H-1}, S_{1-3}, and S_{3-5} (for the case shown on the block diagram in Figure 2). Then the departing second train will move along the block sections L_{bs1}, L_{bs2} and L_{bs3}. As the first train moves to the signal box, information will come from signaling points 5, 7, 9, 11 and so on. This leads to change in indications of subsequent signals S_{7-5}, S_{9-7}, S_{11-9} and so on. The system identifies a need to switch on or off certain signaling points, which are determined on the basis of traction calculations for another train length.

Conclusion

The study shows and justifies the possibility of changing the traffic capacity of a railway section at significantly different lengths of trains that move along the block. The schematic diagram of the proposed automatic block signaling system and its operation algorithm have been developed. By implementing the proposed traffic control algorithm for trains moving along the block, where signaling points and the signal box share information between each other through direct and reverse data transfer, it is possible to optimize traffic control processes for trains of arbitrary length and maximize the traffic capacity, while maintaining the required level of traffic safety.

At present, according to a planned schedule, specialists are preparing terms of reference for hardware and software implementation of the proposed automatic block signaling system using the accepted methodology for designing automation and remote control equipment in railway transport [12].

References

1. E. Masson, M. Barbinean, *Wireless Communication for Railway Application* (Springer, 2017).
2. The Railway Technical Website, Railway Technical, Available at: http://www.railway-technical.com/bookspapersarticles/railway-technical.com/ (February 15 2018).
3. Transport Canada, Rail Safety – FAQs, Available at: https://www.tc.gc.ca/eng/railsafety/railsafety-faq-969.html (February 1, 2018)
4. I.M. Kokurin, Proceedings of International Science and Practice Conference "Transport of Russia: Problems and Prospects", **Vol. 2**, 67-72 (Saint Petersburg, 2016). (In Russian)
5. P.A. Muginshtein, M.M. Mekhedov, Vestnik of the Railway Research Institute, **Vol. 75(1)**, 3-11 (2016).
6. I.G. Tilk, *Novye ustrojstva avtomatiki i telemehaniki zheleznodorozhnogo transporta* [New automation and telemechanics devices of railway transport] (Ural State University of Railway Transport Publ., Yekaterinburg, 2010). (in Russian)
7. 660301. Regulations on automatic block signals location and defining lengths of block sections on the lines with automatic cab signaling (Saint Petersburg, 2003). (in Russian)
8. Optimization of transportation process optimization. Materials of The Board meeting of Science and Technology Council of the Ministry of Railway Transport of the RF, Zheleznodorozhnyj transport [Railway transport], 1, 2-4, (2001). (in Russian)
9. M.K. Jain, Average speed of freight train over Indian Railways, Available at: https://www.railelectrica.com/status-of-train-speeds-over-indian-railways/average-speed-of-freight-train-over-indian-railways/ (February 09, 2017).
10. I.G. Tilk, V.V. Lyanoy, M.A. Krivda, B.S. Sergeev, World of Transport and Transportation 4, 26-33, (2005). (in Russian)
11. I.G. Tilk, V.V. Lyanoy, M.A. Krivda, B.S. Sergeev, RU Patent 2288126 (2006). (in Russian)
12. V.V. Sapozhnikov, I.M. Kokurin, V.A. Kononov, *Jekspluatacionnye osnovy avtomatiki i telemehaniki* [Operational foundations of automatics and telemechanics] (Marshrut, Moscow, 2006). (in Russian)

Optimization flow model for handling car flows at the marshalling yard

Alexander Alexandrov[1,*], *Alexander* Galkin[1], *Elena* Timukhina[1], and *Nikolai* Tushin[1]

[1]Ural State University of Railway Transport, 620034 Yekaterinburg, Russia

Abstract. Mathematical modeling is widely used in studies of operational planning in railway transport. Mainly heuristic algorithms and simulation modeling is used in short-term planning at marshalling yards. There is an opportunity to improve the quality of planning using strict optimization models. The objective of the study was to find a way to optimize the multi-terminal transport flows of the complex structure by the example of operational planning for handling car flows at the marshalling yard. The process model was built on the basis of Mixed Integer Linear Program (MILP) method. The article provides the mathematical setting and describes results of calculations of the reference example. The LpSolve application package was used. The technological effect is estimated through checking the optimal solution on the simulation model.

Introduction

A linear programming device is traditionally used in solving problems of optimal transport flows management. However, the most developed formulations of the transport problem and the general problem of linear programming do not always allow taking important technological limitations into consideration. Some restrictions may require modeling of logical relationships with conditions of the "either-or" type. Such conditions can be taken into consideration by means of binary variables (taking value 0 or 1). In this case, the problem goes into the category of mixed integer linear programming (MILP) problems.

Publications with examples of the use of various MILP task settings to solve practical problems in management of transport flows have often appeared in recent years [1, 2].

The paper [1] is devoted to compilation and updating of set schedules in the railway network in the southern region of Switzerland. The results showed that the proposed MILP allows finding the optimal solution quite quickly in many cases.

Work [2] is considering an alternative mode of delivery of goods using the urban railway infrastructure. Instead of using trucks to transport goods, the possibility of using the existing suburban railway network is being explored. The MILP model is proposed to minimize the waiting time for daily deliveries. Numerical experiments have shown that the model is able to provide solutions for cases of moderate dimension in a very short time.

See the survey of studies related to the application of various models to solve planning problems in railway systems in [3] and [4].

* Corresponding author: alalexan@gmail.com

© The Authors, published by EDP Sciences. This is an open access article distributed under the terms of the Creative Commons Attribution License 4.0 (http://creativecommons.org/licenses/by/4.0/).

Among research works of Russian authors aimed at studying the applicability of MILP to solve problems in the railway industry, a detailed study [5] shall be referred to. It is devoted to building models and methods for solving problems arising in planning of freight railway transport. Depending on the restrictions on locomotives, load-carrying capacity of sets, various algorithms for solving the problems of forming sets and traffic schedules for freight sets are proposed. The main difference from the problems of this article is the scale, i.e., a more distant planning horizon, a fundamentally larger object of management and a substantially smaller number of details of the structure and the technology of handling the transport flow at marshalling yards.

The objects of management at marshalling yards are sets and groups of cars in them. The flow of sets at the stage of breaking-up is transformed into a multitude of car flows that follow individual tracks of the marshalling yard. The transport problem of linear programming cannot adequately display such complex structure. This problem is solved by using simulation modeling [6, 7]. In this case, it is possible to take into consideration various technological limitations, but strict optimization is not available. In this case, the authors see a good opportunity for applying MILP.

The objective of the study is finding a way to optimize the multi-terminal transport flows of the complex structure by the example of operational planning for handling car flows at the marshalling yard. It is necessary to minimize the time of cars staying at the station and ensure departure of sets according to the specified schedule. The authors used the MILP to build the model. To validate the model, the data from a real marshalling yard was used, and the solution was tested on a simulation model that functions in the automated control system (ACS) of the marshalling yard. The problem formulated in the article has not been solved earlier with the use of the apparatus of mixed integer linear programming.

Research methods

It is proposed to use the method of mixed integer linear programming for building the operational planning model for handling car flows at the marshalling yard. The description of the model is built in accordance with the methodology described in [8]. At the first stage, we will define the boundaries of the system simulated and the structure of the model. A flowchart will be used for this purpose. We will select the stages of handling the sets and the car flows at the phases of preparation for breaking-up, breaking-up and accumulation as blocks of the process.

The block "Waiting for preparation for breaking-up" is intended for displaying unproductive idle time due to employment of the survey team. The number of these blocks is limited by the number of receiving tracks. The block "Preparation for breaking-up" simulates the main operation at the station receiving yard. Availability of the block "Waiting for breaking-up" block is due to the mismatch between the rhythms of the subsystem of preparation for breaking-up and the subsystem of breaking-up. The "Breaking-up" block displays the handling capacity of the sorting hump through the technological interval of the hump. The "Accumulation" block reproduces the process with the same name. The number of these blocks corresponds to the number of set destinations formed by the station.

The work of the first pair of blocks in the model is in many ways fundamentally identical to the second pair of blocks. To shorten the descriptive part and reduce the number of components of the balance equations and the objective function, we will confine ourselves to describing the functioning of three types of the last blocks. The type of the abbreviated block diagram of the process of handling car flows at the marshalling yard is shown in Figure 1.

This scheme is a static mapping of the model structure. Planning also involves considering the process, taking into consideration how it proceeds over time. This is implemented by increasing the dimensionality of the model in accordance with the number of clock cycles of the calculation period. The duration of the hump technological interval is used as the clock cycle. This parameter is defined as the average time spent on breaking-up of one train. The calculation period is connected with the current planning horizon of 4 hours. For example, if the hump technological interval is 15 minutes, then the calculation period is 16 cycles. The description of the principles and examples of transformation of the static network into a dynamic one can be found in [9, 10]. We will add additional index *t*, $T = [1, T]$ corresponding to the cycle of the calculation period into the notation of flows in the scheme (Fig. 1).

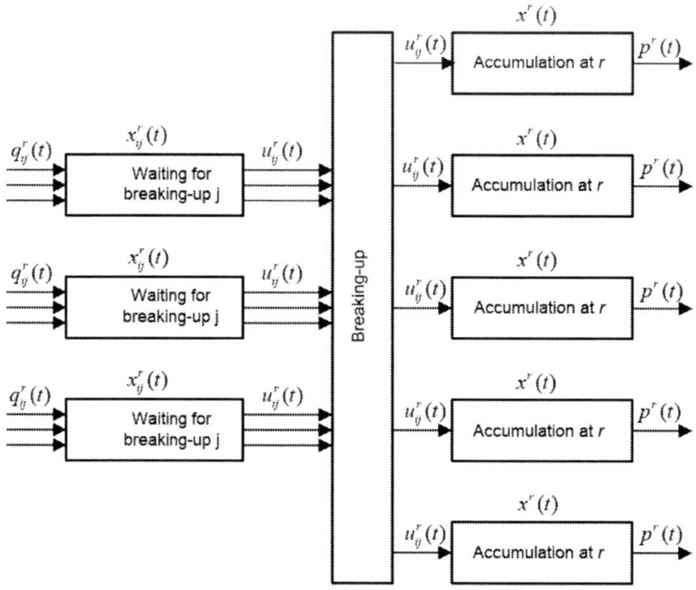

Fig. 1. Block diagram of the car flow handling at the marshalling yard.

Let us list the variables that we will use when writing the objective function and constraints:

$q_{ij}^r(t)$ – model input. The number of cars of destination *r* in the *i*-th set, which comes from the "Preparation for breaking-up" block. These values are the source data.

$x_{ij}^r(t+1)$ is the required variable. The number of cars of destination *r* in the *i-th* set, which is included into the *j-th*block "Waiting for breaking-up" within cycle *t*;

$u_{ij}^r(t+1)$ is the required variable. The number of cars of destination *r*, which, after breaking-up of the *i-th* set of the *j*-th block "Waiting for breaking-up" goes to block "Accumulation at *r*" by the cycle commencement $(t+1)$;

$x^r(t+1)$ is the required variable. The number of cars of destination *r*, which stayed at block "Accumulation at *r*" during cycle *t*;

$p^r(t+1)$ is the model output. The number of cars of destination *r*, which leaves the system at the end of system *t*. These values are the sourse data and they are meaningfully associated with the departure of sets according to the schedule.

The flow from the model input or from the "Waiting for breaking-up" block can get into the "Breaking-up" block or be delayed in the "Waiting for breaking-up" block. This circumstance shifts the problem to the category of mixed integer linear programming problems. The use of binary Boolean variables is required.

Let $y_{ij}(t)=\{0,1\}$ determine if there is delay of the i-th set in the j-th block "Waiting for breaking-up". In this turn, $z_{ij}(t)=\{0,1\}$ determines the result of taking the resolution of sending the i-th set from the j-the block "Waiting for breaking-up" to the "Breaking-up" block. In order to select only one of the two possible alternatives, the constraint of the following type should be used:

$$y_{ij}(t) + z_{ij}(t) = 1 \tag{1}$$

Next, let us write down constraints of the balance equations type.

$$\square\ r \mid y_{ij}(t-1)\, x_{ij}^{r}(t) + q_{ij}^{r}(t) - z_{ij}(t)\, u_{ij}^{r}(t+1) - y_{ij}(t)\, x_{ij}^{r}(t+1) = 0 \tag{2}$$

$$\square\ i,j,t \mid \sum_{r=1}^{R} q_{ij}^{r}(t) = Q_{ij}\,, \tag{3}$$

where Q_{ij} is the general value of the i-th set on the input into the j-th block "Waiting for breaking-up".

The following two restrictions will ensure breaking-up with entire trains. If there are no such restrictions, car groups will arrive in blocks "Accumulation at r" in random order from different tracks within one clock cycle t, which contradicts the actual technology of breaking-up in entire trains.

$$\square\ i,j,t \mid \sum_{r=1}^{R} u_{ij}^{r}(t+1) = z_{ij}(t)\, Q_{ij} \tag{4}$$

$$\square\ i,j,t \mid \sum_{r=1}^{R} x_{ij}^{r}(t+1) = y_{ij}(t)\, Q_{ij} \tag{5}$$

The following limitation will ensure the balance of cars in blocks "Accumulation at r":

$$\square\ r \mid x^{r}(t) - p^{r}(t+1) + u_{ij}^{r}(t+1) - x^{r}(t+1) = 0 \tag{6}$$

Restrictions on the throughput of arcs that represent the structure of a mathematical formulation and the non-negativity of variables are standard for this kind of problem, and they will not be presented here.

The objective function is the total cost of handling the car flows in the simulated system. It must be minimized.

$$\Omega = \sum_{i=1}^{I}\sum_{j=1}^{J}\sum_{r=1}^{R}\sum_{t=1}^{T} c_{ij}^{\ r} x_{ij}^{\ r}(t) + \sum_{i=1}^{I}\sum_{j=1}^{J}\sum_{r=1}^{R}\sum_{t=1}^{T} l_{ij}^{\ r} u_{ij}^{\ r}(t+1) + \sum_{r=1}^{R}\sum_{t=1}^{T} m^{r} x^{\ r}(t+1)\,, \tag{7}$$

where c_{ij}^{r}, l_{ij}^{r}, m^{r} are unit costs for one car of a certain purpose in one clock cycle at the respective handling stage. It is known that the operating costs for railway transport are proportional to the time required. In the simplest form, the listed unit costs can be taken as equal to one. Substantially, this will mean that for all sets and destinations at all stages of handling, priority is not taken into consideration. By changing these values, for example, by increasing the cost of idle time in the "Waiting for breaking-up" blocks, conditions for speedy movement of cars to the marshalling yard will be created. If this is done only for individual *r* sets, they will complete the accumulation at the marshalling yard earlier than others. The order of breaking-up will be changed. Thus, the model is able to reproduce the real methods of controlling car flows handling. Methodological principles of solving mixed integer linear programming problems can be found in many sources [8, 11-13].

Study results

The numerical test case was solved using the LP SOLVE software on a PC with an Intel Core I7-4790K processor. The size and structure of the model display the structure and technology of the Kamensk-Uralsky regional marshalling yard and has the following parameters: the number of variables is 841, the number of limitations is 585. The average calculation time was 386 seconds in a series of 30 calculations simulating the work of the yard for 5 days. Validation of the solution of the optimization problem was performed on the simulation model used in the automated control system by the marshalling yard [6]. Convergence of results of both types of models suggests that the optimization model behaves like a real system. The simulation model was also used to conduct experiments for simulation of planning based on the principles that guide the dispatcher in their work. The results of this simulation were used for comparison with the first series of calculations.

The technological effect, which is the basis of economic efficiency, can be assessed by improvement of such important indicator of the marshalling yard operation as the accumulation parameter. Decrease in the value of the accumulation parameter from 9.6 to 8.9 indicates that the decisions to choose the order of breaking-up of the formulations that the model proposes are more efficient.

Conclusion

An important feature of the proposed MILP optimization model is that it managed to correctly display the complex structure of the transport flow and its transformation while handling at the marshalling yard. With that, the time of cars staying at the marshalling yard is minimized and scheduled departure of sets is ensured.

It is possible to use this model in the automated control system of the marshalling yard, which will increase the level of certainty of a complex transport system, improve the natural and economic performance.

When moving to the study of larger marshalling yards with more than sixteen tracks, the volume of input information and the dimension of the problem itself will be increased substantially. It will be necessary to develop algorithms for automated generation of the initial data package for the problem. It will also be necessary to pay attention to optimizing the structure of the model itself and searching for effective solution algorithms for large-dimensional problems. These issues determine the direction of future research.

References

1. F.F. Khoshniyat, J.T. Krasemann, *17th Workshop on Algorithmic Approaches for Transportation Modelling, Optimization, and Systems (ATMOS 2017)*, 10, 1-17 (2017)
2. W. Behiri, O. Ozturk, S. Belmokhtar-Berraf, *6th International Conference on Information Systems, Logistics and Supply Chain*, 2, 1-8 (Bordeaux, France, June 1 – 4, 2016).
3. V. Cacchiani, D. Huisman, M. Kidd, L. Kroon, P. Toth, L. Veelenturf, J. Wagenaar, Transportation Research. Part B: Methodological, **63,** 15–37 (2014).

4. R.M. Lusby, J. Larsen, M. Ehrgott, D. Ryan, OR spectrum, **33(4),** 843–883 (2011).
5. A.A. Lazarev, E.G. Musatova, E.R. Gafarov, A.G. Kvaracheliya, *Teorija raspisanij. Zadachi zheleznodorozhnogo planirovanija* [Scheduling theory. Tasks of railway planning] (Moscow, 2012). (in Russian)
6. A.E. Alexandrov, P.A. Kozlov, Zheleznodorozhnyj transport [Railway transport], **9,** 65-67 (2003). (in Russian)
7. A.E. Alexandrov, S.V. Surin, Transport of the Urals, **4,** 66-70 (2016). (in Russian)
8. B.A. Murtagh, *Advanced Linear Programming: Computation and Practice* (McGraw-Hill Intarnetional Book Company, 1981).
9. D.R. Ford, D.R. Fulkerson, *Flows in Networks* (Princeton University Press., New Jersey, 1962).
10. P.A. Kozlov, S.P. Milovidov, Izvestija AN SSSR. Tehnicheskaja kibernetika [Engineering Cybernetics], **5,** (1983). (in Russian)
11. A.H. Land, A.G. Doig, *Econometrica,* **28,** 497-520 (1960).
12. R.S. Garfinkel, G.L. Nemhauser, *Integer Programming* (Willey, New York, 1972).
13. V.L. Beresnev, E.Kh. Gimadi, V.T. Dementyev, *Ekstremal'nye zadachi standartizacii* [Extreme problems of standardization] (Nauka, Novosibirsk, 1978). (in Russian)

Modeling of large railway polygons

Yelena Timukhina[1,*], *Petr* Kozlov[2], *Vitaly* Kolokolnikov[1], and *Nikolay* Tushin[1]

[1]Ural State University of Railway Transport, 620034 Yekaterinburg, Russia
[2]STRATEG Scientific-Production Holding, 101000 Moscow, Russia

Abstract. When large junctions of railway polygons are studied, detailed modeling is subject to some limitations. Therefore, it is necessary to develop appropriate tools. This paper presents an aggregate (macromodeling) technique for necks and yards of railway stations. Results of calculations based on aggregate models are highly consistent with results of detailed modeling, which confirms the applicability of this modeling method to railway polygons. The proposed principles were implemented on the basis of the IMETRA simulation system. The resulting polygon model makes it possible to determine the total throughput of a polygon and to identify bottlenecks that slow down car traffic.

1. Introduction

At present, simulation modeling is the most adequate and accurate method for designing railway stations. However, stations operate in close relationship with adjacent stations, lines and polygons. Therefore, it is required to model not only separate stations, but also junctions, sections and entire polygons. It is extremely difficult to use detailed modeling for this purpose. It is necessary to develop a new modeling method that will reduce the amount of input information and a data array for calculations, without significant detriment to the adequacy of the model.

Simulation modeling of stations was first proposed by professor V. A. Persianov in the 1960s [1]. Despite the scarce computer resources available at that time, V. A. Persianov, together with professor N. S. Uskov, came up with some interesting findings. Since then, much progress has been made in this area [2–7].

Simulation modeling of stations and polygons differs in terms of objectives and nature [8]. A station model is usually aimed at assessing a specific development project. Therefore, it should be as detailed as possible and provide a sufficient set of indicators to determine not only the overall throughput and capacity, but also the role of each structural element. At present, the ISTRA system is the most developed imitation system in this area [9]. However, it is difficult to extend this approach to modeling of polygons. We need about 600–700 thousand strings to fully describe the model of a large station with all operations, implementation options, devices involved in each option and their operating parameters. A polygon may include several hundred stations, including dozens of large ones, thereby producing a huge, difficult-to-process array.

* Corresponding author: ENTimuhina@usurt.ru

© The Authors, published by EDP Sciences. This is an open access article distributed under the terms of the Creative Commons Attribution License 4.0 (http://creativecommons.org/licenses/by/4.0/).

The objective of the study is a different one. In a new problem statement, it is necessary to determine the overall throughput of the polygon, while aggregating its bottlenecks. If these are stations that slow down the car traffic, it is enough to know involved necks and yards, without identifying specific switches. However, at the second stage, when it is necessary to reorganize a particular station, detailed modeling should be used.

2 Principles of macromodeling

2.1 Neck macromodeling technique

The aim of macromodeling is to take into account only throughput of a neck in the model without further detailing. In a functional approach, the key parameter of the neck is the number of possible parallel movements. These movements are numbered. Each movement is managed by a certain group of switches. It is kind of a *virtual* service channel. Train receiving and dispatching operations or shunting movements are served by some virtual channels. Thus, throughput of necks is taken into account, even though in aggregate form.

Unlike a separate switch, the channel has an explicit meaningful purpose — it enables one additional parallel movement [10]. It is the number of parallel movements that will determine possible maneuverability, and, hence, potential throughput of the neck (Fig. 1).

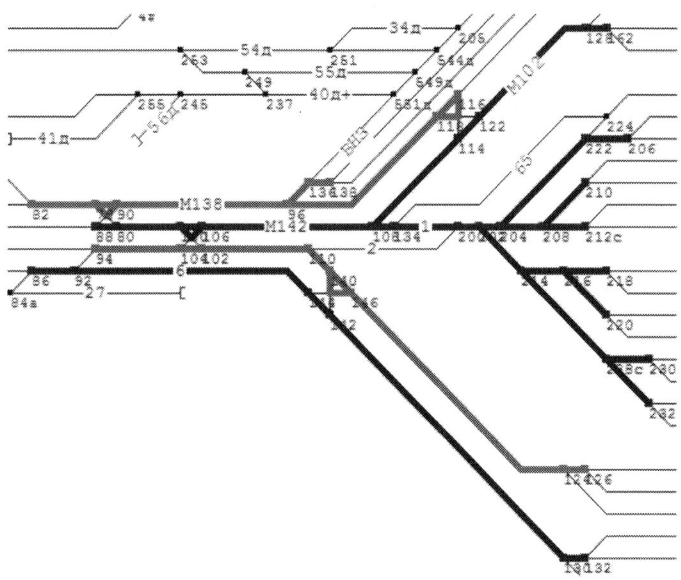

Fig. 1. Structural channels in the neck of the Karymskaya station.

However, the real throughput implemented for selected process conditions may differ from the potential one. The smaller the average number of involved channels per operation is, the closer they will be to each other and, hence, the better the technology will fit the structure.

To verify the validity of the proposed approach, it is necessary to compare operating parameters of necks on the basis of detailed and aggregate models. In this case, the number of delays in throats is the key factor as well. Comparative calculations for several stations show a good coincidence between the results (Fig. 2). Thus, the proposed principles can also be applied to the construction of polygon models.

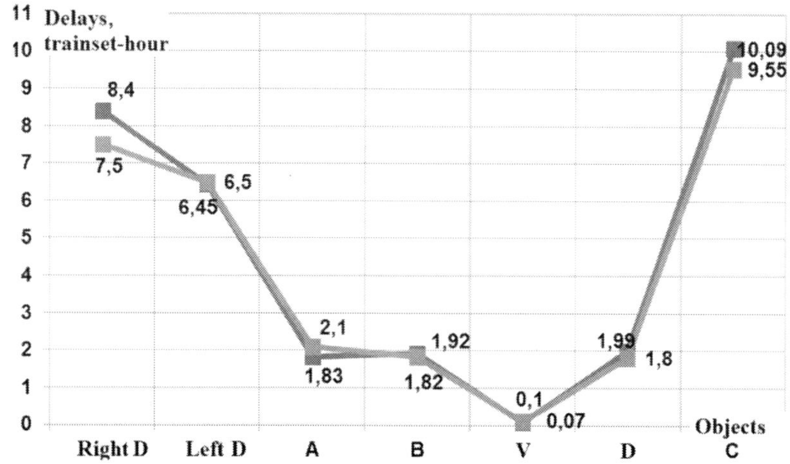

Fig. 2. Delays in throats: blue – in the micromodel, red – in the macromodel.

2.2 Macromodeling of yards

In our case, we use the ultimate functional capacity of the yard (i. e. the capacity at which its functionality is still maintained), rather than the total physical capacity of tracks, as an input parameter for modeling yards. Naturally, a difference between the functional capacity and the physical capacity will vary depending on type of a yard. In this case, coincidence of delays due to yards and the time of stay of trains or cars in yards are used as criteria.

The comparative calculations based on the detailed and aggregate models of various stations show that the results almost coincide with each other.

2.3 Outputs

Based on the proposed principles of macromodeling, the IMETRA imitation system was developed [11]. Using this system, we constructed a model of the Kuzbass–Ust-Luga polygon (283 stations). Based on the outputs, it is possible to assess the performance of the entire polygon and to study the influence of individual factors.

The estimated period was ten or more days. The outputs include a car passing pattern of the polygon (Table 1) and an actual train schedule (Fig. 3). In addition, operations of locomotives with each train are visualized.

Table 1. Delays of Trains by Type.

subprocess	graphically	per day	number	per operation
71 НЕЧ		1191:51	7091,6	0:10
71 ЧЕТ		1124:51	7405,6	0:09
66 НЕЧ		914:57	5068,7	0:10
66 ЧЕТ		315:49	1756,6	0:10
58 ЧЕТ		297:00	1382,1	0:12
100 ЧЕТ		250:40	1587,1	0:09
58 НЕЧ		235:18	837,4	0:16
100 НЕЧ		57:21	266,9	0:12
85 НЕЧ		51:48	275	0:11
ЛКМ		13:20	44,9	0:17
приг ЧЕТ		0:18	32	0:01
Пасс НЕЧ		0:15	25	0:01
приг НЕЧ		0:04	20	0:01
Пасс ЧЕТ		0:00	0	0:00

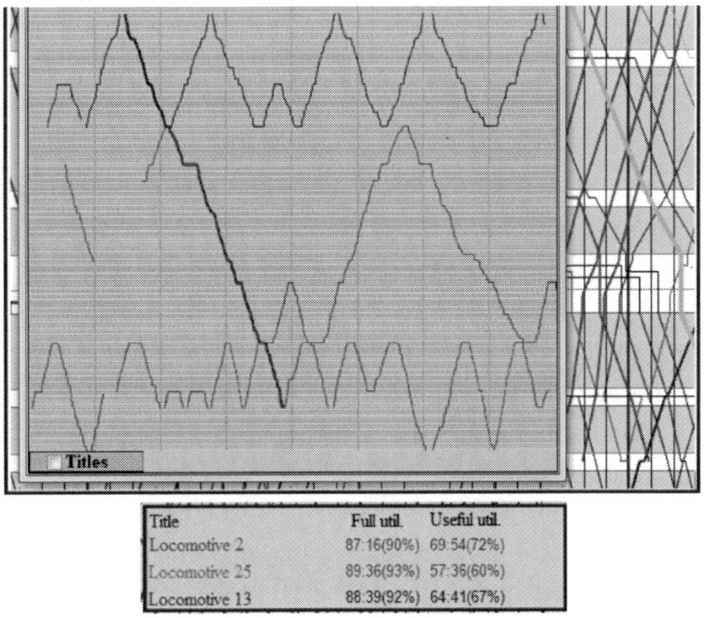

Fig. 3. An executed traffic schedule with parameters of locomotive utilization.

For the purpose of the analysis, the progression of train traffic should be estimated in more detail by calculating the following parameters:

- average speed of car traffic on each railway line;
- running and sectional speeds in all sections, etc.

The layout of the polygon below shows stations and sections that cause train delays (Fig. 4).

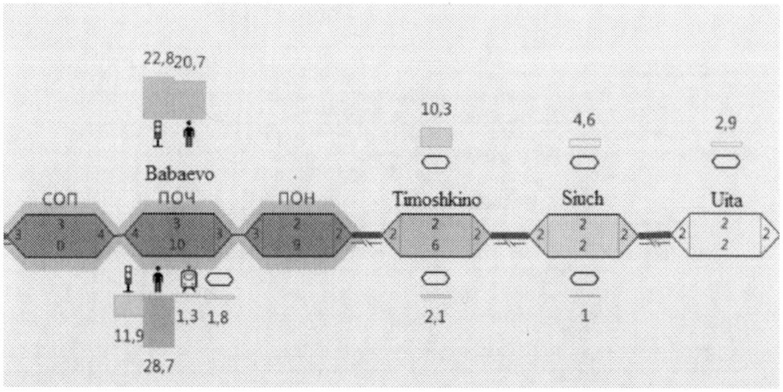

Fig. 4. Delays of trains at stations.

Additional delays (except for delays at passing points) are shown for wayside stations. The traffic graph shows that intermediate stations are subject to irregular conditions (Fig. 5).

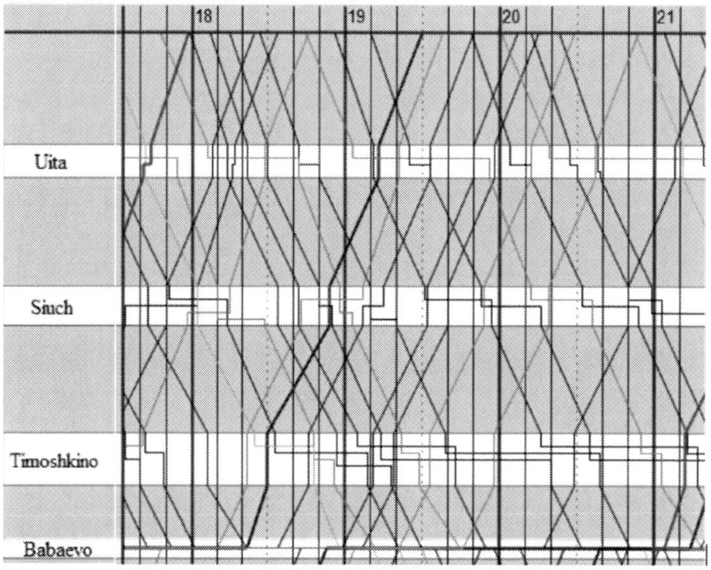

Fig. 5. Delays of trains at wayside stations.

Thus, optimal train schedules constructed by the Elbrus system (developed by the Scientific Research Institute of Railway Transport) usually cannot be implemented in real conditions. The model clearly demonstrates why particular trains and sets of cars are idle at technical stations (average values per train: at the top in one direction, at the bottom in another direction) (Fig. 6).

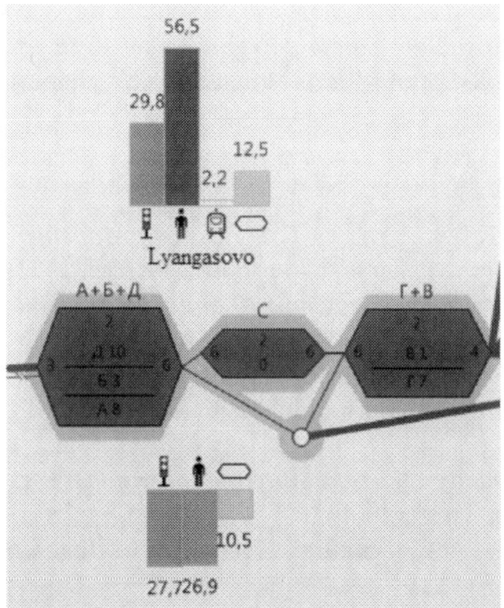

Fig. 6. Delays of trains at technical stations.

Delays are distributed as follows:

- through fault of yard crews – 56.5 min and 26.9 min;
- absence of a locomotive – 2.2 minutes;
- impossibility to start a ready-to-depart train – 29.8 min and 27.7 min;
- including due to lack of tracks at the next technical station – 12.5 min and 10.5 min.

Delays due to locomotives vary from section to section, while their effective utilization does not exceed 50% of the total utilization time (Fig. 7).

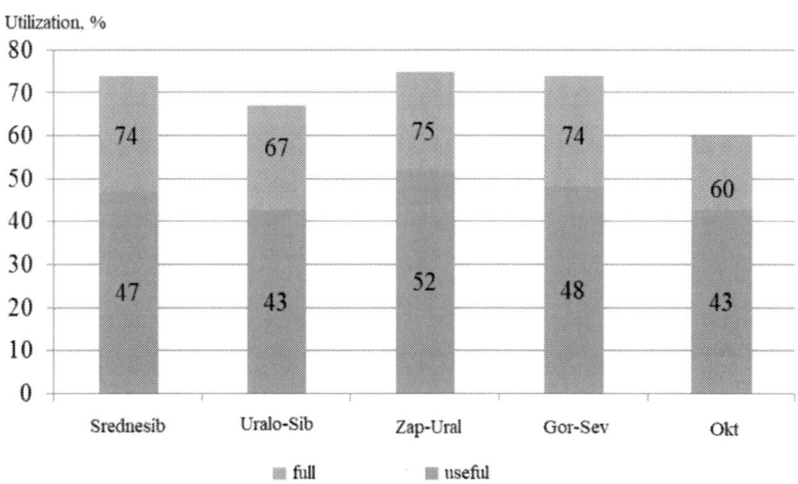

Fig. 7. Full and effective utilization of locomotives.

3. Conclusion

The railway network is struggling to cope with increasing train traffic. It needs to be intensively developed and, therefore, requires multi-billion dollar investments. Simulation modeling is the most appropriate tool for evaluating their effectiveness. The macromodeling method developed by the authors makes it possible to assess the operational efficiency and development of railroad polygons by imitation [12]. In the future, it is necessary to build a *single polygon model* from eastern to western borders of Russia and assess possible options for its structural and technological development.

References

1. V.A. Persianov, K.Yu. Skalov, N.S. Uskov, *Modelirovanie transportnyh sistem* [Modeling of transport systems] (Transport, Moscow, 1972). (in Russian)
2. B. Shmidt, *Iskusstvo modelirovanija i imitacii: Vvedenie v imitacionnuju sistemu Simplex 3* [Modeling and Simulation: An Introduction to the Simplex 3 Simulation System] (St. Petersburg, 2003). (in Russian)
3. N. Adamko, V. Klima, P. Marton, International Journal of Civil Engineering, **8**, 58-67 (2010).
4. G. Medeossi, *Capacity and reliability on railway networks: a simulative approach*/ (Anno accademico, Triest, 2009).
5. A.E. Aleksandrov, A.V. Shipulin, Transport of the Urals, **4**, 67-71 (2011). (in Russian)
6. I.M. Kokurin, V.S.Timchenko, Bulletin of the Emperor Alexander I St. Petersburg State Transport University, **1**, 15-22 (2013). (in Russian)
7. V.S. Timchenko, K.E. Kovalev, D.I. Khomich, *Imitacionnoe modelirovanie na zheleznodorozhnom transporte* [Simulation modeling in railway transport] (LAMBERT Academic Publishing, Saarbruecken, 2017). (in Russian)
8. A.E. Aleksandrov, Doctoral thesis, Ural State University of Railway Transport, Yekaterinburg, 2008. (in Russian)
9. V.Yu. Permikin, Thesis of Candidate of Sciences, Ural State University of Railway Transport, Yekaterinburg, 1999. (in Russian)
10. P.A. Kozlov, V.S. Kolokolnikov, Transport of the Urals, **3**, 3-7 (2017). (in Russian)
11. P.A. Kozlov, I.O. Naboychenko, V.Yu. Permikin, Zheleznodorozhnyj transport [Railway transport], **3**, 26-29 (2016). (in Russian)
12. P.A. Kozlov, V.S. Kolokolnikov, O.V. Osokin, Zheleznodorozhnyj transport [Railway transport], **6**, 12-16 (2018). (in Russian)

Development of approach to improvement of urban traffic flow diagram

Andrey Burlutsky[1,*], *Galina* Pushkareva[1], and *Elena* Kirgisarova[1]

[1]Tomsk State University of Architecture and Building, 634003 Tomsk, Russia

Abstract. The result of generalized analysis of Russian and foreign studies focused on urban transportation systems demonstrate that the existing methods of forming schemes of passenger transport routes only partially account interaction of transport flows and urban highways. Usually, insufficient attention is paid to optimization criteria that allow performing comprehensive analysis of rationality of transport route schemes. It is defined that speed is one of the key optimization criteria for transport systems that accounts specific feature of traffic flow organization on a street network of a big city and its state with regard to the use of traffic. An approach to reasonable scheduling of route scheme reorganization was developed basing on the routing experience, it allows accounting the factors that defines technical state of a road network and characteristics of transport flows.

Introduction

The activities of a modern major city is determined by its infrastructure, one of the key elements of which is street network and passenger transport operation on its territory. High social significance of urban passenger transport shall be emphasized, it is implemented in providing freedom of movement for citizens and reducing commuting time.

Today's level of transport infrastructure development does not allow meeting transportation needs of the population completely. The primary reason for it is drop in the rates of construction, reconstruction and overhaul of transportation infrastructure objects. The acute transportation-related problems are observed in major cities and metropolises, planning schemes of which were designed long ago. In these conditions, insufficiently developed road and transport infrastructure results in actual commuting time exceeding the permissible threshold value [1, 2]. This leads to violation of the basic principle of urban transport systems formulated by a French architect Le Corbusier as follows: "No city can grow faster than its transport does".

Due to the increase of citizens' economic activity that causes growth of their transport mobility, daily use of automobiles becomes more attractive. At the same time, passenger cars are characterized by low carrying capacity and significant traffic lane space occupied. This indicates inefficiency of using such passenger transport for stable and massive work-related movements that occur in certain time periods. However, all citizens' transitions obviously cannot be managed by public transport alone. It shall be noted that passenger cars

* Corresponding author: abura124@yandex.ru

© The Authors, published by EDP Sciences. This is an open access article distributed under the terms of the Creative Commons Attribution License 4.0 (http://creativecommons.org/licenses/by/4.0/).

have equal importance in organization of transportation, since they provide significant amount of cultural and social mobility of urban population [3].

Considerable growth of car ownership level peculiar to cities of Western Europe and the USA after the World War II provoked serious crisis processes accompanied by aggravation of transport situation. Back then, specialists realized that urban highways constructed before massive appearance of cars didn't comply with the traffic parameters. Further on, many American scientists confirmed the necessity to change the adopted European way of cities development that provides growth of public transport system [4–6].

According to the specialists' estimates [7, 8], Russia is more than 20 years behind the developed countries by the level of transport infrastructure development, repeating past mistakes of the western countries and facing the same problems. Project solutions currently designed in Russia mostly support interests of car owners who provide no more that 40% of the entire passenger traffic [3, 9].

Many researchers [4, 5, 7, 8, 10–13] note that selection of reasonable route schemes is one of the most issues for organization of public transport operation. Commuting time within the city largely depends on level of route scheme quality. Therefore, route scheme shall be considered along with street and road network of the city.

Scientists all over the world deal with the issues of bus route schemes improvement starting with the 1930th. The key studies in the field of design of urban public transport system belong to A. Aleksandrov, L. Bronstein, A. Zilbertal, V. Larioniv, A. Polyakov, D. Samoilov. Development of scientifically proven methodologies for designing bus route schemes is studied in the works of B. Gerominus, D. Dzhumaev, M. Antoshvili, V. Buneev, G. Varelopulo, I. Spirin, E. Safronov, M. Khrushchev [3], F. Glik [5], S. Olkhovsky [11] and V. Yavorsky. Among foreign studies, special interest is caused by the issued of modeling of public transport network [14].

Analysis of the routing experience demonstrated that provision of the existing methods of optimal routing schemes design require clarification as they do not account technical parameters of urban streets and roads. For the above reasons, further development of approach to reforming th route scheme with the reference to the highway system operation is considered a relevant issue.

Research methods

Based on the analysis of requirements to operation of urban public transport which are presented in detail in scientific literature, the key principles of route schemes optimization were developed (Fig. 1) [9].

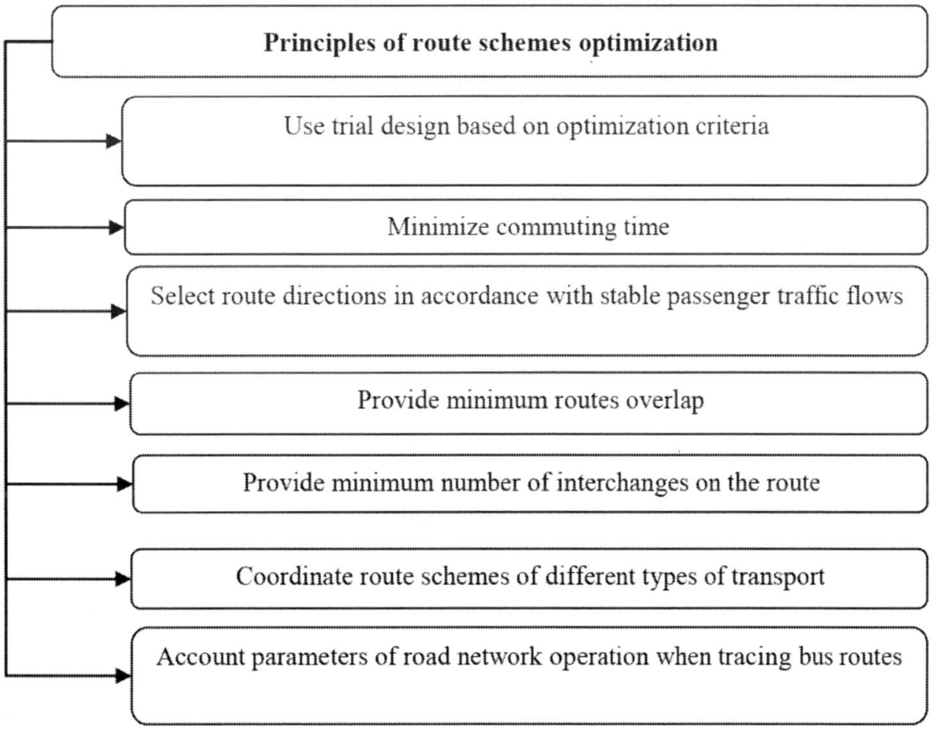

Fig. 1. Principles of route schemes optimization.

Representation of the set objective as a number of operational efficiency criteria is one of the key stages of studying a system of urban passenger transport. The most effective method enables searching solutions based on one crucial criterion with transition of the rest criteria in the category of limitations. In general form, it can be put as follows [9]:

$$\begin{cases} X \to \text{extrem} \\ Y_1^{\min} < Y_1 < Y_1^{\max} \\ \dots \\ Y_n^{\min} < Y_n < Y_n^{\max} \end{cases}, \qquad (1)$$

where X - the crucial criterion defined on the basis of expert evaluations;
Y - multitude of second tier criteria sufficient for complete description of the role of the studied object.

The optimization criteria for certain routes and route schemes accepted in the study are presented in Table 1. According to the majority of scientists, commuting time of citizens can be taken as a key optimality criterion. It should be mentioned that the standard for work-related commuting time are settled in the existing regulatory document [15].

Taking into account multicriterion nature of routing task, the approach to selecting the most rational solution shall be presented in the following form [9]:

for route scheme

$$\begin{cases} t_{av} \to \min \\ K_r^{min} < K_r < K_r^{max} \\ \delta_r^{min} < \delta_r < \delta_r^{max} \\ K_i^{min} < K_i < K_i^{max} \\ K_{i\,pub}^{min} < K_{i\,pub} < K_{i\,pub}^{max} \end{cases};$$

for certain route

$$\begin{cases} t_{av} \to \min \\ l_{min} < l_r < l_{max} \\ K_i < K_i^{max} \\ K_{occ} > K_{occ}^{min} \\ I_{rp} < I_{max} \end{cases}. \quad (2)$$

Table 1. Optimization criteria for passenger transport route schemes.

Optimization of optimization	Criterion of optimization	Rational limits of criteria variation
route schemes	Average commuting time of a citizen $t_{av\,pub}$	$t_{av\,pub}$ <40 min
	Coefficient of interchanges K_i	1.15< K_i <1.30
	Route coefficient K_r	2.0<K_r<3.0
	Density RN δ_r	1.5<δ_r<2.5
	Coefficient of indirectness of traffic on a route network $K_{i\,pub}$	$K_{i\,pub}$<1.25
bus route	Average commuting time of a citizen t_{av} RT	–
	Route length l_r	regular 15-30 km circular up to 40 km
	Coefficient of available places occupancy K_{occ}	K_{occ}>0.5
	Road pavement condition index I_{rp}	I_{rp}<3.0
	Coefficient of indirectness of traffic on a route K_r	K_r<1.25

Among the existing approaches to improving current route scheme the method of successive approximations to the optimum variant studied by F. Glik [5] should be noted. This approach has been developed in the works of S. Olkhovsky [11] and V. Yavorsky. They proposed more detailed dependences and algorithms that account a number of additional criteria when correcting the route network. These ideas were taken as a basis of the method [9] proposed in this paper.

The studied method is based on the analysis of the mobility plan for transportations that are not served by routes included in initial basic frame. Next step in the design of a new prospect route consists in selection of its foundation that corresponds to the most straight chain from the table of unimplemented connections with the highest value of passenger flow. Further actions include building up the considered foundation by adding the most suitable sections. All connections that partially overlap with the route foundation are considered, later they become elements for building several variants of superposed chains. By building-up connections to the initial chain one successively moving towards the supposed destination points. The process of building-up connections is repeated for each superposed chain which shall now be considered as a new route foundation. Based on the obtained tree of chains a set of variants of the designed route is formed (Fig. 2). As a result of directed search the mot reasonable variant which accounts optimization criteria is selected (Table 1), later is will be included in the rational route scheme.

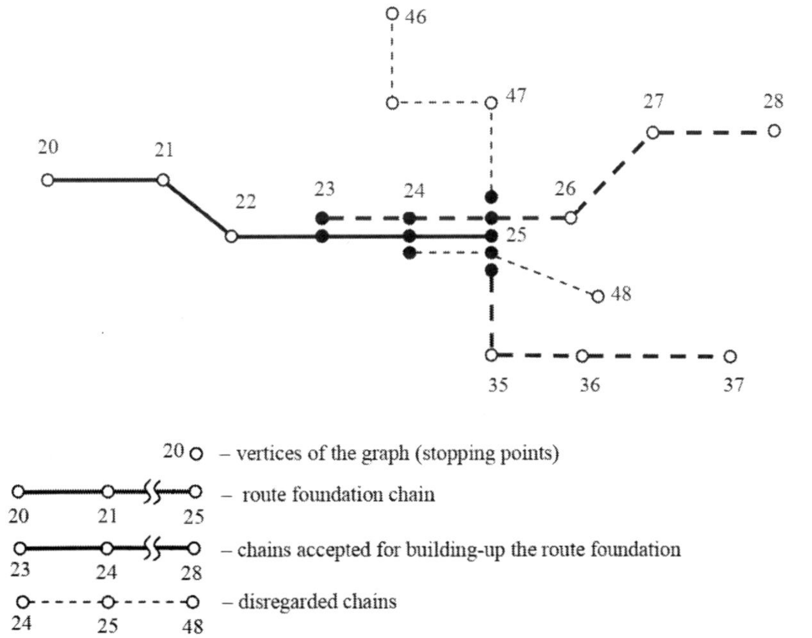

Fig. 2. Formation of variants of superposed chains.

The most rational variant of the studied route is determined in accordance with the adopted optimality criterion, among which are: average commuting time of a citizen t_{av}, route length l_r, coefficient of indirectness of traffic on a route network $K_{i\ pub}$, Coefficient of available places occupancy K_{occ}. The procedure of inclusion on the initial frame of a new route is repeated until all possible transportations are implemented. The desired number of interchanges between the disconnected districts shall not be more than 1. The process of designing a new route scheme is considered complete in case it fully complies with all the required conditions.

Results

Due to using combined analysis and directed variants selection it is possible to obtain a single route scheme variant, the parameters of which are close to that of the optimum variant. Formation of various route scheme variants can be based on alternative scenarios of urban transport network development. The most preferable route scheme variant is selected on the basis of the above optimality criteria. Commuting time of citizens is considered the most important criterion.

The main stages of route formation, as well as building-up of a rational route scheme with the account of highway network development are presented in Figures 3-4.

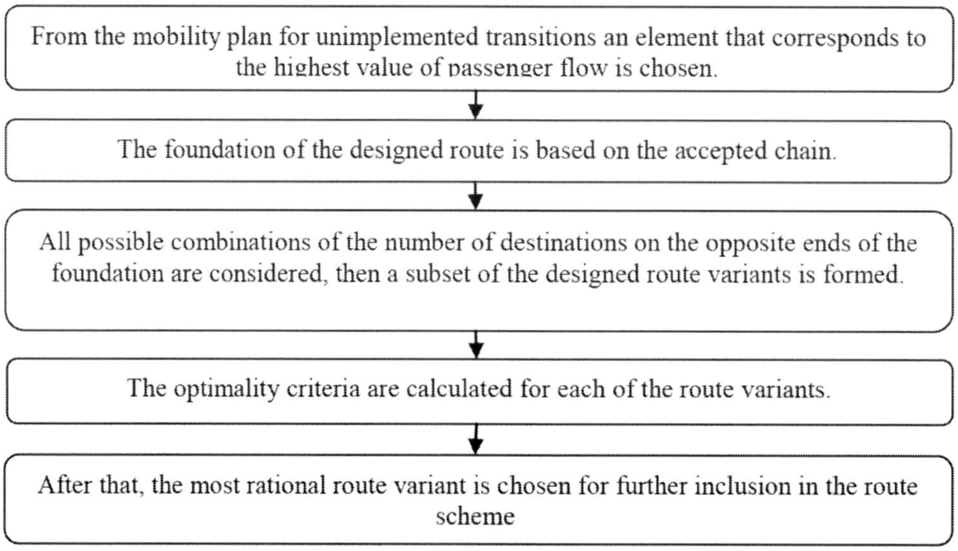

Fig. 3. Succession of actions of passenger route design with the account of technical condition of the road and street network of a city.

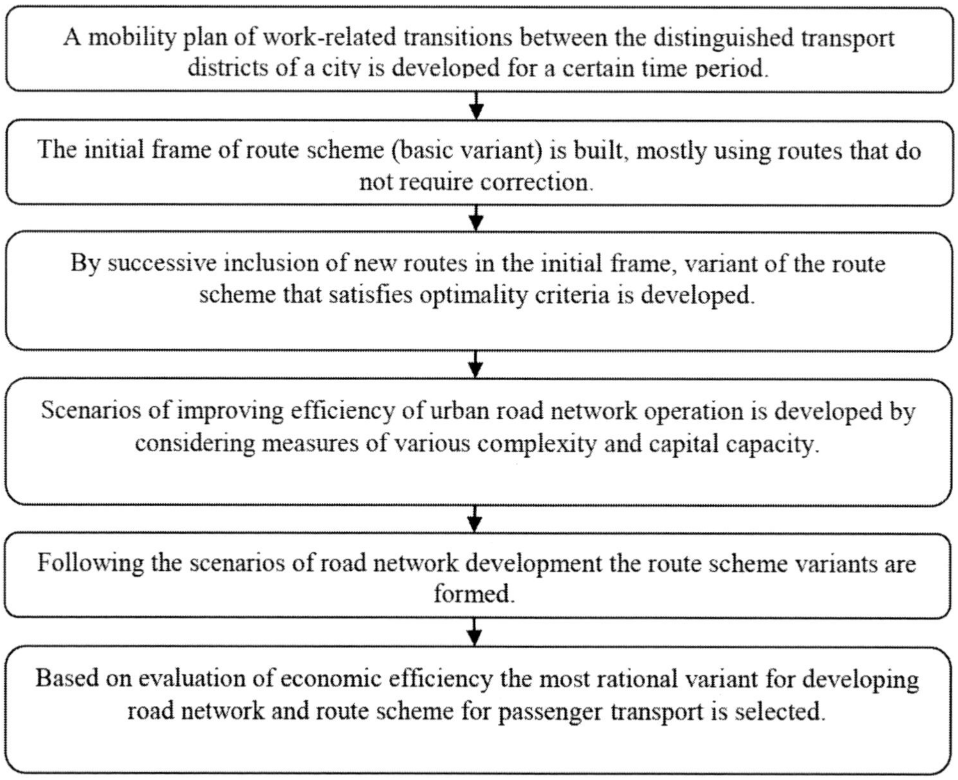

Fig. 4. Succession of actions of passenger route design with the account of improvement of operational parameters of the road and street network of a city.

Conclusion

Taking into account the accumulated routing experience,the approach to improvement of bus route scheme for a big city is developed in relation with operational condition of road and street network. Compared to the previously designed methods, the proposed approach accounts optimality criteria that allow comprehensive evaluation of route scheme efficiency. The essence of the approach consists in connecting individual sections of transport network and successive designing of competing route variants, one of which will then be included in the rational route scheme. At the final stage of the proposed algorithm alternative variants of rational route schemes are developed on the basis of scenarios for urban transport infrastructure development. This method will ensure increase in the traffic flow movement speed and as a result decrease in indirect commuting time. Further research will be focused on specification of dependences and calculation algorithm for movement speed of various types of passenger transport. Besides, further studies will suggest more complete account of factors that determine operational condition of road and street network, and parameters of transport flows, as well as their combination.

References

1. V.M. Buneev, V.I. Novoselov, N.N. Putilova, *Jeffektivnost' gorodskogo passazhirskogo transporta: metody ocenki i obosnovanija* [Urban passenger transport efficiency: evaluation and substantiation methods] (NGAVT, Novosibirsk, 2008). (in Russian)
2. I.S. Efremov, *Teorija gorodskih passazhirskih perevozok* [Theory of urban passenger transportations] (Vysshaya Shkola Publ., Moscow, 1980). (in Russian)
3. M.V. Khrushchev, *Metody obshhej i lokal'noj marshrutizacii avtobusnogo transporta v gorodah* [Methods of general and local routing of urban bus transport] (GUU Publ., Moscow, 1999). (in Russian)
4. Vukan R. Vuchic, *Transport v gorodah, udobnyh dlja zhizni* [Transportation for livable cities] (Territorija budushhego, Moscow, 2011). (in Russian)
5. F.G. Glik, *Interaktivnoe konstruirovanie marshrutnoj sistemy gorodskogo passazhirskogo transporta* [Interactive design of route system of urban passenger transport] (Budivel'nik, Kiev, 1987). (in Russian)
6. A.A. Burlutsky, V.I. Korenev, U.U. Guseva, Vestnik of TSUAB, **1** (2018). (in Russian)
7. M.R. Yakimov, U.V. Trofimenko, *Transportnoe planirovanie: formirovanie jeffektivnyh transportnyh sistem krupnyh gorodov* [Transport planning: building efficient transport systems for major cities] (Logos Publ., Moscow, 2013). (in Russian)
8. A.Y. Mikhailov, I.M. Golovnykh, *Sovremennye tendencii proektirovanija i rekonstrukcii ulichno-dorozhnoj seti gorodov* [Modern trends in design and reconstruction of urban road and street networks] (Nauka Publ., Novosibirsk, 2004). (in Russian)
9. A.A. Burlutsky, *Obespechenie jeffektivnosti funkcionirovanija dorozhnoj seti krupnogo goroda na osnove ucheta ee vzaimodejstvija s potokami passazhirskogo transporta (na primere g. Tomska)* [Ensuring operational efficiency of road networks in major cities based on accounting its interaction with passenger transport flows, example of Tomsk] (Tomsk, 2015). (in Russian)
10. M. Vol, B. Martin, *Analiz transportnyh sistem* [Analysis of transport systems] (Transport Publ., Moscow, 1981). (in Russian)

11. S.Y. Olkhovsky, *Modelirovanie funkcionirovanija i razvitija marshrutizirovannyh sistem gorodskogo passazhirskogo transporta* [Modeling of operation and development of route schemes for urban passenger transport] (SIBADI Publ., Omsk, 2001) (in Russian)
12. V.U. Renkin, P. Klafi, S. Khalbert, *Avtomobil'nye perevozki i organizacija dorozhnogo dvizhenija* [Automobile transportation and organization of traffic] (Transport Publ., Moscow, 1981). (in Russian)
13. S.A. Vaksman, N.M. Gerasimov, I.A. *Slepukhina, Informacionnye tehnologii v upravlenii gorodskim obshhestvennym passazhirskim transportom: monografija* [Information technologies in urban public transport management: monograph] (Yekaterinburg, 2012). (in Russian)
14. S. Dimitrov, A. Ceder, S. Chowdhury, M. Monot, Transportation Planning and Technology, **Vol. 40** (5), 592-610 (2017).
15. SP 42.13330.2011 *Gradostroitel'stvo. Planirovka i zastrojka gorodskih i sel'skih poselenij. Aktualizirovannaja redakcija SNiP* [Urban development. Planning and development of urban and rural areas. Revised edition of SNiP 2.07.01-89* (Moscow, 2011). (in Russian)

Movement of a railway car rolling down a classification hump with a tailwind

Khabibulla Turanov[1,*], and *Andrey* Gordienko[1]

[1]Ural State University of Railway Transport, 620034 Yekaterinburg, Russia

Abstract. The purpose of this paper is to calculate kinematic parameters of a railway car moving with a tailwind for designing a classification hump. The calculation of kinematic parameters is based on the d'Alembert principle, and the physical speed and distance formula for uniformly accelerated or uniformly decelerated motions of a body. By determining a difference between two components — gravitational force of a car and the resistance force of all kinds (frictional resistance, air and wind resistance, resistance from switches and curves, snow and frost resistance), which take place at different sections of a hump profile, the authors calculated the car acceleration at various types of car resistance, as well as time and speed of its movement. Acceleration, time and speed were plotted as a function of the length of a hump profile section. The research results suggest that permissible impact velocities of cars can be achieved by changing profiles of projected hump sections or by using additional hump retarders.

Introduction

A review of studies dedicated to dynamics of cars rolling down humps [1–7] and the applicable design guidelines for classification facilities [8] suggest that there is no method for determining kinematic parameters of a car moving along the entire length of hump profiles, including sections with retarder positions (RP). For example, studies [3–8] focus on designing a hump profile by determining the hump height from its apex to the end of the first retarder position (RP1), then from the beginning of RP1 to the end of the second retarder position (RP2) and, finally, from the beginning of RP2 to the end of the yard retarder position (RP3). Results of the calculation are considered to be valid if a car moving from the hump apex leaves RP3 and reaches the calculation point located 50 m away from RP3.

Studies [1–8] use Galileo's formula that determines the speed of freely falling bodies taking into account the inertia of rotating masses $v = \sqrt{2g'h}$ (see the minuend in formula (8), and formula (9) in [8]). In [1], Galileo's formula is combined with empirical formulas that take into account the resistance arising from rolling wheels along the rail and/or the running resistance (see formula (1) in [1]), as well as resistances that arise when a car passes curves of railway sections (see formula (2) in [1]) and switches (see formula (3) in [1]).

* Corresponding author: khturanov@yandex.ru

© The Authors, published by EDP Sciences. This is an open access article distributed under the terms of the Creative Commons Attribution License 4.0 (http://creativecommons.org/licenses/by/4.0/).

In [1], the total energy of the car is determined as a sum of kinetic energy E_0 and potential energy E_p, kJ: $E_0 + E_p$, where $E_0 = M(v_0)^2\rho/2$ (where M is the car weight, *t*; v_0 is the initial speed, m/s; ρ is the wheel rotation correction factor) and $E_p = gMh_{hump}$ (where h_{hump} is the required hump height, m).

It is commonly known [9] that the total energy remains constant: this state is called the law of conservation of energy. In [1], in contrast to the law of conservation of energy, the total energy $E_0 + E_p$ is equated to the work of a projected gravitational force component ($G\sin\psi$) of the moving car, i.e. the law of conservation of energy is violated (see page 293 in [9]).

The total energy in [1] is assumed to be equal to the sum of works done by all resistance forces, including those arising when the car moves between the hump apex and the reference point (100 *m* beyond the tangent point) A_r, passes a curved track section A_c and collides with switches A_s. Otherwise, $E_0 + E_p = A_r + A_c + A_s$ (see the mathematical expression (6) in [1]). This contradicts the work-energy theorem that defines a change in kinetic energy for a constrained material point in a finite form: $\Delta E = |A_{r,c,s}|$, where the work of the resistance forces $|A_{r,c,s}| = -A_{r,c,s}$ must have a negative sign [9]. Any effort to determine the required hump height h_{hump} using relation (6) in [1] is quasi-scientific.

Studies [3–8] use the Galileo's formula ($v = \sqrt{2g'h}$) in combination with resistances of all kinds, i.e. with the main (net train) resistance (see (4.9) in [8]), air and wind resistances (see formula (4.10) in [8]), snow and frost resistances (see formula (4.11) in [8]), resistances arising when the car passes switches (see (4.13) in [8]) and curved track sections (see formula (4.14) in [8]).

The application of the Galileo's formula is invalid ($v = \sqrt{2g'h}$) since it is applicable only to the ideal constraint, while resistances of all kinds are classified as non-ideal constraints [9]. These physically incompatible concepts seem to be widely used in the literature, for example, in the same formula for estimating hump heights and rolling-down speed of a car, both at high-speed sections and retarder positions of the hump. This approach is fundamentally wrong and unacceptable [10, 11]. As noted in [10, 11], the rolling-down speed of a car along the entire hump profile length, including sections with retarder positions [1-8], has not yet been determined.

Taking this into account, studies [10, 11] describe in detail a simplified method for constructing a mathematical model of the car movement along the hump profile, while [11, 12] provide specific calculations as examples. A reasonable approach to determining the longitudinal profile of the inclined hump part has remained a problem over many years. Authors of available studies [3–8] tend to normalize the rolling-down speed for each section of the inclined part (Table 4.7 in [8]) and then calculate the average time of movement, without taking into account the nature of movement and the real meaning of related physical processes.

The purpose of this study is to illustrate how the time and speed of the car movement along the entire length of the hump profile can be calculated using a simplified procedure. Using a known value of the car acceleration, it is necessary to find t_k, during which the car moves at a specified initial speed v_0 to the end of the tested hump section. Based on a known value of t_k, the speed $v(t_k)$ of the car leaving any hump section k can be determined.

Research methods

Previously, the engineering problem of determining the kinematic parameters (acceleration, time and speed) of the car moving along the hump profile was solved using the fundamental law of dynamics for non-ideal constraints (d'Alembert principle), as well as speed and distance formulas of elementary physics. The car speed on segments with retarder positions was found subject to the assumption that the hump retarder was used to the fullest extent (i.e. full stop of the car). Based on these findings, a refined method was proposed to calculate kinematic parameters of car movement on sections of longitudinal hump profiles [10, 11].

The proposed method makes it possible to determine efficient shunting conditions and efficiently combine powers of retarder positions. This ensures that permissible car impact velocities established for classification yards by the applicable operating rules will be maintained. Based on the developed refined method, the authors developed a program for calculating kinematic parameters of car movement on sections of longitudinal hump profiles [12]. The program is designed to calculate car accelerations, speeds and time on sections of longitudinal hump profiles. Operating parameters of humps are used as input data for the program.

The program is adapted to real current conditions under the assumption that any geometric parameters (grade $\boldsymbol{i_k}$, section length $\boldsymbol{l_k}$) of any hump section $\boldsymbol{k}$ are easily adaptable, e.g., to weather conditions.

Input data and results

Using the calculation program mentioned above [12], we studied the influence of the hump profile grade and placement of the third retarder position on a curved track on kinematic parameters of a car rolling down the hump. The calculated data are presented below.

The following shunting conditions were considered: (1) movement of a very bad runner[1] with a tailwind; (2) powers of retarder positions (RP1, RP2 and RP3) are used to the fullest extent; where RP1 and RP2 include length wheelbase (WhB), breaking zone (SB) and break release zone (RS), whereas RP3 includes only breaking zone (SB) and break release zone (RS); (3) the third retarder position (RP3) is located on straight or curved track sections.

First we consider the case with a concave hump profile (e.g., 35 ‰ on the first high-speed section (HS1), 18 ‰ on the second high-speed section (HS2), 13 ‰ on RP1, 10 ‰ on the intermediate section (IS), 10 ‰ on RP2, 1.2 ‰ on the switch zone (Sw), 1.0 ‰ on the first classification track (CT1), 0.6 ‰ on the second classification track (CT2), and the third retarder position located on a straight track section.

The calculated data are summarized in Table 1 in a form convenient for constructing the characteristic curves for acceleration $\boldsymbol{a_k}$, time $\boldsymbol{t_k}$ and speed $\boldsymbol{v_k}$ of a car moving on each section $\boldsymbol{l_k}$ of the inclined hump part, i.e. for $\boldsymbol{a_k = f(l_k)}$, $\boldsymbol{t_k = f(l_k)}$ and $\boldsymbol{v_k = f(l_k)}$).

Table 1. Calculated kinematic parameters of a car rolling down the hump, with the third retarder position on a straight track section.

Sections of the inclined hump part	**Elements of sections of the inclined hump part**	l_k	i_k	h_k	a_k	t_k	v_k	
		Input values		**Calculated values**				
		m	‰	*m*	*m/s*²	*s*	*m/s*	*km/h*
	HA	–		–	–	–	1.7	6.12
HS1	HS1	39.924	35	1.396	0.372	10.779	5.708	20.55
HS2	Before Sw	54.935	18	1.666	0.205	13.294	6.224	22.41
	After Sw	73.569		2.001	0.20	16.156	6.795	24.46

[1] The very bad runner means a car with a calculated gravitational force of 220 kN and main specific resistance of 0.8.

RP1	WhB	81.87	13	2.109	0.156	17.361	6.983	26.18
	SB	95.212		2.125	-2.037	20.761	0.057	0.205
	RS	102.57		2.239	0.156	30.98	1.652	5.95
IS	Before Sw	122.571	10	2.439	0.127	39.98	2.792	10.05
	After Sw	143.842		2.649	0.121	46.64	3.596	12.95
RP2	WhB	154.243	10	2.753	0.127	49.398	3.945	14.2
	SB	158.15		2.791	-2.067	51.298	0.019	0.067
	RS	174.843		2.959	0.127	67.456	2.065	7.435
Sw	Before Sw1	190.843	1.2	2.978	0.04	74.692	2.357	8.49
	Sw1	216.533		3.009	0.033	84.858	2.697	9.71
	Sw2	237.533		3.034	0.033	92.305	2.943	10.6
	Sw3	261.533		3.063	0.033	100.115	3.2	11.53
CT1	CT1	320.713	1.0	3.122	0.038	116.926	3.837	13.81
RP3	SB	326.963	1.5	3.127	-2.15	118.626	0.182	0.657
	RS	330.977	straight section	3.144	0.041	137.884	0.969	3.487
CT2	CT2	**385.213**	0.6	**3.173**	0.034	**170.539**	2.094	7.537

Abbreviations in Table 1: RS is the remaining section with retarder positions. The research results for the third retarder position (RP3) located on the straight section suggest that, when approaching the calculation point (CP), the car has a speed of $v_{eCP} \approx 2.1$ m/s (or ≈ 7.5 km/h). It should be noted that at $v_{eCP} \approx 2.1$ m/s, the average car speed is equal to $v_{eCPm} \approx 1.53$ *m/s*, which is less than the permissible average car speed on the second classification track (CT2), i.e. $[v_{eCP}] = 2.0$ m/s.

Thus, the specified shunting conditions will not allow the car to achieve the rated speed when approaching to a group of cars in the hump yard (5 km/h) [8]. Using the values in Table 1, variation of the car acceleration over the entire length of the track lk are plotted as a function of tailwind of a small value Frwx, subject to the resistance force of all kinds Fr. (Fig. 1).

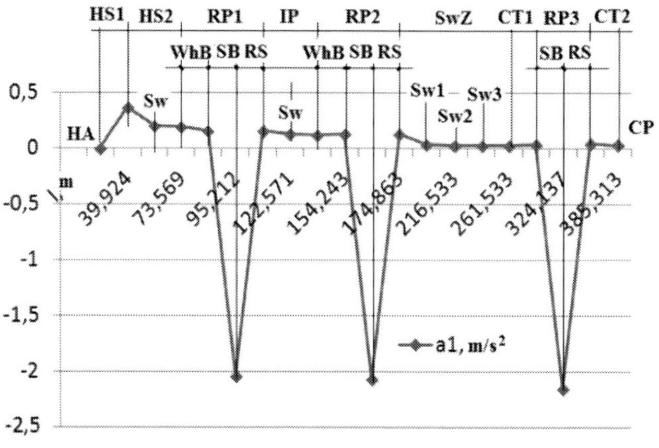

Fig. 1. Variation of acceleration when the car is rolling down the hump, with the third retarder position on a straight track section.

The abbreviations in Figure 1 are similar to those in Table 1. From Figure 1, it is clear that, on sections with retarder positions RP1, RP2 and RP3, the car has uniform deceleration with negative values, i.e. $a_{rp1} < 0$, $a_{rp2} < 0$ and $a_{rp3} < 0$ (where $|a_{rp1}| = -a_{rp1}$, $|a_{rp2}| = -a_{rp2}$, and $|a_{rp3}| = -a_{rp3}$).

Les us write the variation of the car acceleration, which is graphically presented above, in mathematical form. Assume that the car is retarded on the first retarder position (RP1), which is used to the fullest extent:

$$a_{\text{тр}1}(t) = f(t) = \begin{cases} f(\tau_5) = a_{\text{whb}} & \text{under } t < \tau_5, \\ f(t) = \quad f(\tau_5) = -a_{1\text{т}} & \text{under } \tau_5 \le t \le \tau_6, \\ f(\tau_6) = a_6 & \text{under } t > \tau_6; \end{cases} \tag{1}$$

Similar to the characteristic curve $a_k = f(l_k)$, characteristic curves $t_k = f(l_k)$ (Fig. 2), $v_k = f(l_k)$ (Fig. 3) were plotted using the values from Table 1.

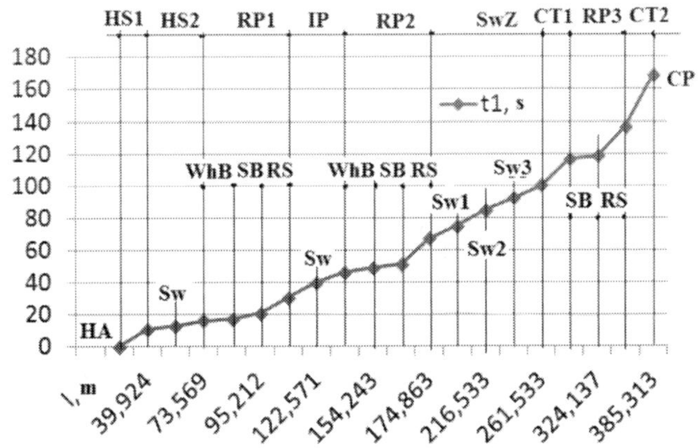

Fig. 2. Variation of the time of car movement on the hump inclined part.

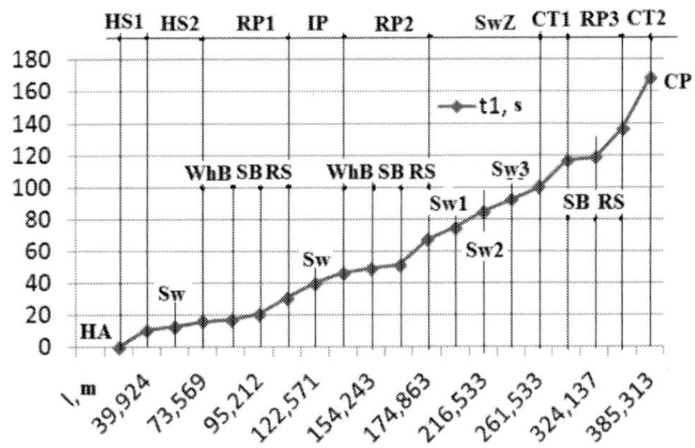

Fig. 3. Variation of the car speed on the hump inclined part.

From Figure 3 it is clear that the car speed falls to almost zero in the retardation zones where linear acceleration values are negative (Fig. 1). This is due to the fact that all retarder positions are used to the fullest extent.

Let us present the calculated kinematic parameters of the car rolling down the hump, with the third retarder position on a curved track section and grade increased to 2 ‰, as shown in Table 2.

Table 2. Calculated kinematic parameters of a car rolling down the hump, with the third retarder position on a curved track section.

Sections of the inclined hump part	Elements of sections of the inclined hump part	l_k	i_k	h_k	a_k	t_k	v_k	
		Input values		Calculated values				
		m	‰	*m*	m/s^2	*s*	*m/s*	*km/h*
	HA	–		–	–	–	1.7	6.12
HS1	HS1	39.924	35	1.396	0.372	10.779	5.708	20.55
HS2	Before Sw	54.935	18	1.666	0.205	13.294	6.224	22.41
	After Sw	73.569		2.001	0.20	16.156	6.795	24.46
RP1	WhB	81.87	13	2.109	0.156	17.361	6.983	26.18
	SB	95.212		2.125	-2.037	20.761	0.057	0.205
	RS	102.57		2.239	0.156	30.98	1.652	5.95
IS	Before Sw	122.571	10	2.439	0.127	39.98	2.792	10.05
	After Sw	143.842		2.649	0.121	46.64	3.596	12.95
RP2	WhB	154.243	10	2.753	0.127	49.398	3.945	14.2
	SB	158.15		2.791	-2.067	51.298	0.019	0.067
	RS	174.843		2.959	0.127	67.456	2.065	7.435
Sw	Before Sw1	190.843	1.2	2.978	0.04	74.692	2.357	8.49
	Sw1	216.533		3.009	0.033	84.858	2.697	9.71
	Sw2	237.533		3.034	0.033	92.305	2.943	10.6
	Sw3	261.533		3.063	0.033	100.115	3.2	11.53
CT1	CT1	320.713	1.0	3.122	0.038	116.926	3.837	13.81
RP3	SB	324.137	2.0	3.129	-2.145	118.626	0.191	0.687
	RS	335.313	curved section	3.350	0.046	136.856	1.024	3.69
CT2	CT2	**385.313**	0.6	**3.650**	0.034	**168.658**	2.12	7.63

The calculated data presented above for the third retarder position (RP3) located on the curved section suggest that, when approaching the calculation point (CP), the car has a speed of $\mathbf{v}_{\mathbf{eCP}} \approx 2.12$ m/s (or ≈ 7.63 km/h). It should be noted that at $\mathbf{v}_{\mathbf{eCP}} \approx 2.12$ m/s, the average car speed is equal to $\mathbf{v}_{\mathbf{eCPm}} \approx 1.57$ m/s, which is less than the permissible average car speed on the second classification track (CT2), i.e. $[\mathbf{v}_{\mathbf{eCP}}] = 2.0$ m/s.

By comparing Tables 1 and 2, we can conclude that an increase in the grade of the third retarder position and its location on the curved track section slightly influence the impact velocity of cars in the hump yard (7.537 km/h and 7.63 km/h).

For the case where the third retarder position is located on the curved track section, the total length of the inclined hump part from the hump apex up to calculation point is equal to $\mathbf{L}_{\mathbf{cr}} \approx 385.31$ m (versus $\mathbf{L}_{\mathbf{straight}} \approx 385.21$ m). The total time of car movement $\mathbf{t}_{\mathbf{tot.cur}} \approx 168.7$ s (versus $\mathbf{t}_{\mathbf{tot.straight}} \approx 170.6$ s). This is consistent with the data in Table 1. The characteristic curves $\mathbf{a}_\mathbf{k} = \mathbf{f}(\mathbf{l}_\mathbf{k})$, $\mathbf{t}_\mathbf{k} = \mathbf{f}(\mathbf{l}_\mathbf{k})$ and $\mathbf{v}_\mathbf{k} = \mathbf{f}(\mathbf{l}_\mathbf{k})$, plotted according to the data in Table 2 , are similar to those based on the data from Figures 1–3.

Moreover, the shunting conditions considered above will not allow the car to achieve the rated speed when approaching to a group of cars in the hump yard [8].

Permissible impact velocities under the specified conditions can be achieved either by changing the profile of separate sections in the inclined hump part, or by using additional car retarders.

Conclusion

The proposed refined method for calculating kinematic parameters of cars moving along longitudinal profiles of humps and the related calculation program make it possible to determine efficient shunting conditions. Using the calculation program, the authors studied the influence of the profile grade and the location of the third retarder position on kinematic parameters of cars moving along longitudinal profiles of humps, and presented the results of these studies. When the third retarder position is located on both straight and curved track sections, the rated speed of a car approaching a group of cars in the hump yard cannot be achieved. Permissible impact velocities under the specified conditions can be achieved either by changing profiles of separate sections in the inclined hump part, or by using additional car retarders.

Relying on the parameters calculated according to the simplified procedure, including the known distance traveled by the car along the entire length, e.g. the 1RP section of the hump l_{rp}, and the calculated uniform deceleration of the car $a_{0\text{rp}1}$, the authors calculated the braking time $t_{\text{rp}1}$ and the braking distance $l_{\text{rp}1}$ of the car in the section with retarder positions. Based on a value of $t_{\text{rp}1}$, the authors determined the car speed in the section with retarder positions at the time when the rail brake was released $v_{\text{rb}}(t_{\text{rp}1})$, i.e. when the car left the retarder positions of this section. The results of these studies can be used to calculate and design classification humps.

References

1. J. Prokop, Sh. Myojin, Memoirs of the Faculty of Engineering, Okayama University, **Vol. 27**, 2, 41 – 58 (1993).
2. S. Zarecky, J. Grun, J. Zilka, Transport Problems, Provlemy Transportu, **Vol. 3**, 4, 87 – 95 (2008).
3. V. Bobrovsky, D. Kozschenko, A. Dorosh, E. Demchenko, T. Bolovanovska, A. Kolesnik, Transport Problems, Provlemy Transporty, **Vol. 3**, Issue I, 147 – 155 (2016).
4. V.M. Rudanovskiy, I.P. Starshov, V.A. Kobzev, Bulletin of Transport Information, 6 (252), 19 – 28 (2016). (in Russian)
5. Yu.O. Pozojskiy, V.A. Kobzev, I.P. Starshov, V.M. Rudanovskiy, Bulletin of Transport Information, 2 (272), 35– 37 (2018). (in Russian)
6. V.N. Obraztsov, *Stancii i uzly, ch. II* [Stations and nodes, Part II] (Transzheldorizdat, Moscow, 1938). (in Russian)
7. V.I. Apatcev, Yu.I. Efimenko, *Zheleznodorozhnye stancii i uzly* [Railway stations and nodes] (Moscow, 2014). (in Russian)
8. Pravila i normy proektirovanija sortirovochnyh ustrojstv na zheleznyh dorogah kolei 1 520 mm [Rules and design standards for assorting works on railways of gauge 1,520 mm] (TEHINFORM, Moscow, 2003). (in Russian)
9. S.P. Timoshenko, D. Yung, *Inzhenernaja mehanika* [Engineering mechanics] (Mashgiz, Moscow, 1960). (in Russian)
10. Kh.T. Turanov, A.A. Gordienko, Mir transporta [World of Transport and Transportation Journal], **14**, 4 (65), 86 – 91 (2016). (in Russian)
11. Kh.T. Turanov, A.A. Gordienko, Certificate of official registration of the computer program, No. RU 2017614017 of 05.04.17 (2017). (in Russian)

Influence of operating firing field technologies on operational performance parameters

Aleksandr Kazakov[1], and *Anton* Suprunovskiy[2,*]

[1]Matrosov Institute for System Dynamics and Control Theory, 664033 Irkutsk, Russia
[2]Irkutsk State Transport University, 664074 Irkutsk, Russia

Abstract. At present, introduction of operating firing field technologies is one of the urgent tasks of the Russian railway transport, as their use can significantly improve operational performance parameters. The factors and conditions of transition to operating firing field control system for operational performance are investigated in this paper. It provides the analysis of the problems that arise during the work of the operating firing field and proposes measures for their elimination. Methods of mathematical and computer modeling using the author's software product were used. A new approach to multilevel simulation of the work of a transport operating firing field has been developed, which involves the use of the mathematical apparatus of multiphase queuing systems.

Introduction

Russian Railways JSC is performing purposeful work for transition from the regional principles of traffic control to arrangement of train traffic in operating firing field in the network. Implementation of a new transportation process model must ensure improvement of operational performance parameters. Unified control of train flows in the operating firing field allows accelerating the traffic. It is possible to arrange an efficient logistics technology with this control type. This approach will allow managing loading and movement of cargo flows to large unloading centers and seaports [1].

The problem of estimating efficiency of the main transportation process indicators arises when moving to the operating firing field railway control system. The difficulty consists in consideration of influence of various factors in the context of their close interconnection. The problem of accounting operating costs when changing the boundaries of operating firing fields determines the need to use methods of mathematical estimates and forecasts. It is necessary to take into consideration fulfillment of the controllability conditions by such large system as the "transportation process" to solve the problem of selecting the boundaries of a control operating firing field when determining the number of operating firing fields.

The next problem is arrangement of an optimal system for building the areas of circulation of locomotive crews within the boundaries of the operating firing fields created. When allocating boundaries of operating firing fields, it shall also be necessary to take into

* Corresponding author: as.irgups@gmail.com

© The Authors, published by EDP Sciences. This is an open access article distributed under the terms of the Creative Commons Attribution License 4.0 (http://creativecommons.org/licenses/by/4.0/).

consideration the distribution of tag control centers. The specifics of location of locomotives technical inspection points should also be taken into consideration. The criteria for creating operating firing fields were defined (see below) to solve the problems identified in the course of selection of operating firing fields boundaries. The following authors also worked on this topic: E. A. Sotnikov, A. N. Baushev, A. T. Osminin.

In determining the boundaries of operating firing fields formation, E. A. Sotnikov proposes to use the calculation methods [2]. On the basis of such methods, A. T. Osminin proposes variant of calculation of the number of operating firing fields.

Professor Osminin proposes calculation of the number of operating firing fields in the railway network by using mathematical approach. The purpose is to build the operating firing field coverage with the maximum flow connectivity and the maximum balance based on actual data on the flows of loaded cars.

As a result of the calculations, maps of the railway network with the optimal location of the operating firing fields boundaries were compiled. Variants with 5 and 6 operating firing fields were proposed [2].

The purpose of this work is to develop a conceptual approach to determine the efficiency of application of operating firing field technologies in the railway network. The following shall be necessary: to consider the criteria of transition to the operating firing field control system of the transportation process; to study the possibility of reducing the operating costs for the transportation process by improving the performance of performance indicators; to study existing problems at performance of operating firing field technologies.

The task that must be solved to achieve this goal is selection of the mathematical apparatus for simulating performance of the operating firing fields system. The mathematical model must provide an opportunity to predict performance of the system at various input parameters, including the transport flow characteristics [3]. The model will allow estimating the efficiency of improving operational performance of the transportation process. It is proposed to use a multilevel stochastic model to achieve this objective in this paper. The number of levels can be arbitrarily large, however, first, the problems discussed can be described with the help of models with a number of levels of not more than three; second, an increase in the number of levels makes the model very difficult to study [4]. A similar approach was earlier applied by the authors, in particular, for simulation of transportation and logistics systems at the regional level [5].

Operating firing field creation criteria

The analysis of performance conditions of the transportation process for the last 50 years makes enables to give a clear definition of the transportation process control operating firing field. *A transportation process control operating firing field* shall mean a set of sections of the network that have a single technology of traction rolling stock performance. When servicing common cargo flows, the identity of the production cycles is revealed and their improvement is achieved [6].

The study of factors and conditions for transition to the operating firing field control system for operational performance of the railway network makes it possible to establish the following basic criteria for the operating firing fields created [6]:

1. Ensuring technological completeness of the transportation process for arrangement and promoting the cars and train traffic within operating firing fields.
2. Creation of a flexible system for building locomotive circulation areas and work areas for locomotive crews within the transportation process control operating firing fields.
3. Rationalization of the development and implementation of plans for repair and construction works on the main directions of the railway network.
4. Ensuring favorable conditions for large handling areas and adjacent approaches.

5. Ensuring convenient conditions for arrangement local performance with large flow of cars at operating firing fields.
6. Providing opportunities for railways to perform social functions related to arrangement of passenger traffic in all types of communications.

Operational performance parameters in arrangement of operating firing fields

Introduction of operating firing field technologies makes it possible to improve the quality of freight traffic and to reduce the company expenses by improving the conditions for controlling the transportation process. With that, the level of fulfillment of the main qualitative indicators of operational performance is increased and the idle time of trains and locomotives at technical stations is reduced. This is achieved by improving the quality of operational train planning by the following indicators:

- increase in sectoral speed due to increased rhythm and uniformity of train traffic;
- reduction in the number of trains that have been left behind by traffic, which must proceed to seaports and other large unloading points, through the use of logistics technologies in regulating loading and advancement of trains at operating firing fields;
- reducing the risks of violation of delivery deadlines due to a reduction in the number of trains left behind by traffic and an increase in the sectoral speed;
- improving the use of locomotives by reducing their idle time at technical stations pending the implementation of maintenance operations (TO-2) and reducing the mileage of empty runs.

Quantification of the impact of operating firing field technologies on performance indicators is of great interest. However, the values of the latter are affected by a large number of random factors [7], therefore, this task is very complicated and has not yet been solved.

Justification of selection of the study method

There is also a significant uncertainty in behavior of large system called "transportation process in the operating firing field" caused by the following factors: technical and operational failures; changing requirements and actions of clients; conditions of interaction between independent control subsystems; weather conditions; employees' errors; other impacts on the course of the transportation process.

All this makes it extremely difficult to build a rigorous common mathematical model for solving the problem under consideration, which, apparently, should be stochastic (statistical, see below) [8]. Logical analysis can be used as an alternative to mathematical simulation and expert assessments of the impact of operating firing field technology on the change in the values of performance indicators can be carried out. However, this approach is quite costly and is not universal.

Thus, despite the existing difficulties, the most promising study method is mathematical simulation using the probabilistic (stochastic) approach. We will also use other methods of systems analysis, such as analysis and synthesis, decomposition and aggregation (see the next section), in the course of the study.

Changes in operational performance parameters with the use of operating firing field technologies

Let us consider the reasons and the nature of changes in indicators of operational performance at transition to operating firing field technologies. Idle time of trains and locomotives at technical stations. With introduction of operating firing fields technologies, the train traffic occurs more regularly due to the following:

- elimination of inter-track junctions with exception of the delivery period impact;
- preventing thickening of the working cars fleet in certain operating firing fields areas, particularly on approaches to ports;
- planning the passage of trains within the boundaries of the operating firing field, not railways.

It is known that processing of trains upon arrival and breaking-up depends on the uniformity of arrival of trains to classification yards. A uniform flow reduces the idle time of trains and cars. This applies to transit trains that are not processed. Besides, improvement of locomotive scheduling for trains makes it possible to reduce idle times while waiting for delivery of locomotives and finished trains [9].

The performance indicators are significantly improved with the use of operating firing field technologies. First of all, idle time for various operations is reduced. This is associated with the improvement in conditions of arrangement of locomotives turnover. Reducing the idle time for performing station operations also reduces the duration of holding of the station tracks, which causes their freeing. The number of freed tracks can be determined on the basis of the reduction in the time of occupying the station tracks. Freeing of arrival and departure tracks improves the maneuverability of railway operating firing fields and improves arrangement of operational performance. Reducing the idle time to departure from stations due to more regular train flows during the day provides more efficient use of the operating time of locomotives and locomotive crews. Increasing the uniformity of train traffic with the transition to operating firing field technology provides reduction in duration within daily periods, when freight trains pass in a more condensed manner. The analysis of the size of transfer of trains on inter-track junctions for the first and the second half of the day shows that freight traffic increases noticeably during the period from 6 a.m. to 6 p.m. [10].

Thus, it can be seen that performance indicators are indeed significantly increased when implementing the operating firing field technology. On the contrary, operational costs are reduced and labor productivity indicators are increasing.

Mathematical model

Selection of the mathematical apparatus for simulation of operating firing field technologies for controlling the transportation processes is determined by the following two principal circumstances. First, as already noted, considerable uncertainty exists in the system caused by various technical, operational and economic factors. Second, the three-level control of the transportation process is practiced in the operating firing field system. In this situation, the use of a three-level stochastic model, which is a multiphase queuing system from the mathematical standpoint, is evident [11].

Let us review system of random values $S, X_1, ..., X_n, Y_1, ..., Y_m$, which has the following structure:

1. "input" – random value S (first level);
2. "intermediate" – random vector $\vec{X} = (X_1, ..., X_n)$ (second level);

3. "output" – random vector $\vec{Y} = (Y_1,...,Y_k)$ (third level).

These random variables can be either discrete or continuous.

Depending on the value of random variable S at the first level, the distribution laws of random variables of the second level are defined. $X_i = X_i(S), i = 1,...n$. In their turn, the laws of distribution of random variables of the third level depend on the values that random variable S 0x1 and random vector $\vec{X}$ take. $Y_j = Y_j(S, X_1,...,X_k), j = 1,...k$.

With that, S actually performs as the initial data and in certain cases its values may be set or uniquely determined from additional conditions; $\vec{X}$ is the vector of auxiliary parameters; $\vec{Y}$ is the vector of the main characteristics of the process studied, which are of interest from the simulation standpoint. It can easily be seen that the model considered is indeed a three-level model. The number of levels can be increased if necessary. However, the study becomes much more complicated with introduction of each new level [11].

The study of the model built is only possible using numerical methods. First of all, these are the Monte Carlo methods [12]. To summarize this section, it should be noted that the technique proposed earlier in [13] can be used to establish the boundaries of a particular operating firing field.

Operational performance parameters of the railway operation in conditions of operating firing field technologies

The Eastern Operating Firing field (EOD) is currently becoming the key region for the social and economic development of Russia in the context of activation of the eastern vector of the country's economic development. It is necessary to create real instruments that give a positive impulse to the entire transportation process for more efficient control of the operational performance of the EOD. One of such instruments is a unified model for planning performance indicators. First of all, planned values for the operating control center (OCC) of the EOD shall be established and then, they shall be established for the EOD railways. Due to this, the basic principles of the transportation process operating firing field control are preserved. This approach will allow arranging the through passage of trains with setting the uniform weight norms, reducing the number of idle periods at technical stations, reducing costs.

Let us review the results of operation for 2017. Table 1 contains the main indicators of operational performance of the entire EOD and the indicator for the railways within it.

Table 1. Operation indicators for 2017.

Indicators	Planned	Actual	+/-
Sectoral speed (km/hour)	39.7	39.9	0.2
Locomotive productivity (thousand gross tons-km)	2,249	2,261	12
Average train weight (tons)	3,969	3,984	15
Daily locomotive run (km)	723	728	5
Average loading (thousand tons) per day	563.8	568.7	4.9

Based on the results of 2017, the main performance indicators for implementation of operating firing field technologies are in the positive trend. The average train weight was increased by 15 tons, the average daily locomotive run was increased by 5 km, the locomotive productivity grew by 12 thousand gross tons-km.

The criterion for efficiency of introduction of operating firing field technologies is fulfilling the operational performance indicators: freight turnover, share of shipments delivered within the standard period, average delivery rate of freight shipments in loaded cars, average delivery rate of freight shipments in containers, route speed of a freight train, fulfillment of the freight trains schedule, implementation of the plan for unloading at port stations, implementation of the plan for delivery of trains to port stations, average daily capacity of locomotives, average train weight in tons, average daily locomotive run, quality of the arrangement of infrastructure repair works, the provision of "windows" in accordance with the directive schedule.

It is necessary to perform a preliminary scenario simulation of the EOD performance for efficient implementation of these criteria. For this purpose, it is planned to develop its simulation model based on the approach of mathematical simulation of operating firing field technologies proposed in the previous section.

Results

The following has been determined in the course of the study performed:

1. Introduction of operating firing field technologies is a promising direction for development of the Russian railway transport in general and the eastern services operating firing field in particular.
2. It is necessary to perform scenario simulation of operation of the operating firing field to determine its quantitative parameters.
3. The operating firing field is influenced by a large number of random factors, due to which its mathematical model must have the probabilistic (stochastic) nature.
4. The use of the apparatus multilevel (multiphase) queuing systems for simulation is viewed as the most promising approach in the conditions described above.

Conclusion

The prospects for development of operating firing field technologies are based on arrangement of the transportation process control within the boundaries of the railway network with the efficient use of the capacity and carrying capacity of the infrastructure, traction resources and technical means to support the transportation process. At the same time, the following functions must be performed in the operating firing field: a) control on the basis of logistic train traffic control principles; b) redistribution of car flows by directions in accordance with the shift and daily plan for train and cargo operations, the traffic schedule and the train formation plan. Based on the local conditions, a set of basic indicators of operational performance can be supplemented and modified to take into consideration the development of a system of key performance indicators of the Russian Railways JSC holding company. The mathematical model allows more detailed consideration of the relation between the operating firing field technologies control level and estimation of the effect on the state of the system when input flows change.

Further development of the studies must be related to improvement of the mathematical model and its software implementation in the form of the operating firing field simulation model with subsequent verification of the model on actual data. When implementing this idea, the tools will be obtained that will allow performing scenario simulation of application of operating firing field technologies in railway transport.

The research was performed with the financial support of the Russian Foundation for Basic Research within the scope of research project No.18-07-00604.

References

1. E. Kreutzberger, R. Konings, Research in Transportation Business and Management, **Vol. 19,** 83–96 (2016).
2. A.T. Osminin, Bjulleten' Objedinennogo uchenogo soveta OAO RZD [Bulletin of the Joint Scientific Council of Russian Railways JSC], 2, 42–56 (2017). (in Russian)
3. F.A. Haight, *Mathematical Theories of Traffic Flow* (NY-London Academic Press, 1963).
4. G. Bolch, S. Greiner, H. de Meer, K.S. Trivedi, *Queueing Networks and Markov Chains. Modeling and Performance Evaluation with Computer Science Applications* (NY Wiley & Sons, 2006).
5. I.V. Bychkov, A.L. Kazakov, A.A. Lempert, D.S. Bukharov, A.B. Stolbov, Automation and Remote Control, **Vol. 77,** 332–343 (2016).
6. A.T. Osminin, E.A. Sotnikov, A.N. Baushev, Zheleznodorozhnyj transport [Railway transport], 6, 21–27 (2017). (in Russian)
7. E.A. Sotnikov, Zheleznodorozhnyj transport [Railway transport], 3, 4–8 (2018). (in Russian)
8. G.J. Hahn, S.S. Shapiro, *Statistical Models in Engineering* (NY Wiley & Sons, 1994).
9. D.Yu. Levin, Dispetcherskie centry i tehnologija upravlenija perevozochnym processom [Dispatching centers and control technology of the transportation process] (Marshrut, Moscow, 2005). (in Russian)
10. B.S. Kerner, *Introduction to Modern Traffic Flow Theory and Control* (Springer, Berlin, 2009).
11. C. Kim, A. Dudin, O. Dudina, S. Dudin, European Journal of Operational Research, **Vol. 235,** 170–179 (2014).
12. C. Graham, D. Talay, *Stochastic Simulation and Monte Carlo Methods, Mathematical Foundations of Stochastic Simulation* (Springer, 2013).
13. A.L. Kazakov, A.A. Lempert, International Journal of Artificial Intelligence, **Vol. 13**, 200–210 (2015).

Controlled atmosphere GMAW welding of transportation vehicles and production machines parts made from 30MnB5 steel

Evgeny Ivanayskiy[1,*], *Aleksei* Ishkov[2], *Aleksandr* Ivanayskiy[3], and *Iakov* Ochakovskii[1]

[1]Polzunov Altai State Technical University, 656049 Barnaul, Russia
[2]Altai State Agricultural University, 656049 Barnaul, Russia
[3]"Emissiia" LLC, 656067 Barnaul, Russia

Abstract. The paper studies the influence of shielding gas on the composition and the structure of weld joint metal of 30MnB5 steel applied in essential parts of automobiles and tractors. The welding was performed in inert, oxidizing and reducing atmospheres. It was established that TIG welding with argon used as shielding gas did not provide the required mechanical properties when using conventional welding materials. Carbon dioxide during MAG welding caused partial burning of alloying elements. Carbon monoxide used as shielding gas was proved to form reducing atmosphere enabling to obtain chemical composition close to the base metal composition. Metallographic examinations were carried out. The obtained results provided full-strength weld, as well as the required reliability and durability of welded components and joints.

Introduction

Boric steels are getting wider use in manufacture of various types of wheeled and caterpillar vehicles for production of wear resistant cover plates, knives, caterpillar tracks, liner and screen plates, crushing units and other details. Composition and properties of these steels are defined by the requirements of EN 10083, along with the national standards elaborated on their basis. Steels are characterized by low hardness after rolling, they are easy to mold and cut, thus enabling manufacturing complex parts and products. Quenching and tempering provide high strength combined with good notch toughness, high wear resistance and resistance to mechanical loading. Along with that, welding of these steels not only changes the chemical composition of the weld joint but also softens the heat-affecting zone subjected to thermal cycle.

A number of research works were devoted to different combinations of welding materials used for Boric microalloyed steels welding. The authors of [1] suggest using conventional welding wire Sv-08G2S (Russian grade) with addition of 0.005 % Boric suitable for welding in carbon dioxide (CO_2). Production technology of these wires was elaborated, however data on the composition and properties of the weld joint was not provided. Other research [2] indicates positive influence of Boric content >0.002% on the

[*]Corresponding author: 609185@mail.ru

© The Authors, published by EDP Sciences. This is an open access article distributed under the terms of the Creative Commons Attribution License 4.0 (http://creativecommons.org/licenses/by/4.0/).

steel microstructure. L.N. The research [3] was focused on the properties of weld joints made from low-carbon steel 10G2FB (Russian grade) by flux-cored wire with Boric. The Boric content in the weld joint amounted to 0.0025%...0.0065%. Orlov et al. [4] determined that Boric microalloying of weld joint through flux was insufficiently reliable due to low metallurgic activity of Boric oxide in the welding flux. Authors suggested using special flux-cored wires providing Boric content in the weld joint metal of up to 0.0065%. Larger Boric content indicated crack formation in the weld joint.

All welding methods mentioned above, as well as manual arc welding use CO_2 as shielding gas. It is known [5] that high temperature causes dissociation of carbon dioxide into carbon, carbon monoxide and oxygen which are dissolved in a fluxed molten weld pool or recombined in colder areas of the arc into carbon dioxide. The generated free oxygen reacts with alloying elements forming oxides [6]. Studies [7, 8] demonstrate that active oxidation of carbon dioxide and alloying elements from drops takes place during melting and arc transfer of molten metal. The oxidation velocity increases along with the increase in oxidation capacity of the environment [7]. The loss of alloying elements occurs both due to oxidation and due to evaporation from the surface of the drop. The ratio between the content of evaporating and oxidizing element is determined by the content of oxygen in the gas phase and the welding mode [8].

In the view of the above mentioned, the objective was defined as selection of shielding gas which does not cause oxidation of alloying elements. Currently [9] for these purposes either inert gases (Ar and He), or reducing atmospheres containing inert gases and hydrogen are used.

The purpose of this study is to investigate various methods of electric-arc welding of parts of transportation vehicles and production machines made from Boric microalloyed steels. The research novelty consists in application of reducing shielding atmosphere based on carbon monoxide (CO) to prevent burning of alloying elements.

Materials and methods

The material used in the research is 30MnB5steel, which is a replacement of 65G steel. Chemical composition of the base metal of weld joints made by various welding methods can be found in Table 1.

Steel was welded using Sv-08G2S welding wire. The obtained specimens were further water quenched from the temperature 880...900°C. Microstructure, hardness and microhardness of various parts of weld joints were investigated.

In order to study the behavior of alloying elements during welding chemical analysis was conducted using DFS-500 optical emission spectrometer. Theoretical studies of possible chemical reactions ongoing at temperatures higher than the melting temperature were conducted based on the methods described in [10], and the reference data from the website [11].

Experiment and results

According to the data of manufacturer [12] conventional welding technologies with low-hydrogen welding materials can be applied for 30MnB5 steel. Initially for manufacturing parts of transportation vehicles and production machines MAG (Metal Active Gas) welding was used which is the most common method of industrial welding. However, substantial drop in operational life of the equipment was noted. It was found that after quenching hardness of the base material was 46...48 HRC and hardness of the weld joint metal was 32...34 HRC. Chemical analysis (Table 1) showed that in the weld joint decrease in the content of carbon (C), manganese (Mn) and Boric (B) took place, and some increase in the content of silicium (Si), apparently due to its transition from the welding wire.

Table 1. Results of chemical analysis (on the side of weld bed which is melted the last).

Chemical composition, % wt								Notes
C	Si	Mn	Cr	Cu	B	S	P	
0.348	0.225	1.259	0.015	0.044	0.003	0.0069	0.0085	30MnB5 Steel base metal
0.120	0.617	1.109	Trace levels	0.104	Trace levels	0.0058	0.0079	Welding in CO_2 atmosphere
0.072	0.456	1.093	Trace levels	0.061	Trace levels	0.0059	0.0071	Welding in Ar atmosphere
0.178	0.692	1.268	0.010	0.131	0.002	0.0097	0.0072	Welding in CO atmosphere

TIG welding was applied to reduce burning of the alloying elements. Argon (Ar) was used as shielding gas. Chemical composition of weld metal can be also seen in Table 1. It should be noted that in all cases chemical composition was determined from the side of weld joint reinforcement.

Generally, when applying manual argon-arc welding a significant decrease in the content of almost all alloying elements was observed (Table 1). The hardness of the joint metal after quenching was <20 HRC (Fig. 1). Microhardness of the quenched specimens was measured along the section of the weld joint, and metallographic analysis of the metal structure was conducted. It was established that the argon-arc welded specimens had sufficient structural inhomogeneity. The core zone had typical martensite structure with hardness value of 41…47 HRC. In the mid-zone of the weld joint one could observe the structure of upper bainite with release of accicular ferrite. Therefore, the decrease in the value of material hardness up to 30…20 HRC occurred depending on the place of measurement. This can be explained by low mixing coefficient of the base and electrode metal where there were no Boric and the carbon content did not exceed 0.11% [13].

Upper zones of the weld joint had hardness < 20 HRC. The metal coincided with the unalloyed low-carbon steel in its composition and had Widmanstatten structure containing pearlite grains with accicular precipitates of ferrite and rounded grains of ferrite. Separate zones with the structure of upper bainite were observed. The velocity of cooling was insufficient for the formation of martensite structure. In these conditions the absence of active chemical reactions between the molten weld pool and inert gas shielding atmosphere is suggested.

Thus, it was found that application of MIG/MAG technologies and TIG welding does not provide the required properties for parts of transportation vehicles and production machines.

It is known that heating of welding arc causes dissociation of carbon dioxide with release of atomic oxygen, for that reason these atmospheres are considered to be oxidizing (1, 2).

$$2CO_2 \leftrightarrow 2CO + O_2 \tag{1}$$

$$2CO \leftrightarrow 2C + O_2 \tag{2}$$

Along with that, CO possesses explicit reducing properties and is widely used in metallurgical industry for metal reduction from oxides. The use of CO during welding was restrained by its harmful biological effect. The authors in [14] propose pre-heating of monoxide at the temperature higher than the flashpoint resulting into its burning in the air atmosphere with the formation of harmless CO_2 (2).

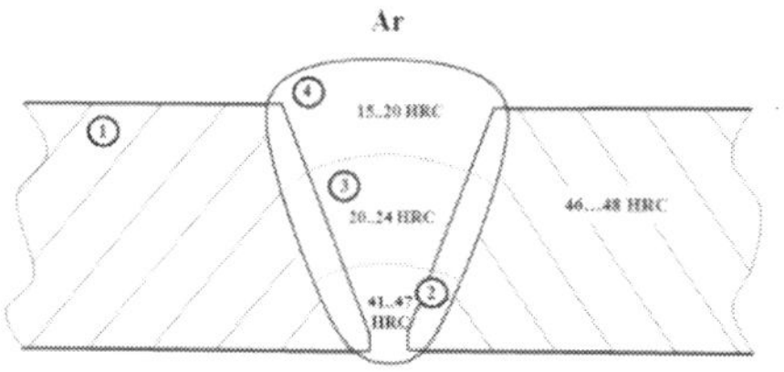

a)

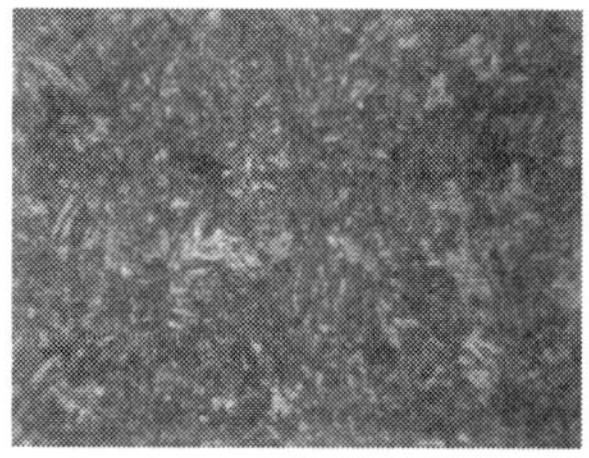

b) ×500

c) ×500

d) ×500

Fig. 1. The scheme of weld joint of 30MnB5 steel welded in CO_2 atmosphere (a) and microstructure of the zone 2 (b), 3 (c), 4 (d).

Gibbs thermodynamic potential calculations ΔG demonstrated that such alloying elements as Cu, Ni, Co, Mo, W, Cr, Mn, Si, B, within the temperature range 1500…3500°K do not react with CO. Alternately, the oxide reduction reactions of the mentioned elements will take place except for Si and B.

Welding of specimens from 30MnB5 steel was conducted in the reducing atmosphere on conventional equipment for mechanized welding in active gases atmosphere. CO was used instead of CO_2. The improved burner provided heating of the fed carbon monoxide up to the temperature of 870…900°K. As it can be seen from Table 1 the content of C, Si, Mn, Cr and Cu in the joint metal increased. This proves that these elements are not burned during welding in CO atmosphere. Therefore, the hardness of the joint metal also increased up to 32…43 HRC depending on the zone of weld joint (Fig. 2).

The weld joint after quenching had martensite microstructure in the lower zone, ferrite-martensite in the middle part and bainite in the upper part. Quenching structures were formed in spite of the decrease in carbon content due to mixing of the base and electrode metals.

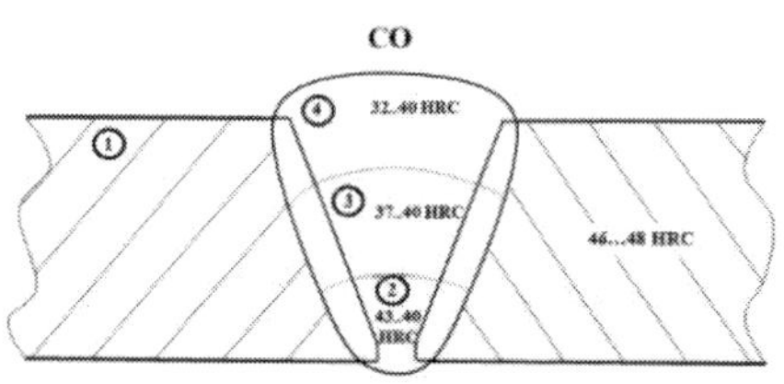

a)

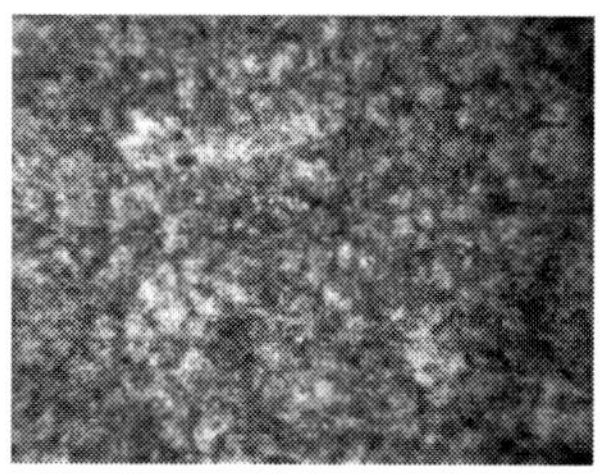

b) ×500

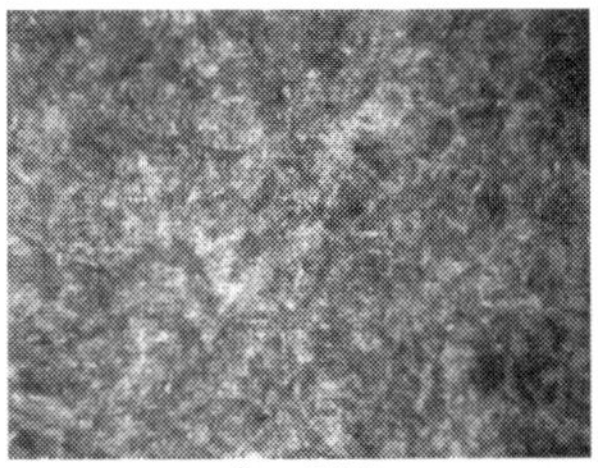

c) ×500

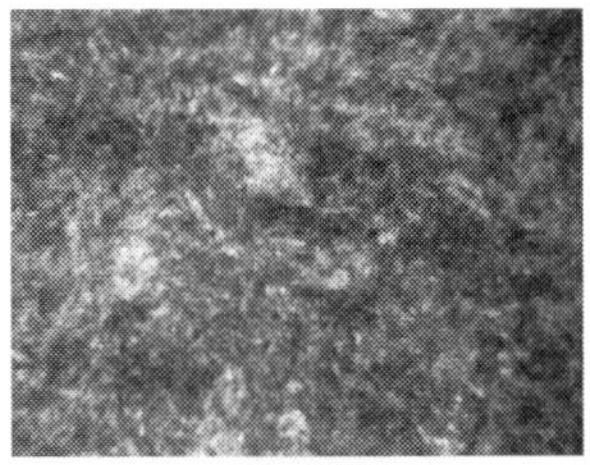

d) ×500

Fig. 2. Scheme of the weld joint from 30MnB5 steel welded in CO atmosphere (a) and microstructure of the zone 2 (b), 3 (c), 4 (d).

Use of carbon monoxide shielding atmospheres during arc welding enables to broaden significantly the application area of alloyed wires during mechanized welding. The recommended gas atmosphere provides stable arcing and good formation of weld joint.

Conclusion

It was established that the parts of transportation vehicles and production machines made from Boric microalloyed steels when using the most common welding methods have zones of lower hardness which reduce their operational life. Using carbon monoxide as shielding gas prevents burning of alloying elements and enables to provide the required mechanical properties. Application of reducing atmospheres during mechanized welding allows broadening the application area of alloyed welding wires.

References

1. A.M. Nesterenko, A.B. Sychkov, V.I. Sukhomlin, Vestnik of Nosov Magnitogorsk State Technical University, No. 3, 30-32 (2012) (in Russian).
2. V.V. Parusov, A.B. Sychkov, I.V. Derevyanchenko, M.A. Zhigarev, Vestnik of Nosov Magnitogorsk State Technical University, No. 1(9), 15-17 (2005) (in Russian).
3. L.I. Faynberg, A.A. Rybakov, A.N. Alimov, R. Rozert, Avtomaticheskaya svarka [Automatic welding], **5,** 20-25 (2007) (in Russian).
4. L.N. Orlov, M.G. Sharapov, V.L. Volynets, Sudostroenie [Ship construction], **5,** 54-57 (2010) (in Russian).
5. Lincoln Electric, Gas Metal Arc Welding. Product and Procedure Selection, available at: http://www.lincolnelectric.com/assets/global/Products/Consumable_MIGGMAWWires-SuperArc-SuperArcL-56/c4200.pdf.
6. S. Noland, Select the right argon/CO_2 blend for your weld requirements. Practical welding today, 9/10, (2015).
7. P.A. Norin, N.I. Malyshev, S.V. Rushchits, Svarochnoe proizvodstvo [Welding production], **7,** 4-6, (1980) (in Russian).
8. P.A. Norin, N.I. Malyshev, Svarochnoe proizvodstvo [Welding production], **2,** 21-23 (1982) (in Russian).
9. W. Lucas, Shielding gases for arc welding and cutting, available at: https://www.twi-global.com/technical-knowledge/published-papers/shielding-gases-for-arc-welding-and-cutting-may-2001.

10. A.V. Ishkov, V.V. Ivanayskiy, N.T. Krivochurov, V.F. Aulov, D.V. Koval, A.V. Sokolov, V.A. Novozhenov, A.V. Novozhenov, Izvestiya of Altai State University, **3 (83),** 199-203 (2014) (in Russian).
11. www.sciencebysimulation.com, Chemical reaction modeling and simulation app, available at: https://www.sciencebysimulation.com/chemreax/Analyzer.aspx.
12. METINVEST, Gorjachekatanyj tolstolistovoj prokat iz borsoderzhashhej stali marki 30MnB5 dlja zakalki i otpuska [Hot rolled thick-sheeted plate from boron steel of grade 30MnB5 for hardening and tempering], available at: https://sales.metinvestholding.com/upload/sales/technical_brochures/16/30MnB5_RU.pdf (in Russian).
13. GOST 2246–70. Welding steel wire. Specifications (Moscow, 1993) (in Russian).
14. E. Ivanayskij, A. Ivanayskiy, RU Patent 2570609 (2015) (in Russian).

Systems analysis of the issue of ensuring reliable operation of vehicles

Ivan Tikhii[1,*], and *Viktor* Kashkovsky[1]

[1]Irkutsk State Transport University, 664047 Irkutsk, Russia

Abstract. The paper describes relevance of the issue of ensuring reliable operation of vehicles for providing the required level of economic efficiency and safety of transportations via transport systems. Systems analysis method is used for solving the scientific problem. The place of vehicles is defined in the general classification of technical systems on the basis of systems analysis. The study proposes to divide the criteria of operational efficiency in accordance with the groups of properties of technical objects and shows their interrelation. As a result of the study, the generalized structure of integrated complexes of on-board equipment (ICOE) of vehicles is formed. Analysis of ICOE properties and their effect on the complex reliability is performed from the standpoint of systems approach is performed. Theoretical substantiation is provided for the necessity and the possibility of implementing the principles of survivability and fault tolerance of ICOE to ensure their effective use. The application of mutual control structures for the organization of on-board computer system diagnostics as a central part of ICOE is substantiated.

Introduction

Achieving and maintaining the required level of efficiency of transport systems has been and remains an important scientific and practical problem, due to the high importance of technological processes of transportation of goods for the development of the economy. The problem has a complex nature, since operational efficiency of vehicles is defined by multiple factors. For technical systems, reliability represents one of the key factors , for that reason a big part of studies is dedicated to the issues of providing the required efficiency level with regard to reliability and safety criteria.

Methods and techniques of solving this problem were mostly developed by various research and design teams for vehicles of a certain type on the basis of the account of their individual construction peculiarities and properties. At the same time, presently, due to the use of various technologies (including information ones) and cutting-edge design solutions while designing vehicles for different purposes, they gained common properties as systems.

This statement defines the necessity and rationality of using systems analysis method for selecting and substantiating the effective solution to the studied problem based on the adequate presentation of vehicles' properties and application conditions (limitations).

* Corresponding author: tiviv@list.ru

© The Authors, published by EDP Sciences. This is an open access article distributed under the terms of the Creative Commons Attribution License 4.0 (http://creativecommons.org/licenses/by/4.0/).

Research methods

First, let us define the object and the subject of study in accordance with the key principles of systems approach; it shall be done by specifying general statements on the studied topic.

Object of study. All objects of engineering activity, (without applying for universality of the given classification), are reduced to the following groups: - technical objects (technical products):

- technical systems;
- technical complexes;
- organizational and technical systems;
- ergatic systems (man-machine systems).

At present, the technical literature, including the normative one, widely uses the concept of technical product, which combines structural features of technical objects, systems and complexes of various types and purposes. The *technical system*, like any other system, is understood as a set of interrelated elements united by common operational purposes. The term *complexes* is usually used to refer to complex systems that differ in the number of tasks to be solved for their purpose, the heterogeneity of its elements, a large number of objects, involving their integration into separate subsystems.

Transport systems considered in the study can be classified by organizational characteristic to the so-called large systems having a hierarchical multilevel structure, the components of which at different levels are represented by all of the above types of objects and systems.

In this paper, the transport systems are divided into two components: technical and organizational-methodical, the technical component is chosen for further study. From the technical component of the transport system, the actual vehicles (locomotives, airplanes, cars, etc.) are distinguished, which form a park of similar objects according to the concepts of the theory of state control.

In general, the classification of objects of engineering activity involves their division into two levels: technical objects (TO) and technical systems (TS), depending on the objectives of the study. So, if the knowledge of interval characteristics of the object properties without studying its structure is enough to obtain the result, then it is presented as a TO. Otherwise, it is presented as a vehicle, which is a set of interrelated elements (subsystems). The extent and methods of division,as well as the range of distinguished components are determined not only by the objectives of the study, but also by the methods of their achievement. Therefore, this study uses the general formulation of the object of study as a generalized concept of vehicle.

Subject of study. The concept of efficiency in general and, in particular, the functioning of technical objects can be defined as the degree of performance of functions the object is designed to perform, which depends on the state of TO. The paper [1] proposes and justifies the concept of the state of a technical object, and the paper [2] formulates is as follows: *a form of manifestation of its qualitative certainty, characterized by the degree of compliance of the parameters of the properties and characteristics of the system of existence of this object with the established requirements defined in time and space.*

The presented definition is adapted to the solution of the problems of TO state management, as it reflects not only the semantic content of the concept, but also outlines the method of assessing this state.

In this definition, the system of existence of technical objects (SETO) is a set of the technical object itself, the associated systems and the environment involved in the process of existence. These characteristics should be divided in accordance with the structure of the SETO into: essential properties of technical objects, related systems, environment and the process of existence.

For technical objects, a common specification is a complex of interrelated essential properties: constructability, functionality, reliability, safety, efficiency, ergonomics, environmental friendliness. Here: constructability involves characteristics of shape, size, etc., the change of which leads to a change in the state of TO; functionality denotes the number and type of functions performed in accordance with the purpose of TO; reliability is interpreted in accordance with GOST 27.002-89 [3] and the other properties are used in their conventional sense.

This division of the whole complex of essential properties TO into particular properties allows presenting the complex concept of TO effectiveness as the degree of achievement of the operational goals according to the criteria of constructability, functionality, reliability, safety, efficiency, ergonomics and environmental friendliness. By the same criteria it is possible to divide ways and methods of increasing operational efficiency of functioning TO, which in most cases have different effects on the result.

Thus, the main attention of this study is focused on the development of a method to improve the efficiency from the standpoint of the criteria of vehicles reliability and safety. At the same time, taking into account the complexity of the concept of TO effectiveness, the proposed solutions will be also evaluated by other criteria.

To solve the task, let us analyze some properties of vehicles as systems, in accordance with their classification proposed in [4] and developed in [5, 6].

Integrity and openness. The properties of integrity and openness should be correlated with the (large) transport system based on a distinctive feature – transportation of people and goods in different environments (earth, water, air, space).

The internal heterogeneity (the distinctiveness of parts) allows singling out means of transport from a large system into a separate subsystem (a park of similar objects).

Structuredness. In turn, modern vehicles, regardless of their type, are technical systems of varying degrees of complexity, consisting of several subsystems, united by a hierarchical structure. For example, aircraft at the top level of the hierarchy consists of airframe, engine and on-board equipment systems. The on-board equipment includes subsystems, including power supply, control, navigation, radar and communication, life support, etc. Due to the significant difference in the types of subsystems included in the on-board equipment, it is classified as an integrated technical complex. At the same time, the integration of the equipment is carried out on the basis of common computing resources [7, 8]. The typical structure of the aircraft integrated complex of on-board equipment (ICOE) is shown in Figure 1.

The given structure is the implementation of general trends in development of ICOE based on the deep integration of systems and generalization of software and hardware resources. Such structural solutions are driven by the increasing need to increase the functionality of the equipment while seeking to reduce its cost and operating costs. That is, in terms of system analysis, there are increasing requirements to improve the efficiency of on-board equipment on the criteria of functionality and efficiency. The possibility to fulfill these requirements is provided by the state-of-the-art level of technological development and the hardware components of microchip equipment.

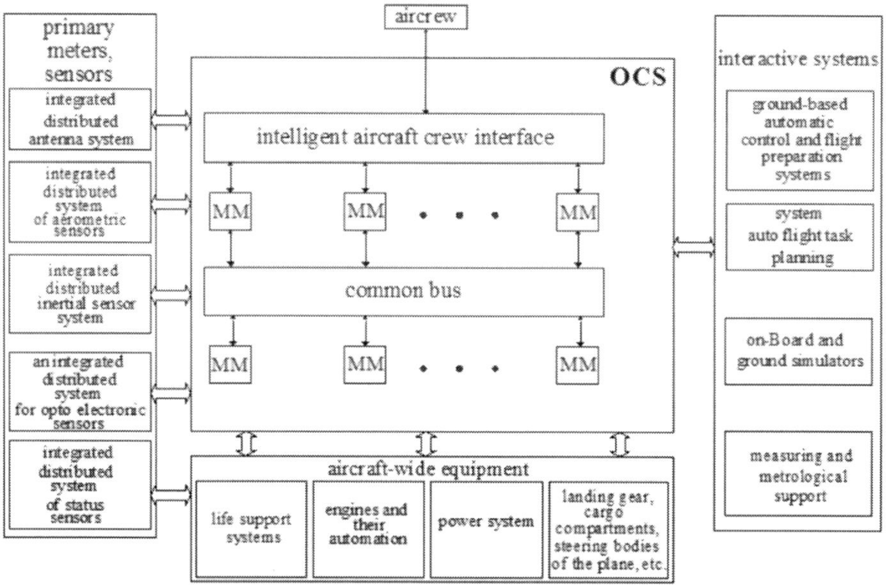

Fig. 1. Typical structure of ICOE.

While exploring the property of structuring, we present a set of on-board equipment consisting of two main parts: the central part, which is the on-board computer system (OCS), and the peripheral, which includes all the rest subsystems specialized to perform individual functions.

The on-board computer system consists of microprocessor modules (MM) and preform functions of overall control, control and transfer of information between the equipment units. According to the architecture, modern multi-component computing systems are distributed, i.e. the control functions are distributed between the modules of the system, and a significant degree of autonomy of the modules is achieved while maintaining a sufficient level of connectivity [9].

Functionality. In studying the properties of ICOE functionality from the standpoint of reliability, it is important to distinguish the functions of individual subsystems based on different degrees of impact on the safety of transport, and for on-board computing systems- the important function is implementation of self-control of individual modules.

Variability. The variability property of ICOE as a system by the criteria of reliability and safety is primarily connected with stochasticity of the processes of reliability components variation and degradation of the structure caused by these processes.

Emergence. Unification of all computing resources in a distributed microprocessor OCS allows organizing the process of diagnosing the status of system components, additionally to the function of self-control,

As a fundamental property of all systems, inherence characterizes consistency, compatibility, adaptability to the environment and is of particular interest for the studied problem. For artificial systems, which include ICOE, inherence determines the degree (quality) of the performing given functions, that is, the efficiency of the systems.

In accordance with the general principles of the systems approach [7], the process of evaluating effectiveness of the systems can be formally represented by the scheme (Fig. 2).

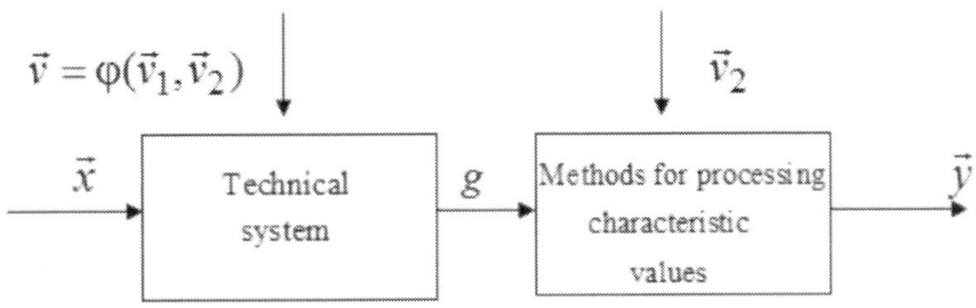

Fig. 2. Experiment as a system.

The analytical process for determining efficiency can be described as $\vec{y} = F[\psi(\vec{x}, \varphi(\vec{v}_1, \vec{v}_2))]$, where ψ - the law of the system operation; F - methods of data processing; $\vec{x}$ - the perturbation vector (properties of the system); $\vec{v} = \varphi(\vec{v}_1, \vec{v}_2)$ - the control vector; $\vec{v}_1$, $\vec{v}_2$ - vectors of controlled and uncontrolled parameters (constraints); φ - the function of formation of the law of experiment control; $\vec{y}$ - the vector of the results of the experiment to determine the efficiency.

In this statement of the research problem, the efficiency of the system is determined by finding the vector $\vec{y} \subset A$ in the set area A and its values (the system becomes fully observable) and is achieved by specifying the vector $\vec{v}$, F and ψ (Fig. 3.): Conditions for the system observability: for $\vec{y} \subset A$ (A – set range of values):

1. for $\vec{v}_2 = const$ $\psi = const$,
2. for $\vec{v}_2 = \text{var}$, ψ_0 corresponds to F_0; ψ_1 corresponds to F_1;

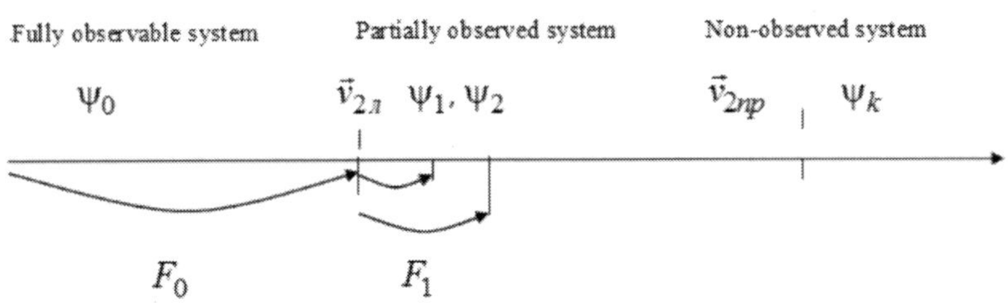

Fig. 3. System monitoring areas.

Under the operating conditions of the system, failure to comply with the $\vec{v}_2$ restrictions leads to a change in ψ and thus to the emergence of a new ψ_1 system, emergent to the original ψ_0. In this case, the system is shifted to the area of partial observation or becomes unobservable. Therefore, changing the ψ transformation in the law of operation requires an adequate change in the F transformation.

Results

Thus, the operational efficiency, in accordance with the principles of a systems approach, shall be understood as the degree of adaptability of the ICOE to performing its tasks in compliance with all assumptions and limitations related to operation. With regard to such a complex and multifaceted system as the ICOE, they form a rather extensive set of interrelated conditions (limitations), the meeting which is necessary to achieve the required efficiency.

In this statement of the problem of efficiency improvement, the solutions techniques can be divided into three groups:

- *removal or lowering the level of limitations;*
- *adaptation of the system to existing limitations;*
- *a combination of the first two methods.*

The choice of methods is determined by the properties of the system under study. Let us show this by the example of the problem to be solved.

Based on the objectives of this study, from the whole set of restrictions only those destabilizing factors are chosen that directly affect the efficiency of the system in terms of reliability and security. In this case, they can be divided into two groups of factors:

- external impact of natural (environmental parameters) and artificial (damaging factors) origin;
- internal impact caused by the mutual negative influence of the system elements.

Ensuring the inherence of ICOE to external destabilizing effects requires giving the complex the properties of survivability, which is especially important for systems used in extreme conditions of emergency situations and military actions. Internal destabilizing factors for ICOE are most often represented by electromagnetic compatibility problems, as well as mechanical effects in the form of shocks, vibrations, pulsations and acoustic noises. In these cases, providing the necessary level of inherence of the complex requires attributing to the complex additional properties of fault tolerance, in addition to the use of highly reliable elements.

To implement the properties of survivability and fault tolerance in ICOE, it is required to provide a solution to two main tasks:

- determination of the type of state (diagnosis) of the system and
- its restoration at the selected level of degradation.

The solution of these problems is carried out by the corresponding subsystems also under limited conditions. Thus, system recovery is based on the existing level of redundancy in the system and the division of system functions by the degree of security impact.

If the system of diagnostics is represented as a set of the object of diagnosis, diagnostic device and the process of diagnosis, the main limitation in the system operating under the influence of destabilizing factors, will be a high probability of failure (damage) of the diagnostic device.

This limitation can be removed by organizing the mutual control structures (MCS) in multiprocessor computing systems, which are the central part of the ICOE (the method was proposed and developed in [10, 11, 12, 13, 14]). The method involves determination of the technical state of OCS by the results of mutual test checks of each other's state performed by the operating modules of the system (the module is understood as a separate computer), at the same time it remains possible to obtain a reliable diagnosis even in the presence of the failed modules in the structures of mutual control.

When using the ICS method, it is necessary to take into account the limitations on the diagnostic model used, which suggest a high probability of non-constant outflow situations. These situations are caused by failures, intermittent failures, incompleteness of checking tests, communication failures, changes in the outflow situation during the diagnostic cycle. The most complete account of these limitations is provided by the authors of model proposed in the study "On diagnosing outflow situations of various types in computing systems" [15].

Conclusion

Thus, the study analyses the properties of the ICOE as a system functioning under the influence of external and internal destabilizing factors (limitations), with the use of systems approach. Based on the identified properties of the system, the direction for solving the problem of ensuring the effective operation of ICOE vehicles based on the criteria of reliability and safety is justified. This direction provides attributing the properties of fault tolerance and survivability to the system, along with the use of highly reliable elements. At the same time, the degree of implementation of these properties is ensured by the use of mutual control structures and is set based on the required performance indicators of a particular vehicle.

The obtained results are unique and can be applied for ensuring fault tolerance of integrated technical complexes and systems of various type and purpose.

References

1. I.I. Tikhii, V.V. Kashkovsky, Modern Technologies. System Analysis. Modeling, **Vol. 4** (48), 134 - 139 (2015). (in Russian)
2. I.I. Tikhii, V.V. Kashkovsky, L.V. Arshinsky, FJEC, **Vol. 103**, Issue 7, 1103 – 1113 (2018).
3. GOST 27.002 – 2015. Dependability in technics. Terms and definitions (Standartinform, Moscow, 2016). (in Russian)
4. F.P. Tarasenko, *Prikladnoj sistemnyj analiz* [Applied System Analysis] (KNORUS, Moscow, 2010). (in Russian)
5. V.N. Kozlov, *Sistemnyj analiz, optimizacija i prinjatie reshenij* [System analysis, optimization and decision making] (Prospekt, Moscow, 2016). (in Russian)
6. V.N. Volkova, *Sistemnyj analiz informacionnyh kompleksov* [System analysis of information systems] (Lan', St. Petersburg, 2016). (in Russian)
7. E.A. Fedosov, V.I. Kasyanchuk, Radioelectronic technologies, 1, 66-71 (2015). (in Russian)
8. I.M. Saidumarov, A.A. Umarov, R.G. Zakirov, Tehnika. Tehnologii. Inzhenerija [Equipment. Technologies. Engineering], 1, 20-24 (2016). (in Russian)
9. S.G. Bobkov, Vysokoproizvoditel'nye vychislitel'nye sistemy [High Performance Computing Systems] (НИИСИ РАН, Москва, 2014). (in Russian)
10. F.P. Preparata, G. Metze, R.T. Chien, IEEE Trans. EC, **Vol. 16**, 6, 848-854 (1967).
11. F. Barsi, F. Crandoni, P. Maestrini, IEEE Trans.EC, **Vol. 25**, 6, 585-593 (1976).
12. I.G. Kuhl, S.M. Reddy, IEEE Trans. Comput., 12. 1012-1024 (1984).
13. P.P. Parhomenko, Automation and Remote Control, 5, 126-135. (2009). (in Russian)
14. V.A. Vedeshenkov, Control Sciences, 6, 55-60 (2016). (in Russian)
15. I.I. Tikhii, V.V. Kashkovsky, Instruments and Systems: Monitoring, Control, and Diagnostics, 11, 35-42 (2009). (in Russian)

Analysis of research on the impact of electromagnetic fields and the degree of their automation

Nikolay Filippenko[1,*], *Alexandr* Lipchitz[1], and *Sergey* Kargapoltzev[1]

[1]Irkutsk State Transport University, 634076 Irkutsk, Russia

Abstract. In spite of the significant amount of scientific publications on the impact of fields on structural properties of nonmagnetic materials, investigations of structures of materials subjected to electromagnetic actions are relevant. The purpose of the paper is review and analysis of the state-of-the-art developments on the impact of electromagnetic fields that differ in power and nature. Analysis of the studied outputs enabled to conclude that direct contactless inertia-free effect on the material structure and dynamics of its defects at various levels. It was defined that the use of automated systems of research process management is difficult.

Introduction

Competitiveness and reliability of machines and mechanisms is a vital task of modern industry. Its solution is based on research of methods that enable to create a structure with specified physical and mechanical properties, which is possible due to the fields of different nature. the goal of this article is the analysis of scientific and practical information in the field of the modification of various materials with the help of electric and magnetic fields and methods for their control.

Modern studies in the domain of electromagnetic fields and their effects [1-8] confirm that with the help of low-power fields, a direct contactless effect on the structure of the material and the dynamics of its defects at various levels is possible. They also ave strong effect on the dynamics of various defects in structural materials. Such active impact of fields results in a change in the macroproperties of the material and the operational properties of the product [9]. In a number of works [10-12] it is noted that processing by electromagnetic fields (EMF) is characterized by low energy costs. Thus, for example, typical energy values transmitted to one atom in a crystal lattice with some parameter a in commonly used fields are the following magnitudes in sequence:
in magnetic field (MF)

$$\Delta W \approx \mu_B B \approx 10^{-4} эB \tag{1}$$

in electric field (EF)

$$\Delta W \approx eEa \approx 10^{-4} эB \tag{2}$$

* Corresponding author: ifpi@mail.ru

© The Authors, published by EDP Sciences. This is an open access article distributed under the terms of the Creative Commons Attribution License 4.0 (http://creativecommons.org/licenses/by/4.0/).

in pulse current field

$$\Delta W \approx j^2 \rho a^3 \approx 10^{-4} эB \quad (3)$$

in force field under deformation

$$\Delta W \approx E' \ \varepsilon^2 a^3 \approx 10^{-3} эB \quad (4)$$

and thermal field

$$\Delta T = 100K, \Delta W \approx kT \approx 10^{-2} эB \quad (5)$$

Here: μ is the Bohr magneton, e is the elementary charge, ρ is the specific resistivity, k is the Boltzmann constant, E is the energy, E′ is Young's modulus.

In any real material, defects reduce the degree of its symmetry, locally redistribute the electron density, which causes the emergence of long-range macroscopic electric and magnetic fields [9]. In ideal material, EF and MF can cause ordering in dipole and magnetic moments and phase transitions. Point defects and their interaction with dislocations are an important factor. For example, if a defect has a dipole or magnetic moment and an elastic anisotropy, its orientation in the EF and MF will cause a decrease in the flow stress in some planes and an increase in others. In metals, the change in the state of the electron gas in EF and MF can affect the plastic properties due to the effect of electron-dislocation interaction. The nature of the interaction between dislocations and fields depends on the nature of the field: the EF can exert a force action on the charged dislocation cores, and the non-uniform MF can exert a force action on the particles possessing a magnetic moment. Dislocations in various crystals (ionic, covalent, metallic) cause an increased magnetic susceptibility [9-10].

As for the effect of EMF on macrodefects and the sample as a whole, the difference in the density of EMF energy in adjacent elementary volumes of the sample or on the surface causes the emergence of electrodynamic forces. It shall be noted that the flowing current causes warming up, which leads to the emergence of thermal influences and stresses.

In addition, a number of related phenomena that have been reduced to a significant influence of MF on various physical and mechanical and other characteristics of nonmagnetic materials have been found.

Great attention was immediately paid to the work of V.I. Alshits with his colleagues [11]. It described a contradictory phenomenon, at first glance: the stimulation of the motion of dislocations in NaCl single crystals. The action was introduced by a weak impact of a constant MP. Further studies in this field have shown that the magnetoplastic effect leads to a decrease in the yield point, a decrease in the microhardness and internal friction of various single-crystal materials.

According to [12], some effects (EMF) manifest themselves under EMF action only, whereas others can be reversible and irreversible (Fig. 1). It is assumed that non-equilibrium in the structure (crystal) ensures high sensitivity to of the impact of even insignificant EMF pulses.

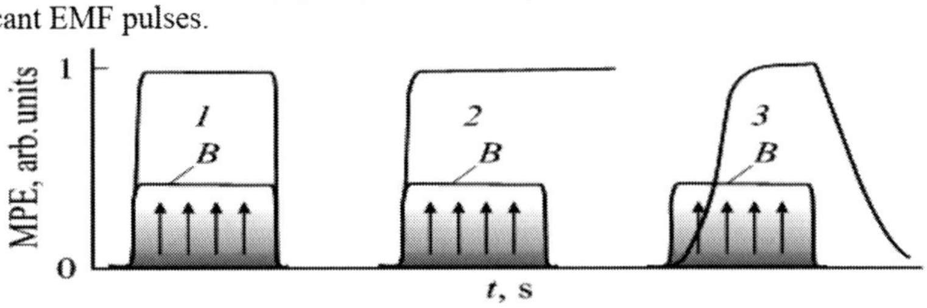

Fig. 1. Three main types of behavior of non-magnetic materials in MEP: 1 - in situ effects arising from the action of EMF, 2 – irreversible post-effects, 3 - aftereffect with slow relaxation and latent period after disconnection.

The studies [6, 10, 13-14] describe investigations of the effect of a weak constant magnetic field on the collision of an electron on the mechanical properties of various nonmagnetic crystals (NaCl, CsI, etc.) and metals (Zn, Al). In these studies it is noted that with an increase in the exposure time of the samples in the MF, the mean dislocation path length L grew linearly; and when the temperature was varied, the path length L practically did not change. When the sign of the field is reversed, the direction of dislocation motion did not change, so the possibility of explaining the effect by the action of ponderomotive forces or a vortex electric field was excluded. Investigation of the influence of MF applied when the indenter was introduced into bismuth crystals, demonstrated increase in microhardness [15]. The opposite results were obtained for aluminum [16, 17], it was determined that exposure to a magnetic field reduces the microhardness of aluminum. It is found that creep under conditions of an external magnetic field results in a decrease in the average size of the pits of a ductile fracture by more than 2 times. Obtaining more accurate results requires improvement of the control system for high-frequency processes, however, the study confirms significant increase in the material strength.

Experimental studies of the change in the strength characteristics of samples of PA-66 polyamide in high-frequency EMF in [18] were made in accordance with regulatory requirements. After specially simulated operating conditions, corresponding to the real conditions of Western and Eastern Siberia, the samples were placed in the EMW field for a short time. The results of full-scale tests are shown in the diagrams (Fig. 2, 3). Analysis of the obtained data proves that the strength characteristics of PA-66 polyamide samples, after HF treatment, in some cases exceeded their original values. Practical implementation of restoration process of the used polyamide products is only possible in the presence of automated system of electrothermic control which depends on the automated system for sample state control.

In [19], the authors propose a method for ionizing nitriding instrumental steels in crossed electric and magnetic fields. As a result, it was found that the effect of EMF results in an increase in the microhardness by approximately 6 times.

In [20, 21], the authors propose a method for softening the materials of the crystal structure, which involves the action of the main and additional EMF. The achieved softening result in this case is associated with the effect of external magnetic field affects on the material containing magnetic grains (magnetite) or minerals with a piezoelectric effect (quartz). Also, because of the heterogeneity of the properties of the materials that make up the sample and the presence of water in the micropores.

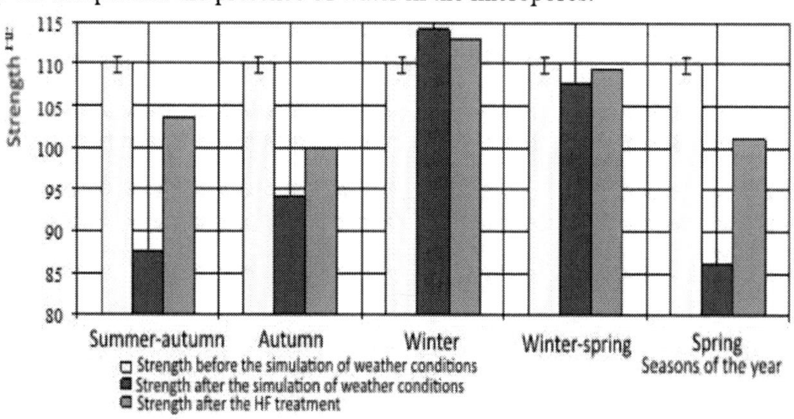

Fig. 2. Results of hardness measurements of samples.

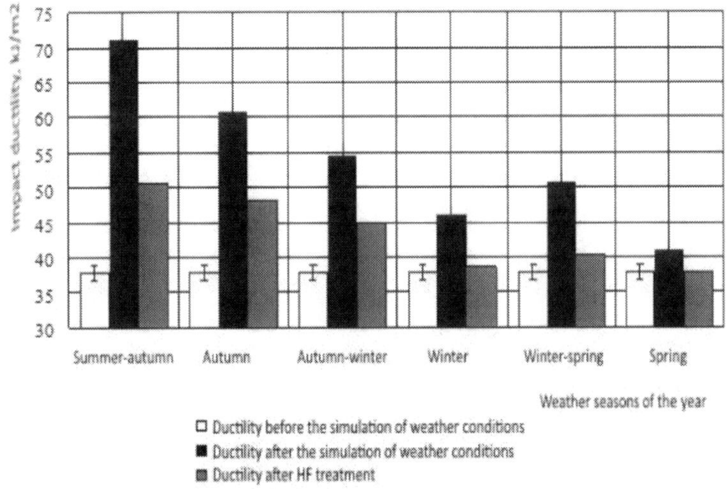

Fig. 3. Results of measurements of impact ductility of samples.

Thus, relying on the arguments of the presented papers, it can be concluded that the effect of force fields on materials is reduced to the following:

1. the given literature review demonstrates complex and multifaceted impact of EMF on various materials;
2. the emerging macroscopic effects of EMF action are the result of influence on all structural and hierarchical levels of the material;
3. threshold character of post-effects of MF effect and saturation of MPE exist;
4. MF changes the ratio of the factors that affect physical and mechanical properties in a special way;
5. EMF occurs in non-equilibrium structures;
6. there are several channels of influence of EMF on the structure and properties of the material;
7. EMF induces multistage relaxation processes of the defect structure, some of which are unique;
8. strong and weak EMF influences various objects in the material;
9. EMF causes a change in the properties of materials of different magnetic nature, which enables to use EMF treatment to modify both magnetic and nonmagnetic materials;
10. lack of automated systems for control, regulation and selection of processing modes in EMF prevents from completely solving specific scientific and production tasks and obtaining a given set of properties.

Conclusion

The results of the study prove the reality of the effects of EMF influence on the mechanical properties of many materials.This creates a foundation for a radically new highly sensitive and high-resolution method of electromagnetic spectroscopy. It was found that HF treatment, including weak and pulse one, can in some cases replace a much longer and energy-intensive heat treatment techniques. The study showed that the developed schemes and physical models of EMF impact can be applied in magnetobiology and biochemistry [22]. However, it must be mentioned that because of the lack of automated control systems for the above processes, the described techniques and methods of EMF impact presently cannot have a wide use.

A number of studies [23-24] conducted at Irkutsk State Transport University (Russia) prove the possibility of organizing automated EMF control systems on the basis of amperometric technique. They provide algorithms of control of high-frequency electromagnetic action, both for the purpose of basic research and for a number of technological operations of treating polar construction materials (practical value).

Taking this method and control algorithms as a foundation, the topic for further study is development of a universal automated control system for EMF impact on polymer and composite materials of various nature.

References

1. Yu.A. Osipyan, S.I. Bredikhin, V.V. Kveder, N.V. Klassen, V.D. Negriy, V.F. Petrenko, I.S. Smirnova, S.A. Shevchenko, E.A. Shteynman, S.Z. Shmurak, *Elektronnye svojstva dislokacij v poluprovodnikah* [Electronic properties of dislocations in semiconductors] (Moscow, 2010). (in Russian)
2. V.A. Lavrentyev, S.G. Kalganova, *Problemy elektrojenergetiki* [Problems of electric power industry], 133-136 (2008). (in Russian)
3. Yu.A. Klimov, V.M. Maslovskiy, K.V. Kholodnov, Elektronnaja tehnika [Electronics engineering], **3**, 5(144), 22 (1991). (in Russian)
4. A.G. Kadmenskiy, S.G. Kadmenskiy, M.N. Levin, V.M. Maslovskiy, A.V. Chernyshev, Pisma v zhurnal tehnicheskoj fiziki [Applied Physics Letters], 19(3), 41 (1993). (in Russian)
5. M.N. Levin, Yu.O. Lichmanov, V.M. Maslovskiy, Pisma v zhurnal tehnicheskoj fiziki [Applied Physics Letters], 20(4), 27 (1994). (in Russian)
6. K.M. Salikhov, Y.N. Molin, R.A. Sagdeev, A.L. Buchachenko, *Spin Polarization and Magnetic Effects in Radical Reactions* (Elsevier, Amsterdam, 1984).
7. A.L. Buchachenko, R.Z. Sagdeev, K.M. Salikhov, *Magnitnye i spinovye jeffekty v himicheskih reakcijah* [Magnetic and spin effects in chemical reactions] (Nauka, Novosibirsk, 1978). (in Russian)
8. A.L. Buchachenko, Chem. Rev., **95**, 7, 2507 (1995).
9. A.V. Lipchitz, A.G. Larchenko, N.G. Filippenko, *Transportnaja infrastruktura Sibirskogo regiona* [Transport infrastructure of the Siberian region]: Proceedings of the 5th International scientific conference (Irkutsk, March 31 – April 4, 2014). (in Russian)
10. Yu.I. Golovin, Tambov University Reports. Series: Natural and Technical Sciences, **Vol. 1**, Issue 1, 3-20 (1996). (in Russian)
11. V.I. Alshic, E.V. Darinskaya, T.M. Perkalina, A.A. Urusovskaya, Physics of the Solid State, **Vol. 29**, 2, 467-470 (1987). (in Russian)
12. Yu.I. Golovin, Physics of the Solid State, **Vol. 46**, 5, 769-803 (2004). (in Russian)
13. N.I. Burlaka, *Novye zadachi sovremennoj mediciny* [New problems of modern medicine]: Proceedings of the III International scientific conference, 11-13 (St. Petersburg, Dec. 2014). (in Russian)
14. V.I. Alshic, E.V. Darinskaya, E.A. Petrzhik, Physics of the Solid State, **Vol. 35**, 2, 320-322 (1993). (in Russian)
15. Yu.I. Golovin, R.B. Morgunov, S.E. Zhulikov, Crystallography Reports, **Vol. 43**, 4, 689-693 (1998). (in Russian)
16. S.I. Popov, A.V. Lipchitz, N.G. Filippenko, *Transportnaja infrastruktura Sibirskogo regiona* [Transport infrastructure of the Siberian region]: Proceedings of the 3rd International scientific conference, 430–437 (Irkutsk, Russia, May 13–17, 2013). (in Russian)

17. K.N. Ramazanov, V.V. Budilov, R.K. Vafin, Strengthening technologies and coatings, 5, 39-42 (2010). (in Russian)
18. P.P. Ananyev, S.A. Goncharov, E.L. Belchenko, V.P. Stupnikov, Patent EA 003853B1 (2003). (in Russian)
19. Yu.I. Golovin, Physics of the Solid State, **Vol. 46**, Issue 5 (2004) (in Russian)
20. T.G. Prokhorova, S.S. Khasanov, L.V. Zorina, L.I. Buranov, V.A. Tkacheva, A.A. Baskakov, R.B. Morgunov, M. Gener, E. Canadell, R.P. Shibaeva, E.V. Yagubskii, Adv. Funct. Mater., 13, 5, 1 (2003).
21. A.V. Komshina, A.S. Pomelnikova, Nauka i Obrazovanie [Science and Education], ФС 77-48211, 09 (сентябрь, 2012). (in Russian)
22. N.G. Filippenko, A.V. Lipchitz, A.Ya. Mashovich, Modern Technologies. System Analysis. Modeling, **Vol. 2** (30), 193-198 (2011). (in Russian)
23. A.V. Lipchitz, S.I. Popov, N.G. Filippenko, A.G. Larchenko, Modern Technologies. System Analysis. Modeling, **Vol. 2** (38), 152-157 (2013). (in Russian)
24. A.V. Lipchitz, N.G. Filippenko, A.G. Larchenko, Modern Technologies. System Analysis. Modeling, **Vol. 5**, 41 (2014). (in Russian)

Quality assurance and control system for railway track tamping

Andrey Ilinykh[1,*], *Alexey* Manakov[1], *Andrey* Abramov[1], and *Sergey* Kolarzh[1]

[1]Siberian Transport University, 630049 Novosibirsk, Russia

Abstract. Ensuring stable parameters of a railway track after bringing it into a design position is a key measure of quality for evaluating completed repairs. Identifying quality criteria for sleeper tamping using a special rolling stock is a high-priority problem for a railway track infrastructure. This problem is complicated by a large choice of ballast compaction, leveling and finishing machines, totaling more than 30 types. The paper presents results of theoretical studies aimed at assuring and controlling the quality of tamping by multi-purpose track machines. The factors that determine the stability of railway track parameters in operation were identified. The track repair processes were analyzed. The operating factors that are essential for developing qualitative process parameters were identified for various types of track machines. Based on the findings of these studies, a quality assurance and control methodology was developed for railway track repair and maintenance operations.

1. Introduction

During operation of a railroad track, assembled rails and sleepers are under train loads, which are transferred to the ballast layer and cause its elastic and permanent deformations. Over time, deformations are accumulated and, as a rule, unevenly distributed along the track length. The stability of a repaired railway track is determined by resistance of sleepers to longitudinal and lateral shifts, as well as by track settlement, and depends mainly on the quality of two operations: track leveling and tamping [1].

The quality of leveling is determined by requirements for the accuracy of positioning a railway track in terms of level, longitudinal section and plan. Quantitative values of these requirements are established and determined by applicable technical regulations [2–3]. They are used in designing instrumentation systems, track leveling devices and automation equipment of track machines. These parameters can be monitored during the operation of track leveling, tamping and lining machines (track renewal trains), thereby controlling the quality of work.

The quality of track tamping is primarily determined by the degree of ballast compaction under sleepers, which should be sufficient not only to hold assembled rails and sleepers in a leveled position, but also to ensure their stability in further operation. Recommended degrees of ballast compaction were established through modeling [4–6] and confirmed by a number of experimental studies [7–8]. According to these studies, a

* Corresponding author: asi80@ngs.ru

© The Authors, published by EDP Sciences. This is an open access article distributed under the terms of the Creative Commons Attribution License 4.0 (http://creativecommons.org/licenses/by/4.0/).

necessary and sufficient degree of compaction for ballast thickness H will be reached if the relative settlement of the layer is $E \geq (0.15 \div 0.17)H$.

As shown by field tests of tracks [9], even modern track machines with their capacity and operating speed can ensure only $E = (0.11 \div 0.13)H$. First of all, this suggests that selected operating modes of tamping machines are inefficient and not controlled in operation. At present, these parameters cannot be monitored during operation of machines due to the lack of monitoring techniques and appropriate instruments. Another important factor that makes it difficult to assure the quality of track tamping is a dependence of degree of ballast compaction on such factors as ballast contamination and porosity, height to which a track is raised, and ballast thickness. These factors lead to a scientific problem that has not been solved yet: a constant change in the density of a ballast section due to a change in its structure. These changes do not allow using a generally accepted indicator for estimating the quality of tamping — relative ballast settlement E.

Scientists have proposed various solutions to this problem, e. g. adding polyurethane fillers [10] or rubber crumb [11] to ballast, or stabilizing the ballast section with a geogrid [12]. All these solutions have not come into wide use due to the complexity and high cost of related technologies. The greatest effect can be achieved by establishing the dependence of changes in the ballast structure and density on vibration parameters.

The purpose of the presented theoretical research is to determine the dependence of quality indicators of ballast compaction on the operating factors of tamping machines in different operating conditions. The theoretical research results can be used to address a high-priority problem of the railway track infrastructure — to develop a quality assurance and control methodology, as well as related tools for track tamping.

2 Theoretical data

2.1. Physical basis of stone ballast compaction

The initial stage of ballast operation under load corresponds to the stabilization period T_1. By the end of this period, a stabilized ballast state is achieved, and the ballast section becomes capable to take operational loads for a long time. In this phase, the current state of ballast is characterized by relative settlement E_Y, which does not exceed its limit value E_n.

As soon as the ballast reaches the limit state ($E_Y \approx E_n$), it completely loses the ability to be compacted, while achieving the maximum bearing capacity. If a load on the ballast section does not exceed the limit values, it remains stable for a long time, thereby moving to a steady flow stage T_2 [13].

The third ground flow stage T_3 is a stage of destruction [13]. First, the accumulation rate of plastic deformations is increased without significantly destructing the ballast body (pre-repair period). This process is followed by viscous destruction of the ballast body and a rapid loss of its bearing capacity.

Let us consider a stone ballast layer, which, at the initial time point, has a thickness H_H. As a result of force action, a new thickness of the compacted layer becomes equal to H_Y. The state of the ballast layer to and prior compaction can be characterized by settlement parameters ΔH_H and ΔH_Y. If we assume that the ultimate loose state of the ballast layer is characterized by thickness H_0, its relative settlement for the initial and compacted states, respectively, will be determined by the following relations:

$$E_H = \frac{\Delta H_H}{H_0} = \frac{\Delta V_H}{V_0};\ E_Y = \frac{\Delta H_Y}{H_0} = \frac{\Delta V_Y}{V_0}, \quad (1)$$

where ΔV_H, ΔV_Y is the decrease in the ballast volume before and after its compaction from the ultimate loose state; V_0 is the ballast volume in the ultimate loose state assumed as the base.

The ballast layer is transformed from the pre-compacted state to the compacted state by tamping padding techniques. It can be said that the track machine "adds" the following value to the relative layer settlement:

$$E_M = \frac{\Delta H_Y - \Delta H_H}{H_0} = \frac{\Delta V_Y - \Delta V_H}{V_0} = E_Y - E_H. \tag{2}$$

In other words, the relative track settlement is an additive value since it is accumulated and determined relative to the same base state.

The relative settlement can be estimated not only through the ratio between ballast volumes in various states (i.e. at the macro level), but also at the level of particles interacting with each other. For this purpose, two parameters are used: porosity n and void ratio ε.

$$n = \frac{V_n}{V_c + V_n}; \; e = \frac{V_n}{V_c}, \tag{3}$$

where V_c is the volume of crushed stone filled with grains, m^3; V_n is the volume of crushed stone filled with air, m^3.

These two indicators of stone compaction can be connected to each other by the following relations:

$$\varepsilon_Y = \frac{n_Y}{1 - n_Y} = \frac{\rho_c}{\rho_Y - 1} = \varepsilon_0(1 - E_Y) - E_Y = \frac{n_0 - E_Y}{1 - n_0}; \tag{4}$$

$$E_Y = \frac{\Delta V_Y}{V_0} = \frac{\varepsilon_0 - \varepsilon_Y}{1 + \varepsilon_0}, \tag{5}$$

where ε_0, ε_Y are void ratios of crushed stone in ultimate loose and compacted states, respectively; n_0, n_Y are porosities of crushed stone in ultimate loose and compacted states, respectively; ρ_c, ρ_Y are the density of the material of particles and bulk density of the compacted crushed stone, respectively.

The formulas (1) ... (5) show that the quality of ballast tamping can be estimated by two key indicators: the void ratio ε and the relative ballast settlement E. According to GOST [14], the porosity of crushed stone is n_0=0.42÷0.45 in the ultimate loose state and n_n=0.36÷0.37 in the ultimate compacted state. The void ratios calculated by the formulas (4) and (5) are ε_0=0.724÷0.818 in the ultimate loose state and ε_n=0.563÷0.587 in the ultimate compacted state. Thus, the relative settlement of the crushed stone ballast in the ultimate compacted state is E_n=0.18÷0.25.

2.2. Quality indicators of stone ballast compaction

Since there is an ultimate compacted state of the ballast E_n, its stabilization process can be modeled through saturation of the compaction indicator accepted for consideration — relative settlement E_Y. The accumulation of the relative ballast settlement E_Y can be described by the following expression:

$$E_Y = E_H + \frac{E_n}{\sqrt{1+\left(\frac{E_n}{K_E T}\right)^2}}, \tag{6}$$

where E_H is the initial relative settlement of the ballast obtained by static compression (in our case, it occurs under the load of wheelsets of tamping machines in operation); E_n is the ultimate relative settlement for a specific force action; K_E is the rate of rise of the relative settlement from the beginning of the force action; T is the load integrally accumulated by the ballast during the cyclic action of the vibrating surface, kPa:

$$T = \frac{\omega t}{2\pi}\sum_{i=1}^{m} p_i, \tag{7}$$

where ω is the angular vibrational frequency, rad/s; t is the time of action of the vibrating surface on the ballast, s; i are cycles of oscillations (i=1, 2, …, m).

In each compression cycle, the ballast is elastically deformed and accumulates inelastic deformations. Under the influence of inelastic deformations, the structure becomes more ordered and concentrated. In the next cycle, it is necessary to apply more pressure to cause inelastic deformation. The ultimate pressure (kPa) at which the ballast material begins to deform inelastically can be calculated by the following formula:

$$p = q \cdot |\ln(2\varepsilon - 1)|, \tag{8}$$

where ε is the void ratio of the ballast; q is the experimental coefficient (q_0=(0.3÷0.5)·10^3 kPa for the loose ballast; q_n=(0.6÷0.8)·10^3 kPa for the compacted ballast. At $\varepsilon > 0.5$, intermediate values of the coefficient q can be determined by linear interpolation.

The rise of the bearing capacity will be limited to the maximum pressure p_{max} that can be reached by the vibrating surface of the machine, and the ultimate relative settlement of the ballast E_n. If $p_{max}<p_n$ (p_n is the pressure (kPa) above which the ballast structure is destroyed, then the relative settlement of the compacted ballast will be $E_Y<E_n$, and no further compression will occur. This means that the ballast layer can take this load, while being elastically deformed.

2.3 Performance of tamping machines

The number of vibration actions N on a compacted material can be used as an indirect indicator of the achieved degree of ballast compaction.

$$N = \upsilon t, \tag{9}$$

where υ is the oscillation frequency of the working tool, Hz.

Regardless of a design of tamping tools used in leveling and tamping machines, they process the ballast in the same way — by compacting the material through vibratory impact. The experimental data [15] show that, on average, the most intensive ballast compaction takes place in the first 3–4 seconds in cyclic machines and 5–6 seconds in continuous machines. Then the process begins to decay.

It should be noted that, even with the same number of vibration actions, the degree of compaction may vary. The greatest effect is achieved at certain values of vibratory tamping parameters, which are characterized by the coefficient K [16]:

$$K = \frac{v_o}{2\pi\upsilon A}, \tag{10}$$

where v_o is the ballast compaction rate, mm/s; A is the oscillation amplitude of the working tool, mm.

If K=0.08÷0.12, the working tool has an effective vibratory impact on the material to be compacted during the oscillation period. This is explained by the fact that, being redistributed more efficiently, ballast grains are moved to a more stable position, and as a result, a track becomes more stable as well.

At K>0.12, the interaction of the working tool with the ballast changes significantly. Vibrocompression of the material takes place. As shown by studies [15–16], the degree of ballast compaction caused by this action is significantly lower as compared to vibratory impact.

Even if the efficient operating mode is chosen for cyclic leveling and tamping machines, their productivity is reduced by at least 1.5 times. In order to improve the quality of sleeper tamping, the double ballast compaction technique is used in practice, which also leads to a decrease in the productivity of these machines.

Thus, operators always face a dilemma: either to choose high productivity of machines and poor quality of sleeper tamping, or conversely: to ensure a stable track condition after repair while performing less work in the same time.

2.4 Setting objectives for developing the quality assurance and control system for ballast tamping

The theoretical framework of stone ballast compaction considered above shows that force actions on the ballast generate some multifactorial processes. Parameters of these processes are usually stochastic and difficult to describe by mathematical models.

By analyzing the methods and designs of working tools used in sleeper tamping, the following should be noted. In their efforts to improve working members, as well as leveling and tamping processes, engineers have almost exhausted the possibilities of improving a combination of performance characteristics, such as the quality of sleeper tamping and high productivity. Therefore, it is very important to use working tools with efficient vibratory tamping parameters on all types of machines and to follow operating procedures.

When choosing operating modes for leveling and tamping machines, it is necessary to take into account such parameters as the actual state of the ballast layer, types and number of machines used, and a sequence of their operations. In order to assure the quality of ballast tamping, it is necessary to check operating modes of leveling and tamping machines, first of all, ballast compaction rate, oscillation frequency of the working tool, and the duration of vibration action.

3. Quality assurance and control system for ballast tamping

According to the objectives set above, the quality assurance and control system for ballast tamping was developed on the basis of the existing software and hardware system "Status Monitoring System", designed for acceptance control of track machines after maintenance and repair, and remote status monitoring of track equipment in operation. The Status Monitoring System includes calibrated and certified instruments that can measure technical parameters of track machines with high accuracy. A set of sensors can be configured and expanded, thereby making it possible to select the necessary range of parameters measured by the system. The Status Monitoring System is equipped with a 3G module designed for real-time remote transmission of measured parameters [17–19].

Quality of track tamping is controlled using performance assessment tools for track equipment. The Status Monitoring System is based on a relationship between performance parameters of track machines and track stability parameters, shown in Figure 1.

Performance parameters of track machines are monitored by a set of sensors. The number of sensors depends on a range of monitoring tasks. During this study, it has been found that at least three parameters should be monitored for the purposes of quality control: ballast vibrocompression rate, oscillation frequency of the working tool, and the duration of vibration action.

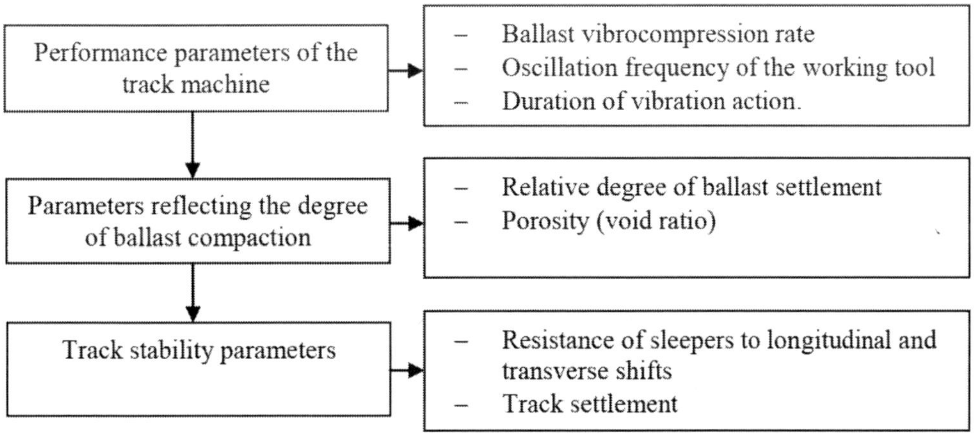

Fig. 1. Relationship between performance parameters of tamping machines and track stability parameters.

The tamping quality control system was tested in real conditions using Duomatic 09-32 track machine at one of linear facilities of the Ural Track Machine Operations Directorate. During the operation of the machine, vibration parameters were read from the sensors installed on tamping units and then compared with the required values calculated from the relations (6)–(10). Further, the parameters of actual ballast settlement and ballast density were estimated and compared with the required values. The difference varied from 8 to 26%.

4. Conclusion

Based on the theoretical research, a dependence of changes in the ballast structure and density on vibration parameters was established. The practical test showed that these dependencies can be used to designate operating modes of tamping machines in order to provide the necessary quality indicators for ballast compaction. The accuracy of results depends mainly on how accurately the initial state of a ballast layer is determined.

As a result of the research, the authors developed a theoretical framework that can be used to develop a software and hardware system for remote quality control of track operations. Widespread adoption of this system will significantly reduce maintenance cycles of railway tracks by maximizing the track stability.

Determining ballast compaction parameters for various track operating conditions remains an open question and needs to be further studied. Thus, the further development of this research area should be aimed at determining the necessary density and structure of the ballast layer in different track operating conditions to ensure its maximum stability.

References

1. B. Indraratna, H. Khabbaz, W. Salim, D. Christie, Ground Improvement, 3, 91–101 (2006).
2. STN C 01-95. Zheleznye dorogi kolei 1520 mm [Railways with gauge 1520 mm] (Ministry of Railways of Russian Federation, Moscow, 1995). (in Russian)
3. Tehnicheskie uslovija na raboty po remontu i planovo-predupreditel'noj vypravke puti [Technical specifications on repair works and preventive maintenance of the track] (Moscow, 2003). (in Russian)
4. M. Lu, PhD thesis, University of Nottingham, 2008.
5. N. Trung Ngo, B. Indraratna, C. Rujikiatkamjorn, Computers and Geotechnics, 55 (January), 224-231 (2014).
6. B. Indraratna, Li-Jun Su, C. Rujikiatkamjorn, Canadian Geotechnical Journal, (February), 322-326 (2011).
7. S. Lobo-Guerrero, L.E. Vallejo, Granular Matter, 8, 195–204 (2006).
8. B. Indraratna, F. Asce; S. Nimbalkar, D. Christie, C. Rujikiatkamjorn, J. Vinod, Journal of Geotechnical and Geoenvironmental engineering, (July), 907-917 (2010).
9. M.E. Bona, The effect of straightening and grinding of welds on track roughness, QUT Thesis (Masters by Research), Queensland University of Technology, 16180, (2017).
10. A. Keene, J. Tinjum, T. Edil, Geotechnical Engineering Journal of the SEAGS & AGSSEA, **Vol. 45**, 1 (March), 67-73 (2014).
11. M. Sol-Sanchez, N. Thom, F. Moreno-Navarro, M. Rubio-Gamez, G. Airey, Construction and Building Materials, 75, 19–24 (2015).
12. B. Leshchinsky, Geo-Frontiers, ASCE 2011, 4693–4702 (2011).
13. B. Indraratna, S. Nimbalkar, D Christie, The performance of rail track incorporating the effects of ballast breakage, confining pressure and geosynthetics reinforcement, 8th International Conference on the Bearing Capacity of Roads, Railways, and Airfields, London, 5-24 (2009).
14. GOST 7392-2002. Crushed stone of solid rocks for railway ballast. Specifications (Standartinform, Moscow, 2002). (in Russian)
15. G.P. Zadorin, Railway Track and Facilities, 11, 22-24 (2007). (in Russian)
16. V.M. Popovich, V.M. Bugaenko, *Putevye mashiny* [track machine] (Zheldorizdat, Moscow, 2007). (in Russian)
17. A.L. Manakov, S.A. Kolarzh, Transport of the Urals, 1(52), 57 - 60 (2017). (in Russian)
18. N.A. Maslov, Chief Mechanical Engineer, 12, 27-34 (2016). (in Russian)
19. A.D. Abramov, N.A. Maslov, Chief Mechanical Engineer, 10, 48-53 (2015). (in Russian)

MATEC Web of Conferences **216**, 03005 (2018) https://doi.org/10.1051/matecconf/201821603005
Polytransport Systems-2018

Calibration method for a strain-gauge measurement system based on bidirectional rail loading

Andrey Kolomeets[1,*], and *Tatyana* Sych[1]

[1]Siberian Transport University, 630049 Novosibirsk, Russia

Abstract. At present, all railways tend to increase the speed of passenger trains and axle loads in transportation of goods. These processes contribute to the improvement of rolling stocks and railway infrastructures. At the same time, there is a need to maintain a high level of safety in transportation. Therefore, experimental research and feasibility studies of the existing monitoring solutions are of the highest priority. Being experimental in nature, this study is aimed at increasing the reliability of the strain-gauge method in measurement of dynamic forces transferred from the wheel to the rail in real operating conditions. Rail strains were experimentally studied under bidirectional loading using a special-purpose impact device. Results of this research are presented in the paper. An experimental measuring section was created for recording loads. Strain gauges were installed on rails in several cross-sections. Rails were loaded with a special-purpose device, which was designed to adjust a loading force and shift a contact point. The structure of the loading device and its basic features are described in the paper.

Introduction

Defects of wheel tread surfaces have a negative impact on track superstructures and undercarriage of rolling stock. Growing freight traffic and increasing capacities of freight cars lead to accelerated deterioration of wheelsets and, therefore, failures of rolling stock. Systems for monitoring rolling stock in motion are developed and implemented to early detect wheelsets with wheel tread defects. Wheel tread monitoring systems are based on recording the forces transferred from wheels to rails. The strain gauge method is one of the most promising ways of recording these forces. It is based on measurements of rail strains under a passing train.

Operators and owners place high demands on operating conditions and safety of their rolling stocks. Repair stops of cars lead to delays in delivery and, therefore, economic losses. In this connection, it is important to ensure reliable measurement results and avoid rejection of defect-free wheelsets during strain-gauge monitoring.

Specialists of the Siberian Transport University (Novosibirsk) have been engaged for a long time in developing the strain-gauge method to monitor wheel tread defects in freight

* Corresponding author: andreykolomeec@yandex.ru

© The Authors, published by EDP Sciences. This is an open access article distributed under the terms of the Creative Commons Attribution License 4.0 (http://creativecommons.org/licenses/by/4.0/).

cars [3, 9, 13]. In collaboration with the Chaplygin Siberian Scientific Research Institute of Aviation (SIBNIA), they improve measuring equipment, study methodological aspects of monitoring, and test the method in operation [5, 6, 14].

While moving along the rail, trains with wheel tread defects produce impact interaction in the wheel–rail system. This impact interaction is usually complex and involves both vertical and horizontal forces. Due to this, it is necessary to estimate strains of rail webs caused by simultaneous application of horizontal and vertical forces. The purpose of the paper is increase the reliability of strain-gauge monitoring aimed at detecting wheel thread defects of freight cars in motion. The scientific novelty of the study is in estimating strains of rail webs under simultaneous loading of rails with vertical and horizontal forces.

Research methods

In order to increase the reliability of monitoring results, strain-gauge sections and measuring equipment are calibrated under operating conditions. There are two types of calibration depending on predefined forces applied to the rail – static or dynamic. The calibration methods based on static forces have several modifications. Figure 1 shows the most common calibration schemes for strain-gauge sections in which static forces are used (Fig. 1a and b) and dynamic forces (Fig. 1c).

For calibration of the strain-gauge section according to the first scheme (Fig. 1a), a special-purpose expanding device is used [1]. It is fastened to the rail foot on both sides. A hydraulic or mechanical jack is placed between the upper support and the rail. Static forces are measured by an electrical dynamometer. An advantage of this calibration scheme is the mobility of the expanding device. Due to this, calibration can be conducted at any point of the measuring section. This calibration scheme does not take into account the stiffness of the rail support. The contribution of this stiffness to results of rail strain measurements can reach 10% [2, 4].

It is a challenging task to calibrate the strain-gauge section, while taking into account the stiffness of the rail base in real conditions. The study [3] proposes a calibration scheme in which a hydraulic or mechanical jack is placed between a cross beam of a car and rail (Fig. 1b). This calibration procedure requires a freight car or a flat car with cargo of known weight. Strains are measured using a mechanical dynamometer with a dial gauge or an electric dynamometer. A clear advantage of this calibration procedure is the fact that the rail rests against the ballast layer and strain measurements take into account the stiffness of the rail base.

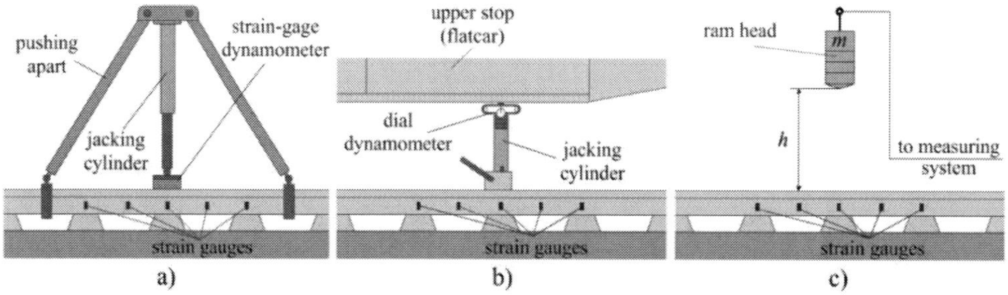

Fig. 1. Calibration schemes for the strain-gauge section with: a) static force applied from the expanding device; b) static force applied to the cross beam of a loaded freight car; c) dynamic force applied from the special-purpose impact device.

Calibration of the strain-gauge section with dynamic force is subject to the third scheme (Fig. 1c). The calibration procedure is based on a special impact device of known weight, which is dropped onto the rail from a certain height. Timing parameters of the impact are recorded, while the force of impact is determined indirectly. An advantage of this calibration method is that it is mobile and does not require additional tools or devices. A disadvantage is that it cannot be used to identify a point of application of dynamic force (eccentricity). In case of significant eccentricity, there is a moment of force that leads to flexural (lateral) strains of rail webs.

The common drawback of the schemes described above is that they cannot be used to estimate strains of the rail from horizontal (lateral) forces. In real operating conditions, lateral forces are created by pressing a wheel flange against the rail. This study proposes a method for calibrating the strain-gauge section using a special-purpose loading device. The device applies a static force to the rail in two directions (Fig. 2).

The loading device (Fig. 2) is placed on the rail on a special holding platform 6. A horizontal (lateral) force is applied by a horizontal hydraulic cylinder 7 of model DU10P100. The force is limited to 218 kN (22.2 tf) in the vertical direction and to 110 kN (11.3 tf) in the horizontal direction. The vertical hydraulic cylinder 2 (model DU20P100) rests against a cross beam of a loaded flat car from above and against a special adjustable support 6 from below. The lower support of the vertical hydraulic cylinder can be used to adjust a point of application of force by displacing it relative to the middle line of the rail head surface. The point of application of force can be changed by displacing an elastic roller installed between the rail and the support 6. This adjustment allows vertical forces to be applied with different eccentricity.

The horizontal hydraulic cylinder 7 in the base rests against the compensation beam 8, while the rod of the hydraulic cylinder rests against the rail head with glued strain gauges 5. The point of impact for the horizontal hydraulic cylinder is not adjustable.

Fig. 2. Photo of the special-purpose device for bidirectional rail loading: 1 – cross beam of a loaded flat car; 2 – vertical hydraulic cylinder; 3 – high-pressure hoses; 4 – compensation support of the vertical hydraulic cylinder; 5 – strain gauges; 6 – vertical cylinder support; 7 – horizontal hydraulic cylinder; 8 – compensation beam of the horizontal cylinder.

Two independent manual hydraulic pumps NRG-7010, connected to hydraulic cylinders by high-pressure hoses 3, are used to create pressure in hydraulic cylinders. The pressure is monitored by pressure gauges MA100VU63. The pressure gauges are installed directly on hand-operated hydraulic pumps. The force transferred to the rail is estimated on the basis of pressure gauge readings.

The experimental studies were conducted at a testing ground of the Siberian Transport University by using a high-speed microprocessor strain-gauge system Dynamika-3 with a sampling frequency of up to 64 kHz. The testing ground has a measuring section with wire strain gauges PKS -12-200 glued to a neutral axis of the rail web (Fig. 2, pos. 5). The strain gauges are oriented so that vertical strains can be recorded.

Rails were loaded with vertical and horizontal forces gradually and with pauses in pressure injection. Pauses in loading are necessary for recording the pressure in the system and calculating the force in order to determine a force-strain relationship.

Experimental data and results

Figure 3 presents the dependences of relative strains on time, determined experimentally by loading the rail only with lateral forces. The rail was loaded intermittently (Fig. 3a) with an increment of 18 kN. The maximum load was 54 kN, as measured by the hydraulic pressure gauge. Symmetric strains were estimated in two cross-sections. The first cross-section is located at the point of application of force. The second section is located at a distance equal to half the distance between two sleepers. In these sections, symmetric strains were equal to zero throughout the entire experiment. This suggests that the vertical force does not have any influence (Fig. 3a, pos. 1, 2). Curves 3 and 4 are based on antisymmetric strains (half-difference) recorded during the experiment. For the cross-section in the sleeper zone, when the strain gauges were directly below the loading device, the recorded maximum strains were equal to 300 ppm (curve 4, Fig. 3a). For the cross-section located at a distance equal to half the distance between two sleepers, the strain was decreased by three times to 100 ppm (curve 3, Fig. 3a).

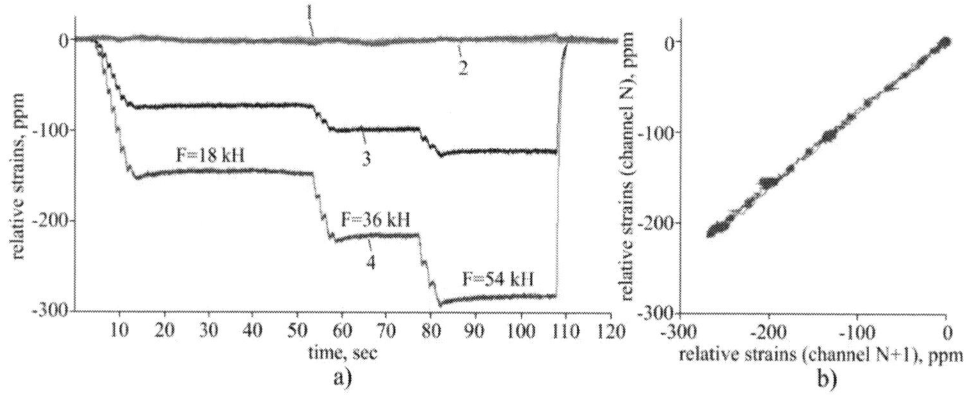

Fig. 3. Graphs representing (a) dependencies of symmetric (1, 2) and antisymmetric (3, 4) strains on time; (b) correlation of readings from one pair of strain gauges when only the lateral force is applied to the rail.

The asymmetric arrangement of strain gauges in the recording system on inner and outer sides of the rail affects the reliability and accuracy of measurements [5–6]. In order to assess the effect of asymmetry, it is proposed to estimate a relationship between pairs of readings from strain gauges. A deviation of this relationship from the linear one suggests that there is a significant difference between bases of the gauges across the height of the rail. Figure 3b shows a correlation graph for readings from the strain gauges located in the cross-section under load. The coefficient of correlation for this pair of strain gauges was 0.999, thereby suggesting that the strain gauges were positioned with a high accuracy.

In the second part of the study, only vertical forces were applied from the loading device [7–14]. Figure 4 shows the experimentally determined dependences of relative strains on time. These strains were recorded when the rail was loaded only with vertical force in a single cross-section, which was directly under the load in the sleeper zone. The rail was loaded intermittently as well. Areas with constant values of strains can be identified on the graph. These constant values were ensured by holding the rail at a certain system pressure. As in the first experiment, the increment of force was constant – 18 kN. The maximum load in the vertical direction was reached at 108 kN. The dependence of antisymmetric strains (Fig. 4a, pos. 1) is not consistent. At the first stage of the experiment, antisymmetric strains increased up to +20 ppm. Then the distribution of strains in the rail web and the bending moment changed the sign. The strains gradually decreased up to -20 ppm. "Jumps" of values could also be observed at the end of each symmetric strain area (Fig. 4a, pos. 2), especially in the first part of the experiment until a load of 54 kN was reached. When only vertical forces were applied, the coefficient of correlation for the values recorded by one pair of strain gauges was equal to 0.97.

Figure 4b shows a dependence of symmetric relative strains of the rail web on the applied vertical force. The dependence is linear. The deviation from the linear law estimated by the least squares method is less than 5%.

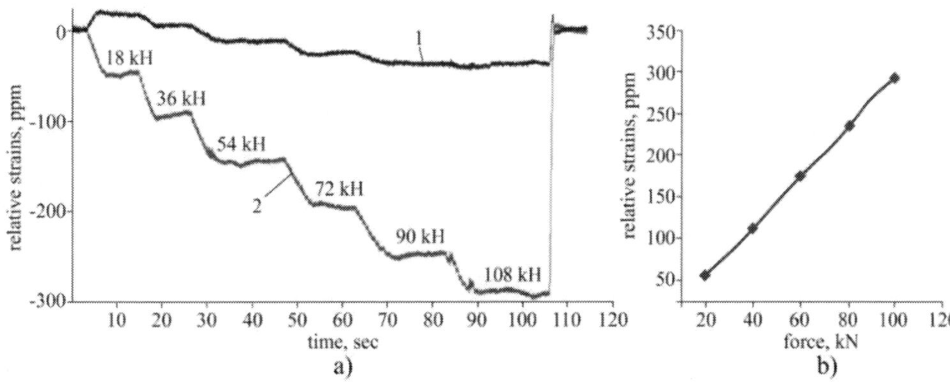

Fig. 4. Dependencies of (a) antisymmetric (1) and symmetric (2) strains on time; (b) symmetric relative strains on the vertical force applied to the rail.

Conclusion

The paper considers the most common calibration schemes for strain-gauge monitoring sections in the wheel–rail system, and describes their features and limitations. The critical factors for this practical task are boundary conditions and local fastening of devices on the rail, which will determine the accuracy of calibration results. The proposed device of new design can be used for bidirectional loading of rails and adjusting the loading force. In addition, it allows a device–rail contact point to be fixed and adjusted. The calibration procedure takes into account the stiffness of the rail base.

Dependences of symmetric and antisymmetric strains on lateral and vertical forces were determined. When a lateral force is applied, the effect of symmetric strains is minimal (within the margin of error) and can be judged from antisymmetric strains. When a vertical force is applied, the dependence of symmetric strains of the rail web on the recorded force is linear throughout the range, with an accuracy of 0.95. This level is sufficient to calibrate the monitoring section. In this case, the effect of antisymmetric flexural strains caused by rail canting and eccentricity of the applied vertical force (which is usual for any practical task) does not exceed 6.9%.

In the future, it is planned to conduct experiments at different stiffness values of the rail base. In order to assess the effect of asymmetric positioning of strain gauges on measurement of symmetric and antisymmetric strains, a series of experiments will be conducted on a specially prepared measuring section. Strain gauges will be glued to rails with a displacement relative to their neutral lines.

References

1. Wheel Condition Monitor (WCM) / Trackside Intelligence Pty Ltd (TracklQ) (King William St, Kent Town, 2007).
2. K. Sekuła, P. Kołakowski, *Proceedings of ISMA 2010 including US201* (2013).
3. S.A. Bekher, A.O. Kolomeets, Journal of Physics: Conference Series, **671** (2016).
4. Precise Diagnosis of Wheel Defects and Vehicle Weights, Signal and System Technik, **8** (2012).
5. S.A. Bekher, L.N. Stepanova, A.O. Kolomeets, A.A. Popkov, RU Patent 2625256 (2016). (in Russian)
6. L.N. Stepanova, S.I. Kabanov, E.Yu. Lebedev et al., RU Patent 2499237 (2013). (in Russian)
7. GOST P 52728–2007. Method of strain-and-temperature measurements in situ. General requirements (Standartinform, Moscow, 2007). (in Russian)
8. GOST P 55050–2012. Railway rolling stock. Permissible exposure norms to the railway track and test methods (Standartinform, Moscow, 2013). (in Russian)
9. S.A. Bekher, A.S. Kochetkov, The Siberian Transport University Bulletin, **17** (2007). (in Russian)
10. A.N. Baybakov, K.I. Kuchinskiy, S.V. Plotnikov et al., Modern problems of science and education, 6 (2013). (in Russian)
11. K.V. Eliseev, Nauka i Obrazovanie [Science and Education], **4** (2014). (in Russian)
12. A.Ya. Kogan, *Dinamika puti i ego vzaimodejstvie s podvizhnym sostavom* [The dynamics of the track and its interaction with the rolling stock] (Transport, Moscow, 1997). (in Russian)
13. A.S. Kochetkov, Thesis of Candidate of technical sciences, Tomsk Polytechnic University, Tomsk, 2011. (in Russian)
14. S.A. Bekher, L.N. Stepanova, A.S. Kochetkov, RU Patent 2480711 (2013). (in Russian)

Dynamic loading in monitoring of brittle objects by acoustic emission method

Artem Popkov[1,*], and *Anton* Kochetkov[1]

[1]Siberian Transport University, 630049 Novosibirsk, Russia

Abstract. Acoustic emission monitoring requires applying a force to an object. In most cases, special-purpose loading devices are used for this process; however, they are subject to some operational limitations. Dynamic loading of a controlled object makes it unnecessary to use loading devices and put the object out of operation. The purpose of the study is to develop a technique of acoustic emission monitoring under dynamic loading. The paper describes results of experiments with impact loading of a glass sheet with a crack. It proposes a method for separating the total flow of acoustic emission signals into stationary groups that are typical for different acoustic emission sources.

Introduction

The capability to selectively detect defects developing under load is traditionally considered to be one of the key advantages of acoustic emission monitoring [1–3]. The acoustic emission method may provide the best results in testing brittle materials, in which risks of defects are more dependent on the stress concentration factor than on sizes. In this case, loading is a complex process aimed at bringing the material to the stress state that provokes the development of defects, while preventing the structure from complete destruction. Pressure vessels and apparatuses are controlled through hydraulic or pneumatic tests [4]. Stress-strain state of parts, assemblies and structural elements is created with special-purpose loading devices [5]. When monitoring structures under dynamic loads, creating conditions for defect development is a non-trivial problem. Impact loading, which can locally reproduce a high level of mechanical stresses and strains, is a promising solution to this problem.

Acoustic emission patterns associated with elastic impact are detailed in [6, 7]. However, as related to the detection of emerging defects, acoustic emission, which accompanies crack propagation processes after damping of oscillations, is of more practical interest. The resulting regularities serve as the basis for creating monitoring systems for objects operating under dynamic or impact loads [8].

The paper is aimed at creating a technique for detecting cracks in brittle materials loaded with an elastic impact using the acoustic emission method.

* Corresponding author: zabagy@gmail.com

© The Authors, published by EDP Sciences. This is an open access article distributed under the terms of the Creative Commons Attribution License 4.0 (http://creativecommons.org/licenses/by/4.0/).

Research Methods

Experimental studies were carried out on a 3-mm thick glass sheet with dimensions of 200×300 mm (Fig. 1). The sample was placed horizontally on damping pads [9]. Impacts with steel balls of 12 mm in diameter and weighing 7 g, freely falling from a height of 1 m, were used for loading the sample. The direction and location of each impact was chosen in such a way as to prevent repeated impact of the ball on the sample after the first rebound [10]. An 8-mm long crack opposite the long edge of the sheet was used as an artificial defect.

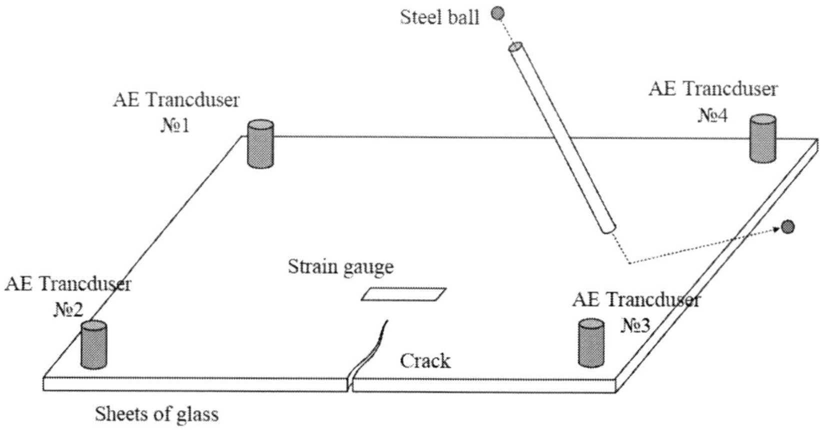

Fig. 1. Experimental scheme.

Acoustic emission signals were recorded by a digital acoustic emission diagnostic system STsAD 16.03 (No. 18892-10 in the State Register) [11, 12] with a recording threshold of 5 μV. Four acoustic emission transducers with a bandwidth of 0.1–0.7 MHz were installed in the corners of the sample at a distance of 10 mm from the edge. Coordinates of acoustic emission sources were determined using planar location algorithms based on the difference between times of arrival of the signals to the transducers, which form a rectangular piezo antenna.

Experimental data and results

The amplitude distribution of the signals (Fig. 2) is described by the exponential distribution law with an average amplitude of 20 μV at the preamplifier input. The discrimination threshold u_0 = 5 μV allows about 70% of the total number of signals to be recorded. Signals associated with processes at the top of the crack, whose amplitude is within a range of 100 to 800 μV (significantly higher than the average) are identified in the flow. The share of these signals varies from 10 to 12%, while the probability of such signals calculated for the exponential distribution does not exceed 0.1%

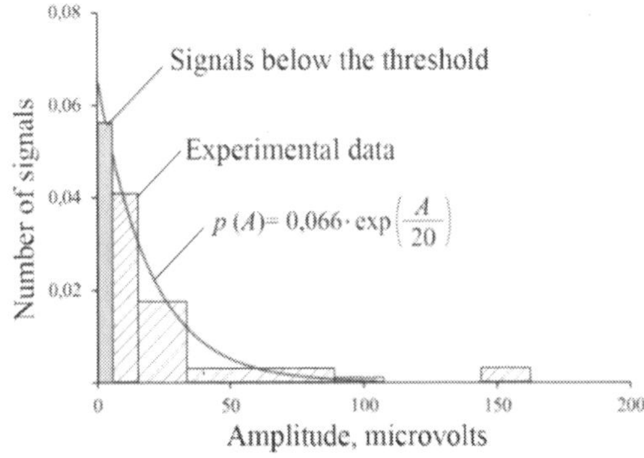

Fig. 2. Distribution of the relative number of acoustic emission signals by amplitude.

The amplitude distribution of the signals corresponds to the exponential distribution with an average amplitude at the preamplifier input equal to 20 μV. At the same time, groups of signals whose time interval substantially exceeds the average time between signals within the group are identified in the total flow of acoustic emission signals. In order to detect and identify the beginning and end of signal groups, it is proposed to use the ratio of time intervals K_B and K_E, whose values indicate the beginning and end of the group, respectively (Fig. 3):

$$K_B = n \cdot \frac{t_m - t_{m-1}}{t_{m+n} - t_m}, \tag{1}$$

$$K_E = n \cdot \frac{t_{m+1} - t_m}{t_m - t_{m-n}}, \tag{2}$$

where t_m is the recording time of the mth acoustic emission signal, n is the number of signals for estimating the average value of the time interval. The critical ratio of time intervals between signals with a given significance level q for an arbitrary value n is determined by the formula:

$$K_{cr} = n\left(\sqrt[n]{\frac{1}{q}} - 1\right).$$

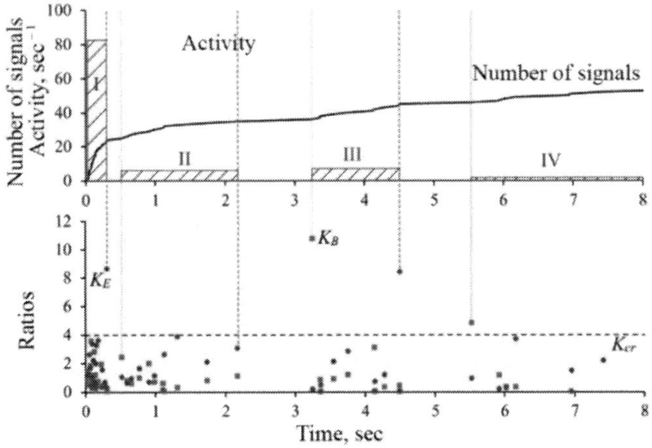

Fig. 3. Time dependence of the number of acoustic emission signals and the average activity of signal groups, identified by ratios of time intervals K_B and K_E.

The dynamic loading, implemented through an elastic impact on the surface of the monitored object, brings the object to the stress-strain state. Recorded events of acoustic emission are localized not only in the impact zone but also in a growing crack zone.

The impact loading of the cracked object causes a residual elastic deformation associated with the displacement of the crack edges in the form of longitudinal shear. This process is accompanied by the destruction of crack edges and produces discrete acoustic emission.

The recorded acoustic emission is a non-stationary process: signals are emitted in groups that significantly differ from each other in terms of activity (by 10–50 times). The time intervals between acoustic emission signals within a group are described by an exponential distribution. Based on the ratio of time intervals between signals to their average value, a method for detecting stationary signal groups has been proposed.

Conclusion

As a result of the studies described above, the authors have found a number of regularities that can be used to identify acoustic emission signals produced by destruction processes in the crack zone. The authors also developed the experimental scheme for studying processes caused by dynamic loading in objects made of brittle materials. The obtained results can be used to study behaviors of structural elements made of materials susceptible to brittle fracture.

References

1. V.V. Muravyev, L.N. Stepanova, A.E. Kareev, Defektoskopija [Russian Journal of Nondestructive Testing], **1**, 63–68 (2003). (in Russian)
2. V.V. Muravyev, O.V. Muravyeva, Deformatsiya i razrushenie materialov [Deformation and destruction of materials], **1**, 24–29, (2016). (in Russian)
3. L.N. Stepanova, E.Yu. Lebedev, A.E. Kareev, V.N. Chaplygin, S.A. Katarushkin, Russian Journal of Nondestructive Testing, **7**, 455-461 (2004).
4. Z. Nazarchuk, *Acoustic emission. Methodology and Application* (Springer, 2017).
5. W. Hwang, S. Bae, J. Kim, S. Kang, N. Kwag, B. Lee, Nuclear Engineering and Technology, **47**, 454-460 (2015).
6. P. Mazal, F. Vlasic, V. Koula, Procedia Engineering, **133**, 379-388 (2015).
7. S. Sengupta, A.K. Datta, P. Topdar, Lat. Am. J. Solid Struct., **12**, 8 (2015).
8. F. Qiu, G. Dai, Y. Zhang, Insight – Non-Destructive Testing and Condition, **59**, 653-358 (2017).
9. S.A. Bekher, Thesis of Candidate of sciences, Siberian Transport University, Novosibirsk, 2004 (in Russian)
10. S.A. Bekher, T.V. Sych, A.A. Popkov, Method of calibration of acoustic emission transducers, RU Patent 2650357 (2018).
11. GOST R ISO 22096-2015. Condition monitoring and diagnostics of machines. Acoustic emission method (Moscow, 2016). (in Russian)
12. GOST R 55047-2012. Technical diagnostics. Without standards calibration of equipment for measuring the stress-strain state of structural materials. General requirements (Moscow, 2017). (in Russian)

Capabilities of acoustic methods in testing of interference-fit joints

Anna Ryzhova[1,*], *Sergey* Bekher[1], and *Aleksey* Bobrov[1]

[1]Siberian Transport University, 630049 Novosibirsk, Russia

Abstract. Tightness of joints on railway wheelsets is controlled by instruments based on a shrink fit method. To date, the shrink fit method has been replaced by an interference fit method. As a result, standard values of tightness have doubled. Therefore, there is an urgent need to upgrade and develop new methods for testing interference-fit joints. A promising solution is to use acoustic methods based on influence of material properties on propagation patterns of elastic waves. The purpose of this study is to evaluate the possibility to test fixed detachable joints by acoustic methods. Reference samples of interference-fit joints with known interference fits (29, 72 and 126 μm) were designed and produced. Experimental tests of samples and wheelset axles with inner bearing rings were conducted by a pulse-echo method and a method of free oscillations. The authors developed a procedure for determining the equivalent thickness of oil clearance using the proportionality factor of echo amplitude and sequence number of echo signals. When testing reference samples and loose bearing rings, frequency responses of the signals were obtained.

Introduction

Wheelsets with axle assemblies are the most important elements of undercarriage in railway cars. The wheelset manufacturing technology implies using fixed detachable joints made by the interference-fit method. Due to insufficient strength of these joints, which is partly associated with a loose inner bearing ring, axle assemblies of wheetsets may fail during operation.

At present, the interference fit of the inner bearing ring onto an axle journal is determined before installation of the axle assembly. Special devices are used to measure diameters of seating faces of the ring and axle in loose state. Based on a difference in diameters, the interference fit is estimated. However, measurement errors, scuffing from press fitting, and rotation of the ring during operation can deteriorate the quality of fit. In order to ensure traffic safety, reduce downtime of trains and cut costs of unscheduled repairs, these joints should be subject to complete inspection.

Acoustic methods described in [1–6] are the most advanced approach to testing interference fits. The ultrasonic method is based on a dependence of the reflection coefficient of ultrasonic waves at the joint interface on the tightness of fit [7]. The method

* Corresponding author: annalodo@yandex.ru

© The Authors, published by EDP Sciences. This is an open access article distributed under the terms of the Creative Commons Attribution License 4.0 (http://creativecommons.org/licenses/by/4.0/).

of free oscillations is aimed at exposing a test part to a mechanical shock, and then measuring self-frequencies and the number of oscillation cycles over a time interval with a special instrument. Based on measured parameters, a mean value of interference fit is determined. The method was experimentally tested in [8] for testing joints of bronze bushings with cylindrical bodies with a diameter of 70 mm and bushings with articulated connecting rods with an interference fit of 30 to 120 μm. The amplitude of recorded waves is significantly affected by deviations between shapes of real and nominal surfaces, defects in test joints, and variations in surface roughness of joined parts. Therefore, the techniques need to be refined and verified for each specific type of joints.

The purpose of the paper is to study how the interference fit of an inner bearing ring onto an axle journal influences propagation patterns of acoustic waves. Unlike conventional methods for testing interference-fit joints, the proposed approach is based on a combination of active and passive acoustic methods. In this approach, the pulse-echo method is used for the local control of the tightness of fit, while the method of free oscillations is responsible for the integrated control of the entire joint. A dependence of informative parameters of diagnostic signals on interference fit was determined on the basis of reference samples. Influence of interfering factors was determined on the basis of real parts.

Research methods

The capabilities of the echo-pulse method (Fig. 1a) and the method of free oscillations (Fig. 1b) for testing interference-fit joints were experimentally studied on samples with a known interference fit [9] and on real parts.

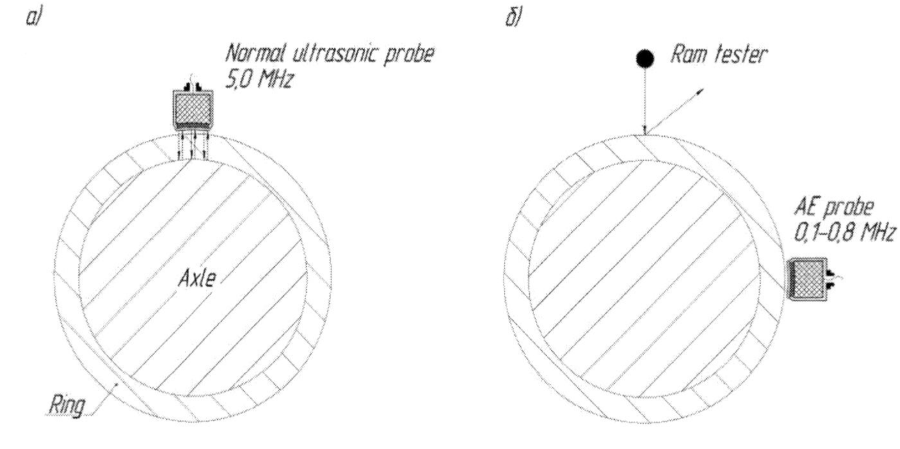

Fig. 1. Test diagrams for fixed detachable joints between a ring and an axle: a — pulse-echo method, b — method of free oscillations.

In case of the ultrasonic testing method, the thickness of a clearance between the ring and the shaft is used as an informative parameter. It determines acoustic properties of the interface between two media and represents the tightness of the fit of joined parts. For active control of interference-fit joints, a straight-beam single element transducer with an operating frequency of 5.0 MHz was used to generate and receive ultrasonic waves. The transducers were connected to a USD-50 multipurpose pulse-echo flaw detector (State Register No. 52657-13). The ring –axle joint was scanned radially from the running surface of the bearing ring (Fig. 1a). A series of echo pulses re-reflected from the inner and outer cylindrical surfaces of bearing rings were recorded. A_1, A_2, .., A_n (Fig. 2). The amplitude of the nth pulse is satisfactorily described by a linear relationship with the proportionality factor α:

$$A_n = \alpha \cdot n \tag{1}$$

where α is the proportionality factor, which is determined by the attenuation coefficient, thickness of the ring, coefficients of reflection from the entry surface and interface between two media, as well as by a clearance between the ring and the shaft, dB; n is the number of echo pulse.

The experimentally determined proportionality factor α makes it possible to estimate the thickness of the contact layer of the joint using the known dependencies [10–12]. Other things being equal, the thickness of the layer characterizes the mechanical stress in joined parts:

$$Lg(R_g) = \frac{\alpha_\Delta - \alpha_0}{20}, \tag{2}$$

$$R_g = \frac{\left(\frac{z_1}{z_2} - \frac{z_2}{z_1}\right)^2}{4\,ctg\left(\frac{2\cdot\pi\cdot h}{\lambda_2}\right) + \left(\frac{z_1}{z_2} + \frac{z_2}{z_1}\right)^2}, \tag{3}$$

where R_g is the coefficient of reflection from the ring–clearance–shaft interface; α_Δ and α_0 are the proportionality factors for the reference sample with interference fit Δ and for the loose ring, respectively; z_1 is the acoustic impedance of the ring material (steel), which is equal to $46\ MPa \cdot s/m$; z_2 is the acoustic impedance of the clearance medium (oil), which is equal to $1.3\ MPa \cdot s/m$; h is the thickness of the clearance, m; λ_2 is the length of the acoustic wave in the second medium, m.

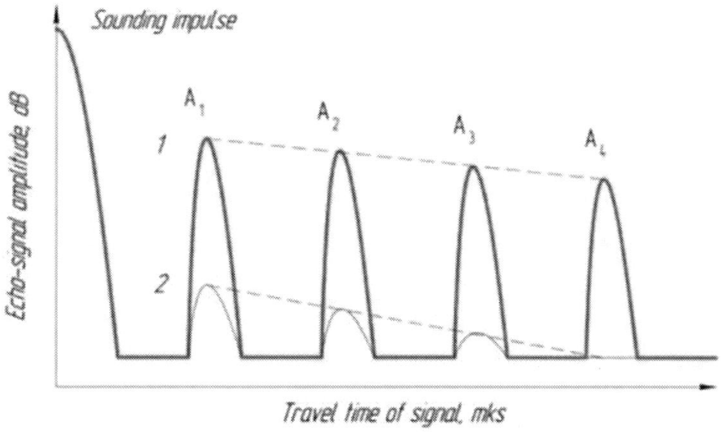

Fig. 2. A-scan with a series of re-reflected pulses: 1 – loose rings, 2 – sample with an interference fit of 72 μm.

In experiments with the passive control method, oscillations were excited by shock action with steel balls weighing 9 g, freely falling from a height of 0.2–0.4 m inside a guide tube. The resulting oscillations were recorded with a GT-300 acoustic emission transducer. Signals were digitized by a Tektronix TDS 2014 oscilloscope and processed with special-purpose software. The spectral composition of the signals and its response to changes in the interference fit were analyzed.

Experimental data and results

Figure 2 shows a typical A-scan of an ultrasonic flaw detector with a series of re-reflected pulses recorded in a loose ring and a sample with an interference fit of 72 μm. The logarithm of the signal amplitude depends linearly on the pulse number with a correlation coefficient of more than 0.98. Proportionality factors for different values of interference fit were calculated by the least-squares method (Fig. 3). The minimum slope (1.9 dB) of the characteristic curve is observed for the loose bearing ring. The maximum slope (6.3 dB) is observed for the reference bearing sample with an interference fit of 126 μm. For samples with a wide range of interference fits from 29 to 126 μm, the proportionality factors varies slightly — from 5.3 to 6.3 dB.

The proportionality factors obtained at a repair depot do not correspond to the data determined with the samples. The difference can be attributed to the state of the seating face, which distorts the relationship of the proportionality factor for the amplitude of re-reflected pulses and the sequence number with interference fit.

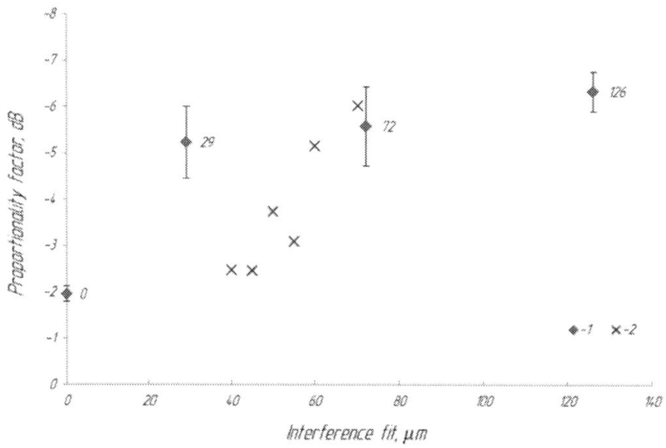

Fig. 3. Dependence of the proportionality factor on the interference fit: 1 — reference samples, 2 — real parts.

Spectral compositions of the signals recorded by the self-oscillation method on the loose ring and the reference sample significantly differ from each other (Fig. 4). The frequency response in interference-fit joints does not contain low-frequency components with a frequency of less than 15 kHz. The spectral lines in the region from 15 to 33 kHz also differ substantially. The width of the spectral lines measured at half-height is 0.1 kHz.

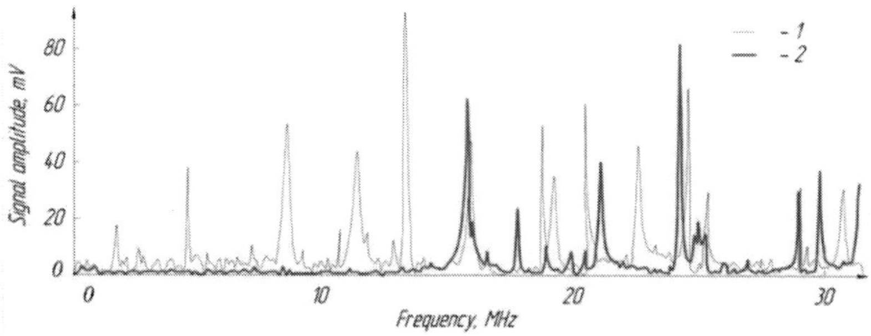

Fig. 4. Frequency responses of the signals received by an acoustic sensor for 1 – loose ring, 2 – sample with an interference fit of 72 μm.

The quality assessment of the joint by the passive method can be performed only if the position of the spectral lines changes with change in the interference fit. This is due to changes in acoustic and geometric parameters of the ring mounted onto the axle, as well as the transparency of the axle– ring interface. In turn, these changes influence the frequency response of free oscillations arising from the impact [13]. Figure 5 shows the frequency responses of signals recorded on the ring mounted on the axle with an interference fit of 29 and 72 μm. The most significant shift of the spectral lines occurs in the high-frequency region (24 kHz or more), which can be used to estimate the interference fit.

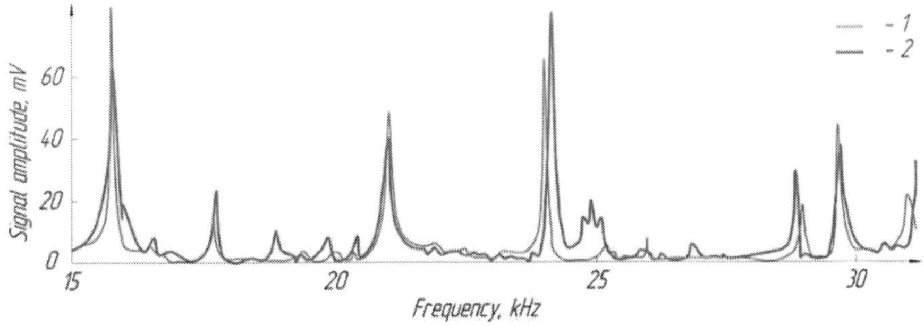

Fig. 5. Frequency responses of the signals received by an acoustic sensor for 1 – sample with an interference fit of 29 μm, 2 – sample with an interference fit of 72 μm.

Conclusion

The studied passive and active techniques aimed at controlling the tightness of interference fit of bearing rings onto an axle journal can be used to detect joints with a low interference fit of 29 μm or less. The active pulse-echo method is based on indirect estimates of the thickness of contact layer using measured amplitudes of echo signals reflected from the joint interface. Using the reference samples with an interference fit of 29, 72 and 126 μm, the authors experimentally determined proportionality factors for amplitudes of echo pulses with their ordinal numbers 5.23, 5.58 and 6.34 dB. The calculated thicknesses of the oil contact layer in the joint are 0.31, 0.27 and 0.22 mm. In the conditions of a car repair depot, the deviation of the axle surface from the cylindrical shape has a significant effect on the thickness of the clearance and, therefore, on acoustic parameters of the joint. Consequently, the ultrasonic method is sensitive not only to interference fit, but also to out-of-roundness, conicity and surface roughness of parts.

In case of the passive method, the informative parameters for estimating the interference fit are self-frequencies in the range of 15 to 30 kHz. The characteristic width of the peaks measured at half-height is 0.1 kHz, which corresponds to the spectral shift with a change in the interference fit from 29 and 72 μm. The considered methods make it possible to detect joints with low interference fit. In order to increase the reliability of control procedures, further studies should be aimed at reducing the influence of interfering factors on the accuracy of interference fit control, through the use of a multifrequency pulse-echo method or optimization of the impact technique in the method of free oscillations.

References

1. V.V. Muravyev, V.A. Strizhak, L.V. Volkova, A.V. Pryakhin, Lokomotiv [Locomotive], 5, 39-41(2014). (in Russian)
2. I. Solodov, J. Bai, S. Bekgulyan, G. Busse, Appl. Phys. Lett, 99, 211911 (2011).

3. L.N. Stepanova, E.S. Tenitilov, S.A. Bekher, Defektoskopija [Russian Journal of Nondestructive Testing], 9, 49–55 (2009). (in Russian)
4. A.G. Belonogov, S.A. Rodionov, A.M. Shanaurin, Defektoskopija [Russian Journal of Nondestructive Testing], 7, 90-92 (2004). (in Russian)
5. K.-Y. Jhang, International Journal of Precision Engineering and Manufacturing, **Vol. 10** (1), 123-135 (2009).
6. I.I. Kozyatnik, T.V. Muravyev, Siberian Transport University Bulletin, **12**, 73-81 (2005). (in Russian)
7. V.P. Ivannikov, A.V. Kabakova, Industrial laboratory. Diagnostics of materials, **81(9)**, 49-53 (2015). (in Russian)
8. B.A. Glagovskiy, I.B. Moskovenko, *Nizkochastotnye akusticheskie metody kontrolja v mashinostroenii* [Low-frequency acoustic methods of control in engineering] (Mashinostroenie, Leningrad, 1977). (in Russian)
9. A.O. Ryzhova, S.A. Bekher, A.L. Bobrov, "The acoustic waves propagation laws in the force-fit connections for test of the interference fit", JPCS (to be published).
10. V.V. Muravyev, O.V. Muravyeva, A.V. Platunov, *Akusticheskaja tenzometrija i strukturoskopija tonkih stal'nyh provolok* [Acoustic tensometry and structuroscopy of thin steel wires] (ISTU Publishing House, Izhevsk, 2016) (in Russian).
11. V.A. Troitskiy, V.Yu. Popov, *Ul'trazvukovoj kontrol' svarnyh soedinenij* [Ultrasonic inspection of welded joints] (Feniks, Kazan, 2010) (in Russian).
12. L.M. Brekhovskikh, *Volny v sloistyh sredah* [Waves in layered medium] (Nauka, Moscow, 1973). (in Russian)
13. Yu.V. Lange, *Akusticheskie nizkochastotnye metody i sredstva nerazrushajushhego kontrolja mnogoslojnyh konstrukcij* [Acoustic low-frequency methods and nondestructive inspection aids of multiply construction] (Mashinostroenie, Moscow, 1991) (in Russian).

Optimization of technical solutions for pilot hole drilling in soil

Boris Danilov[1,*], and *Boris* Smolyanitskiy[2]
[1]N.A. Chinakal Institute of Mining, Siberian Branch, Russian Academy of Sciences, 630060 Novosibirsk, Russia
[2]Siberian Transport University, 630049 Novosibirsk, Russia

Abstract. The paper discusses approaches to improvement of equipment for borehole drilling with a predetermined trajectory in construction of underground utility systems and facilities. Piercing method allows implementing dry drilling of boreholes with small diameter using simple technical equipment. The methods used when preparing the research are analysis, generalization, and experimental research methods. Outcomes of the research include evidence that increase in performance of vibro-impact piercing is possible not only due to higher impact energy, but also due to optimization of interaction between the operating tool and soil. Combination of dynamic action by impact pulses and static forces applied to the drilling equipment enables to enhance performance of impact pulse action and increase the drilling speed. Accuracy of the borehole trajectory can be provided by using dynamic stabilizers or correcting the drilling direction due to asymmetrical tool shape in combination with the torque moment of a drilling equipment. The study formulates requirements to design of a drilling unit for directed pilot hole drilling by dynamic piercing method. The design of an improved pneumatic tool installed in front of the drill string and equipped with asymmetrical front head is described. Experimental research results are given on the process of a borehole drilling using the described tool.

Introduction

Borehole drilling in the rock mass is an important part of the upstream technologies for mineral deposits. Boreholes are widely used in underground development for utilities installation without opening daylight surface, roof bolting, installing pile foundations, reinforcing soil structures and other technological processes [1]. In underground development, borehole drilling is mostly performed in soil. Since soil compaction may occur under mechanical action, such methods as piercing and direct push techniques are widely practiced, which are based on static or dynamic driving of an operating tool into soil without rotation [2]. Due to simplicity and efficiency these techniques became the basis of trenchless technologies for underground utilities installation on the early stage of their development.

* Corresponding author: bbdanilov@mail.ru

© The Authors, published by EDP Sciences. This is an open access article distributed under the terms of the Creative Commons Attribution License 4.0 (http://creativecommons.org/licenses/by/4.0/).

The main drawbacks of these techniques are poor performance and insufficient accuracy of borehole location in the defined underground area. For that reason, in recent times trenchless technologies are mostly connected with horizontal directional drilling (HDD) [3, 4]. Effective control of the installation trajectory with HDD equipment is achieved by using asymmetrical drill, and ground breaking is performed hydraulically. The latter condition empirically proved this technique inappropriate for urban use. Drilling mud is supplied in the borehole under pressure, it inevitably causes geometric inconsistencies while borehole forming which are hard to control. Such inconsistencies lead to daylight surface subsidence which is totally unacceptable when installing utilities under roads, highways and other constructions [5, 6].

Therefore, the task for developing trenchless technologies consists in increasing performance and accuracy of borehole location in the defined underground area with compliance to safety requirements for adjacent infrastructure and natural environment. Methods based on impact techniques of borehole formation are the most promising. They potentially enable to significantly increase drilling speed without the increase of operational resources of technical equipment [7]. However, impact machines are the source of vibrations and noise and therefore the preferable direction of the technology development is achievement of the effect not by increasing the impact energy of the machines, but due to optimization of interaction between the operating tools and soil [8]. These processes are insufficiently studied, while having high potential for increasing performance of impact pulse action for moving the operating tool [1]. Using these potential reserves will enable to significantly improve technical and economic parameters of the studied technological processes and develop novel mixed technologies combining different drilling methods.

Research methods

In the process of study the following methods were used: analysis, comparison, consolidation of information, experimental research and parameters measurement. This set of chosen methods can be explained by the fact that soils possess a wide range of physico-mechanical properties, and to obtain complete and reliable information on the process of interaction between the operating tool and soil both theoretical and experimental methods are required. Analysis of the existing borehole drilling techniques and equipment allows distinguishing peculiarities of technological processes and assessing their improvement possibilities. As a result of consolidation of this information the directions and perspectives for trenchless technologies were substantiated. Efficiency of the suggested solutions was experimentally verified, the obtained results are formulated in the conclusions.

Analysis of specific features of technological processes that take place in the modern dry drilling equipment with no fluid used demonstrates that in most cases borehole is formed in two stages. At the first stage a pilot hole with a small diameter is drilled which sets the required trajectory. After that it is reamed up to the required diameter by further drilling. In some cases, third stage is carried out which includes extraction of casing, mostly metal one, and installation of a kelly made of plastic, reinforced concrete, etc.

This principle is used in operation of auger drilling units which recently got a new development impulse due to solving the issue of drilling trajectory control. Typically, it is provided by preliminary drilling of a pilot hole with a small diameter [9]. Such units have an operating tool for piercing a pilot hole with a predetermined trajectory, a rotary drilling tool for further reaming and a screw conveyor for soil excavation, as well as drivers for operating tool, casing and kelly. The most widespread are the following models and brands: Richmond, WIR, Astec Underground, Bohrtec and Herrenknecht, HEB 1 and Taifun by Schmidt, Kranz & Co., GmbH, Perforator, etc.

The first stage - pilot hole drilling - is carried out using piercing method from the entry pit (Fig.1) where a hydraulic jack is installed which presses soil into the drill pipe with a wedge bit. When pressing the drill pipe the wedge provides deviation from the direct trajectory. This deviation is recorded by a control device and is eliminated by reverse rotation of the wedge inclined surface during the drill pipe penetration. The occurring deviation is compensated in the same manner. Pressing of a drill pipe is carried out until the bit reaches the intake pit. The process is controlled by a laser control system. In spite of a slightly wavelike trajectory, the borehole usually reaches the predetermined area.

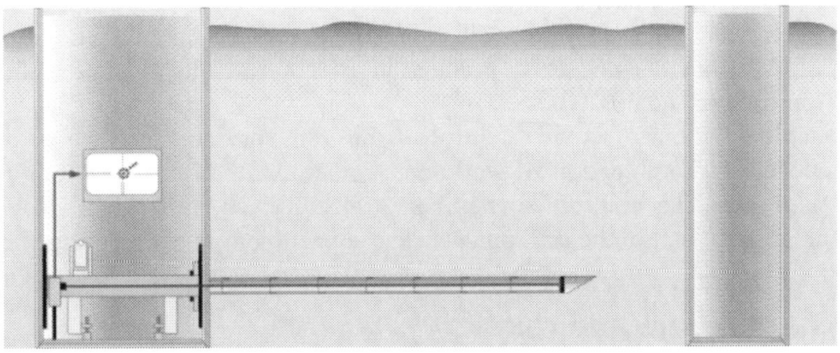

Fig. 1. Drilling of a pilot hole in compacting soil without drill string rotation.

It shall be noted that such pilot hole drilling method is only applicable for compacting soils. Its main drawback is high energy consumption while forming a borehole space due to static manner of pressing action [10].

Vibro-impact piercing is the simplest and rather efficient method which was developed in the 1970s - 1980s, when reliable pneumatic impact machines called pneumodrifts were designed at the Institute of Mining, Siberian Branch of the Russian Academy of Sciences [11]. Controlled pneumodrift independently moving in the soil enables to avoid using drilling unit at the first stage of technological process, which provides considerable cut of operational costs.

An important requirement when drilling a borehole in compacting soil for installing underground utilities in most cases is its straightness and reaching the predetermined area. However, both static and dynamic operating tools almost always have certain deviations from the set direction. The main reason for that being inhomogeneity of soil, among many others.

Accuracy of borehole drilling can be achieved by extending the length of calibrating section of the operating tool, for example, pneumodrift, or by its equipment with stabilizers (Fig.2) [11].

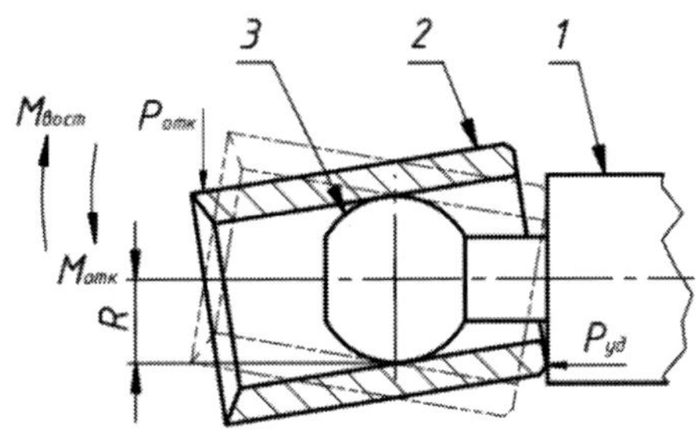

Fig. 2. Principle of operation of a dynamic stabilizer: 1 – body of pneumodrift; 2 – cylinder; 3 – round support.

The principle of operation of a stabilizer is the following: when the action that causes deviation occurs the plug rotates to a specified angle about the pneumodrift axis. In this case a stabilizing moment occurs caused by eccentric action of impact load which tends to bring the plug in its initial position and the pneumodrift - to the set direction. Use of stabilizers enables to expect higher accuracy of drilling direction, especially for boreholes of small length (25-30 cm). For longer boreholes the efficiency of such method decreases due to progressive increase of error [11].

The most effective solution of the drilling accuracy issue consists in providing technical means for controlled change of drilling trajectory of the operating tool in soil. It can be independently moving pneumodrifts that are capable of changing drilling trajectory by operator's command [12, 13], as well as static borehole piercing equipment (Fig.1). However, today there is no serial production of controllable pneumodrifts which are currently represented by prototypes.

Reasonable solution to provide control of the trajectory and increase of the borehole piercing speed is a combination of static and dynamic action on the operating tool that forms a pilot hole. To control the borehole trajectory, an impact action tool shall be installed in the front part of the drill pipe, such as a pneumodrift with a wedge bit.

Experimental data and results

The studies [8, 14] demonstrate that a combination of static and dynamic actions applied to the tool that penetrates soil enables to enhance the forward movement by impact pulse actions and to reduce its return caused by elastic component of soil response after impact pulse action. As a result of calculations, the authors defined the dependency for the movement rate of the operating tool with a head installed on the front part of a pneumodrift and forming the hole of 325 mm in diameter on the static action applied to the pneumodrift body transmitted via drill string. The energy of impact pulses is 600 J and the frequency of pulses is 5 Hz.

The calculation was based on the known solution of the task of equilibrium state of annular soil layer with core loaded cavity suggested by Prof. Dr. A.L. Isakov for describing the dynamics of the tool movement while borehole reaming [15, 16].

The solution was obtained witht he following assumptions:

1. Plane section hypothesis is applied when describing the process of soil cavity expansion, i.e. it is assumed that the movement trajectory of the compacting soil particles lies in the planes perpendicular to the axis of reamed borehole.

2. Under pulse loading soil compaction from initial to final density occurs in a jumplike manner under the pressure that reached some critical value. Behind the compaction wave front soil behaves like a plastically deformed body.

At the first stage the distance of the operating tool movement under single action of the impact pulse was defined, then movement rate was defined with the account of impact actions frequency.

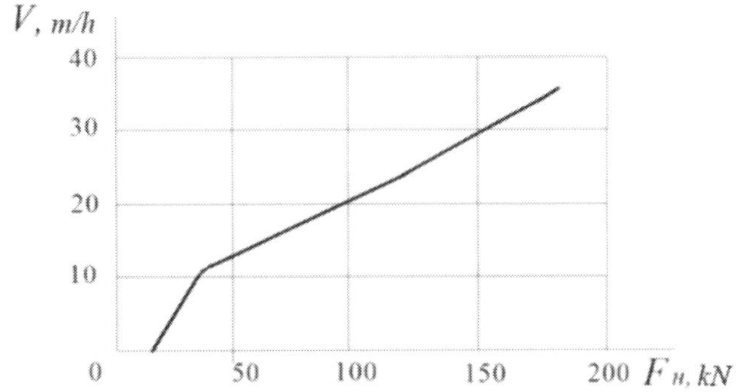

Fig. 3. Dependency of tool penetration rate on static action for various structure of impact energy.

The defined dependency is graphically represented in Figure 3. It is seen that the movement of operating tool is observed only for some initial value of static load, below this level the impact pulse energy is insufficient for overcoming the elastic component of soil resistance. Consequently, plastic deformation of soil is impossible to occur. Under further growing static action the drilling rate soars as the efficiency of impact pulse actions increases due to lower uncompensated share of elastic soil response. As soon as static action reaches the value of 35-40 kN the intensity of drilling rate growth significantly decreases. In this zone static action completely compensates for soil elastic response and all impact pulse energy is spent on plastic deformation of soil and forward movement of the tool. Here the capability of increasing impact efficiency is exhausted. Further increase of rate occurs less intensively and is caused exclusively by growing static action.

For the purpose of experimental verification of the results obtained with ИП-4603 serial pneumodrift an operating tool was produced for pilot hole drilling by directed piercing. To perform that the front side of pneumodrift installed in a drill string was equipped with a wedge bit. The rear part of the body was retrofitted to provide connection with the drill string. The joint is an important element of the drilling equipment which transmits static axle load and torque to the operating tool. Special spline connection was developed which enables axle mobility of the pneumodrift in relation to drill string. It allows preventing the possibility of transmitting impact pulses to the drill string, destruction of this connection or pneumodrift body, as well as reversing the impact mechanism when changing the direction of a drilling unit for easier reverse motion.

Design scheme of the operating tool with the use of retrofitted ИП-4603 pneumodrift is presented in Figure 4.

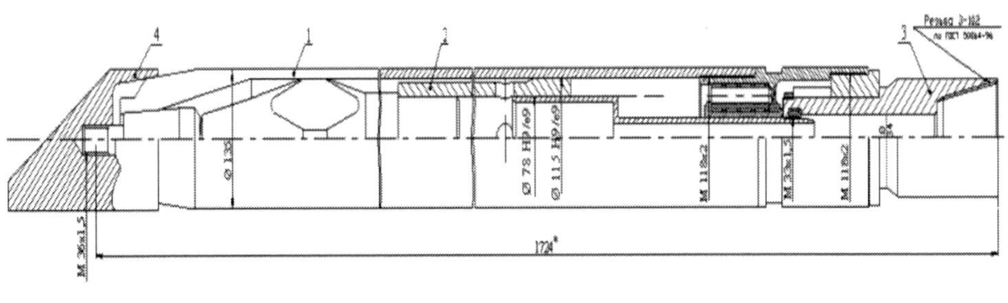

Fig. 4. Operating tool for pilot hole combined drilling: 1 – body; 2 – striker; 3 – joint; 4 – deflecting mechanism.

Experiments were preformed on the "Green Hill" testing ground of Institute of Mining, Siberian Branch of Russian Academy of Sciences. At the first stage of experiments pilot holes were drilled using directed dynamic piercing method in combination with static load. It was determined that the amount of static load can be reduced up to 2 times in comparison with static piercing method. This fact significantly simplifies the task of drilling machine bolting and allows reducing its power. The tendency of drilling rate change for various combinations of impact power and static load was revealed both experimentally and by calculations. However, the amount of effect obtained in all experiments appeared to be smaller by 25-30%.

Analysis of the obtained results demonstrates that important factors for high borehole drilling rate are amount of static and pulse load, as well as the rate of drill string forward movement. The rate shall be sufficient for the elastic deformation phase of soil to finish within the pause between two impacts. Then, all energy of impact pulse will perform useful work on plastic deformation and forward movement of the tool.

The process of interaction between the pneumodrift body and soil was previously studied at the Institute of Mining, Siberian Branch of the Russian Academy of Sciences [17], as a result a dependency was obtained for movement of the operating tool body under impact pulse action and after it (Fig.5).

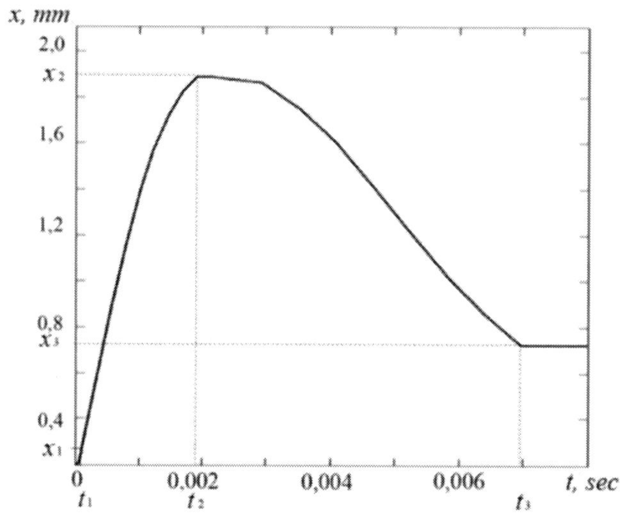

Fig. 5. Dependency of pneumodrift movement distance on the time of impact action: t_1 – end time of impact action and start of movement; t_2 – end time of forward movement; t_3 – end time of return.

The graph shows that the process of pneumodrift movement has mostly dynamic nature. Within the period of 0.002 sec the movement distance is 1.75 mm, and the average rate is 0.9 m/sec. After the impact action finishes the body stops under the effect of soil elastic response and return movement begins. To enhance impact efficiency the tool shall be moved forward before the next pulse impact begins. This way, a pneumodrift shall move approximately 1 mm forward due to static action. With impact frequency of 5 to 10 Hz it shall cover this distance for 0.2 – 0.1 sec. Consequently, the rate shall be within the range of 0.005– 0.01 m/sec.

The simplest and the most efficient solution of the stated problem consists in using an intermediate element like elastic linkage for connecting the drill string and the operating tool. The main function of this element is preliminary storage of deformation energy in pauses between impacts and output of this energy for moderation of elastic soil response immediately after the impact.

During field experiments with the suggested design it was determined that it enables to drill pilot holes in compacting soil using a combination of force actions with the capability of compensation of the trajectory deviation up to 0.1 m on the length of less than 2 m. This result is accepted for solving practical tasks.

Conclusion

Piercing is the simplest and the most technologically advanced technique of pilot hole drilling. The results of this research showed that significant increase in the borehole drilling rate using vibro-impact operating tool is achieved due to simultaneous application of pulse impact and static loads. This effect is obtained without increase in impact pulse energy by enhancing efficiency of its operation. For experimental verification and assessment of the expected effect the operating tool based on serial pneumodrift was designed and retrofitted for operation with a drilling unit. The experiments demonstrated that such technology enables implementation of highly efficient method of vibro-impact piercing and provides accuracy of a borehole location in the defined underground area due to control and corrections in the trajectory while drilling. This proves high perspective of development of such technology. In order to provide complete implementation of its capabilities further research on the process of interaction between the operating tool and soil are required aimed at decreasing impact energy losses on elastic deformation of soil.

References

1. B.B. Danilov, B.N. Smolyanitskiy, Journal of Fundamental and Applied Mining Sciences, **Vol. 2**, 1, 104-113 (2014). (in Russian)
2. B. Maidl, L. Schmid, W. Ritz, M. Herrenknecht, *Hardrock Tunnel Boring Machines* (Ernst & Sohn, Berlin, 2008).
3. G. Deng, A. Yao, Proceedings of the 19th EGU General Assembly, EGU2017, (Vienna, Austria, 23-28 April, 2017).
4. K. Fallwell, Tunnels and Tunnelling International, (June), 45-50 2015).
5. A.P. Rybakov, *Osnovy bestranshejnyh tehnologij* [Fundamentals of trenchless technologies] (Press-Buro, Moscow, 2005). (in Russian)
6. C. Kummerer, Proceedings of the XVI European Conference on Soil Mechanics and Geotechnical Engineering, ECSMGE 2015, **2** 619-624 (2015).
7. B.B. Danilov, B.N. Smolyanitskiy, Proceedings of the Research-to-Practice Conference "Safety and Efficiency Problems of geo-resources development in present conditions", 195 - 201 (Perm, 2014). (in Russian)
8. B.N. Smolyanitskiy, B.B. Danilov, *Polytransport Systems*: Proceedings of the VIII International Scientific and Technical Conference, 718-723 (STU Publ., Novosibirsk, 2014). (in Russian)
9. E. Schey, J. Chae, Proceedings of the Pipelines 2013 Conference, 875-883 (2013).
10. W. Norhaliza, B. Ismail, A.T.S. Azhar, N.J. Nurul, *IOP Conf. Series: Materials Science and Engineering*, **136,** 012018 (2016).
11. K.S. Gurkov, V.V. Klimashko, A.D. Kostylev, V.D. Plavskikh, K.K. Tupitsyn, *Pnevmoprobojniki* [Pneumodrifts] (Novosibirsk, 1990). (in Russian)
12. Allied Hole-Hog underground piercing tools, (Allied Steel & Tractor Products Inc., 1982).
13. B.B. Danilov, D.O. Cheshchin, *Polytransport Systems*: Proceedings of the VIII International Scientific and Technical Conference, 724-728 (STU Publ., Novosibirsk,, 2014). (in Russian)

14. B.B. Danilov, A.S. Kondratenko, B.N. Smolyanitskiy, A.S. Smolentsev, Fiziko-tehnicheskie problemy razrabotki poleznyh iskopaemyh [Journal of Mining Science] 3, 57 – 64 (2017). (in Russian)
15. A.L. Isakov, A.K. Tkachuk, Fiziko-tehnicheskie problemy razrabotki poleznyh iskopaemyh [Journal of Mining Science], 2 (2000). (in Russian)
16. A.L. Isakov, A.E. Zemtsova, Fiziko-tehnicheskie problemy razrabotki poleznyh iskopaemyh [Journal of Mining Science], 3, 95 – 100 (1998). (in Russian)
17. A.A. Repin, Dinamics and Strength of Mining Machines, 160 – 161 (2001). (in Russian)

Methods of determination of forces in the "wheel-rail" system

Tatyana Sych[1,*], and *Andrey* Kolomeets[1]

[1]Siberian Transport University, 630049 Novosibirsk, Russia

Abstract. Increase in the volume of heavy traffic on railways updates the requirements for ensuring transportation safety in conditions of continuous increasing in axle loads on the track. The purpose of the study is to review methods for determining the dynamic forces arising from interaction between the wheel and the rail during rolling stock movement. The numerical method is used to determine the values of relative strain of the rail web at the transducers locations. Model verification and estimation of the calculation accuracy for several methods of determining forces in the "wheel-rail" system has been performed. Methods for determining the loads arising in the wheel and rail system, as well as the results of calculating the three load components were obtained. Simulation tests of the proposed forces control method have been performed.

Introduction

In conditions of growing freight turnover, the task of reliable monitoring of dynamic forces affecting the track and caused by rolling stock on the network of railways is becoming increasingly important [1]. This problem is especially relevant in connection with increase in axle loads and introduction of heavy rolling stock around the globe [2-4]. Safety of traffic of freight and passenger rolling stock is directly related to timely identification of operational defects in the parts of rolling stock and track. Dynamic forces trigger development of fatigue cracks and are the cause of derailments, accidents and destructions [5].

Excessive dynamic forces cause progression of rail defects and development of fatigue cracks in the unsprung part of the carriage. Standard [6] with the norms of permissible effect on the track and test methods was introduced in the Russian Federation. There are various ways to determine these forces, but the number of studies on assessing the methods reliability is insufficient. It raises the need for research on the metrological support of methods for determining forces in the "wheel-rail" system.

Systems of continuous monitoring of wheel-rail interaction parameters have become widespread recently. These systems may use optical or laser sensors to determine the geometry of parts, maximum deflections, and strain sensors. In all cases, indirect information about the process is recorded, on the basis of which the decision is made on

* Corresponding author: tatyna979@mail.ru

© The Authors, published by EDP Sciences. This is an open access article distributed under the terms of the Creative Commons Attribution License 4.0 (http://creativecommons.org/licenses/by/4.0/).

(non)admissibility of dynamic loads acting on the part. In accordance with [6], the methods for determining lateral and vertical forces transmitted from the wheel to the rail are strain gages on the rails, and strain gages on wheels with the frequency of recording of 250 Hz. It is proposed to use the Schlumpf method [7] to determine lateral forces. A lot of methods for recording information have been developed, but metrological support of the methods is necessary for their wide application, reliability and accuracy of calculations.

Thus, the main purpose of the study is to analyze the stress-strain state of the rail when the wheel of the rolling stock is acting on it and metrological support of the methods of registering forces in the "wheel-rail" system. Reliable definition of lateral and vertical forces will help improve traffic safety, increase the service life of rails and carriage parts.

Research methods

The most common and investigated are the following two methods of placing sensors on the rail web to record the train load. The first method considered is the Schlumpf method, which is set forth in [6]. It uses a tensometric circuit assembled on the rail web, by which lateral forces are measured by the difference in the opposite bending moments occurring in the rail web under the action of lateral forces. Several measuring cross-sections of the rail can be used, in each four strain gages are installed (Fig. 1). The strain gages are placed on the rail web in pairs from external and internal side, one pair located at point z_1 and z_2 is higher than the neutral axis of the rail cross-section, the second pair located at point z_3 and z_4 is lower than that level.

The second method suggests using two measuring transducers in each section of the rail in the middle of the web near the y–y′ neutral axis (Fig. 1). The transducers are oriented vertically [8], half-sum and half-difference of deformations are used for calculations, the data is recorded in several measuring cross-sections. There are alternative methods as well [9]. Computer and numerical methods can be used to perform detailed analysis of the state of the wheel and rail during their interaction for various arrangements of the primary transducers [10-13].

This study uses the finite-element rail model (type P65) with the cross-section in accordance with GOST R 51685 created for calculation, the model length was 6 m. The simulation was performed in the SolidWorks software environment. An elastic base simulating the supports (Fig. 2, pos. 2) through equal intervals L was set according to the length of the rail (Fig. 2, pos. 1). The vertical component of elastic base E comprised 10^9 to 10^{12} (N/m)/m^2.

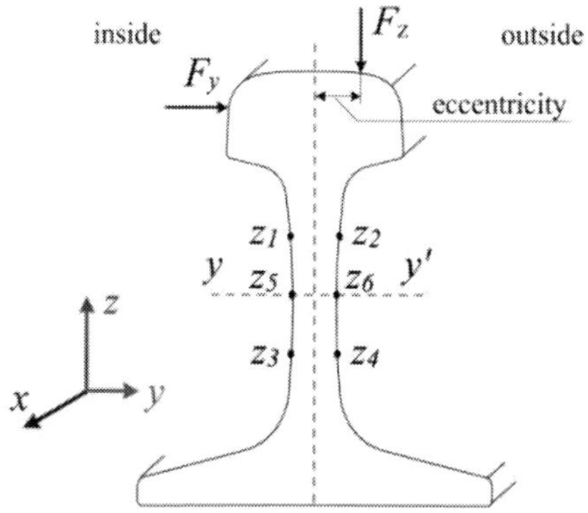

Fig. 1. Layout for determining the effect of force factors on the rail from the train load. F_z is vertical force, F_y is lateral force, *e* is displacement in the cross-section (eccentricity).

The strained state of the rail was studied with vertical force F_z=100 kN and zero eccentricity e=0 mm, the measuring cross-section for $L/2$. These results will be used hereafter for comparison with other calculation options. The maximum local deflection in the force application area was 110 million^{-1}. Calculations for the model were compared for different boundary conditions. The discrepancy between the calculation results for fixing the face with rigid embedding and hard edge sealing calculated using the relative error formula (1) was 0.05%. In (1): $s(y-y_1)$, $s(y)$ are root-mean-square deviations of calculation results with two different parameter values y or y_1, million^{-1}. The error in the calculation between the results obtained with a rigid edge seal and the roller was 0.4%. With that, the effect of the fixing variant has a local nature at the model edges.

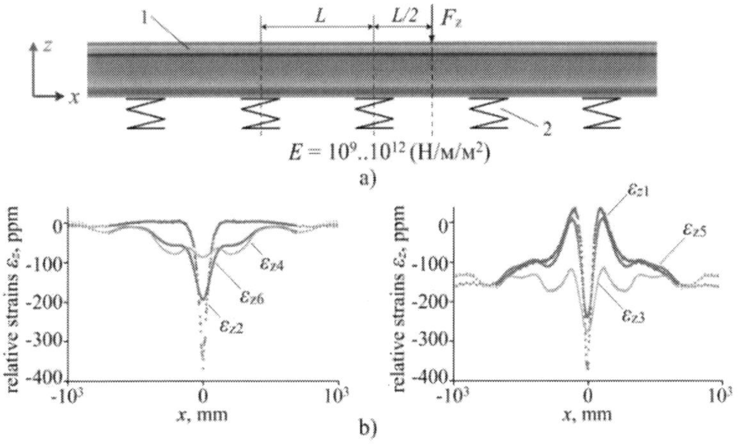

Fig. 2. Mathematical rail model: a is the finite element rail model; b are the results of calculating the relative strain of the rail web near the neutral axis for F_z = 100 kN,
F_y = 0, e = 10 mm, E = 10^9 N/m/m^2.

$$\delta = \frac{s(y-y_1)}{s(y)} \cdot 100\% \, , \tag{1}$$

With a decrease in the minimum dimensions of the finite elements from 5 mm to 2.5 mm, the discrepancy in the calculation results was 0.82%. The type of the load applied was varied to verify the model: when the point force was varied into force distributed along the edge, the discrepancy between results was 0.14%. In case of replacement of the point force with the force distributed in an area, the discrepancy between results was increased to 1.7 %.

In operation, the force is irregularly acting on the wheel due to wobble, rolling of the wheel onto the ridge, and its squeezing. Elimination of the effect of this displacement on the calculation results will be important, since eccentricity causes occurrence of bending moment. Large values of the bending moment, in turn, cause additional errors in calculation of forces. In the second experiment, the point force in the model was displaced from the central point along the y axis by the value of e=10 mm. Figure 2, b demonstrates distribution of relative strains ε_{z1}, ε_{z2}, ε_{z3}, ε_{z4}, ε_{z5}, ε_{z6} along the edges on both sides of the rail in accordance with numbering (Fig. 1). The half-sum of the relative strains in each rail web node (symmetrical strains) is calculated from the external and internal sides of the rail, their value is compared with the calculated results for each node in the first experiment with e=0. For comparison of two dependencies (the first one being the dependency of distribution ε_{z6} along the rail length at F_z=100 kN, e=0 mm, the second one was obtained by calculation of symmetrical strains ε_{z5} and ε_{z6}), discrepancy between them was found equal to 0.96% (1). In the course of the study, the results of the lateral load application were analyzed, separately and in combination with vertical force. When applying the lateral force equal to F_y=25 kN, F_z=0, e=0, where F_y=1/4F_z, as compared to the first experiment, relative strains of the rail web ε_{z6} reach the maximum of 75 million^{-1}, the model elasticity is associated with less flexural rigidity in the lateral force direction.

Results

After verification of the model, two ways of registering the rail strains were compared, which were discussed in the first section, and an estimate of the accuracy of forces calculation was made. The "RZD-2016" method [2] based on the principle of independence of the forces and the registration of data by strain gauge z_1 … z_4, like in [6], is widespread in the Russian railways. Forces are calculated with effect matrices that connect the forces acting on the rail to the stresses in the places where strain gages are fixed:

$$\varepsilon_i = g_{i,j} \cdot f_j \quad (2)$$

where ε are relative strains, g is the obtained matrix of coefficients, f are the loads applicable in the system, i, j are matrix coefficients. The $g_{i,j}$ coefficient matrix is obtained in the course of calibration of the system with a specific combination of forces, which takes into consideration vertical component, lateral force, and bending moment.

$$V = \begin{bmatrix} V^0 & V^1 & V^2 & V^3 \end{bmatrix} \quad (3)$$

where V^0… V^3 are columns of values of relative strains of tension sensors from one to four for various load types. To study the accuracy of this method, the calculated values of strains at different eccentricity of vertical force e from 10 to 24.5 mm. Dependency of relative strains ε_z on e has been built. It has linear nature for each of the four tension sensors (Fig. 3). The calculated vertical error of determination of vertical force F_z comprised from 1.1 to 6.7% for e=10 mm and e =24.5 mm, respectively, which confirms the impermissible increasing of error with increasing of eccentricity for this method. The assumption was verified suggesting that the error can be caused by the asymmetry of forces in the third and fourth gage experiments, when independent columns with positive and negative value e are obtained in matrix V. For each of the curves *R1*…*R4* coefficients were calculated in the equation of function $k_{i,1..4}$. These results allow simulating the systems with deliberately set displacement d. The columns of the effect matrices (3) were recalculated, and the calculated maximum error for artificial simulation of the eccentricity asymmetry was not more than 1.159% for d = 2 mm. The sensitivity was compensated for each channel with the help of coefficients to reduce the error. When multiplying V_3 in (3) by coefficient k_3 equal to 0.9773295, the error in determination of F_z is reduced to (-6.624·10^{-6} %) with compensation for V_2 in (3) with k_2,=0.977645, the error is equal to (-6.81·10^{-6} %). For this method, any deviation of the system from the conditions during calibration causes an unacceptable increase in errors.

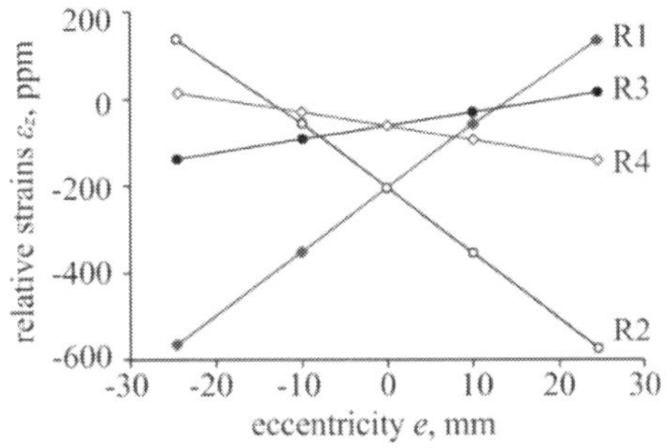

Fig. 3. Dependency of relative strains at the strain gages installation locations on value *e*.

The study of the effect of the sub-rail base rigidity E on the calculation accuracy became the second important section of the work. Rigidity E affects redistribution of rail strains, and, accordingly, the accuracy of forces determination [14]. Figure 4 represents distribution of strains ε_z along the edges on the height of the rail web on two sides of the rail at F_z=100 kN, e=10 mm, E=10^9 (N/m)/m^2. Local reduction in compressive strains (Fig. 4, b) is caused by change in the rail web in this section. Figure 5 shows the results obtained for simulation rail load (F_z=100 kN, F_y=0, e=0) and E variations from 10^8 to 10^{12} (N/m)/m^2. With a change in rigidity, relative strain curves ε_z have non-linear distribution along web height z, where $z \in (44.5\ldots129.9)$ mm. Let us consider the site close to the neutral axis, where the web thickness is equal to 9 mm and the curves are linear with the accuracy of 0.95% (Fig. 5, b). It can be seen from the Figure that with variation in the rigidity of the under-rail base by five orders of magnitude, the neutral axis changes its height within the following limits: for variation of rigidity from 10^8 to 10^9(N/m)/m^2, neutral axis has the coordinate of z=81.523 mm. At this point, relative strains ε_z do not change values (-109 million^{-1}), for $E \in 10^9\ldots10^{10}$(N/m)/m^2, the neutral axis coordinate is increased to z=84.492 mm, at ε_z =-113 million^{-1} within the specified rigidity change limits. With further increase of E, the neutral axis coordinate will be increased up to the value z=91.465 mm, the strains will comprise ε_z =125 million^{-1}. Even if the load is symmetrically applied in the cross section, if the rigidity E is varied within two orders of magnitude, the neutral axis can significantly change its coordinate between 3 and 7 mm. When studying models with lateral forces, the distributions shown in Figure 5 change the character, the neutral axis rotates in the plane of the rail section. The value of displacement of the neutral axis characterizes the accuracy rate when installing strain gages. The errors resulting from displacement of the installation points of strain gages are calculated, and the norms for their installation are provided in [15].

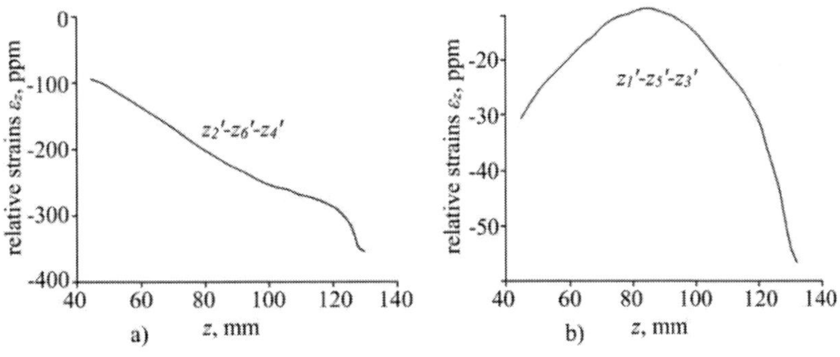

Fig. 4. Distribution of relative strains ε_z by the rail web height from two sides; a – along the edge z_2'-$z6'$-$z4'_6'$-$z4'_4'$; b –along the edge z_1'-z_5'-z_3'.

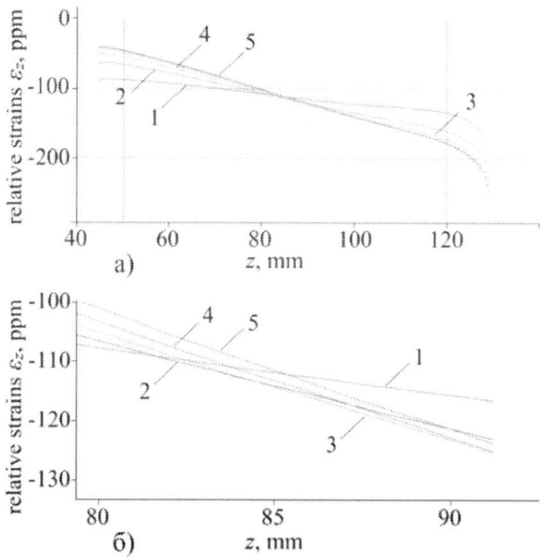

Fig. 5. Distribution of relative strains ε_z by the rail web height from the external side: a – along the entire rail web height; b – at the linear section, ***1*** – at E=10^8(Н/м)/м^2, ***2*** – E=10^9 (N/m)/m^2, ***3*** – E=10^{10} (N/m)/m^2, ***4*** – E=10^{11} (N/m)/m^2, ***5*** – E=10^{12} (N/m)/m^2.

Conclusion

At present, rolling stock of the new type is being introduced both in Russian Railways JSC and abroad. In this connection, the problem of reliable estimation of the effect of loads on the railway track is highly relevant. Development of measuring equipment for certification of vehicles with application of theoretical approach can significantly improve the quality of measurements. Monitoring systems must work within a wide amplitude range with permissible errors when recording different types of load. The results of the work can be used for metrological support of such systems.

One of the most important factors for accuracy of measurements remains the choice of the strain recording method, which will be least affected by the influencing factors. For this purpose, the analysis of effect of various factors in calculation of loads by the two most common methods was performed using the numerical model. The stress-strain state of the rail under the load of two types and redistribution of deformations with a change in rigidity of the under-rail base was estimated. The effect of displacement of strain registration points on the calculation results was discussed, which was the case with asymmetric installation of the primary transducers along the rail web height. These results can be used to select the data registration method, improvement and detailed study of new methods, as well as metrological support of dynamic forces monitoring systems in the "wheel-rail" system.

References

1. S.A. Bekher, A.O. Kolomeets, L.N. Stepanova, A.S. Kochetkov, Kontrol'. Diagnostika [Testing. Diagnostics], 7, 68-72 (2016). (in Russian)
2. V.A. Gapanovich, Zheleznodorozhnyj transport [Railway Transport], 10, 10–15 (2016). (in Russian)
3. P.A. Ivanov, Zheleznodorozhnyj transport [Railway Transport], 10, 16–18 (2016). (in Russian)

4. D.N. Losev, Transport Innovation, **4** (22), 9-10 (2015). (in Russian)
5. I.I. Galiev, V.A. Nekhaev, V.A. Nikolaev, Izvestia Transsiba [Journal of Transsib Railway Studies], 1, 107–112 (2012). (in Russian)
6. GOST P 55050-2012. Railway rolling stock. Permissible exposure norms to the railway track and test methods (Standartinform, Moscow, 2013). (in Russian)
7. V.S. Kossov, A.A. Lunin, D.A. Knjazev, M.V. Timakov, Vestnik transporta Povolzhya, **4** (58), 63–68 (2016). (in Russian)
8. S.A. Bekher, L.N. Stepanova, A.O. Kolomeets, A.A. Popkov, RU Patent 2625256 (2016). (in Russian)
9. D.R. Ahlbeck, H.D. Harrison, The Shock and Vibration Digest, **12** (10), 31-41, (1980).
10. L. Bocciolini, A. Bracciali, L. Di Benedetto, R. Mastandrea, F. Piccioli, Proceedings of the Second International Conference on Railway Technology: Research, Development and Maintenance, ed. by J. Pombo (Civil-Comp Press, Stirlingshire, Scotland, 2014).
11. A.V. Favorskaya, N.I. Khokhlov, V.A. Miryakha, Bjulleten' Obyedinennogo uchenogo soveta OAO RZhD [Bulletin of the Joint Scientific Council of JSC Russian Railways], **Vol. 1,** 49-63 (2018). (in Russian)
12. M. Bogdevicius, R. Zygiene, G. Bureika, S. Dailydka, Vehicle System Dynamics 54 (5), 689–705 (2016).
13. A.A. Shabana, J.R. Sany, Nonlinear Dynamics, **Vol. 26,** Issue 2, 179–212 (2001).
14. DIN EN 14363-2016. Railway applications – Testing for the acceptance of running characteristics of railway vehicles – Running Behaviour and stationary tests; German version 04.30.2016.
15. S.A. Bekher, T.V. Sych, A.O. Kolomeets, A.S. Kochetkov, The Siberian Transport University Bulletin (to be published).

Simulation of wheel heating when drum braking

Aleksander Mironov[1], *Pavel* Shalupina[2,*], *Aleksander* Pavlyukov[2], and *Ivan* Dobychin[2]

[1]"Infoteks AT" LLC, 620017 Yekaterinburg, Russia
[2]Ural State University of Railway Transport, 620034 Yekaterinburg, Russia

Abstract. Application of heating control systems is rational for effective prevention of thermal-mechanical damages of the wheels and brake shoes of rolling stock. These systems enable to perform diagnosis of brake equipment elements and to evaluate the effectiveness of drum braking process in terms of wheel heating. The present study aims to assess wheel heating when drum braking and to define the most informative zones and threshold control values for heating control systems. Heating evaluation is conducted using finite element method under different braking modes. Research results are given as heating patterns in solid-rolled wheel of freight car; the influence of the air distributor mode on the wheel heating is considered, the most informative zones for heating control are identified.

Introduction

Heating control systems (HCS) are effective means to detect pre-failure conditions of brake equipment and prevent thermal-mechanical damages of brake system elements. They are widely used at the railroads of Russia and in European Union countries [1], the USA [2], Canada [3], and India due to operating principle of rolling stock brake system. Friction brakes are applied on rolling stock to control the travel velocity; their basic operating principle lies in conversion of the mechanical energy of motion into thermal energy due to friction. Multiple freight cars apply drum brakes, where brake shoes press against wheel thread to decelerate the motion of the vehicle.

Starting from the 1960s, brake shoes made from polymer composites became commonly used at the railroads. Compared to cast-iron brake shoes, composite shoes possess lower weight, more consistent friction coefficient at the whole velocity range and high operational life. However they differ by a number of significant drawbacks. The first experience of using brake shoes made from 6KV-10 composite showed that the average number of wheel pairs with surface damages increased by 10 times. For the first time in maintenance the problem appeared when wheel wear products were carried over the adjacent surfaces of brake shoes made from polymer composites [4]. Due to that the braking process was accompanied by excessive wear and occurrence of defects of thermal-mechanical nature. Despite ongoing enhancement of the polymer composition for brake shoes, their basic problem still remains which is the low value of thermal conductivity and therefore increased thermal load on the wheels. Studies have shown that 95-97% of heat

*Corresponding author: p.shalupina@gmail.com

© The Authors, published by EDP Sciences. This is an open access article distributed under the terms of the Creative Commons Attribution License 4.0 (http://creativecommons.org/licenses/by/4.0/).

generated during braking is dissipated by wheels; while brake shoes from polymer composites dissipate only 3-5% of heat (cast-iron brake shoes dissipate over 10-15%) [5].

Low thermal conductivity of polymer composites and increased thermal load on the wheels along with the common failures taking place when working with automatic brakes of rolling stock to a large extent increase the damage rate of the wheels and brake shoes. The cases of automatic braking equipment failure in Russian railroads amount to 39% out of the total number of failures, in absolute numbers it is 3809 cases of failure in 2017. Such high value is also conditioned by a significant number of thermal-mechanical damages of the wheels, such as voids, wheel flats, weld-on deposits and circumferential wear [6].

HCS allow performing diagnosis of braking equipment elements and evaluate the effectiveness of braking process by heating of friction surfaces. Their working principle is based on the emission phenomenon – any body having the temperature higher than the absolute zero (-273.15°C) emits electromagnetic waves. The intensity and wave length depends on the body temperature according to Planck's equation and Wien's law [7]. A challenging issue while developing HCS is defining accurate and proper information and the heating degree of braking system elements. Whereas the ultimate purpose of HCS application is reduction of operating expenses of railroads, defining proper threshold values and control zones on the braking system elements is a primary objective.

Therefore the present study aims to deliver information in the field of threshold values and thermal control zones of wheels in freight car to develop HCS. The first stage of this objective is appropriate to be solved by means of simulation modeling. The heating process of solid-rolled wheels of freight car during braking by composite brake shoe was investigated in the present paper by finite element analysis. The essential difference of this study from the previously conducted ones [2, 8, 9] consists in the development of full-scale model corresponding to the real wheel structure and brake shoe. Such approach enables to clarify the pattern and degree of wheel heating during different braking modes.

Materials and methods

The heating process during braking was investigated on the example of solid-rolled wheel and brake shoe from polymer composite. The model of solid-rolled wheel corresponds to Russian National State Standard GOST 10791-2011 with the tread diameter of 950 mm. Based on solid models of freight car wheel, and brake shoe made from polymer composite (Fig. 1) their finite element models were developed using solid finite elements of hexahedral and tetrahedral shapes.

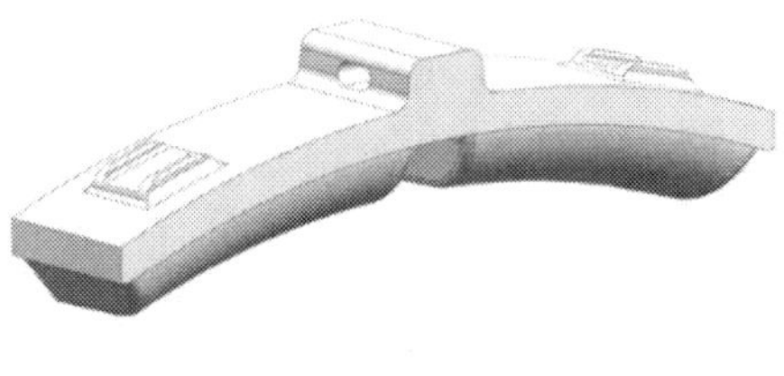

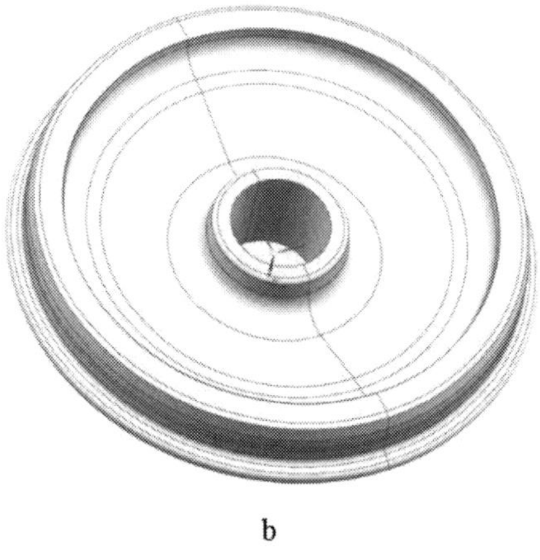

a b

Fig. 1. Solid models of wheel and brake shoes: a – solid model of brake shoe made from polymer composite, b – solid model of wheel.

 https://doi.org/10.1051/matecconf/201821603010

Part of the finite element model is shown in Figure 2 as an example.

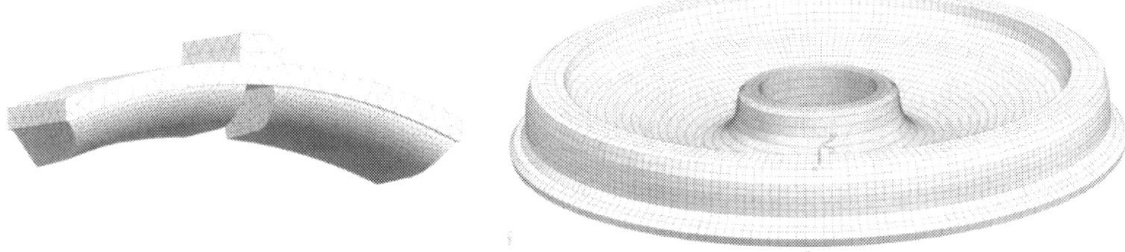

a b

Fig. 2. Finite element model: a – Finite element model of brake shoe from polymer composite (number of nodes – 3,036), b – Finite element model of the wheel (number of nodes – 42,224).

The developed model takes into account the number of parameters given in Table 1.

Table 1. Parameters considered in simulation.

Simulation specification	Notation	Dimensions	Numeric value		
1. Materials properties:			Solid-rolled wheel	Brake shoe	
- density	ρ	kg/m^3	7850	2100	
- Young's modulus	E	Pa	$2.1\cdot10^{11}$	$1.0\cdot10^{11}$	
- Poisson's ratio	v	-	0.28	0.3	
- thermal capacity	C_P	J/kg·K	486	430	
- heat transfer coefficient	k	W/m·K	7920	-	
- linear expansion coefficient	α	$10^{-6}\cdot K^{-1}$	11.6	30	
			Air distributor mode		
			Empty	Average	Loaded
2. Compressive force acting on brake shoe:	F_N	tf	0.82	1.48	2.4
3. Ambient temparature	T_{amb}	°C	20		
4. Axial load	q_0	kN	245		

Contact area between solid-rolled wheels and brake shoe from polymer composite is about $0.29\ m^2$. The change in friction coefficient in the contact between solid-rolled wheel and brake shoe is taken into account depending on motion velocity according to the known empirical dependencies.

During drum braking heat flow goes into the wheel through the wheel tread contacting with the brake shoe. It is changed in a complex manner and it depends on the specific braking force $b(t)$ at each moment of time t, velocity of train car $\vartheta(t)$, axial load of train car q_o and friction surface of brake shoe A [8, 9]:

$$q(t) = \frac{b(t)\vartheta(t)q_o}{A}. \tag{1}$$

Mathematical model applied to define the heat flow density, suggests that heat flow $q(t)$ grows nonlinearly from zero to maximum when brake cylinders are filled with compressed air. Since the pressure in brake cylinder is increased up to a maximum point the train velocity and heat emission decrease up to zero. Mathematical model takes into account the fact that during braking the heat flow $q_1(t)$ is directed into brake shoe, while the heat flow $q_2(t)$ - into the wheel rim. Part of heat given as heat flow $q_3(t)$ is released into the environment. The value of each heat flow is defined according to the following dependencies:

$$q_1(t) = \alpha \cdot q(t), \tag{2}$$

$$q_2(t) = (1-\alpha) \cdot q(t), \tag{3}$$

$$q_3(t) = \alpha'(t)[T_2(0,t) - T_c], \tag{4}$$

where α - part of the heat flow directed into the brake shoe (heat flow sharing coefficient), for composite brake shoe $\alpha = 0.05$; $\alpha'(t)$ – heat exchange coefficient, $W/m^{3} \cdot {}^\circ$; $T_2(0,t)$ – temperature of wheel tread in the moment of time t, °C; T_c – ambient temperature, °C.

Results

In order to evaluate heating of solid-rolled wheel and brake shoe during braking design modes were formed. They consider earlier defined simulation parameters and mathematical model of defining heat flow density (Table 2). For each of the operating modes of air distributor and the type of applied brake shoe the assessment of wheel heating is conducted while braking with different initial velocities and duration.

Table 2. Design modes to evaluate wheel and brake shoe heating.

Modes	Velocity of forward movement of rail car, km/h	Braking time, s
I	120…0	60
II	100…0	300
III	15	1200

Modes I and III are regulated by "Rules…" [10]. For each of the accepted design modes eigenvalues of heat flow density are calculated in each of the moments of time t. Figure 3 indicates simulation results given as heating patterns for short-term I mode and III mode, corresponding to the situation of maintaining constant velocity at the long down grade.

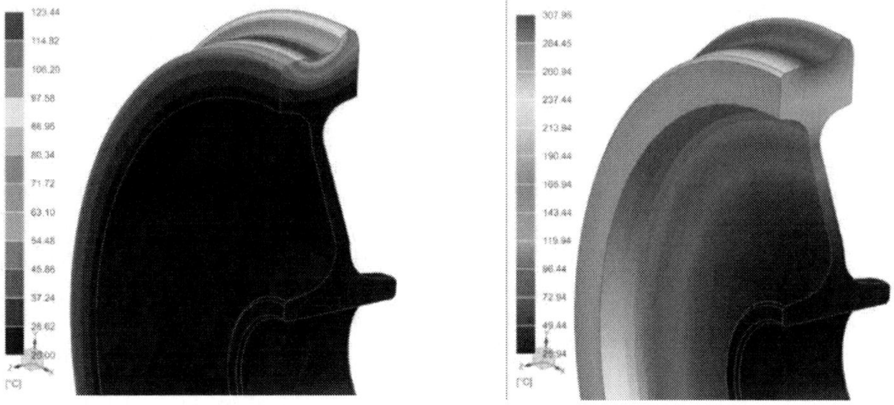

a b

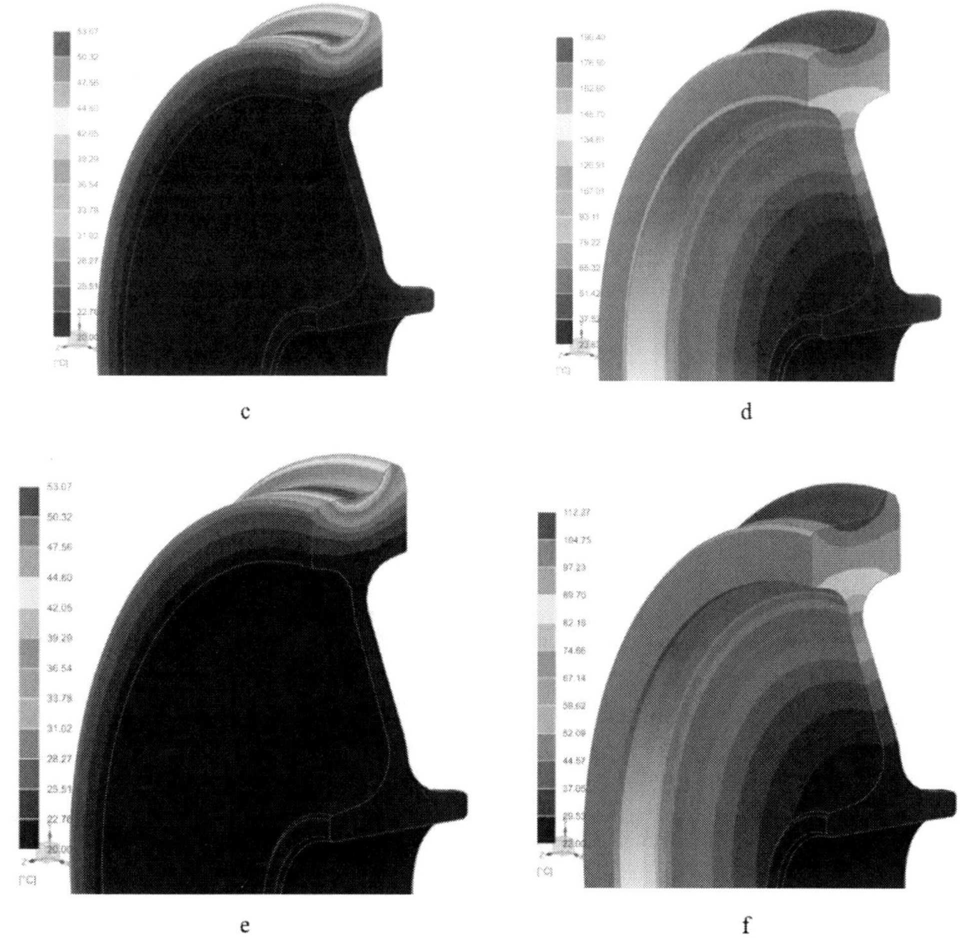

Fig. 3. Heating patterns by different braking modes (loaded mode of air distributor): a – mode I (loaded), b – mode III (loaded), c – mode I (average), d – mode III (average), e – mode I (empty), f – mode III (empty).

Simulation results show that during short-term braking heating occurs mainly in the wheel rim. The temperature of disc part of the wheel (in the junction of the rim and the disc) changes insignificantly and it is about 25-30°C (mode I). The temperature of the hub during short-term braking scarcely changes. In case of long-term braking more homogenous heating of the wheel with significant growth of the rim temperature up to 305°C is observed when using composite brake shoes. The obtained results correlate well with the known studies [11, 12]. It is obvious that the most informative thermal control zone for HCS application is the zone of wheel profile. In that case it is rational to orient IR optics of HCS on the surface of the wheel rim from the internal or external side. It is necessary to consider the lowering of the rim height due to the wheel wear while operation.

Therefore, solving the task of selection of IR-optics orientation to control wheels has two options: orientation of IR-optics into the point lying at the contact line of the wheel and the rail or in the point located above the rim on the disc. The first option provides control of the zone which describes heating of the wheel most informatively. Such orientation enables to separate heating of the solid-rolled wheel during short-term braking. However, at the same time possibility of getting alarm signal from HCS appears in case of using emergency braking, as in this zone it is possible to reach the threshold control values during emergency braking. The second option with IR-optics orientation into higher point on the disc enables to define effectively the wheel overheating, as in this zone intensive temperature growth will occur. At the same time due to relatively slow heating such orientation will allow avoiding alarm signals from HCS in case of short-term or emergency braking.

Conclusion

The study on assessment of wheel heating when drum braking was conducted by means of finite element analysis. The developed full-scale models of solid-rolled wheels and brake shoe enabled to define the working temperatures of solid-rolled wheels for different braking modes with high accuracy. Full-scale heating patterns obtained from simulation allowed preliminary indicating the most informative zones of heating control on the wheel. Results of this investigation may become the basis for designing new HCS and enhancing the existing ones. The next stage in elaborating information support for HCS is conducting experimental study to evaluate heating of the wheels of train cars in operation, as well as validation of the model to evaluate wheel heating when braking developed in this study.

References

1. E. Eisenbrand, Rail Technology Review Special: Wayside Train Monitoring Systems, 2-11, (2011).
2. J. Roberda, D. Sammon, B. Madrill, *Using Wheel Temperature Detector Technology to Monitor Railcar Brake System Effectiveness* (Washington, U.S. Department of Transportation, 2013).
3. WWW-BST-TSB-GC-CA, Railway Investigation Report R99T0031, available at: http://www.bst-tsb.gc.ca/eng/rapports-reports/rail/1999/r99t0031/r99t0031.pdf (May 1, 2018).
4. A.Ye. Pavlyukov, O.V. Cherepov, P.I. Shalupina, Herald of the Ural State University of Railway Transport, 4, 4-11 (2017). (in Russian)
5. S.M. Zakharov, *Kontaktno-ustalostnye povrezhdenija koles gruzovyh vagonov* [Contact fatigue damage of the freight wagon wheels] (Intekst, Moscow, 2004). (in Russian)
6. Regional Center of Innovation Technologies, Klassifikator neispravnostej vagonnyh kolesnyh par i ih elementov [Defects classification of wagon wheel pairs and their elements, available at: http://www.rcit.su/techinfo51.html (May 1, 2018). (in Russian)
7. L.Z. Kriksunov, *Spravochnik po osnovam infrakrasnoj tehniki* [Handbook of the basics of infrared technology] (Sovtskoe radio, Moscow, 1978). (in Russian)
8. E.Ye. Galay, Abstract of a thesis of Candidate of sciences (Gomel, 2018). (in Russian)
9. A.V. Savrukhin, A.N. Neklyudov, R.A. Efimov, Mir transporta [World of transport and transportation], 5, 22-37 (2014). (in Russian)
10. Normy dlja rascheta i proektirovanija vagonov zheleznyh dorog MPS kolei 1520 mm (nesamohodnyh) [Norms for the calculation and design of railroad cars of the Ministry of Railways with gauge 1520 mm (non-self-propelled)] (Ministry of Railways, Moscow, 1996). (in Russian)
11. A.A. Mironov, V.L. Obraztsov, A.Ye. Pavlyukov, Transport of the Urals, **4**, 24-29 (2008).
12. K. Mitura, R. Faja, Železn. techn. **3**, 175-184 (1980).

Forecast model for estimating the service life of a diagnosed object based on the Neyman–Pearson method

Sergey Barsukov[1,*], and *Sergey* Pakhomov[1]

[1] Irkutsk State Transport University, 664074 Irkutsk, Russia

Abstract. The paper is aimed at developing a forecast model for estimating the service life of a diagnosed object based on the Neyman–Pearson method. It presents a procedure for selecting necessary and sufficient number of diagnostic indicators using the forecast model. The technique has been tested on the basis of a power transformer with a liquid dielectric. A condition-based operation strategy has been proposed for the transformer. According to this strategy, the iron impurity content in the dielectric liquid (oil) of the transformer should be measured every year of operation. Based on the forecast model, it is possible to calculate the variation of average risk (R) and a threshold value of iron impurity content in the transformer oil (k_0) for each year of operation. Using these parameters, a reliable forecast model can be constructed to estimate the remaining service life of the transformer. The obtained relationships make it possible to identify a scientifically grounded stage in the service life of a diagnosed object, at which the number of measurable diagnostic indicators (indicators that are necessary for assessing the real technical condition of equipment) can be minimized.

Introduction

At present, two traditional approaches to preventive maintenance of equipment are used [1–4]: the scheduled maintenance system (service life-based maintenance) and maintenance according to the current technical condition (condition-based maintenance). The key difference between these approaches is in different grounds for determining the frequency and scope of maintenance for a diagnosed object. There is a clear trend towards introducing the principle of condition-based maintenance for different units, assemblies and structural elements. For this purpose, numerous studies and experiments are carried out to expand a range of systems and assemblies operated under this strategy.

The primary objective of the transition to the condition-based maintenance strategy [1–5] is to improve the reliability of equipment and reduce maintenance costs. The implementation of the condition-based maintenance strategy requires a sufficient number of informative diagnostic indicators to assess the real technical condition of a diagnosed object and predict its operability.

* Corresponding author: bars_irkutsk@mail.ru

© The Authors, published by EDP Sciences. This is an open access article distributed under the terms of the Creative Commons Attribution License 4.0 (http://creativecommons.org/licenses/by/4.0/).

The operating time of any system, as well as the scope and frequency of preventive maintenance work is determined by threshold values of monitored parameters (diagnostic indicators) [6]. In order to reliably diagnose the technical condition of a system, the maximum amount of information about monitored parameters should be used. This diagnostic method minimizes the probability of a wrong decision. However, the related monitoring systems would be overloaded with sensors, while diagnostic programs would be very cumbersome and time-consuming. This reduces the economic efficiency of equipment. In this regard, it is important to take a science-based approach by identifying diagnostic indicators and then selecting, among them, the minimum number of indicators that are necessary and sufficient to reliably diagnose the technical condition of a system (remaining service life). In this case, both a diagnosed object and monitoring facilities will be as simple and effective as possible.

Therefore, the studies in which forecast models are constructed to estimate the remaining service life of a diagnosed object are of current interest [7–11]. In addition, there is a need for methods that make it possible to reduce the number of measured parameters, which are necessary and sufficient to reliably diagnose a monitored system [12].

The purpose of this study is to develop a tool (procedure) that can be used to reliably assess the current condition of a monitored object. Based on a reliable diagnosis of the technical condition, it is possible to introduce a condition-based preventive maintenance strategy.

The novelty of the study is in presenting the forecast model that, unlike the existing forecast models, is designed to estimate the remaining service life of a diagnosed object by year of operation. The forecast model is based on the Neyman–Pearson method. It also focuses on estimating how the average risk of a wrong decision concerning the technical condition of a diagnosed object varies from year to year.

Research methods

There are statistical methods that can be used to recognize indicators [1–3, 13–15] and, therefore, set limits to making a decision about the technical condition of a diagnosed object. In addition, these methods allow possible diagnostic errors to be quantified. Danger of a wrong diagnostic decision is quantified through average risk assessment. For this purpose, it is necessary to determine a probability density of a particular diagnostic parameter k, which is used to identify whether a diagnosed object is serviceable (D_1) or unserviceable (D_2).

Let us introduce the following notations:

k is the output performance parameter of a diagnosed object;

k_0 is the threshold value of the output performance parameter.

The parameter k_0 indicates a degree of serviceability of equipment:

- at $k < k_0$ $k \in D_1$, a diagnosed object is serviceable;

- at $k > k_0$ $k \in D_2$, a diagnosed object is unserviceable (defective).

Thus, these inequalities are a quantitative measure of the remaining service life of a diagnosed object. Figure 1 shows values of the probability density of a diagnostic parameter k for two statuses of a diagnosed object. In real systems, the probability densities $f(k/D_1)$ and $f(k/D_2)$ usually have a common area. Selecting a threshold value k_0 is subject to a certain risk that the current technical condition will be misdiagnosed.

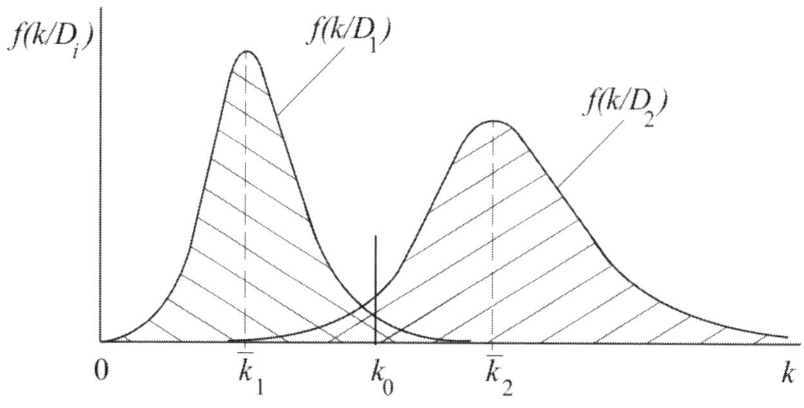

Fig. 1. Probability density of the diagnostic indicator k for two statuses of a diagnosed object. $\bar{k}_1$ and $\bar{k}_2$ are the average values (mathematical expectations) of the diagnostic indicator k.

A wrong diagnostic decision (magnitude of the average risk) is defined as a sum of probable events:

$$R = C_{21} \cdot P(H_{21}) \cdot \int_{k0}^{\infty} f(k / D_1) \cdot dk + C_{12} \cdot P(H_{12}) \cdot \int_{-\infty}^{k0} f(k / D_2) \cdot dk\,, \qquad (1)$$

where $P(H_{21})$ is the probability of a false alarm; a serviceable diagnosed object is recognized as defective: a diagnosed object is serviceable (real condition of a diagnosed object – D_1), but the parameter k exceeds its threshold value ($k > k_0$);

$P(H_{12})$ is the probability of a missed defect; a defective diagnosed object is recognized as serviceable (real condition of a diagnosed object – D_2), but the parameter k is less than its threshold value ($k < k_0$);

C_{21} is the cost of a false alarm; C_{12} is the cost of a missed defect.

Based on the Neyman–Pearson method, the probability of a missed defect will be minimized at a specified allowable level of false alarm probability.

Results

The method for selecting the necessary and sufficient number of diagnostic indicators based on the Neyman–Pearson method was tested on the basis of a power transformer with a liquid dielectric. A conventional maintenance procedure of the power transformer is based on preventive maintenance (service life-based operation).

The condition of the transformer is assessed by measuring the iron impurity content in its dielectric liquid (oil) (parameter k):

– if $k < k_0$, $k \in D_1$ (the transformer is recognized as serviceable);

– if $k > k_0$, $k \in D_2$ (the transformer is recognized as unserviceable).

In this case, k_0 is the threshold value of the iron impurity content in the transformer oil. According to the maintenance schedule, the diagnostics of the transformer is carried out every five years of operation on the basis of the iron impurity content in the transformer oil. In order to implement the condition-based maintenance strategy of the transformer, it is proposed to measure the iron impurity content in the tank oil every five years of operation, rather than every year.

Figure 2 shows the calculated probability density of the diagnostic parameter k by year of operation with serviceable D_1 and unserviceable D_2 conditions of the transformer. The figure also shows a distribution of the threshold parameter k_0, which allows the remaining service life of the transformer to be assessed in real time.

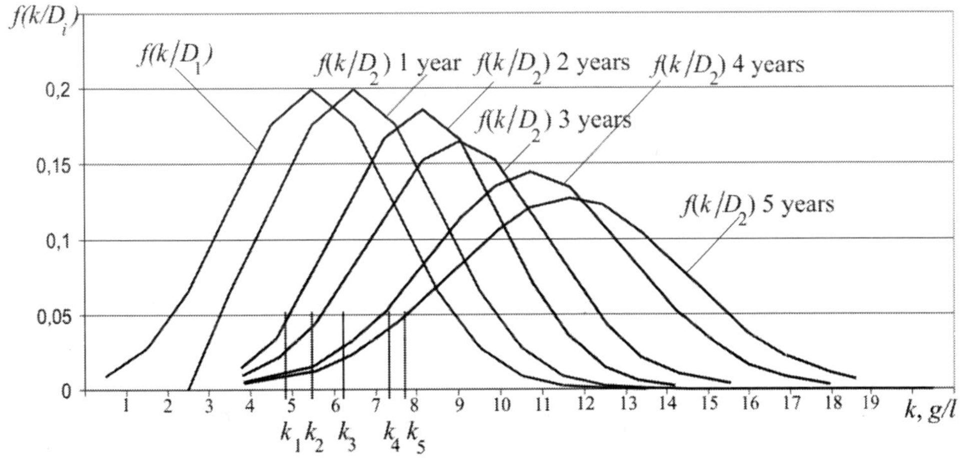

Fig. 2. Variation of the probability density of the diagnostic parameter k by year of operation of the transformer, $k_1, \ldots, k_5$ is the distribution of the threshold parameter k_0 by year of operation of the transformer.

Figure 3 presents the variation of the false alarm and missed defect probabilities calculated on the basis of the Neyman–Pearson method, as well as the magnitude of the average risk by year of operation. The obtained characteristics make it possible to construct a reliable forecast model for estimating the remaining service life of a diagnosed object by varying the threshold parameter k_0. By estimating a threshold value of the average risk $R_{\max}^{add}$ of a wrong decision concerning the technical condition of the transformer, it is possible to identify a scientifically grounded stage in the service life of a diagnosed object, at which the number of measurable diagnostic indicators (indicators that are necessary for assessing the real technical condition of equipment) can be minimized.

The calculations performed for the diagnosed object demonstrate that, starting from the second year of operation, the risk of a wrong decision concerning the condition of the transformer decreases to an acceptable value. Quantitatively, this is justified by the fact that, starting from the second year of operation, the average risk R falls below the accepted threshold value $R_{\max}^{add} = 0.6$. By reducing the probability of a wrong decision concerning the condition of the transformer to the acceptable value, it is possible to reduce the number of measurable diagnostic indicators, without detriment to a reliable diagnosis of its technical condition.

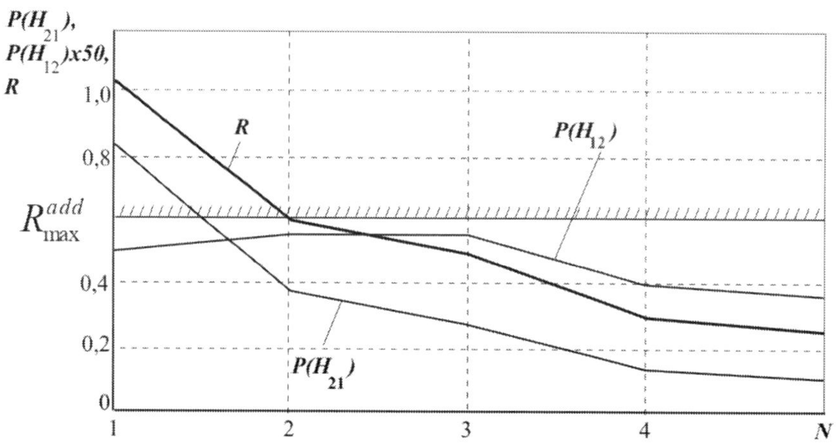

Fig. 3. Variation of the false alarm probability $P(H_{21})$, probability of a missed defect $P(H_{12})$ and average risk R by year of operation (N) of the power transformer.

Conclusion

The forecast model for estimating the service life of a diagnosed object has been constructed on the basis of the Neyman–Pearson method. The developed model can be used to introduce a condition-based preventive maintenance strategy. Based on the forecast model, the variation of the average risk of a wrong decision concerning the technical condition of the transformer R has been calculated by year of operation. By comparing the average risk R with the estimated threshold level of risk, $R_{\max}^{add}$ it is possible to identify a scientifically grounded stage in the service life of a diagnosed object, at which the number of measurable diagnostic indicators (indicators that are necessary for assessing the real technical condition of equipment) can be minimized.

References:

1. V.S. Malkin, *Tehnicheskaja diagnostika. Uchebnoe posobie* [Technical diagnostics. Textbook] (Lan' Publ., Moscow, 2013). (in Russian)
2. A.M. Safarbaklov, A.V. Lukyanov, S.V. Pakhomov, *Osnovy tehnicheskoj diagnostiki detalej i oborudovanija. Uchebnoe posobie. Ch.1* [Fundamentals of technical diagnostics of parts and equipment. Textbook, part 1] (Irkutsk State Transport University Publ., Irkutsk, 2007). (in Russian)
3. Y.D. Sibikin, M.Y. Sibikin *Diagnostika i tehnicheskoe obsluzhivanie jelektroustanovok potrebitelej. Uchebnoe posobie* [Diagnostics and maintenance of electric consumer units. Textbook] (Moscow, 2016). (in Russian)
4. A. B. Shelkov, *Problemy upravlenija bezopasnost'ju slozhnyh sistem, materialy XXIII mezhdunarodnoj konferencii* [Proceedings of XXIII international conference "Problems of safety management of complex systems"], 2016, (3). (in Russian)
5. GOST B23743 – 1988, GOST B20570 – 1988, GOST B20436 – 1988. Flight safety, reliability, controllability and repairability (Goscomizdat SSSR Publ., Moscow, 1988). (in Russian)
6. V.S. Viktorova, A.S. Stepanyants, *Modelirovanie i analiz kontroleprigodnosti bortovyh sistem samoletov* [Modeling and analysis of controllability of on-board

airplane systems] (Dependability Publ., 2007). (in Russian)
7. V.I. Dubrovin, V.A. Klimenko, Matematichni mashini i sistemi [Mathematical machines and models], **4** (2010). (in Ukraine)
8. A.A. Dubov, Occupational Safety in Industry, **3** (2003). (in Russian)
9. V.N. Ksendzov, G.A. Dyko, S.P. Murashko, Nadjozhnost' i kontrol' kachestva [Reliability and quality control], **10** (1988). (in Russian)
10. H.M. Chen, B. Vidakovic, N.D. Mavris, Technological Forecasting and Social Change, **1** (2004).
11. N.V. Lubkov, Institut problem upravlenija im. V.A. Trapeznikova RAN, XII Vserossijskoe soveshhanie po problemam upravlenija VSPU [Proceedings of XII All-Russian Conference on Control Issues at V.A. Trapeznikov Institute of Control Sciences of Russian Academy of Sciences] (Moscow, 2014). (in Russian)
12. N.R. Tarnurr, L.W. Stanton, *Quantitative Forecasting Methods. The Duxbury Series in Statistics and Decision Sciences* (Boston, PWS-KENT Publishing Company, 1989).
13. I.V. Lyubimov, S.A. Meshkov, *Statisticheskie metody kontrolja kachestva i nadezhnosti tehnicheskih sistem* [Statistical methods of control of technical systems quality and reliability] (Baltic State Technical University Publ., Saint Petersburg, 2010). (in Russian)
14. N.S Loginova, S.V. Barsukov, S.V. Pakhomov, Model' prognozirovanija resursa tehnicheskogo objekta (sistemy) na osnovanii diagnostirovanija metodom minimal'nogo riska [Proceedings of VI Science and Practice Conference "Youth of the XXI century", Model of forecasting technical object resources based on minimum risk diagnosis] (Far East Federal University, Vladivostok, 2017). (in Russian)
15. Y.D. Sibikin, M.Y. Sibikin, *Diagnostika i tehnicheskoe obsluzhivanie jelektroustanovok potrebitelej. Uchebnoe posobie* [Diagnostics and maintenance of electric consumer units. Textbook] (Moscow, 2016). (in Russian)

Use of computer software for technical training at rail car repair shops

Artem Popkov[1,*], and *Sergei* Bekher[1]

[1]Siberian Transport University, 630049 Novosibirsk, Russia

Abstract. Currently, there is a clear trend towards updating technical regulations and improving control technologies in the field of maintenance and repair of car assemblies and parts. Therefore, there is a need for software and hardware that will provide updated information to specialists of car repair shops in a timely manner. This study is aimed at creating a computer-based network training system that will increase the effectiveness of training and reliability of results. The paper describes methods for verifying and identifying training results based on an analysis of user's behavioral parameters. As a result of the research, the authors have developed a system that can verify training results with a probability of more than 95%.

Introduction

In recent years, there have been repeated failures of undercarriages on railways of the Russian Federation. One of their causes are fatigue defects that have not been early detected because specialists at car repair enterprises lack professional experience and knowledge [1]. The use of network software will allow specialists to adopt training materials remotely and on-the-job, without interrupting their professional activities, and to keep themselves up to date on the latest changes in technical regulations. At present, e-learning management systems, such as Moodle, Edmodo and Schoology, are widely used. All these systems have extensive functionality, are flexible and customizable, equipped with special modules designed to manage training materials, generate statistics, etc. However, the need of fine tuning for specific demands, lack of high-quality technical support and excessive functionality make technical training systems more difficult to use by specialists of car repair shops.

In case of technical e-learning, it is impossible to guarantee the reliability of learning results [2]. Detection of attempts to falsify results or other types of fraud by trained specialists, e. g., involving a third person to pass training tests, is an acute problem.

Modern researchers mention the user's "digital handwriting" (keystroke and mouse dynamics) — unique quantitative characteristics, also called as behavioral parameters, which are determined during the user's interaction with input/output manipulators [3, 4]. The purpose of the study is to develop a methodology that will allow car repair shops to determine the reliability of training results by analyzing students' behavioral parameters.

[*]Corresponding author: Zabagy@gmail.com

© The Authors, published by EDP Sciences. This is an open access article distributed under the terms of the Creative Commons Attribution License 4.0 (http://creativecommons.org/licenses/by/4.0/).

Use of computer software in training

User's behavioral parameters were studied among specialists of car repair shops. A special-purpose network software product was designed to conduct technical on-the-job training [5]. The most preferred way of implementing the necessary functionality is a client-server architecture [6]. A database managed by MS SQL Server database management system is used to store training materials and results. Its simplified diagram is shown in Figure 1 [7].

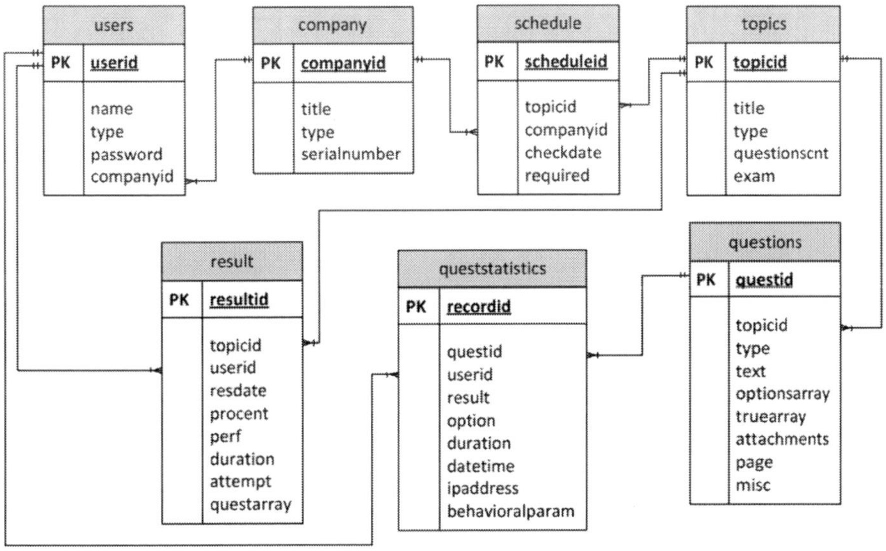

Fig. 1. Simplified diagram of the database.

Car repair shops employ non-destructive testing (NDT) specialists in various elements of the rolling stock. There are special technical regulations and training materials for these specialists [8]. Therefore, the technical training system was designed so that training materials could be hierarchically separated into several independent levels. It enables individual planning of the training process for each business unit.

Training materials include a list of topics, multimedia training aids, and a set of interactive test questions. A specialist responsible for technical training can select necessary topics according to the profile of his/her enterprise, and set key dates for them [9]. The training process has three stages: introduction to training materials, a preliminary test and a final test. When passing a preliminary test, the user has the right to use training materials and can see whether his/her answers are true or not. In the final test mode, the user will not have access to training materials and will see a final result only after completion of the test. A topic is deemed to have been passed if at least 80 percent of questions have been answered correctly both in the preliminary and final tests.

Information about progress for each topic is saved on the server. The training can be continued at any time on a PC with access to a corporate network [10]. Statistics saved in the system include the number of correct and incorrect answers, the number of views of training materials, and time spent on a question by each user.

Depending on the enterprise's profile, training can be conducted in different areas: automatic couplers, automatic brakes, general questions of NDT, bogie monitoring, railway wheel monitoring, and welding operations in repairs of undercarriages. Time spent per question varies slightly for different areas. The average value is eight seconds. It can be concluded that test questions for different training areas are similar in terms of difficulty (Fig. 2).

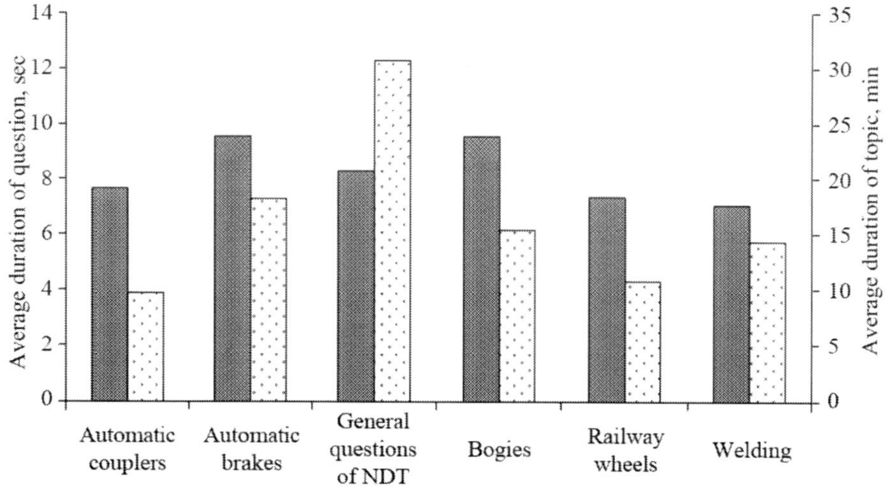

Fig. 2. Distribution of time spent per question and total time of testing per topic in different training areas.

The average time of testing for the topic "general questions of NDT" is 1.5 times or more longer than that for other training areas (Fig. 2). This is due to the fact that there are many questions in this area, used to test the knowledge of technical regulations, and users more often refer to training aids to answer them.

Although the test questions are similar in terms of difficulty, the total time of testing by different users varies. For example, user *A* spends from three to 12 minutes to pass each topic from a set *X*. User *B* spends seven to 18 minutes to pass each topic from the same set *X*. A relationship between times spent on each topic from the set *X* by users A and B is close to linear (Fig. 3). The time of testing by a particular user may depend on many factors: level of attention, knowledge of the topic, etc.

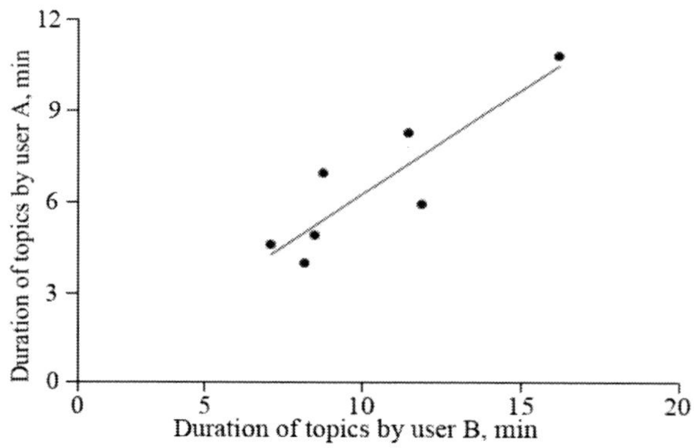

Fig. 3. A relationship between times spent on each topic by users A and B.

However, it is the number of incorrect answers that has the greatest influence on the time of testing. In most cases, a dependence of the time of testing to the number of incorrect answers is linear.

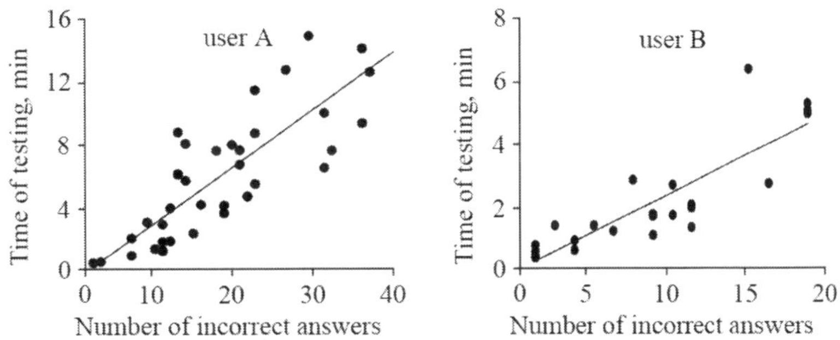

Fig. 4. Dependence of the time of testing on the number of incorrect answers.

Verification of results

The technical training system uses one-step authentication for reusable passwords. The user enters his/her unique ID (login) and reusable password. If the entered data coincides with the reference data stored on the server, authentication is considered to have been passed. This step is followed by authorization of the user and providing the access to relevant training materials and results. This access control system is sufficient for a system that processes publicly available personal data.

If the training is subject to deadlines and supervision, and the user is not personally interested in acquiring the related knowledge and skills, there is a higher probability that results will be falsified. The system cannot deny authorization to user *A* if he/she has entered a correct login and password of user *B*. Therefore, one-step authentication with reusable passwords does not provide sufficient protection against attempts to falsify results.

When interacting with PC input/output manipulators, each user demonstrates his/her own "digital handwriting" with a variety of parameters, such as typing speed, distribution of delays between keystrokes in certain sequences, force and duration of keystrokes and mouse clicks, cursor movement speed, etc. Special-purpose input/output manipulators are required to determine the keystroke force, which makes it impossible to use these parameters in large-scale research [11].

The duration of a right mouse button click during the training process was analyzed as one of behavioral parameters. The duration of a right mouse button click for most users was found to be in the range of 80 to 1000 μs [12]. The analysis of clicks for the entire training session shows that the distribution of their durations varies from user to user (Fig. 5).

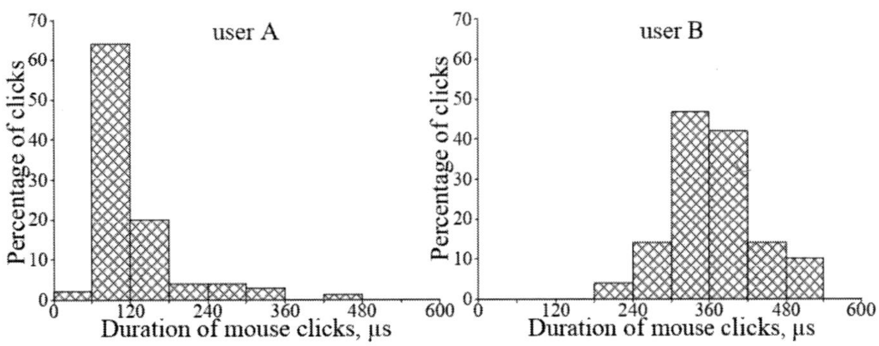

Fig. 5. Distributions of durations of mouse clicks for users A and B.

The analysis of mouse clicks made by the users while passing a set of topics *Y*, shows that the average duration is 110 µs for user *A* and 340 µs for user *B*, which is consistent with the previously determined distributions (Fig. 5). Standard deviations of durations of the clicks made while passing the topics from the set *Y* by users *A* and *B* is within 20 µs, which suggests that there is an insignificant and equal variation of experimental data for different test subjects (Fig. 6).

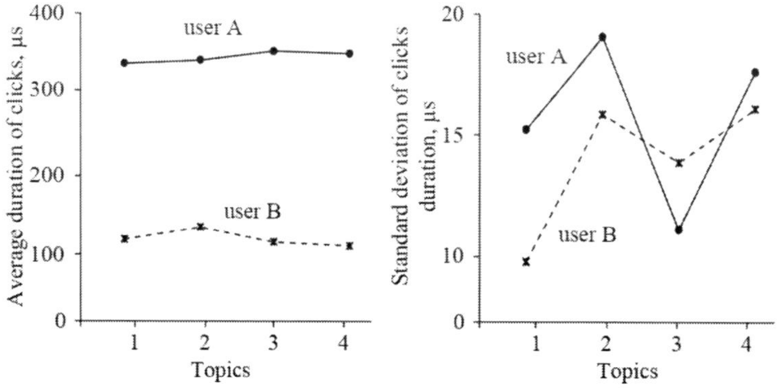

Fig. 6. Average value and standard deviation of duration of clicks in different topics for users A and B.

The duration of mouse click by a particular user *C* is a normally distributed random variable (Fig. 5), for which the arithmetic mean a and the standard deviation σ are determined uniquely and with some accuracy. Therefore, if a value of duration is outside the range $[a - 2\sigma, a + 2\sigma]$, there is a 95 percent probability that the click does not belong to analyzed user *C*. If only one click is outside the confidence interval, it is impossible to judge whether results are falsified or not. If, however, all clicks made while passing a particular topic differ from user's typical values, results are considered to have been falsified (Fig. 7).

By analyzing training results of NDT specialists, the authors identified five of 27 available topics in which results were falsified through involving third-party users in passing a test. Throughout the entire technical training system, the number of attempts to falsify results does not exceed 1% of the total number of results.

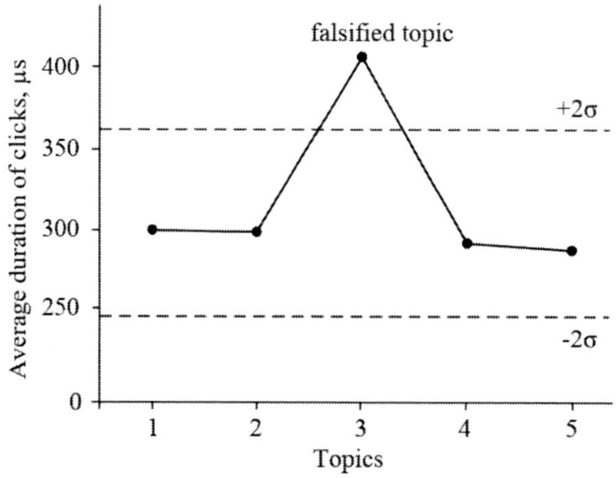

Fig. 7. Average duration of mouse clicks in different topics, including a topic with falsified results.

In practice, it is possible that different users will have the same durations of mouse clicks. In addition, the parameters described above are influenced by a number of factors, such as user's fatigue levels, equipment, etc. Therefore, it is reasonable to use a set of several different behavioral parameters to detect falsified results more accurately.

Conclusion

Based on the results of the study, the authors proposed a system architecture to increase the efficiency of technical training by using solutions that reduce the time of training. Reducing the time of technical training will provide more time for primary activities and, therefore, increase the labor productivity of specialists at car repair shops.

The proposed technique can be used for detecting attempts to falsify training results with a probability of 95%. Specialists of one of the tested enterprises falsified more than 20% of results. Throughout the entire training system, the number of attempts to falsify results does not exceed 1% of the total number of results. By expanding a range of behavioral parameters to be analyzed, it is possible to identify the user's digital handwriting (keystroke and mouse dynamics). It is expected that revealed patterns of behavioral parameters will be used to identify users and determine his/her current status.

References

1. V.S. Vorobyev, R.M. Bryzgalova, I.B. Repina, Nauka i transport [Science and transport] 3, 42–46 (2012). (in Russian)
2. S. Fuicu, M. Popa, D. Dobrilovic, M. Marcu, R. Bogdan, Brain: Broad Research in Artificial Intelligence and Neuroscience **8** (1), 52-58 (2017).
3. A. Mahfouz, T. Mahmoud, A. Eldin, Journal of Informational Security and Applications **37**, 28-37 (2017).
4. M. Biasutti, Computers&Education **12**, 158–171 (2017).
5. L. Collins, X. Liang, The Turkish Online Journal of Distance Education **15**, 268-281 (2014).
6. M. Adame, M. Matysek, M. Barinova, *MATEC Web of Conferences* **125**, 02058 (2017).
7. GOST P 43.0.11-2014. Informational ensuring of equipment and operational activity. Database in technical activities (Moscow, 2015) (in Russian)
8. GOST 12.0.004-2015. Occupational safety standards system. Organization of training for safety and health at work. General requirements (Moscow, 2017). (in Russian)
9. H. Peration, *Open and Distance Learning in the Developing World* (Routledge, New York, 2000).
10. A.A. Popkov, S.A. Bekher, Method to testing and/or polling remote users, RU Patent 2625554 (2017).
11. S.A. Bekher, Thesis of Candidate of Sciences, Siberian Transport University, Novosibirsk, 2004 (in Russian)
12. S.A. Bekher, A.A. Popkov, The program of user identification in the process of remote testing. Registration No. 2017610808, 18.01.2017 (Moscow, 2017). (in Russian)

Development of transport systems as one of the areas of Industry 4.0

Konstantin Komarov[1,*]

[1]Siberian Transport University, 630049 Novosibirsk, Russia

Abstract. This article considers the results of research conducted to define the impact of information technology (IT) on the development of regional transport systems (TS) within the subjects of the Russian Federation. The purpose of this paper is to investigate the impact of digitalization on transport systems and to assess its economic consequences. Methods of analytical modelling, ranging and spatial differentiation are used. The differentiated recommendations are offered for cities, agglomerations and regions for assessing the economic consequences of transport digitalization.

1. Introduction

Active introduction of IT is one of the key methods to improve the efficiency of transport systems. These technologies are well-known from monographs, articles and web sources published in various countries and successfully used in practice [1–4]. However, the introduction of IT in various types of TSs is uneven for a number of reasons, including, but not limited to the specificity of the three levels of the TS:

- Local TSs providing basic production activities in the territory;
- regional TSs, providing inter-district exchange of goods [5];
- state (country) TSs [6–7].

Each of these TSs requires the development of appropriate development models that minimize the transport component in the price of the final product. The resulted expenses connected with work of TSs of all levels reach 39%, and full transport costs make up 10% of gross domestic product [1] in economy of Russia. Formation and expansion of unified TS in the Russian Federation takes place on the basis of an evolving system of territorial and local levels. And each of these levels has its own development prospects.

If we talk about the stages of the development of the country's economy in the context of the development of TS ensuring the development of each stage, one can identify three stages here: (1) separation of the transport systems of the former USSR, in which Russia received 59% of the railways, 49% of the motor roads and 74% of the trunk pipelines of the unified transport system of the USSR; (2) the privatization of individual elements of the TS, during which, in particular, more than 100 airlines emerged. In parallel with the process of privatization, a legal framework was established that defines the activity of the transport complex in the market conditions. During this stage (2000-2012), the total passenger

* Corresponding author: komarovkl2015@gmail.com

© The Authors, published by EDP Sciences. This is an open access article distributed under the terms of the Creative Commons Attribution License 4.0 (http://creativecommons.org/licenses/by/4.0/).

turnover for all modes of transport decreased by 23 billion passenger/km. At the same time, it should be noted that the share of traffic in international communications has significantly increased [1]. The current moment can be attributed to (3) the third stage of development of the TS, which began in 2010. The current stage in the development of transport systems requires the development and implementation of a new model of the TS, which should take into account:

- sectoral and territorial structure of production;
- social and demographic situation in the region;
- place of the district in the national division of labour.

At this stage of the TS development it is important to represent the place and role of transport in the process of implementation of the concept of Industry 4.0.

The purpose of this article is to study the state of affairs in the use of information technologies, which are quite successfully used in a number of industries, but which are used in transport systems in a limited way.

The novelty of the study is the application of analytical modelling for regional TSs.

2. Materials and methods

Methods of analytical modelling, ranging and spatial differentiation are used. In this case, analytical modelling involves a qualitative method that allows finding some properties of the solution that optimize the development of the TS. In the absence of functional ratios of the investigated parameters of the transport process, it is advisable to use expert analysis, which allows us to give ordinal estimates of process parameters that can not be directly measured. In this case, the conclusions about the degree of influence of individual parameters of the transport process will be based on the judgments of specialists. The validity and urgency of this methods were widely discussed, in particular, at the conferences "Digital economy and Industry 4.0: Problems and Prospects" INDUSTRY-2017 and "Innovative Clusters in the Digital Economy: Theory and Practice" INPROM-2017 in St. Petersburg.

2.1 The concept of Industry 4.0

In recent years (1990-2016), structural changes occurred in the economic systems of countries all over the world. It has been decided to distinguish three main sectors of the economic system from the point of view of creating added value: industry, agriculture and services, which include transport.

The concept of Industry 4.0 gradually spreads to the whole world. The United States, Japan, China and other developed countries followed the example of Germany. In 2014, a commercial industrial Internet consortium was created in the United States, which included such leaders of the global industry as GE, AT & T, IMB, Intel and others. Japanese companies, along with German ones, are currently leaders in the digitalization of the economy. They have developed digital interoperability that supports end-to-end processes with business partners through a horizontal value chain. This approach can be fully used in transport in the chain: production-storage-loading-transportation-unloading-warehousing. The coordination of actions in this chain will contribute to a significant increase in operational efficiency through reduction of costs, increase in productivity and improvement of the quality of transport work.

Currently, the concept of Industry 4.0 has acquired the meaning of the fourth industrial revolution, which consists of connecting the real world with the virtual one. At the same time, some new complexes appear that carry the meaning of cyberphysical devices that unite the objects of the material world with the virtual world. As a result, some cyberphysical objects emerge that naturally combine into a certain digital ecosystem. The elements of such an ecosystem are robotic production, including "smart stations" as elements of the transformed transport. The concept of Industry 4.0 assumes automation of almost all stages and processes of industrial production, including the transport one. Another feature of the new industrial revolution is that the manufacturer of "smart stations" and all its elements controls the conditions of their operation. It can remotely change settings, including the software in control systems. It also can warn the user in advance about possible disturbances in the operation of devices. At the end of the established service life, the equipment manufacturer shall take the object for disposal.

Apparently, in connection with such an essentially closed cycle of the use of equipment, the concept of Industry 4.0 is usually represented as a mathematical sign of infinity. This symbol symbolizes the continuity of the process of interaction between the equipment manufacturer and the product, and customers [2, 8].

2.2 The features of Industry 4.0

The founders of the concept of Industry 4.0 formulated several principles for its construction.

1. *The principle of compatibility*: the ability of machines, devices, sensors and people to interact and communicate with each other through the Internet of things.

2. *The principle of transparency*: the formation in the virtual world of a digital copy of real objects, as well as systems of functions that repeat everything that happens to a real physical object.

Thus, there is accumulation of quite complete information about all processes and the state of objects and equipment included in the "smart" production. At the same time, it is required to ensure the collection of all information from sensors and transducers in order to generate all information taking into account the features and values of each of the indicators.

3. *The principle of technical support*: the assistance of computer systems to personnel in decision-making in specific situations, based on the analysis and visualization of all available information. The full replacement of people with computers is possible in the future, especially in cases that threaten the health of people.

4. *The principle of decentralization of managerial decisions*: the delegation of some administrative functions to cyber-physical systems. The sense of implementation of the principle is that in all cases where the machine can work without human intervention, a transition to manless technology must be implemented. The person in this case acts as a controller, ready to make a decision in non-standard situations.

In the implementation of these principles in industry and transport, as well as in some other branches of the economy, there will inevitably be a change in the corresponding business processes and business models. For example, instead of focusing on lean production, companies can concentrate their attention on personalization of products, including transportation, as well as on the release of unique products (transportation) in single versions. It is important to note that at the same time the saving principle is maintained, since robot production provides higher product quality and minimization of failures and rejections [3].

3. Results

3.1 Digital intelligent economics

The new trends in technological and economic development of Industry 4.0 dictate the need for change at all levels of evolutionary development. At the first level - the *conceptual one*, the changes are connected with the adoption of managerial decisions. At the *strategic* level, a substantiation of priority directions of development, including the development of program documents, is required.

Currently, a new institutional environment is developed that contributes to innovative development and the emergence of new organizational structures [9]. In Europe, the most important changes in the innovation landscape include, in particular, the creation of European technology platforms. They include 9 platforms connected with information and communication technologies, including 5 platforms in the transport sector.

The technology of creation of the European technological platforms provides for such stages as:

- pooling the interests of stakeholders with a view to formulate a long-term development strategy;
- the development of the Strategic Plan and the Work Program for its implementation;
- implementation of the Strategic research plan using the mechanisms and scientific programs of the EU.

The developed technological platforms have so-called "mirror groups", which should provide a link between the activities of the European platform and the creation of products at the national and regional levels. A number of technological platforms in the EU are already in the third stage: "implementation of the strategic research plan." European single technological platforms unite efforts of private business, scientific and educational organizations, public and state bodies. This approach allows the creation of joint public-private projects (programs).

The fourth industrial-technological revolution led to drastic changes in the economy from micro- and meso levels to the level of the global economy. At the same time, the economy takes more and more new forms - from digital to the cloud one. At the same time, the economy and management of enterprises are faced with contradictions in the innovative development of engineering business. Specialists note the growing significance of the phenomenon of technicalization, digitalization in all spheres of economic life, including human activity. The information technologies form a virtual and augmented reality. At the same time, new stages, levels and problems of production development are observed:

- global challenges associated with the formation of the digital economy;
- digital transformation of industry and transport;
- problems of digitalization in the development of regional and branch economy;
- problems of economics and enterprise management in the digital economy;
- development of modelling tools and the rationale for the development of the digital economy.

3.2 Digital railroads

Speaking of a more specific topic, such as digital railways, the concept of "digital railroad", from the authors' point of view [4], should primarily be based on the use of safety-related devices. This is, as a rule, signaling and communication equipment (SCE). The issues of safety of transportation of goods and passengers on the railways have always been under increased attention [10–11]. It should be noted that the railway signaling system on the basis of "digitalization" already operates in a system of high-speed railways on a landfill with a total length of more than 80,000 km. At the same time, the European Union of Railway Transport has created and well-proven digital railway signalling system based on a special system of standards. The transition from an analog signalling system to the digital one was first implemented on conventional railways in the UK. The specialists of this country believe that the transition to digital modernization of the railway will stimulate the overall stable growth of the country's economy [4].

The initiators of the transition to digital railways say that with this technology, it is possible to regulate technical, technological and economic indicators. In addition, the digital modernization of the railway increases the labour productivity, traffic safety, and customer-orientedness. It can be expected that a reduction in the negative impact on the environment will be achieved [12].

When launching the program of digitalization of railways in the UK, three goals were formulated. The first one is an increase in the number of trains on the existing infrastructure. The second one is the best alignment of traffic schedules. And the third one is more convenience for customers [4]. At the present stage of "digitalization" the authors do not take into account any kind of anomalies, in particular, the disconnection of digital components as a result of natural disasters.

The introduction of digital technologies into the country's transport system, according to experts, will promote more active industrial development and, ultimately, economic growth of the country. With limited financial resources in the industry, priority should be given to financing sectoral transport innovations, for example, the design of high-speed railroads using digital technologies. The most striking example here is the construction of high-speed railway lines, such as Moscow-Kazan, which is planned as part of the future mega-project of the Moscow-Beijing railway line [13]. The implementation of this scale of infrastructure projects is positioned as a priority in the economic policy of the Russian Federation.

In certain sectors of the economy, Russian companies show results at the world level and often have their competitive advantages. The domestic IT companies such as Mail.ru, Yandex, Kaspersky and others create products at the interface of information technology and the transport industry. The products of these companies are not inferior and even go ahead of their Western competitors. Even today's traditional activities (medical care, education, financial services) are transferred to the digital format.

In addition to the above-mentioned features and directions for the development of "digitalization" in the technical and technological aspects of transport systems, it is necessary to take into account the impact of digitalization on the behavior of passengers. According to some experts' estimates, the penetration rate of such devices as smartphones will reach 50% by 2019. The fact that every second passenger or cargo owner will have gadgets, on the one hand, increases the mobility of citizens and on the other - raises the level of control over the movement of the cargo. In addition to widespread smartphones, new types of mobile devices appear, such as smart watches and bracelets, as well as promising virtual reality devices. The intelligent transport management systems receiving the right to use, having being until recently the part of the plots of fantasy novels, become a reality. All of the above will help increase the speed of transport and increase the level of comfort of living in various countries of the world, including, in Russia [13].

As a rule, the authors understand under the digital ecosystem a certain set of participants in economic activity (objects and subjects) and resources. Resources can be combined with a specific target orientation (education, construction, etc.) or industry affiliation. For example, an ecosystem of digital design and production in transport can include educational laboratories of universities, workshops, digital equipment, resources of companies and corporations. All elements of such ecosystems can effectively interact through cloud technologies.

One can say that fast-growing technological innovations create a mobile, virtual, supplemented contradictory world, when it is required in certain situations to weigh the pros and cons. New business processes require the development of technological and new economic thinking in all post- and neo-industrial sectors of the economy. At present, new economic-technological thinking becomes an intellectual part of the transforming economy.

The digitalization as a result of the 4th industrial and technological revolution acquires global scales in the conditions of a changing economy.

4. Conclusion

Currently, the technological and economic aspects of the digitization of transport systems and railways, in particular, are the subject of discussions. The discussion is also taking place at the sites of the EAEC working group on the digital space.

The importance of the topic is determined by

1) determination and specification of directions and structural dynamics of national economic systems in the field of transport;

2) specification of the role of the information technology (IT) sector in structural dynamics in TSs;

3) determination of directions of further researches in the field of convergence of IT and management of electronic (digital) economic subsystem of states and territories.

The construction of a TS management system oriented to a wide exchange of information increases the efficiency of decision making and reduces the probability of error. When developing some schemes of cargo delivery in different climatic zones of the country using several modes of transport for synchronization of actions, it is possible to use a method similar to a "brainstorm", with involment of all participants of the transport process.

The researches conducted have shown that for increase of efficiency and innovative development of the TSs it is necessary to carry out their digitalization and transformation of the economy on the basis of modern tools and mechanisms.

Thus, the proper and effective application of the "large data" technology will play a positive role in optimizing the activities of logistics and transport enterprises in terms of management and decision making, as well as customer service and resource allocation.

References

1. K.E. Gafarova, E.I. Osadchiy, Economy and business: theory and practice 2, 52-55, (2016). (in Russian)
2. V.P. Kupriyanovskiy, D.E. Namiot, S.A. Sinyagov, International Journal of Open Information Technologies **4** (2), 19-25 (2016). (in Russian)
3. M. Hermann, T. Pentek, B. Otto, Design Principles for Industrie 4.0 Scenarios: A Literature Review Working Paper 01 (2015).
4. V.P. Kupriyanovskiy, D.E. Namiot, S.A. Sinyagov, A.P. Dobrynin, Modern Information Technology and IT-education **12** (1), 243-249 (2016). (in Russian)
5. N.S. Nesterova, S.M. Goncharuk, V.A. Anisimov, A.V. Anisimov, *MATEC Web of Conferences* **86**, 05024 (2016).
6. K.L. Komarov, Issues of New Economy **1,** 35-42 (2017). (in Russian)
7. K.L. Komarov, *Politransport systems*: Proceedings of the VIII International Scientific and Technical Conference "Scientific problems of transport projects implementation in Siberia and Far East" (Novosibirsk, 2015).
8. V.P. Kupriyanovskiy, A.P. Dobrynin, S.A. Sinyagov, D.E. Namiot, N.A. Utkin, International Journal of Open Information Technologies **5** (1), 34-49 (2017).
9. K. Chruzik, M. Sitarz, Mechanika **20** (4), 431-437 (2014).
10. K.L. Komarov, A.N. Ser`eznov, V.V. Murav`ev, L.N. Stepanova, E.U. Lebedev, S.I. Kabanov, M.V. Gerashchenko, Russian Journal of Nondestructive Testing **37** (3), 232-237 (2001).

11. R. Brkić, Z. Adamović, Russian Journal of Nondestructive Testing **47** (6), 420-429 (2011).
12. M. Dedík, J. Gašparík, Z. Záhumenská, *MATEC Web of Conferences* **134**, 00009 (2017).
13. T.N. Yudina, State and Municipal Management Scholar Notes. RANEPA 3, 139-143 (2017).

Development of the technical vision algorithm

Pavel Elugachev[1,*], and *Boris* Shumilov[1]

[1]Tomsk State University of Architecture and Building, 634003 Tomsk, Russia

Abstract. The purpose of the work is creation of a set of technical means (switches, sensors) for recognition of transport infrastructure facilities, including development of algorithms for autonomous operation of technical facilities under changing environmental factors. In this work, we used methods for determining the volume of a three-dimensional facilities from the data of photo and video recording of the surrounding situation. The algorithm of technical vision was obtained, which is implemented as a program on a mobile device for recognition by means of stereometry of transport infrastructure facilities and their defects and storage of transport infrastructure defects. The novelty of the research is building of decision algorithms based on devices and sensors that recognize changing road conditions, namely, defects in coverage. The data obtained can be used in the planning of road repairs, in the analysis of traffic accidents by road police, road users for processing complaints, etc.

Introduction

The key component in implementation of a fully autonomous robot capable of performing tasks of collecting road data is the technical vision system [1-2]. Research in this area is performed by Google (USA), in Russia, the research is performed by Kamaz concern and others. The rapid growth in the number of automotive motor vehicles (AMV) in Russia and the world is many times ahead of the pace of road construction. As a result, the road network operates in stressed conditions. The condition of highways, the quality of the road bed surface, the visibility, the width of the roadway, the arrangement of the relevant signs have a significant impact on road safety and define the concept of "road conditions" in their totality. In investigation of road traffic accidents, in most cases it is believed that their main causes are the negligence or mistakes of the driver - the person (incorrect assessment of road conditions), as well as the AMV fault. According to experts, the real impact of road conditions on occurrence of road accidents is from 60 to 80% of cases [3].

The trajectory and speed of the automobile depends on the "road conditions". If a person drives the car, then he or she makes a decision about the driving regimens based on their experience and psychological and physiological state, if the robot is driving, it is orientated on the basis of a set of sensors that allow navigation in space [4]. In the investigation of road accidents involving robots, it is believed that their main reasons are the lack of data on the engineering infrastructure due to the limited action of sensors and

* Corresponding author: Elugachev@mail.ru

© The Authors, published by EDP Sciences. This is an open access article distributed under the terms of the Creative Commons Attribution License 4.0 (http://creativecommons.org/licenses/by/4.0/).

the dynamically changing situation on the road. Creating a database and accessing it in road conditions is not effective, since it slows down the process of data processing and search for necessary solutions, and the dynamically changing road situation causes erroneous decisions in operation of control algorithms. Development of automatic diagnostic systems for evaluation of defects and detection of destructions of the road surface is possible with the use of video cameras and image processing algorithms. However, the problem of the operation of systems based on pure video is their inability to filter out such shading in pictures as road marking elements, smudges from oil and lubricant spills, brake traces, shadows of passing cars, and fresh patches [5].

One of the classical methods of extracting information about the depth of a three-dimensional (3D) object is the method of photogrammetric processing of stereoscopic images of a 3D object obtained from different angles [6-7]. The drawback of traditional digital photogrammetry is the significant involvement of the human operator, as well as the need to pre-scan analog images using high-precision scanners. The use of modern inexpensive photogrammetric methods [8-10] to determine the damage and unevenness of the road surface and structural elements of the road gives a new impetus to the development of digital technologies for the design of road repairs, increasing mobility and lowering the cost of the works.

Research methods

Due to affordability and prevalence of mobile devices (smartphones, unmanned aerial vehicles (drones), etc.), it is proposed to use mobile measurements on a series of successive video shots. The most accessible method can be to determine the amount of damage using markers from video recording [6]. To determine the volume of a three-dimensional object from the photo and video data, it is permissible to apply the method of reconstructing a three-dimensional coordinate vector from two perspective projections forming a stereo pair [11] or a simpler method using orthographic projections. This allows acting without accurate information about the transformation, relying on additional information about the object, which is provided with the presence of markers. From the graphical marks, the elements of the geometric transformations matrix are formed and the three-dimensional coordinates of the object points are determined. Then, the task of determining the volume of the object from its video image is reduced to transformation of the image into a digital volumetric model.

The main stages of the solution are as follows:

- identification of stable features of the video series;
- determination of reference frames;
- localization and definition of typical points of the video frame;
- solution of the inverse problem of photogrammetry;
- obtaining the three-dimensional mathematical model of the object. Further use of this model for expert evaluation and the formation of design estimates.

With the designation of homogeneous geometric coordinates, the transformation of the linear perspective (Fig.1) is represented as a 4x4 matrix:

$$[x \quad y \quad z \quad 1][T'] = [x' \quad y' \quad z' \quad h], \tag{1}$$

where x,y,z are point coordinates in the three-dimensional space, x',y',z' are homogeneous geometrical coordinates of the point, h is the scale factor, T' is the four-dimensional matrix,

$$[T'] = \begin{bmatrix} T'_{11} & T'_{12} & T'_{13} & T'_{14} \\ T'_{21} & T'_{22} & T'_{23} & T'_{24} \\ T'_{31} & T'_{32} & T'_{33} & T'_{34} \\ T'_{41} & T'_{42} & T'_{43} & T'_{44} \end{bmatrix}. \tag{2}$$

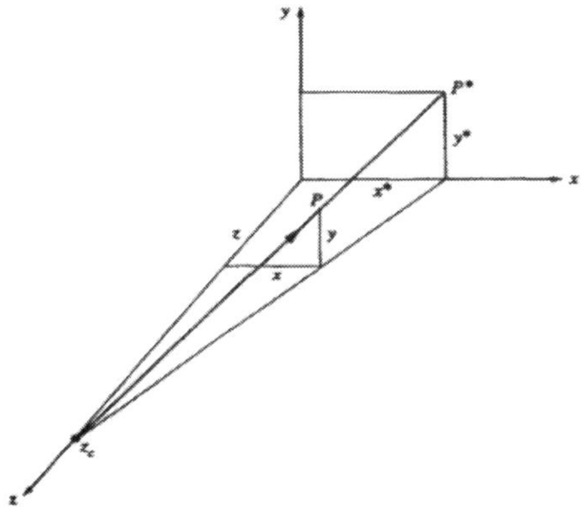

Fig. 1. Perspective projection to the point.

In the course of photographing, the results are projected onto a two-dimensional plane, in this case, on a $z=0$ 0x1 plane by means of the projection transformation

$$[T''] = \begin{bmatrix} 1 & 0 & 0 & 0 \\ 0 & 1 & 0 & 0 \\ 0 & 0 & 0 & 0 \\ 0 & 0 & 0 & 1 \end{bmatrix}. \quad (3)$$

The composition of these two linear transformations gives the following

$$[T] = [T''][T'] = \begin{bmatrix} T'_{11} & T'_{12} & 0 & T'_{14} \\ T'_{21} & T'_{22} & 0 & T'_{24} \\ T'_{31} & T'_{32} & 0 & T'_{34} \\ T'_{41} & T'_{42} & 0 & T'_{44} \end{bmatrix}. \quad (4)$$

As a result, let us put down the transformation in the following form

$$\begin{bmatrix} x & y & z & 1 \end{bmatrix}[T] = \begin{bmatrix} x' & y' & 0 & h \end{bmatrix} = h\begin{bmatrix} x^* & y^* & 0 & 1 \end{bmatrix}. \quad (5)$$

Where x^* and y^* are the coordinates of perspective projection on the picture plane of the photo image $z=0$. After excluding scale factor h, we obtain two scalar equations:

$$\left(T'_{11} - T'_{14}x^*\right)x + \left(T'_{21} - T'_{24}x^*\right)y + \left(T'_{31} - T'_{34}x^*\right)z + \left(T'_{41} - T'_{44}x^*\right) = 0, \quad (6)$$

$$\left(T'_{11} - T'_{14}x^*\right)x + \left(T'_{21} - T'_{24}y^*\right)y + \left(T'_{31} - T'_{34}y^*\right)z + \left(T'_{41} - T'_{44}y^*\right) = 0, \quad (7)$$

Under the assumption of the known $[T], x, y, z$, these equations can be used for direct simulation of the photographing process. If x^*, y^*, x, y, z, are known, then equations (6) and (7) are two equations with 12 unknown elements T'_{ij}. By applying these equations to $n \geq 6$ noncoplanar points in the object space and to their images on the perspective projection, we obtain a homogeneous system of $2n$ equations with 12 unknown values.

To solve the resulting system, let us transfer the terms containing normalizing coefficient T'_{44} to the right-hand side and set value $T'_{44} = 1$. Thus, to find the solution of $[T]$, we obtain the overdetermined system of equations, the matrix of which cannot be inverted, since it is not square. As it is known from the theory of the method of least squares, the best averaged solution can be calculated by multiplying both sides of the matrix equation by the transposed matrix of the system. Then we obtain a system of 11 linear equations with respect to 11 unknown values with a symmetric square matrix. This equation can be solved with the square root method. Thus, the known coordinates are used to determine the transformation generating this perspective projection, for example, a photo.

Finally, the last approach [12] assumes that $[T], x^*, y^*$ is known. In this case, two equations are obtained from three unknown spatial coordinates x, y, z. This is an underdetermined system of equations, so it is impossible to solve it. However, if two perspective projections are known, say, two photographs obtained from different angles, then equations (6 and 7) can be written for both projections. Then we get the following:

$$\begin{aligned}
&\left(T_{11}'^{1} - T_{14}'^{1} x^{*1}\right)x + \left(T_{21}'^{1} - T_{24}'^{1} x^{*1}\right)y + \left(T_{31}'^{1} - T_{34}'^{1} x^{*1}\right)z = x^{*1} - T_{41}'^{1},\\
&\left(T_{12}'^{1} - T_{14}'^{1} y^{*1}\right)x + \left(T_{22}'^{1} - T_{24}'^{1} y^{*1}\right)y + \left(T_{32}'^{1} - T_{34}'^{1} y^{*1}\right)z = y^{*1} - T_{42}'^{1},\\
&\left(T_{11}'^{2} - T_{14}'^{2} x^{*2}\right)x + \left(T_{21}'^{2} - T_{24}'^{2} x^{*2}\right)y + \left(T_{31}'^{2} - T_{34}'^{2} x^{*2}\right)z = x^{*2} - T_{41}'^{2},\\
&\left(T_{12}'^{2} - T_{14}'^{2} y^{*2}\right)x + \left(T_{22}'^{2} - T_{24}'^{2} y^{*2}\right)y + \left(T_{32}'^{2} - T_{34}'^{2} y^{*2}\right)z = y^{*2} - T_{42}'^{1},
\end{aligned} \tag{8}$$

where upper indices 1 and 2 denote the first and the second perspective projection. These equations represent four equations from three unknown spatial coordinates x, y, z. Thus, an overdetermined system of equations is again obtained, and one can apply the methods of least squares and the square root to find the solution.

As a result, the elements of the geometric transformations matrix are formed from the graphical marks and the three-dimensional coordinates of the object points are determined. Thus, the problem is reduced to solving a system of linear equations from which the elements of the transformation matrix are determined. It is enough for the road foreman to make two photos, and send them for further processing.

Isolation of characteristic points of the image and determination of the contour of damage can be performed by one of the known methods of Sobel, Laplace, Kani [13-14]. Availability of local inhomogeneities on defects of natural origin (potholes, rills, holes) makes it expedient to use blob detectors based on the Laplace method [15], for correct identification of interpolation points of a three-dimensional object. With that, availability of a rectangular image table makes it possible to effectively apply the modern theory of shearlets to solve the problems posed [16].

Shearlets were first identified in 2006 as a structure that allows efficient working with multidimensional data. These structures are widely used to suppress noise on images in order to improve visual perception or increase clarity. Within the scope of the task set, shearlets can serve as a pre-processing tool for stereo pair images to facilitate automatic detection of local features of the damage object.

Results

The practical application of the claimed algorithm is quite wide for recording and determination of the actual dimensions of potholes in the road surface. Let us apply the method to a real stereo pair (Fig. 2).

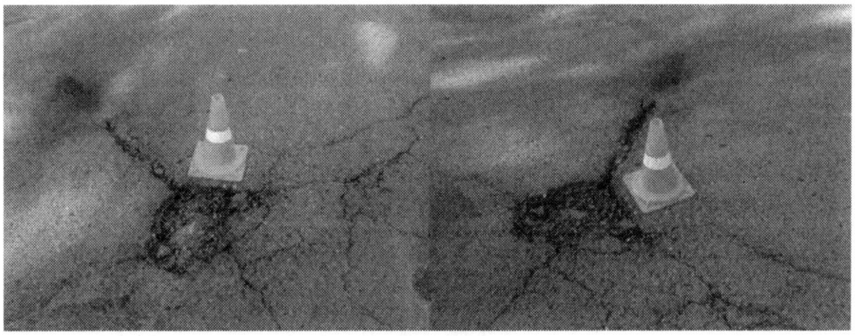

Fig. 2. Stereo pair: road cone against the background of damage to the road surface.

The coordinates of the vertices of the 3D object were measured with a ruler. The coordinates of the corresponding points on the images were recorded in a graphic editor using the mouse. Attempt to restore the 3D coordinates of the vertices of the object gave a good match with the original values. Moreover, it was possible to correct the measurements on the photo and the typing errors when taking samples during the calculations. Given the coordinates of the road surface point on the left and right images, one can estimate the accuracy of the presented technical vision algorithm. In our case, the distance from the tip of the cone to the asphalt coating calculated by the Pythagorean theorem was 31.975 cm, which is 0.078% different from the 32 cm value on the technical data sheet.

Given the features of the image of roadway defects (lack of clear boundaries, presence of foreign objects, insignificance of certain defects), it should be possible to allow "manual" editing. The road foreman must be provided with an interface that allows highlighting typical points by moving the cursor. The algorithm for creating such interface on a smartphone running Android OS is described in [17] (Fig. 3). The algorithm of the program on a smartphone for a road foreman can be as follows: the left and right image of the stereopair is alternately dropped onto the screen of the smartphone, the image of the wire model of the 3D object is superimposed on the image, the characteristic points of the object flash on the model, and the user moves the cursor to select the corresponding point on the photo, after processing both images of the stereo pair in the smartphone memory, linear perspective transformation matrices are formed, then the command is given to the user to select an arbitrary point on each stereo pair image from the corresponding test mode menu (if it is a typical point of the object), or set the mode of verification of the Pythagorean Theorem (if it is a point on the road base), or go to continue working; then a voice command is given to the user to select the next point on each stereo pair image, the distance between points is calculated, then the user is asked to select the third and so on points in each stereo pair picture.

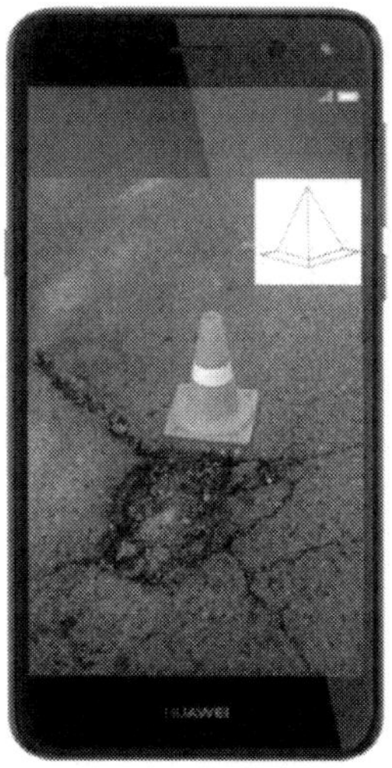

Fig. 3. Image of the program running on the smartphone screen.

As the array of typical image points is replenished, it becomes possible to construct a three-dimensional mathematical model for defects of the road surface. Then, based on the obtained model, the area and the volume of the geometric figure characterizing this particular damage are calculated using the triangulation technology.

Conclusion

The result obtained corresponds to the stated goal of the study. An algorithm for detecting road surface defects based on the photogrammetry method was obtained as a result of the work. The algorithm is implemented in the program for mobile devices, which can be used by road services, traffic police, emergency surveyors in the cases where it is required to establish the size of defects and their location. Further directions of the study may include the analysis of the ways of automating the process of searching for graphic markers and reference points on photo-images, including damaged road surfaces, evaluating ways of managing autonomous mobile robots, analyzing the constantly changing traffic situation and its effect on the percentage of erroneously calculated transport infrastructure defects, as well as further optimization of the proposed stereo matching algorithm.

The research was performed with the financial support of the Russian Foundation for Basic Research and Tomsk Region Administration (project code 16-41-700400 p_a).

References

1. A.A. Boreyko, S.A. Mun, A.F. Shcherbatyuk, Mechatronics, Automation, Control, **8**, Attachment 2-8 (2008). (in Russian)
2. A.V. Vazuev, V.P. Noskov, I.V. Rubtsov, S.G. Carichenko, Izvestiya SFedU. Engineering Sciences, **186,** 121-132 (2016). (in Russian)
3. E.R. Domke, *Rassledovanie i jekspertiza dorozhno-transportnyh proisshestvij* [Investigation and examination of road accidents] (Akademija, Moscow, 2009). (in Russian)
4. A. Pronobis, Ph.D thesis, KTH Royal Institute of Technology, Stockholm, 2011.

5. G. Bao, Ph.D thesis, The University of Toledo, 2010.
6. A.V. Mezhenin, *Metody i sredstva raspoznavanija obrazov i vizualizacii* [Methods and means of pattern recognition and visualization] (ITMO, St. Petersburg, 2012). (in Russian)
7. A.S. Nazarov, *Fotogrammetrija* [Photogrammetry] (TetraSistems, Minsk, 2006). (in Russian)
8. A. Chiuso, P. Favaro, H. Jin, S. Soatto, IEEE Trans. Pattern Anal. Machine Intell, **24**, 523 (2002).
9. A.J. Davison, I.D. Reid, N.D. Molton, O. Stasse, IEEE Trans. Pattern Anal. Machine Intell, **29**, 1052 (2007).
10. R. Tsai, IEEE J. of Robotics and Automation, **3**, 323 (1987).
11. D.F. Rogers, J.A. Adams, *Mathematical elements for computer graphics* (McGraw-Hill, New York, 1990).
12. C. Slama, (ed.), *Manual of Photogrammetry* (American Society of Photogrammetry, Falls Church, Va., 1980).
13. M. Sonka, V. Hlavac, R. Boyle, *Image Processing, Analysis and Machine Vision* (Thomson, Toronto, 2008).
14. Harris affine region detector, Available at: https://en.wikipedia.org/wiki/Harris_affine_region_detector (June 11, 2018)
15. T. Tuytelaars, K. Mikolajczyk, Foundations and Trends in Computer Graphics and Vision, **3,** 177-280 (2007).
16. G. Gao, Y. Liu, D. Labate, Journal of Visual Communication and Image Representation, **32,** 83-94 (2015).
17. S.A. Prokhanov, B.M. Shumilov, A.Zh. Kuduev, K.A. Abdykalykov, Proceedings of Ninth Siberian Conference on Parallel and High Performance Computing (PVV-2017) (October 10–12, 2017, Tomsk, Russia). (in Russian)

AUTHOR INDEX

AUTHOR INDEX